INTERNATIONAL COMMERCIAL COURTS

The book offers a comprehensive analysis of the role, importance and place of international commercial courts in the field of international adjudication from a comparative perspective. In a time where scholarly and academic debates revolve around the issues of the role of law in the post-globalization era, the new international commercial courts seem to be in the position to bridge concerns regarding diminished sovereignty, on the one hand, and the necessity of globalizing dispute resolution, on the other. International commercial courts thus present themselves as the paradigm for the future of adjudication.

Stavros Brekoulakis is Professor in International Arbitration at Queen Mary University of London.

Georgios Dimitropoulos is Associate Professor of Law and Associate Dean for Academic Affairs, Hamad Bin Khalifa University College of Law.

STUDIES ON INTERNATIONAL COURTS AND TRIBUNALS

General Editors
Andreas Føllesdal, University of Oslo
Geir Ulfstein, University of Oslo

Studies on International Courts and Tribunals contains theoretical and interdisciplinary scholarship on legal aspects as well as the legitimacy and effectiveness of international courts and tribunals.

Other books in the series:

Mads Andenas and Eirik Bjorge (eds.) *A Farewell to Fragmentation: Reassertion and Convergence in International Law*

Cecilia M. Bailliet and Nobuo Hayashi (eds.) *The Legitimacy of International Criminal Tribunals*

Amrei Müller with Hege Elisabeth Kjos (eds.) *Judicial Dialogue and Human Rights*

Nienke Grossman, Harlan Grant Cohen, Andreas Føllesdal and Geir Ulfstein (eds.) *Legitimacy and International Courts*

Theresa Squatrito, Oran R. Young, Andreas Føllesdal and Geir Ulfstein (eds.) *The Performance of International Courts and Tribunals*

Robert Howse, Hélène Ruiz-Fabri, Geir Ulfstein and Michelle Q. Zang (eds.) *The Legitimacy of International Trade Courts and Tribunals*

Marlene Wind (ed.) *International Courts and Domestic Politics*

Christina Voigt (ed.) *International Judicial Practice on the Environment: Questions of Legitimacy*

Martin Scheinin (ed.) *Human Rights Norms in 'Other' International Courts*

Freya Baetens (ed.) *Legitimacy of Unseen Actors in International Adjudication*

Shai Dothan *International Judicial Review: When Should International Courts Intervene?*

Silje Langvatn, Mattias Kumm and Wojciech Sadurski (eds.) *Public Reason and Courts*

Daniel Behn, Szilárd Gáspár-Szilágyi and Malcolm Langford (eds.) *Adjudicating Trade and Investment Disputes: Convergence or Divergence?*

Sondre Torp Helmersen *The Application of Teachings by the International Court of Justice*

Daniel Behn, Ole Kristian Fauchald and Malcolm Langford (eds.) *The Legitimacy of Investment Arbitration: Empirical Perspectives*

Eric De Brabandere *International Procedure in Interstate Litigation and Arbitration: A Comparative Approach*

Chiara Giorgetti and Mark Pollack (eds.) *Beyond Fragmentation: Cross-Fertilization, Cooperation and Competition among International Courts and Tribunals*

INTERNATIONAL COMMERCIAL COURTS

The Future of Transnational Adjudication

Edited by

STAVROS BREKOULAKIS

Queen Mary University of London

GEORGIOS DIMITROPOULOS

Hamad Bin Khalifa University

CAMBRIDGE
UNIVERSITY PRESS

CAMBRIDGE
UNIVERSITY PRESS

University Printing House, Cambridge CB2 8BS, United Kingdom

One Liberty Plaza, 20th Floor, New York, NY 10006, USA

477 Williamstown Road, Port Melbourne, VIC 3207, Australia

314–321, 3rd Floor, Plot 3, Splendor Forum, Jasola District Centre, New Delhi – 110025, India

103 Penang Road, #05–06/07, Visioncrest Commercial, Singapore 238467

Cambridge University Press is part of the University of Cambridge.

It furthers the University's mission by disseminating knowledge in the pursuit of education, learning, and research at the highest international levels of excellence.

www.cambridge.org
Information on this title: www.cambridge.org/9781316519257
DOI: 10.1017/9781009023122

First published 2022

A catalogue record for this publication is available from the British Library.

Library of Congress Cataloging-in-Publication Data
Names: Brekoulakis, Stavros L., editor. | Dimitropoulos, Georgios, 1984– editor.
Title: International commercial courts : the future of transnational adjudication / edited by Stavros Brekoulakis, Queen Mary University of London; Georgios Dimitropoulos, Hamad Bin Khalifa University.
Description: Cambridge, United Kingdom ; New York, NY : Cambridge University Press, 2022. | Series: Studies on international courts and tribunals | Includes index.
Identifiers: LCCN 2021056138 (print) | LCCN 2021056139 (ebook) | ISBN 9781316519257 (hardback) | ISBN 9781009010139 (paperback) | ISBN 9781009023122 (ebook)
Subjects: LCSH: Commercial courts. | Commercial law. | Dispute resolution (Law) | BISAC: LAW / International
Classification: LCC K1008 .I58 2022 (print) | LCC K1008 (ebook) | DDC 343.08/7–dc23/eng/20220128
LC record available at https://lccn.loc.gov/2021056138
LC ebook record available at https://lccn.loc.gov/2021056139

ISBN 978-1-316-51925-7 Hardback

CONTENTS

List of Contributors *page* xi
Foreword xvii
LORD THOMAS OF CWMGIEDD, FORMER LORD CHIEF JUSTICE OF ENGLAND AND WALES, PRESIDENT, QATAR INTERNATIONAL COURT AND DISPUTE RESOLUTION CENTRE
Preface xxi

International Commercial Courts: The Future of Transnational Adjudication – An Introduction 1
GEORGIOS DIMITROPOULOS AND STAVROS BREKOULAKIS

PART I **A Contextual Perspective to International Commercial Courts** 27

1 The Role of International Commercial Courts in Commercial Dispute Resolution 29
CHRISTOPHER GROUT AND SIR WILLIAM BLAIR

2 International Commercial Courts: Possible Problematic Social Externalities of a Dispute Resolution Product with Good Market Potential 52
THOMAS SCHULTZ AND CLÉMENT BACHMANN

3 Transnational Adjudication and the Court of Justice of the European Union 73
CHRISTOPHER VAJDA

4 International Commercial Courts: Lessons from International Criminal Tribunals 89
ILIAS BANTEKAS

PART II **Jurisdiction, Applicable Law and Enforcement of Judgments** 113

5 A Comparative Perspective on International Commercial Courts: Jurisdiction, Applicable Law and Enforcement of Judgments 115
JANET WALKER

6 Jurisdiction and Choice of Court Clauses in Favour of International Commercial Courts 158
EVA LEIN

7 The Battle for Jurisdiction through Jurisdictional Requirements: Comparing the Commercial Court of England and Wales, the Singapore International Commercial Court and the Chinese International Commercial Court 176
MAN YIP

8 Harmonization of Commercial Law Based on Common Law: The Role of International Commercial Courts 201
MATEJA DUROVIC AND FRANCISZEK LECH

9 Applicable Laws in the International Commercial Courts of the Gulf 228
FARIS ELIAS NASRALLAH

PART III **Procedure, Function, Organization** 249

10 The Design of International Commercial Courts: From Organizational Hybridity to Functional Interoperability 251
GEORGIOS DIMITROPOULOS

11 Internationalizing Domestic Courts in Europe: A Comparative Analysis on Procedure, Function, Organization 278
MARIEKE WITKAMP

12 The Legitimacy and Ethics of International Commercial Court Judges 299
CATHERINE A. ROGERS

13 Counsel Ethics in Transnational Lawyering: The Case of International Commercial Courts 315
ZACHARY R. CALO

14 The Use of Technology at International Commercial Courts 335
PIETRO ORTOLANI

PART IV **The Interplay between International Commercial Courts and Other Dispute Resolution Fora** 361

15 The Interplay between International Commercial Courts and Ordinary Courts 363
JULIAN BAILEY

16 Private Autonomy in International Commercial Dispute Resolution: International Commercial Arbitration and International Commercial Courts 388
MICHAEL PATCHETT-JOYCE

17 Procedure before International Commercial Courts and Ordinary Courts: A Comparative Perspective 421
GEORGIA ANTONOPOULOU

PART V **International Commercial Courts and Global Governance** 445

18 Hybridity in International Adjudication: How International Are International Commercial Courts? 447
SALVATORE CASERTA AND MIKAEL RASK MADSEN

19 China International Commercial Court: Architecture, Pitfalls and Promises 468
JULIEN CHAISSE AND XU QIAN

20 The Emergence of International Commercial Courts and Dispute Resolution Centres in Frontier Markets: A Perspective from Kazakhstan 489
THE RT. HON. THE LORD WOOLF CH AND CHRISTOPHER CAMPBELL-HOLT

21 Brexit and the Competition of Dispute Resolution Fora in Europe: Whither the Rush to English Courts Post Withdrawal? 501
GEERT VAN CALSTER

22 International Commercial Courts, Dispute Resolution and the Rule of Law 515
SUSAN L. KARAMANIAN

Index 536

CONTRIBUTORS

GEORGIA ANTONOPOULOU is Lecturer in International Commercial Dispute Resolution at Birmingham Law School and a PhD candidate at Erasmus School of Law, Rotterdam.

ILIAS BANTEKAS is Professor of Transnational Law at Hamad Bin Khalifa University and Adjunct Professor at Georgetown University. He has published *International Human Rights Law and Practice* (3rd ed. Cambridge University Press 2020, with L. Oette), *Introduction to International Arbitration* (Cambridge University Press 2015) and *Islamic Contract Law* (Oxford University Press 2022, with J. Ercanbrack et al.).

CLÉMENT BACHMANN is a postdoctoral researcher at the Geneva Centre for International Dispute Settlement (CIDS). He holds a PhD from the University of Geneva (where he wrote a thesis on the legitimation of international arbitration) and is admitted to practise law in Switzerland.

JULIAN BAILEY is a solicitor and partner at White & Case LLP, London. He is a visiting fellow at the Dickson Poon School of Law, King's College London and is Adjunct Professor of Law at Hamad Bin Khalifa University, Doha.

SIR WILLIAM BLAIR is Chairman of the QFC Regulatory Tribunal and Judge of the Qatar International Court. He is also Chair of the Bank of England's Enforcement Decision Making Committee and Professor of Financial Law and Ethics at Queen Mary University of London.

STAVROS BREKOULAKIS is a professor in international arbitration. His academic work includes the leading publications on *Third Parties in*

International Arbitration, Arbitrability, ICCA-Queen Mary Report on Third Party Funding and numerous publications in leading legal journals and reviews. He is the editor-in-chief of CIArb's *International Journal of Arbitration, Mediation and Dispute Management*, general editor of *Journal of International Dispute Settlement* and co-editor of Kluwer's *International Arbitration Law Library* series.

ZACHARY R. CALO is Professor of Law at Hamad Bin Khalifa University and Professor of Law (Adj.) at the University of Notre Dame Australia. A member of McNair Chambers in Doha, Calo also serves on multiple international sports arbitration tribunals and on the Ethics Committee of the International Mediation Institute.

CHRISTOPHER CAMPBELL-HOLT is the registrar and chief executive of the AIFC Court and IAC in the Republic of Kazakhstan.

SALVATORE CASERTA is an Assistant professor of sociology of law and international law at iCourts, the Centre of Excellence for International Courts of the Faculty of Law of the University of Copenhagen.

JULIEN CHAISSE is Professor of Law at the School of Law, City University of Hong Kong, and President, Asia Pacific FDI Network.

GEORGIOS DIMITROPOULOS is Associate Professor of Law and Associate Dean for Academic Affairs at Hamad Bin Khalifa University College of Law.

MATEJA DUROVIC (LLM CANTAB., LLM AND PHD EUI) is a Reader in contract and commercial law and co-director of the Centre for Technology, Ethics, Law and Society at Dickson Poon School of Law, King's College London, UK.

CHRISTOPHER GROUT is Registrar of the Qatar International Court and Dispute Resolution Centre. He is a barrister and deputy district judge in England and Wales as well as a fellow of the Centre for Law and Religion at Cardiff University.

SUSAN L. KARAMANIAN is Dean of the College of Law, Hamad Bin Khalifa University.

FRANCISZEK LECH is a BCL candidate at St Catherine's College, University of Oxford. He holds an LLB from King's College London, where he graduated as a Dickson Poon Scholar for Excellence in Studies. He was previously a research Assistant and a KURF fellow at King's College London.

EVA LEIN is a professor of comparative and private international law at the University of Lausanne and the director of the Comparative Law Centre at the British Institute of International and Comparative Law in London.

MIKAEL RASK MADSEN is a professor of law and the director of iCourts, Centre of Excellence for International Courts, University of Copenhagen.

FARIS ELIAS NASRALLAH is a solicitor of the Senior Courts of England & Wales and specializes in international arbitration with expert knowledge of Middle Eastern laws. He studied at SOAS and the University of Cambridge and in 2019 founded the International Arbitration Working Group within the Max Planck Law network.

PIETRO ORTOLANI is a full professor of digital conflict resolution at Radboud University, the Netherlands.

MICHAEL PATCHETT-JOYCE FCIARB is a barrister, arbitrator and mediator. He practises at 36 Commercial, Grays Inn, London, and will become Head of 36 Commercial in 2022.

XU QIAN is an Associate professor and 'Hundred Talents Program Fellow' at Zhejiang University, Guanghua Law School.

CATHERINE ROGERS is a professor of law at Bocconi University in Milan, with a joint appointment at Queen Mary, University of London. Her teaching and scholarship focus on the intersection of international arbitration, legal ethics and markets for professional services. Catherine was a reporter for the American Law Institute's *Restatement of the U.S. Law of International Commercial and Investor-State Arbitration*, and a co-chair of the ICCA-Queen Mary Task Force on Third-Party Funding in International Arbitration (with William W. Park and

Stavros Brekoulakis). Catherine is the founder of Arbitrator Intelligence, a legal tech startup that seeks to revolutionalize arbitrator selection while promoting transparency, accountability and diversity in arbitrator appointments.

THOMAS SCHULTZ is a professor of law at King's College London, a professor of international arbitration at the University of Geneva, a visiting professor of international law at the Graduate Institute of International and Development Studies, and the editor-in-chief of the *Journal of International Dispute Settlement.* He is the (co-)author of five books.

LORD THOMAS of Cwmgiedd was Judge of the Commercial Court and subsequently Lord Chief Justice of England and Wales. He is President, Qatar International Court, Chairman of the Steering Group of the Standing International Forum of Commercial Courts, an international arbitrator, Chancellor of Aberystwyth University and an Honorary Fellow of HBKU College of Law.

CHRISTOPHER VAJDA QC was the British judge at the Court of Justice of the European Union between 2012 and 2020 (until Brexit). He has now returned to Monckton Chambers, London, to act as arbitrator and to give advice in international disputes. He is a visiting professor of law at King's College, London.

GEERT VAN CALSTER is a member of the Belgian Bar, focussing on international litigation, and a full professor at KU Leuven. His blog at www.gavclaw.com is a well-known portal for developments in European and United Kingdom conflict of laws.

JANET WALKER (CD, BA (HONS), MA, JD, DPHIL (OXON), FCIARB) is Distinguished Research Professor and past Associate Dean at Osgoode Hall Law School, and a chartered arbitrator. She authors *Canadian Conflict of Laws,* the most cited private law work in Canadian courts; and she is the author and general editor of works on civil litigation, complex litigation, comparative procedure and arbitration. She is the chair of the ICC Canada arbitration committee and a member of the scientific advisory board of the Max Planck Institute Luxembourg.

MARIEKE WITKAMP serves as a commercial judge at the court of Rotterdam in the Netherlands. She is qualified in Dutch and Texas law and has more than fifteen years of international legal experience in the Netherlands, Qatar and the United States.

THE RT. HON. THE LORD WOOLF CH is former Lord Chief Justice of England and Wales and former Chief Justice of the AIFC Court in the Republic of Kazakhstan.

MAN YIP is an Associate professor and the director of the Centre for Commercial Law in Asia at Singapore Management University, Yong Pung How School of Law.

FOREWORD

LORD THOMAS OF CWMGIEDD, FORMER LORD CHIEF JUSTICE OF ENGLAND AND WALES, PRESIDENT, QATAR INTERNATIONAL COURT AND DISPUTE RESOLUTION CENTRE

Merchants, financiers and other commercial people have always understood the need for the rule of law exemplified by courts or tribunals that adjudicate fairly and impartially disputes that arise in international trade, finance and investment. Sometimes the ordinary courts can provide this as they did in England under Lord Mansfield when he laid the foundations of modern commercial law. At the end of the nineteenth century, however, discontent with the ordinary courts in the UK, as reflected in the novels of Charles Dickens, occasioned serious consideration of following the continental European model of a *Tribunal de Commerce.* What found favour, however, was the London Commercial Court established as a specialist court by the judiciary. The judges of that court provided speedy and effective justice, worked in harmony with arbitration and continued the development of modern commercial law. Over the following century it became a model others have sought to emulate, though many preferred to resolve their disputes through arbitration and other forms of alternative dispute resolution.

The close of the twentieth century and the first two decades of this century have seen the rapid evolution of international commercial courts in each continent. Governments, urged on by the World Bank, caught up with businesses and finance and realized that without impartial and swift adjudication, it would be difficult to attract investment. The result has been the establishment of courts which provide a cost-effective and speedy means of dispute resolution before a specialist judge with an understanding of trade, finance and commerce. Not only does this provide fair and just decisions, but at the same time it continues the transparent development of the law through open hearings and judgments widely accessible on the Internet.

Although international commercial courts have begun to work closely together and share good practice, particularly since the establishment of the Standing International Forum of Commercial Courts in 2017, what was needed was a work that provided not only a clear description of the developments, but also an analysis of the courts. This book has the aim of explaining why these courts have developed and of providing a clear and systematic analysis of the courts.

That objective is most successfully achieved, in large part because of this book's very wide scope and comprehensive scholarship. Its detailed consideration of courts from those established in Special Economic Zones (largely in the Gulf) to the international commercial courts in China, Singapore, Kazakhstan, France, Germany and the Netherlands is characterized by deep and careful analysis. The willingness to tackle fundamental issues is very welcome. For example, important questions that can arise in the relationship between international commercial courts and the municipal courts of a state are studied and answered. The contribution the courts make to upholding the rule of law is carefully scrutinized. The way in which the courts can harmonize and develop the law is explored, thus addressing a significant lacuna occasioned by the widespread use of arbitration and the consequent need to respect the confidentiality of the decisions made. Another valuable topic is the study of how the courts can give effect to balancing the requirements of public interest in the resolution of international commercial disputes whilst affording protection against the effects of the over-privatization of justice in such disputes. Valuable lessons from the experience of criminal courts are brought together in an insightful chapter as in another chapter is the jurisprudence of the Court of Justice of the European Union's attitude to transnational adjudication.

Practitioners concerned with the day-to-day issues of litigation will find a clear and useful explanation of the issues of jurisdiction, choice of law and enforcement. These important topics are considered in relation to each of the main international commercial courts together with a clear exposition of the procedural rules. It is commendable that a chapter is devoted to the ethics of advocates, for as Chief Justice Sundaresh Menon of Singapore set out in his seminal James P. White lecture in November 2018, this is a central issue for transnational litigation. The use of technology is thoroughly examined; it was the leadership shown by international commercial courts in deploying technology during the pandemic which began in early 2020 that demonstrated how courts could be operated effectively and valuable lessons learnt for the future provision of access to justice.

In short, we should all be grateful to the editors for bringing together so many valuable contributions. These make the book indispensable not only to those who practise in international commercial litigation, but also to those who wish to understand the role of the courts in strengthening the rule of law in international commerce, trade and finance and the contribution the courts can make to a fairer and more prosperous world order.

PREFACE

This edited volume arose out of a joint research initiative of the editors and the organization of a major conference on 'The Promise of Hybrid Dispute Resolution Fora' which was held at Hamad Bin Khalifa University in November 2018. We are grateful to the speakers at our conference many of whom have also contributed to this volume.

The volume is the first comprehensive study of the new dispute resolution institution of International Commercial Courts. With a view to capturing all internal and external aspects of the organization and functions of International Commercial Courts, the volume is divided into five parts. Part I offers 'A Contextual Perspective to International Commercial Courts'. While Part II discusses 'Jurisdiction, Applicable Law and Enforcement of Judgments', Part III deals with 'Procedure, Function, Organization'. Part IV addresses 'The Interplay between International Commercial Courts and Other Dispute Resolution Fora'. Part V concludes with a broader perspective on 'International Commercial Courts and Global Governance'.

We are also thankful to a number of institutions, including our home academic institutions, which supported the original conference through grants and otherwise. We are particularly grateful to the Qatar National Research Fund (QNRF) Conference and Workshop Sponsorship Program (CWSP) for the generous financial support. Almas Lokhandwala enthusiastically and tirelessly supported our conference and book project from its first day until almost its completion. Finally, we are indebted to the whole editorial team of Cambridge University Press for their continuous support and for bringing our book to a timely completion.

Stavros Brekoulakis,
London, UK
Georgios Dimitropoulos
Doha, Qatar
December 2021

International Commercial Courts: The Future of Transnational Adjudication – An Introduction

GEORGIOS DIMITROPOULOS AND STAVROS BREKOULAKIS*

Over the past fifteen years, international adjudication has become one of the most exciting research areas in international law.[1] Before the development of international adjudication as a distinct field, few studies had systematically examined the role and importance of international courts and tribunals. The lack of attention to international adjudication was mainly due to the original design of the international legal order. While the World Court was supposed to be the epicentre of the international legal order in the wake of the two world wars, its jurisdictional set-up as well as the historical development of public international law since its inception did not allow it to play this role.[2]

Indeed, the original model of the 'international court' developed in the twentieth century intended that only disputes between States based on

* The authors would like to thank Sir Rupert Jackson for wonderful comments and Almas Lokhandwala for excellent research assistance. All errors remain ours.

1 This field is also referred to as international dispute settlement; see generally Chester Brown, *A Common Law of International Adjudication* (Oxford University Press 2007); Cesare P. R. Romano, Karen J. Alter and Yuval Shany (eds.), *The Oxford Handbook of International Adjudication* (Oxford University Press 2015); William A. Schabas and Shannonbrooke Murphy (eds.), *Research Handbook on International Courts and Tribunals* (Edward Elgar 2017); Hélène Ruiz Fabri (ed.), Max Planck Encyclopedia of International Procedural Law (MPEiPro) (launched 5 September 2019).

2 See generally Peter Tomka, 'The Role of the International Court of Justice in World Affairs: Successes and Challenges with Special Reference to OAS Member States and the Pact of Bogotá', Statement by H. E. Judge Peter Tomka, President of the International Court of Justice, at the Organization of American States, Lecture Series of the Americas (Thursday, 10 April 2014) www.icj-cij.org/files/press-releases/4/18324.pdf, accessed 1 December 2019.

public international law were to be adjudicated before them. This model did not hold true in practice for very long. International courts had to start adapting to the realities of a globalizing world that was increasingly growing out of traditional divides in international law, including divides between public and private and international and domestic. The move away from divides is reflected in the jurisdiction, the applicable law and the organization of more recently established international courts. International courts started relying increasingly on paradigms from domestic law as well as international arbitration to accommodate a rapidly diversifying and globalizing world.

After World War II, the majority of States engaged in an unprecedented enterprise of multinational law and institution-building which has resulted in a significant body of global regulatory law. Many scholars have argued that this global regulatory law should be viewed as global administrative law. Such a perspective would entail that all global actors, including States, be subject to administrative review against fundamental administrative standards such as transparency, participation, reason giving and accountability.[3] The task of administrative review has been entrusted to a number of international courts and tribunals, including investment treaty tribunals.

These international courts and tribunals are markedly different from old-style international courts.[4] Today, a wide range of new-style international courts and tribunals have emerged with far-reaching powers, including the power to review the validity of administrative decisions, and operate mostly within specialized international regimes.[5] These international courts and tribunals are used not only by States, but – crucially – by a wide range of non-state actors too, including international commissions, institutional actors and private litigants.[6] The new-style international courts and tribunals can significantly influence State behaviour through their pronouncements on international law and by specifying remedies when States violate that law.

At the same time, in a world where cross-border transactions are the order of the day, cases involving such transactions among exclusively

[3] See Benedict Kingsbury, Nico Krisch and Richard Stewart, 'The Emergence of Global Administrative Law' (2005) 68 Law and Contemporary Problems 15.

[4] On a taxonomy of international courts and tribunals, see Cesare P. R. Romano, 'A Taxonomy of International Rule of Law Institutions' (2011) 2 Journal of International Dispute Settlement 241.

[5] On the notion of the international regime see Stephen D. Krasner, *International Regimes* (Cornell University Press 1983).

[6] See Karen J. Alter, *The New Terrain of International Law: International Courts in International Politics* (Princeton University Press 2014).

private parties cannot find recourse to international courts. Instead, international commercial arbitration has become the default jurisdiction for the resolution of disputes in cross-border transactions.[7]

International law has tried to fill this gap with the development and proliferation of international standards for domestic courts, as well as international organizations working in the field of domestic judiciary reform.[8] Still, these initiatives were not in the position to cover the lack of courts addressing cases arising out of complex scenarios of cross-border trade transactions. This gap in international adjudication has ultimately been filled by domestic courts. International commercial courts (ICommCs) are a new species in the field of international – and domestic – dispute settlement.[9] They are domestic courts, on one hand, but are different from the ordinary courts of the jurisdiction from which they stem – a 'difference' characterized by their 'international' character. They are 'international courts', on the other hand, as their composition and the cases before them have an international – that is, cross-border – dimension.[10] International commercial courts are a novel addition to the

[7] See, for example, Walter Mattli, 'Private Justice in a Global Economy: From Litigation to Arbitration' (2001) 55 International Organization 919.

[8] See section 2 of this chapter.

[9] See Denise Huiwen Wong, 'The Rise of the International Commercial Court: What Is It and Will It Work?' (2014) 33 Civil Justice Quarterly 205; Zain Al Abdin Sharar and Mohammed Al Khulaifi, 'The Courts in Qatar Financial Centre and Dubai International Financial Centre: A Comparative Analysis', 46 Hong Kong LJ 529 (2016); Firew Tiba, 'The Emergence of Hybrid International Commercial Courts and the Future of Cross Border Commercial Dispute Resolution in Asia', (2016–17) 14 Loy U Chi Int'l L Rev 31; Sundaresh Menon, 'International Commercial Courts: Towards a Transnational System of Dispute Resolution' (*DIFC Courts Lecture Series* 2015) www.supremecourt.gov.sg/docs/default-source/default-document-library/media-room/opening-lecture–difc-lecture-series-2015.pdf, accessed 1 December 2019; Xandra Kramer and John Sorabji, 'Editorial: International Business Courts in Europe and Beyond: A Global Competition for Justice?' (Special Issue 2019) *Erasmus Law Review*; Sir William Blair, 'The New Litigation Landscape: International Commercial Courts and Procedural Innovations', International Journal of Procedural Law 212 (2019); Pamela Bookman, 'The Adjudication Business' (2020) 45 Yale Journal of International Law 227; Matthew S. Erie, 'The New Legal Hubs: The Emergent Landscape of International Commercial Dispute Resolution' (2020) 60 Virginia Journal of International Law 228.

[10] The main focus of this introduction as well as the whole edited volume is on the new ICommCs established in the past fifteen years as fora distinct from the ordinary courts of the host jurisdictions. These are courts that are domestic but have a comparative advantage in adjudicating private and commercial cross-border disputes. The prime example is the Commercial Court in London, now part of the Business and Property Courts, which are part of the High Court of Justice in London. The Commercial Court has functioned as a domestic court ever since its inception more than a century ago, dealing with all types of disputes arising in the City of London. But the Commercial Court in London has also

field and practice of 'transnational adjudication'.[11] In this new era of transnational adjudication, ICommCs globalize dispute resolution from the bottom in ways further explained later.[12]

The first institutions of this new era of transnational adjudication are the Dubai International Financial Centre (DIFC) Courts, established in 2004.[13] The Qatar International Court and Dispute Resolution Centre (QICDRC) was established in 2009.[14] The Abu Dhabi Global Market (ADGM) Courts followed in 2015.[15] The idea of ICommCs also migrated to Southeast Asia, where the Singapore International Commercial Court (SICC) was also set up in 2015.[16] The Astana International Financial Centre (AIFC) Court is the first ICommC in Central Asia[17] – a region which is trying to keep up with developments in other parts of the continent. China, a country with a long history of international courts of a similar type, followed in 2018.[18] The much-anticipated international commercial courts of the Supreme People's Court of China operate now as the China International Commercial Court (CICC).[19]

A more recent trend emerged in Member States of the European Union (EU) with the creation of similar courts, or chambers within

become an international commercial court – with a far heavier caseload than any of the 'new breed' of ICommCs. Another example is the Hong Kong Court of Final Appeal that has a roster of Permanent and Non-permanent Judges, differentiating between Hong Kong and Overseas Non-permanent Judges; see www.hkcfa.hk/en/about/who/judges/npjs/index.html, accessed 1 November 2020.

[11] We thus consider ICommCs as a new step in the development of international and transnational adjudication, not as public international law courts. For a discussion on what is to be regarded as international adjudication see Cesare P. R. Romano, Karen J. Alter, and Yuval Shany, Mapping International Adjudicative Bodies, the Issues, and Players, in Cesare P. R. Romano, Karen J. Alter and Yuval Shany (eds.), *The Oxford Handbook of International Adjudication* (Oxford University Press 2014).

[12] See also Georgios Dimitropoulos, International Commercial Courts in the 'Modern Law of Nature': Adjudicatory Unilateralism in Special Economic Zones (2021) 24 Journal of International Economic Law 361.

[13] See Dubai Law No. 12 of 2004: The Law of the Judicial Authority at Dubai International Financial Centre, as amended.

[14] See Article 8(3) of the QFC Law – Law No. 7 of 2005 – as amended by Law No. 2 of 2009 (Amending Certain Provisions of the Qatar Financial Centre (QFC)).

[15] See Abu Dhabi Law No. 4 of 2013 concerning Abu Dhabi Global Market, as amended.

[16] See Section 18A, Supreme Court of Judicature Act (Cap 322).

[17] Constitutional Statute no. No 438-V ZRK of 7 December 2015: Astana Financial Services Authority (AFSA); AIFC Court; AIFC International Arbitration Centre (IAC).

[18] See Pär Kristoffer Cassel, *Grounds of Judgment: Extraterritoriality and Imperial Power in Nineteenth-Century China and Japan* (Oxford University Press 2012).

[19] See 'Opinion concerning the Establishment of the Belt and Road International Commercial Dispute Resolution Mechanism and Institutions' (Updated 27 June 2018), http://cicc.court.gov.cn/html/1/219/208/210/819.html, accessed 1 November 2020.

existing court structures.[20] There are now ICommCs in three different Members States of the EU: Germany, France and the Netherlands. The German state of Hesse in January 2018 introduced a special chamber for commercial law cases within the district court of Frankfurt am Main.[21] In February 2018, an agreement was signed between the French justice minister and the head of the Paris Bar Association at the Paris Court of Appeal for the purpose of creating an international chamber within the Paris Court of Appeal.[22] In March 2018, the Netherlands Commercial Court Bill was passed in the Netherlands, amending the Dutch Code of Civil Procedure to provide for the use of English as the language of proceedings within the Netherlands Commercial Court.[23] A failed attempt to set up such a court took place in Belgium, where the Brussels International Business Court (BIBC) never came to fruition, after it had been announced by the Belgian government at the end of 2017.[24]

International commercial courts coexist with ordinary domestic courts as the natural forum of general jurisdiction for all domestic matters. They moreover coexist with arbitration as the private system of adjudication of disputes of a mostly commercial nature. They present themselves as a new forum for the resolution of cross-border disputes in the global competition to attract cases to their jurisdictions. In comparison to previous phases of judicial globalization, domestic jurisdictions and domestic courts are not consumers of international rules but are becoming the rule-setters themselves.

The introduction to this edited book on *International Commercial Courts: The Future of Transnational Adjudication* discusses the proliferation and main features of ICommCs. Section 1 of this introduction explains that the 'pure' international court model has already

[20] See Xandra Kramer, 'The Domino Effect of International Commercial Courts in Europe – Who's Next?' (Conflict of Laws, 20 February 2018) http://conflictoflaws.net/2018/the-domino-effect-of-international-commercial-courts-in-europe-whos-next, accessed 1 November 2020.

[21] See https://ordentliche-gerichtsbarkeit.hessen.de/ordentliche-gerichte/lgb-frankfurt-am-main/lg-frankfurt-am-main/chamber-international, accessed 1 November 2020.

[22] See 'Preconisations Sur la Mise en Place à Paris de Chambres Specialisees pour le traitement du contentieux international des affaires' (3 May 2017), www.justice.gouv.fr/publication/Rapport_chambres_internationales.pdf, accessed 1 November 2020.

[23] See https://netherlands-commercial-court.com, accessed 1 November 2020.

[24] See Chambre des Représentants de Belgique, Projet de loi instaurant la Brussels International Business Court (15 May 2018) www.dekamer.be/flwb/pdf/54/3072/54K3072001.pdf, accessed 1 November 2020.

experienced a great variegation with elements of domestic law as well as arbitration lending several features to international courts. Section 2 presents past efforts to internationalize domestic courts. It is claimed that this trend was part of a larger effort of top-down globalization of domestic judicial systems so that they would facilitate cross-border transactions, and more broadly, a globalized world where goods, capital and companies cross borders more conveniently. Section 3 presents the creation of the new institution of ICommCs that started to proliferate in order to cover the previously existing gap in a world of globalized transactions but without courts adapted to the needs of resolving disputes arising out of these transactions. Section 4 provides an outline of the present edited volume.

0.1 Judicial Globalization and the Proliferation of International Courts

The last quarter of the twentieth century saw a 'juridification' process in the international legal order as legal rules emerged for the regulation of various fields at the level of international governance.[25] One of the most recent and most important phases in this process was that of 'judicial globalization' or 'international judicialization'.[26] Judicial globalization means the creation and proliferation of judicial and quasi-judicial bodies for the adjudication of international disputes.[27] Cesare Romano identifies an international judicial body as one that is:[28] (i) a permanent institution; (ii) established by an international legal instrument, usually a treaty; (iii)

[25] See, for example, Bernhard Zangl and Michael Zürn (eds.), *Verrechtlichung: Baustein Für Global Governance?* (Dietz 2004).

[26] See, for example, Alec Stone Sweet, 'Judicialization and the Construction of Governance' (1999) 32 *Comparative Political Studies* 147; Laurence R. Helfer and Anne-Marie Slaughter, 'Toward a Theory of Effective Supranational Adjudication' (1997) 107 Yale Law Journal 273; Robert O. Keohane, Andrew Moravcsik and Anne-Marie Slaughter, 'Legalized Dispute Resolution: Interstate and Transnational' (2000) 54 International Organization 457; Anne-Marie Slaughter, 'A Global Community of Courts' (2003) 44 Harvard International Law Journal 191; Jenny S. Martinez, 'Toward an International Judicial System' (2003) 56 Stanford Law Review 429; Alter (n. 6).

[27] Accordingly, most international courts were created in the last quarter of the twentieth century; see Christian Tomuschat, 'International Courts and Tribunals', *Max Planck Encyclopedia of Public International Law [MPEPIL]* (Article last updated: February 2011) para. 7 (hereinafter: Tomuschat, International Courts and Tribunals).

[28] Cesare P. R. Romano, 'The Proliferation of International Judicial Bodies: The Pieces of the Puzzle' (1999) 31 N.Y.U. J. Int'L L & Pol 709; see also Tomuschat, International Courts and Tribunals.

relying on international law to resolve cases; (iv) following set rules of procedure; and (v) issuing legally binding judgments. In addition, international courts very often form part of an international organization.[29] The prime example of an international court is the International Court of Justice (ICJ). Apart from permanent bodies, non-permanent bodies have become very common in international law as well, and are usually referred to as arbitral tribunals. These bodies are ad hoc, reflecting the specific configuration of the litigant parties in a specific dispute;[30] they rely on party autonomy more than the permanent international courts do, as the parties have the power to influence the rules of proceedings as well as the nomination of the adjudicators who sit on the tribunals.

The original model of an international court as developed in the post-World War II international legal landscape has undergone many organizational, procedural and other changes. International courts now take a plethora of types, forms and shapes. In traditional international law, international disputes were considered disputes between States, and international courts only admitted cases between States. The *ratione personae* jurisdiction of some international courts has expanded to claims brought forward by individuals.[31] Moreover, international courts were developed as bodies that *ratione iuris* apply international law as defined in Article 38 ICJ Statute, or as specified in the founding documents of the relevant international courts.[32] Several exceptions apply nowadays even to this rule – for example, the hybrid panels in East Timor, Kosovo, Sierra Leone and Cambodia, as well as Bosnia and Herzegovina, apply a mixture of national and international law.[33] Also at the level of procedure, parties are sometimes allowed to modify the rules of the court subject to their agreement.[34] Organizationally, judges appointed to international courts are as a rule 'international judges'. Hybrid criminal courts employ a mixture of national and international staff.

Beyond the 'pure' model of the international court, as reflected in the organization and jurisdiction of the ICJ, other types of international courts have emerged. Paradigms from domestic law as well as arbitration

[29] Tomuschat, International Courts and Tribunals, para. 7.

[30] See ibid., at para. 1.

[31] Ibid., at para. 3 and 56; Karen J. Alter, 'Private Litigants and the New International Courts' (2006) 39 Comparative Political Studies 22.

[32] Tomuschat, International Courts and Tribunals, para. 4.

[33] Laura A. Dickinson, 'The Relationship between Hybrid Courts and International Courts: The Case of Kosovo' (2003) 37 New England Law Review 1059.

[34] See Article 48 of the Rules of the Tribunal of the International Tribunal for the Law of the Sea (ITLOS).

have started filtering into the traditional model of international court adjudication. Accordingly, it is difficult to speak of just one model of international courts.

The emergence of these new-style tribunals has arguably resulted from a different perspective of international law and has deeply affected the concept of national sovereignty: from the traditional perspective that States cannot be obliged to comply, except to the extent States consent to such compliance, to an international rule of law perspective which assumes that States are not above international law and that their acts, including legislative and governmental acts, ought to be reviewed for compliance with international law. Such a perspective of international and global administrative law clashes with traditional concepts of national sovereignty and the principle of democratic legitimacy. According to traditional concepts of democracy, based on theories of social (fictional) contracts, all powers of a State stem from its citizens, who collectively are the only actor that can review State behaviour through national courts (which typically rule in the name of the people) or through national elections. In the global administrative law world, States do not have unfettered power and their behaviour must comply with fundamental principles of international and global administrative law. This proposition may seem to curtail national sovereignty, but it may also reflect the realization that in today's strongly interdependent world, national isolation is not a viable political choice.[35]

0.2 Internationalization of Domestic Dispute Resolution

Apart from the multiplication and the qualitative change of courts within international regimes, there has been a second, less noticed wave of judicial globalization: the development and proliferation of international standards for the organization and function of domestic courts, as well as sometimes specialized international bodies dealing with the organization and operation of domestic courts. This trend has increased exponentially since the 2000s in an effort from international organizations to encourage reforms in domestic court systems. This reform impetus was initiated by an economic condition: while economic transactions had reached an unprecedented volume, institutions adjudicating on disputes arising out of these transactions largely remained domestic.

[35] Alter (n. 6), at 339.

Since the 1980s, international – mostly economic – organizations have become interested in the performance of the justice sector and have promoted judicial reforms in different countries. The World Bank, the International Monetary Fund (IMF) and the Organisation for Economic Co-operation and Development (OECD) are among the most active international organizations in this area. The World Bank, for example, measures the quality of judicial processes and the performance of national justice systems as part of its *Doing Business* indicators.[36] It moreover operates at three different levels in the field of internationalization of dispute resolution:[37] financing stand-alone justice reform projects – that is, projects dedicated exclusively to justice reform; justice projects conducted as part of broader lending projects; financing analytical and advisory work in relation to anti-corruption agencies, ombudsperson offices, legal aid and legal empowerment and human rights protection. To streamline its justice sector activities, the World Bank has developed an overall strategy for justice reform.[38] In addition, the IMF also introduces judicial branch reforms as part of its lending activity; such reforms have also featured very prominently in the context of the more recent activities of the IMF in Europe.[39]

Moreover, a number of non-governmental transnational networks of courts, judges and other judicial institutions have been established with a view to developing standards regarding the independence, accountability and efficiency of national judiciaries. A prominent example is the International Consortium for Court Excellence. The Consortium, established in 2008, is a network of national, regional and international organizations, including supreme courts, district courts, organizations of courts and judges and international organizations like the World Bank. The Consortium has developed the 'International Framework for Court Excellence', including the 'Global Measures of Court Performance', and implementation guidance providing for a voluntary

[36] See World Bank, *Doing Business: Comparing Business Regulation in 190 Economies* (World Bank 2020) https://openknowledge.worldbank.org/bitstream/handle/10986/32436/9781464814402.pdf.

[37] World Bank, *New Directions in Justice Reform: A Companion Piece to the Updated Strategy and Implementation Plan on Strengthening Governance, Tackling Corruption* (World Bank 2012), 3–5.

[38] World Bank (n. 32).

[39] See, for example, Armin von Bogdandy and Michael Ioannidis, 'Systemic Deficiency in the Rule of Law: What It Is, What Has Been Done, What Can Be Done' (2014) 51 CHLR 59.

quality management system that can help courts improve their performance by assessing the quality of justice and court administration.[40]

Commercial courts have created a similar network. On the initiative of Lord Thomas of Cwmgiedd, former Lord Chief Justice of England and Wales and current President of the QICDRC, the Standing International Forum of Commercial Courts (SIFoCC) was formed.[41] The SIFoCC organizes meetings of judiciaries and officials of commercial courts, and it has undertaken a variety of initiatives. The most important of these initiatives is the Multilateral Memorandum on the Enforcement of Commercial Judgments for Money launched in June 2019.[42] International commercial courts from all over the world were some of the first commercial courts to join this network.

0.3 Proliferation of International Commercial Courts

In a world where cross-border transactions are the order of the day, parties until recently could not find recourse to international courts for cases involving such transactions among exclusively private parties.[43] International arbitration instead assumed the role of default jurisdiction for the resolution of disputes of cross-border transactions. The identified gap in international adjudication has given rise to a new species of courts: international commercial courts. On one side, ICommCs are domestic courts as they are creatures of domestic legal orders – but they are different from the ordinary courts of the jurisdiction in which they are situated. On the other side, they are international courts, as their composition as well as the cases they decide have an international dimension. International commercial courts are a novel addition to the system of international dispute settlement as they present an effort to globalize the resolution of disputes in a bottom-up way.[44] Overall, they are creatures of

[40] The International Framework for Court Excellence (2nd Edition, March 2013), www.courtexcellence.com/~/media/Microsites/Files/ICCE/The%20International%20Framework%202E%202014%20V3.ashx, accessed 1 November 2020.

[41] See www.sifocc.org/about-us, accessed 1 November 2020.

[42] Standing International Forum of Commercial Courts, Multilateral Memorandum on Enforcement of Commercial Judgments for Money (June 2019), www.judiciary.uk/wp-content/uploads/2019/06/Multilateral-Memorandum-on-Enforcement.pdf, accessed 1 November 2020.

[43] Cf. also W. Laurence Craig, 'Some Trends and Developments in the Laws and Practice of International Commercial Arbitration' (2016) 50 Texas International Law Journal 699, 700.

[44] See Dimitropoulos (n. 13).

a new form of transnational adjudication that is blind to dichotomies such as domestic/international and public/private.

The following sections offer an account of the various ICommCs that have sprung up all over the world. It then proceeds to discuss the interplay between ICommCs and other potentially competitive dispute resolution fora.

0.3.1 The Global Spread of International Commercial Courts

The contemporary trend of establishing ICommCs started in 2004 in Dubai with the Dubai International Financial Centre (DIFC) Courts.[45] The DIFC Courts are based in the Dubai International Financial Centre,[46] which is one of the several Special Economic Zones (SEZs) in the Emirate of Dubai. The DIFC Courts are now incorporated into the DIFC's Dispute Resolution Authority (DRA). The DIFC Courts have a two-instance structure featuring a court of first instance (CFI) – with a small claims tribunal (SCT) and court of appeal (CA). While the jurisdiction of the DIFC Courts was originally limited to the geographical area of the DIFC dealing with zone-related disputes, Dubai Law No. 16 of 2011 expanded its jurisdiction by allowing the DIFC Courts to hear any domestic or international case and to resolve commercial disputes with the consent of all parties. DIFC Courts have jurisdiction *ratione materiae* over cases governing civil and commercial matters. The law applicable in the SEZ is the applicable law before the Courts, which largely draws on common law principles.[47] The bench has an international composition with a focus on common law judges. Accordingly, the language of proceedings is English.

The State of Qatar established the Civil and Commercial Court of the Qatar Financial Centre with Law No. 2 of 2009 – which amended Article 8(3) of the Qatar Financial Centre Law No. 7 of 2005 – in the institutional environment of the Qatar Financial Centre (QFC), an 'onshore' SEZ.[48]

[45] See generally Michael Hwang, 'Commercial Courts and International Arbitration: Competitors or Partners?' (2015) 31 Arbitration International 193; Jayanth Krishnan, *The Story of the Dubai International Financial Centre Courts: A Retrospective* (Motivate Publishing House 2018).

[46] See Dubai Law No. 9 of 2004 In respect of the Dubai International Financial Centre.

[47] See Alejandro Carballo, 'The Law of the Dubai International Financial Centre: Common Law Oasis or Mirage within the UAE?' (2007) 21 Arab Law Quarterly 91.

[48] See generally Gerald Lebovits and Delphine Miller, 'Litigating in the Qatar International Court' (2015) 28 (1) NYSBA International Law Practicum 54, https://papers.ssrn.com/sol3/papers.cfm?abstract_id=2616475, accessed 1 November 2020.

The Court began to hear cases in the same year. What is now known as the Qatar International Court (QIC)is part of the Qatar International Court and Dispute Resolution Centre (QICDRC), a renaming that took place in 2012. The Qatar International Court itself consists of the QFC Civil and Commercial Court and the QFC Regulatory Tribunal.[49] The Qatar International Court has the First Instance Circuit and the Appellate Circuit. The First Instance Circuit has jurisdiction over civil and commercial disputes arising between parties that have a connection to the QFC. In terms of applicable law, the QIC applies the law of the QFC by default, unless the parties have agreed to the application of the substantive law of a different jurisdiction.[50] Proceedings before the QIC can be held in English by default, or in Arabic.[51] The Court publicizes its decisions in English and Arabic on its website.[52]

Similar developments to those in Dubai and Qatar have more recently taken place in Abu Dhabi and the Abu Dhabi Global Market (ADGM) – an SEZ located in the Emirate of Abu Dhabi that features the ADGM Courts. The ADGM Courts were established in 2013 and have operated since 2015. They also have two instances – namely, a CFI and a CA. In terms of jurisdiction, they hear civil and commercial cases coming out of the ADGM; they moreover have jurisdiction conferred on them by any request, in writing, by the parties to have the CFI determine the claim or dispute.[53] English common law finds direct application according to the ADGM 'Application of English Law Regulations' 2015. The bench has an international composition with a focus on judges with a common law background. The main language of proceedings is English.

Moving beyond the geographical boundaries of the Gulf, the Singapore International Commercial Court (SICC) was established in 2015 as a division of the High Court of Singapore, and as part of Singapore's ongoing effort to become a leading centre for the resolution of international commercial disputes.[54] Chief Justice Sundaresh Menon's

[49] The Regulatory Tribunal has jurisdiction to hear appeals against decisions of the QFC Authority, the Regulatory Authority and other QFC institutions. Its judgments can be appealed before the Appellate Circuit of the Civil and Commercial Court; see Article 8(2) of the QFC Law.

[50] Article 11.1.2 of the QFC Civil and Commercial Court Regulations and Procedural Rules.

[51] Article 3.2 of the QFC Civil and Commercial Court Regulations and Procedural Rules.

[52] See www.qicdrc.gov.qa/the-courts/judgments, accessed 1 November 2020.

[53] Section 16(2)(e) of the ADGM Courts, Civil Evidence, Judgments, Enforcement and Judicial Appointments Regulations 2015.

[54] See generally Andrew Godwin, Ian Ramsay and Miranda Webster, 'International Commercial Courts: The Singapore Experience', 18 Melbourne Journal of

conceptualization of the SICC was inspired by the success of the English commercial court he observed during a visit in the UK in September 2012.[55] Despite being institutionally embedded in the Singapore High Court, the SICC jurisdictional rules are different as the SICC does not hear domestic cases.[56]

Being part of the High Court of Singapore makes the SICC's judgments enforceable as judgments of the Supreme Court of Singapore. Decisions of the SICC may be appealed to the CA of the Supreme Court of Singapore, while parties are allowed to contractually exclude or limit the right of appeal.[57] As opposed to the other courts presented earlier in this introduction, the SICC is not part of an SEZ; the SICC was rather created for the litigation of international disputes by a domestic court.[58] The SICC hears claims that are of an 'international and commercial nature'. International commercial disputes are governed by foreign law with only tenuous connections to Singapore. A case will also be of an international nature sufficient for the SICC to exercise jurisdiction where, even though the parties' respective businesses are situated in Singapore, the parties expressly agree that the subject matter of the claim relates to more than one State.[59] While the parties may by

International Law 219 (2017); Man Yip, 'The Resolution of Disputes before the Singapore International Commercial Court', 65 ICLQ 439 (2016) (hereinafter: Man Yip, The Resolution of Disputes); Quentin Loh, 'Keynote Address: Asia Pacific Insurance Conference 2017' (*SICC*, 18 October 2017), www.sicc.gov.sg/documents/docs/Asia_Pacific_Insurance_Conference_2017.pdf, accessed 1 November 2020; Report of the Singapore International Commercial Court Committee' (*SICC*, November 2013) www.sicc.gov.sg/documents/docs/Annex%20A%20-%20SICC%20Committee%20Report.pdf, accessed 1 December 2019 www.sicc.gov.sg/documents/docs/SingCham_Distinguished_Speaker_Series_-_The_Rule_of_Law_and_the_SICC.pdf, accessed 1 December 2019.

55 See Sundaresh Menon, 'International Courts: Towards a Transnational System of Dispute Resolution' (Opening Lecture for the DIFC Courts Lecture Series 2015, 19 January 2015), www.supremecourt.gov.sg/data/doc/ManagePage/5741/Opening%20Lecture%20-%20DIFC%20Lecture%20Series%202015.pdf.

56 See Sundaresh Menon, 'The Rule of Law and Singapore International Commercial Court' (*SICC*, 10 January 2018), www.sicc.gov.sg/documents/docs/SingCham_Distinguished_Speaker_Series_-_The_Rule_of_Law_and_the_SICC.pdf, accessed 1 November 2020, 11 (emphasis in the original).

57 Singapore International Commercial Court Practice Directions (Effective 20 July 2020), para. 139, www.supremecourt.gov.sg/docs/default-source/default-document-library/rules/singapore-international-commercial-court-practice-directions-v2.pdf, accessed 1 November 2020.

58 Man Yip, The Resolution of Disputes, at 446.

59 According to section 18D of the Supreme Court of Judicature Act, the SICC has jurisdiction to hear an action if the following conditions are satisfied: (a) the action is international and commercial in nature; (b) the action is one that the High Court may

express agreement turn an otherwise domestic claim into an international claim, they cannot by agreement turn an otherwise international claim into a domestic claim.[60] This is to streamline party autonomy towards the SICC and its jurisdiction.[61]

An organizational innovation is that the bench of the SICC comprises two groups of judges: domestic judges – namely, Singapore Supreme Court judges from both the Court of Appeal and the High Court; and 'international judges' from other jurisdictions – both common and civil law.[62] Applicable law is the law of Singapore, and English of course is the language of proceedings of the Court.

The government of Kazakhstan has been leading similar initiatives as the ones in the Gulf region by establishing the Astana International Financial Centre (AIFC) and its AIFC Court.[63] The AIFC Court was formally established in 2015, and started operating in 2018. Following the example of the DIFC Courts, it has a CFI, with a fast-track procedure for small claims, and a CA. The AIFC Court hears standard commercial and contractual disputes adjudicating exclusively all claims arising out of the AIFC and its operations, and other claims in which all parties to the dispute agree in writing to the jurisdiction of the AIFC Court. Applicable law is the AIFC law, which is essentially English common law. The bench of this court is composed as well of international judges with a common law focus. In fact, for the time being the judges are exclusively from the UK. As with the other courts, the language of proceedings is English.

While Asia set the stage for the expanding phenomenon of ICommCs, a new wave of establishment of ICommCs seems to have been set in motion by the political and economic repercussions of Brexit in the EU. These courts are not stand-alone courts per se, but rather chambers within the first and second instance ordinary courts. Since January 2018, a special

hear and try in its original civil jurisdiction; (c) the action satisfies such other conditions as the Rules of Court may prescribe.

60 Tiong Min Yeo, 'Staying Relevant: Exercise of Jurisdiction in the Age of the SICC' (Eighth Yong Pung How Professorship of Law Lecture 2015, Singapore, 13 May 2015) 7–8, http://law.smu.edu.sg/sites/default/files/law/CEBCLA/YPH-Paper-2015.pdf, accessed 1 November 2020.

61 Man Yip, The Resolution of Disputes, at 450.

62 See www.sicc.gov.sg/about-the-sicc/judges, accessed 1 November 2020.

63 See generally Paul Fisher, 'Ambitions for Astana' (Practical Law Construction Blog, 7 March 2018), http://aifc-court.kz/files/85329113713c4735/Practical%20Law%20Construction%20Blog%20-%20Ambitious%20for%20Astana.pdf, accessed 1 November 2020; Ilias Bantekas, 'The Rise of Transnational Commercial Courts: The Astana International Financial Centre Court' (2020) 33 Pace Int'l L. Rev. 1.

chamber for commercial law cases has been operating in the German state of Hesse.[64] It is based in the *Landgericht* (LG) Frankfurt am Main, the district court of Hesse. Hearings are held in English, if so agreed by parties.

A similar development is found in France with the new International Chamber at the Paris Court of Appeal. On 7 February 2018, two agreements were signed between the minister of justice and the head of the Paris Bar Association at the Paris Court of Appeal regarding the procedural rules of the Paris Commercial Court and the Paris Court of Appeals.[65] The agreements specify the exact conditions under which the already existing International Chamber of the Paris Commercial Court that was established in 1995 and the newly established International Chamber of the Paris Court of Appeals (CICAP) should operate to hear international commercial disputes. The agreements apply as of 1 March 2018. The new Chamber allows parties to plead in English, as it features English-speaking judges who may have expertise in common law systems. The written submissions and other procedural documents provided for in the French civil procedure have to be in French;[66] final judgments are also issued in French.[67] This is mostly to facilitate the cassation procedure before the Cour de cassation.

In the Netherlands, the Dutch legislator adopted the Netherlands Commercial Court Bill in March 2018 amending the Dutch Code of Civil Procedure to provide for the use of English as the language of proceedings, and making provision for the 'international commercial chamber' of the Amsterdam District Court and the Court of Appeal, commonly referred to as the Netherlands Commercial Court (NCC).[68]

[64] Jenny Gesley, 'Germany: Regional Court of Frankfurt Establishes English-Speaking Chamber for Commercial Matters' (Library of Congress, 6 December 2017), www.loc.gov/law/foreign-news/article/germany-regional-court-of-frankfurt-establishes-english-speaking-chamber-for-commercial-matters, accessed 1 December 2019.

[65] See Preconisations (n. 23); Emmanuel Gaillard, Yas Benifatemi and Chloe Vialard, 'The International Chambers of Paris Courts and Their Innovative Rules of Procedure' (Sherman & Sterling, 23 April 2018), www.shearman.com/perspectives/2018/04/paris-courts-and-their-innovative-rules-of-procedure, accessed 1 November 2020.

[66] Preconisations (n. 23), at para. 36.

[67] See ibid., at para. 51.

[68] 'CONCEPT: The NCC Rules – Rules of Procedure' (NCC), www.rechtspraak.nl/SiteCollectionDocuments/concept-procesreglement-ncc_en.pdf, accessed 1 December 2019; Annette Scholten, 'An International Netherlands Commercial Court?', 28 February 2017, https://blogs.law.nyu.edu/transnational/2017/02/an-international-netherlands-commercial-court, accessed 1 December 2019; Bob Wessels, 'International Commercial Courts: The Netherlands Is Lagging Behind' (Leiden University, 5 February 2018), http://leidenlawblog.nl/articles/international-commercial-courts-the-netherlands-is-lagging-behind, accessed 1 December 2019; Erik van den Emster, Elske van Amelsfort, Frans van Dijk, 'Restructuring

The NCC District Court and the NCC Court of Appeal started hearing cases at the beginning of 2019.

In October 2017, the Belgian Council of Ministers approved the establishment of the Brussels International Business Court (BIBC) as a first and last instance court, which was supposed to become operational by 1 January 2020, aiming to attract potential conflicts arising from Brexit as well as other international business disputes.[69] The BIBC was designed to allow parties to freely decide the law applicable between them. The language of proceedings was scheduled to be English. Based on the initial plans, this court should have been composed of a president, a vice president, professional judges and 'Judges in the BIBC' – namely, judges expert in international commercial law, university professors or lawyers. It was expected that applicable procedural rules would be not the Belgian Judicial Code, but the United Nations Commission on International Trade Law (UNCITRAL) Arbitration rules. A blow to the establishment of this Court was given by the negative opinion of 4 March 2018 by the Conseil supérieur de la Justice (CSJ) that considered the BIBC unconstitutional.[70] The plans for the BIBC have now been discontinued.

During the nineteenth National Party of the Communist Party of China, the *Opinion concerning the Establishment of the Belt and Road International Commercial Dispute Resolution Mechanism and Institutions* was released by the General Office of the Communist Party Central Committee and the General Office of the State Council.[71] Accordingly, in June 2018, the First International Commercial Court and the Second International Commercial Court of the Supreme People's Court (SPC) were respectively inaugurated in Shenzhen, Guangdong Province – one of the main economic hubs of China as well as an important economic zone for the Maritime Silk Road – and Xi'an, Shaanxi Province – a province with great practical and symbolic

of the Judicial Map: Quality through Collaboration' (NCC, June 2014) www.rechtspraak.nl/SiteCollectionDocuments/Re-structuring-of-the-Judicial-Map.pdf, accessed 1 December 2019.

[69] 'Draft Bill for Brussels International Business Court (German, French)' (Belgium Chamber of Representatives, 15 May 2018), www.dekamer.be/FLWB/PDF/54/3072/54K3072001.pdf, accessed 1 December 2019; Quentin Decleve, 'Draft Bill to Establish Brussels International Business Court' (International Litigation Blog, 22 May 2018), http://international-litigation-blog.com/draft-bill-brussels-international-business-court, accessed 1 December 2019.

[70] See Conseil supérieur de la Justice, Avis d'office – Avant-projet de loi instaurant la Brussels International Business Court (Mars 2018).

[71] See http://cicc.court.gov.cn/html/1/219/208/210/819.html, accessed 1 November 2020.

significance as the starting point of the ancient Silk Road – and started to operate officially.[72] They are referred to as the China International Commercial Court (CICC). The CICC was established by the Supreme People's Court of China (SPC) to adjudicate international commercial cases. The Fourth Civil Division of SPC is responsible for coordinating and guiding the two international commercial courts. In contrast to the majority of ICommCs, its judgments are final and binding on the parties.

In this more mature era of judicial globalization, a geographically widespread proliferation of ICommCs is taking place. However, ICommCs are not international per se in the sense of having been established by international law or with a view to resolving public international law disputes. The courts are actually domestic. But in this case, it is not international law that superimposes rules and standards on the domestic courts. Rather, ICommCs signal a new era in international adjudication, whereby judicial globalization is taking place in a bottom-up way – namely, spearheaded by individual domestic jurisdictions and without recourse to international law. National jurisdictions develop domestic institutions for the adjudication of global cross-border disputes, and produce procedural and substantive rules establishing them as global norms.

This development begs the following questions. Are ICommCs really filling a gap, or have they been established in the hope of attracting cases that would have otherwise ended up in the ordinary domestic courts? Is there any added value to these courts in comparison to the current standard way of resolving international commercial disputes – namely, international commercial arbitration? The next section takes up these questions and discusses whether ICommCs present a new court model that is here to stay.

0.3.2 *The Courts of the Future?*

International commercial courts coexist with the ordinary domestic court system, but also with other hybrid domestic and international forms of dispute resolution like international and local arbitration, mediation and conciliation. This adds further choices for parties who may select a forum to adjudicate their cases from a range of choices within a very competitive international market for the resolution of international and domestic

[72] See Matthew S. Erie, 'The China International Commercial Court: Prospects for Dispute Resolution for the "Belt and Road Initiative"', ASIL Insights (31 August 2018).

disputes, including commercial and investment arbitration as well as national and international courts.

The judiciary is the third branch of government. It thus plays a role in the traditional separation of powers that is acknowledged as the backbone of the operation of any system of government. At the same time, it is a function government offers to citizens for peaceful resolution of disputes. State justice is comprised of domestic federal and local courts that have the power to adjudicate all cases within their territorial jurisdiction.

Justice has faced a trend of privatization with the emergence of arbitration and the various types of alternative dispute resolution (ADR) such as mediation and conciliation. Arbitration was developed to deal with some of the problems of State justice, such as the excessive backlog of cases before national courts, which is actually only becoming worse in times of diminishing public budgets. Arbitration is usually viewed as more efficient and respective of party autonomy; it also usually leads to faster resolution of disputes by avoiding unnecessary litigation, and in a confidential setting that might help to preserve good relations between two individuals or business partners.[73] Additionally, arbitration accommodates cross-border dispute resolution, achieving an equivalent standard of dispute resolution across the world. In arbitration, an arbitral award is final, binding and enforceable in the same way as a court judgment is, and the proceedings are held before an impartial third party. Finally, the Convention on the Recognition and Enforcement of Foreign Arbitral Awards of 1958 (New York Convention) requires courts of contracting States to give effect to private agreements to arbitrate and to recognize and enforce arbitration awards made in other contracting States.

The main difference between arbitration and State justice is the level of formality. Arbitration proceedings are typically private, and the awards are (usually) not publicly available. Moreover, there is no appeal process for arbitral awards; arbitral awards are only reviewable by courts on a limited number of grounds.[74] In addition, arbitration does not produce precedent or case law and thus does not ensure consistency and predictability in a legal order. For these reasons, scholarship is split over whether arbitration should be preferred over State justice in a legal order, with

[73] See, for example, the Decision of High Court in London: Re AI and MT [2013] EWHC 100 (Fam).

[74] See, for example, Article V of the Convention on the Recognition and Enforcement of Foreign Arbitral Awards (New York, 1958).

some theoretical and empirical accounts favouring formal systems of dispute resolution,[75] while others favour the informal approach to dispute resolution.[76]

The new ICommCs seem to be in a position to bridge the two types of dispute resolution, positioning themselves between State/formal and private/informal justice. They are State courts, exhibiting therefore all the advantages associated with State justice; at the same time, they have an international dimension, providing them with some of the advantages of private justice. While arbitrators in international arbitration are generally appointed by the parties to the dispute, in the new fora judges are independently appointed. Moreover, as opposed to international arbitration, proceedings take place in open court, rather than confidentially. Finally, most ICommCs retain the option of appeal. Depending on the needs of the parties and the nature of the cases the new dispute resolution fora might be more suitable than ordinary domestic courts or international commercial arbitration.

International commercial courts have been designed based on accumulated experience in the design of both State and private justice systems. They are a new hybrid, cutting across public and private as well as domestic and international, and they may well become the new paradigm for domestic and international dispute resolution – a new paradigm for the future of adjudication. While these new 'courts of the future' accommodate the transition of justice from a function for citizens to a service for those willing to pay,[77] they are in the position to strike a new balance in the post-globalization world by offering dispute resolution as a service in global competition, while at the same time preserving the sovereign power of the State over the adjudication of disputes.[78] This makes them one of the very first institutions of twenty-first-century globalization. This may also suggest that international commercial courts are here to stay.

[75] See, for example, Owen M. Fiss, 'Against Settlement' (1984) 93 Yale Law Journal 1073, 1075; Harry T. Edwards, 'Alternative Dispute Resolution: Panacea or Anathema?' (1986) 99 Harvard Law Review 668, 675.

[76] Jean R. Sternlight, 'Is Alternative Dispute Resolution Consistent with the Rule of Law? Lessons from Abroad' (2007) 56 DePaul Law Review 569.

[77] See 'Exploring the Courts of the Future in Dubai' – interview with Mark Beer (3 May 2018), https://blogs.thomsonreuters.com/answerson/exploring-the-courts-of-the-future-in-dubai.

[78] See also Georgios Dimitropoulos, 'National Sovereignty and International Investment Law: Sovereignty Reassertion and Prospects of Reform' (2020) 21 Journal of World Investment & Trade 71, 91–2.

0.4 Outline of the Book

This edited volume has five parts. Part I (Chapters 1–4) deals with broader issues surrounding ICommCs offering 'A Contextual Perspective to International Commercial Courts'. Part II (Chapters 5–9) presents issues of 'Jurisdiction, Applicable Law and Enforcement of Judgments' in ICommCs in a comparative perspective. Part III (Chapters 10–14) takes the reader again on a comparative tour of ICommCs, this time dealing with 'Procedure, Function, Organization' of the courts. Part IV (Chapters 15–17) provides a dynamic account of 'The Interplay between International Commercial Courts and Other Dispute Resolution Fora', discussing the relationship between ICommCs, on one side, and ordinary domestic courts and international commercial arbitration, on the other. The aim of Part V (Chapters 18–22) is to offer a general account of the overall relationship between 'International Commercial Courts and Global Governance'.

The first chapter by Christopher Grout and Sir William Blair on 'The Role of International Commercial Courts in Commercial Dispute Resolution' considers the role ICommCs are fulfilling in the field of international commercial dispute resolution – placing a particular emphasis on the role and character of the judiciary and the development of case law, as well as broader issues relating to access to justice. Thomas Schultz and Clément Bachmann in Chapter 2, entitled 'International Commercial Courts: Possible Problematic Social Externalities of a Dispute Resolution Product with Good Market Potential', suggest that ICommCs seem quite likely to become a successful 'product' on the dispute resolution market. But beyond their dispute resolution functions, they are expected to trigger social externalities contributing to the development or reinforcement of a wider social order. While pushback may be possible, the authors claim that this is an area that deserves further study. Christopher Vajda, in Chapter 3 on 'Transnational Adjudication and the Court of Justice of the European Union' explains what bodies constitute a court or tribunal for the purposes of Article 267 of the Treaty of the Functioning of the European Union (TFEU). The chapter concludes with a discussion on how ICommCs in Europe are expected to operate within the judicial system of the EU. Chapter 4, entitled 'International Commercial Courts: Lessons from International Criminal Tribunals', by Ilias Bantekas, claims that ICommCs can learn a lot from international criminal tribunals (ICTs), as ICTs were the first courts to combine domestic and international law in a way that today exemplifies transnational law. International commercial courts follow the same model of justice as ICTs: both wish to attract users and ultimately become financially independent, as well as strive to convince their funders that they are worth the effort and expense. Eventually, both ICTs and ICommCs have to showcase that they are truly legitimate and that they feed into the domestic legal system.

Part II of the book starts with the contribution of Janet Walker on 'A Comparative Perspective to International Commercial Courts: Jurisdiction, Applicable Law and Enforcement of Judgments' (Chapter 5), which studies the features of ICommCs and suggests that these courts have been designed in response to the perceived strengths and deficits of domestic courts in relation to arbitration with a view to maximizing strengths and reducing deficits for courts and, finally, improving their competitive advantages for the community that will eventually request international commercial dispute resolution services. Chapter 6, by Eva Lein, entitled 'Jurisdiction and Choice of Court Clauses in Favour of International Commercial Courts', studies jurisdiction provisions of various ICommCs with a view to showcasing the circumstances under which the courts can be solicited. Focusing on European ICommCs, the chapter discusses choice of court agreements and specific agreements on proceedings in English before an ICommC, as well as rules permitting the transfer of cases to an ICommC. Man Yip, in Chapter 7, entitled 'The Battle for Jurisdiction through Jurisdictional Requirements', analyses whether ICommCs compete for the same kinds of judicial business, and whether their institutional set-up is designed to advance their aspirations. The chapter compares the jurisdictional frameworks of the CICC and the SICC with that of the Commercial Court of England and Wales. It finally showcases that the courts' jurisdictional rules have a lot to say about their strategic interests and competitive advantages. In Chapter 8, on 'Harmonization of Commercial Law Based on Common Law', Mateja Durovic and Franciszek Lech argue that ICommCs possess the features that will allow them to implement a new wave of harmonization of international commercial law – with English common law at the forefront of this effort, which they consider generally desirable both for theoretical and for practical purposes. The structural features of these courts also better position them to effect international commercial law harmonization than domestic courts or arbitral tribunals. Faris Elias Nasrallah, in Chapter 9 on 'Applicable Laws in the International Commercial Courts of the Gulf', zooms into issues of applicable law in the DIFC Courts, the ADGM Courts and the QICDRC, and evaluates jurisdictional differences and the case law of the three ICommCs of the Gulf region. The chapter suggests that the values and symbolic capital attached to applicable law before the Gulf ICommCs can illuminate distinct normative and legal practices developed within the courts, as well as more general processes of hybrid transnational lawmaking.

Part III of the book opens with Georgios Dimitropoulos' contribution on 'The Design of International Commercial Courts' (Chapter 10), which suggests that ICommCs are 'international' in that they perform functions that may be characterized as such. The 'functional internationalism' of ICommCs defines their organizational and procedural design. While ICommCs may be understood as hybrids – between the national and the international, the public and the private, the formal and the informal – the chapter highlights the mechanisms of interoperability between ICommCs, on one side, and domestic courts, international commercial arbitration and international courts and tribunals, on the other. Marieke Witkamp, in Chapter 11, entitled 'Internationalizing Domestic Courts in Europe', discusses the reasons for the establishment of new international chambers in France, Germany and the Netherlands. The author examines how the three European countries place their new ICommCs, studying their procedures, functions and organization. The chapter presents the features that distinguish these courts from their counterparts in Asia as well as from one another by looking at changes in legislation, the use of the English language in procedure, the courts' rules of procedure and their (online) accessibility, as well as their actual function so far. Chapter 12 on 'The Legitimacy and Ethics of International Commercial Court Judges', by Catherine A. Rogers, examines the link between the legitimacy of ICommCs and the ethics rules of their judges. The author argues that the international and cross-cultural context of the courts has an impact on what may be considered appropriate for a judge. The chapter compares various ethical rules on *ex parte* communication between judges and parties or their lawyers, and the cultural differences among legal systems. It finally calls for the development of codes of conduct for ICommC judges.

Zachary R. Calo, in his contribution on 'Counsel Ethics in Transnational Lawyering' (Chapter 13), examines the regulation of counsel within ICommCs. The analysis is done against the background of counsel ethics within international arbitration. The author identifies three approaches to regulating counsel practising before ICommCs, and suggests that this regulatory diversity affords due space to the distinct institutional structures and needs of the various courts. The author concludes by suggesting that procedural harmonization would be imprudent and unnecessary. According to Pietro Ortolani in Chapter 14 on 'The Use of Technology at International Commercial Courts', ICommCs are an ideal breeding ground for new technologies, since cross-border disputes cannot be adequately managed and resolved without the use of information and communications technologies. Hence ICommCs tend to use technology in their procedures with the double goal of maximizing efficiency and enhancing their attractiveness in the market for dispute resolution services. The chapter studies different uses of technology at ICommCs and evaluates the impact of different technologies on ICommC litigation in terms of efficiency and due process, as well as enforceability of judgments.

In Part IV, Julian Bailey discusses in Chapter 15 on 'The Interplay between International Commercial Courts and Ordinary Courts' the interaction between ICommCs and pre-existing national courts. In certain jurisdictions, such as Singapore, the relationship between the courts has been harmonious; in others, such as Dubai, the creation of new fora has led to conflicts between the courts. Bailey considers historical examples of conflicts within the English court system, the nature of ICommCs and clashes between ICommCs and pre-existing national courts. Chapter 16, by Michael Patchett-Joyce, entitled 'Private Autonomy in International Commercial Dispute Resolution', examines the relationship between ICommCs and international commercial arbitration. The author suggests that ICommCs have a complex identity whose utility the market will eventually test. The chapter examines the meaning of autonomy in the context of commercial dispute resolution, as well as the 'imperatives' of international commercial dispute resolution, identifying a business imperative, a political imperative and a jurisprudential imperative. The study of the imperatives highlights the interdependence between ICommCs and international commercial arbitration. The relationship between the two will not be one of hybridity as suggested by many scholars, but rather one of competition and collaboration. Chapter 17, by Georgia Antonopoulou, on 'Procedure before International Commercial and Ordinary Courts' examines the differences in procedure between ICommCs and ordinary courts, focusing primarily on three distinctive features: the cross-border character of the disputes they deal with, the voluntary establishment of their jurisdiction and their arbitration features. The author also makes an overall evaluation of the procedural differences between ICommCs and ordinary courts as well as the potential to enhance the attractiveness of the former over the latter.

Opening Part V, Chapter 18, entitled 'Hybridity in International Adjudication', by Salvatore Caserta and Mikael Rask Madsen poses the question: how 'international' are ICommCs? The authors trace examples of hybridity in international adjudication with a focus on professional, institutional and legal forms of hybridity, and claim that hybridity is a feature of both public international law courts and ICommCs. This is interpreted to suggest that the various forms of transnational adjudication are on a path of convergence at multiple levels. Julien Chaisse and Xu Qian in their contribution on 'China International Commercial Court: Architecture, Pitfalls and Promises' (Chapter 19) discuss the genesis of the CICC and its anatomy and its problematic features, and place the CICC in the broader context of China's economic and regulatory development, in particular with respect to the existing domestic courts as well as the arbitration centres – in China as well as countries that form part of the Belt and Road Initiative. The authors argue that the CICC is indicative of a new stage of regulatory and economic development in the country, which showcases China's ambition to strengthen the rule of law. The Rt. Hon. The Lord Woolf CH and Christopher Campbell-Holt in a contribution entitled 'The Emergence of International Commercial Courts and Dispute Resolution Centres in Frontier Markets' (Chapter 20) state that the establishment of international financial centres has become a common strategy for modernizing states in an effort to attract capital and to generate income from taxes, as well as develop innovative economies – alongside improving the role of states in global governance. Especially the dispute resolution systems of international financial centres can positively contribute to the promotion of foreign investment. The AIFC with its AIFC Court and International Arbitration Centre (IAC) is assisting Kazakhstan to become more competitive regionally and globally, and can serve as a paradigm for other frontier markets, including in Central Asia, to create their own international dispute resolution systems. Geert van Calster, in Chapter 21, entitled 'Brexit and the Competition of Dispute Resolution Fora in Europe', reviews some key points on the impact of Brexit on the competition for dispute resolution in Europe. The author expects litigants to continue resorting to UK courts after Brexit, and UK courts will continue competing with ICommCs. A possible discontinuation of the automatic recognition and enforcement of UK judgments by courts in Europe would give European and other ICommCs an opportunity to attract litigation from the UK. One important condition needs to be satisfied for this to happen: ICommCs will need to ensure sufficient integration within the domestic judicial system. Finally, Susan L. Karamanian in her contribution on 'International Commercial Courts, Dispute Resolution and the Rule of Law' (Chapter 22) examines court rules and adjudicatory practices to assess the influence of ICommCs on the rule of law. By posing the question why certain cases are removed from local courts, the chapter presents the argument that the new ICommCs do promote the rule of law both in the host jurisdictions and in the regions in which they are established, as well as internationally.

PART I

A Contextual Perspective to International Commercial Courts

1

The Role of International Commercial Courts in Commercial Dispute Resolution

CHRISTOPHER GROUT AND SIR WILLIAM BLAIR

1.1 Introduction

The term 'international commercial courts' is a curious one. Certainly, the institutions which are the subject of discussion in this book are courts. The extent to which they are properly characterised as 'international' (whether self-styled by the institutions themselves or referred to as such by commentators) needs some exploration. So too does the extent to which these institutions exclusively deal with commercial matters for, as will be demonstrated, many of these international commercial courts deal with matters which, whilst specialising in commercial law disputes, are in fact much broader than that.

When considering these courts, it is important not to lose sight of the fact that many jurisdictions have specialist 'commercial courts', though the type of work dealt with differs. Typically, these courts deal with domestic disputes, sometimes including relatively low-value disputes. Sometimes they have an important international jurisdiction, as in the case of the Commercial List of the Court of First Instance of the Hong Kong SAR, China. Perhaps the best examples come from New York, in the form both of the state and federal courts, and from London.[1] A number of other important jurisdictions, including France, Germany and the Netherlands, have sought to enhance the international standing of their courts – an example is the Netherlands Commercial Court established in 2019. According to its website, 'Amsterdam has joined the likes of London, Dubai and Singapore when the new Netherlands Commercial Court opens its doors.'[2]

[1] The Commercial Division of the New York State Supreme Court and the United States District Court for the Southern District of New York, which includes Manhattan.

[2] https://netherlands-commercial-court.com, accessed 12 August 2020.

Some of these courts are integrated with the domestic system; others stand apart to a greater or lesser extent. The common characteristic, certainly from the perspective of this chapter, is that the courts all have the same broad purpose – that is, to improve the adjudication of commercial disputes in the jurisdiction concerned, with a view to improving the attractiveness of the jurisdiction for inward investment, and providing the possibility of developing an international legal centre with the court as a centrepiece.

Starting with the characterisation of these courts as 'international', it is undoubtedly the case that the majority of the newly established courts in this arena are styled as such. Examples include the Singapore International Commercial Court ('the SICC'),[3] the China International Commercial Court ('the CICC'),[4] the Dubai International Financial Centre Courts ('the DIFC Courts')[5] and the Qatar International Court ('the QIC'),[6] although, in the case of the latter, it is established in law as the Civil and Commercial Court of the Qatar Financial Centre.[7] Some (much older) courts are recognised as international not because of their name, but because of their expertise in dealing with international cases, the most obvious example being the London Commercial Court (one of England and Wales' Business and Property Courts, and part of the Queen's Bench Division of the High Court[8]). It is unnecessary to provide introductions to each of these courts (as well as others) as this has been done elsewhere in this book.[9]

An issue is the extent to which these courts can truly be characterised as 'international'. Professor Wong has helpfully sought to summarise the scholarly attempt to create a taxonomy for international judicial institutions as follows:

> First, the court must be permanent and exist independently from a particular case or series of cases. Secondly, the court must have been

[3] www.sicc.gov.sg, accessed 12 June 2020.
[4] http://cicc.court.gov.cn/html/1/219/index.html, accessed 12 June 2020.
[5] www.difccourts.ae, accessed 12 June 2020.
[6] www.qicdrc.gov.qa, accessed 12 June 2020.
[7] See Qatar Financial Centre Law, Law No. (7) of 2005 (as amended), Article 8(3).
[8] www.judiciary.uk/you-and-the-judiciary/going-to-court/high-court/queens-bench-division/courts-of-the-queens-bench-division/commercial-court, accessed 12 June 2020.
[9] See, for example, Mateja Durovic and Franciszek Lech's chapter on the 'Harmonization of Commercial Law Based on Common Law: The Role of International Commercial Courts' (Chapter 8) and Janet Walker's chapter on 'A Comparative Perspective to International Commercial Courts: Jurisdiction, Applicable Law and Enforcement of Judgments' (Chapter 5).

> established by an international legal instrument or some international legal acts deriving their force from treaties. Thirdly, in deciding the cases submitted to them, they must resort to international law. Fourthly, they must decide those cases on the basis of rules of procedure, which pre-exist the case and usually cannot be modified by the parties. Fifthly, the outcome of the process much be legally binding. Sixthly, the judges hearing the case must not have been appointed *ad hoc* by the parties, but rather chosen before a case is submitted through an impartial mechanism. Lastly, the international judicial body must decide disputes between two or more entities, of which at least one is a sovereign state or an international organisation.[10]

For reasons which are perhaps self-evident, the courts discussed in this book do not meet these collective requirements. Most notably, they are not established by an international legal instrument, nor is it a requirement that the dispute must involve at least one sovereign state. In addition, whilst some of the courts may well have regard to a variety of jurisprudence and international best practices, they do not routinely apply international law. Why, then, are they characterised as 'international'? One could identify a number of reasons (such as by reference to the judiciary who sit in these courts or the fact that the rules relating to the advocates who can appear before them are usually markedly different from the rules that apply to their 'national' counterparts), but the simple reality is that these new courts have been established to cater for an international audience, primarily parties (and sometimes lawyers as well) beyond nationals of the jurisdiction in which the court is operating. That is not to say, of course, that these international courts are not accessible by nationals; they are, provided, of course, that the dispute falls within a particular court's jurisdiction. But the primary reason they exist is to cater for the needs of the international community. It therefore comes as no surprise that many of these new courts are affiliated with a special area or 'zone' created within the country concerned. For example, the DIFC Courts are associated with the Dubai International Financial Centre, the QIC is associated with the Qatar Financial Centre, and the Abu Dhabi Global Market Courts ('the ADGM Courts') are associated with the Abu Dhabi Global Market.

These courts are not, however, necessarily constrained to dealing with disputes that relate to their affiliated area or zone; the DIFC Courts, for example, have the jurisdiction to 'hear and determine any civil or

[10] D. H. Wong, 'The Rise of the International Commercial Court: What Is It and Will It Work?' Civil Justice Quarterly (2014) 33(2) 205, at 214–15.

commercial claims or actions where the parties agree in writing to file such claim or action with it whether before or after the dispute arises, provided that such agreement is made pursuant to specific, clear and express provisions'.[11]

This is often colloquially referred to as the DIFC Court's 'opt-in' jurisdiction.[12] The QIC has a jurisdiction quite independent from that given to it by the QFC Law in that, where it has been selected as the 'Competent Court', it may perform various supportive and supervisory functions in relation to arbitrations which are seated in the State of Qatar.[13]

Nevertheless, the framework in which these courts are established relates to attracting international investment and business into the respective host country. The ADGM, for example, states that it is an 'innovative, progressive and responsive financial centre transforming the business and finance landscape'. It also purports to be 'uniquely positioned as a gateway into the multi-billion dollar Belt and Road initiative'.[14] Similarly, the Astana International Financial Centre (AIFC) in Kazakhstan (which also has an affiliated court) states that it 'plays a pivotal role in positioning itself as a global centre for business and finance, connecting the economies of Central Asia, the Caucasus, EAEU, West China, Mongolia, [the] Middle East and Europe'.[15] Accordingly, generally speaking, what makes these courts 'international' is the audience they are designed to cater for. As a matter of law, however, they are domestic judicial institutions, albeit with specialist jurisdictions and distinct procedural rules.

Turning next to the commercial nature of these institutions, the London Commercial Court is precisely that – a commercial court. It deals with complex cases arising out of business disputes, both national and predominantly international. There is a particular emphasis on (i) insurance and reinsurance, (ii) banking and financial markets, (iii) commodities, (iv) shipping and (v) arbitration.[16] As one of the authors of this chapter has observed, the court 'has been described as the paradigm for

[11] Law No. (16) of 2011 Amending Certain Provisions of Law No. (12) of 2004 Concerning Dubai International Financial Centre Courts, Article 5(A)(2).

[12] See, for example, the judgment of Steel J in *SPX Middle East FZE (Formerly Invensys Middle East FZE (Apv Division))* v. *Judi for Food Industries* [2013] DIFC CFI 002, at paragraph 4.

[13] See Law No. 2 of 2017 Issuing the Arbitration Law in Civil and Commercial Matters.

[14] https://adgm.com, accessed 12 June 2020.

[15] https://aifc.kz, accessed 12 June 2020.

[16] www.judiciary.uk/you-and-the-judiciary/going-to-court/high-court/queens-bench-division/courts-of-the-queens-bench-division/commercial-court/about-us, accessed 13 June 2020. See also Part 58 of the Civil Procedure Rules.

the new international commercial courts, which are said to have been inspired in part by its success'.[17] This is in no small part due to the international work of the court.[18] That is not to suggest that the court has been the sole focus of these new courts and has been copied and pasted abroad. The nuances of each of these new courts reveal that this is not so. Apart from anything else, not all of these new courts focus solely on what can properly be characterised as commercial law disputes. For example, the jurisdiction of the QIC relates to 'civil and commercial disputes',[19] which, as the jurisprudence of the QIC illustrates,[20] extends to a wide range of issues including (i) banking and finance, (ii) debt recovery, (iii) employment, (iv) immigration, (v) insurance and reinsurance, (vi) insolvency and (vii) regulatory matters.[21] Similar observations could be made in relation to the DIFC Courts,[22] the ADGM Courts[23] and the AIFC Court.[24] The court therefore deals with a much broader range of disputes than its counterpart in London.[25]

That is why the characterisation of these new courts as both 'international' and 'commercial' is in one sense curious. Nevertheless, as this

[17] Sir William Blair, 'The New Litigation Landscape: International Commercial Courts and Procedural Innovation' Journal of Procedural Law (2019) (2) 212–34, at 223.

[18] For example, in relation to the SICC, see Sundaresh Menon, 'International Commercial Courts: Towards a Transnational System of Dispute Resolution', Opening Lecture for the DIFC Courts Lecture Series 2015, available at www.supremecourt.gov.sg/docs/default-source/default-document-library/media-room/opening-lecture–difc-lecture-series-2015.pdf.

[19] See Qatar Financial Centre Law, Law No. (7) of 2005 (as amended), Article 8(3)(c).

[20] Judgments of the QIC are available online at www.qicdrc.gov.qa/the-courts/judgments.

[21] The QIC also acts as an appellate body from decisions of the QFC regulatory tribunal, which has the jurisdiction to 'hear appeals raised by individuals and corporate bodies against decisions of the QFC Authority, the Regulatory Authority and other QFC institutions' – see Qatar Financial Centre Law, Law No. (7) of 2005 (as amended), Article 8(2)(c).

[22] See Law No. (16) of 2011 Amending Certain Provisions of Law No. (12) of 2004 Concerning Dubai International Financial Centre Courts, Article 5.

[23] See, most recently, Abu Dhabi Law No. (12) of 2020 Amending Abu Dhabi Law No. (4) of 2013.

[24] See the Constitutional Statute of the Republic of Kazakhstan on the Astana International Financial Centre, Constitutional Statute No. № 438-V Zrk of 7 December 2015 (as amended), Article 13.

[25] This observation does not apply to the SICC, which has a limited (and specialist) jurisdiction – see the Supreme Court of Judicature Act (Chapter 322, Section 80), Rules of Court (O. 110, r. 7). In relation to the rather curious jurisdiction of the CICC, see the Civil Procedure Law of the People's Republic of China (Revised in 2017), Chapter II. For a comparison of the SICC and CICC, see Z. Huo and M. Yip, 'Comparing the International Commercial Courts of China with the Singapore International Commercial Court' International & Comparative Law Quarterly (2019) 68(4) 903.

chapter seeks to demonstrate, they have a particularly important role to play when it comes to the resolution of commercial (as well as other types of) disputes. Recognising that some of these courts are modelled, to one degree or another, on the 'London model', Section 2 discusses the competitive nature of the courts. Section 3 is a case study of the Qatar International Court and Dispute Resolution Centre. Section 4 considers the importance of locally administered justice, and Section 5 evaluates whether these new judicial institutions complement or compete with arbitration. Section 6 looks at the judiciary which comprise these courts, and Section 7 considers the importance of jurisprudence to the development of commercial law more generally. Section 8 is devoted to the key issue of enforcement, whilst Section 9 looks at various issues relating to access to justice more generally. The threads are then drawn together in Section 10. A key purpose is to assess the overall value these new courts add to the field of commercial dispute resolution.

1.2 The Competitive Nature of the New Courts

It is said that imitation is the sincerest form of flattery. If that is right, it might be said that not only does the London Commercial Court have a lot to be happy about, but so too does the common law system of England and Wales generally. It has been mentioned that the London Commercial Court has inspired some of the new international commercial courts. But it is not just the court that has been of interest. Equally important is the fact that many of these courts operate within legal systems which have drawn, to varying degrees, from the common law system. This is particularly remarkable when it comes to courts operating in countries which historically do not follow the common law model. The DIFC, for example, boasts that it 'is home to an internationally recognised, independent regulator and a proven judicial system with an English common law framework'.[26]

As noted earlier in this chapter, the QFC makes similar claims.[27] Indeed, some (although by no means all) of the substantive law of the QFC is either based on or incorporates the English common law.[28] The

[26] www.difc.ae/about, accessed 14 June 2020.

[27] www.qfc.qa/en?gclid=EAIaIQobChMIuIGkn6qB6gIVygorCh0Tqw0pEAAYASAAEgK6iPD_BwE, accessed 14 June 2020.

[28] The QFC Trust Regulations are particularly interesting in this regard. Article 8 provides that '(1) The common law of Trusts and principles of equity applicable in England and Wales supplement these Regulations, except to the extent modified by these Regulations

ADGM goes further. Its Application of English Law Regulations 2015 provides, subject to certain important caveats, that 'The common law of England (including the principles and rules of equity), as it stands from time to time, shall apply and have legal force in, and form part of the law of, the Abu Dhabi Global Market.'[29] Similarly, the AIFC Court states that it 'provides a common law court system based on the norms and principles of English law for the first time in Central Asia'.[30]

It is not just the substantive law that has been influenced. The procedure that is applied before these courts is often based on the Civil Procedure Rules ('CPR') used in England and Wales since 1999, or the previous codification based on the rules first promulgated in 1883.[31] The Regulations and Procedural Rules of the QIC, for example, have clearly been influenced by the CPR, most notably by the inclusion of the Court's 'Overriding Objective'.[32] However it is noteworthy that the QIC has managed to limit its procedural rules to a mere thirty-seven articles as opposed to the thousands of pages that comprise the CPR.

In addition, judges from England and Wales are present in a number of these courts. The QIC, the DIFC Courts, the SICC, the ADGM Courts and the AIFC Court all have judges from England and Wales. Indeed, at the time of writing, all ten of the AIFC Court judges are from England and Wales, but this will likely change over time.[33]

The London Commercial Court has dedicated premises[34] along with other Business and Property Courts, well-regarded judges and procedural rules, and according to its online 'lead times', as of October 2021, despite the coronavirus pandemic, it has trial dates available as early as April 2022.[35] But it is the perceived success of the court over time as contributing to the success of London as an international commercial and financial centre that has led to its emulation. First and foremost, it is seen as demonstrating that a court which has the confidence of business is an essential part of developing an ecosystem that favours finance and commerce. Second, it is seen as showing how international legal business

or any other Regulations; (2) The statute law of England and Wales applicable to Trusts does not, except to the extent it is replicated in these Regulations, apply in the QFC.'

29 Application of English Law Regulations 2015, Article 1(1).

30 https://court.aifc.kz/an-introduction, accessed 3 August 2020.

31 As is the case in the Hong Kong SAR and Singapore.

32 Civil and Commercial Court Regulations and Procedural Rules, Article 4.

33 https://court.aifc.kz/who-we-are, accessed 14 June 2020.

34 See www.judiciary.uk/you-and-the-judiciary/going-to-court/high-court/the-rolls-building/facilities, accessed 14 June 2020.

35 www.gov.uk/guidance/commercial-court-hearing-and-trial-dates, accessed 20 October 2021.

can become a major economic contributor in its own right. Other centres which have not done so already wish to achieve the same outcome. So to some extent, the courts are in competition. As regards Europe, Brexit has been seen as a commercial opportunity for courts in mainland Europe, though in the broader perspective some consider that it is unlikely that London will be significantly displaced.

1.3 A Case Study: The Qatar International Court and Dispute Resolution Centre

The Qatar International Court was established when the Qatar Financial Centre (QFC) was set up in 2005, under the provisions of the QFC Law of that year. The QFC aims to promote the development of financial business in the State of Qatar. According to the QFC's own material, QFC firms benefit from a legal and judicial framework based on English common law, and an independent court, regulatory tribunal and dispute-resolution centre. This is now known as the Qatar International Court and Dispute Resolution Centre (QICDRC).

As part of its architecture, the QFC has two bodies established under the QFC Law. The first is a civil and commercial court, now the Qatar International Court, which has a jurisdiction set out in Article 8 of the QFC Law. In broad terms, the court has jurisdiction over civil and commercial disputes which arise out of the QFC or the bodies registered there. The second is a regulatory tribunal which has an appeal jurisdiction in respect of certain regulatory decisions and other matters. It became fully operational in 2009 from which time its first cases were decided. Currently judges sit in benches of three with a first instance and, in the case of the court, an appellate jurisdiction – it is hoped in the future to have the necessary amendments to the law to enable single judges to sit at first instance at least in some cases.

Within the QICDRC the two bodies work together, sharing the same premises and registrar. The judges come from diverse parts of the world: from Qatar itself, and also from Cyprus, Hong Kong SAR, China, India, Kuwait, New Zealand, Singapore, South Africa, the UK and the USA. Past judges have come from Australia, France and Japan. The first president of the court was Lord Woolf. He was succeeded by Lord Phillips, who was succeeded by Lord Thomas, the current president – remarkably in terms of the standing of the president, each of these was the Lord Chief Justice of England and Wales. Sir William Blair was the first (and now current) chair of the regulatory tribunal, followed by Michael Thomas QC, followed by Sir David Keene. Taken as a whole, the breadth and seniority of the judges can be seen as a demonstration of international confidence in the QICDRC.

The court also has a mediation and arbitration function.[36] As regards arbitration, Law No. 2 of 2017 Issuing the Arbitration Law in Civil and Commercial Matters provides parties with an option to agree on the 'Competent Court' of the arbitration. The Competent Court may perform various functions including in relation to interim measures, enforcement of awards and appeals. The QIC may be chosen as the Competent Court.

Thus, the QICDRC is conceived as part of the QFC and seen as important for its development. It has this in common with a number of the other courts under consideration, Dubai being an example. But all financial centres emphasise the importance of the legal structures under which they operate, including those with no separate court system such as Casablanca and Mauritius, because such structures are inherent in the nature of a financial centre.

A number of further points should be made which show the wider position. The QICDRC is part of Qatar's judicial system. It was an observer at the United Nations Office on Drugs and Crime's (UNODC) Global Judicial Integrity Network hosted by the chief justice of the State of Qatar. It actively engages with the legal profession in Qatar, and has close relations with the main universities in Qatar. It co-organises the Qatar Law Forum, and in these ways seeks to contribute to the legal system in the state as a whole. In 2020, a law was promulgated establishing a new commercial court in Qatar to provide a judicial platform for the prompt adjudication of commercial disputes within the state.

1.4 Locally Administered Justice

The importance of locally administered justice cannot be overstated. It is of fundamental importance to any legal system that the courts are accessible to those who need them, notably parties, witnesses and lawyers. Between 2010 and 2019, more than half of the courts in England and Wales were closed, with plans to close a further seventy-seven courts by 2025/6.[37] This has led to widespread criticism, particularly among the

[36] See www.qicdrc.gov.qa/mediation/overview, accessed 20 September 2020.

[37] 'Transforming Courts and Tribunals: A Progress Update', National Audit Office, September 2019.

legal community, which has raised fears over access to justice. As the Law Society of England and Wales has made clear, 'We cannot consider a system to deliver justice if it prevents people from using the courts effectively.'[38] Although, in respect of these new international commercial courts, the considerations are slightly different, access to justice remains at their heart. They each recognise that, for reasons which it will be necessary to explore in further detail, they are best placed to resolve certain types of disputes, in particular, for courts affiliated with special areas or zones, as regards the individuals and companies that do business there.

As has been explored, many of these new platforms, such as the QFC and the DIFC, are designed to attract international investment. Part of that attraction includes having a legal and judicial system with which users of these new platforms feel comfortable. If these international commercial courts did not exist, what would be the consequences? First, it is perhaps unlikely that the number of companies which establish within these platforms would be as high as it is at present.[39] Moreover, in the absence of a specialist international commercial court, some other form of dispute resolution procedure would be required. There are various options, including the national courts of the country concerned as in Mauritius, and some form of alternative dispute resolution process, such as arbitration as in the case of the Casablanca Finance City (CFC) – the Casablanca International Mediation and Arbitration Centre (CIMAC) is a long-term project supported by the CFC. It is necessary therefore to say something about the relationship between these new international commercial courts and arbitration.

1.5 International Commercial Courts and Arbitration: Competing or Complementary?

An abundance of material, including academic commentary, exists on the pros and cons of arbitration as a forum for dispute resolution, particularly in the context of disputes that involve parties from different countries. Independence, impartiality and neutrality are often cited as the

[38] www.lawsociety.org.uk/policy-campaigns/articles/court-closures–what-s-changing, accessed 18 June 2020.

[39] As of 18 June 2020, the QFC, for example, had in excess of nine hundred firms established within it, comprising more than thirty-five hundred people and more than USD 20 billion combined total assets under management: see www.qfc.qa, accessed 18 June 2020.

key components, though there are of course others.[40] As s.1(a) of the Arbitration Act 1996 (a statute which extends to England, Wales and Northern Ireland) explains:

> The object of arbitration is to obtain the fair resolution of disputes by an impartial tribunal without unnecessary delay or expense.

The statute recognises that parties should be free to agree how their disputes are resolved subject only 'to such safeguards as are necessary in the public interest'.[41]

A plethora of respected arbitral institutions pride themselves in being able to administer neutral dispute resolution processes. Examples include the International Chamber of Commerce (ICC),[42] the Singapore International Arbitration Centre (SIAC),[43] and the London Court of International Arbitration (LCIA).[44] It is perhaps telling that, in respect of the latter, upon its inauguration in 1892 (when it was known as The City of London Chamber of Arbitration), the *Law Quarterly Review* reported that

> This Chamber is to have all the virtues which the law lacks. It is to be expeditious where the law is slow, cheap where the law is costly, simple where the law is technical, a peacemaker instead of a stirrer-up of strife.[45]

One can perhaps reflect on the extent to which those observations may or may not remain apropos at the present time if cost and expedition are the criteria. Suffice it to note that, when initially established, the provision of arbitration as a forum for commercial dispute resolution was seen to make up for the perceived shortcomings of the courts and the legal system in general. Today, while many of the criticisms once levied at the courts could arguably be said of the arbitral process (in addition to other problems),[46] the fact is that arbitration has become a common and

[40] R. Feehily, 'Neutrality, Independence and Impartiality in International Commercial Arbitration, a Fine Balance in the Quest for Arbitral Justice' Penn State Journal of Law & International Affairs (February 2019) 7(1).

[41] Arbitration Act 1996, s.1(b).

[42] https://iccwbo.org, accessed 22 June 2020.

[43] www.siac.org.sg, accessed 22 June 2020.

[44] www.lcia.org, accessed 22 June 2020.

[45] (1893) IX LQR 86.

[46] See, for example, the joint study of White & Case and Queen Mary University of London, '2018 International Arbitration Survey: The Evolution of International Arbitration'. The study reveals, among other things, that respondents to the survey identified (i) cost, (ii) lack of effective sanctions during the arbitral process and (iii) lack of power in relation to

respected mechanism for the resolution of international commercial disputes.[47]

Accordingly, whilst these new international commercial courts may take some of the cases which hitherto would likely have been resolved by arbitration, it is certainly questionable as to whether they can in any meaningful sense be said to be in competition with the various arbitral institutions around the world. First, as one of the co-authors has noted,

> The idea of courts being in competition with arbitration and with each other for international work would not be universally accepted, because courts are public goods, and their purpose is the administration of justice.[48]

Secondly, as the Chief Justice of the Federal Court of Australia, the Hon. James Allsop, has pointed out, 'the practical reality is that arbitration requires the court system for its efficacy – either as a positive force or by its benign non-interference with arbitral activity'.[49] There can be little doubt that that is right. The court of the seat of the arbitration, when it is required to intervene, plays a critical role in the integrity of the arbitral process. The QIC, for example, can issue interim measures,[50] appoint and remove arbitrators,[51] determine matters relating to the jurisdiction of the arbitral panel,[52] assist the arbitral panel with the taking of evidence (through, for example, the issuance of a witness summons),[53] act (within very limited grounds) as an appellate body[54] and, perhaps most importantly, enforce the award.[55]

It would be misleading, however, to suggest that the primary role of these new international commercial courts was to support and supervise international arbitration. That is patently not the case. They each, as explored

third parties as the top three worst characteristics of international arbitration (see page 8 of the survey).

47 The same study revealed that 99.08 per cent of respondents to the survey said they would likely choose and/or recommend international arbitration to resolve cross-border disputes in the future (see page 8 of the survey).

48 Sir William Blair, 'The New Litigation Landscape: International Commercial Courts and Procedural Innovation' (n. 17) at 219.

49 Hon. James Allsop, 'International Commercial Arbitration: The Courts and the Rule of Law in the Asia Pacific Region' Arbitration (2015) 81(2) 169–75, at 170.

50 Law No. 2 of 2017 Issuing the Arbitration Law in Civil and Commercial Matters, Article 9.

51 Ibid., Articles 11(5) and 13(1).

52 Ibid., Article 16(3).

53 Ibid., Article 27.

54 Ibid., Article 33.

55 Ibid., Articles 34 and 35.

earlier in this chapter, have carefully crafted jurisdiction provisions which allow them to hear commercial (and other) disputes as a trial (and appellate) court. It is therefore necessary to look in more detail at what precisely makes these new courts an attractive dispute resolution forum and the value they add to dispute resolution more generally. As the most notable aspect of international commercial courts is arguably the calibre of the judiciary they tend to attract, it is to that topic that it is now prudent to turn.

1.6 The Judiciary

A perceived advantage of arbitration is the ability to select, to one degree or another, the arbitrators who will be hearing and determining the dispute. Parties can nominate the individual or individuals they consider suited to act as part of the arbitral panel. This has the advantage of, among other things, being able to appoint person(s) who have knowledge and experience of the subject matter at the heart of the dispute.[56] In a court setting, parties cannot, of course, choose or exert influence over the appointment of the judge or judges who hear a particular case. Nevertheless, the members of the judiciary that comprise the international commercial courts are limited in number and, generally speaking, have specialist backgrounds usually relating to diverse aspects of commercial law. Accordingly, parties know that when their disputes are referred to these courts for resolution, they will be determined by expert judges.

Though the CICC has only appointed Chinese judges (albeit it has an International Commercial Expert Committee)[57] and the AIFC Court has only appointed judges from England and Wales,[58] it is a striking feature of the new international commercial courts that they comprise judges from a range of jurisdictions. At the time of writing, the DIFC Courts, for example, have judges from Malaysia, the United Arab Emirates, England and Wales, and Australia.[59] The SICC has judges from Singapore, the USA, Australia, England and Wales, Canada, France, Hong Kong, Japan

[56] This is particularly valuable, for example, in the context of construction disputes. In this regard, see the joint study of Pinsent Masons and Queen Mary University of London, '2019 International Arbitration Survey – Driving Efficiency in International Construction Disputes', which noted, among other things, that 'when appointing arbitrators, the vast majority of respondents valued construction experience above all, echoing the survey's finding that factual and technical complexity is the most defining feature of international arbitration in the construction sector' (at page 5, and see also pages 12–14).

[57] http://cicc.court.gov.cn/html/1/219/193/196/index.html, accessed 23 June 2020.

[58] https://court.aifc.kz/who-we-are/justices, accessed 23 June 2020.

[59] www.difccourts.ae/court-structure/judges, accessed 23 June 2020.

and India.[60] Notably, since its establishment, as pointed out earlier in this chapter, the QIC has been led by three successive former Lord Chief Justices of England and Wales[61] and presently has judges from a range of civil and common law backgrounds, including judges from England and Wales, Qatar, New Zealand, Cyprus, Scotland, Kuwait and South Africa.[62] Accordingly, the judges, quite apart from their individual specialisms, bring with them a wealth of experience and knowledge from various jurisdictions throughout the world. This is likely of comfort to parties involved in cross-border disputes (or cases which may have an 'international flavour') who will not only be satisfied with the expertise of the judges, but who should also have no concerns about partisanship.

It must be pointed out, however, that some parties (or, more accurately, their legal representatives) may find it daunting to appear before these judicial institutions, especially when some of these courts sit in a constitution of three, even at first instance.[63] Such apprehension can be compounded when faced not only with three judges, but with three judges from different jurisdictions. Nevertheless, experience shows that, notwithstanding the diverse backgrounds from which the judges come, there is an effort (whether conscious or unconscious) to seek unanimity of approach and outcome. An illustrative example of this is the fact that, in the eleven years that it has been operating, there has yet to be a dissenting judgment in the QIC.[64] This is so notwithstanding the fact that the QIC's Regulations and Procedural Rules make express provision for dissenting judgments.[65] The importance of consistency in judicial decision-making, and the building up of publicly accessible jurisprudence, is a feature unique to courts worthy of further consideration.

1.7 The Importance of Jurisprudence

Unlike arbitration, commercial courts are quite often concerned not only with the particular case before them at any given time, but also with stating principles. This is particularly the case in the common law system

[60] www.sicc.gov.sg/about-the-sicc/judges, accessed 23 June 2020.

[61] Lord Woolf of Barnes (2009–12), Lord Phillips of Worth Matravers (2012–19) and Lord Thomas of Cwmgiedd (2019–Present).

[62] www.qicdrc.gov.qa/the-courts/overview, accessed 23 June 2020.

[63] The QIC is such a court – see Article 12.2 of the Regulations and Procedural Rules of the Court.

[64] Although there has been one in the QFC Regulatory Tribunal; see *Karim Noujaim v. Qatar Financial Centre Regulatory Authority* [2014] QIC (RT) 1.

[65] Article 32.3.

which is traditionally led by judges. Consequently, commercial courts, like other specialist courts, play a key role in interpreting and developing the law. As Lord Thomas, then the Lord Chief Justice of England and Wales, opined on the occasion of the 2016 BAILII lecture,

> The common law has played a very significant role in that development through its strength, vitality and agility in applying and adapting its principles to changes in trade, commerce and the markets. This great strength of the common law is exemplified in the judgments of the great judges, particularly those in the specialist and appellate courts in London.[66]

Indeed, the importance of the development of the law should not be overlooked. Whilst many people may, for a variety of reasons, feel in some way alienated from the legal system and the operation of the courts, the development of jurisprudence is not only about informing lawyers and judges. It is about ensuring that the law is clear, outcomes can be predicted with a reasonable degree of certainty, and, to put the point colloquially, people know where they stand. It has often been said that in commercial life, the certainty of a rule is more important than its content. The public availability of court judgments allows lawyers to advise their clients in accordance with previously issued judgments, with the consequence that issues that may otherwise have arisen in the future can be avoided and some disputes, which may otherwise have ended up in court or arbitration, can be settled amicably.

There is no reason to suppose these same principles do not apply to international commercial courts. If anything, it is perhaps more important that these new courts develop a consistent body of jurisprudence so that those operating within their jurisdiction are well informed as to the approach the courts will take on various issues. One might go further. Given the high profile of the judges who tend to sit on these courts, the jurisprudence that emanates from them may have implications (in terms of persuasive authority) in other jurisdictions. An example is the recent judgment of the Appellate Division of the QIC in *Leonardo S.p.A* v. *Doha Bank Assurance Company LLC*.[67] In that case, the Court upheld a judgment of the First Instance Circuit, which had found in favour of the Claimant in the sum of €14,619,440.00 in furtherance of demands,

66 Lord Thomas of Cwmgiedd, 'Developing Commercial Law through the Courts: Rebalancing the Relationship between the Courts and Arbitration', The BAILII Lecture 2016 (9 March 2016), paragraph 3.

67 [2020] QIC (A) 1.

found valid by the Court, made under an advance payment guarantee and performance bond. The Appellate Division considered, among other things, the proper approach to Uniform Rules for Demand Guarantees (URDG 758). In doing so it observed that,

> As URDG 758 is intended to be an instrument underpinning international trade and commerce and to harmonise international demand guarantee practice, it is important URDG 758 is not interpreted in a literalistic manner or by adoption of rules of national law. A similar approach to the interpretation of URDG 758 should be adopted as that in relation to the Uniform Commercial Practices (UCP), as like UCP, URDG is a code reflecting the views and practices of the market and is kept under review.[68]

As to the UCP, which applies to analogous instruments – namely, letters of credit, the Court referred to the judgment of the Court of Appeal (Civil Division) of England and Wales in *Fortis Bank S.A./N.V, Stemcor UK Limited* v. *Indian Overseas Bank*,[69] which observed that,

> [A] court must recognise the international nature of the UCP and approach its construction in that spirit. It was drafted in English in a manner that it could easily be translated into about 20 different languages and applied by bankers and traders throughout the world. It is intended to be a self-contained code for those areas of practice which it covers and to reflect good practice and achieve consistency across the world. Courts must therefore interpret it in accordance with its underlying aims and purposes reflecting international practice and the expectations of international bankers and international traders so that it underpins the operation of letters of credit in international trade. A literalistic and national approach must be avoided.[70]

The Court in *Leonardo* anticipated that that approach 'would be adopted by courts worldwide', noting that guarantees 'are the lifeblood of commerce'.[71] The judgment has already been the subject of commentary outside the jurisdiction with one observer opining that,

> We now have two high-profile cases[72] from internationally respected courts that endorse the clarity and simplicity offered by URDG 758 to demand guarantees. It is hoped that this will allay concerns that URDG

[68] Ibid., paragraph 39.

[69] [2011] EWCA Civ 58.

[70] Ibid., at paragraph 29.

[71] At paragraph 41.

[72] The other being the judgment of the Technology and Construction Court (England and Wales) in *Tecnicas Reunidas Saudia for Services and Contracting Co Ltd* v. *Korea Development Bank* [2020] EWHC 968.

> 758 is untested. We could not have a clearer endorsement of the benefits of international adoption of URDG 758.[73]

This particular case example is illustrative of the fact that the jurisprudence of the new international commercial courts is not confined to the jurisdictions with which the individual courts are concerned. On the contrary, a number of judgments may have international influence and, as the case example highlights, with good reason. The success of international commerce depends, to a not insignificant degree, on the harmonisation of the most important matters which impact the efficacy of cross-border trade and dealings. The UCP and the URDG provide good examples of the benefits of consistency of approach across jurisdictions. Whilst the substantive law (and by extension those who operate within it) benefits from this approach, another key area which needs to be considered is in relation to the enforcement of judgments, which is considered next.

1.8 Enforcement

One of the oft-quoted advantages of arbitration is the means by which the resultant awards can be enforced internationally. This is almost entirely down to the successful adoption of the 'New York Convention' by, as of 12 June 2020, 164 State parties.[74] As the introduction to the Convention makes clear,

> The Convention's principal aim is that foreign and non-domestic arbitral awards will not be discriminated against and it obliges Parties to ensure such awards are recognized and generally capable of enforcement in their jurisdiction in the same way as domestic awards. An ancillary aim of the Convention is to require courts of Parties to give full effect to arbitration agreements by requiring courts to deny the parties access to court in contravention of their agreement to refer the matter to an arbitral tribunal.[75]

Whilst a recent study points to a 'perceived gap between the theoretical ease of award enforcement promoted by the provisions of the New York

[73] R. Dupay, 'URDG 758: Finally Tested and It Does What It Says on the Tin', Thomson Reuters, Practical Law Construction Blog (17 June 2020).

[74] The 164th State party being Tonga, where its accession to the Convention took effect on 12 June 2020; see http://newyorkconvention1958.org/index.php?lvl=cmspage&pageid=7&id_news=1025&opac_view=-1, accessed 28 June 2020.

[75] Convention on the Recognition and Enforcement of Foreign Arbitral Awards (New York, 1958), page 1.

Convention and potentially less successful practical experiences of respondents seeking to enforce arbitral awards in various jurisdictions', there can be little doubt that, generally speaking, a party will likely find it easier to enforce a foreign arbitral award than they will a foreign court judgment.[76] At first blush it is perhaps surprising that an award rendered as part of, ordinarily, a private dispute resolution process is more advantageous when it comes to enforcement abroad than a judgment of a State court; this is because of the international treaty in the form of the New York Convention, which in turn was possible to get off the ground because arbitration is by definition consensual. In other words, the parties have agreed to it. This is not necessarily the case in court proceedings.

That having been said, various treaties and conventions do exist concerning the enforcement of foreign court judgments, most notably the 'Hague Choice of Court Convention' and, more recently, the 'Hague Convention on the Recognition and Enforcement of Foreign Judgments in Civil or Commercial Matters', both discussed elsewhere in this book.[77] The latter is not yet in force. The Standing International Forum of Commercial Courts (SIFoCC) established in 2017 is a forum that, 'for the first time, brings together the world's commercial courts'.[78] One of the SIFoCC's achievements has been the production and publication of the Multilateral Memorandum on Enforcement.[79] Courts from around the world (including international commercial courts such as the QIC, DIFC Courts and ADGM Courts) have contributed by detailing the mechanism for the enforcement of foreign court judgments in their respective judicial institutions. Whilst significant variances exist in practice, the unique feature of the document is that it is written by judges. This in itself highlights another important role international commercial courts can play – namely, as institutions that do not operate in silos but rather actively collaborate with their foreign counterparts to discuss areas of mutual interest. A most recent example of this has stemmed from the

[76] '2018 International Arbitration Survey: The Evolution of International Arbitration' (n. 45), page 37.

[77] See Walker, Chapter 5, this volume.

[78] https://sifocc.org, accessed 28 June 2020.

[79] Available at https://sifocc.org/app/uploads/2019/11/Multilateral-Memorandum-on-Enforcement-Nov-2019.pdf, accessed 28 June 2020. The second edition of the Multilateral Memorandum on Enforcement of Commercial Judgments for Money was published in April 2021 (https://s3-eu-west-2.amazonaws.com/sifocc-prod-storage-7f6qtyoj7wir/uploads/2021/04/6.7387_JO_Memorandum_on_Enforcement_2nd_Edition_April2021_WEB.pdf, accessed 20 October 2021).

Covid-19 pandemic, which has caused chaos across the globe. The SIFoCC produced a memorandum which details how member courts are responding to the pandemic and which highlights the importance of maintaining fully functioning courts in times of crises.[80] The memorandum reflects the sharing of different experiences by different courts.

Returning to the role of international commercial courts in the context of enforcement, the enforcement of *foreign* judgments (as opposed to their own judgments) has not been a primary consideration. That said, some courts have not shied away from so doing. In *A4* v. *B4*, the ADGM Court of First Instance enforced an arbitration award made pursuant to an arbitration administered by the London Court of International Arbitration.[81] Whilst both parties were incorporated in Abu Dhabi, there was no evidence before the Court that either of them had a presence in the ADGM. The Court was satisfied that it had jurisdiction, by virtue of Article 56(1) of the Arbitration Regulations, to enforce the foreign award. Nevertheless, Andrew Smith J postulated the following question:

> Should this Court be concerned about whether A4 might be seeking recognition and enforcement of the Award not in order to enforce it against assets in the ADGM, but as a device to have an order of this Court (rather than the Award itself) enforced elsewhere in the UAE, and in particular elsewhere in Abu Dhabi, without having other UAE Courts, including those of the Abu Dhabi Judicial Department ('ADJD'), examine for themselves whether the Award should be recognised and enforced within their jurisdictions?[82]

In answering his own question, the judge concluded that as there was no evidence that B4 *did not* have assets within the ADGM, nor was there any evidence to suggest that B4 *might not* have assets within the ADGM in the foreseeable future, there was therefore no reason to suppose that A4 was simply using the proceedings as a device to obtain a judgment to enforce elsewhere in the UAE.[83] One might find that analysis somewhat artificial in the sense that the absence of proof of assets within the ADGM was more likely to suggest that the party did not have assets within the ADGM as opposed to the contrary. Moreover, the absence of any evidence of assets within the ADGM might lend credence to the argument

[80] See 'Delivering Justice during the Covid-19 Pandemic and the Future Use of Technology' (29 May 2020), available at https://sifocc.org/app/uploads/2020/05/SIFoCC-Covid-19-memorandum-29-May-2020.pdf, accessed 28 June 2020.

[81] [2019] ADGMCFI 0007.

[82] Ibid., paragraph 20.

[83] Ibid., paragraph 23.

that the enforcing party *was* using the proceedings as a device to obtain a judgment which it could then seek to enforce elsewhere in the UAE. Regardless, the judge did make this telling observation:

> I would need little persuasion that it is desirable and, in a general sense, in the public interest that the different Courts of the UAE work together harmoniously and that there be an orderly distribution of jurisdiction between the Courts of Abu Dhabi and more generally of the UAE.[84]

Although the judge did not say so, this appears to be an acknowledgement of the difficulties that have arisen in neighbouring Dubai between the DIFC Courts and the other courts of Dubai as regards the issue of competing jurisdiction, especially in the context of enforcement. This situation led to the establishment of the 'Judicial Committee of the Dubai Courts and the DIFC Courts', discussed in detail elsewhere in this book.[85]

What is unquestionably of importance is that the various international commercial courts can successfully enforce their *own* judgments. If they cannot, their role is significantly diminished. Moreover, it is not helpful to the efficacy of litigation if, having obtained a judgment from a commercial court, the successful party must go to some other court in order to enforce it.

The Regulations and Procedural Rules of the QIC provide, it is suggested, a good example of how enforcement of a particular court's own judgments should operate. As the beginning of Article 34.1 makes clear,

> Any judgment or order of the Court is a judgment or order of the courts of Qatar and capable of enforcement and execution by the courts of Qatar as would be a judgment or order of any other Qatari court.

Article 34.3 gives the QIC the explicit power to enforce its own judgments through a variety of means, including 'by the making of any order that it considers necessary in the interests of justice'. In practice, the enforcement judge of the QIC can enforce QIC judgments through a variety of means (such as freezing orders and the seizure of assets). Moreover, because the QIC is 'a court of Qatar', it is not restricted to assets located within the QFC, but can enforce throughout the State generally.[86] This has enabled the court to issue precautionary freezing injunctions.[87]

[84] Ibid., paragraph 21.
[85] See Julian Bailey's chapter in this volume (Chapter 15) entitled 'The Interplay between International Commercial Courts and Ordinary Courts'.
[86] Article 3.2.
[87] *Blom Bank Qatar LLC* v. *(1) Qatar Asphalt Company WLL and (2) Emile Michel Turk* [2019] QIC (F) 5.

The successful enforceability of the judgments of the international commercial courts is a key component of access to justice considerations, which is the final issue considered in this chapter.

1.9 Access to Justice

In Section 4, the importance of locally administered dispute resolution was noted as a fundamental aspect of access to justice. It is fitting that, in bringing this chapter to an end, further observations are made in respect of the role of international commercial courts in addressing access to justice issues more generally. If one accepts that these courts are primarily catering to the needs of foreign parties operating within the jurisdiction of the particular court in question, it must follow that it has to be ensured that such parties have confidence that their disputes can be resolved in an efficient (and cost-effective) manner and their rights enforced.

In meeting this aim, the powers of the courts are more far reaching than those of private arbitrators. For example, the courts can issue witness summons, join third parties and make findings of contempt – all of which the courts can themselves directly enforce.[88] In another departure from private dispute resolution methods, the international commercial courts have the transparency of court proceedings, with open hearings and publicly accessible judgments. Quite apart from the importance this plays in developing jurisprudence, as discussed in Section 7, it helps boost confidence with certain prospective users.

In this regard, language is a significant issue. An example comes from France following recent reforms. The Paris Commercial Court has specialised chambers dedicated to various matters such as banking, town planning, international disputes and so on. Additionally, two procedural court protocols of 7 February 2018 record the creation of international chambers within the Paris Commercial Court and the Paris Court of Appeal. This means that these two courts will now hear pleadings in English and accept exhibits in English. It is indeed a common thread of the international commercial courts that they conduct their proceedings in English, or at least allow extensive use of the English language – for example, in documentation. In the case of the QIC, its Regulations and Procedural Rules allow proceedings to be conducted in English or Arabic, but judgments are always issued in Arabic (as well as English).[89] One

[88] See, for example, the Regulations and Procedural Rules of the QIC, Articles 10 and 34.
[89] Ibid., Article 3.2.

consequence is that the rules relating to lawyers who can appear before the courts (rights of audience) are usually much broader than national rules, allowing parties to appoint a lawyer of their choosing, regardless of the lawyer's nationality.[90]

Another increasingly common thread among the international commercial courts in enhancing access to justice is through their commitment to pro bono services to help those most in need. For example, the QIC,[91] DIFC Courts,[92] ADGM Courts[93] and the AIFC[94] all make provision for pro bono services in one form or another to assist individuals who cannot afford legal advice and representation. Ensuring that those who would not otherwise be able to seek assistance from a lawyer can do so is a key access to justice consideration; the developing role of the international commercial courts in this regard is certainly worthy of note.

1.10 Conclusion

Speaking about international commercial courts, Professor Lucy Reed, formerly of the National University of Singapore, observed that,

> The courts' constituency will be the subgroup of transnational parties that requires or prefers: appellate rights; permanent rather than ad hoc judges; general transparency, and the related development of commercial jurisprudence that generally public proceedings allow; and, representation by ethical counsel of their choice.[95]

Contemplating some 'normative propositions' on what the vision and mission of international commercial courts might be, Sundaresh Menon, the Chief Justice of Singapore, suggested that their mission should be,

90 For example, Article 29.1 of the Regulations and Procedural Rules of the QIC provides 'The President of the Court or the Judge presiding over the case in question shall have a discretion to determine who shall have rights of audience for that case. However, where no direction has been made in relation to rights of audience, any qualified lawyer who is entitled to appear before the superior courts in the State of Qatar or of any other jurisdiction shall have rights of audience.'

91 www.qicdrc.gov.qa/legal-bureau/pro-bono, accessed 30 June 2020.

92 www.difccourts.ae/probono, accessed 30 June 2020.

93 www.adgm.com/adgm-courts/pro-bono-scheme, accessed 30 June 2020.

94 https://aifc.kz/press-relizy/aifc-law-pro-bono-office, accessed 30 June 2020.

95 Lucy Reed, 'International Dispute Resolution Courts: Retreat or Advance? 10th John E. C. Brierley Memorial Lecture' (2017–18) 4 McGill Journal of Dispute Resolution 129.

> to facilitate international commerce in a flattened world marked by an extremely high degree of economic interconnectedness. They should support international commerce by enforcing bargains and resolving disputes across national boundaries.[96]

They would achieve this, he suggested, through four points: first, through building 'a trustworthy, competent and commercially sensible system to resolve transnational commercial disputes'; secondly, to 'function alongside arbitration and fill in a gap in the suite of transnational dispute resolution mechanisms'; thirdly, to be 'responsive to the needs of the international commercial community'; and fourthly, to 'develop deeper connections amongst commercial courts, and eventually develop a network of such courts'.[97]

It is difficult to argue with that conclusion. Indeed, in many ways it has already been realised. As this chapter has sought to explore, the new international commercial courts are, generally speaking, supporting specialist frameworks established to attract international investment and business into the respective host country. They have, as their main aim, the efficient resolution of commercial disputes, including (although not exclusively) within a transnational context. They complement, it is suggested, national courts and arbitration and, in respect of the latter, provide additional support. Owing to the specialist judiciary which comprises the courts, particular needs of the international commercial community can be met. Finally, as described in this chapter, the Standing International Forum of Commercial Courts has sought to bring together the world's commercial courts (both national and international) in a meaningful and impactful way.

Overall, there is good reason to believe that the emergence of these international commercial courts adds a significant dimension to the resolution of, among other things, commercial disputes which have an international flavour. Because of the reasons behind their establishment and the role they play, the reality is that the international commercial markets will ultimately determine their success and longevity.

96 'International Commercial Courts: Towards a Transnational System of Dispute Resolution' (n. 18), paragraph 66.

97 Ibid., paragraph 67.

2

International Commercial Courts

Possible Problematic Social Externalities of a Dispute Resolution Product with Good Market Potential

THOMAS SCHULTZ AND CLÉMENT BACHMANN*

2.1 Introduction

International commercial courts are likely to work well as a consent-based international dispute resolution mechanism, as something private autonomy will desire, as something serving law's industry. They come across as easy to like, easy to sell, easy to buy. Think of them as something introduced by Jony Ive – the deep, soothing, British-accented voice in Apple's commercials who makes complex technology understandable, oneiric, something that will finally make your life right. Some adjustments, probably, will be needed here and there for the hybrid courts, but overall, they appear likely to be a fine new product of the arbitration industry at large. Hybrid justice has excellent marketing characteristics, making international commercial courts quite alluring 'litigation destinations', as Pamela Bookman puts it.[1] If there existed something like shares of hybrid international commercial courts in general, they likely would be a rather safe investment. Then again, perhaps the shares should not be held for too long.

In the longer run, the wider social implications of privatized dispute resolution might become disruptive and upset the field. Dispute

* An earlier version of this chapter, making some of the same points, was published as Thomas Schultz and Clément Bachman, 'A Wig for Arbitrators: What Does It Add?', in Rita Trigo Trindade, Rashid Bahar and Giulia Neri-Castracane (eds.), *Vers les sommets du droit, Liber Amicorum pour Henry Peter* (Schulthess 2019) 105. This chapter is a substantial revision of that earlier version.

[1] Pamela Bookman, 'The Adjudication Business' (2020) 45 Yale Journal of International Law. Available at: https://digitalcommons.law.yale.edu/yjil/vol45/iss2/1.

resolution mechanisms, international commercial courts and arbitration included, are not *just* dispute resolution mechanisms. Now, in strict twentieth-century black letter, neat logic-oriented, systems-directed, category-focused legal thinking, perhaps they were.[2] In that way of thinking, the parties choose to go to arbitration or to hybrid dispute resolution and, if they choose freely, that is that. Like what happens between consenting adults, it is not legitimately anyone else's business. Arbitrators and the semi-private judges of hybrid courts owe it to the parties to respect their consent and if they do not, there are doctrines, rules and the like to annul the decisions and oppose their enforcement. In more contemporary legal thinking, however, things tend to be different (not, of course, that there is only one form of contemporary legal thinking). There we may try to remember that law, lawyers, legal scholars and dispute settlement institutions exist to serve men and women in communal life; not the reverse, where men and women serve law's neatly logical internal perfection and its makeshift legitimation through self-injected constitutionalization, or even serve law's industry. There, dispute resolution institutions are also institutions which sustain or support a certain social order, with its own cultural features, its own values, norms and beliefs, and its own economic arrangements and distribution of wealth. Once we think of dispute resolution institutions that way, it is hard not to consider that individuals and societies tend to become, generally speaking, ever more likely to react to social orders which edge away from their own cultural and economic aspirations. A simple example is the growing backlash against investment arbitration, which may be understood as a mounting reaction to the social order this form of dispute settlement generates – a reaction that has started to spill over into a guarded attitude towards arbitration in general, into the first

[2] This kind of thinking was epitomized by International Court of Justice Judge Gerald Fitzmaurice. 'The real fault of the lawyers', he insisted, 'is that they have not, as lawyers, been single-minded enough, and have not resisted the temptation to stray into other fields', because 'the value of the legal element depends on its being free of other elements or it ceases to be legal'. Gerald Fitzmaurice, 'The United Nations and the Rule of Law' (1953) 38 Transactions of the Grotius Society 135, 140, 142. Pierre Schlag calls this way of thinking the grid aesthetic: 'Law is pictured as a two-dimensional area divided into contiguous, well-bounded legal spaces. These spaces are divided into doctrines, rules, and the like. Those doctrines, rules, and the like are further divided into elements, and so on and so forth. The subjects, doctrines, elements, and the like are cast as "object-forms". . . . The grid aesthetic is the aesthetic of bright-line rules, absolutist approaches, and categorical definitions.' Pierre Schlag, 'The Aesthetics of American Law' (2002) 115 Harvard Law Review 1047, 1051. In sum, think orthodox twentieth-century private international law scholarship.

signs of a disruption of the overall field of arbitration.[3] A similar pushback may well be fuelled by the rise of hybrid commercial justice. Dispute resolution is not simply something which happens between consenting adults in a closed room (or another closed space, for that matter) and which stays there.

In the first section of this chapter, we will review the main features that give hybrid justice its appeal as a product on the dispute resolution market. We will also show, briefly, how the arbitration industry uses these features in business campaigns and academic discourses advertising hybrid international commercial courts. The second section of the chapter then explains why these features are likely to be more oneiric than real and that the reality is likely more complicated and warrants more caution. This will mean that a strong push in favour of hybrid international commercial courts might eventually trigger a commensurate pushback against privatized dispute resolution in general.

Brutally simplified, the overall cautionary story this chapter tells is this. Too much privatization of justice, through both international commercial courts and international arbitration, may well have problematic social externalities: they may well reinforce a specific social order against which people may well revolt. And this backlash might cause more harm to privatized justice than the short-term benefits these developments might bring to its industry. As Sir William Blair put it, in a slightly different context, 'some of the vast amount written on the subject seems more of a sales pitch than an attempt at analysis'.[4] Pretending and wearing masks may be fine, it may even be intrinsic to dispute resolution, necessary for it, but we should be wary not to get caught in our own game, not to believe it ourselves.[5]

2.2 Appealing Features of Hybrid Justice

Two of the key marketing characteristics of international commercial courts, two of the main features that make them so appealing, revolve around the power and the legitimacy of courts, and the fact that they

[3] See, for instance, Malcolm Langford and Daniel Behn, 'Managing Backlash: The Evolving Investment Treaty Arbitrator?' (2918) 29 European Journal of International Law 551.

[4] William Blair, 'Contemporary Trends in the Resolution of International Commercial and Financial Disputes', Institute of Commercial and Corporate Law Annual lecture delivered at Durham University, 21 January 2016, 4.

[5] Thomas Schultz and François Ost, 'Shakespearean Legal Thought in International Dispute Settlement' (2018) 9 Journal of International Dispute Settlement 1, 12–18.

participate in what is presented as a race to the top in international dispute resolution.

The point about the power of courts is simple: international commercial courts can circumvent the problems of arbitrability and joinder. For instance, the Singapore International Commercial Court has both the authority to resolve non-arbitrable matters (such as special torts arising from contract, and international intellectual property or trust disputes) and the power to join third parties without their consent.[6] Michael Hwang puts it clearly with regard to the question of arbitrability: 'The target client pool of the SICC will be parties which have disputes (actual or potential) with their counterparties, and who do not immediately think of arbitration as an option. They do not wish to have their cases heard by national courts for various reasons, and yet have reservations about certain features of international arbitration. These reservations would include: . . . the restrictions on the scope of arbitration because of the doctrine of arbitrability.'[7] Dalma Demeter and Kayleigh Smith make essentially the same point, but about joinder. International commercial courts, they argue, are '[t]argeting cases where joinder of third parties is required'.[8] The idea is simple: the intended clients of hybrid justice here are those who do not like courts for some reason, but who do not buy into arbitration either, because of questions of scope.

Calling on the image of Jony Ive again, one might think here of customers who do not like computers for some reason, and yet have reservations about smartphones because their screens are too small for what they want to do with them. Give them a smartphone of sorts with a bigger screen. So we have the iPad, a hybrid computer-smartphone. The logic is simple and effective. Marta Requejo Isidro is straightforward about it: 'International commercial courts are public courts. As such, they are apt to provide an "adjudicative offer" in ways arbitrators are not.'[9] Offers that the competition cannot beat. Psychologically (sales strategies owe much to psychology), one might take this one step further and understand international commercial courts as institutions which are appealing because they are less loose, less floating, than some consider

6 Justice Quentin Loh, 'The Limits of Arbitration' (2014) 1 McGill J Disp Resol 66, 81.

7 Michael Hwang, 'Commercial Courts and International Arbitration: Competitors or Partners?' (2015) 31 Arbitration International 193, 196–7.

8 Dalma R. Demeter and Kayleigh M. Smith, 'The Implications of International Commercial Courts on Arbitration' (2016) 33 Journal of International Arbitration 441, 445.

9 Marta Requejo Isidro, 'International Commercial Courts in the Litigation Market' (2019) (2) *MPILux Research Paper Series*, 26.

arbitration to be. All these theories about delocalized arbitration and about arbitration operating within its own transnational legal system are not to everyone's liking; arbitration comes across, to some, as excessively loose. Hybrid justice psychologically brings arbitration back down to earth, to comfortable notions of territoriality, to the fantasies of power and control associated with territory. In this they ride the general societal anti-globalization wave currently in fashion.[10]

Then there is the appeal of the legitimacy of courts. Legitimacy has a number of meanings, so that to situate the argument a first brief discussion of the concept is needed at this juncture, to which we will return. The sort of legitimacy we mean here is one that justifies the creation of new dispute resolution fora, one that justifies the choice of the parties to resort to hybrid justice and the ensuing power of third neutrals over the parties. This sort of justificatory legitimacy relies on standards which resonate with the value orientation of the particular audience to which the thing in question is to be justified. What makes something legitimate, in this particular sense of the concept of legitimacy, is whether this something is attuned to the particular rhetorical sensitivities of the audience for which the something is meant to be legitimate.[11]

Put differently, it is the alignment with trends and the use of signalling buzzwords that marks something as legitimate in that sense. Think of the word 'organic' as a food label. Producing more organic food, allowing supermarkets to use all manner of strategies to sell more of it, is 'legitimate' in that sense, because 'organic' is good and 'chemical' bad, because 'natural' is right and 'manmade' wrong. The ideal product then, from the point of view of the food industry, is one that would barely need to be changed, but could now come with the label 'organic'. Now you pay more for it, because it comes with the label and you feel good about it.

Likewise with hybrid justice – at least to some extent. The signalling buzzword, the elevating label, here, is 'court'. It is a buzzword because it evokes the state, the opposite of privatization. Just as 'manmade', 'technology', 'science' and 'the scientific method' and 'experts' were for a long while markers of civilization and progress, of legitimate developments, and then at

[10] Georgios Dimitropoulos, 'International Commercial Courts in the "Modern Law of Nature": Adjudicatory Unilateralism in Special Economic Zones' (2021) 24 Journal of International Economic Law 361.

[11] For a longer and clearer discussion of these questions, see Thomas Schultz, 'Legitimacy Pragmatism in International Arbitration: A Framework for Analysis', in Jean Kalicki and Mohamed Abdel Raouf (eds.), *Evolution and Adaptation: The Future of International Arbitration*. ICCA Congress Series No. 20 (Kluwer 2020) 25.

some stage shifted to quite the opposite, 'privatization' was for a long while a marker of better, more efficient, more legitimate dispute resolution services, but now seems to be shifting to quite the opposite, rightly or wrongly. Increasing criticism is heaped on arbitration, understood as an epitome of sorts of privatized dispute resolution, as it becomes clear that the ethos of arbitration is very much centred on the arbitration industry itself and mostly pays lip service to external interests and values.[12] In other words, as it becomes clear that arbitration is too 'private', the opposite values become the new standards of legitimacy, and the associated buzzwords become the markers of that legitimacy. 'Court', 'public', 'transparency', 'the state': these are the new trending buzzwords, the new hashtags, the new labels of legitimate dispute resolution services. And, again, the ideal product is one that could be changed just a little but could now come with these new labels. Hybrid justice, in that sense, is a godsend. The arbitration industry's joy is understandable.[13]

So far, then, the simple idea is this: the word 'arbitration' is increasingly a red flag pointing to critical discourses in politics, in the media, in general societal discussions. The corresponding institutional symbolic capital is therefore transferred to its opposite of sorts: courts.

Beyond this simple idea, where one institution's loss in symbolic capital is another's win, insofar as the two institutions are usually presented as opposites, there seem to be at least two reasons why courts, and thus international commercial courts, are credible depositors of the transferred capital, two reasons why they indeed appear more legitimate than arbitration. Both reasons revolve around different forms of public interests – again a symbolical opposite of privatization.

Before we turn to these two reasons why hybrid justice would take more public interests into consideration than arbitration and is thus more legitimate, we should point out that the two reasons seem far more effective in the long run as marketing strategies than the earlier argument that the resolution of private disputes does not, in fact, entail any public interests. The typical argument goes as follows, here in the words of Gary Bell:

> There are instances where arbitral tribunal, in deciding commercial cases must also decide issues of public law and public policy and this may indeed raise issues of legitimacy – why should private individuals

[12] Thomas Schultz, 'The Ethos of Arbitration', in Thomas Schultz and Federico Ortino (eds.), *Oxford Handbook of International Arbitration* (Oxford University Press 2020) 235.

[13] Schultz and Bachman, 'A Wig for Arbitrators', 105–6.

> appointed by non-state entities decide issues of public law and public policy, one may ask. However, in the vast majority of commercial arbitration cases there are no such public law issues. In any event, the SICC as its very name indicates, is about commercial activities, not investments, and it is very unlikely that an investment dispute in which a sovereign state is involved would come to the SICC. Therefore, the legitimacy of the SICC is to be compared to the legitimacy of commercial arbitration which remains rather high.[14]

The red herring here is remarkable, when public interest becomes 'public law and public policy' and then merely 'public law' (which of course, true to the grid aesthetic, omits unorthodox scholarship on the public implications of, for instance, private contract law, which goes back at least to the 1930s[15]). In any event, it seems far more effective, as we will see, to acknowledge the involvement of public interests and then argue that these public interests are properly taken into account.

The two reasons go as follows. First, states are political entities, in the sense that they are instruments of 'who gets what, when, how', as Harold Lasswell would put it, defining politics.[16] They are a mechanism that transforms interest-based inputs (among other types of input) into an authoritative allocation of values (in the sense of things which have value, not in the axiological sense).[17] In that sense, they are a 'political system', in David Easton's understanding of that concept.[18] In fact, every social institution which turns interest-based inputs into an authoritative allocation of values and thus determines who gets what, when, and how is a political system, including arbitration.[19] But the difference between a state as a political system and arbitration as a political system is that states are expected to be open to a far wider array of inputs, to take into account a far wider array of interests. The whole idea of democratic states is that they aggregate a diversity of interests as great as possible, as representative as possible of all the individuals and communities whose values they allocate. As it becomes ever clearer that even the resolution of disputes which are technically of a private nature effectively has an

[14] Gary Bell, 'The New International Commercial Courts: Competing with Arbitration? The Example of the Singapore International Commercial Court' (2018) 11 Contemp Asia Arb J 193, 212.

[15] Morris Cohen, 'The Basis of Contract' (1933) 46 Harvard Law Review 553, 585–91.

[16] Harold Lasswell, *Politics: Who Gets What, When, How* (P. Smith 1950).

[17] David Easton, *A Framework for Political Analysis* (Prentice Hall 1965), 79–83.

[18] Ibid.

[19] Cédric Dupont and Thomas Schultz, 'Towards a New Heuristic Model: Investment Arbitration As a Political System' (2016) 7 Journal of International Dispute Settlement 3.

impact on the allocation of values far beyond the parties to the dispute, it becomes correspondingly clearer that what is needed to resolve these disputes is a 'political system' (in Easton's sense) which is open to the interest-based inputs of, ideally, all those whose values are allocated.

To put this in a way which is comprehensible from within the orthodox dispute resolution ontology: if arbitration caters essentially to 'the commercial community' but has effects on society at large, then it is a less good fit than a dispute resolution mechanism which is part of the state, which is by this token more likely to cater to wider audiences, at least a priori. To put this even more simply, if a dispute resolution mechanism has effects on society at large, then it should be designed as something that structurally reflects the interests of society at large. Courts, because they are part of the state, are precisely that. Arbitration, because it is a business dispute resolution system for business by business, is precisely not that. Or, to offer one last iteration of the same core idea, it is *the extent to which* a dispute resolution mechanism has effects on society at large (because they all do have *some* effect beyond the nominal parties in front of them) which determines *the extent to which* the mechanism should structurally reflect the interests of society at large. If arbitrations are few and far between, we may not need to worry about this, but the more arbitration expands the greater the concern becomes.[20]

Justice Quentin Loh essentially recognized as much in his promotion of international commercial courts. Instead of denying that public interests are at stake, he argued that international commercial courts, because they are courts and because they are thereby part of the state, can precisely handle these public interests appropriately. Here is how he put it. 'When the issue at stake affects the public interest – a more and more common occurrence linked to the proliferation of public-private contracts entered into by States or their emanations and private partners', then, he argues, dispute resolution fora with the name 'court' are a better fit.[21] 'Court', a dispute resolution mechanism by the public for the public, is the buzzword that invokes the oneiric image of public interest considerations.

The second reason why hybrid justice would take more public interests in consideration than arbitration is less important and probably comes straight from societal experiments with investor-state dispute resolution,

[20] Thomas Schultz and Thomas D. Grant, *Arbitration: A Very Short Introduction* (Oxford University Press 2021), chapter 6.

[21] Quentin Loh cited in Isidro (n. 9).

where many advance the understanding that international investment courts would be preferable to investment arbitration. The idea is simply that the more states are involved, the more *state* interests are taken into consideration. Not public interests, then, in the sense of interests of the broader public, but public interests in the sense of the interests of *states.* And not only the particular interests of the particular state involved, but also common state interests. Interests that states share because they are states.

The great thing, for the arbitration industry, about international commercial courts, about hybrid justice, is that these considerations do not have to translate into capitulation. The arbitration industry does not have to make what would be, in Lucy Reed's terms, 'an abject retreat'.[22] The idea of this 'retreat' is that arbitration, as an industry, may have gone too far, may have expanded too far into areas of significant public interest and sensitivity for which it was not meant, precisely because in terms of dispute resolution design it is suboptimal for the integration of public interests.[23]

To understand the dynamics of the situation, it is important to briefly pause here and notice the words just used, both the adjective and the noun: 'an *abject retreat*'. The admission that litigation is a dispute resolution mechanism that is perhaps better suited than arbitration to deal with certain kinds of disputes is presented as 'an abject retreat.' Such conquest language does not seem appropriate coming from the director of a university centre for international law – a research institute by nature meant to promote something nearing objective knowledge. (Consider the equivalent: a director of a university research laboratory in epidemiology who refers, in a scientific publication, to not using a given drug in the treatment of a given disease as an 'abject retreat' for that drug, while he sells this drug himself, directly, in addition to his employment as laboratory director.) Whether this is an instance of the 'post-shame age' in international law which Fuad Zarbiyev describes,[24] or whether this is an instance of what social psychologists call groupthink[25] (something like

[22] Lucy Reed, 'International Dispute Resolution Courts: Retreat or Advance – The 10th John E. C. Brierley Memorial Lecture' (2018) 4 McGill J. Disp. Resol. 129, 136–7.

[23] See a summary of the discussion in Schultz and Grant, *Arbitration.*

[24] Fuad Zarbiyev, 'International Law in an Age of Post-shame' (2020) 9(3) ESIL Reflections. Available at: https://esil-sedi.eu/wp-content/uploads/2020/07/ESIL-Reflection-Zarbiyev-2.pdf.

[25] Cass Sunstein and Reid Hastie, *Wiser: Getting beyond Groupthink to Make Groups Smarter* (Harvard Business Review Press 2014).

'in my circle, which is highly homogeneous, it is fine to say this and I do not know what other circles would say'),[26] or whether this is something yet different may be worth exploring to understand how the field of private and hybrid dispute resolution forms ideas and opinions. But for the time being, in the context of this chapter, it is sufficient to notice the fact.

It is not so, then, with hybrid justice, that the arbitration industry has to give back to traditional litigation the territory it has taken over the past forty years. Quite the opposite. The arbitration industry can harness the rhetorical power of the word 'court', re-legitimize itself, and continue to expand. Quoting Reed again: it is by 'leaving the Arbitration v Courts ... debate' that the arbitration industry can achieve 'the best of all possible worlds'.[27] And the operative word to achieve this is, precisely, 'hybridization'. Something new, something better. 'Hybridization' is like 'transnationalization' or 'harmonization' – it expresses a diffuse sense of finding the right balance, getting the best of both worlds, keeping all the good stuff while getting rid of the bad. To be sure, finding the right balance will hardly stir much public outcry as balance is generally considered an unconditional positive. Notice the irony: while courts and arbitration were often competitors, courts, as an idea, as a symbolic institution, as a socially appealing label, are now used to legitimize (hybrid) arbitration.

Then again, the idea is not simply to fuse litigation and arbitration, just like the iPad has never seriously been intended to do away with laptops and iPhones. The idea clearly is to offer an *additional* product on a competitive market. And an additional product on a competitive market is meant to spur competition. And competition, in turn, is meant to make everyone try a little harder, do a little better. So that, at the end of the reasoning, hybrid justice would make everything a little better – arbitration, litigation and of course itself.

International commercial courts are particularly appealing in that sense because they are the latest innovative product of a competition industry. One should want them the way one wants new technology, an 8 K TV set, an Apple Watch, an electric Harley Davidson. When Chief Justice Michael Hwang underscores the need, now, for 'a serious campaign of overseas marketing',[28] when Justice Anselmo Reyes argues that

[26] See an application to arbitration of groupthink in Myriam Gicquello, 'The Reform of Investor-State Dispute Settlement: Bringing the Findings of Social Psychology into the Debate' (2019) 10 Journal of International Dispute Settlement 561.

[27] Reed (n. 22).

[28] Hwang (n. 7), 197.

'[i]n a more competitive marketplace, costs decrease and efficiency increases',[29] they do not mean new consumer goods; they mean international commercial courts. Dispute resolution fora, in the field's discourse, are primarily portrayed as products to be sold like any other product, plain and simple. Bookman puts it eloquently: 'international commercial courts seem to be engaging in "forum selling"'.[30] And Requejo continues: '[e]xpressions such as forum selling or forum shopping epitomize the consequences of the competition between jurisdictions in terms that evoke the selection or the promotion of a consumer product'.[31] The objective is hidden in plain sight. International commercial courts 'will create a platform to catalyse the further growth of the legal services sector and to expand the scope for the internationalisation and export of [a country's] law'.[32] It brings to mind John Maynard Keynes' famous remark, which is more of an aphorism than he probably thought: as the UK representative in UK-US negotiations on what would much later become the GATT and the WTO, he asked, '[i]sn't our scheme intended to get things done, whereas yours [the United States'] will merely provide a living for a large number of lawyers?'[33] Bookman confirms that this is not so special: 'In other contexts, scholars have noted that lawyers have strong incentives to lobby states to supply new legal "products" that will generate revenues for the lawyers.'[34] So yes, more remuneration is to be had for us, the transnational adjudication gang, in our never-ending race to keep up with the Joneses. And Yves Dezalay and Bryant Garth have made clear that this has worked extremely well in the past: the rise of international arbitration throughout the twentieth century was largely the result of the purposeful creation of a market by the lawyers who directly benefit from it.[35] The entrepreneurial success has to be admired: by some accounts, just investment arbitration,

[29] Anselmo Reyes, 'The Business of International Dispute Resolution', (2017) 4 J. Int'l & Comp. L. 69, 80.
[30] Bookman (n. 1).
[31] Isidro (n. 9), 28.
[32] Report of the Singapore International Commercial Court Committee, November 2013, p. 23.
[33] Robert Skidelsky, *John Maynard Keynes: Fighting for Britain, 1937–1946* (Macmillan 2000), 416.
[34] Bookman (n. 1), citing Jonathan R. Macey and Geoffrey P. Miller, 'Origin of the Blue Sky Laws' (1991) 70 Texas Law Review 347.
[35] Yves Dezalay and Bryant Garth, 'International Commercial Arbitration: The Creation of a Legal Market', in Thomas Schultz and Federico Ortino (eds.), *The Oxford Handbook of International Arbitration* (Oxford University Press 2020) 769.

a comparatively marginal practice, has generated more than US$10 billion in fees for the arbitration industry, with an additional three quarters of a billion each year.[36] The old recipe is likely to work, as legal entrepreneurs (i.e., us) create new legal products, convince the world of a need for such products, and then supply these products. Deborah Hensler and Damira Khatam recognize it plainly: arbitration 'not only supports international commerce, it has *become a business* in itself'.[37] In fact it always, probably, has been.

But there is nothing wrong with that. Quite the contrary: the litigation sales competition is presented as a 'race to excellence'.[38] The typical narrative, as Bookman puts it critically, is that of a '"race to the top" for tribunals to develop the best, most efficient procedures to resolve disputes', where 'these jurisdictions are all striving to provide the 'best' possible dispute resolution, resulting in innovation that can promote choice, customization, and efficiencies'.[39]

To be clear, our argument is not that *the actual political driver* for the development of international commercial courts always is an attempt to take litigation market shares away from other countries and cities. Bookman has compellingly shown that the political motive for the creation of some of these courts is the attraction of greater foreign investment (which, as she points out, is not a plan very likely to work,[40] in the same way that offering investment arbitration to attract foreign investment is not a plan very likely to work) or just standard diffusion effects (i.e., political imitation). Our argument is that *the sales strategy* used to promote international commercial courts relies in part on this idea of instrumental competition, where competition is the instrument,

[36] Cédric Dupont, Thomas Schultz and Merih Angin, 'Double Jeopardy? The Use of Investment Arbitration in Times of Crisis', in Daniel Behn, Ole K. Fauchald, and Malcolm Langford (eds.), *The Legitimacy of Investment Arbitration: Empirical Perspectives* (Cambridge University Press 2020) 258.

[37] Deborah R. Hensler and Damira Khatam, 'Reinventing Arbitration: How Expanding the Scope of Arbitration is Re-shaping Its Form and Blurring the Line between Private and Public Adjudication' (2018) 18 Nev LJ, 381, emphasis added.

[38] 'Turning point or brewing storm, a race to excellence has begun'; see Winnie Jo-Me Ma, 2018 Taipei International Conference: Competitive, Collaborative or Cooperative Relations between Litigation, Arbitration and Mediation? Kluwer Arbitration Blog, 23 October 2018, available at http://arbitrationblog.kluwerarbitration.com/2018/10/23/2018-taipei-international-conference-competitive-collaborative-cooperative-relations-litigation-arbitration-mediation accessed 10 June 2020.

[39] Bookman (n. 1).

[40] Ibid., citing John F. Coyle, 'Business Courts and Interstate Competition' (2012) 53 Wm & Mary L Rev 1915.

the invisible hand guaranteeing ever-improving services and the desirability of the market's top product. Political drivers and (subsequent) sales strategies can differ. Bookman again: '[o]nce they are established, they can begin to adopt other kinds of innovation'.[41]

2.3 Likely Less Appealing Realities

So the main features making hybrid justice appealing as a product on the dispute resolution market are that they are technically courts, and thus have the power and legitimacy of courts as state organs, and that they are the latest innovative product in the race to the top in international dispute resolution. While the power of courts as state organs, allowing international commercial courts to be shielded from questions of arbitrability and joinder, seems indeed to be a fair advantage of hybrid justice, the two other features (legitimacy as courts and latest innovative product) appear to be more rhetorical than real. The reality is likely less appealing. *Likely*, because we do not really know. We do not really know because arbitration and commercial dispute resolution scholarship spends its time doing something else, which is often useful, but really not always, at least not for the commercial dispute resolution institutions themselves, in the societal sense (in the societal sense it does not mean the one, for instance, to be found on avenue du President Wilson in Paris).

We will deal with both the argument of the legitimacy of courts as state organs and the argument of the latest innovative product in one discussion, because in our approach they are linked. They are linked because the argument of the latest innovative product essentially means that international commercial courts promise to deliver what they deliver better, faster, more efficiently. And the cause of concern we see is not with the *how* but with the *what*, with *what* international commercial courts deliver, what they produce, what effects they may have.

At this juncture we need to pick up the discussion we started earlier in this chapter about the concept of legitimacy. In that previous part of the discussion we focused on a notion of legitimacy which draws on rhetorical sensitivities, on the 'wow' effect, on the a priori attraction of certain features of dispute resolution design. In the current part of the discussion we switch to a more substantive notion of legitimacy, because this is the notion of legitimacy which could, eventually, lead to the backlash.

[41] Ibid.

The context of these notions of legitimacy is the assessment of institutions, of their existence, their particular shape, their operations. These are notions of legitimacy used to account for people's support and espousal of institutions, and conversely their disapproval and neglect and attack of them. These positions towards institutions are based, at least partly, on people's assessment and perception of them. People's position on the legitimacy of an institution, in the most ordinary sense of the word, is essentially the sum of their different assessments and perceptions expressed in the binary mode of legitimate/illegitimate. 'The legitimacy' of an institution, in that sense, plays a critical role for its evolution over time, possibly for its life and demise. Importantly, such legitimacy notions are non-Kantian, as it were, in the sense of radically *not* categorical imperatives, they are not universal in the sense of valid throughout space and time: they cannot lead to the identification of intrinsic merits of institutions, of qualities of universal value that institutions would have and that could explain, ensure, justify or augur of their success. Legitimate institutions, in that sense, are always only legitimate to given people at a given point in social space and time; they are always only legitimate in the relative perspective of someone, nothing more. Such notions of legitimacy cannot allow us to argue that an institution is legitimate or illegitimate in the abstract, once and for all, with regard to everyone.

The substantive notion of legitimacy we rely on here focuses on this question: who benefits from a given institution, in the rational-choice theory sense of seeing one's actual interests being furthered but also in the behavioural-economics approach of seeing one's emotional and other non-rational preferences being furthered? Does a given institution, as it currently stands or in the way it evolves, benefit a certain group, community, category of people? How do institutional changes impact the interests and values of all affected people? The assumption behind these questions is simple: people are likely to support institutions they perceive to serve their interests and values, and to oppose, or try to change those which do not. In other words, the inquiry posits a correlation between the values and interests a regime serves and the colouration of its supporters' cluster. The more powerful such a cluster is, the more stable the institution would be.[42]

[42] See Cédric Dupont, Thomas Schultz and Jason Yackee, 'Investment Arbitration and Political Systems Theory', in Thomas Schultz and Federico Ortino (eds.), *Oxford Handbook of International Arbitration* (Oxford University Press 2020) 697.

Let us bring back into the discussion this idea we mentioned in the introduction: arbitration, international commercial courts, and probably all other dispute resolution mechanisms are not only mechanisms which resolve individual disputes. They are also institutions which create or sustain certain social orders. The fact that a number of disputes are resolved through given dispute resolution mechanisms, taken in the aggregate, leads to the enforcement or perpetuation of a certain power structure, certain axiological orientations, certain epistemic choices, the socio-professional positioning of certain actors, a certain type of wealth (re)distribution, certain patterns of relating or behaving. Dispute resolution institutions have social externalities: they increase and decrease certain social inequalities, foster and neglect certain values, spread and shut down certain norms, elevate and sideline certain status groups. And one institution may well create or perpetuate a given social order within the one wider social order, with its specific constellation of groups, values, and authorities, with its own ethos, social layout, and social dynamics.

To be clear, there is nothing theoretically new, or indeed tentative, here: the critical legal studies movement has long shown that law creates a certain social order, and that standard, state-centric and state-produced law tends to maintain the existing nation-based social orders and to reproduce existing power relations.[43]

But, now, how would international commercial courts do this, if they become important enough? What are these power structures, sets of norms and values, understandings of the world that the institution likely promotes? How do the ideological orientations and aesthetic prefigurations of international commercial judges differ from other judges? Do ideologies exist in hybrid justice which are less prevalent or altogether absent in the usual judiciary? Is there a specific arbitration/hybrid justice/private dispute resolution ethos that is not quite as strong at the bar in general? (Answer: attend an arbitration conference; five minutes of observation are enough.) Do the very principles underlying their work differ from those of other judges, or how does the difference impact the resulting social order? In a different context, Joost Pauwelyn conducted a well-known study showing that investment arbitrators are 'from Mars' ('Star Arbitrators', 'high-powered, elite jurists with a much deeper level of expertise and experience as compared to the average WTO panelist', with

[43] See for instance Duncan Kennedy, 'Legal Education and the Reproduction of Hierarchy' (1982) 32 Journal of Legal Education 591.

a self-centred, jostling and excluding personality) while WTO panellists are 'from Venus' ('Faceless Bureaucrats', 'diplomats or ex-diplomats, often without a law degree and mostly with relatively little experience', with a discreet and bureaucratic but inclusive personality), and how radically this changes the rules they make, the values they advance, the interests they promote.[44]

The inquiry could go further, and quite a bit: judges and lawyers in court have, so much should be obvious, certain constraints when they mentally reconstruct the world, when they apprehend reality, when they translate reality into the legal language used in court.[45] (Simply think of the difference between 'truth' and 'judicial truth' to see the point.) And thereby they 'legislate reality', as Pierre Schlag puts it, from a particular perspective.[46] As should also be obvious, legal academics have an altogether different set of constraints, typically vastly looser (though not on every point), when they reconstruct legal realities, when they explain legal phenomena, as they can use a whole array of ideational universes (types of ideas and references, ways of reasoning, objectives to attain, etc.) that judges and lawyers in court are simply not allowed to use in their profession.[47] Put differently, judges and academics have vastly different cosmogonies, different principles that undergird and filter how they reconstruct the world mentally; how they reconstruct it for their tasks; how they reconstruct it for themselves (think of areas of law neatly ordered to calm the judge's, or indeed the researcher's, own anxieties).[48] The question we should then ask here is this: what are those of private dispute resolution practitioners, or judges on international commercial courts? When arbitrators and hybrid justice judges apprehend the world, what are their incentives and constraints? Brutally simplified, do they wear different Wittgenstein-type glasses when they look at the world than

[44] Joost Pauwelyn, 'The Rule of Law without the Rule of Lawyers? Why Investment Arbitrators Are from Mars, Trade Adjudicators from Venus' (2015) 109 American Journal of International Law 761, 763, 768, 780, 783 (while informative, the study regrettably perpetuates male/female stereotypes: Mars/Venus are of course mythological symbols of masculinity and femininity; that they are to be associated, respectively, with high-poweredness and facelessness is regrettable, even if, knowing the author, the intention was undoubtedly different).

[45] Ana Luísa Bernardino, 'The Discursive Construction of Facts in International Adjudication' (2020) 11 Journal of International Dispute Settlement 175.

[46] Pierre Schlag, *Laying Down the Law: Mysticism, Fetishism, and the American Legal Mind* (New York University Press 1998) 133.

[47] Pierre Schlag, 'A Comment on Thomas Schultz's Editorial' (2014) 5 Journal of International Dispute Settlement 235.

[48] Thomas Schultz, 'Scholarship as Fun', Harvard Journal on the Legal Left, forthcoming.

judges, or anyone else, do?[49] Or, yet more brutally simplified: do arbitrators and international commercial court judges, and the practitioners before them, understand the world differently than judges do?[50] And how would this affect the social order they collectively create?

The problem with commercial arbitration and hybrid justice is that we have no idea; we do not know the first thing. Mostly, we do not ask. But it matters, in the long run. Not to the phenomenologists (they do not mind), but to dispute resolution practitioners, because it matters to society in the long run.

The question has in fact begun to be entertained with regard to arbitration, starting with the simplest and most tangible points: given that the proportion of male arbitrators, out of all arbitrators, is far greater than the proportion of male judges, out of all judges, does arbitration constitute a parallel patriarchal system of justice?[51] Are typically male values more prevalent (i.e., values typically associated with men), more readily enforced in arbitration than they are in comparable court procedures? Does, then, arbitration favour a more male social order? 'Arbitration: big white male justice': this sounds more like slogan than argument, but scores of students in arbitration programs describe it precisely like this. Students should not be treated as sages before the fact, to be sure, but their ingenuousness, or rather their lack of acculturation, may reveal things which we, precisely because we are too acculturated to dispute resolution, have difficulties noticing – like a fish who has difficulties noticing water, as Andrea Bianchi put it in a different context.[52]

[49] Ludwig Wittgenstein, *Philosophical Investigations* (Blackwell 2001 [1953]), §103: 'It is like a pair of glasses on our nose through which we see whatever we look at. It never occurs to us to take them off.'

[50] We hear the objection: 'This is silly! Why would they?' Answer: because they may have a different set of intellectual instruments, of ideologies in Žižek's sense, of preformed opinions, or pre-understandings in Gadamer's sense, or simply ontologies they need to have or adhere to in order to belong to the relevant community, or to 'fit in' in any other way. To make the point from yet a different angle, think of the recent popular book *Factfulness*, which explained that if you believe the world is getting worse on every front, you will reconstruct the daily reality, through selective attention and belief-informed guesses, in a very different manner than if you believe the world is getting better on very many fronts, and you will therefore end up living in a very different mentally reconstructed reality – see Hans Rosling, *Factfulness: Ten Reasons We're Wrong about the World – And Why Things Are Better Than You Think* (Flatiron 2018).

[51] For instance Schultz, 'Ethos' (n. 12).

[52] Andrea Bianchi, *International Law Theories. An Inquiry into Different Ways of Thinking* (Oxford University Press 2016) 1.

But the question of what social order international commercial courts could promote, sustain or create, and who would benefit from it, which group, community and category of people, and how these institutional developments would impact the interests and values of all affected people – these are questions that seem not to be asked, or asked only from a very specific, self-centred perspective. The substantive assessments of international commercial courts have so far essentially been done by us and for us. Our substantive assessment is confined to the interests of our community and of the current users of international commercial dispute settlement, the actors of international trade. The perspective is clear in the existing commentaries: international commercial courts are there to serve the interests of their users, and, as Madame de Pompadour would put it, *après nous le déluge*. The objective is unambiguous: 'Any commercial dispute resolution mechanism is ultimately placed at the service of users,'[53] 'to service the needs of the City of London (financial centre) and the business community'.[54] The nearly exclusive criteria by which these fora are judged are the deserved 'expectations',[55] 'needs'[56] and 'preferences',[57] 'benefits',[58] 'comfort'[59] and 'advantages'[60] of 'international business-to-business actors',[61] and of international 'legal practitioners'.[62] We assess whether these developments benefit our community and where the answer is positive, we work on advertising them, framing these developments in a way that will make them appear attractive to larger audiences. We try to convince others that what is good for us is good for them too. Our language, the words we use, the way we mobilize symbols and use soothing notions such as

[53] Justice Steven Chong, 'The Singapore International Commercial Court: A New Opening in a Forked Path', British Maritime Law Association Lecture, 21 October 2015, 19.
[54] Bell (n. 14), 193, 194.
[55] Reed (n. 22), 132–3, 147.
[56] Sundaresh Menon, 'International Commercial Courts: Towards a Transnational System of Dispute Resolution', Opening Lecture for the DIFC Courts Lecture Series 2015, 42–3; Andrew Godwin, Ian Ramsay and Miranda Webster, 'International Commercial Courts: The Singapore Experience' (2017) 18 Melb J Int'l Law 219, 259; Loh (n. 6), 82; Chong (n. 53), 19.
[57] Hwang (n. 7), 200.
[58] Johannes Landbrecht, 'The Singapore International Commercial Court (SICC) – an Alternative to International Arbitration?' (2016) 34 ASA Bulletin 112, 112.
[59] Loh (n. 6), 82.
[60] Vivian Ramsey, 'The Challenges to International Arbitration' (2017) 19 Asian Dispute Review 54, 57.
[61] Reed (n. 22), 147.
[62] Landbrecht (n. 58), 122.

'hybridization' – this is rhetoric, advertising. Of course, we tend to talk of universal rights, of the general interest, of universal and formal justice. Of course, we seek the best possible solution for all. But it is hard to deny that our substantive assessment is focused on very specific values and interests. We tend to equal the interests of international trade with the general interest, on the ground that global economic growth can only benefit the whole. Critical thoughts, marked as unhelpful, as too complicated, as too theoretical, as party spoilers, are quickly put away.

But let us not get caught in our own game and believe it ourselves. Heartening rhetoric and clever advertisement will delay serious societal scrutiny, but in the long run substantive assessments of the interests and values of others are probably critical. Importantly, the question may prove crucial even if we only cater for the interests of our community: if what we develop, in this case hybrid dispute resolution mechanisms, is not really good beyond for ourselves and negatively impacts states, common interests, society at large, then we should expect a pushback, a backlash from those people, those forces which do not benefit, and possibly suffer consequences, from what we do.

A few related things, taken from neighbouring fields, we do tend to know, and they may justify that we exercise caution. For instance, we tend to know that economic growth does not benefit everyone, that trickle-down economics is 'zombie economics' – dead theories we should realise are dead even if they are still among us.[63] The economic rise of just some categories of individuals is rather likely to increase resentment, and eventually lead to backlash, because of inequity aversion. As Samuel Scheffler puts it, elegantly summarizing a much more complex argument in a simple *New York Times* article, important inequalities compromise people's relations with one another and distort their understanding of themselves: 'The rich may persuade themselves that they fully deserve their . . . wealth and develop attitudes of entitlement and privilege. Those who have less may develop feelings of inferiority and deference, on the one hand, and hostility and resentment on the other.'[64] This does not augur well for legal institutions which increase inequalities – if of course they do, and this is why we should inquire and be cautious until we have inquired. There may also be a more fundamental societal rift looming in the future here: international commercial courts tend to be developed in

[63] John Quiggin, *Zombie Economics: How Dead Ideas Still Walk among Us* (Princeton University Press 2010).

[64] Samuel Scheffler, 'Is Economic Inequality Really a Problem?', *NY Times*, 1 July 2020.

societies which self-identify as societies of equals, but, as Samuel Scheffler puts it, '[t]here is a limit to the degree of economic inequality that is compatible with the ideal of a society of equals'.[65] To be sure, access to privatized and semi-privatized dispute resolution remains a privilege for the few. Arbitration, for instance, may offer justice, but the overwhelming majority of people and companies will never have access to it. If the right to choose one's judge, autonomy, impartiality and efficiency in dispute settlement are so fundamental, and if inequality in access to them amounts to real, social, economic inequality, then dispute resolution mechanisms should not remain luxury goods. The development of hybrid dispute resolution is unlikely to change anything in this respect. It more likely will merely offer new opportunities for the privileged few.

Beyond that, nothing indicates that hybrid court judges will be more representative than the existing pool of international arbitrators, that they will give greater attention to extra-communal interests and values (i.e., interests and values beyond those of the commercial community): the appointment process will not be much more participative, or democratic; the individuals appointed as international commercial judges will probably resemble today's arbitrators very much.[66] In fact, as this new institution is designed to take market shares from local courts, not arbitral tribunals, it would rather further replace local judges in all their diversity with a much more homogeneous global group of commercially oriented dispute resolution individuals.[67]

International commercial courts also are unlikely to take common state interests into particular account – these interests we described earlier as those that states share because they are states, and which are of a common, public nature. Hybrid mechanisms rather place states in direct competition, thus changing the setting from solidarity of interests to competition of interests. States then have an incentive to advance their particular interests as potential hosts of international dispute settlement

[65] Ibid.

[66] Stephan Wilske, 'International Commercial Courts and Arbitration: Alternatives, Substitutes or Trojan Horse' (2018) 11 *Contemp. Asia Arb. J.* 153, 166: *'[The] judges [are] all male, all rather senior and all with a rather British cultural background. Accordingly, whoever expects diversity to be reflected in the composition of the bench should pursue other options.'* Similarly, Hwang (n. 7) 195: '[i]t is interesting to note that, when the first cohort of overseas judges were appointed to the bench of the DIFC Courts, all of them were practising arbitrators, and hence were familiar with arbitration theory and practice.'

[67] On the homogeneity of the arbitration community, see Schultz, 'Ethos' (n. 12).

bodies,[68] to the possible detriment of interests they share with other states – or as Georgios Dimitropoulos would put it, a reclaiming of *national* sovereignty, one state against the other.[69] And an efficient way for a state to be a good host, a good litigation destination, is to grant wide autonomy to potential users: enabling them to shape the procedure, to determine the substantive rules applicable to the merits, and to apply these rules quite freely. We may thus set off a new race to the bottom, a race which will hardly lead to shift the political orientation of international dispute resolution.

Conclusion

There is a limit to how much money can be made with justice, and there is a limit to how much we can privatize it. Curiously enough, perhaps, at least in view of the staggering outpouring of writings on arbitration and other forms of privatized or semi-privatized justice, we barely know where these limits may lie; in fact we have never really asked ourselves that question, not seriously at least. But it is a question we can investigate. If we mean our field well, we *have to*. Because it certainly seems true that privatization or semi-privatization of dispute resolution is not an unqualified positive.

[68] Wilske (n. 66), 156.

[69] Georgios Dimitropoulos, 'National Sovereignty and International Investment Law: Sovereignty Reassertion and Prospects of Reform' (2020) 21 Journal of World Investment and Trade 71.

3

Transnational Adjudication and the Court of Justice of the European Union

CHRISTOPHER VAJDA*

3.1 Introduction: An Overview of the European Union Judicial System

The European Union (EU) judicial system provides a model of how transnational adjudication can work effectively. The EU can trace its origins back to the European Coal and Steel Community (ECSC) treaty covering coal and steel products which came into operation in 1952 and which created the Court of Justice of the European Union (CJEU) to control the legality of actions of the High Authority. In 1958 the treaty establishing the European Economic Community (EEC) came into effect.[1] The jurisdiction of the CJEU was expanded to cover the wider subject matter of the EEC treaty, covering all economic activity other than coal and steel and some aspects of nuclear energy, as well as introducing the procedure for a reference by a national court to the CJEU on a question of interpretation or validity of EU law.[2] A crucial – indeed unique – feature of EU law is that it is interpreted, applied and enforced not only by a transnational court, the CJEU but also by national courts and tribunals in all the Member States of the EU. Unlike the US system, which has separate federal and state courts, the EU has a unitary system where every court of a Member State, within the scope of its jurisdiction, is not only able, but also bound, to apply

* All opinions expressed are personal to the author.

1 Hereinafter called the EEC. However, unless otherwise stated, the expression EU will cover both the EEC and its successor, the European Community.

2 The Euratom treaty, which came into force at the same time as the EEC treaty, deals with nuclear energy issues. The ECSC treaty expired in 2002, so coal and steel now fall within the ambit of the TFEU.

EU law and to disapply any conflicting national law.[3] Central to this system is the procedure pursuant to Article 267 of the Treaty on the Functioning of the European Union (TFEU),[4] whereby a national court or tribunal of a Member State can, and in certain circumstances must,[5] refer to the CJEU a question on the interpretation or validity of EU law that is necessary in order to enable the national court or tribunal to give judgment in the case before it.[6] A national court has no power to declare an EU measure invalid; where it has serious doubts as to the validity of such a measure it must refer the question to the CJEU.[7] Article 267 provides for a system of judicial cooperation between national courts and the CJEU which serves to ensure the uniform interpretation of EU law. It is not therefore surprising that the CJEU has termed Article 267 the keystone of the EU legal order.[8]

[3] See, for example, Case 106/77 *Simmenthal* ECLI:EU:C:1978:49 and Case C-378/17 *Minister for Justice and Equality and the Commissioner of the Garda Síochána* v. *Workplace Relations Commission* ECLI:EU:C:2018:979 at paras. 36–9.

[4] European Union, *Consolidated Version of the Treaty on the Functioning of the European Union*, 13 December 2007, 2008/C 115/01 (hereinafter TFEU).

[5] Article 267(3) TFEU imposes an obligation on courts of final instance to make a reference. The CJEU has interpreted this provision strictly in the sense that such a court is only relieved of such an obligation if the answer would be equally clear, inter alia, to courts in all other Member States; see Case 283/81 *CILFIT* ECLI:EU:C:1982:335 and Case C-416/17 *Commission* v. *France* ECLI:EU:C:2018:811.

[6] This means that the CJEU has no jurisdiction to give an answer to a hypothetical question; see, for example, Case C-439/01 *Cipra and Kvasnicka* EU:C:2003:31 at para. 19.

[7] See Case 314/85 *Fotofrost* ECLI:EU:C:1987:452. Pending the outcome of the reference the national court may grant any necessary interim measures; see Case C-465/93 *Atlanta Fruchthandelsgesellschaft mbH and others* v. *Bundesamt für Ernährung und Forstwirtschaft* ECLI:EU:C:1995:369 (hereinafter *Atlanta*). The national court needs to respect four conditions – namely, that (1) it entertains serious doubts as to the validity of the EU act and, if the validity of the contested act is not already in issue before the CJEU, itself refer the question to the CJEU; (2) there is urgency, in the sense that interim relief is necessary to avoid serious and irreparable damage to the party seeking the relief; (3) it takes due account of the EU's interest; and (4) in its assessment of all those conditions, it respects any decisions of the CJEU or general court ruling on the lawfulness of the regulation or on an application for interim measures seeking similar interim relief at the European Community level.

[8] See *Opinion 2/13* ECLI:EU:C:2014:2454, at para. 176: 'the judicial system as thus conceived has as its keystone the preliminary ruling procedure provided for in Article 267 TFEU, which, by setting up a dialogue between one court and another, specifically between the Court of Justice and the courts and tribunals of the Member States, has the object of securing uniform interpretation of EU law, thereby serving to ensure its consistency, its full effect and its autonomy as well as, ultimately, the particular nature of the law established by the Treaties'; Case C-614/14 *Criminal Proceedings against Atanas Ognyano* ECLI EU:C:2016:514, at para. 36; and Case C-284/16 *Slowakische Republik* v. *Achmea BV* ECLI:EU:C:2018:158, at para. 37 (hereinafter *Achmea*).

This chapter will first focus on the approach of the CJEU as to what judicial bodies fall within the ambit of Article 267. It will then consider the specific question of whether an arbitral tribunal falls within Article 267 before turning to consider the CJEU's approach to the Investor-State dispute settlement mechanism[9] in the Comprehensive Economic and Trade Agreement between the EU and Canada (CETA) as set out in Opinion 1/17.[10] The chapter concludes by considering how the new national commercial courts established in some Member States of the EU are likely to operate within the EU judicial system.

3.2 What Is a Court or Tribunal of a Member State for the Purposes of Article 267 of the Treaty on the Functioning of the European Union?

For a body to be considered as a court or tribunal for the purposes of Article 267 TFEU, the CJEU takes account of a number of criteria such as whether the body in question is established by law, whether it is permanent, whether its jurisdiction is compulsory, whether its procedure is *inter partes*, whether it applies rules of law and whether it is independent.[11]

Where a legal enactment lists the body in question as a national court, that body is considered established by law.[12] As regards permanence, what is important is that the body is a permanent element in the court system even if the body does not itself sit permanently or its composition changes.[13] The criterion of compulsory jurisdiction is satisfied where the jurisdiction of the body is provided for by legislation and its jurisdiction does not depend on the will of parties, as is the case in contractual arbitration.[14] This was the

[9] Hereinafter ISDS.

[10] *Comprehensive Economic and Trade Agreement (CETA) between Canada and the European Union and Its Member States*, signed on 30 October 2016, OJ 2017 L11, P.23 (hereinafter CETA).

[11] See Case C-54/96 *Dorsch Consult Ingenieurgesellschaft mbH* v. *Bundesbaugesellschaft Berlin mbH* ECLI:EU:C:1997:413, para. 23 (hereinafter *Dorsch Consult*); Case C-377/13 *Ascendi Beiras Litoral e Alta and others* ECLI:EU:C:2014:1754, para 23 (hereinafter *Ascendi*); Case C-64/16 *Associação Sindical dos Juízes Portugueses* v. *Tribunal de Contas* ECLI:EU:C:2018:117, para. 44 and Case C-274/14 *Banco Santander* ECLI:EU:C:2020:17, paras. 56–63.

[12] *Ascendi*, at para. 24.

[13] Ibid., at paras 25–6.

[14] Case C-555/13 *Merck Canada* v. *Accord Healthcare* ECLI:EU:C:2014:92, paras. 19–20 and *Ascendi*, fn. 11, at paras. 27–9. On contractual arbitration, see Section 3 of this chapter.

case in *Ascendi* where the taxable person chose to bring legal proceedings before a court of arbitration rather than an administrative court as he was entitled to under national law. As the Advocate General put it, recourse to such a body is 'not contingent on the parties expressing a prior desire to submit disputes to arbitration'.[15] The jurisdiction of the body must be such that its decisions are binding, subject to any appeal.[16] The reference to an *inter partes* procedure and the application of the rule of law means that the basic principles of an adversarial procedure, such as a right to be heard, are to be respected and that the body in question applies rules of law.[17]

The independence of a court or tribunal is of fundamental importance as reflected not only in the case law of the CJEU, but also in both the Treaty on European Union (TEU) and the Charter of Fundamental Rights of the European Union.[18] Article 2 of the TEU provides that the Union is founded on the value of respect for the rule of law. The second paragraph of Article 19(1) of the Charter states that Member States shall provide remedies sufficient to ensure effective legal protection in the fields covered by Union law. The first paragraph of Article 47 of the Charter provides that '[e]veryone whose rights and freedoms guaranteed by the law of the Union are violated has the right to an effective remedy before a tribunal in compliance with the conditions laid down in this Article'. The second paragraph of that Article provides for the right 'to a fair and public hearing before an independent and impartial tribunal'.

The CJEU has held that the concept of independence has two aspects, one external and one internal. The external aspect presupposes, in particular, that the body concerned exercises its judicial functions wholly autonomously, without being subject to any hierarchical constraint or subordinated to any other body and without taking orders or instructions from any source whatsoever, and that it is thus protected against external interventions or pressure liable to impair the independent judgment of its members and to influence their decisions. This means that the members of the body concerned must be irremovable in the sense that, as a general rule, members of the body concerned are entitled to remain in post provided that they have not reached the obligatory retirement age or until the expiry of their mandate where that is for a fixed term. This principle of irremovability is only subject to exceptions warranted by

[15] Para. 28 of the Opinion of Advocate General Szpunar in *Ascendi*, fn. 11, cited with approval by the CJEU at para. 29 of its judgment.

[16] *Dorsch Consult*, fn. 11, at paras. 27–9, and *Merck Canada* at para. 19.

[17] *Ascendi*, fn. 11, at para 30.

[18] Hereinafter the Charter.

legitimate and compelling grounds, such as being unfit for office on grounds of incapacity or serious breach of their obligations, and are applied consistently with the principle of proportionality. Thus, the dismissal of members of a judicial body should be determined by specific rules. The internal aspect of independence is linked to impartiality, which requires objectivity and the absence of any interest in the outcome of the proceedings apart from strict application of the rule of law. This requires rules, in particular, as regards the composition of the body, length of service and grounds for dismissal of its members in order to dispel any reasonable doubt in the minds of individuals as to the imperviousness of that body to external factors and its neutrality with respect to the interests before it.[19]

For a judicial body to be a court or tribunal for the purposes of Article 267 TFEU it must also be 'of a Member State'. In this respect the CJEU has accepted that a court common to a number of Member States such as the Benelux Court of Justice falls within the ambit of Article 267 TFEU, as it ensures the uniform application of legal rules common to the three Benelux States and the procedure before it is a step in the proceedings before the national courts in one of those States.[20]

3.3 Does an Arbitral Tribunal Fall within Article 267 of the Treaty on the Functioning of the European Union and When Can It Apply European Union Law?

In the case of arbitration tribunals, one first needs to consider whether arbitration that arises from an agreement between two parties, that is to say contractual arbitration, falls within the concept of a court or tribunal for the purposes of Article 267 TFEU. In *Nordsee* the CJEU held that

[19] *Banco Santander*, fn. 11, at paras. 58–63. Applying this test, the CJEU found that a Spanish tax tribunal did not satisfy the requirement of independence as there was no special protection from removal from office. First, the general rules applicable to civil servants also applied to members of the tribunal, and secondly, in what was termed the extraordinary appeal procedure, the roles of the appellant tax ministry and the members of that tribunal were conflated so that it was impossible to regard the tribunal as a third party in relation to the tax ministry. In effect the CJEU departed from its earlier judgment in Joined Cases C-110/98 to C-147/98 *Gabalfrisa* EU:C:1999:489 where the CJEU had found that the tax tribunal did satisfy the test of independence. For a case on the other side of the line to *Banco Santander*, see Case C-396/14 *MT Hojgaard and Züblin* ECLI EU: C:2016:347 where the Danish tribunal was considered a court as the majority of its members were members of the judiciary who enjoyed the particular protection granted to members of the judiciary whereas the expert members who were in a minority did not.

[20] Case C-337/95 *Parfums Christian Dior SA* EU:C:1997:517 at paras. 21–3.

contractual arbitration did not fall within the scope of Article 267 TFEU.[21] This was because the relevant parties were under no obligation to refer their disputes to arbitration but had chosen by agreement to do so. Accordingly the arbitral jurisdiction was not compulsory.[22] Furthermore, the national authorities were not involved in the decision to opt for arbitration or called upon to intervene automatically in proceedings before the arbitrator.[23] As a result, the link between the arbitration procedure and the organization of legal remedies through the courts of Member States was not sufficiently close.[24] Subsequently the CJEU held that where a consumer agrees to the standard terms of a supplier, which include an arbitration clause, when purchasing a service the agreement to arbitration is also voluntary and therefore does not meet the compulsory jurisdiction criterion in Article 267 TFEU.[25] It follows that the CJEU has no jurisdiction to entertain a reference for preliminary ruling from such an arbitral tribunal.

Although such an arbitral tribunal is not a court or tribunal within the meaning of Article 267 TFEU, a court of a Member State, when reviewing such an arbitration award, can itself make a reference to the CJEU for a preliminary ruling.[26] *Eco Swiss* v. *Benetton* illustrates this approach.[27] The arbitration awarded Eco Swiss damages for wrongful termination of a contract which Benetton sought to have set aside in a Dutch court on the ground that the underlying agreement was void because it was contrary to EU competition rules. Dutch law, however, provided that an arbitration award could be annulled only on narrow grounds, one of which was if the award was contrary to public policy.[28] The referring court was of the opinion that a breach of EU competition rules did not necessarily entail a breach of public policy, such that it would not always be possible to set aside an award which gives effect to an anticompetitive (and hence void) contract. The CJEU held, however, that EU competition

[21] Case 102/81 *Nordsee Deutsche Hochseefischerei GmbH* v. *Reederei Mond Hochseefischerei Nordstern AG & Co. KG and Reederei Friedrich Busse Hochseefischerei Nordstern AG & Co. KG* ECLI:EU:C:1982:107 (hereinafter *Nordsee*).

[22] Ibid., at para. 11.

[23] Ibid., at para. 12.

[24] Ibid., at para. 13.

[25] Case C-125/04 *Denuit and Cordenier* ECLI:EU:C:2005:69.

[26] *Nordsee*, fn. 21, at paras. 14–15.

[27] Case C-126/97 *Eco Swiss China Time Ltd* v. *Benetton International NV* ECLI:EU:C:1999:269 (hereinafter *Eco Swiss*).

[28] Dutch law reflected the position under the New York Convention on the Recognition and Enforcement of Foreign Arbitral Awards 1958.

law was a 'fundamental provision which is essential . . . for the functioning of the internal market', the breach of which should therefore be considered a breach of public policy. As a result, a court faced with an application for annulment of an arbitral award 'must grant that application if it considers that the award in question is in fact contrary to [that competition] Article'.[29] As the Advocate General observed in *Eco Swiss*, 'the decision not to allow arbitrators to make references for a preliminary ruling under Article [267 TFEU] is in a sense "offset" by the importance the Court attaches to judicial review of arbitration awards'.[30]

Secondly, one needs to consider the case where arbitration is provided for in an international treaty between States for the resolution of disputes involving private investors. This occurs, for example, in a bilateral investment treaty (BIT) between two States whereby investment disputes between investors from one State and the State where the investment is situated are to be resolved by means of arbitration. This is called Investor-State dispute settlement (ISDS).

The question of whether such an arbitral tribunal in an ISDS mechanism can be a court or tribunal of a Member State for the purposes of Article 267 TFEU arose in *Achmea*.[31] In 2004, Slovakia opened up its domestic market to private sickness insurance operators. Achmea, a Dutch investor, entered the Slovak market, but following a change in Slovak law, it was no longer able to distribute its profits. Article 8 of the BIT between the Netherlands and Slovakia provided for arbitration. Article 8(6) stated that 'the arbitral tribunal shall decide on the basis of the law, taking into account in particular though not exclusively: the law in force of the Contracting Party concerned . . . other relevant agreements between the Contracting Parties . . . the general principles of international law'. Achmea brought arbitration proceedings against Slovakia for breach of the BIT. The arbitral tribunal sitting in Germany found in

[29] *Eco Swiss*, fn. 27, at paras. 36 to 37. The CJEU added that the competition rules could be regarded as a matter of public policy under the New York Convention.

[30] Ibid., at para. 30. The foundations of this approach can be traced back to *Nordsee*, fn. 21, at para. 14. 'If questions of [EU] law are raised in an arbitration resorted to by agreement the ordinary courts may be called upon to examine them either in the context of their collaboration with arbitration tribunals, in particular in order to assist them in certain procedural matters or to interpret the law applicable, or in the course of a review of an arbitration award – which may be more or less extensive depending on the circumstances – and which they may be required to effect in case of an appeal or objection, in proceedings for leave to issue execution or by any other method of recourse available under the relevant national legislation.'

[31] See fn. 8.

favour of Achmea. Slovakia then brought proceedings before the German courts to set aside the award on the basis that Article 8 of the BIT was contrary to EU law, including Article 267 and 344 TFEU.[32]

In a seminal judgment the CJEU held that EU law precluded a provision such as Article 8 of the BIT between the Netherlands and Slovakia. As the EU legal order is autonomous from the law of the Member States and from international law, it was for the national courts of the Member States and the CJEU to ensure judicial protection of rights of individuals under EU law. The fact that the arbitral tribunal was required to 'take account in particular of the law in force of the contracting party concerned and other relevant agreements between the contracting parties'[33] meant that there was a risk that it would be required to judge disputes of EU law, as EU law is both 'the law in force of the contracting party concerned' and a 'relevant agreement between the contracting parties'.[34] However, as the arbitral tribunal was situated outside the judicial system of either the Netherlands or Slovakia, it was not a court or tribunal 'of a Member State' and so could not make a reference to the CJEU. The CJEU distinguished this form of arbitration from contractual arbitration as considered in *Eco Swiss* on the basis that contractual arbitration involves voluntary consent by the parties to the arbitration whereas arbitration under a BIT amounted to an agreement by two Member States to remove from the jurisdiction of their own courts disputes which may concern the application or interpretation of EU law which had an adverse effect on the autonomy of EU law.[35] The effect of *Achmea* is that the national courts in EU Member States now have exclusive jurisdiction to determine disputes in intra-EU BITs.[36]

3.4 Investor–State Dispute Settlement in Trade and Investment Agreements to which the European Union Is a Party: Opinion 1/17

Even before the judgment in *Achmea* the EU Commission had been critical of the traditional methods of resolving disputes in trade and

[32] Art. 344 TFEU provides: 'Member States undertake not to submit a dispute concerning the interpretation or application of the Treaties to any method of settlement other than those provided for therein.'

[33] *Achmea* at paras. 40 to 41, fn. 8.

[34] Ibid.

[35] Ibid., at para. 55.

[36] The majority of the Member States of the EU have now given effect to this judgment in an agreement for the termination of BITs between the Member States of the European Union of 5 May 2020, OJ 2020 L 169, p. 1.

investment treaties through arbitration.[37] As a result it pushed for a new form of dispute resolution mechanism which would involve the creation of a permanent investment court. The blueprint for what the Commission has in mind is set out in the Comprehensive Economic and Trade Agreement between Canada and the EU and its Member States,[38] which has been the subject of Opinion 1/17 by the

[37] Former EU trade commissioner Cecilia Malmström stated that '[ISDS] is not fit for purpose in the 21st century. I want the rule of law, not the rule of lawyers. I want to ensure fair treatment for EU investors abroad, but not at the expense of governments' right to regulate.' Cecilia Malmström, 'Investments in TTIP and Beyond: Towards an International Investment Court' (*European Commission Blog*, 5 May 2015), https://ec.europa.eu/commission/2014-2019/Malmström/blog/investments-ttip-and-beyond-towards-international-investment-court_en, accessed 20 August 2019. She also criticized the absence of possibility to appeal errors of law or fact, the lack of legitimacy, accountability and transparency, and that the fragmented system has no coherent multilateral rules on investment protection, nor any permanent structure to resolve investment disputes. Cecilia Malmström, 'The Way ahead for an International Investment Court' (*European Commission Blog*, 18 July 2016), https://ec.europa.eu/commission/2014-2019/Malmström/blog/way-ahead-international-investment-court_en, accessed 20 August 2019. For a contrary view, see Judge Stephen Schwebel, 'The extensive Concept paper attached to [Commissioner Malmström's blog] cites no case illustrative of the rule of lawyers, and no case where the State was forced to change legislation ... If there are awards sustaining the investor's "expectations of profits" they are not cited in the EU's papers'; in Stephen Schwebel, 'The Proposals of the European Commission *for* Investment Protection and an Investment Court System' (Washington, DC, 17 May 2016), http://isdsblog.com/wp-content/uploads/sites/2/2016/05/THEPROPOSALSOFTHEEUROPEANCOMMISSION.pdf, accessed 20 August 2019. Judge Schwebel has served as a judge (World Bank Administrative Tribunal, International Monetary Fund Administrative Tribunal and International Court of Justice), as well as an arbitrator (permanent Court of Arbitration and a plethora of private arbitrations). See Lesley Dingle, 'Judge Stephen Schwebel: International Jurist *Extraordinaire:* A Further Contribution to the Cambridge Eminent Scholars Archive' (2009) University of Cambridge, https://papers.ssrn.com/sol3/papers.cfm?abstract_id=3220499, accessed 20 August 2019. See also Sophie Nappert, 'Escaping from Freedom? The Dilemma of an Improved ISDS Mechanism' (European Federation for European Law and Arbitration Conference, London, 26 November 2015), https://efila.org/wp-content/uploads/2015/11/Annual_lecture_Sophie_Nappert_full_text.pdf, accessed 20 August 2019; and Gloria Maria Alverez et al., 'A Response to the Criticism against ISDS by EFILA' (2016) 33 Journal of International Arbitration 1.

[38] *Comprehensive Economic and Trade Agreement (CETA) between Canada and the European Union and Its Member States*, signed on 30 October 2016, OJ 2017 L11, p. 23 (hereinafter the CETA). Article 8.29 of the CETA provides for the subsequent establishment of a multilateral investment tribunal and appellate mechanism ('the multilateral investment Tribunal'), the establishment of which will bring to an end the operation of the CETA Tribunal and the CETA Appellate Tribunal. Statement No. 36 by the Commission and the Council on investment protection and the Investment Court System, entered into the Council minutes in relation to the signature of the CETA and annexed to Decision 2017/37, OJ 2017 L 11, p. 20 envisages the establishment of an

CJEU.[39] Prior to the conclusion of the CETA, Belgium sought an opinion on the compatibility with EU law of the ISDS mechanism procedure in the chapter of CETA.[40] The key issue raised by Belgium was whether the ISDS provisions in the CETA would be contrary to the autonomy of EU law in the same way as the ISDS provision considered in *Achmea*.

In its opinion the CJEU held that the ISDS provision in the CETA would not be contrary to the principle of autonomy. It was open to the EU to enter into an international agreement that confers on an international court or tribunal the jurisdiction to interpret such an agreement, provided two conditions were fulfilled: first, such bodies do not have the power to interpret any EU law other than that in the agreement itself, and secondly, they do not make awards that might have the effect of preventing EU institutions from operating in accordance with the EU constitutional framework. The first condition was fulfilled on the basis that the CETA provided that the Tribunals[41] had jurisdiction to look at EU law only as a matter of fact. *Achmea* was distinguished on the basis that there the tribunal did have the jurisdiction to interpret or apply EU law and that the BIT there was contained in an agreement between Member States.[42] The CJEU gave a more nuanced answer to the fulfilment of the second condition.[43] The issue here was how, in a particular case, the tribunal would weigh the freedom of the investor to conduct his business against the public interest

Investment Court System, also known under the acronym 'ICS', of which the CETA Tribunal and Appellate Tribunal are to constitute only the first stage. See generally Georgios Dimitropoulos, 'Investor-State Dispute Settlement Reform and Theory of Institutional Design' (2018) 9 Journal of International Dispute Settlement 535, 537–8, and 543–4.

39 Opinion 1/17 *(EU-Canada CET Agreement)*, of 30 April 2019, EU:C:2019:341.

40 Despite what might be suggested by its name, an opinion has the same binding force as a judgment. Article 218(11) TFEU provides: 'A Member State, the European Parliament, the Council or the Commission may obtain the opinion of the Court of Justice as to whether an agreement envisaged is compatible with the Treaties. Where the opinion of the Court is adverse, the agreement envisaged may not enter into force unless it is amended or the Treaties are revised.'

41 There is both a tribunal and an appellate tribunal; see Articles 8.27 and 8.28 of the CETA.

42 Opinion 1/17 at paras. 106 to 136, fn. 39. Article 8.31.1 of the CETA provides that it is to be interpreted according to Article 31 of the Vienna Convention on the Law of Treaties, 'in good faith in accordance with the ordinary meaning to be given to the terms of the treaty in their context and in the light of its object and purpose'. It is also expressly stated at Article 8.31.2 that the tribunal does not have jurisdiction to determine the validity of a domestic measure, and must follow the prevailing interpretation given to the domestic law by the courts or authorities of that party.

43 Ibid., at paras. 137–61.

restriction imposed by the EU. The CJEU concluded that CETA, properly construed, meant that the CETA tribunals had no jurisdiction to call into question the level of protection of the public interest as determined by the EU. On this basis the second condition was also satisfied.

Belgium also raised the question of whether the envisaged ISDS mechanism was compatible with the right of access to an independent tribunal guaranteed by Article 47(2) of the Charter and effective access to justice under Article 47(3) of the Charter. The CJEU held that Article 47 binds the EU when it enters into international agreements that encompass dispute resolution bodies that are primarily judicial in nature.[44] It did not matter that the envisaged CETA tribunals are 'hybrid' in nature, containing characteristics of judicial bodies and traditional ISDS mechanisms. In this regard, the CJEU referred to the rules on the composition of the CETA tribunal and the appellate tribunal, which ensure that members are randomly appointed, rules which are clearly distinct from the rules on arbitration and which give concrete expression to the intention of the parties expressed in the Joint Interpretative Instrument, which states that the 'CETA moves decisively away from the traditional approach of investment dispute resolution and establishes independent, impartial and permanent investment Tribunals, inspired by the principles of public judicial systems'[45]. The provision of an appeal mechanism to ensure consistency in the decisions of the tribunal was also proof of this.[46]

In determining whether the CETA tribunals satisfied the requirement of independence, the CJEU applied the same test as that applied in determining whether a court within an EU Member State satisfied the requirement of independence for the purposes of Article 267 TFEU.[47] On the external aspect of the requirement of independence, the CJEU noted that members of both tribunals are to be appointed for a fixed term, will receive remuneration commensurate with the importance of their duties, and enjoy protection against removal. The CJEU held that the power of the CETA Joint Committee to give interpretations of CETA that are binding on the tribunal did not interfere with the independence of the tribunals on the basis that this power could not be exercised

[44] Ibid., at paras. 190–6. See further Vajda and Mair, 'The Applicability of Article 47 of the Charter of Fundamental Rights to International Agreements to which the Union Is a Contracting Party', in *Evolution des rapports entre les orders juridiques de l'Union européenne, international et nationaux* (Bruylant 2020).

[45] Ibid., at para. 195, citing Point 6(f) of the Joint Interpretative Instrument opinion.

[46] Ibid., at para. 196.

[47] Ibid., at paras. 202–4; see also Section 2.

retrospectively to influence disputes that have already been resolved or brought prior to such an interpretation.[48] Hence the requirement of external independence was satisfied. The CJEU also found that the internal aspect of the requirement of independence was satisfied.[49]

On the question of whether the CETA tribunals provided effective access to justice under Article 47(3) of the Charter, the issue was the size of the financial burden on claimants who are natural persons or small and medium-sized enterprises. The envisaged burdens would be twofold: first paying the totality of the legal costs of the respondent party if the claimant lost, and second paying the costs of the members of the tribunal who have dealt with the dispute. At the time of the opinion no rules were in place to mitigate those financial burdens. However, there was a commitment to introduce easier access for natural persons or small and medium-sized enterprises, which was sufficient for the CJEU to conclude, in the context of considering an 'agreement envisaged' within the meaning of Article 218(11) TFEU, that the CETA complied with the requirement to provide effective access to justice.[50]

3.5 The New National Commercial Courts within the European Union

Three Member States of the EU – namely, the Netherlands, France and Germany – have recently created specialist commercial courts.[51] In all three cases those courts are part of the court system of their respective Member States. This means that such courts are under an obligation to apply EU law and disapply any conflicting national provisions.[52] They are also subject to the obligations in Article 47 of the Charter. This means, in short, that they are obliged to provide an effective remedy for breach of EU law under Article 47(1), to be independent under Article 47(2), and to provide legal aid to those who lack legal resources where this is necessary to ensure access to justice under Article 47(3). While the application of Articles 47(1) and (2) are not likely to cause any particular issue, they may

[48] Ibid., at paras. 232–7.
[49] Ibid., at paras. 238–43.
[50] Ibid., at paras. 205–22.
[51] See in this volume Georgios Dimitropoulos and Stavros Brekoulakis, 'International Commercial Courts' (Introduction), and Marieke Witkamp, 'Internationalizing Domestic Courts in Europe' (Chapter 11).
[52] This is irrespective of whether they are a court or tribunal for the purpose of Article 267 TFEU; see *Banco Santander*, at fn. 11, at para. 78.

be required under Article 47(3) to provide some form of legal aid to litigants seeking a remedy for breach of EU law.[53]

It is likely that those courts will satisfy the requirements of being a court or tribunal for the purposes of making a reference to the CJEU under Article 267 TFEU.[54] They are clearly part of the State system of courts, they are established by law, they are permanent, they will be independent and they will apply rules of law pursuant to an *inter partes* procedure. Nor does the fact that they are an alternative to ordinary courts preclude the criterion of compulsory jurisdiction.[55]

On the assumption that such courts are courts or tribunals for the purposes of Article 267 TFEU, such courts have a discretion rather than an obligation to make a reference for a preliminary ruling to the CJEU on a point of interpretation of EU law. This is because they are not a court of final instance. The International Commercial Chambers of the Amsterdam District Court (NCC District Court) and the Chamber for International Commercial Disputes in Frankfurt are courts of first instance. Appeals lie respectively to the International Commercial Chambers of the Amsterdam Court of Appeal (NCC Court of Appeal) and the OLG Frankfurt (Frankfurt Court of Appeal).[56] Appeals from there lie to Hoge Raad and Bundesgerichtshof (BGH) respectively.[57] In the case of the international divisions of the Paris Commercial Court and the Paris Court of Appeal, an appeal would ultimately lie to the Cour de Cassation.[58]

[53] In Case C-279/09 *DEB*, EU:C:2010:811 the CJEU stated that the notion of legal aid encompasses both assistance by a lawyer and dispensation from advance payment of the costs of the proceedings. The right to legal aid may, in principle, be invoked by legal persons, not just natural persons. To establish an infringement of such a right requires a national court to ascertain 'whether the conditions for granting legal aid constitute a limitation on the right of access to the courts which undermines the core of that right; whether they pursue a legitimate aim; and whether there is a reasonable relationship of proportionality between the means employed and the legitimate aims that it is sought to achieve', at para. 60.

[54] See Section 2.

[55] See *Ascendi* at fn. 11.

[56] See Article 1.3.3 of the Rules of Procedure for the International Commercial Chambers of the Amsterdam District Court (NCC District Court) and the Amsterdam Court of Appeal (NCC Court of Appeal) (on the Dutch law); see Section 12 of the German Federal Courts Constitution Act, as well as Sections 511–41 of the German Federal Coder of Civil Procedure (on the German law).

[57] See Article 398(1) of the Dutch Code for Civil Procedure (on the Dutch law); see Section 12 of the German Federal Courts Constitution Act as well as Sections 542–66 of the German Federal Coder of Civil Procedure (on the German law).

[58] See Tribunal de Commerce de Paris and Barreau de Paris, 'Protocole relatif à la procédure applicable devant la Chambre internationale du tribunal de commerce de Paris – Version

The Cour de Cassation in France and its respective equivalents in the Netherlands and Germany are courts of final instance and hence subject to the obligation to make a reference under Article 267(3) TFEU. The stage of the proceedings at which any reference would be made is likely to affect the language of the case in the reference. If the reference is made by one of the new national commercial courts in the course of proceedings where English is the language of the case, that will also be the language of the case before the CJEU.[59] If, however, a reference is made by a higher court on appeal where English is not used as the language of the proceedings, the language of the reference for both the written and oral procedure will be the same as that used in the national court, although the CJEU can grant a derogation from this rule, but only in respect of the oral procedure.[60]

As regards questions on the validity of an EU measure, these new commercial courts would have no jurisdiction to declare such a measure unlawful.[61] If they have serious doubts on the validity of such an EU measure, they are obliged to make a reference to the CJEU but are entitled, pending the outcome of the reference, to prescribe any necessary interim relief subject to observing the conditions laid down by the CJEU.[62]

In making a reference the national court is entitled to express its view on the answer to the question referred.[63] This means that the new national

française', www.cours-appel.justice.fr/sites/default/files/2019-06/CICAP_Protocole%20barreau%20de%20Paris%20-%20Tribunal%20de%20commerce%20de%20Paris.pdf, accessed 28 July 2020; Cour d'Appel de Paris and Barreau de Paris, 'Protocole relatif à la procédure applicable devant la Chambre internationale de la cour d'appel de Paris – Version française' www.cours-appel.justice.fr/sites/default/files/2019-06/CICAP_Protocole%20barreau%20de%20Paris%20-%20Cour%20d%27appel%20de%20Paris%20-%20Version%20Francaise.pdf, accessed 28 July 2020. For appeals to the Cour de Cassation, see Articles 604 to 639–4 of Title XVI of the French Civil Code.

59 Article 37(3) of the Rules of Procedure of the CJEU of 25 September 2012 (OJ L 265 p. 1), as amended on 18 June 2013 (OJ L 173, p. 65), on 19 July 2016 (OJ L 217, p. 69), on 9 April 2019 (OJ 2019 L 111, p. 73) and on 26 November 2019 (OJ 2019 L 316, p. 103) (hereinafter the Rules of Procedure). Notwithstanding the withdrawal of the United Kingdom from the EU, English remains an official language of the EU as it is one of the official languages of Ireland and Malta; see https://europa.eu/european-union/about-eu/eu-languages_en. (accessed 15 July 2020). In Case C-33/17 *Čepelnik* EU:C:2018:896 a reference was made by an Austrian court which permitted the use of Slovenian and hence Slovenian was also permitted as a language of the case before the CJEU.

60 See also Article 37(3) of the Rules of Procedure.

61 See *Fotofrost* at fn. 7.

62 See *Atlanta* at fn. 7.

63 See paragraph 18 of the Recommendations to National Courts and Tribunals in relation to the Initiation of Preliminary Ruling Proceedings (hereinafter the Recommendations): 'The referring court or tribunal may also briefly state its view on the answer to be given to the questions referred for a preliminary ruling.' OJ 2019 C 380 p. 1.

courts, if they make references to the CJEU, will have the opportunity to influence the development of EU law in commercial law cases. This may be important as the object of the creation of such courts is to attract international commercial litigation, which would otherwise have taken place in other jurisdictions, to those Member States of the EU.[64] While the withdrawal of the United Kingdom from the EU is likely to reduce the influence of the common law on the development of EU law, particularly in the commercial field, the legal systems of three Member States – namely, Ireland, Cyprus and Malta – remain familiar with the common law. As for the CJEU, it operates very much as a common law court. It recognizes the value of judicial precedent,[65] the concept of developing the law through building on or, as the case may be, distinguishing previous case law, and is apt at developing general principles of law.[66] The open-textured nature of many EU legal texts facilitates such an approach. Thus, the CJEU seeks to reconcile the principle of legal certainty with the need for flexibility in a manner similar to a court in a common law jurisdiction.

On a practical matter, a reference by one of these new commercial courts, or by an appeal court will, however, increase the total length of the proceedings. A reference to the CJEU is an additional step in the national proceedings and the average time taken for a reference is just over fifteen months.[67] There is, however, a procedure whereby a case before the CJEU can be expedited[68] or, failing that, given priority treatment.[69]

3.6 Conclusion

It can be seen that the CJEU is a highly experienced transnational court that has been able to establish an impressive and effective system of

[64] See Dimitropoulos and Brekoulakis, 'International Commercial Courts'.

[65] It achieves this by an extensive citation in its judgments of previous case law. While it is able to overrule previous judgments, it does so very infrequently and, in practice, this is reserved to the Grand Chamber. See, for example, Case C-10/89, *CNL-SUCAL* v. *HAG* EU:C:1990:359 and *Banco Santander*, fn. 11, at paras. 54–5.

[66] See, for example, the principle of proportionality which is now common place; see Case C-362/14 *Maximillian Schrems*, EU:C:2015:650, at paras. 91–3, and the principle of fundamental rights, applied in Case 11/70 *Internationale Handelsgesellschaft* EU: C:1970:114, which also became well established in the CJEU's case law and has now been largely incorporated into the Charter of Fundamental Rights.

[67] See CJEU Annual Report on Judicial Activity 2019 at page 15, which gives the figure of fifteen and a half months.

[68] See Article 23a of the Statute of the CJEU and Article 105 of the Rules of Procedure and paragraphs 33–9 of the Recommendations, footnote 63.

[69] See Article 53(3) of the Rules of Procedure.

cooperation on issues of EU law with national courts in the EU Member States, through the preliminary reference mechanism. In a manner similar to that of a common law court, it has not only interpreted a large number of EU legislative texts, but also fashioned a number of important legal principles. The new commercial courts recently established in some of the EU Member States will therefore have the benefit, where appropriate, of being able to apply the large body of CJEU case law and also to ask the CJEU for an authoritative ruling on the interpretation or validity of a new point of EU law, where that is necessary, to enable them to give judgment in a case before them.

4

International Commercial Courts

Lessons from International Criminal Tribunals

ILIAS BANTEKAS

4.1 Introduction

If law is to be meaningful and rational, there must be significant commonalities between even diverse areas of law and regulation. In fact, not only the convergence of discrete legal disciplines, but also the meeting of non-legal fields with law can produce more comprehensive, compelling and useful outcomes. By way of illustration, anthropology has helped to clarify and demystify many areas of law which lawyers took for granted.[1] Concerning intra-law convergence, it is perhaps interesting to note that lawyers, at least at the academic level, are generally disinclined to merge legal fields. At one level this is the result of a lack of expertise, at another level distrust exists between legal disciplines, and at yet another level 'experts' tend to guard their disciplines from being infiltrated by other elements or idea coming from other fields.

It is beyond the scope of this chapter to attempt an overview of existing international courts and tribunals, hybrid, semi-hybrid, international, regional or other.[2] The scholarship and literature on this is immense. It is taken for granted that hybrid international commercial courts (ICommCs) require no definition. For the purposes of this chapter they are judicial bodies that operate in the context of a special economic zone,

[1] For an application in the criminal field, see Ilias Bantekas and Emmanouela Mylonaki (eds.), *Criminological Approaches to International Criminal Law* (Cambridge University Press 2014).

[2] This author is generally in agreement with the typology formulated by Georgios Dimitropoulos in 'The Design of International Commercial Courts' (Chapter 10) in this volume; see also Georgios Dimitropoulos, 'International Commercial Courts in the "Modern Law of Nature": Adjudicatory Unilateralism in Special Economic Zones' (2021) 24 *Journal of International Economic Law* 361.

as specialist chambers that assist arbitral proceedings or as specialist chambers that sit as courts of appeal. Their common characteristic is that they are special – that is, their jurisdiction is not ordinary – and that they are composed of international judges, with their purpose being to attract foreign end users and to provide authority and legitimacy to the foreign investment climate of the host state. International criminal tribunals (ICTs) are judicial entities (but this is not the case for truth commissions or commissions of inquiry) predicated on some form of international agreement and composed wholly or partially of international judges and prosecutors and whose mandate requires them to apply international substantive law.

The idea behind this chapter is that the experience of ICTs can provide helpful lessons to the emerging body of ICommCs. This is because ICTs have been pioneers in a field of regulation traditionally reserved for domestic courts and institutions. The fact that they have flourished through various forms and legal bases (e.g. based in the United Nations Security Council (UNSC), hybrid, treaty-based) clearly demonstrates that the international community is not averse to international judicial mechanisms that add value to their domestic counterparts. In the process, ICTs have not only attracted significant funding, but have also gone on to establish a coherent body of both substantive and procedural criminal law, in a manner that was perhaps unthinkable before the creation of the first ad hoc ICTs in the early 1990s. As a result, those elements that rendered them 'successful' in the eyes of their creators and end users are significant for the emerging landscape of ICommCs. The emphasis in this chapter is on distilling and ascertaining the broader public purpose dimension of ICommCs and applying the pertinent rules to their operations. It is not necessarily assumed that legitimate tribunals, imbedded in the rule of law as reflected in their home state context, will generate more business, but the author does presume that when states act in the public interest, even when setting up ICommCs that aim to attract foreign investors, they convey an additional layer of protection and predictability to both foreign investors and their citizens. The various sections of this chapter compare the practices of ICTs and then juxtapose them against the practices and/or aspirations of ICommCs. At the end of the chapter we set out a general framework of 'public interest' that can be applied to the operation of ICommCs.

The present chapter is structured as follows: Section 2 examines the communicative skills of ICommCs, while Section 3 ascertains their user-friendly aspirations, something fundamental to the operation of any mechanism desirous of a critical mass of end users. Sections 4 and 5 go on to show that in an era when transnational tribunals proliferate, they are all vying for the same sources of funding, which in turn requires them to showcase their values, including legitimacy. Section 6 explains the public purpose dimension of ICommCs, a theme that is central to ICTs and one that is demanded of international tribunals meting out commercial or investment justice, such as investment tribunals. Section 7 offers some concluding thoughts.

4.2 The Communicative Skills of International Commercial Courts

When X competes with Y over scarce resources, X will try to convince its intended audience about the superiority of its service or product. The successful conveyance of this message by X to its intended audience will depend on the quality of the message as well as whether the contents of the message are appealing to its intended audience. One assumes that X took into consideration the key desires of end users, but in many cases the transmitter (i.e. X) may have conflated these with his own intentions and aspirations. It is important to understand the intended meaning of the language conveyed by ICommCs, and this in turn may help us understand what type of decoding they expect their stakeholders/end users to undertake.[3] It may also explain whether the particular ICommC that undertakes to communicate its message expects some degree of interaction or dialogue from its interlocutors. Given that this chapter is not meant to critically expose and analyse the various schools of semiotics and linguistics, the author assumes from the outset that communication is a means by which a system interacts with its external environment and by so doing lends itself to the characterization of an open rather than a closed system.[4] Within information theory a tripartite model of communication was developed. According to this, a *message* is derived from a source, which is then conveyed along a *channel* and from there to a *receiver* that interprets and decodes the message.[5] It is obvious that the

[3] See generally the standard work of Jurgen Habermas, *The Theory of Communicative Action: Reason and Rationalisation of Society*, trans. Thomas McCarthy (Massachusetts Institute of Technology Press 1984).

[4] Norbert Wiener, *Cybernetics: Control and Communication in the Animal and the Machine* (Wiley and Sons 1948).

[5] Claude Shannon and Warren Weaver, *A Mathematical Model of Communication* (Illinois University Press 1949).

effectiveness of communication in this model depends on the reliability and quality of the channel. If the channel conveys the message without distortion (the so-called background noise), assuming it has that capacity, it will reach its receivers in much the same way as it was intended. The meaning, according to this theory, is precisely in the message, but the theory itself may be criticized for failing to take into consideration the variety of contexts and environments inherent in the communicative process.[6] Yet it helps overcome the theoretical distinction between communication and signification, most prominently enunciated by Mounin. Mounin argues that whereas communication involves the intention to convey a message through a sign (e.g. words or actions), the unintended conveyance of a message cannot by implication constitute communication, but something of an inferior character, which he termed 'signification'.[7]

In the context of ICommCs, the message may be conflated by other overriding considerations. By way of illustration, while the creation of the Qatar International Court and Dispute Resolution Centre (QICDRC) may be animated by the State of Qatar as a way of showing how the country and its legal system has progressed, in addition to showcasing Qatar's investor-friendly climate, the first part of the message may be irrelevant to investors or law firms seeking an optimal forum for dispute resolution. This brief foray into communication early on in this chapter is important in understanding how ICTs and ICommCs communicate with their intended stakeholders.

The success of communication depends on the sources of the message, as well as the reasons why and the context in which it is conveyed, as well as the process whereby it reaches its intended receivers. Missing from this equation is the language of the message and the potency of the channels through which it is communicated. When the content of the message is generally ambiguous, difficult to understand although overall very positive, or antithetical to the prevailing views of the majority (or its intended audience), it is usually intentionally distorted when conveyed through the channel. Distortion in this sense is not necessarily tantamount to lying.[8]

[6] This is even more relevant in the case of law, which is characterized by a culture of its own and is actually said to be culturally embedded. Roger Cotterrel, *Law, Culture and Society: Legal Ideas in the Mirror of Social Theory* (Ashgate 2006) 81.

[7] See Bernard Jackson, *Semiotics and Legal Theory* (Routledge 1987) 21–3.

[8] This is not to say that even democratic governments do not lie to their people. Consider, for example, the Spanish government's announcement on the day of the Madrid train bombing of 11 March 2004 that the Basque separatist organization, the Euskadi Ta

Oversimplification or emphasis on positive features as opposed to negative ones will do just as well. The medium of the channel is also responsible for dispersing the meaning of an otherwise straightforward message. The creators of ICommCs may presume that their goals coincide with the aspiration of (all) end users and hence employ financial and business ideas and goals to attract litigants, forgetting that this might limit their legitimacy to the business sector outside the special economic zone, 'national investors', access to justice campaigners and existing end users of arbitration. Unlike the relationship between governments and their people, where the language used is devoid of complexity and specialist legal jargon, the language of communication between ICommCs and end users tends to be more complex. This is because: (a) both possess symmetric knowledge of this language, which means the source will be able to convey the desired message to the recipients; (b) the sophistication of the parties dictates that an appropriate semantic system of communication must be employed in such a way that facilitates meaningful interaction. In the case of asymmetric actors this language is usually somewhere in the middle between metaphors (or parables), which are indirect, but not through the medium of the language of international law, which although direct is perceived as incomprehensible. This intermediate language assumes three general forms: that of political rhetoric, funnelling of particular emotions and the language of money and finances. These roughly correspond to the three faculties of the soul – that is, the rational, the concupiscible (appetitive) and the irascible (θυμικόν).[9] As will be shown in this chapter, whether directly or indirectly, the language of ICommCs, especially those operating in special economic zones, is oblivious to communication theory and on many occasions, although the parties are symmetrical and highly sophisticated, the language and content of the message assumes that their interlocutor is unsophisticated (i.e. by trying to convince experienced litigants to resolve differences in an ICommC simply because it hires top retired judges).[10]

Askatasuna (ETA), was behind the carnage. The reason for blaming the ETA was because general elections were due in three days and the incumbent Zapatero government was well aware that the Spanish public had been opposed to Spain's leading role in the Iraq war, fearing retaliatory terrorist attacks on Spanish territory; see Keith Richburg, 'Spain Campaigned to Pin Blame on ETA: Despite Evidence to Contrary Basque Group Was Focus in Blasts', *Washington Post* (17 March 2004) A1.

[9] See Ilias Bantekas, 'The Metaphysics of Temptation in Eastern Orthodox Monasticism' (2006/7) 4 Theandros 1, at 2.

[10] Consistent with the findings regarding the so-called dialogic models in the field of conversation studies, it is postulated that meaning is conditioned by the interlocutors through the course of their dialogue. Thus, we cannot talk of *meaning* outside the

4.3 User-Friendly Aspirations

International commercial courts aim to fill a particular demand of commercial actors in the sphere of dispute resolution and the same is true *mutatis mutandis* of ICTs. This observation requires some explanation. International criminal tribunals undertake a function that is, or could be, served by domestic courts, which need only expand the ambit of their operations and employ a new albeit small number of additional staff members. This is a long cry from the experience of ICTs, which are massively expensive to operate and manage. The financing of ICTs is derived from the United Nations (UN) budget, other intergovernmental organizations and individual contributions from states. Overworked, understaffed and financially strained prosecutorial and judicial mechanisms would welcome an additional workload in exchange for the lavish financing and privileges of ICTs; hence, ICTs must at all financing cycles be able to 'sell' the added value of their work – as compared to domestic mechanisms – to their financiers.[11]

It is a common argument that ordinary courts are cumbersome, litigation is slow, the courts are overburdened, and delays are inevitable, not always reliable, and, in certain countries, they are also unpredictable. These are among the reasons why alternative dispute resolution (ADR) mechanisms rose to prominence even in industrialized states where the court system is otherwise reliable and the judges are highly respected. Since ICommCs do not generally aim to replace arbitration but rather to: (a) assist it as 'competent courts' where applicable; (b) function as specialist commercial chambers, on par with the London Commercial Court; and (c) function as the judicial arm of a special economic zone, they may be perceived as possessing some of the key characteristics of arbitration, and certainly much more efficient alternatives to ordinary litigation. As specialist litigation chambers they equally have the potential to offer speedier commercial justice, especially if their dockets and

parameters of a particular conversation and its distinct interlocutors. When a conversation commences, it is governed by so-called conversational rules, which are cooperative in nature. The philosopher Paul Grice identified numerous conversational maxims, such as avoidance of information overflow, relevance, brevity, avoidance of ambiguity and obscurity of expression; see Talbot J. Taylor and Deborah Cameron, *Analysing Conversation: Rules and Units in the Structure* (Pergamon Press 1987) 83.

[11] See Dominic Raab, 'Evaluating the ICTY and Its Completion Strategy', (2005) 3 *Journal of International Criminal Justice* 88, who notes that '[i]t was increasingly questioned in the UN General Assembly's Fifth Committee, whether the ICTY (and ICTR) were providing value for money'.

caseloads remain low or selective. For those ICommCs that are an extension of a special economic zone, as is the case with the Qatar Financial Centre (QFC) and the Dubai International Financial Centre (DIFC), the common argument by their creators is that they provide an extra layer of protection to potential investors and hence this in turn necessitates the appointment of prominent judges of international repute. Whether this is true is yet unknown, but it is not generally supported by the relatively small caseload of ICommCs other than the DIFC.

International criminal tribunals have equally aspired to bypass regular criminal courts under the assumption that many are either unable or unwilling to entertain large cases against prominent accused persons. International criminal tribunals with experienced judges and prosecutors are familiar with complex criminal trials involving masses of evidence and the treatment of vulnerable witnesses, and they possess the necessary resources to bring a case to fruition, including by convincing other states to surrender both persons and crucial evidence. International criminal tribunals cater to the greater goals of their financiers, all of which demand that ICTs take on the biggest cases while at the same time satisfying the rule of law, human rights guarantees and legitimacy concerns.[12] That domestic courts may be speedier or cheaper is of little relevance, because in the situations at hand they are unable to satisfy the aforementioned guarantees. The end users in the case of ICTs are not of course investors or private litigants. However, one should view the international community, and particularly its more powerful members, as stakeholders of international criminal justice and the rule of law, which in turn allows them to make critical decisions about the financing of such justice in post-conflict situations. As end users (i.e. financiers with legitimacy concerns) of international criminal justice, they are presented with a plethora of possible mechanisms (e.g. national courts, truth commissions, hybrid tribunals, UNSC-based tribunals, traditional justice, etc.) from which they must choose the most appropriate.[13] Their choice is therefore determined by end user requirement in much the same way as similar choices are made by the end users of ICommCs.[14] The process is similar, although the criteria are different. Although ICTs have gone

[12] See Payam Akhavan, 'The International Criminal Tribunal for Rwanda: The Politics and Pragmatics of Punishment' (1996) 90 American Journal of International Law 501.

[13] See Ilias Bantekas, *International Criminal Law*. 4th ed. (Hart 2010) 402–67.

[14] See Kenneth Anderson, 'The Rise of International Criminal Law: Intended and Unintended Consequences' (2009) 20 European Journal of International Law 331, who

through several cycles from the early 1990s to the late 2010s (as explained in Section 7), their end users have generally been driven by the following criteria: (a) legitimacy concerns, (b) widest possible consensus with target states, (c) fighting impunity even at the highest level and (d) varying support by the international community and retention of linkages with existing international security architecture. End users have not been particularly concerned with: (a) the speed of proceedings, (b) cost, save in a few notable instances or (c) reputation of judges and prosecutors, with minor exceptions.

Overall, the measure of success of the user-friendly nature of ICTs has been their legitimacy and the centrality of the rule of law in their operations, with cost and speed of secondary importance.[15] In equal measure, ICommCs will be deemed to have fared well vis-à-vis their competitors if perceived as the best possible alternatives (in terms of quality of service, reliability, speed and predictability) to regular dispute resolution mechanisms and arbitration. Unlike in ICTs, whose end users are also their creators, the creators of ICommCs must make them attractive for their intended end users. Hence, if the institutions behind ICommCs rely on the reputation of judges and the attraction of the special economic zone within which ICommCs are situated, without simultaneously equipping ICommCs with greater jurisdictional competence, speedy execution powers and other qualities, their intended end users will find other mechanisms that better satisfy their needs and aspirations.[16]

4.4 Competing for Revenue with Other Institutions

It follows from the previous section of the chapter that end users' preferences dictate the expansion, growth and ultimately the viability of

questions to what degree the proliferation of ICTs supplanted or crowded other aspects and institutions of international law.

15 Although the meaning of 'user friendly' is implicit in this chapter, a brief explanation may be warranted. The term refers to all those qualities that direct stakeholders/financiers (states and international organizations) require from ICTs; these include speedy trials, legitimacy, accurate historical records, fair trials and many others. Hence, 'user-friendly' in this context does not encompass the expectations of the accused, counsel or ICT staff.

16 The QICDRC, for example, enforces its judgments through the appointment of an enforcement judge; otherwise, as is the case elsewhere, the winning party would have to enforce its hybrid dispute resolution forum (HDRF) judgment and seek enforcement in the regular courts. The same is true in respect of freezing of assets or other similar injunctions which fall within the power of the QICDRC and in respect of which the parties would be forced to apply to the regular courts; see 'Qatar International Court and Dispute Resolution Centre' (*QICDRC*), www.qicdrc.com.qa, 10 January 2019.

dispute resolution mechanisms, assuming of course that this can be communicated in the right way. There is no doubt that dispute resolution is a multibillion-dollar industry and several actors have a stake in this. It generates money both directly and indirectly. Direct stakeholders are law firms, judges, arbitrators, arbitral institutions and law schools,[17] and the communication between these stakeholders displays some, but not all, of the qualities associated with autopoietic systems – namely, systems capable of reproducing and maintaining themselves.[18]

Dispute resolution may be viewed as an investment service, but also as an indirect route for other forms of investment in a given country. The establishment of an arbitral institution and specialist judicial mechanism for the enhancement of the arbitral proceedings (in the form of a 'competent court'), in addition to adding an extra layer of investment protection in a special economic zone, would constitute foreign investment if undertaken by a non-national as it is a profitable business in its own right.[19] When the DIFC and QFC courts are set up and operated on the basis of public resources they do not qualify as investments, but they are aimed at attracting other foreign investment into the country, as one among several incentives inherent in such special economic zones. International commercial courts of this nature, hence, compete among each other and with the ordinary courts of other nations for the attraction of foreign direct investment (FDI), as well as revenue from the litigation of disputes (whether in form of court fees, lawyer fees, etc.). Although ICommCs may receive their financing solely from subsidization, they ultimately need to compete with similar institutions around the world, including arbitral tribunals (even if they are not arbitral tribunals themselves) under the promise of effective, speedier and quality dispute settlement.

[17] See Andrew L. Friedman and Samantha Miles, *Stakeholders: Theory and Practice* (Oxford University Press 2006); Robert Phillips, *Stakeholder Theory and Organisational Ethics* (Berrett-Koehler 2003).

[18] Communication is in fact central to autopoietic systems, in the sense of internal constructions of information based on their respective code. In the case of transnational judicial mechanisms set up and operated by a closed number of entities and intended for use by particular end users (states, large corporations), the code is predicated on the distinction between lawful and unlawful and it serves as the basis for producing international rules. Therein, the three elements of communication (i.e. information, utterance and understanding) are present, albeit the mode of addressing is reversed, in that it is the addressee controlling the sender through anticipation of utterance. See Niklas Luhmann, *Social Systems*, trans. John Bednarz (Stanford University Press 1995) 143.

[19] See Teresa Garcia-Reyes and Michael McIlwrath, 'Arbitration Institutions: Five Things Your Website Must Do to Attract Cases' (*Kluwer Arbitration Blog*, 17 January 2018), http://arbitrationblog.kluwerarbitration.com/2018/01/17/mike, accessed 10 January 2019.

International criminal tribunals resemble ICommCs in a number of ways. Firstly, potential host countries for ICTs realize that staff salaries and operational costs will benefit the local economy immensely, as well as their secondary economies.[20] Secondly, once an ICT is set up, its staff and the local economy have a significant interest in ensuring that it is continuously financed by its donors, even to the detriment of competing institutions. By way of illustration, once the permanent International Criminal Court (ICC) was set up, it was clear that the lifeline of the International Criminal Tribunal for the former Yugoslavia (ICTY) and the International Criminal Tribunal for Rwanda (ICTR) was limited. Even so, those with a financial stake in the ICTY made significant efforts to keep it alive until 2017. International criminal tribunals may further use their jurisdictional powers to divert cases from local criminal courts to their dockets, if by doing so they can retain their existing budgets. Moreover, given that ICTs are expensive to run, if the international community decides to fund them, it will necessarily divert or limit financial resources destined for aid or capacity building elsewhere. Such outcomes are unwelcome and call upon the legitimacy of ICTs and the motives underlying their finances.

It is important that ICommCs exhibit a healthy dose of legitimacy. They should provide a clear picture of their aims vis-à-vis their competitors and should set a clear timeline of becoming self-funded. Under no circumstances should they divert critical finances from the country's legal system in order to sustain elitist practices, while at the same time the legal system is underfinanced and access to justice is limited.[21] Moreover, ICommCs should be used as best-practice paradigms for the target country's legal system as a whole. They should feed their best practices into the legal systems, rather than being selectively exceptional.

4.5 Legitimacy and Value for Money Concerns

It has been argued that international adjudication is a 'law-based way of reaching a final decision' and that the 'law-based nature of adjudicative decision-making distinguishes adjudication from other processes, such

[20] Janet Anderson, 'The Hague, the ICC and the Economic Benefits of Being a Centre for Justice' *The Guardian* London, 25 September 2012), www.theguardian.com/law/2012/sep/25/the-hague-international-criminal-court-economic-benefits-justice-capital, 10 January 2019.

[21] For a general overview of this important and overarching right, see Francesco Francioni (ed.), *Access to Justice as a Human Right* (Oxford University Press 2007).

as political decision-making and mediation'.[22] Two legitimacy-based approaches have been advanced in the literature, and these have been adapted in turn to explain the concept of judicial legitimacy from the perspective of international law – namely, sociological (or descriptive) and normative legitimacy.[23] The sociological approach is chiefly concerned with the perception of legitimacy ascribed to a particular judicial institution, whereas the normative approach investigates whether such institution deserves to be regarded as authoritative (or whether its authority is justified). It is evident that both approaches are predicated on external perceptions by relevant constituencies. A court that makes a claim for normative legitimacy is effectively arguing for the 'right to rule,' whereas a claim of sociological legitimacy is perceived as already having that right.[24] Normative legitimacy is prescriptive, whereas sociological legitimacy is agent-relative and subjective.[25] Judicial legitimacy, particularly in the sphere of international law, is inextricably woven around the concept of authority, which ultimately dictates adherence, obedience or even disobedience. Because of the horizontal nature of international law and the juridical equality of states, which itself is based on consent, the legitimacy of domestic courts is different to (as is also its origin) their international counterparts. The source of authority, for example, is directly affected by perceptions as to the legitimacy of the source itself (e.g. the UNSC as creator of tribunals in countries where the UN has allowed grand massacres to take place). In contrast, acts of parliament (or the constitution itself) from which regular courts derive their creation are not under dispute. The same is true of the processes employed by an international tribunal in exercising its powers, as well as the overall outcomes such processes produce.

[22] Cesare P. R. Romano, Karen J. Alter and Yuval Shany, 'Mapping International Adjudicative Bodies, the Issues, and Players', in Cesare P. R. Romano, Karen J. Alter and Yuval Shany (eds.), *The Oxford Handbook of International Adjudication* (Oxford University Press 2014) 4–5.

[23] See, for example, Chris Thornhill and Samantha Ashenden, 'Introduction: Legality and Legitimacy – Between Political Theory and Theoretical Sociology', in Chris Thornhill and Samantha Ashenden (eds.), *Legality and Legitimacy: Normative and Sociological Approaches* (Baden-Baden 2010) 7–12.

[24] Daniel Bodansky, 'The Concept of Legitimacy in International Law', in Rudiger Wolfrum and Volker Roben (eds.), *Legitimacy in International Law* (Springer 2008) 313; Allen Buchanan and Robert Keohane, 'The Legitimacy of Global Governance Institutions', in Lukas H. Meyer (ed.), *Legitimacy, Justice and Public International Law* (Cambridge University Press 2009) 29.

[25] Bodanksy, 'Concept of Legitimacy', 313.

Irrespective of the source of authority of an international tribunal, its legitimacy is guaranteed only where its outcomes and processes are in the public interest – namely, if they adhere to fundamental human rights standards (or whichever of the two generates a higher standard). The same principles should necessarily be applied to assess the legitimacy of ICommCs.[26] However, one cannot artificially divorce source from processes and outcomes, because the source dictates those who sit at the helm of the tribunal and in turn restricts their decision-making autonomy. The source does so, not necessarily by forcing judges to decide in a particular way, but by artificially fragmenting the law or by dictating a choice of law that excludes human rights as an underlying, overarching and primary consideration in all cases.[27]

In terms of their financing, it should be pointed out that tribunals compete for funding not only with other courts, in existence or impending, but also with other pertinent institutions. By way of illustration, ICTs are but one element of an overall transitional justice plan, others being reconstruction of critical infrastructure, capacity building, education and many others. Tribunals that receive funding must show not only that they deliver impeccable outcomes, but also that money spent on them is money well spent. A tribunal must both generate enough resources for its own survival and meet the targets set out by its funders. In the case of ICommCs, their success will be measured by the amount of foreign investment attracted through the availability of such a judicial mechanism and perhaps even by the number of cases decided by ICommCs. It is

[26] Domestic or even hybrid tribunals may equally suffer from the same or similar legitimacy concerns as international tribunals, irrespective of their establishment by parliamentary-type entities in accordance with local laws. See, for example, the concerns against the Special Criminal Court on the Events in Darfur (SCCED), established pursuant to the Sudanese minister of justice's Decision No. 3/2005 (19 January 2005) as amended in November and December 2005. Mbeki Report, AU Doc. PSC/AHG/2(CCVII) (29 October 2009), paras. 215–17; see also Richard A. Duff, 'Blame, Moral Standing and the Legitimacy of the Criminal Trial' (2010) 23 Ratio 123.

[27] See Ole K. Fauchald, 'The Legal Reasoning of ICSID Tribunals: An Empirical Analysis' (2008) 19 European Journal of International Law 301. Significant research has also been undertaken by lawyers using methods and sources from cognitive psychology and behavioural economics, much of which can be applied to analyse the decision-making of international judges and arbitrators, particularly as regards heuristics and the biases debate. See Tomer Broude, 'Behavioral International Law' (2015) 163 University of Pennsylvania Law Review 1099; and more recently on the theory of 'nudges', see Klaus Matis and Avishalom Tor (eds.), *Nudging: Possibilities, Limitations and Application in European Law and Economics* (Springer 2016); see also applied in the field of international adjudication Georgios Dimitropoulos, 'Investor-State Dispute Settlement Reform and Theory of Institutional Design' (2018) 9 Journal of International Dispute Settlement 535.

the opinion of this author that this is only a very narrow view of success, let alone legitimacy. If an ICommC delivers excellent judgments among several elite end users, while at the same time access to justice for the rest of the population is ineffective, courts are understaffed, justice is slow, the legal profession is hindered in its daily work and the revenue generated by the ICommCs does not lead to sustainable human development, the ICommC in question will be considered not only unsuccessful, but also illegitimate.[28] The legitimacy of an institution, therefore, should be assessed by reference to its particular context and environment and not by reference to the institution itself.

The money spent on ICTs is vast, and during its twenty-four years of operation the ICTY alone indicted a mere 161 persons at an average cost of 230 million USD per year (at least during its last ten years of operation).[29] Much more could have been done for the former Yugoslavia with this amount, which mostly went to pay salaries and other operational expenses in the Netherlands. An increasing number of voices are vehemently noting that this money was not well spent and that more could have been done to reconstruct the various republics and reconcile their peoples.[30]

International commercial courts need to set out a detailed account, agreed with their funders, with a detailed set of criteria that spell out successful outcomes. Such outcomes need to be logical and legitimate and should not raise doubts about the criteria used. Legitimacy demands that 'value for money' criteria should not only be limited to the generation of court fees or self-sufficiency in terms of financing, but also extend to wider aims. These may bring local courts to a higher level, promote access to justice, strengthen legal education and link it to the professional market, and perhaps others.

[28] I am here making use of the human development index (HDI) as a standard of achievement – other than legitimacy – because one of the key goals of HDRF is to promote and enhance trade and investment in the host state, which must necessarily be translated into generalized human development. The QFC Court CEO, Faisal Al-Sahouti, according to whom 'we recognise that an integrated legal community, anchored in common standards of dispute resolution in line with the rule of law, is essential to economic growth and prosperity'. See www.qicdrc.gov.qa/news-item/qatar-international-court's-ceo-unveils-plans-expand-jurisdiction-court-cover-entities, accessed 17 October 2021.

[29] 'The Cost of Justice' (United Nations International Criminal Tribunal for former Yugoslavia), www.icty.org/en/about/tribunal/the-cost-of-justice, 10 January 2019.

[30] David Wippman, 'The Cost of International Justice' (2006) 100 American Journal of International Law 861.

4.6 The Emerging Public Purpose of International Tribunals

Prior to the end of the Cold War, the assumption was that conduct produced solely in one state could not give rise to reaction and protest from other states, unless the conduct in question caused injury to these other states. But the concept of injury did not in practice encompass human rights or other violations (e.g. stemming from the laws of internal armed conflict) committed by the state against its own citizens. This artificial assumption no longer holds ground whether in law or in respect of the current perception of the impact (political or legal) of domestic conduct.[31] Indeed, in the era of globalization, even the trade, commercial or consumer practices of one nation can produce an adverse effect on the citizens of other states thousands of miles away.[32] This dense interconnectivity between the conduct of states, or conduct stemming from non-state actors from within a state, which is accepted and regulated by states, requires that it become the subject matter of international law.[33] By extension, the adjudication of disputes concerning such conduct, whether submitted to 'domestic' or international tribunals must also be subject to international law, both procedural and substantive. The 'real' governing law of a dispute regulated within the sphere of international law is ultimately the subject matter of the latter body of law, and no tribunal deciding a pertinent dispute can avoid its application. In the case of ICommCs, this position has already been explained briefly by reference to the assessment of the rule of law as applied against ICommCs.

Of course not all tribunals are willing to compromise their existence or to agitate their creators in order to produce socially just outcomes or construe the obligations of states and non-state actors through a public policy/human rights perspective. The International Court of Justice

[31] Indeed, the creation of the ICTY and the ICTR, as well as subsequent hybrid tribunals, such as that of Sierra Leone, Cambodia, Lebanon and Timor Leste, as well as the vast majority of cases before the ICC, effectively concern domestic conflicts or situations, although it is true that they caused transnational ripples, such as internal displacement and refugee flows, massive human rights violations, regional instability and intervention by third states and intergovernmental organizations. See Bantekas (n. 13) 444–64.

[32] In Bangladesh, for example, the mere consideration by the US Congress of banning products manufactured by child labour led to the dismissal of girls in the textiles industry, many of whom were forced into prostitution by destitute parents. See Jagdish Bhagwati, 'Afterword: The Question of Linkage' (2002) 96 American Journal of International Law 126.

[33] In the case of *Sadiq Shek Elmi* v. *Australia*, CAT/C/22/D/120/1998, UN Committee against Torture (25 May 1999) para. 5.5, the CAT treated members of the Hawiye clan in central Somalia as holding 'effective control'.

(ICJ), even though under intense political pressure, has shown itself willing to stretch the boundaries of the law and expand its jurisdiction against the conduct of states, as in the *Nicaragua* case, where it masterfully evaded the jurisdictional hurdles of the United States by assuming that the UN Charter was effectively reflective of customary international law.[34] The ICJ, in equal manner, makes use of its advisory opinions to infuse a public interest dimension to international law, as in the *Palestinian Wall*[35] and *Nuclear Weapons*[36] advisory opinions, albeit with varying degrees of success. Other tribunals such as the Southern African Development Community (SADC) went as far as risking – and ultimately paying the price – for construing the applicable law in light of human rights and advancing just claims.[37] Yet other international tribunals have simply been labelled 'activist' when embarking and validating human rights considerations in the discharge of their mandates, as has been the case with the Court of Justice of the European Union (CJEU), both in its early caseload,[38] as well as more recently.[39]

Unlike the ICTs addressed in the previous paragraph, which by and large have desisted from fragmenting fundamental human rights

[34] Military and Paramilitary Activities in and against Nicaragua (*Nicaragua* v. *United States of America*) (Merits) [1986] ICJ Rep 14.

[35] Legal Consequences of the Construction of a Wall in the Occupied Palestinian Territory (Wall Case) (Advisory Opinion) [2004] ICJ Rep 136.

[36] Legality of the Threat or Use of Nuclear Weapons (Advisory Opinion) [1996] ICJ Rep 226.

[37] The Southern African Development Community (SADC) tribunal was effectively suspended following its judgment in *Mike Campbell (Pvt) Ltd and Others* v. *Republic of Zimbabwe* (2/2007) [2008] SADCT 2 (28 November 2008), in which it held that the complainant's eviction from his land was unlawful and a form of discrimination against white people.

[38] See, for example, Case 41/74 *Van Duyn* v. *Home Office* [1974] ECR I-1338, where the European Court of Justice (ECJ) held that public policy restrictions to freedom of movement should be predicated on 'personal conduct'. Fundamental rights arising from an expansive interpretation of EU have crystallized into distinct rights in the EU legal order, beyond the rights enshrined in the EU Charter of Fundamental Rights.

[39] The CJEU emphasized in Joined Cases C-8/15 P to C-10/15 P *Ledra Advertising and Others* v. *European Central Bank*, [2016] paras. 59 and 67, that the EU Commission must 'refrain from signing an MoU whose consistency with EU law [which implicitly encompasses fundamental rights] it doubts'. While reaffirming the non-applicability of the EU Charter of Fundamental Rights to the European Stability Mechanism (ESM), as originally expounded in Case C-370/12 *Thomas Pringle* v. *Government of Ireland* [2012] ECR I-1 (the *Pringle* case), it made it clear that 'the Charter is addressed to the EU institutions, including when they act outside the EU legal framework. This is a clear message by the CJEU that EU institutions are not at liberty to function outside the legal framework of the EU Charter and in this manner to opt out of intra-EU human rights obligations'.

(including socio-economic rights) and justice claims from the law applicable to the dispute before them,[40] investment tribunals have largely taken a different approach to their mandate. A similar approach (i.e. inclined towards fragmentation) would no doubt be assumed by specialized tribunals set up to deal with disputes of a very particular nature, such as sovereign debt, or indeed the work of ICommCs, as their creators would endow them with specific powers within a very narrow mandate.[41] Moreover, any judge or arbitrator called on to assume a judicial function in the context of such specialized tribunals would be unlikely to expand their mandate as any 'dangerous' candidates would have been eliminated beforehand by those financing such a tribunal.

4.6.1 *Working in Partnership with Other Mechanisms as 'Public Purpose'*

International criminal tribunals were originally seen as hostile to local courts, but over time this proved to be wrong. International criminal tribunals could only prosecute some cases and showed no interest for minor executioners, for which local courts in the target country where crimes were committed were better suited, in addition to the exercise of universal jurisdiction by other foreign courts.[42] At some point it became apparent that ICTs should be part of a larger pyramid where they should act as standard setters by prosecuting those in the highest echelons of authority. Below in the pyramid it was critical that local courts be empowered to take on the many thousands of cases still available, with the necessary resources to handle their caseloads effectively within the framework of the rule of law. In some cases, truth commissions were set up and it took some time to reconcile the work of the courts and ICTs with such truth commissions.[43] It is now generally agreed that truth commissions play a significant role as transitional justice mechanisms and that they are better suited to 'write' the history of a conflict and the crimes committed therein and that it is preferable that 'local ownership'

[40] This author does not view the overall claims in *Germany* v. *Italy (Greece Intervening)* (Jurisdictional Immunities of the State) [2012] ICJ Rep 99, as compromising justice claims. This is because the particular claim can be exercised through inter-State adjudication or unilateral state action by the public authorities of the claimant.

[41] See Ilias Bantekas, 'A Human Rights-Based Arbitral Tribunal for Sovereign Debt' (2018) 29 American Review of International Arbitration 1.

[42] Bantekas (n. 13) 429–32.

[43] Ibid., 445–60, 467–73.

of processes, judicial or otherwise, be strengthened in transitional justice situations.[44] This allows for better healing and reconciliation between all interested parties.

The lesson for ICommCs is that they should strive to work with other, at least local, justice institutions and not become isolated from these. A hybrid court isolated from the justice processes of the rest of the target state breeds resentment, fails to satisfy legitimacy concerns and may ultimately fail to convince investors that the special economic zone in question is predictable, and the same is true in respect of its laws and dispute resolution processes. In countries where the rule of law is strong, justice institutions, even in times of crisis, serve the interests of justice and this is an enticement for foreign investors.[45] Where an ICommC is exceptional in its operation to all other justice processes in the country (including its substantive and procedural rules), such exceptionality will breed a feeling of insecurity. By way of illustration, if in order to entice FDI in a special economic zone, its laws discard certain public policy principles that strictly apply in the ordinary laws of the country,[46] there is no guarantee that with the spread of public unrest over such exceptionality that the special economic zone's laws will not be aligned with the state's ordinary laws.[47] The only real guarantee for foreign investors as to the long-term security of their investments is the spread of the rule of law to all the institutions in the host state from a top-bottom approach.

[44] Steven Ratner and Jason Abrams, *Accountability for Human Rights Atrocities in International Law* (Oxford University Press 1997) 196; Priscilla Hayner, 'Fifteen Truth Commissions 1974 to 1994: A Comparative Study' (1994) 16 Human Rights Quarterly 597.

[45] The impact of special economic zones on the rule of law in the target country has received little attention. See Madeleine Martinek, *Experimental Legislation in China between Efficiency and Legality: The Delegated Legislative Power of the Shenzen Special Economic Zone* (Springer 2018), which discusses the improvement of the legal design of experimental regulations in special economic zones by striking a balance between the pursuit of rapid socio-economic progress on one hand, and the increasing need and will to govern by the rule of law on the other.

[46] By way of illustration, articles 169, 170 and 107 of the Qatari CC set out good faith as a foundational principle of contract law. In equal measure, *pacta sunt servanda* is set out in the Quran, as follows: 'Those who fulfill the agreements they make in Allah's name and do not break their pledges' (al-Ra'd, 13:20).

[47] Compare the situation whereby the application of good faith in the common law (as the basis for the governing law of HDRF) with the mandatory character of good faith in the Gulf states; compare also the imposition of the death penalty in Rwanda with life imprisonment as the highest possible penalty before the ICTR. See Bantekas (n. 13) 412.

4.6.2 *The Pitfalls of Institutionalization for Public Purposes*

International commercial courts are creatures of broad institutionalization frameworks. They are part of a permanent institutional framework and their financiers in fact desire to render them not simply permanent institutions but invest them with a perception of constitutional court-like appearance. The idea is that investors in a special economic zone will not be impressed by a tribunal possessing jurisdiction under the ordinary laws of the state, or be staffed by local judges dispensing commercial justice under local standards. The institutionalization of ICommCs is not necessarily a negative phenomenon as long as the ultimate aim is to facilitate dispute resolution as this is achieved under the best possible transnational commercial practices. The institutionalization of an ICommC may render it self-referential, indifferent to the particular type of commercial justice sought by its end users, slow and potentially also rigid in its approach to fast-changing commercial circumstances. Just like every newly established exceptional (transnational) court or tribunal, ICommCs need to strike a delicate balance between taking on many cases in their early years (which they would not necessarily accept in their more mature years) in order to establish a coherent body of case law, from assuming a constitutional or semi-constitutional character once they have proven their value to end users.

Unlike other permanent and semi-permanent international courts and tribunals, including ICTs, whose institutionalization empowers judges to explore varying degrees of judicial activism, ICommCs cannot easily be drawn to such activism, although as shall be explained they are required to act within the broader framework of international law and not simply their narrow mandate. The activism of ICommCs may be beneficial for the 'improvement' of otherwise anachronistic principles, but it is on the basis of such principles that legal counsel advise their clients and if a commercial tribunal is held in the conscience of counsel to be a 'rebel' choice of forum clauses will make no mention of it. This result is clearly irrespective of the quality of the forum's judgments and decisions. International criminal tribunals have struggled with their activism. To the degree that a particular area of international law was antiquated, imprecise and not in touch with customary international law and general principles of law, a fair degree of judicial activism was not only undisputed, but welcome.[48] In cases where the activism was antithetical to state

[48] See Fuad Zarbiyev, 'Judicial Activism in International Law: A Conceptual Framework for Analysis' (2012) 3 Journal of International Dispute Settlement 247; Mark Dawson,

practice, but otherwise laudable and consistent with academic scholarship, it was well received by the international community and later even transformed into treaty law.[49] On the contrary, tribunals mired with compromises from their very outset and whose bench was not composed of well-known lawyers have not fared well and have generally fallen into relative obscurity. This has been the case with the hybrid tribunals for Cambodia, East Timor, Kosovo, Iraq and Bosnia-Herzegovina, among others, even if none of these have been particularly activist. But, even those with reputable judges, such as the Special Tribunal for Lebanon, have been resisted in their activism. The latter's finding that terrorism is a crime under international law, rather than a transnational (or treaty-based) crime, has been fiercely resisted in scholarly works and state practice.[50] In some rare instances, as is the case with the SADC tribunal, activism (even if absolutely consistent with international law as in the case at hand) is even the reason for dismantling the tribunal.

4.6.3 *Institutionalization That Furthers the Public Purpose Aims of International Commercial Courts*

A particular form of activism consists of courts adding one or more additional functions to their existing mandate. These additional mandates are not necessarily vexatious or imbalance the rights of parties, but one has to question whether they divert the courts' attention from their primary subject matter and whether ultimately the courts should not overstep their mandates, even if there is no other institution to fill in the identified gap. The following subsections will identify some types of activism of the nature just described as practised by ICTs. At the close

Bruno de Witte and Elise Muir (eds.), *Judicial Activism at the European Court of Justice* (Edward Elgar 2013).

49 By way of illustration, the ICTY in the *Tadic* Appeals Jurisdiction judgment held that war crimes committed in non-international conflicts incurred international, rather than purely domestic, criminal liability and hence were crimes under international law. See ICTY, *The Prosecutor* v. *Dusko Tadić*, IT-94-1-AR72, Appeals Chamber Decision on the Defence Motion for Interlocutory Appeal on Jurisdiction (2 October 1995). This was a radical departure from the accepted wisdom at the time, but within three years it was so well entrenched that it found its way into the Statute of the International Criminal Court (ICC).

50 See Ben Saul, 'Legislating from a Radical Hague: The United Nations Special Tribunal for Lebanon Invents an International Crime of Transnational Terrorism' (2011) 24 Leiden Journal of International Law 677.

of this section, a brief subsection will provide some examples of ICommC institutionalization that promotes public purpose objectives.

4.6.3.1 Historiography and Timeline of Conflict

International criminal tribunals regularly venture into setting out a historical record. This has aptly been demonstrated in the case of the former Yugoslavia, Rwanda, Sierra Leone, Cambodia and elsewhere. It is clear that ICTs must look to the recent history of the conflicts in which crimes within their jurisdiction take place in order to assess the warring groups, their motives, their organization, the place of victims and ultimately to create a timeline of events and fit the evidence within that timeline.[51] Although the accumulation of all these elements does not directly serve to write a history of the target country and its people, but rather to set the background and the evidence for subsequent criminal trials, the authority of an international tribunal, especially those set up by the UN, provides an authoritative narrative. Such a narrative is clearly not a comprehensive account of the relevant history, nor is it written with all points of view in mind (particularly since those perceived as falling within the group of perpetrators will be disinclined from participating in the trials). However, the group which is favoured from the tribunal's historical narrative will be inclined to use this as the only official record of events. This may be dangerous, and if an authoritative historical record is to be recorded during a transitional period, then it is essential that an ICT operate alongside a locally owned truth commission. History should be written locally (certainly with assistance as to its evidence from ICTs) and not be imposed by external forces.

4.6.3.2 Giving Voice to Victims

This is an equally laudable objective and is closely connected to the historiography 'function' of ICTs. While it is in the interests of justice that victims have a voice, the notion of 'victims' in post-conflict situations typically encompasses only persons from the target group, but not those originating from the group of the major aggressors.[52] Such persons are never viewed as victims. Moreover, such persons are further victimized in several other ways, particularly by being excluded from subsequent international aid efforts; may not be regarded as fleeing prosecution and hence be denied asylum; and be perpetually categorized as

[51] Bantekas (n. 13) 29.
[52] Ibid.

'genocidaires' or aggressors, without the possibility of differentiating themselves from those with whom they share racial, religious or other characteristics.

4.6.3.3 Contribution to Healing

Healing the scars of violent conflict is not a monolithic exercise. It cannot come about by a single event or through a combination of isolated acts and events. Those working professionally in international criminal justice assume that criminal adjudication has the power to heal wounds and contribute (to a large degree) to reconciliation between the various feuding communities.[53] The problem with this assumption is that the healing argument emanating from ICTs is sophisticated and may, and typically does, divert resources from other processes, such as truth commissions, human development and others back to ICTs.

4.6.3.4 Fortifying Local Justice Institutions

International criminal tribunals do and can fortify the reconstruction of local courts, but the disparity of resources is so vast, as is the level of legal and other training between members of ICTs and local courts, that assistance is not pragmatic. International criminal tribunals generally conduct some outreach programs, perhaps even basic training, but the assumption is that the case law of ICTs directly feeds into the case law of local courts. It is difficult to see how this is in fact possible when there is no serious plan when setting up an ICT to empower local courts to slowly build up their expertise to ultimately take up the role of ICTs. International criminal tribunals have little incentive to raise the level and profile of their local characters if this entails sharing scarce financial resources.

4.6.3.5 Transitional Justice

Transitional justice is an umbrella term encompassing actions, judicial and otherwise, the aim of which is to uphold the rule of law in a chaotic post-conflict situation. Transitional justice starts during or after conflict and ends when the target country enters into general stability.[54] Clearly, ICTs represent one perspective of transitional justice – namely, upholding the justice process and the rule of law. At the same time, however, it is

53 Ibid., 14, 30.

54 See Colleen Murphy, *The Conceptual Foundations of Transitional Justice* (Cambridge University Press 2017), and the classic work by Ruti G. Teitel, *Transitional Justice* (Oxford University Press 2002).

dangerous to view ICTs as the most important mechanism in the reconstruction or reconciliation process of a war-torn country, and the sophisticated advocacy of ICTs may lead to the diversion of resources destined for critical infrastructure or reconciliation, as these are not visible to external stakeholders.

4.6.4 *Examples from International Commercial Court Practice and Potential Applications*

Although the headings of ICT practice set out earlier do not correspond to the work of ICommCs, their (limited) activism has enhanced public purpose objectives. A few illustrations are apt. The QFC Court is meant to apply QFC law and regulations, as well as the law set out by the parties in their contractual relationships,[55] albeit in practice the Court relies predominantly on common law principles and case law, not only because these are more familiar to the majority of the judges, but also because English law is predominant in the majority of transnational commercial agreements. In *Leonardo Spa* v. *Doha Bank Assurance Co LLC*, the QFC Court had to deal with demand guarantees under the Uniform Rules for Demand Guarantees, which were adopted by the International Chamber of Commerce in 1991. Even so, the Court went on to examine the nature of such guarantees by reference to English case law.[56]

A second function of ICommCs concerns the application of uniform rules in a manner that promotes their international character. A point in hand is article 7 of the Vienna Convention on the International Sale of Goods (CISG). Given the prominence of this treaty, the relatively uniform case law from around the world and the flexibility of ICommCs to apply the parties' choice of law – save where it conflicts with public policy – ICommCs are generally free to engage in transnational judicial dialogue, as well as to promote the uniformity and international character of the CISG.[57]

[55] Arts. 7 and 8, Appendix 6 of the QFC Law. This is also spelt out in art. 11 of the Court's Regulations and Procedural Rules, while art. 4 of the latter enunciates the principle of 'overriding objective' of the Court, which is to 'deal with all cases justly'.

[56] *Leonardo Spa* v. *Doha Bank Assurance Co LLC*, Case 3/2019, judgment of 5 September 2019, paras. 42ff.

[57] Ronald J. Krotoszynski, '"I'd like to Teach the World to Sing (In Perfect Harmony)": International Judicial Dialogue and the Muses – Reflections on the Perils and the Promise of International Judicial Dialogue' (2006) 104 Michigan Law Review 1321.

Finally, ICommCs may cooperate with other international actors and/or courts with a view to promoting legitimate outcomes, or assisting transnational judicial procedures. By way of illustration, the QFC Court may act as 'competent court' in respect of arbitral proceedings seated in Qatar.[58] In addition, the QFC Court signed a memorandum of understanding (MoU) with the International Centre for Settlement of Investment Disputes (ICSID) in June 2019 and among the aims the QFC will serve as a conduit to enforce judgments at the international level.[59]

4.7 Ante Conclusion: Necessary Elements of Public Interest-Based International Commercial Courts

The key idea underlying this chapter is that the historiography and operation of ICTs can provide some guidance to ICommCs, chiefly because the financiers of both expect specific results, absent which there is little or no incentive to retain them. While the creators of judicial mechanisms until the mid-to-late 1990s were content solely with the adjudicatory functions of these mechanisms, since the end of the Cold War this is no longer sufficient. Legitimacy is as important, if not more, than the prosecutorial function of ICTs. For prosecutors, judges, counsel and all those involved in the UN and the host state, it is pointless if all those accused are captured and effectively prosecuted at the expense of legality and legitimacy. The entire process would be tainted to such a degree that no one would lend any credence to the procedure. What is more, the financiers would have no hesitation abandoning this project for another one around the corner, whether the ICC, a UN-based tribunal, a hybrid tribunal, a truth commission, national prosecution or other. Given that there is no shortage of available mechanisms and suitors, financiers, typically states and international organizations, are keen to 'invest' their financial resources into a mechanism that would not only provide substantive criminal justice, but will moreover sustain a legacy that is respected universally. It is exactly because of this that some ICTs fared far better than others, with several ignored almost completely in scholarly writings.

[58] Law No. 2 of 2017 Promulgating the Civil and Commercial Arbitration Law, art. 1.

[59] See www.qicdrc.com.qa/enhancing-qatar%E2%80%99s-arbitration-sector-new-international-partnership.

The lesson for ICommCs is simple. In the pursuit of their commercial objectives they should not lose sight of broadly defined legitimacy concerns. Commercial justice is as important as criminal justice, but at the same time the ordinary commercial justice meted out by lower courts in the forum stated should not be sidelined in favour of an elite mechanism. International commercial courts should operate in the public interest and not against the interests of the wider stakeholder community in which they exist. The notion of public interest should never fall below the standards typically associated with fundamental civil, political and socio-economic rights.[60]

[60] The precise formulation of such standards has become much easier with the introduction and extensive use of human rights indicators and benchmarks in respect of all human rights. See David McGrogan, 'Human Rights Indicators and the Sovereignty of Technique' (2016) 27 European Journal of International Law 385.

PART II

Jurisdiction, Applicable Law and Enforcement of Judgments

5

A Comparative Perspective on International Commercial Courts

Jurisdiction, Applicable Law and Enforcement of Judgments

JANET WALKER

5.1 Introduction

In recent decades, as the parties to international commercial disputes and their advisors have become more sophisticated in choosing the fora for resolving their disputes, there have emerged a number of international commercial courts (ICommCs) to compete with arbitration in the lucrative international dispute resolution market.[1] To understand how each of these courts is designed to respond to the demand for the particular needs in dispute resolution in their sphere of operation, it is helpful to consider the approaches taken to issues of their jurisdiction, the applicable law and the enforcement of judgments. This functional comparison highlights the way in which each of these aspects has been designed to address the limitations of national court procedure that otherwise might prompt the parties to choose arbitration. It also highlights efforts to maximise the competitive advantages inherent in choosing national courts over arbitration.

In respect of the jurisdiction of ICommCs, a number of questions arise for parties considering one or another of the courts examined here. If the parties wish, as a result of their contract negotiations, to designate the court as the forum for the resolution of their disputes, will this choice be

[1] Stephan Wilske, 'The Global Competition for the "Best" Place of Arbitration for International Arbitrations: A More or Less Biased Review of the Usual Suspects and Recent Newcomers' (2008) 1(1) Contemporary Asia Arbitration Journal 21; Janet Walker, 'The London Principles and Their Impact on Law Reform' (2018) 84(2) Arbitration 175; "International Dispute Resolution in the 21st Century: The Role of National Courts" Canadian Council on International Law, *Looking Ahead: International Law in the 21st Century* (New York: Kluwer, 2001) 95.

respected by the court in question? If, in the absence of designating the court in their contract, one party commences an action in the court and the other party wishes to accept this choice of forum, will the court be able to accept jurisdiction? If the court is able to exercise jurisdiction over the parties that have accepted its jurisdiction, does it have the capacity to join additional parties, or to add claims to the dispute over which it has jurisdiction? Is the court able to exercise further bases of jurisdiction to assist parties or potential parties?

In respect of applicable law, it must be remembered that international commercial dealings were, at one time, a function of the effective application of English commercial law, with two important consequences: first, that the English Commercial Courts were the preferred place for resolving those disputes; and, secondly, that the effectives of international dispute resolution in other fora around the world depended on the skill with which the court or tribunal and the counsel could apply English commercial law. Over time, the increasing sophistication of the international business community has led to an interest in adopting a wider variety of applicable laws. This has diversified the range of potentially applicable laws and increased the relevance of the skill of courts or tribunals and counsel in applying those other laws. Accordingly, again, these features of ICommCs will be considered from the perspective of the parties choosing to provide for dispute resolution in those courts.

Finally, in respect of the enforcement of judgments, a key competitive advantage of international arbitration has been the widespread enforceability of arbitral awards in comparison with the patchwork of local and regional legal provisions for the international enforcement of national court judgments. This chapter explores the various means by which national courts are working to address this historic limitation in the dispute resolution facilities that they provide.

Before embarking on the comparative analysis of these three features of international courts, it will be helpful to have a brief overview of each of the courts to be considered.

5.2 Overview of the International Commercial Courts

The international courts to be considered in this chapter include:

- Business and Property Courts of England and Wales (Commercial Court and Technology and Construction Court) (UK)[2]

[2] 'Civil Procedure Rules' (Ministry of Justice), www.justice.gov.uk/courts/procedure-rules/civil, accessed 1 August 2019; 'The Commercial Court Guide' (HM Courts and Tribunals Service,

- Singapore International Commercial Court (SICC)
- Commercial courts in the Gulf Region and in Central Asia, including Dubai International Financial Centre Courts (DIFC Courts), Qatar International Court and Dispute Resolution Centre (QICDRC), Abu Dhabi Global Market Courts (ADGM Courts) and Astana International Financial Centre Court (AIFC Court)
- Chinese International Commercial Court (CICC)
- Commercial courts in Europe, including the Netherlands Commercial Court (NCC) and the International Chamber of the Paris Courts (Paris Chambers).

It is helpful to begin the comparison with a brief introduction to each court to place it in the larger context of the emerging array of options for international dispute resolution.

5.2.1 English Commercial Court and the Technology and Construction Court

The English Commercial Court is the original specialised court for international commercial matters. Although it is different from the other international courts considered in this chapter, it is worth including in the comparison as it set the benchmark for the kind of international dispute resolution to which the newer courts have aspired. Since its establishment by the City of London in 1895, it has supported London as an international financial and commercial centre with specialist commercial judges capable of handling complex disputes efficiently.[3] Seventy per cent of its caseload[4] consists of international disputes not involving a UK party.[5] The Court has a broad remit over commercial matters, and it is the principal supervisory court for international arbitration.

The Commercial Court's companion court, the Technology and Construction Court (TCC), has judges who are experienced in

2017), https://assets.publishing.service.gov.uk/government/uploads/system/uploads/attachment_data/file/672422/The_Commercial_Court_Guide_new_10th_Edition_07.09.17.pdf, accessed 1 August 2019.

[3] 'Commercial Court' (United Kingdom Courts and Tribunals Judiciary), www.judiciary.uk/you-and-the-judiciary/going-to-court/high-court/queens-bench-division/courts-of-the-queens-bench-division/commercial-court, accessed 26 October 2018.

[4] On the types of claims before the English Commercial Court see 'Civil Procedure Rules and Practice Directions', Part 58, Rule 58.1 (Ministry of Justice), www.justice.gov.uk/courts/procedure-rules/civil/rules/part58, accessed 26 October 2018.

[5] 'UK Legal Services 2016' (TheCityUK, 2016) 20, www.thecityuk.com/assets/2016/Reports-PDF/618d27dbbd/UK-Legal-services-2016.pdf, accessed 26 October 2018.

construction and large-scale commercial disputes and are capable of handling factually complex matters.[6] They use robust case management practices, including conducting case management conferences to encourage settlement.[7] When matters go to trial, the TCC decisions are publicly available and therefore contribute to the jurisprudence.[8]

These two courts comprise the Business and Property Courts' specialist civil jurisdiction of the courts of England and Wales. Their strength is enhanced by their historic link with London arbitration, notably but not limited to the London Court of International Arbitration (LCIA) and the London Maritime Arbitration Association (LMAA). The Business and Property Courts are 'international' not so much because they adapted their bench, procedure or law to an external international standard, but because they themselves have set the standard for international commercial litigation.[9]

5.2.2 *Singapore International Commercial Court*

The Singapore International Commercial Court (SICC) was established as a division of the High Court to build on Singapore's success as an Asian arbitration hub to increase the international caseload of the Singapore courts.[10] The SICC has twenty-six sitting Singapore judges,

[6] See 'Technology and Construction Court' (*HM Courts & Tribunal Service*) www.gov.uk/courts-tribunals/technology-and-construction-court, accessed 26 October 2018; 'Annual Report of the Technology and Construction Court 2013–2014' (*Judiciary of England and Wales*, 2015), www.judiciary.uk/wp-content/uploads/2015/05/technology-construction-court-ar-2013-14.pdf, accessed 26 October 2018; 'The Lord Chief Justice's Report 2017' (*Judiciary of England and Wales*, 2017), www.judiciary.uk/wp-content/uploads/2017/09/lcj-report-2017-final.pdf, accessed 26 October 2018.

[7] 'Annual Report of the Technology and Construction Court 2013–2014' (*Judiciary of England and Wales*, 2015), www.judiciary.uk/wp-content/uploads/2015/05/technology-construction-court-ar-2013-14.pdf, accessed 26 October 2018.

[8] Available at 'England and Wales High Court (Technology and Construction Court) Decisions' (*BAILII*), www.bailii.org/ew/cases/EWHC/TCC, accessed 26 October 2018.

[9] In that regard, the courts in New York, particularly under the leadership of the United States District Court for the Southern District of New York, have similarly aspired to attract transnational commercial litigation by maintaining high standards in the field.

[10] 'Singapore International Commercial Court' (Singapore International Commercial Court), www.sicc.gov.sg, accessed 26 October 2018; 'Supreme Court of Judicature Act – Rules of Court' (*Attorney-General's Chambers*) (Chapter 322, Section 80, R5, Order 110), https://sso.agc.gov.sg/SL/SCJA1969-R5?DocDate=20181221, accessed 1 August 2019; Andrew Godwin, Ian Ramsay and Miranda Webster, 'International Commercial Courts: The Singapore Experience' (2017) 18(2) Mel J Int'l L 219. A 2013 report on the court can be found at 'Report of the Singapore International Commercial Court Committee' (*Singapore International Commercial Court*, 29 November 2013), www.sicc.gov.sg/docs/default-source

and sixteen retired judges and senior arbitrators from overseas, two of whom are from civil law countries. Foreign lawyers may register to appear before the SICC, and the court is free to depart from the local rules of evidence if the parties agree. The SICC increases the range of options for parties by offering the opportunity to have disputes adjudicated by a panel of experienced commercial judges from Singapore and retired judges from a range of other civil and common law jurisdictions in a court-based forum.[11] This is intended to contain rising costs and to address the potential for inconsistency of decisions and jurisprudence, the lack of appellate review, and the inability to join third parties.

5.2.3 *International Commercial Courts in the Gulf Region and Central Asia*

For business conducted in the Middle East and Central Asia, there is an increasing attraction to resolving disputes within the region but in the tradition of the English Commercial Court. Accordingly, in 2004, the Dubai International Financial Centre (DIFC) was established to operate in a 'unique legal and regulatory framework' with its own laws and courts, within a free financial zone located in Dubai, with its own civil and financial administration systems.[12] The DIFC Courts are independent and based on the English common law system, and they seek to provide certainty, flexibility and efficiency in commercial matters.[13] The proceedings are conducted in English and the judgments are rendered in English with the majority of cases involving at least one foreign party. As of 2011 foreign parties are free to choose the DIFC Courts even for matters unconnected to the United Arab Emirates (UAE). Seven out of

/about-sicc/annex-a-sicc-committee-report.pdf, accessed 26 October 2018. Practice directions may be found at 'Singapore International Commercial Court Practice Directions' (*Supreme Court of Singapore*, 30 December 2016), www.supremecourt.gov.sg/rules/practice-directions/singapore-international-commercial-court-practice-directions, accessed 26 October 2018.

11 On recent appointees see 'Judges' (Singapore International Commercial Court, last updated 14 June 2018), www.sicc.gov.sg/about-the-sicc/judges, accessed 20 September 2020.

12 'DIFC Courts' (DIFC), www.difccourts.ae, accessed 26 October 2018; 'Dubai International Financial Centre' (DIFC), www.difc.ae, accessed 26 October 2018; DIFC Court Law – DIFC Law No. 10 of 2004; Law on the Application of Civil and Commercial Laws in the DIFC – DIFC Law No. 3 of 2004; Law of the Judicial Authority at Dubai International Financial Centre – DIFC Law No. 12 of 2004 as amended by Law No. 16 of 2011; Rules of the Dubai International Financial Centre Courts 2014 (RDC 2014).

13 Michael Hwang, 'Commercial Courts and International Arbitration: Competitors or Partners?' (2015) 31 Arb Int 193, 198.

ten of the judges are from outside the region, including retired judges from the UK, Singapore, Malaysia and Australia.

The QICDRC[14] similarly operates within an enclave of English common law specialising in international civil and commercial disputes arising in or from the Qatar Financial Centre (QFC).[15] It is staffed by leading jurists from Qatar and by leading retired judges from the UK, Germany, New Zealand and India with a background in civil and common law. The court administers arbitrations and permits parties to nominate it as the court of the seat in agreements that designate the QFC as the seat of the arbitration.[16] The QFC also has an independent regulatory tribunal to serve as a specialist appeals tribunal established under the laws of the QFC. This tribunal hears appeals by individuals and corporate entities against decisions of the QFC authority, its regulatory body and other QFC institutions.[17] The QFC registry is responsible for case management and assists users with filing, court practices and procedural queries; and it has advanced courtroom technology, which supports video-conferenced hearings.[18] Hearings are held in English unless the parties apply to have them heard in Arabic, and non-Qatari lawyers generally may gain rights of audience. The judges of the QFC may also be appointed as arbitrators, and the court administers arbitrations.

The ADGM Courts[19] have jurisdiction over commercial and civil disputes connected to the ADGM, including domestic and international

[14] 'Qatar International Court and Dispute Resolution Centre' (QICDRC), www.qicdrc.com.qa, accessed 26 October 2018.

[15] 'QFC Regulations' (*Qatar Financial Centre*), www.complinet.com/qfcra/display/display.html?rbid=1557&element_id=3, accessed 1 August 2019; 'About Us – QFC Law No. 7 of 2005' (*Qatar International Court and Dispute Resolution Centre*), www.qicdrc.com.qa/about-us, accessed 26 October 2018.

[16] 'Dispute Resolution Clause' (*Qatar International Court and Dispute Resolution Centre*), www.qicdrc.com.qa/arbitration/dispute-resolution-clause, accessed 26 October 2018.

[17] 'The Tribunal Overview' (*Qatar International Court and Dispute Resolution Centre*), www.qicdrc.com.qa/tribunal/overview, accessed 26 October 2018.

[18] 'e-Court' (*Qatar International Court and Dispute Resolution Centre*), www.qicdrc.com.qa/the-courts/e-filing, accessed 26 October 2018.

[19] 'Law No. (4) of 2013 – Concerning Abu Dhabi Global Market' (*Abu Dhabi Global Market*), www.adgm.com/-/media/project/adgm/legal-framework/documents/abu-dhabi-legislation/abu_dhabi_law_no_4_of_2013.pdf, accessed 1 August 2019; 'Financial Services and Markets Regulations' (*ADGM*, 2015), http://adgm.complinet.com/en/display/display_main.html?rbid=4503&element_id=3945, accessed 1 August 2019; 'ADGM Courts, Civil Evidence, Judgments, Enforcement and Judicial Appointments Regulations 2015' (*ADGM*, 2015), http://adgm.complinet.com/net_file_store/new_rulebooks/a/d/ADGM_Courts_Regulations_17Dec2015.pdf, accessed 1 August 2019; 'Application of English Law Regulations 2015' (*ADGM*, 2015), http://adgm.complinet.com/en/display/

financial transactions and employment disputes.[20] The parties may opt in to or opt out of the ADGM Courts. The ADGM Courts are largely based on the English judicial system with a physical and electronic registry that supports their operations and hearings in Abu Dhabi and around the world. The ADGM Court Rules are contained in a single statute with additional guidance in the Court Regulations and Practice Directions to promote transparency. Hearings are conducted in English and documents are submitted in English.

The judiciary is comprised of eminent retired international jurists. Foreign lawyers can apply to represent parties before the court. The court also has an arbitration centre and arbitration regulations based on the United Nations Commission on International Trade Law (UNCITRAL) Model Law. Under the regulations, the ADGM judges are authorised to serve as arbitrators. The ADGM Court has partnered with the International Chamber of Commerce International Court of Arbitration, which has a representative office there. This enables parties to commence arbitrations there under the ICC Rules. The ADGM Courts have a memorandum of understanding with the Abu Dhabi Court for reciprocal enforcement of judgments and decisions.

The AIFC Court[21] is a common law court system for civil and commercial disputes based in Astana (now 'Nur-Sultan')[22] and operating within the AIFC. It hears cases relating to the AIFC claims in which the

display_main.html?rbid=4503&element_id=2, accessed 1 August 2019; 'Divisions and Jurisdiction (Court of First Instance) Rules 2015' (*ADGM*, 2015), http://adgm.complinet.com/en/display/display_main.html?rbid=4503&element_id=5648, accessed 1 August 2019; 'ADGM Court Rules' (*ADGM*), http://adgm.complinet.com/en/display/display_main.html?rbid=4503&element_id=5647, accessed 26 October 2018.

20 Henry Quinlan, Adam Bradshaw and Charlotte Leith, 'Abu Dhabi Global Market Courts: Framework, Procedures and First Judgment Summary' (*DLA Piper Middle East*, 1 March 2018), https://uk.practicallaw.thomsonreuters.com/w-013-7809?transitionType=Default&contextData=(sc.Default)&firstPage=true&comp=pluk&bhcp=1, accessed 26 October 2018.

21 'Constitutional Statute of the Republic of Kazakhstan on the Astana International Financial Centre 2015 (amended in 2017)' (*AIFC*), http://aifc-court.kz/legislation, accessed 1 August 2019; 'AIFC Court Regulations' (*AIFC*, 5 December 2017), http://laws.aifc.kz/files/3c79917a4b9e44f2/3.%20Legislation%20-%20AIFC%20Court%20Regulations%202017.pdf, accessed 1 August 2019; 'AIFC Court Rules 2018' (AIFC), https://laws.aifc.kz/files/adb6b118a86f4a55/3.%20Legislation%20-%20AIFC%20Court%20Rules%202018.pdf, accessed 1 August 2019.

22 In 2019, the city of Astana was renamed 'Nur-Sultan'. Accordingly, the name of the Financial Centre and Court may also be amended. See 'Nursultan: Kazakhstan Renames Capital Astana after Ex-president' *BBC* (London, 20 March 2019), www.bbc.com/news/world-asia-47638619, accessed 24 October 2019.

parties to the dispute agree in writing to its jurisdiction. It is independent of the local judicial system and has its own court of final appeal, and its own procedural rules, including a special fast track for small claims. The AIFC Court decisions are enforceable throughout Kazakhstan. The judges of the AIFC Court are leading common law judges with strong reputations for impartiality and incorruptibility.[23]

By operating in Dubai, Qatar, Abu Dhabi and Nur-Sultan within autonomous legal and civil justice systems based on the English civil justice system, these ICommCs serve an important role in these regions in supporting international commercial dispute resolution, and particularly arbitration, for transnational matters involving local parties and projects.

5.2.4 China International Commercial Court

One of the newest of the ICommCs is the China International Commercial Court (CICC).[24] The CICC is a permanent branch of the Supreme People's Court of China (SPC) with branches in Shenzhen (for the Maritime Silk Road) and Xi'an (for the Silk Road Economic Belt), and it has a jurisdictional relationship with the SPC and the lower courts. The CICC provides mediation, arbitration and litigation in a range of matters: matters in excess of RMB 300 million where the parties consent; matters within the jurisdiction of the Higher People's Court that it seeks to have the CICC decide; international commercial matters that have a nationwide impact; and other matters that the SPC considers appropriate for determination by the CICC.[25] The CICC also has jurisdiction over

[23] 'About the AIF Court' (*AIFC*), https://aifc-court.kz, accessed 1 August 2019.

[24] 'Building the Judicial Guarantee of International Commercial Court "Belt and Road" Construction: An Exclusive Interview with Gao Xiaoli, Vice President of the Fourth Civil Division, The Supreme People's Court, PRC' (*China International Commercial Court*, 19 March 2018), http://cicc.court.gov.cn/html/1/219/208/209/774.html, accessed 1 August 2019; 'Provisions of the Supreme People's Court on Several Issues Regarding the Establishment of the International Commercial Court' (*CICC*, 27 June 2018), http://cicc.court.gov.cn/html/1/219/199/201/817.html, accessed 1 August 2019; 'Procedural Rules for the China International Commercial Court of the Supreme People's Court (For Trial Implementation)' (CICC, 5 December 2018), http://cicc.court.gov.cn/html/1/219/208/210/1183.html, accessed 1 August 2019; Civil Procedure Law of the People's Republic of China (Revised in 2017)' (*CICC*, 29 June 2017), http://cicc.court.gov.cn/html/1/219/199/200/644.html, accessed 1 August 2019; Susan Finder, 'Update on China's International Commercial Court' (*Supreme People's Court Monitor*, 11 March 2018) < . . . . . . > accessed 1 August 2019.

[25] Disputes are international where one or both of the parties is foreign, regularly resides outside of PRC, where the subject matter is outside the territory of the PRC and where the facts impact relations that occur outside the territory of the PRC.

applications for interim measures in support of arbitrations and the enforcement of arbitral awards. The CICC does not hear investor-state disputes or state-to-state trade disputes.

The CICC was established to hear international commercial cases in a timely and fair manner, including through the use of new information technologies and reduced formalities for foreign evidence. The court aims to promote stability, fairness, transparency and convenience as well as coherence between mediation, arbitration and litigation. Cases are heard in panels of three or more specialised judges selected by the SPC from among the senior judges of the SPC who are fluent in English, and who have the benefit of technical experts selected from a committee comprised of Chinese and foreign experts. The counsel who appear before it are local counsel. Decisions of the CICC are not appealable, but an application may be made to retry a matter by the SPC.[26]

As with the ICommCs in the Gulf Region, the CICC seeks to provide within mainland China an alternative to the local People's Republic of China (PRC) courts or arbitration commissions for international matters involving foreign and PRC parties that is acceptable to a broader range of parties.

5.2.5 *Commercial Courts in Europe*

In response to the changes in the composition of the European Union (EU), a number of European centres are establishing courts that seek to adopt the role once served almost exclusively by the English Commercial Court.[27] One such court is the Netherlands Commercial Court (NCC), which opened in 2018.[28] The court specialises in complex international commercial cases and it hears matters submitted to it by the parties either in their commercial agreement or after the dispute has arisen. Tribunals consist of three experienced judges chosen for their specialist knowledge of the law, their experience with similar disputes, their familiarity with

[26] Provisions of the Supreme People's Court on Several Issues Regarding the Establishment of the International Commercial Court (n. 24).

[27] Described as 'Brexit Wannabe Profiteers' in Stephan Wilske, 'International Commercial Courts and Arbitration: Alternatives, Substitutes or Trojan Horse' (Taipei International Conference on Arbitration and Mediation, Taipei, August 2018)

[28] 'A First Guide to Commercial Litigation in the Netherlands' (*Netherlands Commercial Court*), https://netherlands-commercial-court.com, accessed 26 October 2018; Rules of Procedure for the International Commercial Chambers of the Amsterdam District Court (NCC District Court) and the Amsterdam Court of Appeal (NCC Court of Appeal) (NCC Rules of Procedure).

commercial legal practice and their knowledge of legal English. Proceedings are conducted in English, and the court seeks to be more cost-effective than arbitration or litigation in common law jurisdictions by applying efficient Dutch approaches to procedure.

In 2010, the Commercial Court of Paris established an international and European chamber (Paris Chamber) for complex commercial cases, in which documents may be submitted and evidence may be presented in English or another foreign language. Matters commenced in the Commercial Court of Paris that were suitable for this special chamber would be assigned to it by the court. More recently, in 2018, an international chamber was also created in the Paris Court of Appeal so that matters involving one or more foreign entities or the application of foreign law could be heard in ICommCs both at first instance and on appeal. While the procedure in these chambers continues to be based on the French procedures and hearings are conducted in French, the process is open to be adapted to maximise efficiency, to establish clear timetables and to increase the role of testimonial evidence.[29]

In 2018, Frankfurt established the International Chamber for Commercial Matters at the Regional Court for parties who consent to have matters heard before it.[30] The Belgian government also developed a plan to establish the Brussels International Business Court (BIBC) in 2020[31] for parties from different states or those with international matters who agree to have their matters heard there. The procedure for cases

[29] Emmanuel Gaillard, Yas Banifatemi and Chloe Vialard, 'The International Chamber of the Paris Courts and Their Innovative Rules of Procedure' (*Shearman and Sterling*, 23 April 2018), www.shearman.com/perspectives/2018/04/paris-courts-and-their-innovative-rules-of-procedure, accessed 26 October 2018; 'Protocol Relating to the Procedure before the International Chamber of the Paris Commercial Court' (*Cour D'Appel De Paris*, 21 February 2018), www.coursappel.justice.fr/sites/default/files/201806/CICAP_EnglishVersion_Protocole%20barreau%20de%20Paris%20-%20Tribunal%20de%20commerce%20de%20Paris.pdf, accessed 1 August 2019; 'Protocol relating to the Procedure before the International Chamber of the Paris Court of Appeal' (*Cour D'Appel De Paris*, March 2018), www.cours-appel.justice.fr/sites/default/files/2019-04/Traduction%20en%20anglais%20du%20protocole%20CCIP-CA%20-%20V4%20.pdf, accessed 1 August 2019.

[30] Burkhard Hess, 'The Justice Initiative Frankfurt am Main 2017' (*Conflict of Laws.net*, 31 March 2017), http://conflictoflaws.net/2017/the-justice-initiative-frankfurt-am-main-2017-law-made-in-frankfurt, accessed 26 October 2018.

[31] Guillaume Croisant, 'The Belgian Government Unveils Its Plan for the Brussels International Business Court (BIBC)' (*Kluwer Arbitration Blog*, 25 June 2018), http://arbitrationblog.kluwerarbitration.com/2018/06/25/the-belgian-government-unveils-its-plan-for-the-brussels-international-business-court-bibc, accessed 26 October 2018; 2nd Draft Bill – CHAMBRE DES REPRÉSENTANTS DE Belgique (Doc. 54 3072/011), www

was to be based on the UNCITRAL Model Law on International Commercial Arbitration with cases heard in English and presided over by a professional judge and two ad hoc judges, potentially from other countries. In 2019, the bill was withdrawn at the behest of the leading political party, leaving the establishment of the BIBC to be determined based on future elections.[32] However, the design of the court is worth mentioning in anticipation of the plans that may emerge in other places in Europe. In this regard, the European Parliament has commissioned a study for the possible launch of a European Commercial Court.[33]

Together with the provision of specialised bilingual commercial judges, the NCC, the Paris Chambers and the emerging courts elsewhere in Europe seek to draw business from the English Commercial Court following Brexit and the consequential changes to the EU – changes that were hoped to leave these courts alone integrated into the European legal system following the departure of the United Kingdom.

5.3 Jurisdiction

A critical aspect of the ICommCs' attractiveness to international commercial parties concerns the nature and scope of their jurisdiction. The jurisdiction of courts differs in fundamental ways from arbitration, and there are a number of ways in which the international courts' jurisdiction have been fashioned to highlight and enhance their attractiveness to the anticipated user groups. It is, therefore, important to know whether an ICommC chosen by the parties will, in fact, be available to them when a dispute arises and will have the kind of jurisdictional reach necessary to handle their matters effectively.

In nominating one of the ICommCs, the parties will need to investigate, as a matter of the internal structure of the civil justice system in which the ICommC is based, whether the dispute that emerges between them will be accepted in the ICommC that they nominate. The

.dekamer.be/FLWB/PDF/54/3072/54K3072011.pdf; www.lachambre.be/FLWB/PDF/54/3072/54K3072001.pdf, accessed 21 October 2021.

32 See Charles Price and Sebastian Popijn, 'Problems for the Brussels International Business Court' (*Legal Knowledge Portal*, 7 May 2019), https://legalknowledgeportal.com/2019/05/07/problems-for-the-brussels-international-business-court, accessed 1 August 2019.

33 Giesela Ruehl, 'Towards a European Commercial Court?' (*Conflict of Laws.net*, 11 August 2018), http://conflictoflaws.net/2018/towards-a-european-commercial-court, accessed 26 October 2018.

admissibility of their dispute might be affected by its size or nature. However, in principle, since the jurisdiction of these courts has been fashioned to attract international commercial parties, it is likely that they will accept most such matters. Therefore, this question is not addressed further in this chapter.

Accordingly, the first question of jurisdiction concerns the capacity of each of the ICommCs to accept the cases of parties who choose them. If these courts are to be successful in attracting international commercial disputes, their jurisdiction must include cases involving foreign parties and, perhaps even disputes arising elsewhere. This issue will be considered under the heading 'Where Both Parties Choose the Court'.

The second question concerns the ability of the court to accept disputes between parties where it has been chosen as the forum in advance of the dispute and when it is chosen following the emergence of a dispute. On one hand, it is important for sophisticated parties who wish to negotiate their preferred dispute resolution format and forum for the business relationship to be confident that they will benefit from the bargain. This will occur only if the court they choose can accept jurisdiction over the disputes they have submitted to it in advance. On the other hand, there are situations in which, without previously having entered into an agreement to submit disputes to a particular forum, a defendant is amenable to accepting the plaintiff's choice of forum upon receipt of the notice of proceeding. In this situation the parties' consent will not be evidenced by a prior written agreement. This basis for jurisdiction will be considered under the second heading, 'Where the Defendant Accepts the Plaintiff's Choice of Court'.

Each of these ways of consenting to a court's jurisdiction – by agreement or by appearance – is important. Accepting jurisdiction over disputes on the basis of a forum selection clause provides ICommCs with a key benefit enjoyed by those who choose international commercial arbitration. Accepting jurisdiction over disputes where the defendant simply appears to defend in the absence of a formal agreement to the court's jurisdiction provides parties with a benefit that goes beyond that, which is commonly available in many situations in international commercial arbitration.

A third question of jurisdiction involves the capacity of ICommCs to join additional parties and claims, with or without the unanimous consent of the parties.[34] As the parties to international commercial dealings

[34] Hwang (n. 13) 193, 195; Thomas Bathurst, 'Benefits of Courts such as the Singapore International Commercial Court (SICC)' (Sydney Arbitration Week, Sydney, 21 November 2016) p. 7, www.supremecourt.justice.nsw.gov.au/Documents/Publications/Speeches/2016%20Speeches/Bathurst%20CJ/Bathurst_20161121.pdf, accessed 1 August 2019.

have moved beyond discrete transactions to more complex arrangements, the importance of this kind of jurisdiction has increased. In international commercial arbitration, half of the ICC's new cases involve three or more parties;[35] in the 2018 Queen Mary University of London (QMUL) Survey, 39 per cent of respondents identified the lack of power in relation to third parties as one of the worst features of international arbitration,[36] making it one of the top three complaints about arbitration.[37] Arbitral institutions have worked for many years to develop joinder and consolidation mechanisms to provide, to the extent possible, a means to address the challenges of multiparty disputes. In particular, they have done so by enlarging the institutions' or tribunals' powers to order joinder in the following circumstances: where the parties consent; where the arbitrations arise from the same arbitration agreement; where the relief sought in each dispute arises from the same transaction; and where the dispute arises in connection with the same legal relationship.[38] However, a comprehensive solution remains elusive.

In considering the jurisdiction of ICommCs over added parties and claims as a feature weighing in favour of choosing them, it is important to note that the international enforceability of the resulting judgment against parties added without their consent may be limited. However, for ICommCs the judgment will almost certainly be enforceable in the forum of the ICommC in question, and the impact of the adjudication on all the relevant parties, as well as whatever international effect the judgment may have in the particular circumstances, could meet the needs of

[35] 'Full 2016 ICC Dispute Resolution Statistics Published in Court Bulletin' (*International Chamber of Commerce*, 31 August 2017), https://iccwbo.org/media-wall/news-speeches/full-2016-icc-dispute-resolution-statistics-published-court-bulletin, accessed 26 October 2018.

[36] '2018 International Arbitration Survey: The Evolution of International Arbitration' (*Queen Mary University of London and White & Case*, 2018) 10, www.whitecase.com/sites/whitecase/files/files/download/publications/qmul-international-arbitration-survey-2018-18.pdf, accessed 26 October 2018.

[37] Ibid.

[38] ICC Rules 2012 arts 7, 10; ICC Rules 2017 arts 7, 10; Swiss Arbitration Rules 2012 arts 4.1, 4.2; HKIAC Arbitration Rules 2013 arts 27, 28; CIETAC Rules 2015 arts 18, 19; SIAC Rules 2016 r 7; SIAC Rules 2016 (at 1 August 2016) r 8.9; ACICA Arbitration Rules 2016 arts 14, 15. SCC Arbitration Rules 2017 arts 13–15; 'Proposal on Cross-Institutional Consolidation Protocol' (*Singapore International Arbitration Centre*, 19 December 2017), http://siac.org.sg/69-siac-news/551-proposal-on-cross-institution-consolidation-protocol, accessed 26 October 2018; Gordon Smith, 'Comparative Analysis of Joinder and Consolidation Provisions under Leading Arbitral Rules' (2018) 35(2) J Int'l Arb 173.

the parties invoking it. This basis for jurisdiction will be considered under the heading 'Jurisdiction over Additional Claims and Parties'.

Finally, many courts accept jurisdiction over matters with strong connections to the forum even in the absence of the defendants' consent. In most cases, they do so knowing that the judgment will be enforceable in the territory of the forum even if it will not be recognised elsewhere. Nevertheless, as with jurisdiction over added parties, this can be an important area of jurisdictional competence that is not readily available in international commercial arbitration and that may be an attractive feature for users. This basis for jurisdiction will be considered under the heading 'Other Bases of Jurisdiction'.

5.3.1 *Where Both Parties Choose the Court*

It is now widely recognised that the choice of forum for dispute resolution can have important consequences for the effectiveness of other terms of the parties' agreements and may be a key bargaining point. It is crucial, therefore, to know whether this choice will be accepted by the nominated court. Does the local law governing the ICommC's jurisdiction permit the court to accept cases simply on the basis that the parties have chosen it – or must there be other connections with the forum? What restrictions might local law place on the parties' choice of court?

5.3.1.1 English Commercial Court and the Technology and Construction Court

Parties who adopt English law as the governing law of their contract may be able to bring claims in the English Commercial Court and the Technology and Construction Court (TCC), provided that they meet the ordinary jurisdictional requirements of the courts.[39] Under these requirements they may serve parties in the UK with the notice of proceeding without any special arrangements and they may serve parties with the notice of proceeding outside the country in a range of different circumstances contemplated in Part 6 of the Civil Procedure Rules. These include service abroad without permission for defendants in Europe under the Brussels Regulation and those in countries that are parties to the Hague Choice of Court Convention, as well as service abroad for defendants domiciled in the UK. They also include service abroad in

[39] Under the umbrella designation of the 'Business and Property Courts of England and Wales'.

a variety of situations where the court gives permission, including where the parties' contract 'contains a term to the effect that the court shall have jurisdiction to determine any claim in respect of the contract'.[40]

5.3.1.2 Singapore International Commercial Court

The Singapore International Commercial Court (SICC) accepts jurisdiction based on the parties' agreement where it is on decisive terms. A jurisdiction agreement nominating the SICC, unless expressly providing otherwise, is interpreted as exclusive and as importing the obligation to carry out the resulting judgment without undue delay, and the waiver of recourse in a foreign tribunal or court against the judgment insofar as recourse can validly be waived.[41]

5.3.1.3 International Commercial Courts in the Gulf Region and Central Asia

Dubai – The DIFC Court of First Instance may determine civil or commercial claims where the parties agree in writing before or after the dispute arises, provided that the agreement is made pursuant to specific, clear and express provisions. In addition, the Court of First Instance may determine any civil or commercial claim falling within its jurisdiction where the parties agree in writing to the jurisdiction of another court, but the other court has dismissed the claim for lack of jurisdiction. However, the Court of First Instance may not determine civil or commercial claims in respect of which a final judgment has been rendered by another court.[42] It has also been suggested that parties should be able to submit to the jurisdiction of the DIFC Courts in other circumstances as well, based on another provision of Dubai law, which establishes that a submission to the DIFC courts in a contract shall be effective.[43]

[40] 'Civil Procedure Rules r 6.36 and Practice Direction 6.36(d)' (*Ministry of Justice*), www.justice.gov.uk/courts/procedure-rules/civil/rules/part06, accessed 1 August 2019.

[41] Note 10, 18F.

[42] 'DIFC Law No 16 of 2011' (*DIFC*), www.difccourts.ae/2011/10/31/law-no-16-of-2011-amending-certain-provisions-of-law-no-12-of-2004-concerning-dubai-international-financial-centre-courts, arts 5A(2) and (3), accessed 1 August 2019.

[43] DIFC Law relating to the Application of DIFC Laws, DIFC Law No. 10 of 2005, art. 13(1); Michael Hwang, 'The Courts of the Dubai International Financial Centre: A Common Law Island in a Civil Law Ocean' (DIFC Courts, 1 November 2008), www.difccourts.ae/2008/11/01/the-courts-of-the-dubai-international-finance-centre-a-common-law-island-in-a-civil-law-ocean, accessed 1 August 2019.

Qatar – The relevant provision for jurisdiction based on the parties' agreement in the QICDRC is more principle-based. It states that consistently, and in accordance with fundamental international principles and international best practice, the Court will take into account the expressed accord of the parties that the Court shall have jurisdiction.[44] However, it is important to note that, in practice, the QICDRC is designed primarily as a dispute resolution facility for matters connected to Qatar and does not aspire to a broader range of cases as does, for example, the DIFC Court.

Abu Dhabi – The ADGM Court of First Instance is a superior court of record in Abu Dhabi that has jurisdiction, in addition to that conferred on it by the ADGM Founding Law, applicable Abu Dhabi law, and regulations, where there is a request, in writing, by the Parties to have the Court of First Instance determine the claim or dispute. Where the ADGM Courts would otherwise have jurisdiction, the Parties may 'opt out' in their contracts.[45]

Astana – In Kazakhstan, for civil and commercial matters, the AIFC Constitutional Statute 2015 provides that the AIFC Court has exclusive jurisdiction over disputes transferred to it by agreement of the parties.[46] The AIFC Court Regulations 2017 clarifies that this includes civil or commercial disputes arising from transactions, contracts, arrangements or incidences, and disputes involving parties who are not registered in the AIFC and who have opted in by agreeing to give the Court jurisdiction before or after the dispute arose.[47]

5.3.1.4 China International Commercial Court

Parties to a contractual or property dispute may select the People's Court at the place connected with the dispute (e.g. where the plaintiff or

[44] 'QFC Regulations' (QFC) art. 9.2, www.complinet.com/qfcra/display/display.html?rbid=1557&element_id=3, accessed 1 August 2019.

[45] 'ADGM Courts, Civil Evidence, Judgments, Enforcement and Judicial Appointments Regulations 2015' (ADGM), http://adgm.complinet.com/net_file_store/new_rulebooks/a/d/ADGM_Courts_Regulations_17Dec2015.pdf, accessed 1 August 2019, https://uk.practicallaw.thomsonreuters.com/w-0137809?transitionType=Default&contextData=(sc.Default)&firstPage=true&comp=pluk&bhcp=1, accessed 21 October 2021.

[46] AIFC Constitutional Statute 2015 (AIFC) art. 13.4(3), https://aifc-court.kz/legislation, accessed 1 August 2019.

[47] AIFC Constitutional Statute 2017 (AIFC), https://aifc-court.kz/legislation, art. 26(2) and (3) accessed 1 August 2019.

defendant is domiciled, where the contract is executed or to be performed or where the subject matter of the dispute is located), provided that this is consistent with the court structure and restrictions for exclusive jurisdiction within the Chinese civil justice system.[48]

Where the dispute is for more than 300,000,000 Chinese yuan, the parties to international commercial cases may seek permission for the matter to be heard in the CICC; and the CICC may hear cases that have a nationwide significance and cases involving applications for preservation measures in arbitration,[49] for setting aside or enforcement of international commercial arbitration awards,[50] and cases the Supreme People's Court considers appropriate to be tried by the International Commercial Court.[51]

5.3.1.5 Commercial Courts in Europe

Amsterdam – Where a particular legal relationship is not subject to the jurisdiction of the Subdistrict Court or the exclusive jurisdiction of any other chamber or court, and the parties have designated the Amsterdam District Court as the forum to hear their case or the Amsterdam District Court has jurisdiction to hear the action on other grounds. The parties may also agree in writing to submit the proceedings to the NCC in English.[52]

Paris – The jurisdiction of the Paris Chambers may be based on the parties' agreement in a matter otherwise within the courts' jurisdiction.[53]

[48] 'Civil Procedure Law of the People's Republic of China (Revised in 2017)' (CICC, 29 June 2017) art. 34, http://cicc.court.gov.cn/html/1/219/199/200/644.html, accessed 1 August 2019.

[49] Ibid., art. 14.

[50] Ibid., art. 11.

[51] Ibid., art. 2.

[52] 'Rules of Procedure for the International Commercial Chambers of the Amsterdam District Court (NCC District Court) and the Amsterdam Court of Appeal (NCC Court of Appeal)' (*Netherlands Commercial Court*, December 2018) art. 1.3.1, www.rechtspraak.nl/SiteCollectionDocuments/ncc-procesreglement-en.pdf, accessed 1 August 2019 [hereinafter NCC Rules of Procedure].

[53] Translations of the relevant protocols may be found at 'The International Chamber of the Paris Courts and Their Innovative Rules of Procedure (Unofficial English Translation)' (*Shearman and Sterling*), www.shearman.com/perspectives/2018/04/paris-courts-and-their-innovative-rules-ofprocedure?utm_source=Mondaq&utm_medium=syndication&utm_campaign=LinkedIn-integration#utm_source=Mondaq&utm_ medium=syndication&utm_campaign=inter-article-link, accessed 1 August 2019.

Brussels – According to the draft legislation for the BIBC,[54] and the commentary on it[55] in international commercial disputes (i.e. between parties based in different jurisdictions, or where a substantial part of the commercial relationship is to be performed in a third country, or governed by foreign law) and where the parties frequently used a language other than French, Dutch or German in their commercial dealings, the parties may choose the BIBC provided that they do so prior to the crystallisation of their dispute.[56]

Frankfurt – Since January 2018, the Frankfurt international chamber has sought to recover some of the caseload that has migrated to arbitration in recent years by maintaining a special 'international commercial chamber' within the court system. The parties' choice of this court will be respected, provided that the case does not fall within the jurisdiction of another chamber of the District Court Frankfurt/Main, and the case is international.

5.3.2 *Where the Defendant Accepts the Plaintiff's Choice of Court*

Just as it is critical to the effectiveness of international commercial courts that they be accessible to knowledgeable commercial parties who wish to arrange for their dispute resolution by nominating these ICommCs in their agreements, so too may it be important for the courts to be accessible to parties who agree to submit disputes to them without previously having designated them.

One difference between the jurisdiction of common law courts and that of their civil law counterparts in disputes involving foreign defendants is that, generally speaking, common law courts will review their own jurisdiction over the parties only when it is challenged by one of the parties. Accordingly, even where the court might not have jurisdiction on any of the other bases considered in this chapter, the commencement of the claim in the court by the plaintiff and the acceptance by the defendant of the court's jurisdiction by defending the claim on the merits will be

[54] 'Projet De Loi – instaurant la Brussels International Business Court' (*Chambre De Représentants*, 10 December 2018), www.dekamer.be/FLWB/PDF/54/3072/54K3072011.pdf, accessed 1 August 2019; 'Projet De Loi – instaurant la Brussels International Business Court' (*Chambre De Représentants*, 15 May 2018) www.lachambre.be/FLWB/PDF/54/3072/54K3072001.pdf, accessed 1 August 2019 (the legislation was provisionally withdrawn in May 2019).

[55] Croisant (n. 31).

[56] Ibid.

sufficient to result in a judgment regarded as binding on the defendant. In civil law courts, a court's jurisdiction often must comply with that set out in its constitutive legislation. As just mentioned, in the case of the BIBC, this would not appear to have included situations in which a defendant informally accepted the plaintiff's choice of the BIBC following the emergence of the dispute.

5.3.2.1 English Commercial Court and the Technology and Construction Court

Where a foreign defendant files an acknowledgement of service but makes no application during the next twenty-eight days to dispute the court's jurisdiction, the defendant is treated as having accepted that the court has jurisdiction to try the claim.[57]

5.3.2.2 Singapore International Commercial Court

Where the defendant makes an appearance in the courts in Singapore without disputing the court's jurisdiction or contending that Singapore is not a proper forum for the dispute, the defendant is treated as having submitted to the court's jurisdiction.[58]

5.3.2.3 International Commercial Courts in the Gulf Region and Central Asia

Dubai – While the Dubai law providing for the jurisdiction of the DIFC does not appear to have a provision specifically addressed to the implicit acceptance of the court's jurisdiction by appearing and defending on the merits, the law does provide for jurisdiction where the parties agree to it in writing after the dispute arises.[59]

Qatar – If a party wishes to contest the jurisdiction of the QICDRC, the party must notify the Registry and the claimant within fourteen days of service of the claim form, file an application notice with supporting evidence, and serve it on the other party or parties within fourteen days of the notification. Following this, the Court will give directions as to

[57] Note 40, Part 11(5).

[58] Note 41, Rule 7.6.

[59] 'DIFC Law No 12 of 2004' (*DIFC*, 2004), www.dfsa.ae/Documents/Dubai%20Law%20No%2012%20of%202004.pdf, accessed 1 August 2019, as amended by 'Law No. 16 of 2011' (*DIFC*, 2011), www.difccourts.ae/2011/10/31/law-no-16-of-2011-amending-certain-provisions-of-law-no-12-of-2004-concerning-dubai-international-financial-centre-courts, accessed 1 August 2019.

how the jurisdiction application is to be determined, including as to any evidence to be filed.[60]

Abu Dhabi – Where a defendant files an acknowledgement of service in the ADGM Court but makes no application during the next twenty-eight days to dispute the court's jurisdiction, the defendant is treated as having accepted that the court has jurisdiction to try the claim.[61]

Astana – If the defendant files an acknowledgment of service in the AIFC and does not make an application disputing the Court's jurisdiction within fourteen days, the defendant is treated as having accepted that the Court has jurisdiction to try the claim.[62]

5.3.2.4 China International Commercial Court

Where a party does not raise any objection to the jurisdiction of the CICC in the case and responds to the claim and enters a defence, the party is deemed to have accepted the jurisdiction of the People's Court to which it has been submitted, unless this jurisdiction violates a provision regarding the jurisdiction of the particular court within the PRC court system or some other provision for the exclusive jurisdiction of another court.[63]

5.3.2.5 Commercial Courts in Europe

Where a defendant does not challenge the jurisdiction of the Amsterdam District Court or the Amsterdam Court of Appeal, as the case may be, or the alleged agreement for proceedings to be before the NCC District Court or NCC Court of Appeal in English, prior to any defences on the merits, the court may direct that the defendant's right to do so is waived. If the defendant makes such a motion, it does not need to file a defence on the merits. The motion may be made in Dutch, in which event the further proceedings and the decision on this point will be in Dutch.[64] In the case of the

[60] Note 42, arts. 19.1–19.3.

[61] 'Abu Dhabi Global Markets Court Procedure Rules' (*ADGM*, 2016) art. 38(4) and (5), www.adgm.com/-/media/project/adgm/courts/documents/forms-and-fees/court-of-first-instance/adgm-court-procedure-rules-2016-updated-25-february-2019.pdf, accessed 1 August 2019.

[62] 'AIFC Court Rules 2018' (AIFC, 2018) Rule 8.5 https://laws.aifc.kz/files/adb6b118a86f4a55/3.%20Legislation%20-%20AIFC%20Court%20Rules%202018.pdf, accessed 1 August 2019.

[63] Note 48, art. 127.

[64] Note 52, art. 6.3.

international commercial chamber of the District Court Frankfurt/Main, the parties must declare their agreement to the jurisdiction of the chamber before the deadline for the statement of defence has expired and indicate their willingness to proceed in English without interpreters.

5.3.3 *Jurisdiction over Additional Claims and Parties*

One feature that ICommCs emphasise in promoting their use is their capacity to join and consolidate claims, with or without the unanimous consent of the parties.[65] As discussed earlier, this is a significant area of jurisdictional competence which has eluded international commercial arbitration.

5.3.3.1 The English Commercial Court and the Technology and Construction Court

The English Commercial Court and the TCC may order a person to be added as a new party if it is desirable for the court to resolve all the matters in dispute in the proceedings before it, or if there is an issue involving the new party and an existing party which is connected to the matters in dispute in the proceedings, and it is desirable to add the new party so that the court can resolve that issue. The Court also has the authority to remove a party if it is not desirable for that person to be a party to the proceedings, and to substitute a new party for an existing party if the existing party's interest or liability has passed to the new party and this will enable the court to resolve the matters in dispute in the proceedings.[66] Furthermore, all persons jointly entitled to a remedy must be parties unless the court orders otherwise, and if any of them does not agree to be a claimant, that person must be made a defendant.[67] The rules for adding, removing and substituting parties also include mechanisms for ensuring that all parties receive appropriate notice and that suitable directions are made for the proceedings as a result. Special provisions are made for adding or substituting parties after the end of a relevant limitation period.[68] Robust rules for handling multiparty cases are particularly important for the TCC in its remit to handle

[65] Note 34.
[66] Note 40, r 19.1(1)–(4).
[67] Ibid., r 19.2.
[68] Ibid., r 19.3, 19.4.

construction disputes involving interconnecting contracts and many parties.[69]

5.3.3.2 Singapore International Commercial Court

The SICC procedure similarly addresses issues of joinder in situations of string contracts where it may be necessary to add relevant parties who do not consent. The SICC may order the joinder and consolidation on application from a party or on its own motion; and in the case of a state or sovereign of a state, joinder may occur where the state has submitted to the jurisdiction of the SICC.[70]

5.3.3.3 International Commercial Courts in the Gulf Region and Central Asia

Dubai – The DIFC Court may, if it considers it appropriate, join any party to an action or proceeding.[71] Part 21 of the DIFC Court Rules makes detailed provision for counterclaims and claims for contribution and indemnity from parties to be added to the proceeding. Accordingly, the Rules provide for the addition both of parties and of claims to ongoing proceedings.[72] These include, where required, provisions for the permission of the DIFC Court, notice, the delivery of documents and other relevant considerations.

Qatar – The QICDRC may, at any stage of the proceedings give directions: permitting the amendment of the claim form or of any statement of case; adding or substituting any party or parties; permitting or requiring any party to provide further information in relation to its case.[73]

Abu Dhabi – Parties and claims may be added to an ongoing matter with the ADGM Court's permission.[74] In addition, the Court may direct the service of a non-party who may be affected by a claim or judgment and

[69] 'Technology and Construction Court' (*HM Courts and Tribunal Service*), www.gov.uk/courts-tribunals/technology-and-construction-court, accessed 26 October 2018.

[70] 'Rules of Court Order 110'(*SICC*) r 9, www.sicc.gov.sg/legislation-rules-pd/rules-of-court, accessed 1 August 2019.

[71] 'DIFC Law No. 10 of 2004' (*DIFC*, 2004), art. 33(2), www.difc.ae/files/1914/5448/9176/Court_Law_DIFC_Law_No.10_of_2004.pdf, accessed 1 August 2019.

[72] 'Rules of the Dubai International Financial Centre Courts 2014' (*DIFC*) Parts 20, 21, www.difccourts.ae/court-rules/part-21-counterclaims-and-other-additional-claims, accessed 1 August 2019.

[73] Note 15, art. 24.

[74] Note 61, Part 7, r 56.

the party, who will be bound by the judgment or order, may apply to participate.[75]

Astana – The AIFC Court may join any party to an action or proceeding.[76] Parties may be removed, added or substituted in existing proceedings on the application of an existing party or a person wishing to be added, or on the Court's own initiative.[77]

5.3.3.4 China International Commercial Court

The CICC Procedural Rules permit the parties to apply at the pretrial conference to add or amend claims, to consolidate actions, and to join additional parties.[78]

5.3.3.5 Commercial Courts in Europe

Taking the NCC as an example, joinder and consolidation were anticipated as an important feature of its jurisdiction,[79] as indicated by the provisions for adding third parties for contribution and indemnity or any other purpose allowed by law.[80]

5.3.4 Jurisdiction over Claims Connected with the Forum

One further feature of the jurisdiction of the ICommCs that should be mentioned for the sake of completeness is that, as with other courts of law, their jurisdiction is not limited to situations in which the parties have accepted their jurisdiction but extends to situations in which the plaintiff commences a claim in a dispute that has close ties to the forum. This may be the case in respect of claims brought on the basis of events occurring in the forum or of losses suffered in the forum. The circumstances in which this form of jurisdiction is exercised are extensive, and they vary from one court to the next. In common law systems, the circumstances are

75 Ibid., Part 7, r 58.

76 'AIFC Court Regulations 2017' (AIFC, 2017) Article 27(2)(h), http://laws.aifc.kz/files/3c79917a4b9e44f2/3.%20Legislation%20-%20AIFC%20Court%20Regulations%202017.pdf, accessed 1 August 2019.

77 Note 62, Part 12.

78 'Procedural Rules for the China International Commercial Court of the Supreme People's Court (For Trial Implementation)' (*CICC*, 5 December 2018), ch 5, http://cicc.court.gov.cn/html/1/219/208/210/1183.html, accessed 1 August 2019.

79 'The NCC Rules – Concept' (Netherlands Commercial Court, June 2017) arts 6.4, 6.5, www.rechtspraak.nl/SiteCollectionDocuments/concept-procesreglement-ncc_en.pdf, accessed 1 August 2019.

80 Note 52, art. 6.4.

often set out in lists authorising service of defendants outside the jurisdiction, and in civil law systems, they are often described in the civil code or the code of civil procedure.

As with matters involving non-consenting parties, the judgments will often not be enforceable internationally. However, where local enforcement is the objective of the proceeding, this form of jurisdiction will be an attractive feature of the ICommC.

5.4 Applicable Law

English commercial law and common law procedures have been important forces in advancing international commerce and dispute resolution for generations. For this reason, in some regions of the world, such as the Gulf Region and Central Asia, the capacity of courts to depart from the local law and procedure and to apply English commercial law and manage common law proceedings skilfully has been an important feature of their attractiveness.

However, in more recent years, as the international community has broadened and diversified, so too has the range of laws adopted in commercial dealings expanded and so too has adopting civil law techniques in resolving disputes emerged as a potentially attractive alternative. With this diversification of preferred applicable laws and procedures, it has become important for courts to demonstrate their capacity to apply these laws and to employ these dispute resolution techniques in the disputes before them. Accordingly, this section describes the ways in which the 'specialised courts' have sought to excel in the application of English commercial law and, subsequently, and more recently, to demonstrate their capacity to apply a range of laws effectively; and the ways in which courts have sought to promote the dispute resolution techniques that they offer as a means attracting cases.

5.4.1 English Commercial Law

5.4.1.1 English Commercial Court and the Technology and Construction Court

London's importance as a dispute resolution forum is so well established that few now reflect on its foundation. At the opening conference of London's first 'International Dispute Week' in 2019, the first session began with a discussion of the history of London's success. London's success was said to be due, not primarily, or at least, initially, to the leadership of the English Commercial Court or to the strength of the English bar, but to the attractiveness of English commercial law in maximising party autonomy and securing the specificity of contractual terms.

Clearly, the leadership of the English Commercial Court and the strength of the legal profession have been critical in promoting London's success, but these were cast in a supporting role to English commercial law. As the Commercial Court Guide explains: 'Alongside its work nationally, the great preponderance of the work of the Commercial Court is international. Commercial parties worldwide bring their cases to the Court through choice. English Law is a global business law as a result of choice.'[81] The City UK Legal Services Report adds to this as follows:

> Through this workload the Court is asked to reach decisions that ensure that English common law continues to develop, always ready to provide a framework in law in a fast-changing business world. The Court is frequently asked to interpret commercial documents in wide international usage, or to show how the law works in the context of new forms of trade or transaction. The Court further takes responsibility for expert judicial oversight and support of arbitration, including international arbitration seated in London. In combination these roles contribute to confidence, stability and certainty through the rule of law.[82]

Accordingly, it would seem that the initial success of London as a centre for dispute resolution came as a result of the once unique opportunity that dispute resolution in London provided for parties to assure themselves of the effective application of English commercial law. In time, this supported the development of dispute resolution processes in London as an independent reason for choosing the English Commercial Court or the TCC for international disputes. Indeed, the widely accepted strengths of the English bar and bench have made their members sought after in dispute resolution the world over, particularly where the parties have chosen English law to govern their contract.

The attraction of English commercial law has prompted other ICommCs, such as the DIFC, QICDRC, ADGM and AIFC, to adopt English law as the basis for dispute resolution in order to attract parties who wish to have the benefit of English commercial law in dispute resolution conducted in the

[81] Note 2.

[82] 'Legal Excellence, Internationally Renowned: UK Legal Services 2018' (*TheCityUK*, 2018), www.thecityuk.com/assets/2018/Reports-PDF/86e1b87840/Legal-excellence-internationally-renowned-UK-legal-services-2018.pdf, accessed 1 August 2019.

region. It has also been a formative influence in the approach to the applicable law taken in centres such Singapore.

5.4.1.2 Singapore International Commercial Court

As a common law legal system, Singaporean commercial law is founded on English commercial law. The leading English precedents continue to be consulted, but the common law in Singapore has been developed autonomously by Singapore judges. There is, nevertheless, a desire to promote the SICC as a court that is genuinely capable of applying English commercial law and the best of the common law from around the world. To do so, the SICC has staffed its bench with a number of senior retired judges and leading arbitrators from England and Wales and other common law countries, and it has relaxed the restrictions that otherwise exist to permit foreign lawyers greater rights of audience than they would have in other Singapore courts.

5.4.1.3 International Commercial Courts in the Gulf Region and Central Asia

Dubai – In 2004, the UAE Constitution was amended to authorise the federal government to enact laws to establish Financial Free Zones exempt from federal, civil and commercial laws and regulations of the UAE.[83] However, laws concerning the criminalisation of money laundering and the UAE Penal code continue to apply.[84] The exemptions enable the DIFC Court to operate as a common law court within what is otherwise a civil law system. Accordingly, the Dubai law for determining the governing law[85] provides that DIFC Court Law applies notwithstanding any federal law on civil or commercial matters and that, subject to local regulatory requirements and the parties' choice to the contrary, the

[83] 'Constitutional Amendment No. 1 of 2003' (*Dubai Financial Services Authority*, 10 January 2004) art. 121, www.dfsa.ae/Documents/Constitutional%20Amendment%20No%201%20of%202003.pdf, accessed 1 August 2019; 'Federal Law No. 8 of 2004' (*DFSA*, 27 March 2004), art. 3 www.dfsa.ae/Documents/Federal%20Law%20No%208%20of%202004.pdf, accessed 1 August 2019; Alejandro Carballo, 'The Law of the Dubai International Financial Centre: Common Law Oasis or Mirage within the UAE?' (2007) 21 Arab Law Quarterly 91, 95.

[84] 'Federal Law No. 4 of 2002' (International Money Laundering Information Network), www.imolin.org/doc/amlid/United_Arab_Emirates/Federal-Law-No.4-2002-English.pdf, accessed 1 August 2019.

[85] 'DIFC Law No. 3 of 2004' (DIFC, 2004), www.difc.ae/files/9214/5448/9184/Law_on_the_Application_of_Civil_and_Commercial_Laws_in_the_DIFC_DIFC_Law_No._3_oF_2004.pdf, accessed 1 August 2019.

default law to be applied is based on the laws of England and Wales.[86] The DIFC Court Law also provides for the appointment of judges with a common law background, reinforcing an appearance of independence of both the judicial and legal systems from those of Dubai.[87]

Qatar – The procedures of the QICDRC are based on international best practices, modelled to a significant extent on those practiced in England and Wales.[88] Thus, the QICDRC also operates in a special enclave under 'international common law', which allows the judges to draw from precedents across the common law world.[89] The proceedings are usually conducted in English but, as Arabic is the official language of the state, under the QICDRC regulations, the parties are also entitled to conduct proceedings in Arabic if they wish to do so.[90]

Abu Dhabi – English law is the foundation of the civil and commercial law of the ADGM and the ADGM Courts and its judiciary are modelled broadly on the English Judicial System.[91] Pursuant to the Application of English Law Regulations 2015, the ADGM Court makes English common law, including equity, directly applicable in the ADGM, along with many well-established English statutes on civil matters. Furthermore, the Financial Services and Markets Regulations establishes the legislative and regulatory framework for financial services in the ADGM and is modelled on the UK's Financial Services and Markets Act 2000. In this way, like the DIFC and the QICDRC, the ADGM Courts operate within an independent common law framework[92] with English common law (including the rules and principles of equity) directly applicable in the ADGM.[93] Further guidance is drawn from Scottish and Australian federal law.[94]

86 Ibid., art. 8.2(e).

87 'DIFC Law No. 10 of 2004' (DIFC, 2004) art. 9, www.difc.ae/files/1914/5448/9176/Court_Law_DIFC_Law_No.10_of_2004.pdf, accessed 1 August 2019.

88 'e-Court-QICDRC' (*National Association for Court Management*), https://nacmnet.org/wp-content/uploads/QATAR_Final-Submission.pdf, accessed 1 August 2019.

89 Neil Rose, 'Qatar: A Centre for "Quality" International Dispute Resolution?' *The Guardian* (London, 14 December 2010), www.theguardian.com/law/2010/dec/14/qatar-international-dispute-resolution-law, accessed 1 August 2019.

90 Note 15, art. 3.2.

91 'English Common Law' (*ADGM*), www.adgm.com/adgm-courts/english-common-law, accessed 1 August 2019.

92 Ibid.

93 Ibid., Application of English Law Regulations 2015.

94 ADGM Courts, Civil Evidence, Judgments, Enforcement and Judicial Appointments Regulations 2015 (n. 19).

Astana – The Astana Council Resolution governing the activities of the AIFC Court is based on the principles and legislation of the law of England and Wales and the standards of leading global financial centres,[95] provided that they are consistent with the public order and policy of the Republic of Kazakhstan.[96] The AIFC Court is authorised to take into account its own precedents and those of other common law jurisdictions,[97] and the judges are required to have significant knowledge of the common law and experience as a lawyer or judge in a common law system, and to be able to speak and write in the English language.[98] In addition, the Court may provide common law courses and accreditation for lawyers and judges.[99]

5.4.1.4 China International Commercial Court

The China International Court (CICC) was established to support the international dispute resolution arising from the Belt and Road Initiative and not specifically to serve as an enclave of common law dispute resolution. Accordingly, the CICC does not often apply English law or use English common law procedures. It does, however, have capacity to apply the common law where the parties have chosen it by agreement.

5.4.1.5 Commercial Courts in Europe

Amsterdam – In the NCC, the applicable substantive law is determined by reference to the rules of Dutch private international law. Subject to the unanimous request of the parties that the proceedings be conducted in Dutch, they are conducted in English.[100] As English is

[95] AIFC Constitutional Statute 2015 (AIFC), https://laws.aifc.kz/storage/files/47ba42d60f3e4766/Unofficial%20English%20translation%20of%20the%20Contitutional%20Statute%20On%20the%20AIFC%20as%20amended%20.pdf, accessed 1 August 2019. Article 13: Astana Council Resolution, On the Court of Astana International Financial Centre.

[96] 'AIFC Court Regulations 2017' (AIFC, 5 December 2017), art. 29(1)(b), http://laws.aifc.kz/files/3c79917a4b9e44f2/3.%20Legislation%20-%20AIFC%20Court%20Regulations%202017.pdf, accessed 21 October 2021.

[97] Note 46, art. 13(6).

[98] Note 96, art. 12(6).

[99] Ibid., art. 12(6)(f).

[100] Note 28, art. 2.1.1. For substantive law, H. C. S. Warendorf, Richard Thomas, I. Curry-Sumner, Marius Josephus Jiita, Colin Longhurst and Peter Kell, *Warendorf Dutch Civil and Commercial Law Legislation* (Deventer: Wolters Kluwer, 2014) is the prescribed source for English-language terminology.

commonly spoken in the Netherlands as a second language, it appears to be unnecessary to make special provision for anglophone judgess and the judges are selected from the local judiciary. The procedural rules provide flexibility, allowing proceedings to be conducted either in the civil law tradition, or in a manner more similar to proceedings in common law jurisdictions or international arbitration. This flexibility seeks to make the proceedings more familiar to international parties.[101]

Paris – The Paris chamber does not aim primarily to provide dispute resolution in the English common law tradition but emphasises its capability of applying foreign law more generally.[102]

Brussels – The draft legislation, which was based on the UNCITRAL Model Law, would permit the application of foreign law, including English commercial law.[103]

Frankfurt – This chamber aims primarily to provide dispute resolution in English (with judgments rendered in German), and is capable of applying foreign law generally, but in other respects operates as an integral part of the existing court system.

5.4.2 *The Application of Other Foreign Laws*

5.4.2.1 English Commercial Court and the Technology and Construction Court

Although the Commercial Courts in London may have risen to prominence through expertise in the application of English commercial law, they are regularly called upon to apply other laws and they have developed a rich jurisprudence concerning the process for doing so.[104] Indeed, the expertise of the Commercial Court in applying foreign law is one of the features emphasised in its claim to be a leading international court. This strength is to be placed in the context of the use of English language in the proceedings. While the use of English is sufficiently attractive to the parties in many international cases to be adopted in

[101] 'Stibbe Book on the Netherlands Commercial Courts Published' (*Stibbe*, 8 March 2019), www.stibbe.com/en/news/2019/march/stibbe-book-on-the-netherlands-commercial-court-published, accessed 1 August 2019.

[102] Protocol relating to the Procedure before the International Chamber of the Paris Commercial Court (n. 29); Protocol relating to the Procedure before the International Chamber of the Paris Court of Appeal (n. 29).

[103] Croisant (n. 31).

[104] Note 2, C1.3(f); Richard Fentiman, *Foreign Law in English Courts* (Oxford: Oxford University Press, 1998).

many of the non-anglophone courts considered in this chapter, it is the only language available for the proceedings in the Commercial Court, with witnesses and others testifying through interpreters and counsel pleading in English.

5.4.2.2 Singapore International Commercial Court

Like the English Commercial Court, the Singapore International Commercial Court (SICC) seeks to provide the parties with dispute resolution in accordance with their preferred law. In accordance with the standard common law procedure, foreign law is pleaded and then proved by an expert. In the Singapore courts, primary sources of evidence can be introduced directly, but it is preferable for there to be expert to provide guidance on the interpretation of the various legal sources provided. Alternatively, in the SICC, parties may apply to have foreign law determined on the basis of the submissions of counsel provided that counsel are competent to submit on the relevant questions of foreign law.[105] When this occurs, the SICC is authorised to consider the legislation and decisions of the courts of the country in question.[106]

The SICC is supported in its application of foreign law in two ways. First, there is a departure from the standard restriction to local counsel to permit foreign counsel to apply for rights of audience.[107] Secondly, the court is staffed by an international bench[108] and, to date, at least one international judge has been assigned to each case.[109]

5.4.2.3 International Commercial Courts in the Gulf Region and Central Asia

Dubai – Under the law constituting the DIFC Court, the parties are free to depart from the default application of the common law to seek the

[105] Note 10, s. 18L; n. 10, Singapore O 110 r 25; *BCBC Singapore Pte Ltd* v. *PT Bayan Resources TBK* (Supreme Court of Singapore, 9 January 2019), www.supremecourt.gov.sg/news/case-summaries/bcbc-singapore-pte-ltd-and-another-v-pt-bayan-resources-tbk-and-another, accessed 1 August 2019.

[106] Ibid., O 110 r 26.

[107] Note 10, 18M; 'Representation by Foreign Lawyers' (*SICC*, 10 January 2019), www.sicc.gov.sg/guide-to-the-sicc/representation-by-foreign-lawyers, accessed 1 August 2019.

[108] 'Judges' (*SICC*), www.sicc.gov.sg/about-the-sicc/judges, accessed 1 August 2019.

[109] 'Legal Profession Act (Cap. 161)' (Attorney General's Chambers, 1 June 2009) Part IVB, https://sso.agc.gov.sg/Act/LPA1966, accessed 1 August 2019; Andrew Goodwin, Ian Ramsay and Miranda Webster, 'International Commercial Courts: The Singapore Experience' (2017) 18 Melbourne Journal of International Law 2.

application of some other law.[110] The formula for determining the law to be applied requires the court to consider the potentially applicable laws in sequence as follows:

(a) so far as there is a regulatory content, the DIFC Law or any other law in force in the DIFC; failing which,
(b) the law of any Jurisdiction other than that of the DIFC expressly chosen by any DIFC Law; failing which,
(c) the laws of a Jurisdiction as agreed between all the relevant persons concerned in the matter; failing which,
(d) the laws of any Jurisdiction which appears to the Court or Arbitrator to be the one most closely related to the facts of and the persons concerned in the matter; failing which,
(e) the laws of England and Wales.[111]

The DIFC Court's ability to offer dispute resolution in accordance with other laws is supported by a bench comprised in the majority of non-UAE judges – from the UK, Singapore, Malaysia and Australia. It should be noted in respect of all the Gulf Region courts considered that the application of common law or some other law is without prejudice to the continuing application of local regulatory laws and laws of public order.

Qatar – The QFC Regulations provide a similar hierarchy of applicable laws, beginning with the non-derogable local laws and regulations, including those protecting local consumers, followed by the law that the parties have chosen subject to its consistency with the Qatari public order and public policy.[112] As in Dubai, the ability to apply foreign law is supported by a bench primarily comprised of common law judges from abroad.

Abu Dhabi – The default law for the ADGM Court is English common law, but a party may introduce foreign law on notice to the other party with supporting documentation.[113] The foreign law must be proved by a suitably qualified expert.[114] The bench of the ADGM Court consists of judges from England, Australia, New Zealand and Hong Kong.

110 Hwang (n. 43).
111 Note 85, art. 8(2).
112 Note 15, art. 11.1.
113 ADGM Court Rules (n. 19), r 117.
114 ADGM Courts, Civil Evidence, Judgments, Enforcement and Judicial Appointments Regulations (n. 19), art. 73.

Astana – The hierarchy of applicable laws prescribed for the AIFC are as follows:

(a) the AIFC Constitutional Statute, AIFC Regulations including the AIFC Court Regulations, and AIFC Court Rules;
(b) such law as is agreed by the parties, although it will not do so if such law is inconsistent with the public order or public policy of the Republic of Kazakhstan; or
(c) such law as appears to the Court to be the most appropriate in the facts and circumstances of the dispute.[115]

The AIFC is also authorised to take guidance from the jurisprudence in common law countries in matters of procedure.[116] The application of foreign law, particularly common law, is supported by the requirement that judges have significant knowledge of the common law and experience as a lawyer or judge in a common law system and fluency in spoken and written English.[117]

5.4.2.4 China International Commercial Court

The applicable law pursuant to the Law of the People's Republic of China on the Laws Applicable to Foreign-related Civil Relations[118] authorises the CICC to apply the law chosen by the parties, the contents of which may be determined by evidence:

(1) provided by the parties;
(2) provided by the legal expert from China or abroad;
(3) provided by the institution rendering law finding services;
(4) provided by the member of the International Commercial Expert Committee;
(5) provided by the central authority of the other contracting party that has entered into a judicial assistance treaty with China;
(6) provided by the Chinese Embassy or Consulate in the relevant country;

[115] Note 47, art. 29(1).

[116] Ibid., art. 29(2).

[117] Ibid., art. 12.

[118] 'Law of the People's Republic of China on the Laws Applicable to Foreign-Related Civil Relations' (*National People's Congress*, 28 October 2010) art. 7, https://asadip.files.wordpress.com/2010/11/law-of-the-application-of-law-for-foreign-of-china-2010.pdf, accessed 1 August 2019.

(7) provided by the Embassy of the relevant country in China;
(8) other reasonable ways to find foreign law.[119]

The CICC does not have international judges, but instead the bench is comprised of senior judges from the SPC. These judges are said to be familiar with international law and can speak both Chinese and English. In addition, the SPC has an international committee of experts comprised of both Chinese experts and foreign experts coming from many different countries. There are thirty-one experts, each serving a four-year term.[120]

5.4.2.5 Commercial Courts in Europe

Amsterdam – The NCC applies Dutch procedure, including in particular the Code of Civil Procedure. The applicable substantive law is determined by reference to the rules of Dutch private international law.[121]

Paris – The preamble to the protocols establishing the procedure before the Paris chambers state that the judges are all fluent in English and that the disputes referred to it will be of an international commercial nature, particularly those involving the application of European or foreign law.[122] Foreign counsel may apply to represent parties; and, in the Commercial Court, parties may submit exhibits in English without translation and witnesses may testify in English, but with translation.[123]

5.5 Enforcement of Judgments

5.5.1 Introduction: Cross-Border Enforcement

For many international transactions and projects, there is a need to ensure that the decisions can be enforced outside the forum. The

[119] Provision on Several Issues concerning the Creation of International Commercial Courts (n. 24), art. 8.

[120] 'Law of the People's Republic of China on the Law Applicable to Foreign-Related Civil Relationships (Excerpts)' (CICC, 28 October 2010), http://cicc.court.gov.cn/html/1/219/199/200/649.html, accessed 1 August 2019.

[121] 'Code of Civil Procedure' (*Dutch Civil Law*), art. 1.2.1, www.dutchcivillaw.com/civilprocedureleg.htm, accessed 1 August 2019.

[122] Protocol relating to the Procedure before the International Chamber of the Paris Commercial Court (n. 29); Protocol relating to the Procedure before the International Chamber of the Paris Court of Appeal (n. 29).

[123] Protocol relating to the Procedure before the International Chamber of the Paris Commercial Court (n. 29), art. 2.

places where enforcement is desired will include places where the parties are based, or where their assets are located, especially where these are different from the place where the contract is to be performed or the place where the parties agree that disputes are to be resolved.

This is an important reason parties choose international arbitration as a method of dispute resolution. With the participation of nearly 170 states in the New York Convention, arbitral awards have considerable assurance of being enforced around the world. The current options for enforcing court judgments, by comparison, are an uncertain patchwork of possibilities that vary from country to country, often based on the various laws of the recognition and enforcement of foreign judgments in the countries of enforcement.

In many countries, there are no mechanisms for recognising and enforcing judgments issued in other countries without revisiting the merits of the dispute, or the possibilities for enforcement are limited to judgments from countries specified in local legislation or regulations. Nevertheless, an overview of the various international arrangements for enforcement is helpful in assessing when the available mechanisms for cross-border enforcement of judgments is likely to be sufficient to serve the needs of the parties.

As a preliminary note, though, it should be borne in mind that court judgments are always enforceable locally. If the parties resolve their disputes in the place where the judgment is to be enforced, either by agreeing to the courts of that place in their contract, or by the defendant accepting the plaintiff's choice of those courts, the issue of cross-border enforcement will not arise. This is particularly helpful where the judgment concerns title to land or some other issue on which only the local courts may pronounce.

However, the local enforceability of court judgments is helpful only if the local courts are able to meet the needs of the parties. This is one of the reasons, for example, for the creation of the ICommCs in the Middle East and East Asia. International enforcement of judgments, although potentially significant in some situations, may not be the principal reason for parties to choose these courts. In some situations, these ICommCs may be chosen in preference both to the local courts and to arbitrations seated in the region.

5.5.2 *The Hague Choice of Court Convention: Where the Parties Have Chosen the Court*

Where there may be a need to enforce a judgment in a place other than the place where it is issued, the parties will benefit in their choice of a court, including an ICommC, from knowing the extent to which that court's judgments will be enforceable through an international arrangement, whether of a multilateral or a bilateral nature.

Potentially, the most significant of these international arrangements is the Hague Choice of Court Convention.[124] This Convention creates an obligation on the part of the courts of Member States, subject only to a narrow range of exceptions, to recognise and enforce judgments issued by Member States' courts where the parties have chosen the designated court as their exclusive forum for dispute resolution. The Convention applies to civil and commercial agreements (i.e. not consumer or employment agreements) and it excludes from its scope a number of other contracts that might be described as other than civil and commercial in nature.[125]

When it was concluded, the Choice of Court Convention was hailed as the national court equivalent to the New York Convention. It was promulgated in 2005 and came into force in 2015, with the coming into force of the Convention in the Member States of the European Union. Singapore joined the Convention in 2016, and the United Kingdom has put in place arrangements for its membership to continue independently of the European Union.[126] The United States and China are signatories but have yet to ratify the Convention.

Accordingly, for the ICommCs based in the countries in which the Choice of Court Convention is in force, including the English Commercial Courts, the SICC, the NCC, the Paris Chambers and the BIBC, judgments relating to disputes in which the parties have exclusive jurisdiction agreements selecting their courts will be enforceable throughout the Member States to the Convention. This is a point that distinguishes them from their counterparts in the Gulf Region, Eastern Europe and China.

[124] 'Convention of 30 June 2005 on Choice of Court Agreements' (*Hague Conference on Private International Law*, 1 October 2015), www.hcch.net/en/instruments/conventions/full-text/?cid=98, accessed 1 August 2019.

[125] Ibid., art. 2 (2).

[126] 'UK suspends accession to Hague Choice of Court Convention' (*Herbert Smith Freehills*, 1 April 2019), https://hsfnotes.com/brexit/2019/04/01/uk-suspends-accession-to-hague-choice-of-court-convention, accessed 1 August 2019.

5.5.3 *The Hague Judgments Convention*

The Convention on the Recognition and Enforcement of Foreign Judgments in Civil or Commercial Matters, concluded on 2 July 2019, greatly expands the enforcement available under the Hague Choice of Court Convention.[127] While it similarly excludes matters that are not civil or commercial in nature, it is not confined to matters in which the parties have chosen the court that issued the judgment as their exclusive forum for dispute resolution.

The Hague Judgments Convention extends the bases of jurisdiction on which judgments become enforceable in a number of ways. First, it includes courts designated in non-exclusive choice of court agreements,[128] courts that the defendant has accepted after the matter was commenced even if the parties had not previously designated the court in an exclusive jurisdiction agreement,[129] and courts chosen by the person against whom the judgment is sought to be enforced.[130] The Convention also includes judgments against counterclaimants where the counterclaim arose out of the same transaction or occurrence as the main claim unless the main claim was filed merely to avoid preclusion.[131]

Secondly, the Convention applies to judgments issued by courts in the place of the defendants' habitual residence. Where the defendant is a natural person, this is the place where the defendant has the principal place of business and where the claim on which the judgment is based arose out of the activities of that business.[132] Where the defendant is not a natural person, the habitual residence is (a) the place of the statutory seat; (b) the place under the law of which the entity was incorporated or formed; (c) the place where it has its central administration; or (d) where it has its principal place of business.[133] This extends to situations in which the defendant maintained a branch, agency or other establishment without separate legal personality in the state of origin at the time that person became a party to the proceedings in the court of origin, and the

[127] 'Convention of 2 July 2019 on the Recognition and Enforcement of Foreign Judgments in Civil or Commercial Matters' (*Hague Conference on Private International Law*, 2019), www.hcch.net/en/instruments/conventions/full-text/?cid=137, accessed 1 August 2019.

[128] Ibid., art. 5.1(m).

[129] Ibid., either expressly – art. 5.1(e) – or by arguing on the merits before the court of origin without contesting jurisdiction within the timeframe provided in the law of the state of origin – art. 5.1(f).

[130] Ibid., art. 5.1(c).

[131] Ibid., art. 5.1(l).

[132] Ibid., art. 5.1(b).

[133] Ibid., art. 3(2).

claim on which the judgment is based arose out of the activities of that branch, agency or establishment.[134]

Thirdly, the Convention applies to judgments issued by courts in the place where the contractual obligation in issue was performed, or should have been performed, in accordance with (i) the agreement of the parties or (ii) the law applicable to the contract in the absence of an agreed place of performance, unless the activities of the defendant in relation to the transaction clearly did not constitute a purposeful and substantial connection to that state.[135]

Fourthly, the Convention applies to judgments in non-contractual claims arising from death, physical injury, damage to or loss of tangible property, and the act or omission directly causing such harm occurred in the state of origin, irrespective of where that harm occurred.[136]

Fifthly, the Convention applies to judgments from courts concerning the validity, construction, effects, administration and variation of voluntary trusts where the courts were chosen in the trust or where they were the courts in the place of administration of the trust.[137]

As with the Hague Choice of Court Convention and the New York Convention, the grounds on which the result may be challenged on enforcement are few and are exhaustively described in the Convention.[138] While the Hague Judgments Convention will, in time, become an important instrument for the enforcement of court judgments, it has only recently been concluded and will become effective between Member States only as they join and as it comes into force.

5.5.4 Standing International Forum of Commercial Courts

In addition to these initiatives on the part of the Hague Conference, the courts that aspire to broaden their international caseloads have established the Standing International Forum of Commercial Courts (SIFoCC), which shares best practices to keep pace with commercial change and to serve business and markets better. The forum also seeks to join forces to make a stronger contribution to the rule of law and to stability and prosperity worldwide, and to support

[134] Ibid., art. 5.1(d).
[135] Ibid., art. 5.1(g).
[136] Ibid., art. 5.1(j).
[137] Ibid., art. 5.1(k).
[138] Ibid., art. 7.

developing countries in their efforts to offer effective commercial dispute resolution to attract investment. Twenty-five countries with established and newer ICommCs accepted the invitation from Lord Thomas, former Lord Chief Justice of England and Wales, to have their senior jurists participate in the first meeting in 2017. The value of the collaboration was readily recognised and there have been annual meetings of the forum since.

During that time, the SIFoCC has undertaken a series of projects, one of the first of which was to prepare the Multilateral Memorandum on Enforcement of Commercial Judgments for Money, which explains the procedures for the enforcement of commercial money judgments by the courts of one jurisdiction obtained in the courts of another jurisdiction.[139] According to Lord Thomas, the chair of the SIFoCC Steering Group, the memorandum 'shows to users the readiness of the world's commercial courts to enforce one another's judgments'.[140]

5.5.5 *Regional and Bilateral Regimes*

In addition to these multilateral conventions, regional conventions establish judgment recognition and enforcement regimes among Member States. Among the most significant of these is the Brussels I Regulation,[141] which applies to Member States of the European Union, and its related regime, the Lugano Convention,[142] which extends to European countries that are not members of the European Union.[143]

The English Commercial Courts have benefited from membership in the Brussels system through the membership of the United Kingdom in the European Union. Much has yet to be clarified in the years to come about the role of the Brussels I system going forward now that the United Kingdom has left the European Union.

[139] www.sifocc.org/wp-content/uploads/2019/11/Multilateral-Memorandum-on-Enforcement-Nov-2019.pdf

[140] www.sifocc.org/2019/06/24/multilateral-memorandum-on-enforcement

[141] 'Regulation (EU) 1215/2012 on Jurisdiction and the Recognition and Enforcement of Judgments in Civil and Commercial Matters' (*EUR-Lex*, 12 December 2012), https://eur-lex.europa.eu/LexUriServ/LexUriServ.do?uri=OJ:L:2012:351:0001:0032:en:PDF, accessed 1 August 2019.

[142] 'The Lugano Convention on Jurisdiction and the Enforcement of Judgments in Civil and Commercial Matters' (*EUR-Lex*, 1 January 2010), https://eur-lex.europa.eu/legal-content/EN/ALL/?uri=CELEX%3A22007A1221%2803%29, accessed 1 August 2019.

[143] Denmark, Iceland, Norway and Switzerland. https://eur-lex.europa.eu/legal-content/EN/ALL/?uri=CELEX%3A22007A1221%2803%29

5.5.5.1 English Commercial Court and the TCC

Beyond the forward-going arrangements within Europe, bilateral arrangements are covered in the Administration of Justice Act and the Foreign Judgments (Reciprocal Enforcement) Act. These mainly cover former and current Commonwealth countries and include Crown states such as the Isle of Man and Jersey. Bilateral treaties also exist with countries such as Canada, Australia and Israel.[144]

5.5.5.2 Singapore International Commercial Court

In addition to its implementation of the Choice of Court Convention,[145] Singapore has a multilateral arrangement with courts from other Commonwealth countries[146] and with Hong Kong and the PRC.[147]

Furthermore, the SICC and the DIFC have signed various memoranda of guidance with other leading courts and newly established international courts.[148] These courts include the Commercial Court (Queen's Bench Division) of England and Wales, the Supreme Court of New South Wales, the Federal Court of Australia, the Supreme Court of Singapore, the High Court of Kenya (Commercial and Admiralty Division), the Ras Al Khaimah courts, the UAE Ministry of Justice, the US District Court Southern District NY, the UAE Ministry of Justice (Department of International Cooperation) and the Supreme Court of the Republic of Kazakhstan.[149]

[144] Andrew Bartlett and Ashley Morgan, 'Enforcement of Judgments and Arbitral Awards in the UK (England and Wales): An Overview' (*Thomson Reuters Practical Law*), https://uk.practicallaw.thomsonreuters.com/6-619-3495?transitionType=Default&contextData=(sc.Default)&firstPage=true&comp=pluk&bhcp=1#co_anchor_a174733, accessed 1 August 2019.

[145] 'Choice of Court Agreements Act' (*Singapore Statutes Online*, 8 June 2016), https://sso.agc.gov.sg/Acts-Supp/14-2016/Published/20160608?DocDate=20160608, accessed 1 August 2019.

[146] 'Reciprocal Enforcement of Commonwealth Judgments Act – Chapter 264' (*Singapore Statutes Online*, 30 March 1987), https://sso.agc.gov.sg/Act/RECJA1921, accessed 1 August 2019 (gazetted countries currently include Australia, New Zealand, Malaysia, Pakistan, Hong Kong (for judgments obtained up until 30 June 1997), Brunei, Papua New Guinea and India (except the states of Jammu and Kashmir)).

[147] Ibid. This Act applies to the Hong Kong Special Administrative Region of the People's Republic of China (HKSAR) (judgments on or after 1 July 1997).

[148] 'Enforcement of Money Judgments' (*Singapore International Commercial Court*, 14 June 2018), www.sicc.gov.sg/guide-to-the-sicc/enforcement-of-money-judgments, accessed 26 October 2018.

[149] 'DIFC Enforcement Guide 2016' (DIFC, 2016), www.difccourts.ae/wp-content/uploads/2018/01/ENFORCEMENT-GUIDE-2016-AW.pdf; https://iclg.com/prac

5.5.5.3 International Courts in the Gulf Region and Central Asia

Dubai, Qatar, Abu Dhabi – The UAE and Qatar are party to the Riyadh Convention,[150] which provides for the enforcement of judgments without examination of the merits, and to the GCC Judgments Convention.[151] The UAE is also party to many bilateral legal and judicial cooperation treaties.[152] These treaties apply in the ADGM Courts by virtue of ADGM Courts Regulations.[153] ADGM Courts have also entered into memoranda of understanding with the UAE emirate of Ras Al Khaimah; Hong Kong, England and Wales, Singapore, Australia and the state of New South Wales.[154]

Astana – Kazakhstan is a party to the Minsk Convention on Legal Assistance[155] and to the Kiev Convention on Settling Commercial Disputes.[156] In addition, Kazakhstan has entered into bilateral legal assistance treaties with Lithuania,[157] North Korea, Turkey,[158] China, Vietnam, India, Pakistan, Mongolia and United Arab Emirates, for mutual recognition and enforcement of the judgments of the courts of those states.[159]

tice-areas/enforcement-of-foreign-judgments-laws-and-regulations/united-arab-emirates, accessed 1 August 2019.

150 Riyadh Convention on the Judicial Cooperation between the States of the Arab League 1983. See 'Litigation: Enforcement of Foreign Judgments in Qatar' (*Al Tamimi and Company*, 4 April 2019), www.lexology.com/library/detail.aspx?g=1f76c5f2-feaf-40da-8922-6e8db6e4983d, accessed 1 August 2019.

151 Gulf Cooperation Council (GCC Judgments Regime) for the Execution of Judgments, Delegations and Judicial Notifications (1996); n. 147, 4e ; 'United Arab Emirates: Enforcement of Foreign Judgments 2019' (*ICLG.com*, 2019), https://iclg.com/practice-areas/enforcement-of-foreign-judgments-laws-and-regulations/united-arab-emirates, accessed 1 August 2019.

152 See https://gettingthedealthrough.com/area/46/jurisdiction/33/enforcement-foreign-judgments-2019-united-arab-emirates, accessed 20 September 2020.

153 Civil Evidence, Judgments, Enforcement and Judicial Appointments Regulations 2015 (n. 19), section 170.

154 Note 20; Al Tamimi and Company (n. 150).

155 Minsk Convention on Legal Assistance and Legal Relations in Civil, Family and Criminal Matters 1992.

156 Kiev Convention on Settling Disputes Related to Commercial Activities 1992.

157 Treaty between the Republic of Kazakhstan and the Republic of Lithuania on Legal Assistance and Legal Relations in Civil, Family and Criminal Matters 1994.

158 Treaty between the Republic of Kazakhstan and the Turkish Republic on Legal Assistance in Civil Matters 1995.

159 Lyailya Tleulina, 'Recognition and Enforcement of Foreign Judgments and Commercial Arbitration Awards in Kazakhstan' (2015) Legal Insight, no. 6(42), http://aequitas.kz/upload/files/150812_Recognition_of_Foreign_Judgements.pdf, accessed 1 August 2019.

5.5.5.4 China International Commercial Court

In January 2019, China signed a judgments convention with Hong Kong which creates a bilateral agreement that provides greater clarify and certainty for recognition and enforcement of judgments between Hong Kong and mainland China.[160] This arrangement also applies to the enforcement of judgments of Macau and Taiwan. In addition, China has bilateral treaties for judgment enforcement with many Belt and Road countries and other nations.[161]

5.5.6 *Other Bases of Enforcement*

Moving beyond the various treaty arrangements in place for the recognition and enforcement of awards, the availability of enforcement is subject to the law of the country in which the enforcement of a judgment is sought and not that of the country in which the ICommC is located. However, it is worth noting that common law countries (which may include both traditional common law countries such as those in North America, the English Commercial Court and the TCC, the SICC,[162] and the commercial courts in the Gulf Region and Central Asia[163]) will enforce foreign judgments on the basis of the common law rules. In general, they will enforce a final foreign judgment on the merits of the dispute where it is for an ascertainable sum of money and not for taxes, fines or penalties, provided that the foreign court had international jurisdiction according to its local rules and the judgment was not

160 Arrangement on Reciprocal Recognition and Enforcement of Judgments in Civil and Commercial Matters between the Courts of the Mainland and of the Hong Kong Special Administrative Region.

161 See http://cicc.court.gov.cn/html/1/219/199/202/index.html, accessed 20 September 2020; https://digitalcommons.lmu.edu/cgi/viewcontent.cgi?referer=https://www.google.com/&httpsredir=1&article=1744&context=ilr, accessed 20 September 2020.

162 Adeline Chong, 'Recognition and Enforcement of Foreign Judgments in Asia' (*Asian Business Law Institute*, 2017), https://ink.library.smu.edu.sg/cgi/viewcontent.cgi?article=4454&context=sol_research; www.out-law.com/en/topics/dispute-resolution-and-litigation/enforcement/enforcement-of-foreign-judgments-and-arbitration-awards-in-singapore, accessed 1 August 2019; 'Singapore: Enforcement of Foreign Judgments 2019' (*ICGL.com*, 2019), https://iclg.com/practice-areas/enforcement-of-foreign-judgments-laws-and-regulations/singapore, accessed 1 August 2019.

163 DIFC: Judicial Authority Law (DIFC Law 12/2004) art. 7(6); DIFC Court Law (DIFC Law 10/2004) art. 24(1)(a); *DNB Bank ASA* v. *Gulf Eyadah Corporation & Gulf Navigation Holding* PJSC (CA/007/2015); 'Litigation: Enforcement of Foreign Judgments in DIFC' (*Al Tamimi and Company*), www.lexology.com/library/detail.aspx?g=373132be-7f5a-4aee-bf5b-acafc5b0ac24, accessed 1 August 2019.

procured by fraud or in a manner contrary to natural justice, or its enforcement would be contrary to public policy.[164] Elsewhere, the enforcement of judgments may depend on reciprocity, such as is the case for Qatar[165] and Kazakhstan[166] and China.[167]

5.6 Conclusion

The rapid growth in international business in the last half of the twentieth century fostered a market-based approach to dispute resolution that promoted international commercial arbitration and encouraged national courts to develop means to compete for the economic benefits associated with providing international dispute resolution services. The emergence of ICommCs has responded to the heightened standards of commercial parties by providing them with alternatives to arbitration for resolving their international commercial disputes that address some of the historic deficits of national

[164] Subject to some exceptions; for example, in recent years, the foreign judgments have been directed to the Dubai courts to determine their enforceability under UAE law, limiting the judgments enforceable under the common law regime in place in the DIFC Courts.

[165] Commercial and Civil Procedure Code – Law No. 13 of 1990, arts. 379–81 (reciprocity has been established between Qatar and Germany and the United States); Nicolas Bremer, 'Seeking Recognition and Enforcement of Foreign Court Judgments and Arbitral Awards in the GCC Countries' (2016–17) 3 McGill Journal of Dispute Resolution 37.

[166] 'Kazakhstan Civil Procedure Code 2015' (*Ministry of Justice*, 31 October 2015), http://adilet.zan.kz/eng/docs/K1500000377, accessed 1 August 2019 (unofficial English translation) provides for enforcement based on reciprocity where a formal mechanism has been established. This has not yet occurred, but there are instances of Kazakhstan courts recognising and enforcing English judgments; see Bakhyt Tukulov and Asker Konysbayev, 'Litigation and Dispute Resolution: Kazakhstan 2016' (Mondaq, 26 August 2016), www.mondaq.com/x/521882/Arbitration+Dispute+Resolution/Litigation+Dispute+Resolution+Kazakhstan+2016, accessed 1 August 2019.

[167] For the enforcement of CICC judgments elsewhere, a party may apply directly to the foreign court or seek foreign judicial assistance through a PRC court based on a treaty or on the principle of reciprocity: Civil Procedure Law of the People's Republic of China (Revised in 2017), art. 280; enforcement of a foreign judgment may similarly be sought through application to a PRC court or by way of judicial assistance Civil Procedure Law of the People's Republic of China (Revised in 2017), arts. 281, 282; recognition and enforcement may be granted subject to a finding that the judgment or ruling contradicts the basic principles of the law of the People's Republic of China or violates state sovereignty, security or the public interest. See Song Jianli, 'Recognition and Enforcement of Foreign Judgments in China: Challenges and Developments' (*CICC*, 30 August 2018), http://cicc.court.gov.cn/html/1/219/199/203/1048.html, accessed 1 August 2019.

courts and that maximise their inherent competitive advantages over arbitration. This chapter has considered, as a matter of dispute resolution design, the approaches taken in the leading ICommCs to questions of jurisdiction, applicable law and the enforcement of judgments as a means of serving the dispute resolution needs of businesses, and of remaining competitive in the international marketplace for dispute resolution.

6

Jurisdiction and Choice of Court Clauses in Favour of International Commercial Courts

EVA LEIN

6.1 Introduction

In recent years, the creation of specialist international commercial courts (ICommCs) has become popular across various jurisdictions in Asia and Europe. It can be considered that 'the first few decades of the twenty-first century are likely to be recalled . . . as decades in which national courts . . . were revitalised to re-establish their attractiveness to those engaged in international commerce'.[1] Jurisdictions that recently introduced ICommCs range from China (China International Commercial Court (CICC)), to Singapore (Singapore International Commercial Court (SICC)),[2] to the Netherlands (Netherlands Commercial Court (NCC)), Paris and Frankfurt.[3] In Brussels, discussions on a hybrid form of a self-standing international business court have currently come to a halt as the planned ambitious and unusual set-up of this court faced increasing criticism as to its impartiality and independence.[4] In Zurich and

[1] J. Walker, 'International Dispute Resolution in the 21st Century: The Revitalization of National Courts', in Canadian Council on International Law (ed.), *Looking Ahead: International Law in the 21st Century* (Canadian Council on International Law 2002) 95.

[2] Hong Kong Court of Final Appeal (1997), Dubai International Financial Centre Courts (DIFCC) (2006), Qatar International Court (2010), Singapore International Commercial Court (SICC) (2015), Abu Dhabi Global Market Courts (2016), Chinese International Commercial Courts (CICC) (2018); Astana International Financial Centre Courts (2018).

[3] Netherlands Commercial Court (NCC) (2018), International Chamber of the Paris Court of Appeal (2018), International Chamber for Commercial Matters, Landgericht Frankfurt (2018). Similar initiatives include Hamburg, Mannheim and Stuttgart. See also M. Requejo Isidro, 'International Commercial Courts in the Litigation Market' (2019) MPILux Research Paper Series 2019 (2) (www.mpi.lu).

[4] Brussels International Business Court (BIBC). The draft legislation is available at www.lachambre.be/FLWB/PDF/54/3072/54K3072001.pdf; see also E. Peetermans and P.

Geneva, on the contrary, the creation of an international commercial court or of specific commercial chambers has only recently been put on the agenda.[5]

The comparison of these courts with each other and with commercial courts following a long tradition such as New York, Dublin or in particular the popular London Commercial Court,[6] is in many ways premature as the record of their performance is not sufficient yet to allow for a solid comparative assessment.[7] This is especially true for European courts which have only started operating in the past few years. The novelties created by these specialised courts in the area of jurisdiction and procedure will need to be tested in practice in the coming years. Further, the comparison to a court such as the London Commercial Court will be flawed, as the latter also deals with domestic commercial cases. It is nonetheless interesting to reflect on their set-up and structure from a comparative perspective and to follow the first cases brought before these jurisdictions. One key to the success of these courts will be the extent to which the English language can be used for the proceedings, the submission of documents and the judgment itself.[8]

Lambrecht, The Brussels International Business Court: Initial Overview and Analysis (www.erasmuslawreview.nl/tijdschrift/ELR/2019/1/ELR-D-18-00025.pdf); G. van Calster, 'The Brussels International Business Court: A Carrot Sunk by Caviar', in X. Kramer and J. Sorabji (eds.), *International Business Courts* (International Eleven 2019), at 107ff.; Bill establishing the Brussels International Business Court, Parl. St./Doc. parl. (Parliamentary Documents): Kamer/Chambre (Belgian House of Representatives) 54, 3072/001; 'Verslag van de eerste lezing namens de commissie voor de Justitie'/'Rapport de la première lecture fait au nom de la commission de la Justice' (Report on the first reading on behalf of the Justice Committee), Parl. St./Doc. parl. (Parliamentary Documents): Kamer/Chambre (Belgian House of Representatives) 54, 3072/007; 'Verslag van de tweede lezing namens de commissie voor de Justitie'/'Rapport de la deuxième lecture fait au nom de la commission de la Justice' (Report on the second reading on behalf of the Justice Committee), Parl. St./Doc. parl. (Parliamentary Documents): Kamer/Chambre (Belgian House of Representatives) 54, 3072/010.

[5] See E. Lein, 'International Commercial Courts in Switzerland: The Roadmaps for Geneva and Zurich', in X. Kramer and J. Sorabji (eds.), *International Business Courts* (2019), at 115ff. See also G. David, Konkurrenz zu privaten Schiedsgerichten, Plädoyer 1/2021, p. 12 ff.; Haut Comité Juridique de la Place Financière de Paris, Préconisations sur la mise en place à Paris de chambres specialisees pour le traitement du contentieux international des affaires (www.justice.gouv.fr/publication/Rapport_chambres_internationales.pdf).

[6] www.judiciary.uk/wp-content/uploads/2020/02/6.6318_Commercial-Courts-Annual-Report_WEB1.pdf

[7] But see, for instance, E. Themeli, 'International Commercial Courts Competition in Europe: A Litigation Experience Approach', in X. Kramer and J. Sorabji (eds.), *International Business Courts* (2019), at 273ff.

[8] See also Georgios Dimitropoulos, 'The Design of International Commercial Courts: From Organizational Hybridity to Functional Interoperability', Chapter 10 in this volume.

It must be noted that, although generally referred to as 'international commercial courts', many of these new courts, including the SICC, the CICC and all of the operating ICommCs in Europe, are international chambers at the level of the first and often also the second instance of a specific court within the national jurisdictional system. Contrary to the courts created for the resolution of disputes arising from activities within special economic zones (SEZs) such as the Dubai International Financial Centre (DIFC) Courts,[9] the Qatar Financial Centre (QFC) Courts,[10] the Abu Dhabi Global Market (ADGM) Courts[11] and the Astana International Financial Centre (AIFC) Courts,[12] they are mere divisions of existing courts. While their composition might be quite different (the SICC, for example, operates with foreign judges from common and civil law jurisdictions) and they follow different rules and fee structures, they have no autonomy as self-standing courts. Similarly, the First and Second Chinese International Commercial Court (CICC), established in 2018 by the Supreme People's Court (SPC), are international chambers embedded within the existing court system, adjudicating international commercial cases.[13] This distinction is not necessarily apparent from their denomination as ICommCs, but it is relevant to the issues of jurisdiction addressed in this chapter.

Taking the example of Paris – the French Tribunal de Commerce, the oldest court in the French judiciary,[14] has been operating an international chamber for more than twenty-five years.[15] But to further facilitate access to the French commercial judiciary for international litigants and to enhance the attractiveness of the capital as *Place juridique de Paris*,[16] the Cour d'Appel followed in April 2018 and opened an

[9] Dubai International Financial Centre court; Dubai Law No. 12 of 2004 in respect of the Judicial Authority at Dubai International Financial Centre.

[10] The Civil and Commercial Court of the Qatar Financial Centre, Article 8(3) QFC Law No. (7) of 2005.

[11] Abu Dhabi Law No. (4) of 2013 and Law No. (12) of 2020.

[12] Constitutional Statute No. 438-V ZRK of 7 December 2015.

[13] The CICC was established in Shenzhen and Xi'an, respectively. It follows a 'first instance being final' principle: CICC judgments are binding on the parties and cannot be appealed. The Fourth Civil Division of SPC coordinates and guides the two international commercial courts.

[14] Established in 1563; see J. P. Royer, J. P. Jean and B. Durand, *Histoire de la justice en France* (2016), at 717; J. Sorabji and X. Kramer, 'Introduction, The International Business of Courts', in X. Kramer and J. Sorabji (eds.), *International Business Courts* (2019), at 1.

[15] The international chamber established in 1995 was merged in 2015 with the European Union Law Chamber originally created in 1999.

[16] H. Boutinon-Dumas and B. Deffains, *La place juridique de Paris* (2019), at 29.

international chamber of second instance. These chambers are either referred to as the International Chamber of the Tribunal de Commerce or the Cour d'Appel, but also described as the ICCP (or in French CCIP), the 'International Commercial Court of Paris',[17] regulated by two separate protocols[18] and 'quasi-autonomous, self-regulated with a hybrid and specific procedure'.[19] Similarly, the NCC is not an independent court. The NCC District Court and the NCC Court of Appeal are chambers of the Amsterdam District Court and the Amsterdam Court of Appeal, respectively.[20] Likewise, the SICC is a division of the Singapore High Court, and its procedural framework is set out in the Supreme Court of Judicature Act (SCJA)[21] and in Order 110 of the Singaporean Rules of Court.[22]

In contrast, the Belgian Brussels International Business Court (BIBC) was envisaged as a true self-standing court with an international panel of expert-judges – a novum in the Belgian court system, presenting elements of a court and an arbitral tribunal alike, bringing together international expertise in one court. However, this hybrid autonomous nature of the BIBC has caused a heated internal jurisdictional debate around 'two-class' court system and halted its process of establishment for the moment.[23]

[17] See also E. Jeuland, 'The International Chambers of Paris: A Gaul Village', in X. Kramer and J. Sorabji (eds.), *International Business Courts* (2019), at 65.

[18] Protocol on Procedural Rules Applicable to the International Chamber of the Paris Commercial Court, available at www.cours-appel.justice.fr/sites/default/files/2018-06/CICAP_EnglishVersion_Protocole%20barreau%20de%20Paris%20-%20Tribunal%20de%20commerce%20de%20Paris.pdf. Protocol relating to procedural rules applicable to the International Chamber of the Court of Appeal of Paris, available at www.cours-appel.justice.fr/sites/default/files/2019-04/Traduction%20en%20anglais%20du%20protocole%20CCIP-CA%20-%20V4%20.pdf.

[19] See also Jeuland, 'The International Chambers of Paris', at 65.

[20] See Art. 1.1.1. NCC Rules 2020 (www.rechtspraak.nl/SiteCollectionDocuments/NCC-Rules-second-edition.pdf).

[21] Supreme Court of Judicature Act (2007), ch. 322.

[22] See on the SICC also Andrew Godwin, Ian Ramsay and Miranda Webster, 'International Commercial Courts: The Singapore Experience', 18 Melb. J. Int'l L. 219 (2017); and M Yip, 'The Singapore International Commercial Court: The Future of Litigation?', in X. Kramer and J. Sorabji (eds.), *International Business Courts* (2019), at 129 (136).

[23] The BIBC was not, however, planned as an ad hoc court. See the proposed Art. 73(3) of the Belgian Judicial Code and the Opinion of the Belgian Council of State, Parl. St./Doc. parl. (Parliamentary Documents): Kamer/Chambre (Belgian House of Representatives) 54, 3072/001, at 103. See also E. Peetermans and P. Lambrecht, 'The Brussels International Business Court: Initial Overview and Analysis', ELR September 2019, No. 1.

The nature of certain ICommCs as divisions of existing courts has an impact on the question of transfer jurisdiction but also on the choice of forum as, technically, jurisdiction lies with a court and not with its chambers. The usual way in which these 'courts' can be solicited would therefore be via an internal referral to the international division of the national court having jurisdiction. The question that arises in practice is, therefore, whether and how the parties can tailor a choice of court clause in such a way that they can guarantee that their case is heard by the 'international commercial court'. This chapter addresses both the question of when cases are transferred to an international chamber or ICommC and whether and how the parties can determine in a choice of court agreement that the case should be heard by an ICommC.

6.2 Subject Matter Jurisdiction

International commercial courts are set up across different jurisdictions as specialist decision-making bodies dealing with international commercial cases. Specific national legislation or court protocols regarding ICommCs usually provide detailed provisions on their subject matter jurisdiction, but follow slightly different approaches as to how jurisdiction is established and especially as to when a case is deemed 'commercial' and 'international'. The approach followed by the different rules of court put in place for ICommCs can be more or less flexible in that respect.

6.2.a 'International Commercial Cases'

As a general rule, access to ICommCs will be granted for 'international commercial disputes' or 'disputes related to international contracts', but the relevant provisions can add more precise criteria as a precondition for jurisdiction. The SICC or the Frankfurt international chamber refer rather generally to 'international commercial disputes',[24] and the NCC refers to 'a civil or commercial matter that concerns an international dispute'.

The Dutch definition in Art. 1.3.1. (b) of the NCC Rules 2020, for instance, is understood rather broadly and covers not only cases in which one or more of the parties are domiciled in a foreign jurisdiction, but also

[24] See M. Lehmann, '"Law Made in Germany": The Export Engine *Stutters*', in X. Kramer and J. Sorabji (eds.), *International Business Courts* (2019), pp. 83–106.

disputes involving a relevant cross-border interest (e.g. where shareholders, employees or revenue are located in or linked with foreign jurisdictions). The term 'civil or commercial matter' in Art. 1.3.1. (a) is equally broad and is to be understood as opposed to criminal or administrative cases (contractual disputes, but also claims in tort, property disputes, or intellectual property, antitrust/competition cases, technology disputes, construction or corporate matters).[25]

The proposed Art. 576/1(3) of the Belgian Judicial Code defines international matters before the BIBC in accordance with the United Nations Commission on International Trade Law (UNCITRAL) Model Law and requires that (a) the parties either have their places of business in different States; or (b) that a substantial part of the obligations of the commercial relationship or the place with which the subject matter of the dispute is most closely connected is or are situated outside the State where the parties have their place of business; or (c) that the information required to resolve a dispute is located abroad. The BIBC's competence would extend to all international civil and commercial cases which are not subject to special jurisdiction rules, such as bankruptcy cases.

The protocols setting up the Paris chambers refer (each in a slightly different way) to 'disputes that involve international commercial interests' or to 'transnational commercial disputes',[26] and in particular 'to those to which provisions of a foreign law or EU law apply' (Art. 1.1 CITCP Protocol).[27] The definitions for both protocols are then further refined: According to Art. 1.1 CITCP Protocol, transnational commercial disputes include (but are not limited to) international commercial contracts and the termination of commercial relations, transport, unfair competition, anticompetitive commercial practices, transactions in financial instruments and market standard master agreements, as well as financial contracts, instruments and products. The latter topic has gained particular importance for Paris as a new financial hub, since the European Banking Authority has transferred its seat from London to Paris in reaction to Brexit, and since the International Swaps and Derivatives Association (ISDA) has adapted its Master Agreement to include a version based on French law and the jurisdiction of French

[25] Art. 1.3.1 (a) NCC Rules 2020.

[26] Tribunal de Commerce de Paris (CITCP), Art. 1.1 CITCP.

[27] The English translation does not quite coincide with the French version: 'litiges de nature économique et commerciale de dimension internationale et notamment ceux dans lesquels s'appliquent ou sont susceptible de s'appliquer, des dispositions de droit européen ou de droit étranger').

courts.[28] The International Chamber of the Cour d'Appel de Paris (CICAP) has jurisdiction over 'disputes that involve international commercial interests' (*litiges qui mettent en jeu les intérêts du commerce international*), which includes appeals over decisions on transnational commercial disputes rendered by the CITCP in the first instance (Art. 1.3), but also any other case having an international dimension, such as cases relating to international arbitration, including actions to set aside French arbitration awards or actions denying recognition and enforcement of an international arbitration award (Art. 1.1 in fine). The CICAP jurisdiction provision is broader than its CITCP counterpart.

6.2.b International and Domestic Cases

Some commercial courts do not limit their competence to international cases, but deal generally with all commercial cases independent from their international or domestic character (see e.g. Dublin or London; see also Dubai or Abu Dhabi, which have a rather broad jurisdiction over civil and commercial disputes relating to their free zones).[29]

Jurisdictions such as London or Dublin list and define the subject areas within which the commercial court operates, without limiting their jurisdiction to international cases.[30] The internal distribution of cases is then further refined – see, for example, the financial list in the courts of England and Wales according to which specialist judges get assigned to specific cases involving financial transactions.[31] The new commercial court in Stuttgart, for example, has first-instance jurisdiction over large commercial civil proceedings, in particular disputes concerning company law, corporate acquisitions and economically significant business-to-business (B2B) disputes with an amount in dispute of €2,000,000 or more, regardless of their international or domestic character.

[28] See www.isda.org/2018/07/03/isda-publishes-french-and-irish-law-master-agreements.

[29] See also Section 6.5, 'Other Jurisdictional Grounds'.

[30] See, for example, CPR 58: '[C]ommercial claim' means any claim arising out of the transaction of trade and commerce and includes any claim relating to – a business document or contract; the export or import of goods; the carriage of goods by land, sea, air or pipeline; the exploitation of oil and gas reserves or other natural resources; insurance and re-insurance; banking and financial services; the operation of markets and exchanges; the purchase and sale of commodities; the construction of ships; business agency; and arbitration.

[31] www.judiciary.uk/you-and-the-judiciary/going-to-court/high-court/courts-of-the-chancery-division/financial-list/financial-list-context

For the differentiation between international and domestic cases, it is interesting to draw a comparison to SEZ ICommCs. Looking at the example of Abu Dhabi, the ADGM Courts have jurisdiction over commercial and civil disputes connected to the ADGM, including domestic and international financial transactions and employment disputes.[32] Parties need to express in their contracts that they wish to opt out of the jurisdiction of the ADGM Courts if these would have jurisdiction, but parties can also opt in to the jurisdiction of the ADGM Courts where the dispute has no connection to the ADGM.[33] Similarly, the DIFC Courts have jurisdiction over all cases relating to the DIFC, even where the links with the DIFC may be weak.[34] They also follow an opt-in system which allows for cases to be brought to the DIFC Courts that may have no connection to the DIFC.[35]

6.2.c *Party Agreement on the Nature of the Case*

While the terms 'international' and 'commercial' are clearly defined in the rules of court of many ICommCs, others provide some flexibility in the determination of the international and commercial character of a case.

Interestingly, Singapore allows both the international commercial nature of a claim and its commercial character to be subject to an express agreement of the parties. Order 110 Rule 1 contains definitions of both an international claim and the commercial nature of a claim. A claim is international in nature if the parties have their places of business in different States; or in offshore cases, where none of the parties have their places of business in Singapore; or if at least one party has its place of business in a different State from that in which the place of performance of a substantial part of the obligations is located or the State with which the subject matter of the dispute is most closely

[32] Section 16 of the ADGM Courts Regulations. This refers to cases where disputes involve the ADGM or its authorities or establishments, disputes which arise out of transactions conducted in whole or part in the ADGM, or incidents which have occurred in the ADGM.

[33] See Section 16 (2)(e) of the Regulations; H. Quinlan, A. Bradshaw and C. Leith, 'Abu Dhabi Global Market Courts: Framework, Procedures and First Judgment Summary', https://content.next.westlaw.com/Document/Ieb4d63e22b5911e89bf099c0ee06c731/View/FullText.html?originationContext=docHeader&contextData=(sc.Default)&transitionType=Document&needToInjectTerms=False&firstPage=true.

[34] See Section 6.5, 'Other Jurisdictional Grounds'.

[35] See Art. 5 Dubai Law No. 12 of 2004.

connected.[36] However, according to Order 110 Rule 1 (2)(a)(iv), a claim is also international if the parties have expressly agreed that the subject matter of the claim relates to more than one State.

Similarly, to define the commercial nature of a claim, Order 110 Rule 1 para. 2(b) refers to its subject matter, which needs to arise from a relationship of commercial nature, whether contractual or not, including (but not limited to) a list of standard transactions (e.g. supply of goods, distribution, agency, carriage, banking and finance etc.).[37] The parties can also expressly agree that the subject matter of the claim is commercial in nature.[38]

This flexible party autonomy-based approach acknowledges that the definition of the term 'commercial nature', but even more so of the international character of a dispute, can be problematic and cause some doubt in the individual case. Parties wishing to subject their dispute to the SICC can expressly clarify both notions and avoid any interpretation difficulties where the categorisation of a case might be less straightforward. The policy decision behind this approach is to facilitate bringing a case before the SICC and ultimately to enhance the number of cases the SICC is dealing with.[39]

The downside is that an approach that is very flexible bears the risk of defeating the purpose of an ICommC. When the definition of the international and/or the commercial nature of a case is overstretched by the parties, cases will be brought before a specialist court although the level of specialisation of an ICommC would not be required. This can lead to a new form of forum shopping.

6.2.d. Value of the Claim

In some instances, the value of the case also has an impact on the jurisdiction of an ICommC, and some commercial courts only deal

[36] Order 110 Rule 1 para. 2(a).

[37] These are: any trade transaction for the supply or exchange of goods or services; distribution agreement; commercial representation or agency; factoring or leasing; construction works; consulting, engineering or licensing; investment, financing, banking or insurance; an exploitation agreement or a concession; a joint venture or any other form of industrial or business cooperation; mergers and acquisition; carriage of goods or passengers by air, sea, rail or road; or in personam intellectual property disputes.

[38] Order 110 Rule 1 para. 2(b)(iii).

[39] See also Section 6.4, 'Transfer Jurisdiction'; Godwin et al., International Commercial Courts: The Singapore Experience, 18 Melb. J. Int'l L. 219 (2017); A Reyes, Recognition and Enforcement of Interlocutory and Final Judgments of the Singapore International Commercial Court, 2 J. Int'l & Comp. L. 337 (2015).

with high-value cases in which the value of the case exceeds a certain threshold – for instance, Dublin (€1,000,000),[40] New York ($500,000),[41] and China (300,000,000 Chinese yuan),[42] as well as London (internal distribution to specialist judges in financial cases involving more than £50,000,000).[43] Other jurisdictions do not provide for any threshold, such as the currently discontinued project to establish the BIBC.

6.3 Choice of Court Agreements in Favour of International Commercial Courts

International commercial courts are usually not mandated to act solely because the subject matter of the dispute is an international commercial case. Most procedural rules and protocols provide that ICommCs must derive their competence from an express agreement of the parties. Whether this agreement is a classical choice-of-court agreement determining a court or the courts of a specific State (which is the case for self-standing courts such as the AIFC Court), whether such clause implies an agreement over the intervention of its specialised international division (see e.g. the SICC), or whether it needs to extend beyond the standard choice-of-forum clause and cover other elements (see e.g. the NCC) depends on the respective jurisdiction.

Parties should be aware of the differences between clauses determining the jurisdiction of specialised chambers and clauses selecting a self-standing ICommC. Taking the example of the AIFC Court, the choice-of-court clause is a standard clause:

> Any dispute, whether contractual or non-contractual, arising out of or in connection to this contract, including any question regarding its existence, validity, or termination, shall be subject to the exclusive jurisdiction of the AIFC Court. The language to be used in the proceedings shall be English. This contract is governed by [insert the law to be applied].[44]

40 Article 1, Order 63A of the Superior Courts Rules, version 29 April 2019.

41 Section 202.70, Rules of the Commercial Division of the Supreme Court.

42 Article 2, Provisions of the Supreme People's Court on Several Issues regarding the Establishment of the International Commercial Court (2018).

43 There is no minimum value for claims that require particular expertise in the financial markets, or claims that raise issues of general importance to the financial markets. See CPR 63A.1(2). For an overview see also L'attractivité de la Place de Paris, Lamy, Droit des Affaires, Supplement Octobre 2019, at 10.

44 See https://court.aifc.kz/model-clauses.

In contrast, taking the example of the Netherlands, the parties need to extend their choice to include further elements. A matter can be submitted to the NCC where the Amsterdam District Court or Amsterdam Court of Appeal has jurisdiction, the action is an international civil or commercial dispute, and the parties have 'expressly agreed in writing that proceedings will be in English before the NCC'.[45] This means that first, private international law (PIL) rules determine the jurisdiction of the Amsterdam District Court or the Amsterdam Court of Appeal *either* based on a choice-of-court clause *or* based on default PIL rules such as, for instance, the general jurisdiction rule at the defendant's domicile; and second, that the parties need to express their agreement with two particular points to have their case heard before the NCC: they need to agree to take their case to the NCC and to use the English language as the basis of the proceedings. This agreement can be reached before or after the dispute arises and can therefore either be combined with a classical choice-of-court clause in a contract if the matter is contractual or can be made once the lawsuit is brought to the Amsterdam District Court or Amsterdam Court of Appeal based on default jurisdictional rules of the Brussels I Regime. This allows tort claims to be brought to the NCC where a prior choice-of-court clause is infrequent. But it also for jurisdiction over collective actions or over applications seeking a declaration that a collective Wet collectieve afwikkeling massaschade (WCAM) settlement is universally binding, provided there is jurisdiction in the Netherlands.[46]

It should be highlighted again that a choice of the Amsterdam District Court or Court of Appeal alone does *not* amount to a choice of the NCC. Proceedings before the NCC run in a different language and according to a different fees system, which cannot be forced upon the parties. In contractual cases at least, its jurisdiction needs to be based on an express choice of court, combined with a clear choice of the NCC and of proceedings in English. The model (exclusive) jurisdiction clause recommended by the NCC reads as follows:

> All disputes arising out of or in connection with this agreement will be resolved by the Amsterdam District Court following proceedings in English before the Chamber for International Commercial Matters

[45] NCC Rules, Second Edition 2020, Art. 1.3.1 (d).

[46] WCAM, Dutch Act on Collective Settlements, Law of 23 June 2005, Stb. 340. See articles 7:907–10 BW (Burgerlijk Wetboek/ Dutch Civil Code), articles 1013–18a BRv (Wetboek van Burgerlijke Rechtsvordering/ Dutch Code of Civil Procedure).

("Netherlands Commercial Court" or "NCC District Court"), to the exclusion of the jurisdiction of any other courts. An action for interim measures, including protective measures, available under Dutch law may be brought in the NCC's Court in Summary Proceedings (CSP) in proceedings in English. Any appeals against NCC or CSP judgments will be submitted to the Amsterdam Court of Appeal's Chamber for International Commercial Matters ('Netherlands Commercial Court of Appeal' or 'NCCA'). The NCC Rules of Procedure apply.[47]

Similarly, the jurisdiction of the Paris chambers (CITC and CICA) can result from a contractual clause conferring jurisdiction to the courts within the judicial authority of the Paris Court of Appeal (article 1. 2 CICAP), with a clear reference to the international chambers. The recommended model clause reads as follows:

All disputes arising out of or relating to this contract, including questions relating to the performance, interpretation, validity, breach or termination thereof, shall be subject to the [exclusive] jurisdiction of the International Chamber of the Paris Court of First Instance (Tribunal de commerce de Paris), and all appeals from any decision of such court shall be subject to the [exclusive] jurisdiction of the International Chamber of the Paris Court of Appeals (Cour d'Appel de Paris).[48]

There is no specific agreement on the use of English for the Paris chambers, as the English language is only partly permitted. Procedural acts are drafted in French, submissions can be made in English, and the judgment is rendered in French with English translation.[49] To which extent the proceedings are conducted in English depends therefore on the specifics of the case and is agreed as proceedings go along, rather than in the forum selection clause itself.

A much more flexible approach has been adopted in Singapore. If the parties choose to litigate there, a forum agreement in favour of the Singaporean High Court is 'to be construed as including an agreement to submit to the jurisdiction of the SICC' provided it was concluded on or after 1 October 2016, unless a contrary intention appears in the agreement.[50] The Singaporean High Court can therefore transfer suitable cases to the SICC, even where the parties had not themselves considered bringing the case before the SICC.[51] Again, the Singaporean Rules of

47 www.rechtspraak.nl/English/NCC/Pages/clause.aspx
48 Wording suggested by www.parisplacededroit.org.
49 See Art. 2 of the CITCP Protocol; Art. 2,3 of the CICAP Protocol.
50 See Rules of Court, Order 110, rule 1 (2)(ca).
51 See Section 6.4, 'Transfer Jurisdiction'.

Court send a clear message in favour of proceedings before the SICC. When putting these favourable rules in context with the 2005 Hague Choice of Court Convention which was swiftly ratified by Singapore, the message to the parties is clear: Singapore has the ambition to attract disputes to its modern and specialised litigation centre.

Finally, it should be noted that the BIBC was conceived as a proper stand-alone business court and as per the original plans depended on the parties' willingness to submit to its jurisdiction. This explains why it would only have had the power to act with the parties' consent – either expressed in a previously concluded choice of court clause or in a consensual referral agreement.[52]

Based on these considerations, it is important that the parties are made aware of how to draft their choice-of-court clauses when they wish to submit cases to an ICommC. It is not common in a choice-of-court agreement to select a division within a specific court. According to Article 25 Brussels I bis Regulation, the parties wishing to determine jurisdiction have to agree that 'a court or the courts of a Member State' are to have jurisdiction to settle any disputes which have arisen or may arise in connection with a particular legal relationship. Similarly, Art. 3 (a) of the Hague 2005 Convention defines an exclusive choice-of-court clause as a clause in which the parties determine 'the courts of one Contracting State or one or more specific courts of one Contracting State' to the exclusion of the jurisdiction of any other courts. But if only a specific court is chosen, and not its international division, the parties' wish to litigate before an ICommC will depend on an internal referral or transfer mechanism which allows the case to go before its international division. The example of the Dutch model clause designating the NCC is a good model for the form such choice would need to take. While it could be questioned whether the choice of a division within a specific national court is a valid choice under the Brussels I bis or Hague 2005 regimes, this is unlikely to cause a practical issue in the

[52] Article 576/1(2) of the proposed amendment to the Belgian Judicial Code: 'The parties' consent is demonstrated by an agreement or a provision of an agreement in which the parties resolve to submit to the BIBC all or certain disputes which have arisen or which may arise between them in respect of a defined legal relationship, whether contractual or not, or by the referral by another Belgian, foreign or international court or tribunal, including an arbitral tribunal, in which the parties' consent to the referral is declared.' Cf. also Art. 7 UNCITRAL Model Law, which has been an inspiration for the BIBC rules. See Exposé des motifs (Explanatory Memorandum), Parl. St./Doc. parl.: Chambre (Belgian House of Representatives) 54, 3072/001, at 23.

aforementioned jurisdictions which have taken the policy decision to promote specialist international litigation centres by creating modern ICommCs.

6.4 Transfer Jurisdiction

Jurisdiction of an ICommC can also be founded on an internal transfer. The question raised is whether such transfer requires the agreement of the parties or whether it is possible to refer cases *ex officio*. The latter point raises some concerns given that some ICommCs provide for proceedings entirely in English instead of in the jurisdiction's usual language or for a charge of higher fees. The question arises whether a transfer without consent constitutes a risk for the recognition and enforcement of the judgment abroad.

The Brussels I bis Regulation does not address the issue of transfer of cases. According to Art. 45(3) Brussels I bis, the Regulation does not allow for a review of the jurisdiction of the court of origin unless there is a conflict with provisions on weaker party protection or exclusive jurisdiction rules.[53] Article 8(5) of the Hague 2005 Convention, on the contrary, addresses the issue of recognition and enforcement of judgments given by a court of a Contracting State pursuant to a transfer of the case from the chosen court in that Contracting State. Article 5(3) Hague 2005, which guarantees the jurisdiction of the chosen court, provides that a choice of court by the parties neither affects rules on the subject matter or value of the claim – Article 5(3)(a), nor the internal allocation of jurisdiction among the courts of a Contracting State – Article 5(3)(b). [54] However, where the chosen court has discretion as to whether to transfer a case, due consideration should be given to the choice of the parties.

[53] Article 45 (1)(e) Brussels I bis Regulation.

[54] Article 5 Hague Convention 2005 – Jurisdiction of the Chosen Court

(1) The court or courts of a Contracting State designated in an exclusive choice of court agreement shall have jurisdiction to decide a dispute to which the agreement applies, unless the agreement is null and void under the law of that State.
(2) A court that has jurisdiction under paragraph 1 shall not decline to exercise jurisdiction on the ground that the dispute should be decided in a court of another State.
(3) The preceding paragraphs shall not affect rules:
   a) on jurisdiction related to subject matter or to the value of the claim;
   b) on the internal allocation of jurisdiction among the courts of a Contracting State. However, where the chosen court has discretion as to whether to transfer a case, due consideration should be given to the choice of the parties.

Article 8(5) of the Convention takes this scenario into account. Where the chosen court had discretion with regard to the transfer of a case to another court, recognition or enforcement of the judgment may be refused against a party who objected to the transfer in a timely manner in the State of origin. Whilst the provision concerns transfer between courts, and technically not between divisions within a court, the consent of the parties should be sought in all transfer cases. Basing the transfer on a consent of the parties reduces the risk of a potential refusal of recognition and enforcement of a judgment rendered by an ICommC.

European jurisdictions tend to respect the parties' wishes and require the parties' consent, where they did not already expressly choose to litigate before the ICommC, but where they only agreed in advance on the competence of the court or jurisdiction 'hosting' the ICommC.

For example, the Frankfurt ICommC does transfer international commercial cases internally, but not without the consent of the parties and provided that there is no other specialised chamber that should be solicited. According to the internal distribution plan (*Geschäftsverteilung 2021*) of the *Landgericht Frankfurt am Main*,[55] proceedings which fall under the jurisdiction of a Chamber for Commercial Disputes and not under the special jurisdiction of another Chamber (such as e.g. antitrust and unfair competition) will be referred to the Chamber for International Commercial Disputes if the case concerns an international matter and the parties declare before the expiry of the deadline for the statement of defence that they would like the oral hearings to be conducted in English, without the need for an interpreter. The judgment will be issued in German, as the current legal framework in Germany does not allow for it to be drafted in English.

It should be noted that there is no cost issue involved in such transfer as the proceedings before the International Chamber follow the general rules applicable to proceedings before the German courts. Costs depend on the value of the dispute and will be determined by the Chamber after consulting the parties and follow the loser pays principle.

The NCC also requires the parties to the proceedings to have expressly agreed in writing for proceedings to be held in English before either the NCC District Court or the NCC Court of Appeal.[56] A transfer without consent of the parties is not possible.

[55] https://ordentliche-gerichtsbarkeit.hessen.de/sites/ordentliche-gerichtsbarkeit.hessen.de/files/GVP%202021_06.01.2021_ohne%20TV-.pdf, p. 41 J.I.

[56] Art. 1.3.1, Art. 1.3.3 (b) NCC Rules 2020.

On the contrary, the SICC rules allow in certain cases for a transfer of cases from the Singapore High Court to the SICC without the parties' express consent. According to Order 110 Rule 7(2)(b), the SICC has jurisdiction over cases transferred to it. Order 110 Rule 12 provides for a transfer of proceedings to the SICC which were commenced in the High Court or in the General Division, provided that certain requirements are met. According to Rule 12(4), a case may be transferred from the General Division to the Court only if the General Division considers that the case is an international commercial case for which it is more appropriate to be heard in the SICC, and either a party has, with the consent of all other parties, applied for the transfer in accordance with Rule 13; or the General Division, after hearing the parties, orders the transfer on its own motion. This means that certain cases can be transferred *ex officio*, which has an important practical impact on the caseload of the SICC. Given that Singapore is a signatory of the Hague 2005 Convention, this option should, however, be used with caution in light of Article 8(5) Hague 2005.

Cases brought before the CICC are either cases in which the parties have chosen the jurisdiction of the Supreme People's Court, but also first instance international commercial cases subject to the jurisdiction of Higher People's Courts, in which the latter consider that cases should be tried by the SPC.[57] Likewise, the CICC would, via transfer, handle first-instance international commercial cases with a significant nation-wide impact or other international commercial cases that the SPC considers appropriate to be tried by the CICC. Consequently, in many instances, the jurisdiction of the CICC is based on a discretionary transfer decision, independent of the consent of the parties. Similar to Singapore, this will show in the caseload of the CICC as compared to cases brought before European ICommCs which are operating a consensus-based jurisdictional regime.

6.5 Jurisdiction Based on Other Grounds

It should also be highlighted that for some ICommCs jurisdiction can be based on grounds other than a party choice or a transfer. Examples are the Qatar International Court (QIC) and the DIFC Courts, which not only take jurisdiction based on the parties' choice, but also on a rather

[57] Provided that the value of the dispute is more than 300,000,000 Chinese yuan; see also Article 34 Civil Procedure Law.

broad basis, where cases relate to their financial centres. According to Art. 9 of the Qatar Financial Centre Civil and Commercial Court Regulations and Procedural Rules, the QIC has jurisdiction in civil and commercial disputes with a strong link to the QFC (e.g. disputes arising from transactions, contracts, arrangements or incidences taking place in or from the QFC; disputes between QFC institutions and other entities established therein), but also in civil and commercial disputes involving entities outside the QFC or residents established in the State of Qatar.

As to the DIFC, jurisdiction is granted broadly and over cases with links that go beyond the financial centre itself or that have rather weak links with the DIFC. Article 5 of the Law No. 12 of 2004 in respect of the Judicial Authority at Dubai International Financial Centre Cases grants exclusive jurisdiction to the DIFC first-instance court in cases of civil or commercial claims in which only one party has links with the DIFC. This means that the court will have exclusive competence over a case involving a DIFC-based claimant, but in which the defendant is based outside the DIFC – Article 5(1)(a). It is also considered a sufficient jurisdictional link when a dispute arose out of or relating to a contract that has been solely 'partly concluded' in the DIFC – Art. 5(1)(b). As a result, the DIFC courts can take jurisdiction on a rather broad basis, far beyond the jurisdictional reach of European ICommCs.

6.6 Conclusion

Although ICommCs are often presented and marketed as self-standing courts, the Europe-based courts, the SICC and the CICC are mere international divisions of existing first- and often also second-instance courts. This distinguishes them from courts created for SEZs – the DIFC Courts, QIC, ABGM Courts, and AIFC Courts. The jurisdictional grounds on the basis of which ICommCs operate are different across jurisdictions, but parties generally opt in to their jurisdiction by an express choice of court agreement. Whether this agreement can be a classic choice-of-court clause, or whether it needs to expressly extend to the specific international division of a national court and contain an express agreement on the use of English as language for the proceedings, depends on the respective system. Some jurisdictions provide for jurisdiction of ICommCs based on grounds other than a choice of court, including notably an internal transfer. Whether the latter is possible only with or also without the consent of the parties depends again on the jurisdiction in question. The ICommC jurisdiction rules in Asia but also in the Middle East follow a more flexible and broad approach than their European counterparts, and this will also be reflected in the courts' caseload. Contractual parties wishing to subject their dispute to an ICommC are advised to carefully reflect upon the wording of their jurisdiction clauses when they draft their contract to make sure they avoid any ambiguities.

7

The Battle for Jurisdiction through Jurisdictional Requirements

Comparing the Commercial Court of England and Wales, the Singapore International Commercial Court and the Chinese International Commercial Court

MAN YIP

7.1 Introduction

The rise of modern international commercial courts (ICommCs) is a game changer for dispute resolution. The thriving success of the Commercial Court of London was the source of inspiration for the creation and design of a number of the modern ICommCs.[1] Notably, many countries create ICommCs to enhance their reputation as a centre for commercial law and of commerce, in order to substantially boost the national economy.[2] These ICommCs, by positioning as themselves as user-centric and innovative litigation mechanisms, inevitably compete for judicial business.[3] However, the so-called competition has never been properly analysed. Are these courts competing for the same kinds of judicial business? Are their jurisdictional frameworks strategically designed to advance their ambition?

This chapter seeks to answer these two questions by comparing the jurisdictional frameworks of three notable ICommCs: the Commercial Court of England and Wales, the Singapore International Commercial Court (SICC) and the Chinese International Commercial Court

[1] A number of the ICommCs in Europe have been inspired by the Commercial Court of England and Wales. See X. Kramer and J. Sorabji, 'International Business Courts in Europe and Beyond: A Global Competition for Justice?' (2019) Erasmus Law Review 1.

[2] Ibid., 3; G. Dimitropoulos, 'International Commercial Courts in the "Modern Law of Nature": Adjudicatory Unilateralism in Special Economic Zones' (2021) 24 Journal of International Economic Law 361.

[3] See also G Vos, 'A View from the Business and Property Courts in London' (2019) Erasmus Law Review 10.

(CICC). Through an examination of the reasons for the creation of the ICommCs and their jurisdictional frameworks, the analysis will show that the CICC has very different objectives from the other two ICommCs under examination. The CICC, created as a judicial safeguard of the development of the Belt and Road Initiative, is keen to pursue international and commercial disputes which are connected to China and which affect Chinese interests. It is not clear that its conservative framework appeals to the international business community. The SICC, in contrast, is designed to pursue all types of international and commercial claims. It was created to enhance Singapore's reputation as a premier dispute resolution hub and in turn to boost the national economy. Whilst its framework is marked by both internationalisation and party autonomy, its attractiveness to litigants would only increase once it has established a track record. The Commercial Court of England and Wales, by comparison, is a more traditional form of ICommC. It was created simply as a commercial court to take in both international and domestic commercial claims, but it has grown to become a favoured choice of forum for international commercial litigation. Its appeal and competitiveness lie in a number of crucial factors: its location in a leading international financial centre, its track record of excellence, the sophistication of English law and the international portability of its judgments.

The chapter is structured as follows: Section 7.2, by way of background, considers the reasons for the creation of the three ICommCs and their respective objectives; Sections 7.3, 7.4 and 7.5 scrutinise and compare the jurisdictional frameworks of these three ICommCs; and 7.6, drawing from the preceding analysis, discusses the role and relevance of internationalisation and party autonomy – hallmark features of an ICommC – in the jurisdictional frameworks of the Commercial Court of England and Wales, the SICC and the CICC.

7.2 Background

It would be apposite to start by briefly considering the reasons for the creation of the three ICommCs under comparison and their objectives. To be clear, all courts are national courts, and not truly independent 'international' courts. They are regarded as 'international' in the sense that their subject matter jurisdiction comprises exclusively of or is focused on international commercial claims, or their caseload comprises predominantly of such disputes.[4]

7.2.a The Commercial Court of England and Wales

The Commercial Court of England and Wales was established in 1895 as a division of the Queen's Bench in response to the demands in London and the business community for a specialist tribunal presided over by experienced judges who could decide commercial disputes expeditiously and economically. The Commercial Court of England and Wales, which has jurisdiction over a wide variety of claims relating to the transaction of trade and commerce, has been described as 'arguably ... the most successful Commercial Court in the world'.[5] Its success has contributed significantly to the prosperity of Britain and to the much-admired sophistication of English commercial law.

From 1 October 2019, the Commercial Court of England and Wales is formally brought under the collective title of the Business and Property Courts of England and Wales.[6] There are two main reasons for the restructuring exercise.[7] First, it is a response to the increasing competition for international judicial business from other jurisdictions that have invested substantially in developing their own versions of the commercial court. In particular, the 'uncertainties of Brexit' are perceived to have intensified the regional competition as other jurisdictions in Europe jostle for a windfall benefit.[8] Second, the restructuring is meant to decentralise the domestic disputes from the Rolls Building in London to the regional Business and Property Courts so as to enhance access to justice for domestic litigants. The restructuring, however, does not otherwise substantively change the way the Commercial Court of England and Wales operates in practice.[9]

[4] The different courts define 'international' disputes differently (see discussion under Sections 7.3, 7.4 and 7.5).

[5] M. Hwang, 'Commercial Courts and International Arbitration: Competitors or Partners?' (2015) 31 Arbitration International 193, 197.

[6] See further M. Ahmed, 'A Critical Review of the Business and Property Courts of England & Wales', in X. E. Kramer and J. Sorabji (eds.), *International Business Courts: A European and Global Perspective* (Eleven 2019) 21.

[7] Ibid., 25–6.

[8] Sir Geoffrey Vos, Chancellor of the High Court, Lecture to the Faculty of Advocates, 'The UK Jurisdictions after 2019', *The Judiciary of England and Wales* (20 June 2017), at 6.

[9] *Mezvinsky* v. *Associated Newspapers Ltd* [2018] EWHC 1261 (Ch), at [17]. Ahmed, 'A Critical Review of the Business and Property Courts of England & Wales', 31.

The caseload of the Commercial Court of England and Wales is generally international in nature. In 2018–19, it issued 830 claim forms and 1,450 hearings were listed.[10] In that same period, its international[11] caseload remained stable at about 75 per cent of its total business.[12] A recent study reports that in the year ending in March 2020, 'the Commercial Court has heard cases involving parties from seventy-two countries with the top nationalities being Kazakhstan, Russia, United States, Cyprus and Singapore'.[13] However, unlike the SICC or the CICC, the Commercial Court of England and Wales is not specifically established or designed to attract only *international* commercial disputes. That said, the decentralisation of domestic commercial disputes from the Rolls Building to the regional courts would allow the Commercial Court of England and Wales to be even more focused on international commercial disputes in practice.

7.2.b The Singapore International Commercial Court

The idea of a Singaporean ICommC was announced in January 2013 by Chief Justice of Singapore Sundaresh Menon. Chief Justice Menon drew inspiration from the success of the Commercial Court of England and Wales which he witnessed during his visit in September 2012. As he recounted:[14]

> The London experience suggests that arbitration and commercial courts are not competing players in a zero-sum game. Rather, there is room for co-existence and development of these two systems of dispute resolution.

[10] See the *Commercial Court Report 2018–2019*, p. 10, available at www.judiciary.uk/wp-content/uploads/2020/02/6.6318_Commercial-Courts-Annual-Report_WEB1.pdf (accessed on 2 September 2020).

[11] According to the *Commercial Court Report 2018–19* (ibid., p. 10), a case is classified as 'domestic' where 'the subject matter of the disputes between the parties is related to property or events situated within the UK, and the parties are based in the United Kingdom relative to the dispute'.

[12] Ibid., p. 10.

[13] 'London Remains No. 1 for Resolving International Commercial Disputes' (Law.com International, 24 August 2020): www.law.com/international-edition/2020/08/24/london-remains-no-1-for-resolving-international-commercial-disputes/ (accessed on 4 September 2020).

[14] S. Menon, 'International Commercial Courts: Towards a Transnational System of Dispute Resolution' (19 January 2015), at para. 10, available at www.supremecourt.gov.sg/docs/default-source/default-document-library/media-room/opening-lecture–difc-lecture-series-2015.pdf (accessed on 4 September 2020).

The legal services sector was growing rapidly in Singapore and it would be strategic to develop the dispute resolution sub-sector.[15] The establishment of an international commercial court would enhance Singapore's reputation as a premier dispute resolution hub which is already well known for arbitration[16] and is actively promoting mediation.[17] More particularly, the SICC pre-launch feasibility study recommended the creation of the SICC as a response to the perceived need for 'a neutral and well-regarded dispute resolution hub in the region', as a result of the growth of cross-border trade and commercial activities in Asia.[18]

The SICC was established as a division of the Singapore High Court. Its procedural framework has been described as 'a careful marriage between litigation and arbitration',[19] and is characterised by a greater degree of 'internationalisation' and scope for party autonomy than the traditional litigation framework.[20] At the date of writing, in all of the cases that have come before the SICC, at least one of the parties was based in Asia and/or one or more of the events were connected with Asia.

7.2.c The Chinese International Commercial Court

The CICC was established three and a half years after the SICC, on 29 June 2018. It comprises two international commercial courts (one in

[15] Z. Hamzah, 'Positioning Singapore As Asia's Legal Capital', *The Straits Times*, 16 January 2015, available at www.straitstimes.com/opinion/positioning-singapore-as-asias-legal-capital (accessed on 8 February 2019). In the same commentary, it was reported that the growth rate of Singapore's legal sector outstripped that of the overall economy.

[16] The Singapore International Arbitration Centre has been highly successful, setting an all-time record with 479 new case filings in 2019. See 'SIAC Sets a New Record in 2019' (8 April 2020), available at https://siac.org.sg/images/stories/press_release/2020/[Press%20Release]%20SIAC%20Sets%20a%20New%20Record%20in%202019.pdf (accessed on 4 September 2020).

[17] *Report of the Singapore International Commercial Court Committee* (November 2013) (hereafter the 'SICC Committee Report'), available at www.sicc.gov.sg/docs/default-source/modules-document/news-and-article/-report-of-the-singapore-international-commercial-court-committee-_90a41701-a5fc-4a2e-82db-cc33db8b6603-1.pdf (accessed on 4 September 2020).

[18] Ibid.

[19] S. Chong, 'The Singapore International Commercial Court: A New Opening in a Forked Path' (21 October 2015), at para. 5.2, available at www.supremecourt.gov.sg/Data/Editor/Documents/J%20Steven%20Chong%20Speeches/The%20SICC%20-%20A%20New%20Opening%20in%20a%20Forked%20Parth%20-%20London%20(21.10.15).pdf (accessed on 4 September 2020).

[20] See further M. Yip, 'The Singapore International Commercial Court: The Future of Litigation?' (2019) Erasmus Law Review 82.

Shenzhen and the other in Xi'an) designed to hear international commercial disputes, particularly those arising in connection with the Belt and Road Initiative (BRI).[21]

Given the differences in legal systems and cultures between the BRI countries and their internal political and/or legal issues, the resolution of commercial disputes in the national courts of the different BRI countries could likely lead to very different and inconsistent outcomes – a risk that might undermine China's ambition for the BRI.[22] Proceeding from such concerns, in October 2014, the Central Party of China set out a broad strategy for overcoming the anticipated legal challenges in a communiqué which contained a paragraph under the heading 'Strengthening Foreign-Related Legal Work'.[23] The said paragraph mentioned the use of legal means to safeguard China's sovereignty, security and development interests. The legal means to implement the said strategy – that is, a very preliminary concept of the CICC – was finally formulated in January 2018 in a document entitled 'Opinion concerning the Establishment of the Belt and Road International Commercial Dispute Resolution Mechanism and Institutions'.[24] Specifically, it stated that international commercial courts would be established.

In pursuance to this initial design, the CICC was launched about five months later as a division of the Supreme People's Court, the apex court of the land, and is structured to provide one-stop-shop dispute resolution services: litigation, arbitration and mediation.[25] For the purpose of this chapter, the focus is on the jurisdictional framework of the litigation aspect of the CICC. Nearly a year after its launch, the CICC held an open hearing of its first case in April 2019.[26]

[21] http://cicc.court.gov.cn/html/1/219/193/195/index.html (accessed on 4 September 2020)

[22] Z. Huo and M. Yip, 'Comparing the International Commercial Courts of China with the Singapore International Court' (2019) 68 ICLQ 903, 907. See further N. Zhao, 'The CICC: An Endeavour towards the Internationalization and Modernization of Chinese Courts', in X. Kramer and J. Sorabji (eds.), *International Business Courts: A European and Global Perspective* (Eleven, 2019) 159, 160–3.

[23] 'Communiqué of the 18th Central CPC held the Fourth Plenary Session' (People's Daily Online, 23 October 2014), available at http://news.12371.cn/2014/10/28/ARTI1414492334767240.shtml (accessed on 4 September 2020).

[24] http://cicc.court.gov.cn/html/1/219/208/210/819.html (accessed on 13 October 2020)

[25] For a detailed analysis of the CICC, see Huo and Yip, n. 22; W. Cai and A. Godwin, 'Challenges and Opportunities for the China International Commercial Court' (2019) 68 ICLQ 869; H. Jiang, 'China's International Commercial Court: A Dispute Settlement Mechanism for the Belt and Road Initiative' (2020) 39 CJQ 47.

[26] T. Liu, 'The China International Commercial Court in (CICC) in 2018', available at http://cicc.court.gov.cn/html/1/219/208/209/1316.html (accessed on 4 September 2020).

This discussion sets the background against which to evaluate whether the jurisdictional frameworks of the three specialist courts are strategically designed to advance their objectives. We now turn to consider the jurisdictional frameworks of these three courts in turn.

7.3 The Jurisdictional Framework of the Commercial Court of England and Wales

7.3.a Commercial Claims

The Commercial Court of England and Wales has jurisdiction over 'commercial claims', which are widely defined under Part 58.1(2) of the Civil Procedure Rules as 'any claim arising out of the transaction of trade and commerce and includes any claim relating to' a list of commercial matters: a business document or contract; the export or import of goods; the carriage of goods by land, sea, air or pipeline; the exploitation of oil and gas reserves or other natural resources; insurance and re-insurance; banking and financial services; the operation of markets and exchanges; the purchase and sale of commodities; the construction of ships; business agency; and arbitration.[27]

7.3.b International Jurisdiction

As it is unclear what the precise post-Brexit jurisdictional regime of the English courts will be, the discussion in this section focuses on the current jurisdictional rules of the Commercial Court of England and Wales.

7.3.b.1 Recast Brussels I Regulation

Currently, the recast Brussels I Regulation[28] (Regulation) is the main legislative text that determines the jurisdiction of the English court (including the Commercial Court of England and Wales) over proceedings concerning civil and commercial matters[29] commenced on or after

[27] In 2018–19, about 30 per cent of the Commercial Court's work comprised matters arising out of arbitration; see *The Commercial Court Report 2018–2019*, n. 10, p 7.

[28] Regulation (EU) 1215/2012 of the European Parliament and of the Council on Jurisdiction and the Recognition and Enforcement of Judgments in Civil and Commercial Matters (Recast). The Regulation has a territorial scope. The Brussels Convention applies to certain non-Regulation territories of Member States. The Lugano II Convention, the members of which are the European Union, Switzerland, Norway and Iceland, mirrors the original Brussels I Regulation.

[29] See the Regulation, art. 2. The Regulation does not apply to a range of matters, including bankruptcy, proceedings relating to the winding up of insolvent companies or legal persons, judicial arrangements, compositions and analogous proceedings, as well as

10 January 2015.[30] The Regulation sets out the rules on jurisdiction allocation in civil and commercial matters and conditions for the reciprocal recognition and enforcement of judgments between the European Union (EU) Member States. The regime is applicable to selected matters involving defendants who are not domiciled in a Member State.[31]

A full exposition of the operation and hierarchy of the jurisdictional rules of the Regulation goes beyond the constraint of this chapter and may be obtained from any major treatise on English private international law.[32] For a comparison with the jurisdictional regimes of the SICC and the CICC, generally, the English court has jurisdiction in the following circumstances and order of consideration:[33]

i. Where the English court has been conferred exclusive jurisdiction pursuant to Article 24 of the Regulation (for example, land-related claims).
ii. Subject to Article 24 of the Regulation, where the defendant has entered an appearance before the English court.[34]
iii. Where the English court has been identified to have jurisdiction pursuant to Articles 10–16 (claims arising out of a contract of insurance); Articles 17–19 (claims arising out of a consumer contract); Articles 20–23 (claims arising out of an individual contract of employment).
iv. Regardless of the domicile of the parties, where there is a jurisdiction agreement[35] in favour of the English court.[36]
v. Where the defendant is domiciled in England and Wales.

arbitration. The subject matter scope of the Regulation is therefore not coterminous with the subject matter jurisdiction of the Commercial Court of England and Wales, although there is a very substantial overlap.

30 For proceedings commenced before this date, see the original Brussels I Regulation (Council Regulation 44/2001 on Jurisdiction and the Recognition and Enforcement of Judgments in Civil and Commercial Matters). See also Lugano Convention 2007, the members of which are the European Union, Switzerland, Norway and Iceland.

31 See Articles 17, 20, 24 and 25 of the Regulation.

32 See, for example, A. Briggs, *Civil Jurisdiction and Judgments*, 6th ed. (Informa 2015), 34–9.

33 As a matter of English civil procedure, where the English court's jurisdiction is directly conferred by the Regulation, service out of jurisdiction is permitted as of right: see Civil Procedure Rules (CPR), r 6.33.

34 The Regulation, art. 26.

35 Article 25(1) provides that the chosen court has exclusive jurisdiction unless parties have agreed otherwise.

36 The Regulation, art. 25.

vi. Where the defendant is domiciled in another European Union Member State, the English court may be conferred jurisdiction under Articles 7–9.[37]

vii. Where the defendant is not domiciled in England and Wales or another European Union Member State, the traditional common law rules on jurisdiction would apply.[38]

A key advantage of suing in the Commercial Court of England and Wales, as a result of the applicability of the Regulation, is that the resulting judgment could be easily recognised and enforced in the Member States of the EU. This would be a crucial consideration for a claimant involved in a dispute with a defendant whose assets are located within the EU.

7.3.b.2 The Common Law Rules

The interface between the Regulation and the common law rules is rather complex. The common law rules are brought into play where: (1) the claim falls outside of the subject matter scope of the Regulation; and (2) the Regulation, pursuant to Article 6, points to the application of the common law rules.

At common law, essentially, the English court's jurisdiction is based on the service of process. The claimant has a right to serve the claim form on the defendant if he is present in England. The defendant who has been served while in England may contest that the English court, whilst having jurisdiction over him, ought not to exercise its jurisdiction as the claim should be tried in a more appropriate forum. This is determined based on the *forum non conveniens* principles enunciated by Lord Goff in the case of *Spiliada Maritime Corp* v. *Cansulex, Ltd* (*Spiliada* principles).[39] Where the defendant is overseas, the claimant will need to obtain the English court's permission to serve the claim form on the defendant out of jurisdiction.[40] In order to obtain permission, the claimant must establish that: (1) there is a good arguable case that the claim falls within one (or more) of the jurisdictional gateways set out in the Civil Procedure Rules, Practice Directions 6B para. 3.1; (2) there is a serious issue to be tried; and (3) England is the proper forum for the hearing of the claim, which is

[37] For example, pursuant to art. 17(1), where the claim relates to a contract, the English court has jurisdiction if the contractual obligation is to be performed in England and Wales.

[38] The Regulation, art. 6.

[39] [1987] AC 460.

[40] The exception is where the defendant has appointed a solicitor within jurisdiction to accept service on his/her behalf: see CPR, r 6.7.

determined in accordance with the *Spiliada* principles.[41] The English court also has jurisdiction over a defendant who has submitted to its jurisdiction.

Whilst a number of the jurisdictional heads do not furnish sufficiently strong connections with England as a forum, the 'proper forum' requirement ensures that the dispute is sufficiently connected to England.[42]

7.3.b.3 Hague Convention on Choice of Court Agreements

The Hague Convention on Choice of Court Agreements (HCCCA) entered into force in the Member States of the EU (except Denmark) on 1 October 2015.[43] The HCCCA prescribes a system of rules on the enforcement of exclusive choice-of-court agreements concluded in civil and commercial matters in international cases and the recognition and enforcement of judgments resulting from proceedings based on such agreements. The HCCCA regime operates on three basic rules.[44] First, the chosen court must hear the case. Second, the non-chosen court must refuse to hear the case. Third, the judgment from a chosen court, subject to exceptions, must be recognised and enforced in other Contracting States. The jurisdiction agreement provisions in the Regulation 'have been aligned' with the HCCCA to 'ensure better coordination and to secure the consistent enforcement of jurisdiction agreements both within the EU and globally'.[45] If there is any actual incompatibility between the two instruments, the HCCCA provides that it shall take precedence over the Regulation, save where all parties are resident in EU Member States or where a judgment issued by a court of a EU Member State is sought to be recognised or enforced within the EU.[46]

7.3.b.4 Brexit and Uncertainties

The Regulation will no longer apply to the UK after Brexit.[47] It is not clear what will apply in its place. The UK's plan is to accede to the Lugano

[41] *Seasconsar Far East Ltd* v. *Bank Markazi Jomhouri Islami Iran* [1994] 1 AC 438.

[42] A. Arzandeh, '"Gateways" within the Civil Procedure Rules and the Future of Service-Out Jurisdiction in England' (2019) *JPIL* 516.

[43] Denmark deposited its instrument of accession to the HCCCA on 30 May 2018.

[44] https://assets.hcch.net/docs/89be0bce-36c7-4701-af9a-1f27be046125.pdf (accessed on 13 October 2020)

[45] M. Ahmed and P. Beaumont, 'Exclusive Choice of Court Agreements: Some Issues on the Hague Convention on Choice of Court Agreements and Its Relationship with the Brussels I Recast Especially Anti-suit Injunctions, Concurrent Proceedings and the Implications of Brexit' (2017) 13 JPIL 386, 390.

[46] HCCCA, art. 26(6).

[47] The Regulation continues to apply in relation to proceedings commenced before the end of the implementation period on 31 December 2020. See further Mr Justice Butcher, 'Commercial Jurisdiction: The Pattern of the Past and the Shape of the Future', 2020

Convention 2007, which mirrors the original Brussels I Regulation and is therefore similar in many respects to the Regulation. It applied to join the Lugano Convention 2007 on 8 April 2020, but it has yet to receive the EU's approval of its application. To ensure continuity in the application of the HCCCA after Brexit, the UK deposited its instrument of accession to the HCCCA on 28 September 2020.[48] The HCCCA will be significant in protecting the English courts' jurisdiction and the enforceability of its judgments post-Brexit, especially if the EU does not approve the UK's application to join the Lugano Convention 2007.[49] The uncertainties ahead may affect the popularity of the Commercial Court of England and Wales as the forum of choice for the resolution of international commercial disputes.

7.3.c *Transfer Jurisdiction*

In respect of international commercial claims, the claimant can choose to commence proceedings in the Commercial Court. Where the claim has been commenced in another court in the English judiciary, an application may be made for the case to be transferred to the Commercial Court or the Commercial Court may order for the proceedings to be transferred to the commercial list.[50] In general, the court hearing an application for the transfer of proceedings is to decide based on whether the court to which the proceedings are transferred is the more appropriate venue for the adjudication of the claim(s) and judicial expertise is a critical factor in the 'appropriateness' test.[51]

7.4 The Singapore Commercial Court's Jurisdictional Framework

The SICC hears claims that are of an 'international' and 'commercial' nature which the Singapore High Court may hear and try in its original

Lords Goff and Hobhouse Memorial Lecture (28 March 2020), available at www.judiciary.uk/publications/speech-by-mr-justice-butcher-commercial-jurisdiction-the-pattern-of-the-past-and-the-shape-of-the-future (accessed on 14 October 2020).

48 The UK deposited an instrument of accession on 28 December 2018 on the basis of a 'no-deal Brexit', which it withdrew subsequently.

49 The other Contracting States to the HCCCA are the EU (including Denmark), Mexico, Montenegro and Singapore. China, the Republic of North Macedonia, Ukraine and the USA have signed but have yet to ratify the HCCCA.

50 Practice Directions 58, para. 4.

51 *Mezvinsky*, above n. 9, at [22].

civil jurisdiction and which also satisfy the conditions prescribed in the Rules of Court.[52] As of 1 November 2018, the SICC is conferred jurisdiction[53] 'to hear any proceedings relating to international commercial arbitration that the High Court may hear' under the International Arbitration Act.[54] The SICC's supervisory jurisdiction over international commercial arbitration is not, however, relevant to the present analysis. The remaining discussion will thus focus on the SICC's general jurisdiction over international and commercial claims.

The Rules of Court go on to specify that the SICC has jurisdiction in three scenarios. First is where there is a written jurisdiction agreement in favour of the SICC, and the parties are not seeking any form of prerogative relief.[55] Second is where the case is transferred from the High Court to the SICC.[56] Third is where there is an originating summons issued under Order 52 of the Rules of Court for leave to commit a person for contempt in respect of any SICC judgment/order.[57] The following discussion focuses on the first two scenarios, which are the primary ways through which disputes are brought before the SICC. The discussion now turns to the SICC's subject matter jurisdiction.

7.4.a International and Commercial Claims

A claim is characterised as 'international' in nature if:[58]

'(i) the parties to the claim have their places of business in different States;

(ii) none of the parties to the claim have their place of business in Singapore;

(iii) at least one of the parties to the claim has its place of business in a different State from –

[52] Supreme Court of Judicature Act (Cap 322, Rev Ed 2007), s18D (*a*) and (*b*) (hereafter the 'SCJA'). These claims must also satisfy other requirements prescribed in the subsidiary legislation, the Rules of Court (Cap 322, R5).

[53] SCJA, s 18D(2) read with Rules of Court, Order 110, rule 57(1).

[54] Cap 143A, Rev Ed 2002. These applications include stay of proceedings, interim measures, challenges to arbitrators, challenges to awards, recognition and enforcement of awards, and appeals on ruling of jurisdiction and subpoenas.

[55] Rules of Court, Order 110, rule 7.

[56] Ibid., rule 12.

[57] Ibid., rule 7(2)(b).

[58] Ibid., rule 1(2)(*a*) (emphasis added).

(A) the State in which a substantial part of the obligations of the commercial relationship between the parties is to be preferred; or
(B) the State with which the subject of the dispute is most closely connected; or

(iv) the parties to the claim have *expressly agreed* that the subject matter of the claim relates to more than one State'.

A claim is considered 'commercial' in nature where:[59]

'(i) the subject matter of the claim arises from a relationship of a commercial nature, whether contractual or not, including (but not limited to) any of the following transactions:
(A) any trade transaction for the supply or exchange of goods or services;
(B) a distribution agreement;
(C) commercial representation or agency;
(D) factoring or leasing;
(E) construction works;
(F) consulting, engineering or licensing;
(G) investment, financing, banking or insurance;
(H) an exploitation agreement or a concession;
(I) a joint venture or any other form of industrial or business cooperation;
(J) a merger of companies or an acquisition of one or more companies;
(K) the carriage of goods or passengers by air, sea, rail or road;

(ii) the claim relates to an *in personam* intellectual property dispute; or
(iii) the parties to the claim have *expressly agreed* that the subject matter of the claim is commercial in nature'.

Of note is the legislative provision for parties' express agreement that the claim is of an international and commercial character. This makes it easier for parties to choose the SICC as the forum for dispute resolution, particularly where the claims are not conventionally commercial or international in character. Parties neither have to deal with overly technical definitions nor convince the court their claims come within a plain

[59] Ibid., rule 1(2)(*b*) (emphasis added).

or sensible interpretation of the terms. Party autonomy may thus be said to be an undergirding principle of the SICC's jurisdictional framework.

7.4.b Service out of Jurisdiction

Service of legal process on overseas defendants not only notifies them of the proceedings; it also establishes the extraterritorial jurisdiction of the Singapore High Court. The SICC's cases, being international in character, are likely to involve many overseas defendants. Where proceedings are commenced in the SICC pursuant to a written jurisdiction agreement, departing from the procedure for service out of jurisdiction for the High Court, leave of court to serve out of jurisdiction is dispensed with.[60] This simplified procedure makes it more convenient and less costly for a plaintiff to sue an overseas defendant in the SICC. In view that the defendant has by agreement submitted to the jurisdiction of the SICC, the SICC takes the more enlightened (and defensible) view that extraterritorial jurisdiction in such circumstances cannot be regarded as 'exorbitant'.

7.4.c Written Jurisdiction Agreement

Where the SICC's jurisdiction is founded on a written jurisdiction agreement, the SICC may only decline to assume jurisdiction where 'it is not appropriate' for it to hear the claim.[61] This is essentially a discretionary exercise. However, the SICC cannot refuse to assume jurisdiction on the sole ground that the action is 'connected to a jurisdiction other than Singapore'.[62] In determining whether it is appropriate for the SICC to hear an action, it shall have regard to the international and commercial character of the court.[63] This is a departure from the *forum non conveniens* principles that are applicable to proceedings before the Singapore High court.[64]

[60] Ibid., rule 6(2).

[61] Ibid., rule 8(3) provides that the SICC shall have regard to the 'international and commercial character' of the dispute in exercising its discretion.

[62] Ibid., rule 8(2).

[63] Ibid., rule 8(3).

[64] For a comparison of the SICC regime and the traditional Singapore High Court regime, see M. Yip, 'The Resolution of Disputes before the Singapore International Commercial Court' (2016) 65 ICLQ 439, 440–4.

The assumption underlining the *forum non conveniens* doctrine is that an action is tried with the greatest convenience and lowest costs at a forum with which it has the most substantive connections. Such an assumption does not apply in the SICC for two reasons.[65] First, many of the advantages of trying the action in a foreign forum with which it has the most substantive connections are neutralised by the international and commercial character of the SICC. For example, where the action is governed by foreign law, the litigants have the benefit of applying for foreign lawyer representation,[66] the appointment of an international judge who is trained or familiar with the relevant foreign law,[67] and the possibility of determining foreign law based on submissions. Second, the parties have submitted to the jurisdiction of the SICC by way of a jurisdiction agreement. Therefore, the parties should not be heard to complain that the dispute has few or no connections with Singapore, as these are factors that are generally foreseeable at the time the agreement was entered into.[68] The SICC approach is not revolutionary. It is a natural extension of the common law approach towards an exclusive jurisdiction agreement: the agreement will generally be upheld save where the defendant is able to demonstrate exceptional circumstances amounting to 'strong cause', justifying the breach of agreement.[69] Foreseeable factors at the time the agreement was made are accorded limited weight in the 'strong cause' test,[70] which is said to be 'rooted in considerations of party autonomy and commercial certainty'.[71] By comparison, the SICC approach is even more deeply rooted in considerations of party

[65] See *SICC User Guides* Note 1 (Jurisdiction), available at www.sicc.gov.sg/docs/default-source/legislation-rules-pd/sicc-user-guides-31jan19.pdf (accessed on 4 September 2020). *SICC User Guide* is a non-binding reference resource.

[66] In fact, foreign lawyer representation is mainly granted in 'offshore' cases. An offshore case is a case which has no substantial connection to Singapore: see Rules of Court, Order 110, rule 1(1).

[67] This is, however, not decided by the parties.

[68] A. Chong and M. Yip, 'Singapore as a Centre for International Commercial Litigation: Party Autonomy to the Fore' (2019) 15 JPIL 97, 109.

[69] *Vinmar Overseas (Singapore) Pte Ltd* v. *PTT International Trading Pte Ltd* [2018] 2 SLR 1271 at [71] (*Vinmar*).

[70] Ibid., at [72].

[71] Ibid. In the case of a non-exclusive jurisdiction agreement, if the chosen court is a Singapore court and the proper law of the contract is Singapore law, the 'strong cause' test is applicable (*Shanghai Turbo Enterprises Ltd* v. *Liu Ming* [2019] 1 SLR 779 at [88]). If the chosen court is a foreign court, the *forum non conveniens* principles enunciated in *Spiliada Maritime Corp* v. *Cansulex Ltd* [1987] AC 460 would apply and the jurisdiction clause is just one of the factors considered (*Orchard Capital I Ltd* v. *Ravindra Kumar Jhunjhunwala* [2012] 2 SLR 519 at [12] and [30]).

autonomy and commercial certainty. In fact, the rules on the SICC's grounds for declining to assume jurisdiction do not appear to draw a distinction between an exclusive jurisdiction clause and a non-exclusive jurisdiction clause.[72]

As is clear from the rules concerned with consensual jurisdiction, the SICC's primary objective is to compete with other fora for dispute resolution business, especially cases that would not otherwise be heard by the Singapore High Court by reason of insubstantial connections. The strategy is to promote Singapore as a *neutral* dispute resolution forum to litigants: connections with the forum are thus downplayed. Proceeding from this objective, the SICC rules on the construction of jurisdiction agreements are pro SICC. Save where there is wording to the contrary, a written jurisdiction agreement is presumed to be exclusive in nature.[73] Where parties' jurisdiction agreement to submit disputes to 'the jurisdiction of the High Court is concluded on or after 1 October 2016', save for contrary provision, it is to be construed as including a submission to the SICC.[74]

7.4.d *Transfer of Proceedings from the High Court*

Whilst the written jurisdiction agreement is envisaged as the primary way in which cases will be brought before the SICC in the long run, in the short to medium term, the SICC's docket is expectedly to comprise predominantly transfer cases from the High Court. The business community and their legal advisors would be hesitant to insert SICC jurisdiction clauses into their contracts unless and until the SICC is a tried-and-tested dispute resolution mechanism.

Transfer of proceedings between the High Court and the SICC is a matter of internal allocation of jurisdiction. A case that falls outside the purview of the HCCCA may be transferred from the High Court to the SICC if the following criteria are satisfied:[75]

i. It concerns international and commercial claims;
ii. The parties are not seeking any form of prerogative relief;

72 Cf. Chong and Yip, n. 68, 111–12. The authors argue that the concept of 'appropriateness' under Rules of Court, Order 110 rule 8(1) should, out of respect for party autonomy, apply a calibrated approach.

73 SCJA, sections 18F(1)(*a*), 18F(2).

74 Rules of Court, Order 110, rule 1(2)(*ca*). 1 October 2016 is the date on which the Choice of Court Agreements Act 2016, the implementing legislation of the Hague Convention on Choice of Court Agreements, came into force.

75 Rules of Court, Order 110, rule 12(4).

iii. It is more appropriate for the case to be heard in the SICC; and
iv. Either all parties consent to the transfer or the High court orders the transfer of proceedings on its own motion after hearing the parties.

If the case falls within the scope of the HCCCA, nearly the same requirements apply, save that no transfer of proceedings can be made unless *all parties consent to the transfer*, whether the transfer is initiated pursuant to a party's application or on the Singapore High Court's own motion. This difference caters to the requirement under Article 5(3) of the HCCCA that in exercising internal allocation of jurisdiction between the courts of a Contracting State, 'due consideration should be given to the choice of the parties'.[76] Although the transfer of non-HCCCA cases from the High Court to the SICC does not require consent from all parties, the High Court should be slow to transfer proceedings in cases where all parties object to the transfer. To do otherwise would be perverse to the hallmark principle of the SICC – party autonomy. Indeed, it has been argued that the assessment of whether it is more appropriate for the case to be heard in the SICC should include considerations such as the international elements of the case and the SICC's capabilities to cater to them, as well as parties' consent to the transfer.[77]

More interestingly, where the question of transfer of proceedings is raised at the jurisdictional stage before the Singapore High Court has determined whether to exercise jurisdiction, the Singapore Court of Appeal has confirmed that the possibility of a transfer would be a relevant factor in the *Spiliada* inquiry and specifically, 'the presence of the SICC and its capabilities are potentially relevant' to the analysis.[78] This approach essentially utilises the SICC's unique features to neutralise the advantages of having a claim heard in a foreign forum. Importantly, it will have the effect of indirectly helping to steer cases to the SICC and therefore Singapore.

[76] See also HCCCA, art. 8(5); and Chong and Yip, n. 68. Chong and Yip argue that this higher threshold may be justified by the policy objective of ensuring that the resulting SICC judgments will be straightforwardly recognised or enforced in other Contracting States.
[77] Chong and Yip, n. 68, 109. If a majority of the parties consent to the transfer, it would be more appropriate for the case to be transferred to the SICC.
[78] *Rappo* v. *Accent Delight International Ltd* [2017] 2 SLR 265 at [116].

7.5 The Chinese international Commercial Court's Jurisdictional Framework

The jurisdictional rules of the CICC are set out the SPC's Judicial Interpretation entitled 'Provisions of the Supreme People's Court on Several Issues concerning the Establishment of the International Commercial Courts'.[79] Its preamble emphasises that the CICC shall, amongst others, 'provide services and protection for the "Belt & Road" construction' according to relevant Chinese laws and judicial practice.

Pursuant to Article of 1 of the Judicial Interpretation of the CICC, the CICC has jurisdiction over five types of cases:

(i) First-instance international commercial cases in which the parties have chosen the jurisdiction of the SPC pursuant to Article 34 of the Civil Procedure Law and the quantum in dispute exceeds RMB 300 million;
(ii) First instance international commercial cases which although subject to the jurisdiction of the Higher People's Courts, the Higher People's Courts consider more appropriate to be tried by the CICC and, for which permission for transfer has been obtained from the SPC;
(iii) First-instance international commercial cases that have a significant nationwide impact in China;
(iv) Cases involving applications for preservation measures in arbitration and for the setting aside or enforcement of international commercial arbitration awards within the CICC one-stop shop; and
(v) Any other international commercial cases that the SPC considers appropriate to be tried by the CICC.

7.5.a International Commercial Cases

Putting aside its supervisory jurisdiction over arbitration, the CICC's subject matter jurisdiction is limited to international commercial disputes. Within the CICC regime, a claim is 'international' in nature if: (1) either or both parties is/are foreign individuals, foreign enterprises or organisations, stateless persons; (2) either or both parties has/have habitual residence outside the territory of China; (3) the subject matter of the

[79] Hereafter the 'Judicial Interpretation on the CICC'. The English version is available at http://cicc.court.gov.cn/html/1/219/208/210/817.html (accessed on 14 October 2020).

dispute is outside the territory of China; or (4) the legal facts that created, changed or terminated the commercial relationship at issue occurred outside the territory of China.[80] The term 'international' within the CICC regime is thus defined by reference to China. As has been noted, this is the original definition for the term 'foreign' used by the SPC but which has been reformed to introduce a measure of flexibility. It would thus seem curious, at first blush, that the CICC should adopt a dated definition for the term 'international'. However, as the primary objective of the specialist court is to safeguard Chinese interests, a conservative, inward-looking definition is unsurprising, albeit unfitting for a modern international commercial court which the CICC claims to be.[81]

Unlike the term 'international', which is defined in the Judicial Interpretation on the CICC, there is no official prescribed meaning for 'commercial' in the CICC regime. Some guidance was provided by Justice Liu Guixiang, a senior judge of the SPC, during a CICC press conference held on 28 June 2018. He said the CICC's caseload shall comprise civil and commercial disputes between equal subjects, but it shall exclude two types of disputes: (1) disputes between States on investment/trade issues; and (2) disputes between the host State and the investor on investment law issues that are to be settled through existing international dispute settlement mechanisms.[82] It may thus be surmised that 'commercial' is intended to be widely construed by the CICC in practice.

7.5.b Consensual Jurisdiction

Unlike the SICC framework, a jurisdiction agreement in favour of the CICC is not by itself sufficient to confer jurisdiction on the CICC pursuant to Article 1(i) of the Judicial Interpretation on the CICC.[83] Two further requirements must be satisfied. First, Article 34 of the Civil Procedure Law requires, amongst others, that the dispute has an *actual connection* to China – that is: (a) it is the place of the defendant's domicile; (b) it is where the contract was performed; (c) it is where the contract was signed; (d) it is the place of the plaintiff's domicile; or (e) it is the place where the subject matter of the claim is located.

[80] Ibid., art. 3.
[81] See discussion around note 23. See also Cai and Godwin, n. 25, 871.
[82] See Huo and Yip, n. 22, 917–18.
[83] This jurisdictional rule applies to both exclusive jurisdiction agreements and non-exclusive jurisdiction agreements. See further Zhao, n. 22, 166.

Second, the quantum in dispute must exceed RMB 300 million. In other words, parties may only submit claims of economic significance to the CICC. Claims of lower quantum may be resolved in the lower Chinese courts, foreign courts or via other forms of dispute resolution.

These two requirements clearly indicate that the CICC is designed to pursue international disputes which are connected to China and which involve high-value claims. In view that the CICC is established to protect Chinese interests and to safeguard the development trajectory of the BRI, such a design is unsurprising.[84] At the same time, these two requirements also reveal that party autonomy has a far more limited role in the CICC, as compared with the SICC and the Commercial Court of England and Wales.

7.5.c Transfer Jurisdiction

Article 1, sections (ii), (iii) and (v) of the Judicial Interpretation on the CICC are concerned with internal allocation of jurisdiction between the CICC and other Chinese courts. Interestingly, in contradistinction to Article 1(i), none of the aforesaid grounds stipulate a minimum claim quantum. Further, the phrase 'significant nationwide impact in China' under Article 1(iii) is vague and requires more clarification. The term 'appropriate' under Article 1(v), as a condition for transfer of proceedings to the CICC, is also nebulous. To avoid inconsistent interpretation, more official guidance should be given as to when it would be 'appropriate' to transfer proceedings to the CICC. Overall, it would appear that a transfer of proceedings to the CICC would depend on the SPC's exercise of discretion. As the CICC is a division of the SPC, it is very likely that the SPC would take the legal, political, practical and financial significance of the dispute as a critical factor.

7.6 Internationalisation and Party Autonomy

7.6.a Internationalisation and International Commercial Courts

Compared to the more recently created SICC and the CICC, the Commercial Court of England and Wales is an example of a *traditional* international commercial court. It is traditional or 'old school' because it is an archetype of court specialisation, and court specialisation – for

[84] See Huo and Yip, n. 22, 922–3.

example, in technology, family law, etc. – is nothing novel.[85] It is not specifically designed to pursue only *international* commercial dispute business, unlike the SICC and the CICC. Its subject matter jurisdiction is not limited to that. That said, in practice, the Commercial Court of England and Wales has succeeded in attracting a large volume of international commercial dispute business. The success and appeal of the Commercial Court of England and Wales are based on its sophisticated procedural rules, a long-standing history of excellence in legal services and judicial expertise, the popularity of English commercial law as the chosen governing law of commercial contracts and the enforceability of its judgments within the EU.[86]

The SICC and the CICC, which may be regarded as modern adaptations of the specialist courts, to varying degrees seek to foster their attractiveness and success based on the 'internationalisation' of their respective litigation frameworks.[87] As Dimitropoulos puts it, the modern ICommCs are a 'new and explicitly internationalized form' of the domestic court through which the jurisdictions that have established these ICommCs seek to domesticate international dispute resolution.[88] Both the SICC and the CICC are marketed as specialising in the resolution of international commercial claims. To establish their expertise in this specialisation, both courts have allowed the involvement of international jurists. The SICC has appointed foreign jurists (known as international judges), together with local judges, on the SICC panel.[89] More conservatively, the CICC constituted the 'International Commercial Law Expert Committee' to support the CICC's work. The membership of the Committee comprises experts in international law, commercial law and the law of their home country from both the People's Republic of China (PRC) and foreign

[85] P. K. Bookman, 'The Adjudication Business' (2020) 45 Yale Journal of International Law 227.

[86] Ahmed, 'A Critical Review of the Business and Property Courts of England & Wales', 31. See also www.judiciary.uk/you-and-the-judiciary/going-to-court/high-court/queens-bench-division/courts-of-the-queens-bench-division/commercial-court/about-us (accessed on 2 September 2020).

[87] See G. Dimitropoulos and S. Brekoulakis, 'Introduction', this volume; G. Dimitropoulos, Chapter 10, this volume; G. Dimitropoulos, 'International Commercial Courts in the "Modern Law of Nature"', n. 2.

[88] G. Dimitropoulos, 'National Sovereignty and International Investment Law: Sovereignty Reassertion and Prospects for Reform' (2020) Journal of World Investment & Trade 71, at 93.

[89] www.sicc.gov.sg/about-the-sicc/judges (accessed on 4 September 2020)

jurisdictions.[90] These experts may act as mediators or assist in the CICC litigation by offering expert opinions on issues or law, as well as provide advice on the revision of the CICC rules and development plans and SPC's judicial interpretations and judicial policies.

7.6.b Party Autonomy: The Jurisdiction Agreement

In relation to the global competition for dispute resolution business, Butcher J observes extrajudicially that '[p]arties are increasingly able and willing to choose and courts around the world are increasingly willing to fill the demand'.[91] The jurisdiction agreement is a means through which parties exercise their choice. The effect of a jurisdiction agreement on an international commercial court's jurisdiction indicates that court's willingness to fill the demand of allowing litigants to pick their forum for dispute resolution.

The jurisdiction agreement is a basis for conferring jurisdiction under the jurisdictional regimes of all three courts under comparison. However, as discussed earlier, in respect of the CICC, the presence of a jurisdiction clause is not by itself sufficient to confer jurisdiction. Parties are only allowed to submit to the CICC international commercial claims beyond RMB 300 million which have an actual connection to China. The CICC is therefore not keen on pursuing just *any* international commercial claims. That the CICC is a division of the SPC (the highest appellate court in China) may supply the explanation. Although the SPC has jurisdiction to hear first-instance claims in limited circumstances, it has never exercised its trial jurisdiction since its establishment in 1949.[92] An exception has been made in respect of the CICC which hearings are presided by SPC judges. Therefore, only cases of significance (for example, cases of financial significance or cases with nationwide impact) and closely connected to China are allowed to consume the resources of the CICC. It is also these cases which are likely to be intertwined with Chinese interests. Such a conservative and restrictive jurisdictional framework is unlikely to appeal to the international business community.

[90] 'The Supreme People's Court Established the International Commercial Expert Committee', available at http://cicc.court.gov.cn/html/1/219/208/209/981.html (accessed on 4 September 2020).

[91] Mr Justice Butcher, 'Commercial Jurisdiction : The Pattern of the Past and the Shape of the Future', n. 47.

[92] Civil Procedure Law (2017) Amendment, art. 20.

On the other hand, the Commercial Court of England and Wales and the SICC are far more willing to simply let parties to international commercial disputes exercise their choice: a jurisdiction agreement is a sufficient basis to confer jurisdiction. More particularly, in respect of the Commercial Court of England and Wales, an international commercial case would most likely fall within the scope of the Regulation and a valid jurisdiction agreement in favour of the English court would confer *exclusive* jurisdiction, unless the parties have provided to the contrary. The effect of a jurisdiction agreement is further strengthened by Article 31(2) of the Regulation, which provides that where the jurisdiction of the chosen court is seized, 'any court of another Member State shall stay the proceedings' until the chosen court declares that it has no jurisdiction under the agreement. Article 31(3) continues to provide that where the jurisdiction of the chosen court has been established, 'any court of another Member State shall decline jurisdiction' in favour of the chosen court. Article 31 was introduced as a measure to counter 'Italian torpedo' tactics of the defendant who might launch proceedings in a non-chosen court first, so as to delay or frustrate proceedings in the chosen court by taking advantage of the 'first-seized' rule in the original Brussels Regulation.[93] The jurisdictional rules of the Regulation are not, however, devised to strategically position the Commercial Court for the pursuit of international commercial disputes business. They are devised to ensure a harmonised approach to jurisdiction amongst the Member States of the European Union, so that there is a harmonised approach to the recognition and enforcement of judgments from the courts of the European Member States (see Part III of the Regulation). That being the case, the effect of the applicable harmonised regime to the Commercial Court of England and Wales is that it is particularly poised to attract dispute business connected to the European Union or where the claimant would need to enforce the Commercial Court's judgment within the European Union.

In respect of the SICC, its jurisdictional rules are designed with the intention of enhancing the court's appeal to the international business community. Its aim is to become the choice neutral forum for dispute resolution. Therefore, its rules on assumption of jurisdiction downplay the significance of connections to Singapore. Nor do they explicitly distinguish between an exclusive jurisdiction agreement and a non-exclusive jurisdiction agreement, giving room to suggest the jurisdictional effect of a non-exclusive

[93] See *Erich Gasser GmbH* v. *MISAT Srl* C-116/02, [2003] ECR I-1693.

jurisdiction agreement is elevated to that of an exclusive jurisdiction agreement in the SICC regime. Whilst its jurisdictional framework is innovative and generally well designed, the SICC is a relatively new dispute resolution mechanism. The international business community is likely to take a 'wait and see approach' as the SICC builds its track record.

7.6.c Transfer Jurisdiction and Party Autonomy

The rules on the transfer of proceedings to the international commercial court also indicate the extent to which the court is willing to allow parties to choose where they wish to resolve their disputes. If the rules enable a transfer of proceedings to be made easily without consideration of parties' consent, this may facilitate the direction of international commercial disputes to the international commercial court. However, it would hurt the reputation of the international commercial court and the image of the national court system of which the international commercial court is part of. In the long run, it may reduce the overall volume of international commercial disputes business for the nation. Here, the rules of the SICC and the CICC provide sharp contrast. The SICC's rules on transfer of proceedings either requires consent (HCCCA cases) or incorporates consent as a basis for transfer (non-HCCCA cases). The CICC's rules, on the other hand, do not explicitly require consent.[94] As discussed earlier, whether a transfer will be made to the CICC appears to depend very much on the SPC's exercise of discretion.

7.7 Conclusion

It is still early days to comment on the success and sustainability of the SICC and the CICC. What is clear, from the analysis proffered in this chapter, is that the CICC is keen on pursuing international commercial disputes that are connected to China and that affect Chinese interests, whereas the SICC is designed to court all types of international and commercial claims. The Commercial Court of England and Wales, although not specifically designed to attract international judicial business, is particularly poised to do so, given its situation in a leading financial centre, the sophistication of English law, a track record of

[94] At the date of writing, China, a signatory to the HCCCA, has yet to ratify it. When the HCCCA becomes law in China, the Chinese law on internal transfer of proceedings in respect of HCCCA cases is likely to take into account parties' account on account of art. 8(5).

excellence and the advantages of a harmonised approach towards jurisdiction and the recognition and enforcement of judgments under the Regulation. Importantly, the jurisdictional rules are not the only key determinant of a court's success. The international portability of its judgments is an even more significant factor. Further, the winds of change are sweeping across the world, such as the uncertainties of the post-Brexit United Kingdom, the international role and image of China and the future cohesiveness within the Association of Southeast Asian Nations. It remains to be seen how these ICommCs will evolve to overcome geopolitical challenges.[95]

[95] In January 2019, Chief Justice Menon announced that 'a body of procedural rules for the SICC' has been developed to 'facilitate international commercial litigation' which would incorporate 'international best practices from a variety of dispute resolution mechanisms and legal traditions'. See S. Menon, Opening of the Legal Year 2019, 'Response by Chief Justice Sundaresh Menon' (7 January 2019), [21], available at www.supremecourt.gov.sg/Data/Editor/Documents/chief-justice-sundaresh-menon–address-at-the-opening-of-the-legal-year-2019.pdf (accessed on 4 September 2020).

8

Harmonization of Commercial Law Based on Common Law

The Role of International Commercial Courts

MATEJA DUROVIC AND FRANCISZEK LECH

8.1 Introduction

Since antiquity legal fragmentation has been an obstacle to trade. Cicero bemoaned the 'one law at Rome, another at Athens, one now, another hereafter' and urged for 'one everlasting and unalterable law [to] govern all nations for all time'.[1] This remark is not as quixotic as it may appear at first blush. Since divergence of legal norms and trade customs proved an impediment to profit, there has been a continuous pressure for commercial law to coalesce around a corpus of universal principles of trade custom. In fact, we can trace such developments to medieval Europe, where traders themselves began developing the original *lex mercatoria*.[2]

Today, as commerce becomes more globalized than ever before, the need for a consistent body of global commercial law is perhaps more pertinent. Especially in the aftermath of the Covid-19 pandemic, as litigation concerning cross-border disputes and insolvencies is bound to explode, courts with a markedly transnational, commercial expertise offering efficient and impartial dispute resolution fora are especially attractive.[3] It shall be argued that the traditional dispute resolution mechanisms, in particular litigation before national courts, or international arbitration, are inadequate to

[1] Cicero, *Da Republica* (III Book).

[2] See John Linarelli, 'Global Legal Pluralism and Commercial Law', in Paul Schiff Berman (ed.), *Oxford Handbook on Global Legal Pluralism* (Oxford University Press 2019), 3–15, available at https://papers.ssrn.com/sol3/papers.cfm?abstract_id=3285315, accessed 16 November 2019.

[3] The Hon. Chief Justice Sundaresh Menon, 'International Commercial Courts in the Post-pandemic Era' (10 March 2021) Opening Remarks at the Singapore International Commercial Court Symposium 2021, available at https://file.go.gov.sg/opening-address-cj-sicc-symposium.pdf, accessed 9 May 2021, [8], [12].

promote genuine harmonization of international commercial law. However, international commercial courts (hereinafter 'ICommCs') are bodies that have great potential to act as the engines behind a new wave of explanatory harmonization of commercial law, anchored in the norms of English common law.[4] The ICommCs enjoy a range of advantages compared to the other methods of dispute resolution, and they are consequently better placed to develop a coherent and universal corpus of international commercial law.

International commercial courts are originally domestic courts tasked to settle international commercial law disputes. Despite the name, *international* commercial courts remain part of the national legal systems from which they derive their jurisdiction – they are not truly international courts in the same way the International Court of Justice and the International Criminal Court are.[5]

Before discussing in detail the ICommCs and their role in harmonizing the law of international commerce, Section 8.2 will discuss the main tenets of international commercial law. Section 8.3 then explains how and why English common law became omnipresent in the world of transnational transactions. Section 8.4 discusses the meaning, justification and methods of legal harmonization, while Section 8.5 describes the individual ICommCs and how they interrelate to create this network capable of fuelling a harmonization effort. Section 8.6 discusses why ICommCs are substantially better placed to affect the convergence of commercial law around the world. Section 8.7 draws all the threads together in the conclusion.

8.2 International Commercial Law

At its broadest commercial law can be stated to encompass 'those laws that relate to markets, commerce and the rights relating to them'.[6] Correspondingly, commercial courts deal with disputes relating to markets, commerce and related rights,[7] while *international* commercial courts

[4] The Hon. Chief Justice Sundaresh Menon, 'International Commercial Courts: Towards a Transnational System of Dispute Resolution' (2015) Opening Lecture for the DIFC Courts Lecture Series, [55].

[5] Menon (2015) (n. 4), [17].

[6] Firew Tiba, 'The Emergence of Hybrid International Commercial Courts and the Future of Cross Border Commercial Dispute Resolution in Asia' (2016) 14(1) Loy U Chi ILJ 31, 35.

[7] The Rt. Hon. The Lord Thomas of Cwmgiedd, 'Dubai: Commercial Justice in the Global Village' (2016) Dubai International Financial Centre Academy of Law Lecture, available at www.judiciary.uk/wp-content/uploads/2016/02/LCJ-commerical-justice-in-the-global-village-DIFC-Academy-of-Law-Lecture-February-2016.pdf, [13], accessed 16 November 2019.

apply rules and laws that pertain to international (or transnational) markets and commerce. Throughout the present contribution we take international commercial law to mean rules and laws, not being of any national origin, applicable to transfer of goods and services across jurisdictions by international merchants, aimed at defending the interests of international commerce.[8]

International commercial law has a long history of harmonization. As observed, in the early Middle Ages, merchants from different jurisdictions began developing shared customs, which were enforced by specialist merchant courts.[9] This came to be known as *lex mercatoria*. This decentralized legal system based on custom did not survive the rise of the nation states, which, eager to assert their legal authority, deracinated *lex mercatoria* and substituted their own national rules in its stead.[10] Only under the Bretton Woods system after World War II did cross-border trade begin to flourish to such a degree that a return to some form of universal, mercantile legal framework was necessitated.[11] The 1990s saw an unprecedented wave of transnational commerce, fuelled by the collapse of the Soviet Union and the push for globalization. In this context 'operating in jurisdictional silos' became 'unworkable for the modern commercial lawyer', making it crucial that lawyers and the judiciary alike adopt a transnational outlook.[12] This is the historical exordium to the rise of the ICommCs.

The boom of globalization only exacerbated the need for a coherent body of international commercial law. Legal divergence serves as an obstacle to trade and potentially a barrier to entry. Thus, there is strong pressure from the mercantile community to simplify and unify rules and regulations.

8.3 The Role of the Common Law

English 'common' law is at the forefront of this harmonization process. Several factors help to explain its pre-eminence.[13] Indeed, it has been

[8] Anne Martin, Eric Locquin, Laurence Ravillon and Hélène Tourard, 'Chronicle of Informal Sources of International Commercial Law' (2008) 1 International Business Law Journal 92, 92.

[9] Razeen Sappideen, 'Harmonizing International Commercial Law through Codification' (2006) 40(3) Journal of World Trade 425, 426.

[10] Ibid., 426.

[11] Ibid., 427.

[12] The Hon. Chief Justice Sundaresh Menon, 'Transnational Commercial Law: Realities, Challenges and a Call for Meaningful Convergence' [2013] Sing JLS 231, 231.

[13] Used in juxtaposition to civil or continental legal systems.

seen as the modern natural law of international economic law.[14] First, the world's major financial hubs are New York and London, each applying common law. Additionally, many of the more recently emerging trading hubs such as Singapore or Hong Kong SAR also have common law systems. In fact, there has been a strong global trend to utilize common law principles of laissez-faire in the regulation of commerce.[15]

International commercial courts opt for English law because of its widespread usage, 'certainty, stability, predictability, independence and expertise of the judiciary, the commerciality and reliability of the court decision and for the willingness of judges to endorse contractual bargain struck between commercial parties'.[16] As early as the eighteenth century, Lord Mansfield argued that 'the law of merchants, and the law of [England] is the same', illustrating the absorption of the commercial common sense and the principles of *lex mercatoria* into English law.[17]

To begin with, common law is the most widespread legal system in the world, with more than 30 per cent of the world's population living under a version of common law.[18] As the newly established ICommCs fight for their foothold in the global dispute resolution market, it is natural that they should focus on the most proliferated legal system because that exposes them to the greatest number of potential 'clients'. Additionally, the omnipresence of common law means there will be a wealth of legal principles to apply, and due to the high reliance on English law by commercial actors, and the corresponding high number of commercial disputes concerning English law, there is a steady stream of jurisprudence.[19]

Next, English law has historically adopted a pragmatic approach to developing its commercial law. English law had 'no rule of law to prevent persons from making *any bargain* they pleased'.[20] Although subsequent

[14] Georgios Dimitropoulos, 'International Commercial Courts in the "Modern Law of Nature": Adjudicatory Unilateralism in Special Economic Zones' (2021) 24(2) Journal of International Economic Law 361–79.

[15] Roy Goode, 'Rule, Practice and Pragmatism in Transnational Commercial Law' (2005) 54 (3) ICLQ 539, 540.

[16] Tiba (n. 6), 52.

[17] *Pillans* v. *Van Mierop* (1765) 3 Burr 1663, 1668.

[18] Sweet & Maxwell, 'English Common Law Is the Most Widespread Legal System in the World' (20 November 2008), available at www.sweetandmaxwell.co.uk/about-us/press-releases/061108.pdf, accessed 16 November 2019, 1.

[19] A recent study found that 48 per cent of commercial practitioners and in-house counsel preferred English law as the governing law of the contracts; see Tiba (n. 6), 52.

[20] *Halsbury's Laws of England* (5th ed., 2012) vol. 91, para. 13 (emphasis supplied). See also *Calcutta and Burmah Steam Navigation Co Ltd* v. *De Mattos* (1863) 32 LJQB 322, 328 (Lord Blackburn).

developments mean such a broad proposition is not entirely true today, English law remains receptive to the needs of merchants, thanks to the fact that previous generations of English lawyers put pragmatism over principle.[21] Generally, compulsory legal rules are rare in English common law and everything is permitted, unless expressly prohibited by law.[22]

Another key commercial advantage of English common law is its flexibility, both juridical and procedural. Lord Burnett, the Lord Chief Justice, argued 'the common law is both accessible and flexible. It is predictable and consistent. It can react swiftly to new developments in the commercial and financial world'.[23] In a similar tone, Lord Briggs, Justice of the UK Supreme Court, has argued that the flexibility of English common law is bound to become more accentuated after Brexit, when it is freed from the constraints imposed upon it by EU law.[24] Lord Briggs' colleague from the Supreme Court bench, Lord Hamblen, emphasized that procedural flexibility, on top of legal flexibility, serves to minimize delay and expense and thus presents English law as a desirable forum for commercial disputes.[25]

Not only is the English legal system flexible, it is impartial too. In fact, the Singaporean Chief Justice Menon, the *animus* behind the Singaporean International Commercial Court (SICC), has argued that the crucial reason for London's success is the fact that it can provide impartial adjudication even in disputes which involve an English business and a foreign party.[26]

The rise of multinational corporations anchored in the United States or the UK was accompanied by the expansion of US and UK law firms,

[21] Lady Brenda Hale, 'Principle and Pragmatism in Developing Private Law', Cambridge Freshfields Lecture (29 March 2019), 2, available at www.supremecourt.uk/docs/speech-190307.pdf), accessed 16 November 2019; although Lady Hale goes on to argue that currently judges do and should reason by principle.

[22] Public-Private-Partnership Legal Resource Center, 'Key Features of Common Law or Civil Law Systems' (6 September 2016), available at https://ppp.worldbank.org/public-private-partnership/legislation-regulation/framework-assessment/legal-systems/common-vs-civil-law, accessed 16 November 2019.

[23] Lord Burnett (Lord Chief Justice), 'English Law on the World Stage' (8 May 2019) Speech at the London International Disputes Week, available at www.judiciary.uk/wp-content/uploads/2019/05/20190508-LIDW-English-Law-on-the-World-Stage-For-publication.pdf, [2], accessed 16 November 2019.

[24] Lord Briggs, 'Dispute Resolution in Uncertain Times', PRIME Conference (22 January 2018), available at www.supremecourt.uk/docs/speech-180122.pdf, [17], accessed 18 September 2019.

[25] Lord Hamblen, 'The Commercial Court: Past, Present, and Future', Annual Combar Lecture (13 October 2020), available at www.supremecourt.uk/docs/speech-201013.pdf, accessed 9 May 2021, 6.

[26] Menon (2015) (n. 4), [39].

which preferred using the legal system they were accustomed to, resulting in a great proportion of commercial contracts around the world having English law governing clauses. The widespread presence of English common law means 'any new financial centre *must* . . . adopt common law legal structure' in order to attract investors by providing familiar structures to such businesses.[27]

Alas, the dominant legal platform for international trade has been English common law. Consequently, financial centres 'from New York to Dubai' take notice of developments in the English legal system.[28] This in turn positions the norms of English law as the coalescing force for international commercial law and establishes English common law as a likely vehicle for the harmonization of the new *lex mercatoria*.

8.4 Harmonization

It is argued that ICommCs will drive the harmonization of international commercial law centred on English common law. Yet one could doubt the need for harmonization. Surely the existence of a body of international commercial law, to which we referred earlier in this chapter, presupposes an international community of merchants relying on some ascertained corpus of shared norms, which would mean 'the mercantile law . . . is the same all over the world. From the same premises, the same conclusions of reasons and justice must universally be the same'.[29]

This view is overly simplistic. While perhaps the overarching principles of commercial law remain broadly similar around the globe, substantive law does not, meaning a market actor who intends to offer goods or services across borders still faces a matrix of different laws. The lack of harmonization begs the question of why it should be desirable to harmonize commercial law.

8.4.1 Merits of Harmonization

The primary reason usually cited is that harmonization lowers the cost of international business by predictability and certainty of applicable legal

[27] Zain Al Abdin Sharar and Mohammed Al Khulaifi, 'The Courts in Qatar Financial Centre and Dubai International Financial Centre: A Comparative Analysis' (2016) 46(2) HKLJ 529, 530 (emphasis supplied).

[28] Lord Hamblen (n. 25), 16.

[29] *Pelly* v. *Royal Exchange Assurance Co* [1558–1774] All ER Rep 405, 408 (Mansfield LCJ).

rules.[30] In the absence of harmonization, parties have to expend resources to collate information about the applicable foreign laws, bear the cost of compliance, and factor in the possible costs of dispute resolution in an unfamiliar forum, as well as the cost of navigating the differences.[31] One should also add the cost of legal advice on foreign and unfamiliar elements of law.[32]

Consequently, harmonization can lead to greater economic efficiency, which could translate into lower prices for end consumers. While the truth of the assumption that harmonization of commercial law leads to lowering of the costs of doing business is being challenged, it can be accepted that harmonization, if resulting in lower costs, and removal of obstacles to trade, is desirable.[33]

Apart from lowering costs, harmonization may also work to reduce the 'home advantage' of the parties. As mentioned before, one of the attractions of the London Commercial Court is the fact that foreign litigants do not feel at a disadvantage before the court.[34] Correspondingly, if established rules of international commerce are applied by international courts, then the advantage of the 'home' litigant is diminished without the need of the states to cede sovereignty and give up the indirect protection of their nationals, which they would be in any case reluctant to do.[35]

Harmonization may be also perceived as a goal in itself. Justice Ramesh of the Singapore Supreme Court urged full and comprehensive harmonization in order to facilitate transnational commerce.[36] The argument is that unharmonious laws are an impediment to trade, and since we want to eliminate unnecessary barriers to commerce, harmonization is a goal in and of itself.[37]

[30] Tiba (n. 6), 51–2.

[31] Kannan Ramesh J, 'International Commercial Courts: Unicorns on a Journey of a Thousand Miles' (2018) Conference on the Rise of International Commercial Courts, [5].

[32] Christian Twigg-Flesner, 'Some Thoughts on the Harmonisation of Commercial Law and the Impact of Cross-Border Transactions', in Christian Twigg-Flesner and Gonzalo Villalta Puig (eds.), *Boundaries of Commercial and Trade Law* (Sellier European Law Publishers 2011) 103, 104.

[33] Goode (n. 15), 555: 'To the extent that domestic laws are dispositive there is little empirical evidence that they constitute a significant impediment to cross-border business and quite a strong view from industry that they do not.'

[34] Menon (2015) (n. 4), [39].

[35] Tiba (n. 6), 37.

[36] Ramesh (n. 31), [11].

[37] Goode (n. 15), 554.

This argument is not convincing.[38] Surely harmonization merely as an intellectual exercise is not desirable.[39] Indeed, harmonization for its own sake diminishes regulatory competition, which may have beneficial effects. As the judiciary themselves recognize, regulatory competition 'keeps everyone on their toes'.[40] Hence harmonization is not a goal per se – it is rather a worthy objective in the much larger drive for economic efficiency and free trade.

There are three main avenues of legal harmonization: (1) the legislative method, (2) the explanatory method and (3) the contractual method.[41] The legislative method entails the passing of model laws or international conventions by international bodies. Sappideen lists a number of such efforts, including those led by UNIDROIT, UNCITRAL and ICC resulting in documents such as the UN Convention on International Sale of Goods (Vienna Convention 1980) or the Hamburg Rules 1978 on Carriage of Goods by Sea.[42]

The explanatory method involves a coherent interpretation of established rules and customs across various jurisdictions. It is this method that ICommCs will greatly boost. Justice Ramesh has argued three things must take place so as to enhance the viability of the explanatory method to effect convergence of commercial law – namely, (a) rules relating to recognition and enforcement of foreign judgments must be strengthened; (b) the rules of procedure[43] in commercial dispute resolution must be harmonized; and lastly (c) a consistent stream of coherent jurisprudence from various courts must be present. It is argued that ICommCs precisely achieve those postulates, hence why ICommCs have such great potential to harmonize commercial law around the world.

The last method of harmonization is the contractual method. This method is also quite straightforward: it entails commercial actors

[38] See Luc Thévenoz, 'Intermediated Securities, Legal Risk and the International Harmonisation of Commercial Law' (2008) 13 Stanford Journal of Law, Business and Finance 384, 450.

[39] Twigg-Flesner has argued that the 1983 UNIDROIT Convention on Agency in the International Sale of Goods was undertaken simply as a jurisprudential challenge to solve the differences between the civil law and the common law systems: Twigg-Flesner (n. 32), 111.

[40] Lord Burnett LCJ (n. 26), [5]; Menon (2013) (n. 12), 246.

[41] Busola Omosalewa Akinyera (2015) 'An Analysis of the Methods of Harmonisation of International Commercial Law and Why Many Areas of Commercial Law Remain Unharmonised', University of West London Paper, available at https://papers.ssrn.com/sol3/papers.cfm?abstract_id=2790547, 3–8, accessed 16 November 2019.

[42] Sappideen (n. 9), 427–8.

[43] See Tiba (n. 6), 52.

including boilerplate provisions in their contracts that establish the role of the most effective rules to their contract. The courts of the financial centres can play a crucial role here because through attracting commercial actors to subject themselves to their jurisdiction, and then in turn promulgating coherent, commercially feasible jurisprudence, harmonization will occur purely by diffusion.

8.5 International Commercial Courts

We can finally draw the seemingly unconnected threads of this discussion together. The institution that lies at the nexus of apparent superiority of English common law in governing commerce over other legal systems, the need and methods of harmonization and the establishment of truly transnational commercial law is the international commercial court.

This concept, truly revolutionary in the early years of the second decade of the twenty-first century, has ceased to be a 'unicorn' and has become a common sight around the world.[44] The Standing International Forum of Commercial Courts (SIFOCC) (the innovative association of commercial courts around the world that has held its two first conferences in recent years promoting cooperation) lists as its members thirty-nine courts from thirty countries across five continents, including established players such as the Supreme Court of Delaware and the Commercial Court division of the English and Welsh High Court and newcomers such as the Astana Financial Centre Court and the International Chamber of the Paris Court of Appeal.[45] The proliferation of international commercial courts is best captured by Le Gal and Raynaud speaking of the Dubai International Financial Court: 'At its early stage, [the court] was compared to a "Common Law island in a Civil Law ocean". Some 13 years later, one may wonder whether the island has not turned into an archipelago.'[46]

A development that spurred the establishment of ICommCs was the introduction of special economic zones (SEZs). Special economic zones are a 'demarcated geographic area contained within a country's national boundaries where the rules of business are different from those [in the country]'; they have been adopted in many jurisdictions across the globe

44 Ramesh (n. 31), [1].

45 SIFOCC, 'Member Courts' (2019) at www.sifocc.org/countries, accessed 16 November 2019.

46 Jean-Francois Le Gal and Iris Raynaud, 'The Success of the DIFC Courts: When Common Law Makes Its Way into a Civil Law Region' (2017) 4(2) IBLJ 289, 290.

in order to attract foreign investment.[47] In fact, many of the ICommCs considered in the present chapter, such as the ones in Qatar, Abu Dhabi, Dubai or Nur-Sultan, were created to support an SEZ, only later allowing parties unconnected to the SEZ to opt in to their jurisdiction.[48] Given the goal of the SEZ – attracting foreign investment – an effective and impartial institution for dispute resolution was seen as a necessary pillar of that goal. Additionally, creating ICommCs in such zones shielded the states from additional costs – lack of an effective forum for dispute resolution might prompt frustrated investors to seek legal redress in investor-state arbitration, which is more costly than procedures at the ICommCs. Hence, these institutions can be seen as an intrinsic element of a successful SEZ.[49]

The early ICommCs were designed as courts specialized in 'deciding international commercial disputes and are therefore particularly well suited to develop the jurisprudence of international commercial law'.[50] Their procedure is adapted from the best practices of the established commercial courts with a detectable influence of international arbitration. The judiciary of ICommCs is comprised of eminent judges with an international background and an acute understanding of the world of commerce.[51] The ICommCs generate direct economic benefits by attracting investments while also creating indirect benefits in the form of reputational gain and diffusion of the substantive law of the forum state, in turn increasing the demand for legal services.[52] Consequently they have been adopted by states at various stages of economic development as an instrument of kick-starting or retaining their international financial competitiveness.

The characteristic features of ICommCs which set them apart from traditional courts and tribunals include: (1) dealing with cross-border disputes with at least one foreign applicant; (2) an international bench – presence of the so-called international judges who are not lawyers from that jurisdiction; (3) right of audience for foreign counsel; (4) proceedings in English; (5) publicly available judgments – setting these

[47] Teresa Cheng, 'Special Economic Zones: A Catalyst for International Trade and Investment in Unsettling Times?' (2019) 20(1) Journal of Trade and Investment 31, 35.

[48] Tiba (n. 6), 48.

[49] Ibid., 58.

[50] Menon (2013) (n. 12), 250.

[51] Menon (2015) (n. 4), [17].

[52] S.I. Strong, 'International Commercial Courts in the United States and Australia: Possible, Probable, Preferable?' (2021) 115 AJIL Unbound 28, 32.

ICommCs apart from international arbitration; (6) availability of confidentiality, but not as confidential as arbitral proceedings; (7) a right to appeal based on merits; and (8) the ability to join third parties.[53] These are merely characteristics, not necessary conditions. As we shall see, not all of these features are present in *all* of the ICommCs. In a sentence, these courts are 'bespoke commercial courts characterised by stature, excellence and efficiency'.[54] The best way to illustrate their typology, as well as to inform our discussion of how they drive harmonization, is to consider examples.

8.5.1 London Commercial Court

The London Commercial Court (LCC) was established in 1895 as a subdivision of the Queen's Bench Division of the High Court of Justice. Its establishment followed years of dissatisfaction from within the judiciary that the courts were losing business to international arbitration.[55] Unlike the Singapore or Dubai ICommCs, it was not originally intended to focus on international commercial disputes.[56] Its popularity amongst commercial litigants (domestic and foreign) can be explained by reference to: (i) competence and experience of its judges; (ii) flexible procedure; (iii) available pool of legal service providers with renowned expertise;[57] (iv) sensitivity towards commercial needs; (v) rule of law and independent judiciary.[58] The LCC accepts commercial litigations even when the dispute does not have an actual relation to the United Kingdom. Indeed, 80 per cent of the cases before the LCC have at least one party outside the jurisdiction of the UK.[59]

Evidently, the fact that this court was the progenitor of ICommCs explains the harmonizing potential of English law. Indeed, the fact that many ICommCs attempt to mimic the rules and procedures of the LCC

[53] Stephan Wilske, 'International Commercial Courts and Arbitration: Alternatives, Substitutes or Trojan Horse?' (2018) 11(2) Contemporary Asia Arbitration Journal 153, 157–9.
[54] Ramesh (n. 31), [2].
[55] Lord Hamblen (n. 25), 5.
[56] Wilske (n. 53), 160.
[57] Man Yip, 'The Resolution of Disputes before the Singapore International Commercial Court' (2016) 65(2) ICLQ 439, 445.
[58] Gary F. Bell, 'The New International Commercial Courts: Competing with Arbitration – The Example of the Singapore International Commercial Court' (2018) 11 Contemp Asia Arb J 193, 194.
[59] Tiba (n. 6), 36.

illustrates the potential of English common law to be the platform on which the international commercial law will be built.

The attractiveness of London as a dispute resolution forum has been somewhat cooled by Brexit. Paris, Frankfurt and Amsterdam have all set up English-speaking tribunals in an attempt to scoop up some of the business that would normally end up before the LCC. Importantly, after Brexit, UK courts are likely to be precluded from the mutual recognition of judgments regime, which will result in extra costs and delays for litigants trying to enforce an English judgment in another Member State.[60]

8.5.2 Singapore International Commercial Court (SICC)

The SICC was launched in 2015 as a division of the Singapore High Court, which is part of Singapore Supreme Court.[61] The objective of the court was 'to grow the legal services sector and to expand the scope for the internationalisation and export of Singapore law'.[62]

The SICC does not hear domestic commercial cases. Its bench comprises both domestic and international judges, and its rules of procedure are more similar to modern international arbitral rules.[63]

In terms of jurisdiction, the unique thing about the SICC is that it *only* hears cases that are both commercial and international:[64] its jurisdiction covers many facets but most importantly actions 'international and commercial in nature' and actions 'the High Court may hear and try in its original civil jurisdiction'.[65] An amendment in 2018 added that the SICC may hear 'any proceedings relating to international commercial arbitration' that could be heard by the High Court.[66] Furthermore, the legislation specifies that a jurisdiction clause nominating the SICC entails the submission to the 'exclusive' jurisdiction of the SICC, and to waive the right to recourse to 'any court or tribunal outside Singapore against any judgment or order of the [SICC]'.[67] The criteria of internationality[68]

[60] Ibid., 160.

[61] Supreme Court of Judicature Act 1970 (Singapore), s 18A; see Tiba (n. 6), 47.

[62] Tiba (n. 6), 45.

[63] Man Yip (2016) (n. 57), 445.

[64] Andrew Goodwin, Ian Ramsay and Miranda Webster, 'International Commercial Courts: The Singapore Experience' (2017) 18(2) Melbourne Journal of International Law 219, 221.

[65] Supreme Court of Judicature Act 1970 (Singapore), s 18D(1).

[66] Ibid., s 18D(2).

[67] Ibid., s 18F.

[68] Rules of Court (O 110, r 2(a)).

and commerciality[69] of the action, as prescribed by the Rules of Court, are interpreted broadly,[70] giving the SICC a rather wide jurisdiction in an effort to boost up its involvement and to facilitate transmissions of cases from the High Court to the SICC.

Moving from jurisdiction to the composition of the bench, of the forty-three judges, twenty-three are from Singapore (including Chief Justice Menon, four judges of appeal, and eighteen High Court judges). Of the twenty international judges, there are representatives of the United States,[71] the UK,[72] Australia,[73] France,[74] Canada,[75] Hong Kong,[76] India[77] and Japan.[78] Most of the international judges come from common law jurisdictions. Additionally, the composition of the bench neatly illustrates the nature of the court, still firmly entrenched in the court hierarchy of Singapore, but with a stress on leading foreign expertise.

In terms of procedure, the SICC possesses a few idiosyncratic features that make it more adept at resolving international commercial disputes. Unlike the Singaporean High Court, court proceedings in the SICC *may* be made confidential, particularly if the case is an 'offshore case'.[79] Interestingly, however, under Rule 31, the SICC must '[d]espite any order [of confidentiality] ... direct that a judgment made by the Court may be published in law reports and professional publications if the Court considers the judgment to be of major legal interest'.[80] The rationale is a desire that the SICC be able to contribute to the jurisprudence of international commercial law and provide a source of *lex mercatoria*.[81] The procedural rules of the SICC are marked by the flexibility so desired by international market participants: procedure may be modified by the

[69] Ibid., O 110, r 2(b).
[70] Man Yip (n. 61), 448.
[71] Justice Carolyn Berger, previously a justice of the Delaware Supreme Court.
[72] Lord Neuberger and Lord Mance from the Supreme Court, Sir Bernard Rix from the Court of Appeal, Sir Henry Bernard Eder, Sir Jeremy Cooke and Sir Vivian Ramsey from the High Court, as well as Simon Thorley QC.
[73] Justice Robert French (Federal Court of Australia), Justice Patricia Bergin (formerly Supreme Court of New South Wales), Justice Roger Giles (formerly Supreme Court of New South Wales) and Justice Dyson Heydon AC QC (formerly Court of Appeal of New South Wales).
[74] Justice Dominique T. Hasher (Supreme Judicial Court of France).
[75] Justice Beverly McLachlin PC (formerly Chief Justice of Canada).
[76] Justice Anselmo Reyes (Court of First Instance Hong Kong).
[77] Justice Arjan Kumar Sikri (Supreme Court of India).
[78] Justice Yasuhei Taniguchi.
[79] Ibid., 239.
[80] Rules of Court (O 110, r 31(1)).
[81] Goodwin et al. (n. 64), 240.

parties, like in arbitration, right to appeal may be waived and foreign law may be established by submissions.[82] Another aspect Menon CJ believed makes the SICC an especially attractive forum for disputes after the Covid-19 crisis is the fact that it has a strong construction and insolvency acumen on the bench, and Singapore's new consolidated insolvency legislation.[83] Indeed, as Southeast Asia's massive infrastructure sector deals with the disputes arising from the impacts of Covid, the local ICommCs seem like prime candidates to attract this new wave of litigation.

In conclusion, the structure and procedure of the SICC position it to 'actively serve as a platform for the development and harmonisation of substantive commercial laws, practices and ethics'.[84]

8.5.3 *Dubai International Financial Centre Courts (DIFCC)*

The DIFCC is a court authority of the Dubai International Financial Centre (DIFC), an SEZ established in the city of Dubai in 2004. The Emirate of Dubai gave the DIFC authorities 'complete autonomy' to create their own civil and commercial law separate from the laws of Dubai and the United Arab Emirates (UAE), meaning the zone is 'physically located within Dubai, [but] the laws of Dubai and the UAE do not generally apply, or where DIFC law takes precedence over Dubai and UAE laws'.[85]

Thanks to amendments in the UAE Constitution[86] and Dubai law, the DIFC can pass its own secondary regulations, allowing it to form its own commercial code to the best standards of world's major financial jurisdictions and laws.[87] The DIFC laws applied by the DIFCC are essentially a transplant from English common law.[88] The DIFCC applies the DIFC laws or the governing law of the contract, so long as the governing law does not 'conflict with public policy and public morals'.[89]

[82] Ramesh (n. 31), [23].
[83] Menon (2021) (n. 3), [11].
[84] Ramesh (n. 31), [29].
[85] Ahmed M. Almutawa and A. F. M. Maniruzzaman, 'The UAE's Pilgrimage to International Arbitration Stardom: A Critical Appraisal of Dubai as a Centre of Dispute Resolution Aspiring to Be a Middle East Business Hub' (2014) 15(2) Journal of World Investment & Trade 193, 202.
[86] Article 121 of the UAE constitution.
[87] Al Abdin Sharar and Al Khulaifi (n. 27), 536.
[88] Tiba (n. 6), 44.
[89] Dubai Law No. 12 of 2004 on the Judicial Authority at the Dubai International Financial Centre [DIFCC Law of 2004], Art. 7.

The idea behind the creation of the DIFCC was that 'a capital market could be created in order to provide global businesses with a familiar environment governed by financial regulations and legal rules that are substantially similar to those found in leading common law jurisdictions' – correspondingly the DIFCC applies either the governing law or the 'DIFC's common law', which is heavily based on English law.[90] This is one of the major differences between the SICC and the DIFCC – namely, that unlike the SICC, the Dubai Court was 'established to cater for a new economic zone'.[91]

The DIFCC has a Court of First Instance (CFI), a Court of Appeal (CA) and a Small Claims Tribunal (SCT).[92] The CFI is composed of a single judge and the CA of three.[93] A person may only be appointed as a judge to the DIFCC if they have been a 'holder of high judicial office in any jurisdiction recognized by the Government of the [UAE] and [have] significant experience as a qualified lawyer or judge in the *common law* system'.[94] The proceedings in front of the court are in English,[95] which creates tension with Art. 7 of the UAE Constitution, which provides that the official language of the state, and thus, one would expect, of the courts, is Arabic. The DIFCC, along with other Gulf ICommCs, has been foreseen as a vehicle to advance the growth of Islamic finance by adopting established norms of international commercial law to the instruments of Islamic finance.[96]

In terms of the jurisdiction of the DIFCC, initially it was exclusive to 'civil or commercial cases . . . involving the [DIFC] or any of the [DIFC's] Bodies', civil and commercial cases related to a contract, transaction or an event concluded, executed or taking place in the DIFC.[97] In 2011 this was amended[98] to extend the DIFCC's jurisdiction to cases where 'the parties agree in writing to file such claim or action with it whether before or after the dispute arises, provided that such agreement is made pursuant to

90 Menon (2015) (n. 4), [19].
91 Man Yip (n. 61), 446.
92 DIFCC Law of 2004, Art. 3(1).
93 Ibid., art. 3(3).
94 Tiba (n. 6), 43 (emphasis supplied).
95 Rules of the DIFC Courts 2014 (RDC), Art. 2(2).
96 Ilias Bantekas, 'Transnational Islamic Finance Disputes: Towards a Convergence with English Contract Law and International Arbitration' (2021) JIDS, https://doi.org/10.1093/jnlids/idab008.
97 DIFCC Law of 2004, Art. 5.
98 Dubai Law No. 16 of 2011.

specific, clear and express provisions'.[99] This means claimants no longer need to establish a direct nexus to the DIFC in order for the DIFC Courts to accept jurisdiction.[100] The procedure before the DIFC Courts is 'closely modelled' on the LCC, and the RDC are inspired by the English Civil Procedure Rules 1998 (CPR).[101]

One of the most interesting aspects of the DIFC Courts is the enforcement of their judgments. The DIFCC's judgments are automatically enforced within Dubai's legal system.[102] In the UAE, the DIFCC's decisions are enforced on the basis of an 'execution letter' provided to the parties by DIFCC, on the basis of the Protocol of Enforcement between DIFC and UAE from 2009.[103] The process is not straightforward and is time-consuming.[104] Outside of the UAE, the judgments of the DIFCC can be enforced in several Middle East countries under the Gulf Cooperation Council's (GCC) Convention for the Execution of Judgments, which provides mutual recognition and enforcement of judicial awards between GCC Member States.[105] Consequently, DIFCC judgments have been expressly recognized and enforced, for example, in Kuwait.[106] An innovative solution adopted by the DIFCC is the ability to convert its judgments into arbitral awards, facilitating their enforcement.[107]

8.5.4 Qatar International Court and Dispute Resolution Centre (QICDRC)

The QICDRC was established in 2009 to be the final piece of the State of Qatar's initiative to build a 'world-class international financial Centre' – it is designed to have international standards in dispute resolution and to be part of the Qatar Financial Centre's (QFC) strategy to attract international business and financial services to Qatar.[108] It serves the QFC.

[99] DIFCC Law of 2004 (as amended), Art. 5(2).

[100] Almutawa and Maniruzzaman (n. 85), 205.

[101] Reza Mohtashami and Sami Tannous, 'Arbitration at the Dubai International Financial Centre: A Common Law Jurisdiction in the Middle East' (2009) 25(2) Arbitration International 173, 176.

[102] Wilske (n. 53), 162.

[103] Al Abdin Sharar and Al Khulaifi (n. 27), 547.

[104] Ibid., 547.

[105] Wilske (n. 53), 162.

[106] *Global Strategies Middle East FZE* v. *Aqeeq Aviation Holding Company LCC*: Almutawa et al. (n. 85), 214.

[107] DIFC Practice Direction No. 2 of 2015; Al Abdin Sharar and Al Khulaifi (n. 27), 550.

[108] Wilske (n. 53), 163.

The binding law within the QFC is almost entirely (save for criminal law, which is Qatari) its own QFC law, which is professed to be 'user-/business-friendly'.[109] The body of law promulgated by the QFC is closely based on English common law, once again highlighting the harmonizing potential of English common law as adopted and promulgated by the ICommCs.[110]

The QICDRC applies QFC law and the governing laws of the contracts subject to the dispute, so long as such laws are not inconsistent with the public order of the State of Qatar.[111] The official language is English, though unlike the DIFCC, the court 'will take into account the fact that Arabic is the official language of the State of Qatar', permitting the proceedings to be in Arabic.[112] It is the 'law of Qatar that this Court is applying', although it frequently refers to the commercial principles adopted in other jurisdictions.[113] It becomes apparent that unlike the DIFCC, the Qatar Financial Centre Court (QFCC) does consider the legislation of Qatar where relevant.[114]

Of the twelve judges who sit on the bench, ten are foreign (including the court's president, former Lord Chief Justice, The Lord Thomas of Cwmgiedd), and nine are from common law jurisdictions.[115] The QFCC has jurisdiction to hear: (1) 'Civil and Commercial disputes arising from transactions, contracts, arrangements or incidences taking place in or from the QFC between the entities established therein'; (2) disputes between QFC authorities and QFC-registered entities; (3) disputes arising between QFC-registered entities and contractors and employees unless the QFCC's jurisdiction is excluded and finally; (4) disputes arising from transactions between parties that designate QFCC as the court with jurisdiction.[116]

In terms of enforcement of the QFCC judgments, it is important to stress one nuance that differentiates the QFCC from the DIFCC and that can explain why the QFCC has a closer connection to Qatari law than does its Dubai counterpart. The DIFCC, as we have seen, was established by delegated DIFC law, rather than by the law of the

[109] Al Abdin Sharar and Al Khulaifi (n. 27), 533.

[110] Ibid., 533.

[111] Tiba (n. 6), 44.

[112] Al Abdin Sharar and Al Khulaifi (n. 27), 537–8.

[113] *QFCA* v. *Silver Leaf Capital LLC* [2009] QIC (F) 1, [33].

[114] Al Abdin Sharar and Al Khulaifi (n. 27), 544.

[115] QICDRC, www.qicdrc.com.qa/court-overview-0, accessed 17 November 2019.

[116] Art. 8(3) of QFC Law No. 7 of 2005 as amended by Law No. 2 of 2009 and Law No. 14 of 2009.

Emirate of Dubai or UAE law – on the contrary, the QFCC was established by Qatar law, not the delegated QFC legislature. Accordingly, the QFCC is considered a Qatari court (established by the law of the State of Qatar), and on that basis enforcement of QFCC judgment in Qatar does not have the same complications as the enforcement of DIFCC judgment in the UAE, and hence the enforcement of the QFCC judgment in Qatar is not deemed a judgment of a foreign court (as is a DIFCC judgment in the UAE), making its enforcement substantially easier as regards a party who has its assets in Qatar (or Dubai) but not within the SEZ.[117]

What becomes apparent is that the QFCC followed the path forged by its Dubai forerunner, but not precisely, and there are important differences between them. It is still notable that in terms of their role in harmonizing international commercial law, both these courts play an equally significant and innovative role.

8.5.5 *Abu Dhabi Global Markets Court (ADGMC)*

The ADGMC is a classic instance of an ICommCs, and it provides all the usual aspects: proceedings in English, a foreign bench (the court's president is Lord Hope, ex-deputy president of the UK Supreme Court), etc.[118] An interesting quirk of the ADGMC is that English common law is 'directly applicable' before it, making it the first jurisdiction in the Middle East to truly commit to the hybrid approach.[119] As becomes evident, the crucial difference between the substantive law applied by the Gulf ICommCs, such as the DIFCC, QFCC and ADGMC, as opposed to the SICC, is that English law was directly transposed into their civil legal system for the Gulf ICommCs, whereas the SICC was already a common law jurisdiction.[120]

8.5.6 *China International Commercial Court (CICC)*

The CICC, established in 2018 by the Supreme People's Court of China (SPC), is the first hybrid court dealing with international commercial law matters. It is composed of two branches – in Shenzhen (International Commercial Court No. 1) and Xi'an (International Commercial Court

[117] Al Abdin Sharar and Al Khulaifi (n. 27), 543–4, 547, 549.
[118] Wilske (n. 53), 165.
[119] Ibid., 165.
[120] Tiba (n. 6), 49.

No. 2).[121] The mission of the CICC is to 'handle a broad range of international disputes, in particular commercial and investment disputes related to the Belt and Road Initiative'.[122] The CICC is quite innovative in terms of offering a one-stop-shop for mediation, arbitration and litigation.[123] As regards the jurisdiction of this novel court, the CICC handles cases that satisfy three criteria: (1) have a claim value of more than RMB300 m; (2) are transferred from the Higher People's Court to the SPC; and (3) have a significant impact nationwide.[124]

The CICC offers facilitation in the submission of foreign evidence since the requirement for notarized translation is removed.[125] The CICC judges will be appointed from a pool of the 'SPC's Senior Judges who are experienced with international treaties, conventions and practice and have English working proficiency'.[126] The problem is that judges will not be foreign at all; they will be Chinese judges who speak English. To compensate for this lack of foreign expertise (and correlative judicial independence), the CICC has established the 'Expert Committee' – a body composed of twenty non–People's Republic of China (PRC) nationals[127] who will act as an assistant body, presumably focused on mediating disputes and providing opinions on foreign law.[128] The court applies the PRC Foreign Investment Law.

It has been argued that CICC fails to live up to expectations, and its design architecture betrays a desire to limit foreign participation and maintain strong forum control.[129] The CICC was designed to facilitate disputes with a domestic element, rather than to attract veritably international litigants.

8.5.7 *Astana International Financial Centre Court (AIFCC)*

The AIFCC was established to cater for disputes arising in relation to the Astana International Financial Centre, an SEZ established in Nur-Sultan

121 See Wei Cai and Andrew Goodwin, 'Challenges and Opportunities for the China International Commercial Court' (2019) 68(3) ICLQ 869.
122 Wilske (n. 53), 174.
123 Ibid., 175.
124 Ibid., 175.
125 Wilske (n. 53), 177.
126 Ibid., 177.
127 CICC, http://cicc.court.gov.cn/html/1//219/235/237/index.html, accessed 17 November 2019.
128 Wilske (n. 53), 177.
129 Zhegxin Huo and Man Yip, 'Comparing the International Commercial Courts of China with the Singapore International Commercial Court' (2019) 68(4) ICLQ 903, 935.

(previously called Astana) to attract foreign investors.[130] The law applicable in the AIFC is its own AIFC law under the AIFC Constitution.[131] The AIFC Constitution provides that AIFC law may be 'based on the principles, legislation and precedents of the law of England and Wales and the standards of leading global financial centres' as well as the 'acting law of the Republic of Kazakhstan'.[132] When adjudicating disputes, the court may also 'take into account . . . final judgments of the courts of other common law jurisdictions'.[133]

Lord Wolf is the chief justice of the AIFCC, and the bench is comprised of eight other jurists with an English background, including Prof. Jack Beatson.[134] The rules of the court proclaim that 'all proceedings before the Court shall be conducted in English' and that the documents used or submitted to the Court 'shall be in the English language'.[135] It is apparent that the AIFCC does not bring anything other than the sense of novelty into the world of the ICommCs.

An analysis of the laws of the AIFC reveals that the SEC has adopted legislation which is an 'almost verbatim' transcription of UK legislation.[136] This means the AIFCC will have English lawyers and judges applying what are essentially English laws.

8.5.8 *International Commercial Court of Paris (ICCP)*

On 7 February 2018, two international chambers of the Commercial Court of Paris and the Court of Appeal of Paris were established. The structure comprises the Commercial Court of Paris (Tribunal de Commerce de Paris) and another chamber dealing with appeals of the former's judgments within the Court of Appeal of Paris (Cour d'Appel de Paris). The stated aim of the ICCP is 'to facilitate access to French

[130] Horace Young, Zhanyl Bekmurzayeva, Flora Huang and Dina Suleimenova, 'Institutional Development and the Astana International Financial Centre' (2018) University of Leicester - Leicester Law School Research Paper No. 18-07, available at https://papers.ssrn.com/sol3/papers.cfm?abstract_id=3300104, accessed 17 November 2019, 18.

[131] Constitutional Statute of the Republic of Kazakhstan, No. 438-V of December 2015 on the AIFC Constitution. The AIFC Constitution is available at https://laws.aifc.kz/storage/files/47ba42d60f3e4766/Unofficial%20English%20translation%20of%20the%20Contitutional%20Statute%20On%20the%20AIFC%20as%20amended%20.pdf, accessed 17 November 2019.

[132] AIFC Constitution, Art. 4(1).

[133] Ibid., Art. 13(6).

[134] AIFC, https://aifc-court.kz/justices, accessed 17 November 2019.

[135] AIFC Court Rules 2018, Rules 2.2 and 2.3.

[136] Young et al. (n. 130), 17.

commercial courts for transnational commercial disputes involving large international groups and to enhance the attractiveness of Paris in the choice of jurisdiction'.[137]

The ICCP's jurisdiction may originate from a contractual clause, a revolutionary principle for a French court of justice.[138] The law applied by the court is the governing law of the contract subject to the dispute, or the law stipulated by the parties at the beginning of the proceedings.[139] French 'remains the language of the proceedings', but English can be used at the request of the parties during hearings, as well as for witness statements and submitted documents; judgments of the court are pronounced in French, but on insistence by the parties may be accompanied by an English translation.[140] The bench is composed of ten judges (elected by their peers) who have 'a practice of legal English'.[141] The website of the court however concedes that '[w]ithout necessarily having the practice of the "common law"', its judges have 'competence and quality to judge' on foreign law.[142] The ICCP's rules of procedure demonstrate some common law influences,[143] for example, in that the parties can call expert witnesses to give evidence on which they may be cross-examined.[144]

This turn taken by the French judicial system has of course been 'headline grabbing', attracting some rather acerbic comments from the English legal profession: '[T]he idea that the English courts might establish a chamber to handle French language and French law cases sounds like something from an episode of Monty Python. It's hard to see that the

[137] See the official page of the ICCP at www.cours-appel.justice.fr/paris/presentation-des-chambres-commerciales-internationales-de-paris-ccip#ev, accessed 17 November 2019.

[138] Protocol Relatif à La Procedure Devant la Chambre Internationale de la Cour D'Appeal de Paris of February 2018, available at www.cours-appel.justice.fr/sites/default/files/2019-06/CICAP_Protocole%20barreau%20de%20Paris%20-%20Cour%20d%27appel%20de%20Paris%20-%20Version%20Francaise.pdf, translation available at www.shearman.com/-/media/Files/Perspectives/2018/04/Protocol_relating_to_the_procedure_before_the_International_Chamber_of_the_Paris_Commercial_Court.pdf?la=en&hash=BEE7E9D9833EC33B9DADCFA576972DE8791EA49E, Art. 1(3) accessed 17 November 2019.

[139] Tribunal de Commerce, www.tribunal-de-commerce-de-paris.fr/fr/le-droit-applicable, accessed 17 November 2019.

[140] Tribunal de Commerce, www.tribunal-de-commerce-de-paris.fr/fr/langue-de-la-procedure, accessed 17 November 2019.

[141] Tribunal de Commerce, www.tribunal-de-commerce-de-paris.fr/fr/les-juges, accessed 17 November 2019.

[142] Ibid.

[143] Bell (n. 58), 196.

[144] Wilske (n. 53), 170.

situation in reverse would be taken any more seriously.'[145] Perhaps there is no better testament to the harmonizing effect of English common law than the fact that the French justice system established a court with proceedings in English, modelled on the law and procedure of the English courts.

8.5.9 Netherlands Commercial Court (NCC)

The Netherlands Commercial Court was inaugurated in 2019. The court has two chambers: a district court as a court of first instance and a court of appeal. The NCC specializes in hearing complex international commercial cases. No nexus to the Netherlands is required in order to submit to NCC jurisdiction,[146] and the jurisdiction is based on the parties' consent.[147]

Dutch procedural law is deemed 'efficient, pragmatic and cost-effective', especially when it comes to 'conservatory arrest' (or *Mareva* injunctions),[148] which are more readily available in the Netherlands than in England.[149] Additionally, the Dutch court judgments are 'amongst the most widely enforceable judgments worldwide', thanks to their enforceability in more than thirty jurisdictions.[150] To this, the NCC adds the fact that proceedings and judgments are fully in English, has the ability to tender evidence in French, German, English or Dutch, and boasts a paperless litigation regime.[151]

8.5.10 Frankfurt Chamber for Commercial Matters

On 1 January 2018, the Frankfurt am Main Regional Court opened a special chamber dedicated to commercial matters. This chamber was established to 'create an attractive forum for cross-border disputes of

[145] Stephen Jagush quoted in Alison Ross, 'Paris's English-Speaking Court Meets with Mixed Response, Global Arbitration Review' (15 February 2018), available at https://globalarbitrationreview.com/article/1159078/pariss-english-speaking-court-meets-with-mixed-response, accessed 17 November 2019.

[146] 'Why Litigate in the Netherlands', https://netherlands-commercial-court.com accessed 17 November 2019.

[147] Bell (n. 58), 195.

[148] *Mareva Cia Naviera SA* v. *International Bulkcarriers SA, The Mareva* [1975] 2 Lloyd's Rep 509, and the overview of the history in *Emmott* v. *Michael Wilson & Partners Ltd* [2019] EWCA Civ 219 [38]–[44] (Gross LJ).

[149] NICC, https://netherlands-commercial-court.com, accessed 17 November 2019.

[150] Ibid.

[151] Wilske (n. 53), 171.

English speaking parties, allowing them to benefit from Germany's reliable and expeditious public dispute resolution mechanisms'.[152] Another important reason, was of course that Frankfurt has long been a competitor of London as a European financial hub.[153] The bench consists of one senior judge of the Frankfurt District Court and two business people chosen by the Chamber of Commerce.[154] The proceedings are in English, but the German Code of Civil Procedure is applied.[155]

An initial problem was Art. 184 of the German Courts Constitution (Gerichtsverfassungsgesetz (GVG)), which stated that the communication between German courts and the parties must be in German, which meant that submissions to and judgments of the Chamber were in German, severely restricting its potential to adequately service the needs of foreign litigants.[156] A bill was submitted to the Bundestag to amend the GVG and allow oral proceedings in English, along with court records and judgments, provided there was an 'international element' to the dispute such as a contract in English, and parties' consent to use of English.[157] As of now the bill has not been passed.

This section has outlined the trend of ICommCs appearing on the legal global map from Central Asia, through Southeast Asia and the Middle East, as well as the mature jurisdictions of Europe. Accordingly, given this trend the potential of such institutions to drive the harmonization of international commercial law based on adopted common law principles is unprecedented.

8.6 International Commercial Courts and Harmonization of International Commercial Law

It has been showcased that all ICommCs rely on English common law as the model legal system which they seek to replicate to some extent. The

[152] Ordentliche Gerichtsbarkeit Hessen, 'Chamber for International Commercial Disputes at the Landgericht Frankfurt am Main', (OGH) available at https://ordentliche-gerichtsbarkeit.hessen.de/ordentliche-gerichte/lgb-frankfurt-am-main/lg-frankfurt-am-main/chamber-international, accessed 17 November 2019.

[153] Wilske (n. 53), 172.

[154] OGH (n. 152).

[155] Ibid.

[156] Wilske (n. 53), 173.

[157] Jenny Gesley, 'Germany: Regional Court of Frankfurt Establishes English-Speaking Chamber for Commercial Matters' (6 December 2017) Global Legal Monitor, Library of Congress, available at www.loc.gov/law/foreign-news/article/germany-regional-court-of-frankfurt-establishes-english-speaking-chamber-for-commercial-matters, accessed 17 November 2019.

extent obviously varies, with jurisdictions such as Abu Dhabi or Kazakhstan making English common law directly applicable, while countries such as the Netherlands, Germany or France rely on their own substantive laws, merely tweaking procedural or jurisdictional laws in order to assimilate themselves to the English model. This may thus lead us to the false conclusion that the establishment of ICommCs suggests a clear victory of common law over civil law.

This conclusion should be rejected, for ICommCs are *hybrid* dispute resolution fora. To illustrate, the DIFC Courts, which we saw rely quite heavily on English jurisprudence, still will occasionally apply UAE law; moreover, ICommCs often will apply the governing law of a contract, which can be (and often is) civil law.[158]

English common law, however, is necessarily at the forefront of this new harmonization effort, and will thus have a profound impact on the 'new' international commercial law. The one obstacle that may inhibit the role we envision for the ICommCs is their suppression by or inability to compete with international arbitration.

International commercial courts have been described as a 'careful marriage between litigation and arbitration'.[159] Indeed, it is submitted that ICommCs are substantially better suited to drive a harmonizing agenda in commercial law than is arbitration. Accordingly, it can be said that dispute resolution before these tribunals has the best of both worlds: the flexibility of arbitration and the certainty and precedent of litigation.

To begin with, arbitral awards are not published, which constitutes 'an inherent shackle' for the arbitration's ability to develop a corpus of universal commercial law.[160] Lord Briggs has argued that 'there can be no rule of law unless its development takes place in public, for all to be able to see and learn what the law is, and for academics to be able to apply and proclaim their invaluable criticism of judicial thought processes'.[161]

An arbitral tribunal derives its jurisdiction from parties' consent, hence the award, though persuasive, carries no weight as far as binding precedent to other tribunals.[162] This is an obvious inhibition to developing a coherent stream of case law. To properly lead the harmonization

158 Le Gal and Raynaud (n. 46), 300.

159 Ramesh (n. 31), [2].

160 Ibid., [6].

161 Lord Briggs (n. 24), [31].

162 Peter M. Flanagan, 'Demythologising the Law Merchant: The Impropriety of the *Lex Mercatoria* As a Choice of Law' (2004) 15(9) ICCLR 297, 303.

effort, an institution must not only be sufficiently flexible to accommodate the nature of commercial dispute, but also be in a position to develop a corpus of law.

This is where the ICommCs come in. As we have seen, ICommCs generally publish their judgments, even though most also offer some degree of confidentiality to parties. For example, the SICC can direct a judgment to be published if it is of major legal interest, even where there has been an order of confidentiality of proceedings.[163] The SICC committee has also stressed the need to develop a 'freestanding body of international commercial law', which is best addressed by an international commercial court rather than arbitral tribunals.[164]

Economically, arbitration was initially seen as the more expedient, cheaper alternative to traditional litigation. The ICommCs with their state-of-the-art paperless filings and remote hearings, submissions and teams of experts ready to adjudicate a dispute offer potentially an even cheaper and quicker solution, while guaranteeing the same safeguards to commercial interests.

Another advantage of ICommCs over arbitration is the fact that parties can be joined to proceedings before an international commercial court. When it comes to arbitration, commercial reality, such as string contracts or back-to-back agreements, may result in parallel proceedings concerning essentially the same dispute.[165] The ICommCs being at core domestic courts have the coercive power to join third parties to the proceedings.[166]

In the end, 'despite the sweet talk' of ICommCs and international arbitration being in a state of cooperation rather than competition, both dispute resolution mechanisms are 'fishing in the same pond' of 'international commercial cases with high stakes'.[167] If the ICommCs can attract a portion of the caseload which would ordinarily be resolved by arbitration, then, because of their structural advantages, which are more conducive of coherent harmonization, international commercial law will become more convergent than it would be otherwise. International commercial courts can thus be seen as the solution which integrates the desirable aspects of litigation (published judgments, rights of appeal and the availability of joinder) with the best features of international

[163] Tiba (n. 6), 48.
[164] Goodwin (n. 64), 221–2.
[165] Ramesh (n. 31), [25].
[166] Ibid., [25].
[167] Wilske (n. 53), 181.

arbitration, making them attractive to parties who find both litigation and arbitration undesirable.[168]

As previously argued, due to lack of *stare decisis* and confidentiality of the awards, arbitration is likely to yield different interpretations of a single provision, resulting in a body of transnational commercial law that would be incoherent.[169] In fact, this is particularly so in regards to *inter*national commercial law, as a single rule is interpreted by tribunals and judges (in the conventional courts) from different legal cultures, in different jurisdictions, in different contexts.[170] Accordingly, a network of courts comprised of internationally minded and commercially aware professionals who cooperate to promulgate a coherent stream of jurisprudence might address the obstacles that substantive harmonization faces today.

Next, the ability of ICommCs' potential in harmonizing transnational commercial law must be compared to other methods of harmonization – namely, the legislative method, model laws and international conventions. Such international, 'quasi-legislative'[171] acts are a result of a diplomatic negotiation, which is an 'arduous and time-consuming' process.[172] Additionally, there is still a limited awareness of the commercial actors themselves about the benefits of model laws and conventions.[173] Accordingly, because the harmonization process led by the ICommCs does not involve intergovernmental negotiation, nor particular specialist knowledge by the commercial courts, they are better suited to advance the goals of harmonization.

Lastly, domestic national courts lack the power to apply principles of transnational law such as *lex mercatoria*, which limits their ability to effect the harmonization of a truly international commercial law. For example, in England, the courts have ruled that they do not possess discretion to apply non-national law.[174] Commercial actors are thus prohibited from choosing a transnational legal regime, such as *lex mercatoria*, because such a regime would self-evidently not be a 'national' legal system.[175] The result is that national courts have the possibility (by

[168] Goodwin (n. 64), 223.
[169] Flanagan (n. 162), 303.
[170] Twigg-Flesner (n. 32), 115.
[171] In a sense of being passed by an internationally recognized body – rather than resulting from widespread use or judicial interpretation.
[172] Goode (n. 15), 558.
[173] Twigg-Flesner (n. 32), 108–9.
[174] *Beximco Pharmaceuticals Ltd* v. *Shamil Bank of Bahrain EC* [2004] EWCA Civ 19, [52].
[175] Markus Petsche, 'The Application of Transnational Law (*Lex Mercatoria*) by Domestic Courts' (2014) 10(3) Journal of International Private Law 489, 493.

laying down precedent) to harmonize international commercial law, but cannot apply transnational law (*lex mercatoria*), while international arbitration may apply the principles of *lex mercatoria*, but is inadequate to develop international commercial law.[176]

Accordingly, an institution that lies somewhere in between, such as the ICommCs, with the power to apply the governing law of a contract, even if it is *lex mercatoria*, while also laying down precedent are in the most optimal position to develop the corpus of international commercial law.

8.7 Conclusion

The preceding analysis of the existing ICommCs illustrates that these institutions possess structural elements that position them as the most apposite for driving the harmonization of substantive and procedural international commercial law. Their rules of procedure and jurisdictional remits are designed to facilitate resolution of complex, transnational disputes arising in the mercantile context, while their accommodation within the existing structure of judicial systems augment their power to lay down consistent and coherent precedential jurisprudence that will have a lasting effect on converging the new *lex mercatoria*. As we have shown, this harmonization would be desirable from both the theoretical and, more importantly, practical standpoint, which explains why the development of the ICommCs is significant. Additionally, we have argued that the established principles of English common law, as applied by the ICommCs, will form the underlying bedrock for this more harmonized international commercial law.

In the words of one of the people behind this tidal wave of ICommCs' establishment, Chief Justice Menon of Singapore, a 'network of international commercial courts helmed by a community of renowned international commercial judges can emerge as a very significant platform for the development of a body of consistent jurisprudence [of *lex mercatoria*]'.[177] It is thanks to those courts that perhaps Cicero's vision regarding the law will be true, at least in the limited field of commercial law.

[176] Ibid., 511.

[177] Menon (2015) (n. 4), [55].

9

Applicable Laws in the International Commercial Courts of the Gulf

FARIS ELIAS NASRALLAH

9.1 Introduction

Along the road to nation state independence, various hybrid common law courts, mixed courts and ad hoc tribunals were established throughout the Gulf region. At the turn of the twenty-first century, the most recent incarnations of these dispute resolution forums in the Gulf states took the form of free-zone and financial centre international commercial courts (ICommCs), in the Dubai International Financial Centre (DIFC), Abu Dhabi Global Market (ADGM) and Qatar Financial Centre (QFC). The reach of these jurisdictions, their legislative growth and their corresponding enforcement landscapes have given rise to bodies of court jurisprudence, as well as policy and practitioner attention. Justifiably, these issues raise important questions about managing inter-jurisdictional relations between different national courts,[1] and between national legal systems and international legal orders.[2] By contrast, and amidst wider processes of institutional and legal transplants, the applicable laws within the DIFC, ADGM and QFC courts have generated moderate attention.[3]

The common pursuits of legal certainty and predictability, which often inform the adoption of a particular applicable law, are necessarily balanced against the need for institutional flexibility and party autonomy.[4]

[1] See Julian Bailey, 'The Interplay between International Commercial Courts and Ordinary Courts', Chapter 15 in this volume.

[2] See Georgios Dimitropoulos and Stavros Brekoulakis, 'International Commercial Courts', the introduction to this volume; Georgios Dimitropoulos, 'The Design of International Commercial Courts', Chapter 10 in this volume.

[3] For an overview of DIFC court practice, see Rupert Reed and Tom Montagu-Smith (eds.), *DIFC Courts Practice* (Edward Elgar 2020).

[4] See Alex Mills, *Party Autonomy in Private International Law* (Cambridge University Press 2018) 313–90.

As such, the issue of applicable law, whether chosen by the parties or determined by default in a court having jurisdiction, takes on important functions outside of the courtroom. The inception and implementation of applicable laws are integral to the identity of the free zone and financial centre commercial courts, and therefore influence their inter-jurisdictional and institutional relations.

Focusing on applicable laws in the DIFC, ADGM and QFC courts, this chapter is divided into two main parts. The first part considers the issue of applicable law within the establishment and jurisdictional reach of the DIFC, ADGM and QFC courts. Taking a more contextual view, it is suggested that the values and symbolic capital attached to applicable law can shed light on the distinct normative and legal practices within these forums and processes of hybrid transnational lawmaking generally. The second part compares the applicable laws in the DIFC, ADGM and QFC, assessing the relevant legislation, regulations and lawmaking functions together with a selection of court decisions espoused across these nascent ICommCs.

This assessment reveals that the laws being applied within the DIFC, ADGM and QFC court systems are more nuanced than the uniform and direct application of 'English law'.[5] Instead, each court system engages a diverse set of applicable laws at inception and implementation stages, upon interacting with their host legal systems, and by virtue of the global nature of their disputants. To different extents, the DIFC and QFC courts have developed normative practices and jurisprudence that reflect this legal diversity, while creating a degree of legal certainty as to the applicable laws within these forums. The wholesale adoption of a raft of English legislation in the ADGM marks a departure from the DIFC and QFC approaches, reflecting the transplant of a body of English common law in the image of an Anglo civil code. The extent to which these diverse laws and practices can be harmonised in the DIFC, ADGM and QFC courts will likely influence the future development of similar court models throughout the region.

9.2 Symbolic Capital and Applicable Law

Identifying the applicable law of any ICommC is in principle a straightforward and uncomplicated endeavour, discernible by reference

[5] See generally Georgios Dimitropoulos, 'International Commercial Courts in the "Modern Law of Nature": Adjudicatory Unilateralism in Special Economic Zones' (2021) 24(2) Journal of International Economic Law 361–79.

to establishing laws, legislative rules and growing court jurisprudence within each jurisdiction. Yet, to comprehend the genesis, dimensions and force of applicable laws in the DIFC, ADGM and QFC courts requires a broader legal assessment. Beyond the legislative, judicial and procedural developments within these Gulf jurisdictions, the inception and application of received laws in these ICommCs represent instances of transnational hybrid lawmaking that recalibrate the relationship between national legal systems and international legal orders.[6]

To capture the nature and interdependence of these issues, it is necessary to consider applicable law in tandem with the foundational legal infrastructure within the respective Gulf jurisdictions. Attention must also be paid to the jurisdictional differences and varying transplants of different laws and procedures within the DIFC, ADGM and QFC courts, which are by no means uniform. Conscious of these contextual issues, the following analysis illustrates that the issue of applicable law in the DIFC, ADGM and QFC courts can reveal as much about the symbolic capital of law and the transfer of values as the professional and institutional norms and practices within these nascent jurisdictions. The symbolic capital of these legal transplants is generated out of a struggle between indigenous and received law that is grounded in imperial power relations and administration.

Within the British protectorates of the Trucial States of the Emirates (1820 and 1971) and Qatar (1916–71), British extraterritorial jurisdiction in the Gulf and the application of English law in Anglo-Gulf court forums influenced the pre-independence development of these and other Gulf legal systems.[7] The British courts of the Trucial States of the Emirates, operating under the jurisdictional authority of British Trucial States Orders in Council, comprised ‘the Court for the Trucial States, Chief Court for the Persian Gulf (both first instance courts), Full Court for the Persian Gulf (appeal court), as well as the Joint Court and Joint Court of Appeal, both having jurisdiction in mixed cases involving persons subject to the local court and persons subject to British jurisdiction, while the

[6] Ibid.

[7] See Nathan Brown, *The Rule of Law in the Arab World: Courts in Egypt and the Gulf* (Cambridge University Press 1997); Salim al-Arrayed, *Islamic Law as Administered in British India and in Joint British Courts in the Arabian Gulf, 1857–1947* (al-Ayam Press 2001); and Husain al-Baharna (ed.), *British Extra-Territorial Jurisdiction in the Gulf 1913–1971: An Analysis of the System of British Courts in the Territories of the British Protected States of the Gulf during the Pre-independence Era* (Cambridge Archive Editions 1998).

Joint Court enjoyed jurisdiction in all matters, whether criminal or civil'.[8] According to 'Ali al-Muhairi:

> The law applied by the British courts in the Trucial States was mostly based on the Indian Codes which were applied in India on 14 August 1947. Moreover, several significant acts and codes were listed in the Trucial States Orders in Council, and the Political Resident in the Persian Gulf had the authority to make regulations known as King's Regulations. In making these regulations, certain pieces of Indian legislation, specifically in the field of procedures, were simplified or modified. In addition to these codes and regulations, local custom was also taken into account by British courts.[9]

The establishment of the international financial centre jurisdictions and corresponding court systems in Dubai and Qatar, in 2004 and 2009, respectively, might appear somewhat prescient given the increasing uptake of international commercial courts within established and internationally recognised legal centres.[10] While not immediately apparent to international practitioners, the national jurisdictions within which the Gulf ICommCs were established had long developed and operated under a set of complex and hybrid legal systems.[11] Contrary to common conceptions, the Arabic language local courts of the United Arab Emirates (UAE) and Qatar do not operate entirely under a civil law jurisdiction, but rather an array of secular Arab civil and commercial legislation, underpinned by elements of *Shari'a* (Islamic jurisprudence) as well as local customary law.[12]

[8] 'Ali al-Muhairi, 'The Development of the UAE Legal System and Unification with the Judicial System' (1996) 11(2) Arab Law Quarterly 116–60, 125.

[9] Ibid., 126.

[10] See, for example, the Singapore International Commercial Court established in 2015, the China International Commercial Court established in 2018 and the Netherlands Commercial Court and Frankfurt Chamber for International Commercial Disputes, both established in 2019.

[11] Andrew Dahdal and Francis Botchway suggest that the recent addition of the international commercial court in Qatar 'means that Qatar is quite unique in not only having a mixed or "hybrid" system but actually having a tri-lateral legal system. This is because, in addition to civil and common law, the influence of Islamic Sharī'ah can also be seen as a source of law in the country" (Andrew Drahdal and Francis Botchway, 'A Decade of Development: The Civil and Commercial Court of the Qatar Financial Centre' (2020) 34 Arab Law Quarterly 59, 62 (hereinafter Dahdal and Botchway, 'A Decade of Development').

[12] By way of example, Article 1 of both the UAE and the Qatari civil codes provides for the application of the civil code legislative provisions, Islamic *Shari'a* and customary practice; see UAE Federal Law No. 5 of 1985 (as amended) and Qatari Law No. 16 of 1971 (as amended).

In 2004, the UAE issued federal legislation concerning financial free zones,[13] establishing the DIFC as a financial free zone in Dubai.[14] This followed the earlier enactment of Dubai local legislation establishing the DIFC in 2002.[15] Subsequent Dubai local legislation established the 'Dispute Resolution Authority' in the DIFC,[16] comprising 'The Centre's Courts' and the 'Arbitration Institute' as separate legal personalities,[17] as well as the DIFC Judicial Authority, which in turn established the DIFC Court of First Instance and Court of Appeal.[18] The UAE was the first Gulf country to introduce an economic free zone with its own special legal system, consisting of laws that only applied inside the zone, and a court system whose jurisdiction was initially confined to cases connected to the special economic zone. In the now fabled words of former DIFC Courts Chief Justice Michael Hwang, the court system of the DIFC jurisdiction, largely modelled on the English Commercial Court, represented 'a common law island in a civil law ocean'.[19]

In line with the DIFC model, the Emirate of Abu Dhabi established an English-language international court system within the ADGM free zone at Al Maryah Island in 2013.[20] Like the DIFC courts, the ADGM Courts

[13] UAE Federal Law No. 8 of 2004, Concerning Financial Free Zones.

[14] UAE Federal Decree No. 35 of 2004, Concerning the Establishment of a Financial Free Zone in the Emirate of Dubai.

[15] Dubai Law No. 3 of 2002, Establishing the Dubai International Financial Centre.

[16] Article 3(3)(c) of Dubai Law No. 9 of 2004, Concerning the Dubai International Financial Centre (as amended).

[17] Article 8 of Dubai. Law No. 9 of 2004, Concerning the Dubai International Financial Centre (as amended).

[18] Dubai Law No. 12 of 2004, Concerning the Judicial Authority of Dubai International Financial Centre (as amended).

[19] Michael Hwang, Lecture, 'The Courts of the Dubai International Finance Centre: A Common Law Island in a Civil Law Ocean', at the Lawasia Conference in Kuala Lumpur, Malaysia on 1 November 2008 (www.difccourts.ae/2008/11/01/the-courts-of-the-dubai-international-finance-centre-a-common-law-island-in-a-civil-law-ocean).

[20] Pursuant to Abu Dhabi Law No. 4 of 2013, Concerning Abu Dhabi Global Market. The complex arrangements which led to the creation of these separate jurisdictions within Dubai and Abu Dhabi, themselves representing two of the UAE's seven emirates, are beyond the scope of this chapter. Yet by way of example, under Article 121 of the UAE Constitution, the UAE has exclusive legislative jurisdiction over the 'regulation of the free financial zones, the manner in which they are established, and how far they are excluded from scope of application of the federal legislative provisions'. Article 3 of the UAE Constitution states, 'A member Emirate shall exercise sovereignty over its own territories and territorial waters in all matters which are not within the jurisdiction of the UAE under the Constitution.' Articles 104, 116, 117, 118 and 122 of the UAE Constitution also enshrine the authority of each emirate within the UAE federal system to issue its own laws.

are equipped with a dedicated judiciary drawn from inside and outside the UAE. The DIFC and ADGM are commonly referred to as 'off-shore' jurisdictions, outside of which, the rest of the emirates of Dubai and Abu Dhabi are referred to as 'onshore' or 'mainland' jurisdictions within the UAE.[21] The DIFC and ADGM companies and establishments conducting activities within the UAE, but outside the borders of the free zones, are subject to UAE federal laws, including the civil and commercial federal laws.[22]

In 2005, the QFC was established as an onshore commercial centre within the State of Qatar.[23] The Civil and Commercial Court of the QFC was subsequently established in 2009.[24] As with the QFC Regulatory Authority and the QFC Regulatory Tribunal, the QFC Courts have financial and administrative autonomy from the Qatari state.[25] Consonant with the incremental expansion of the DIFC jurisdiction, first as a conduit for judicial actions taken outside of the DIFC in mainland Dubai,[26] and later as an opt-in jurisdiction for global litigants,[27] the 'QFC Civil and Commercial Court' was transformed into the 'Qatar International Court and Dispute Resolution Centre'

[21] See, for example, Gordon Blanke, 'Navigating Arbitration in the UAE with Dr Gordon Blanke' (Kluwer Arbitration Blog, 13 December 2019, http://arbitrationblog.kluwerarbitration.com/2019/12/13/navigating-arbitration-in-the-uae-with-dr-gordon-blanke).

[22] Article 3(3) UAE Cabinet Resolution No. 28 of 2007, On the Implementing Regulations of UAE Federal Law No. 8 of 2004, Concerning Financial Free Zones.

[23] Qatari Law No. 7 of 2005, Promulgating the Qatar Financial Centre Law.

[24] Qatari Law No. 2 of 2009, Amending Certain Rules of the Qatar Financial Centre Law Issued under Qatari Law No. 7 of 2005. The constitutional basis for the QFC and corresponding court system appears to fall under Article 121(9) of the Qatari Constitution, which entitles the Council of Ministers to 'approve economic projects and the methods of their implementation'.

[25] Article 8(4) of Qatari Law No. 7 of 2005, Qatar Financial Centre Law (as amended by Qatari Law No. 2 of 2009 and Qatari Law No. 14 of 2009) (QFC Law).

[26] In 2009, the Dubai and DIFC courts entered into a protocol of enforcement containing a reciprocal seven-stage process for enforcing judgments, orders and ratified arbitral awards between the two courts. Also, in 2009, the DIFC courts issued two freezing orders in respect of bank accounts outside of the DIFC (*Mohammed Usman Saleem* v. *Oasis Crescent Capital (DIFC) Limited* [2009] CFI 009/2008, Order of 18 February 2009; and *Shereen Aldisi* v. *Orion Holding Overseas Limited* [2009] DIFC ENF 012/2009, Order of 5 August 2009).

[27] In October 2011, pursuant to Article 5(A) of Dubai Law No. 16 of 2011, Amending Certain Provisions of Law No. 12 of 2004, Concerning Dubai International Financial Centre Courts (Dubai Law No. 16 of 2011), the DIFC expanded its jurisdiction in order to allow the DIFC courts to hear disputes from 'anywhere in the world when the contract in question specifies DIFC Courts' jurisdiction (pre-dispute jurisdiction) or when both parties elect to use DIFC Courts to resolve a dispute which has already arisen (post-dispute jurisdiction)' (DIFC

(QICDRC) in 2012 so as to augment its status as a forum for various alternative dispute resolution (ADR) methods as well as traditional litigation.[28] Unlike the DIFC and ADGM free zones and court systems, the QFC and QICDRC operate as 'onshore' financial and judicial organs. Notwithstanding this distinction, applicable law is generally considered a feature of convergence across these jurisdictions, as elucidated in the following summary intended for businesses seeking to establish in the QFC:

> Similar to the QFC, the DIFC is a business centre established in the Emirate of Dubai to attract foreign direct investment. Both the QFC and the DIFC judges seem to apply English-style common law, and therefore, the QFC and the DIFC share many similarities in respect of the treatment of foreign investors setting up within the QFC and the DIFC and the exemption from a number of specific laws such as foreign investment laws.[29]

The prevalent perception is that an antiquated and quintessentially English common law applies uniformly across these three court systems.[30] In the case of the ADGM, this, at least in part, is fuelled by

Courts, *Courts' Activities and Business Plan 2013–2015*, page 10). Under the same legislative instrument, a regime of mutual recognition was established for reciprocal execution of judgments, decisions and orders between the Dubai and DIFC courts (Article 7 of Dubai Law No. 16 of 2011). In January 2012, the DIFC courts issued its first enforcement under the Protocol on Enforcement of Judgments, Letters Regulatory and Judicial Notices issued by the Courts of the Member States of the Arab Gulf Co-operation Council (see the DIFC Courts Press Release, 'DIFC Courts Honour GCC Justice', dated 29 January 2012: www.difccourts.ae/2012/01/29/29-january-2012-difc-courts-honour-gcc-justice).

28 Article 5(1) of the QFC Civil and Commercial Court Regulations and Procedural Rules, issued on 15 December 2010 (QFC Court Rules), states: 'The Court will encourage the parties, whenever it is appropriate to do so, to resolve their disputes by resorting to arbitration or mediation or any other method of alternative dispute resolution.' It is worth noting that in 2012, the government of the Kingdom of Saudi Arabia released plans to establish 'an arbitration court in the United Kingdom to resolve disputes arising out of Saudi Arabia' (Amgad T. Husein and John M. B. Balouziyeh, *A Legal Guide to Doing Business in Saudi Arabia: Legal and Practical Advice on Company Regulations, Labour, Tax, Finance and Dispute Resolution* ((Westlaw Gulf, Thomson Reuters 2013) 197). The DIFC courts established an arbitration division in February 2020 with the mandate of accommodating a growing number of arbitration-related cases.

29 Al Tamimi & Company, 'Setting Up in Qatar Financial Centre (QFC)' (Al Tamimi & Company 2016) 7–8.

30 The development of English common law itself was the product of hybrid adaptations of rules and concepts from various legal traditions. As the eminent British historian Michael Clancy delineates: 'The distinctive style of English common law derived from many sources and traditions: Anglo-Saxon, Norman, ecclesiastical, Roman and Scholastic. The system took the form it did because it developed in the period of the twelfth century Renaissance and it retained that form for centuries thereafter because bureaucracy

representations from within the jurisdiction itself. Under the heading 'English Common Law', the ADGM Courts state: 'ADGM Courts' regulations and supporting rules enshrine ADGM's legal framework of the direct application of English common law,'[31] which is driven by the values and stated aims of 'judicial impartiality, independence and integrity, global enforceability of judgments and orders, to instill confidence, ensure transparency, achieve access to justice, and to compliment arbitration'.[32] With similar aspirations, the DIFC in 2012 entered into a memorandum of understanding with the UAE Institute of Training and Judicial Studies to promote the DIFC's common law judicial system to UAE national advocates.[33] While the QICDRC also expresses 'five core values' of 'justice, teamwork, integrity, service excellence and innovation', its courts and tribunal are presented as judicial bodies that 'operate in accordance with international best practices', with judges drawn from 'a variety of civil and common law jurisdictions, including Qatar, Kuwait, the United Kingdom, Cyprus, Singapore, New Zealand and South Africa'.[34]

Together with the values attached to 'English common law', applicable law embodies other aspects of symbolic capital, which in turn become factors in creating attractive investment environments for international capital. Sophisticated and increasingly cost-conscious global disputants that rely on an array of dispute resolution forums invariably utilise courts, arbitral tribunals and applicable laws which they perceive as offering certainty, predictability and efficiency. Whether accurate or otherwise, the Arabic-language local court systems of the UAE and Qatar and their underlying hybrid applicable laws continue to be perceived by parties and international practitioners as inefficient and unpredictable.[35] As such, and not without friction, local and international arbitration has long bridged

perpetuated it. Hence later lawyers praised as peculiarly English something that was really peculiarly twelfth century and cosmopolitan. ... Its distinctive form was therefore a product of England's close contact with the continent at the time and not in opposition to them' (Michael T. Clanchy, *England and Its Rulers 1066–1272: Foreign Lordship and National Identity* ((Barnes & Noble Books 1983) 137).

[31] www.adgm.com/adgm-courts/english-common-law

[32] Ibid.

[33] DIFC Courts Press Release, 4 March 2012, 'Ministry of Justice Supports DIFC Courts' Promotion of Dubai's Common Law Judicial System to National Advocates' (www.difc courts.ae/2012/03/04/4-march-2012-ministry-of-justice-supports-difc-courts-promotion-of-dubais-common-law-judicial-system-to-national-advocates).

[34] www.qicdrc.gov.qa/overview

[35] On the broader historic relationship between legal transplants of Roman law into the customary legal systems of European countries, see Alan Watson, *The Evolution of Western Private Law*. Expanded edition (Johns Hopkins University Press 2001).

the actual or perceived gaps in industry expertise and other competencies required for handling complex, high-value disputes within or involving the UAE and Qatar.[36] Recognising the central importance of arbitration in the dispute resolution tapestry of these national legal systems, the DIFC, ADGM and QFC jurisdictions each boast complimentary and expanding arbitration and ADR capabilities. Under this guise, the issue of applicable law becomes inextricably linked to arbitration and thereby central to inter-jurisdictional competition between different national court systems to attract commercial and civil disputes.[37]

In the UAE and Qatar, the applicable laws within the DIFC, ADGM and QICDRC take on a broader importance beyond the strict application of law within their respective court forums. As part of voluntary institutional and legal transplants, which broadly reflect English common law rules and practices, the applicable laws in each jurisdiction represent aspects of contemporary institutional and legal development within the Gulf states. Of course, legal systems and particularly newly established jurisdictions, rarely, if ever, develop incommunicado. In the commercial courts of the Gulf, transfers or borrowing of applicable laws give rise to terms such as 'English-style common law' and 'international common law', which in turn we should be prepared to deconstruct. To this end, the

[36] Chibli Mallat has provided a lucid and insightful explanation of the frictions between local judiciaries and arbitrators across the Middle East; see Chibli Mallat, *Introduction to Middle Eastern Law* (Oxford University Press 2007) 345–53.

[37] With a view to the potential risks for failing to harmonise these inter-jurisdictional court systems, Andrew Dahdal and Francis Botchway lucidly state: 'The divergence or similarity in practices can support the progress towards harmonisation in legal regimes – or at least greater co-operation. Distrust, animosity or even just a lack of understanding between these parallel court systems within a state can lead to significant difficulties in the success or failure of the very economic projects that these transnational courts are designed to support. Cooperation is none so more important than in the context of the enforcement of judgements. The ability of a Court to have its judgements enforced is the fundamental measure of a tribunals effectiveness' (Dahdal and Botchway, 'A Decade of Development', 71–2). See also Faris Nasrallah, 'Article 257 of the UAE Penal Code: Inter-jurisdictional Conflict and the Battleground of Arbitration' (2015–17) 19 Yearbook of Islamic and Middle Eastern Law 334–50. For an assessment of recent decisions issued by the Joint Judicial Committee in Dubai, see Harris Bor, 'Joint Judicial Committee', in Rupert Reed and Tom Montagu-Smith (eds.), *DIFC Courts Practice* (Edward Elgar 2020) 34–47. A more recent example of the tensions borne out between indigenous and received institutions in Dubai can be seen through Dubai Decree No. 34 of 2021, Concerning the Dubai International Arbitration Centre (issued on 20 September 2021), which under Articles 4 and 5 abolished two DIFC-based arbitral institutions and transferred their assets, property and employees to the Dubai International Arbitration Centre.

DIFC, ADGM and QFC each represent comparative law laboratories which offer a fascinating basis for future comparative law studies.[38]

9.3 Applicable Laws within the Courts of the Dubai International Financial Centre, Abu Dhabi Global Market and Qatar Financial Centre

This part of the chapter assesses the applicable laws in the DIFC, ADGM and QFC – including a qualitative analysis of relevant legislation, court rules and selected case law espoused in their respective courts. Each boast vastly disparate case traffic, with the DIFC courts being the busiest of the three courts by some distance. By the end of 2019, the DIFC courts were administering 952 active cases.[39] At the time of writing,[40] more than a decade since its establishment, the QICDRC has published a total of 98 judgments in both English and Arabic.[41] The ADGM courts, the newest of the three courts, have to date published a total of 24 judgments, 20 at the Court of First Instance and 4 at the Court of Appeal.[42] The jurisprudence of each court will continue to develop over time and, by virtue of consistent and comprehensive publication, should give rise to more exhaustive assessments of the legal doctrines applied in the respective courts.

(a) Applicable Law in the DIFC Courts

The DIFC courts are established by and function in accordance with DIFC laws and regulations.[43] Pursuant to Dubai local legislation, the

[38] See generally Rene David and John E. C. Brierly, *Major Legal Systems in the World Today: An Introduction to the Comparative Study of Law.* Second edition (Simon & Schuster 1978); Konrad Zweigert and Hein Kötz, *An Introduction to Comparative Law.* Third *edition* (Clarendon 1998); Werner Menski, *Comparative Law in a Global Context: The Legal Systems of Asia and Africa.* Second edition (Cambridge University Press 2006).

[39] DIFC Courts Annual Review 2019, p. 22 (www.difccourts.ae/2020/02/26/difc-courts-annual-review-2019).

[40] 1 November 2020.

[41] For a useful qualitative analysis of the first ten years of QFC court practice, see Dahdal and Botchway, 'A Decade of Development'.

[42] See www.adgm.com/adgm-courts/judgments.

[43] Article 3(1) of Dubai Law No. 12 of 2004, In Respect of the Judicial Authority at Dubai International Financial Centre (as amended by Dubai Law No. 16 of 2011) (DIFC Judicial Authority Law). Article 8(2)(4) of Dubai Law No. 9 of 2004, Concerning the Dubai International Financial Centre (as amended by Dubai Law No. 7 of 2011, Dubai Law No. 14 of 2011, and Dubai Law No. 7 of 2014) (Dubai Law No. 9 of 2004), states that 'The functions of the Centre's Courts shall be determined in accordance with the Centre's

DIFC courts apply DIFC laws and regulations (i) except where parties to the dispute have explicitly agreed that another law shall govern such dispute; and (ii) provided such law does not conflict with the public policy and public morals.[44] Entities operating within the DIFC are of course free to opt in to any other legal jurisdiction when entering contracts, although 'in the event that parties do not do so, the DIFC laws will be applicable by default and they can file a case in the DIFC Courts'.[45]

Dubai local legislation also provides that the laws, regulations and resolutions of the emirate shall not govern the DIFC courts and DIFC bodies and establishment, including their employees and delegates.[46] The UAE federal civil and commercial laws are not applicable in the DIFC courts, although the DIFC and its courts remain subject to all other UAE federal laws,[47] including treaties ratified into UAE law.[48]

The inductive DIFC legislation dealing with applicable law[49] stated its objectives: (i) to provide certainty as to the rights, liabilities and obligations of persons in relation to civil and commercial matters arising in the DIFC; and (ii) to allow persons to adopt the laws of another jurisdiction in relation to civil and commercial matters arising within the DIFC. Article 8(2) of DIFC Law No. 3 of 2004 provides as follows:

(2) The relevant jurisdiction is to be the one first ascertained under the following paragraphs:
  (a) so far as there is a regulatory content, the DIFC Law or any other law in force in the DIFC; failing which,

Laws, and they shall carry out their duties and powers pursuant to the Centre's Laws and the Centre's Regulations.'

[44] Article 6 of the DIFC Judicial Authority Law. Similarly, under the heading 'Laws Applicable in the Centre', Article 13(1) of Dubai Law No. 9 of 2004, states: 'The Centre's Bodies and Centre Establishments shall carry on its commercial activities in accordance with the Centre's Laws and the Centre's Regulations.'

[45] www.difccourts.ae/about-courts-2/difc-courts-jurisdiction

[46] Article 13(2) Dubai Law No. 9 of 2004.

[47] Article 3(2) of UAE Federal Law No. 8 of 2004, Concerning Financial Free Zones.

[48] Article 5 of UAE Federal Law No. 8 of 2004, Concerning Financial Free Zones provides that financial free zones shall not do anything which may lead to the contravention of any international agreements to which the UAE is or shall be a party. This position was conformed by Justice Sir Jeremy Cooke in *Pearl Petroleum Company Limited & Ors* v. *The Kurdistan Regional Government of Iraq* [2017] DIFC ARB 003 (20 August 2017) [para. 19].

[49] DIFC Law No. 3 of 2004, Law on the Application of Civil and Commercial Laws in the DIFC (DIFC Law No. 3 of 2004).

(b) the law of any Jurisdiction other than that of the DIFC expressly chosen by any DIFC Law; failing which,
(c) the laws of a Jurisdiction as agreed between all the relevant persons concerned in the matter; failing which,
(d) the laws of any Jurisdiction which appears to the Court or Arbitrator to be the one most closely related to the facts of and the persons concerned in the matter; failing which,
(e) the laws of England and Wales.

As a fundamentally statutory body of applicable law, DIFC legislation includes laws, regulations, rules, court administrative orders, practice directions and registrar directions, and authoritative guidance notes for court users, which together encompass a vast canvas of civil and commercial activities.[50] The DIFC Authority (DIFCA) and the Dubai Financial Services Authority (DFSA) are responsible for proposing and submitting draft DIFC laws to the president of the DIFC,[51] who is vested with the power to approve and submit draft DIFC laws to the Ruler of Dubai for issuance.[52] Both the DIFCA and DFSA have the power to approve and issue DIFC regulations falling within their respective jurisdictions.[53] Equally, the chief justice of the DIFC courts has the power to approve and issue DIFC regulations relating to the DIFC courts.[54] In 2002, prior to the establishment of the DIFC courts, the DIFC Regulatory Authority mandated a number of prominent international law firms to draft cornerstone DIFC legislation, including the law establishing the regulatory authority itself.[55]

One of the first reported judgments saw Chief Justice Michael Hwang elaborate the flexible approach of the DIFC courts in seeking the most appropriate applicable law to a preferential debts and insolvency dispute.[56] The court rejected adversarial arguments for the default application of UAE and English law on insolvency, finding that these laws 'are

[50] The latest of which being DIFC Law No. 5 of 2020, the DIFC Data Protection Law.
[51] Articles 6(4)(c) and 7(5)(e) of Dubai Law No. 9 of 2004, respectively. It is notable that the boards of directors of both the DIFCA and the DFSA undertake to provide for public comment on draft laws and regulations falling within their respective jurisdictions (Articles 6(4)(d) and 7(5)(g) of Dubai Law No. 9 of 2004, respectively).
[52] Article 5(2) of Dubai Law No. 9 of 2004.
[53] Articles 6(4)(e) and 7(5)(f) of Dubai Law No. 9 of 2004, respectively.
[54] Article 8(5)(a) of Dubai Law No. 7 of 2014, Amending Dubai Law No. 9 of 2004.
[55] www.difc.ae/newsroom/news/difc-regulatory-authority-appoints-leading-law-firms-draft-difc-legislation
[56] *Forsyth Partners Global Distributors Limited & Ors* [2007] DIFC CFI 005/006/007 (30 January 2007).

influenced by the priorities and social conditions within the respective countries, which do not necessarily apply in the DIFC'.[57] The court applied the DIFC insolvency law,[58] despite the absence of DIFC regulations yet to be promulgated in respect of preferential debts.[59] Similarly, in the absence of employment regulations, the DIFC courts applied DIFC employment law to the exclusion of any other law selected by the parties.[60]

In *Pearl Petroleum Company Limited & Ors* v. *The Kurdistan Regional Government of Iraq*,[61] Justice Sir Jeremy Cooke offered an instructive assessment of applicable law in the DIFC courts:

> It is clear that the basis of the law of the DIFC is statutory . . . the DIFC courts are common law courts, the basis of the Courts' jurisdiction lies in the statutes of the UAE and Dubai. [para. 12]

. . .

> Whilst this Court is a common law court, there is no basis for incorporation of a body of substantive 'common law', whatever that may mean, into the substantive law which falls to be applied in the DIFC. . . . Whilst the law of the DIFC is interpreted in accordance with the methodology of the common law and proceeds incrementally, the courts have no power to create law by incorporating some external body of law for which there is no provision in Article 8 of DIFC Law No 3 of 2004. The DIFC creates its own precedents on the basis of the law to be applied under the provisions of the statutory framework. [para. 18]

Perhaps conscious of the hybrid legal landscape in the DIFC, Dubai and throughout the UAE, Justice Cooke pointed out that the jurisdiction of the DIFC courts 'is founded on statutory provision which requires the law of the DIFC to be first applied and only in absentia to move on to the cascading subparagraphs' provisions, of which the last is the law of England and Wales'.[62] While the statutory basis of applicable law within the DIFC courts contributes to legal certainty, this is by no means coterminous with legal uniformity. By way of example, the fact that the

[57] Ibid., [paras. 42 and 43].

[58] DIFC Law No. 7 of 2004, DIFC Insolvency Law.

[59] *Forsyth Partners Global Distributors Limited & Ors* [2007] DIFC CFI 005/006/007 (30 January 2007) [para. 46].

[60] *Rasmala Investments Limited* v. *various Defendants* [2009] DIFC CFI 001–006/2009 (17 February 2009), before Justice Tan Sri Dato Seri Norma Yaakob on appeal from the Small Claims Tribunal.

[61] [2017] DIFC ARB 003 (20 August 2017).

[62] Ibid., [para. 18].

DIFC Real Property Law is modelled on the Torrens land registration system has not corresponded with the direct application of English case law in this area before the DIFC courts.[63] As one practitioner points out, 'the [DIFC] Court is likely to gain more assistance from other Torrens jurisdictions, such as Australia and Singapore'.[64]

Regarding the application of non-DIFC substantive law,[65] parties are required to identify such law and explain the basis of its application within the statement of case.[66] Concerning the rules of evidence, the DIFC courts are permitted to apply rules they consider appropriate to the circumstances.[67] The DIFC courts have been willing to consult foreign laws, particularly the laws of onshore Dubai and the UAE.[68] As stated by Chief Justice Michael Hwang in *Fidel* v. *(1) Felecia (2) Faraz*:

> On non-DIFC UAE law specifically . . . the majority of the current DIFC judges have expertise and experience in UAE law, either as a result of having trained in and practised in UAE law or having sat on tribunals to resolve disputes in accordance with non-DIFC UAE law (e.g. the Dubai World Tribunal). Further, each overseas judge will have had exposure to substantive UAE law from hearing a number of cases in the DIFC Courts involving issues of UAE law.[69]

In *National Bonds Corporation PJSC* v. *(1) Taaleem PJSC and (2) Deyaar Development PJSC*,[70] the DIFC Court of Appeal was tasked with interpreting a contractual reference to the 'laws of Dubai, UAE to the extent

[63] *Vegie Bar LLC* v. *Emirates National Bank of Dubai Properties PJSC DIFC* [2016] CFI 009 (4 September 2019), [paras. 36, 52 and 104]. Justice Omar Al Muhairi stated succinctly, 'As is well-established, DIFC law is quite unlike English law' [para. 77].

[64] Matthew Watson, 'Substantive Law', in Rupert Reed and Tom Montagu-Smith (eds.) *DIFC Courts Practice* (Edward Elgar 2020) 85–124, 112.

[65] Defined under Part 29.132 of the Rules of the Dubai International Financial Centre Courts 2014. Notably, under Part 2.9 of the DIFC Court Rules, the English Interpretation Act 1978 applies for the interpretation of the rules, pending the enactment of the DIFC Interpretation Act.

[66] Ibid., Part 17.45.

[67] Article 50(c) of the DIFC Law No. 10 of 2004 (DIFC Courts Law).

[68] See for example *DIFC Investments LLC* v. *Mohammed Akbar Mohammed Zia* [2017] CA 005 (10 January 2018) [paras. 32–5], where Justice Sir Jeremy Cooke considers the potential impact of onshore Dubai law and certain provisions of the UAE Civil Code.

[69] *Fidel* v. *(1) Felecia (2) Faraz*: [2015] DIFC CA 002 (22 November 2015) [para. 57]. Hwang also identified that 'the composition of the DIFC Courts bench differs radically from that of the English courts by having judges who have expertise in the laws of various jurisdictions, including Singapore, Australia, Malaysia, New Zealand and the UAE (and possibly in the future from other common law jurisdictions)' [para. 56].

[70] [2011] DIFC CA 001 (5 May 2011).

these laws are not inconsistent with the principles of Sharia'.[71] The court found 'with reasonable confidence' that when parties select the 'Laws of Dubai' as the governing law, 'they intend to select either Civil Law Dubai Law, as applied in the non-DIFC Courts, or Common Law Dubai Law, as applied in the DIFC Courts'.[72] The courts applied DIFC law on the basis that the property underlying the disputed agreement concerned a DIFC-located trust, 'a legal institution unknown to the Civil Law administered in the non-DIFC Courts of Dubai but fully applicable under the law administered in the DIFC Courts'.[73]

The DIFC Court of Appeal subsequently departed from this decision due to 'practical difficulties rendering the *Taaleem* approach unworkable in most scenarios',[74] instead, adopting an 'International Approach' encompassed in the 'Fact Doctrine' applied by international commercial courts and arbitral tribunals, which:

> treat all 'law' as 'law', with Counsel making legal submissions on disputed areas of the applicable (or relevant) law, appending expert opinions if necessary, and, in the case of international commercial courts, the court being allowed to take judicial notice of the foreign law in question (the 'International Approach').[75]

(b) *Applicable Law in the Abu Dhabi Global Market Courts*

Following establishment of the free zone, the ADGM's implementing legislation provided that the management and procedures of 'litigation, judgments and all forms of dispute resolution' concerning the ADGM Courts would be determined by an ADGM board of directors' regulation.[76] The ADGM board of directors has the authority to propose and submit draft ADGM laws to the Abu Dhabi executive council for approval.[77] The head of the ADGM registration bureau is tasked with

71 Ibid., [para. 19].
72 Ibid., [para. 39].
73 Ibid., [para. 46].
74 *Fidel* v. *(1) Felecia (2) Faraz* [2015] DIFC CA 002 (22 November 2015) [para. 65]. It is worth noting that more recently, the DIFC Court of First Instance found that an arbitration agreement governed by 'the laws of the United Arab Emirates' equivocated that 'any reference to UAE law must be a reference to UAE Laws applicable in the DIFC' in matters where DIFC courts held jurisdiction (*Gavin* v. *Gaynor* [2015] DIFC CFI 017 (3 April 2016) [para. 67].
75 Ibid., [para. 67].
76 Article 13(4) of Abu Dhabi Law No. 4 of 2013, Concerning the ADGM.
77 Article 6(2) of Abu Dhabi Law No. 4 of 2013, Concerning the ADGM.

proposing draft ADGM regulations to be submitted to the ADGM board of directors for approval,[78] a power and approval mechanism shared by the ADGM financial services regulations bureau on the organisation of financial services,[79] and subsequently granted to the chief justice of the ADGM Courts.[80] As in the DIFC, UAE federal civil and commercial laws are not applicable in the ADGM and ADGM Courts, although they remain subject to all other UAE federal laws, including treaties ratified into UAE law.

While empowered to develop its own laws and regulations, the ADGM in 2015 chose to issue the 'Application of English Law Regulations 2015' (2015 Regulations), giving legal force to and making directly applicable 'the common law of England (including the principles and rules of equity), as it stands from time to time'.[81] The ADGM sought to ameliorate this blanket direct application of English law and statute, against the following caveats: '(a) so far as it is applicable to the circumstances of the ADGM; (b) subject to such modifications as those circumstances require; (c) subject to any ADGM amendment; and (d) any amended or new English law adopted after the date of 2015 Regulations, shall not apply and have legal force in the ADGM, unless expressly enacted under ADGM law'.[82]

Schedule 1 of the 2015 Regulations references forty-seven English legislative instruments, setting out whether each legislative instrument is to be applied in whole or with specific exceptions. It is not clear the extent to which the ADGM Courts are authorised to exercise discretion under caveats (a) and (b) of Section 1(1), and depart from ADGM incorporated legislation. Under Section 3(1) of the 2015 Regulations, the ADGM Courts and tribunals are required to 'administer English common law and equity on the basis that, wherever there is any conflict or variance between the rules of equity and the rules of the common law with reference to the same matter, the rules of equity shall prevail'. The 2015 Regulations represent the most radical legislative import performed across the region's three ICommC jurisdictions. It remains to be seen whether this ambitious and selective legal transplant can provide sufficient flexibility for the ADGM Courts to address the full

[78] Ibid., Article 11(11).
[79] Ibid., Article 12(6).
[80] Article 6(a) of Abu Dhabi Law No. 12 of 2020, Amending Certain Provisions of Abu Dhabi Law No. 4 of 2013.
[81] Section 1(1) of the Application of English Law Regulations 2015.
[82] Ibid., Section 1(1) (a)–(d).

spectrum of civil and commercial activity within the free zone, as well as institutional relations between the ADGM and the onshore UAE legal system.

In its first published judgment, the ADGM Courts directly applied English civil procedure rules and case precedent.[83] In a dispute over a late payment fee as a form of contractual interest, the ADGM Court upheld the application of UAE Federal Law No. 8 of 2017, on value added tax (VAT), in a claim for non-payment of VAT at a rate of 5 per cent.[84] The ADGM Courts have proceeded cautiously, refraining from opining on their jurisdiction to hear civil cases, which relate to ongoing criminal proceedings in the onshore UAE courts.[85] In a similar vein, Justice Sir Andrew Smith determined that whether and how other proceedings are conducted against companies in administration under an ADGM Court 'is, of course, for other Courts in the UAE to decide'.[86] Perhaps by design, the relatively modest number of reported judgments published to date have produced a largely uncontentious body of case law.

(c) Applicable Law in the Qatar Financial Centre Courts

Under established QFC law, any person, company or entity licensed within the QFC shall be subject to 'supervision, regulation and enforcement procedures' provided by QFC laws and regulations.[87] The QFC courts have the power to prepare draft QFC regulations for enactment by the Qatari minister of economy and commerce,[88] subject to the consent and approval of Qatar's Council of Ministers.[89]

The supervision or regulation of any QFC authorised or licensed business falls outside the jurisdiction of Qatari state institutions, and any potentially applicable laws other than QFC laws and regulations shall not apply 'to the extent they are otherwise excluded by, conflict

[83] *Afkar Capital Limited* v. *Saifallah Fikry* [2017] ADGMCFI1, Justice Sir Andrew Smith (26 November 2017). See also *A3* v. *B3* [2019] ADGMCFI 0006, Justice Sir Andrew Smith (25 August 2019) [para. 5].

[84] *Rosewood Hotel Abu Dhabi LLC* v. *Skelmore Hospitality Group Ltd.* [2019] ADGMCFI 0009, Justice William Stone (16 December 2019).

[85] *Karin Berardo* v. *Stumpf Energy Limited* [2018] ADGMCFI1; Justice Sir Michael Burton (1 May 2018) [paras. 5 and 6].

[86] *NMC Healthcare LTD and associated companies* [2020] ADGMCFI 0008, Justice Sir Andrew Smith (6 October 2020) [para. 60].

[87] Article 11(4) of the QFC Law.

[88] Ibid., Article 9(1).

[89] Ibid., Article 8(7).

with or are inconsistent with QFC regulations'.[90] More specifically, QFC laws and regulations apply to 'contracts, transactions and arrangements' between QFC entities, or involving a QFC entity and entities in Qatar but outside of the QFC, unless the parties agree otherwise.[91]

Schedule 6(8) of the QFC Law mandates the QFC courts to apply QFC laws and regulations to the subject matter of the dispute 'unless the parties have explicitly agreed to apply another law provided that such law is not inconsistent with the public order of the State'.[92] Distinct from the DIFC and ADGM courts, the QFC courts are required to apply Qatari Law No. 13 of 1990, the Qatari Civil and Commercial Procedure Law, to matters in which QFC law and court rules are silent.[93] Qatari criminal laws and sanctions apply in the QFC, and compliance with QFC laws and regulations 'shall not constitute an offence or be a breach of any criminal or other law applicable in the State'.[94] By way of specific exclusion, the QFC court and other QFC institutions shall not be subject to Qatari Law No. 26 of 2005, the Tendering and Bidding Law, or any laws replacing it.[95]

Under the heading 'Applicable Law', the QFC Court Rules state that 'the Court shall apply the QFC Law and QFC Regulations, insofar as the same are applicable'.[96] While the parties may agree on the law applicable to the dispute,[97] the QFC courts will not do so in the event such law is inconsistent with the public order or public policy of Qatar.[98] Equally conscious of their cultural environment, Article 4.6 of the Judicial Code of Conduct of the QICDRC states that:

> Justices from overseas are mindful of Qataris' discrete national, religious, social and cultural characteristics and conduct themselves at all times with appropriate sensitivity and respect for local traditions.

[90] Ibid.

[91] Ibid., Article 18(3).

[92] Under Schedule 6(9) of the QFC Law, the QFC courts also apply QFC laws and regulations in any appeals filed against decisions of the QFC Regulatory Tribunal.

[93] Schedule 6(16) of the QFC Law.

[94] Article 18(1) of the QFC Law.

[95] Ibid., Article 18(6).

[96] Article 11.1.1 of the QFC Court Rules.

[97] See *Kampala Management Consultancy Cluster Associates* v. *Reed Personnel Qatar LLC* [2015] QIC (F) 3, where the QFC courts have allowed the parties every opportunity at the outset of proceedings to state whether they expressly agreed to apply another law than QFC law and regulations.

[98] Article 11.1.2(a) of the QFC Court Rules.

A lucid pronouncement of the QFC courts' position on applicable laws came in *Chedid & Associates Qatar LLC* v. *Said Bou Ayash*,[99] an employment dispute concerning non-competition restraint provisions under an employment contract with a QFC registered entity. The QFC court responded vociferously to the defendant counsel's attempt to guide the court by reference to English case law: 'This is not the correct approach.' Led by the president of the court, Lord Phillips of Worth Matravers, the judgment continued:

> QFC Regulations set out detailed codes of employment law and general contract law. Some of the provisions reflect principles of common law, but in many respects conditions in Qatar differ markedly from conditions in England and other common law countries. Where an issue is governed by a QFC Regulation, the correct approach is to apply that Regulation according to its natural meaning and having particular regard to conditions in Qatar. Foreign jurisprudence can sometimes be of assistance, but it should be used sparingly as a last and not a first resort.[100]

Open to the application of foreign laws and jurisprudence, the QFC courts have consistently been receptive to English common law principles and established English law precedent. The QFC courts first published judgment, *QFCA* v. *Silver Leaf Capital Partners LLC*,[101] saw the court interpret the relevant statutory language of QFC insolvency regulations by reference to the English law concept of 'just and equitable ground for the winding up of a company', as well as the Joint Stock Companies Winding Up Act 1848.[102] In *Abdulla Jassim Al Tamimi* v. *Qatar Financial Centre Authority, Qatar Finance and Business Academy and Employment Standards Office*,[103] the QFC court, referred by counsel to a body of English case authority rather than of its own volition, applied the doctrine of *res judicata* as laid down by Lord Sumption in *Virgin Atlantic Airways Limited* v. *Zodiac Seats UK Ltd.*[104]

99 [2015] QIC (A) 2.

100 Ibid., [para. 18]. Article 11.1.2(b) of the QFC Court Rules provides that the QFC courts 'will in any case apply any consumer protection provisions of the QFC Law and QFC Regulations', over and above any party agreement over the application of different laws.

101 [2009] QIC (F) 1.

102 Ibid., [paras. 31 and 32].

103 [2018] QIC (A) 3.

104 [2013] UKSC 46 [paras. 17 to 26].

9.4 Conclusion

Considering Hersch Lauterpacht's classic work, *The Function of Law in the International Community*,[105] Jose Alvarez summarises how Lauterpacht enumerated ways that 'international judges were entitled (indeed duty-bound) to engage in innovative law making . . . to "find" law where no formal law on a point exists' and 'to balance competing principles – all deployed under a canon of "effectiveness" that would embrace the "larger needs of the international community"'.[106] Equally poignant if not somewhat wistful, Ole Lando observed in respect of applicable laws in international commercial arbitration, that:

> Each legal system has many gaps and the most provident legislator cannot close them all. Nor can he prevent new gaps from arising when social conditions change. No legal system provides certain solutions to all problems. . . . They do not consider special circumstances and changing conditions. The legal process is not and can never be a mere syllogism.[107]

Both of these excerpts succinctly reflect the potential scope and limits facing the DIFC, ADGM and QFC courts, including but not limited to applicable law. This chapter has shown that the issue of applicable law encompasses broader legal, historical and institutional questions beyond legislative provisions and the procedural implementation of law. It also suggests that while the values and symbolic capital attached to applicable law are integral to the identity and aspirations of the jurisdictions and commercial courts, the perception that the DIFC, ADGM and QFC courts uniformly and directly apply 'English common law' is overly simplistic at best.

Mindful of the legal context within which the DIFC, ADGM and QFC jurisdictions and court systems are embedded, they have, to different extents, developed their own hybrid legislation consisting of laws, regulations, court rules and other instruments, which apply *de jure* within their respective court systems. Perhaps inspired by international

105 Hersch Lauterpacht, *The Function of Law in the International Community* (Oxford University Press 2011 (first published in 1933)).

106 Jose Alvarez, 'What Are International Judges For?', in Karen Alter Romano and Yuval Shany (eds.), *The Oxford Handbook of International Adjudication* (Oxford University Press 2013) 163–4.

107 Ole Lando, 'The Law Applicable to the Merits of the Dispute' (1 April 1986) 2(2) Arbitration International 104–15, 113.

judicial and arbitration approaches, they have equally incorporated provisions for the application of foreign laws. Whether by design or otherwise, the DIFC, ADGM and QFC jurisdictions and court systems have transplanted and adapted aspects of English common law and procedure to meet the commercial and legal realties within their wider cultural and legal environments.

PART III

Procedure, Function, Organization

10

The Design of International Commercial Courts

From Organizational Hybridity to Functional Interoperability

GEORGIOS DIMITROPOULOS*

10.1 Introduction

International commercial courts (ICommCs) are an institutional innovation in international and transnational adjudication.[1] International commercial courts are specialized private and commercial law courts that coexist with ordinary domestic courts as the default forum of general

* I am most grateful to Stavros Brekoulakis for wonderful comments, as well as Almas Lokhandwala for excellent research assistance. The usual disclaimer applies.

[1] See generally Denise Huiwen Wong, 'The Rise of the International Commercial Court: What Is It and Will It Work?' (2014) 33 Civil Justice Quarterly 205; Zain Al Abdin Sharar and Mohammed Al Khulaifi, 'The Courts in Qatar Financial Centre and Dubai International Financial Centre: A Comparative Analysis' (2016) 46 Hong Kong LJ 529; Firew Tiba, 'The Emergence of Hybrid International Commercial Courts and the Future of Cross Border Commercial Dispute Resolution in Asia' (2016–17) 14 Loy U Chi Int'l L Rev 31; Sundaresh Menon, 'International Commercial Courts: Towards a Transnational System of Dispute Resolution' (*DIFC Courts Lecture Series* 2015), www.supremecourt.gov.sg/docs/default-source/default-document-library/media-room/opening-lecture–difc-lecture-series-2015.pdf, accessed 1 November 2020 (hereinafter: Menon, ICommCs: Towards a Transnational System); Xandra Kramer and John Sorabji, 'Editorial: International Business Courts in Europe and Beyond: A Global Competition for Justice?' (Special Issue 2019) Erasmus Law Review; Juan Carlos Urquidi Herrera, 'International Commercial Courts: Similarities and Disparities' (2019) 40 Business Law Review 232; Sir William Blair, 'The New Litigation Landscape: International Commercial Courts and Procedural Innovations', International Journal of Procedural Law 212 (2019); Pamela Bookman, 'The Adjudication Business' (2020) 45 Yale Journal of International Law 227; Matthew S. Erie, 'The New Legal Hubs: The Emergent Landscape of International Commercial Dispute Resolution' (2020) 60 Virginia Journal of International Law 228; Anthea Roberts, 'Introduction to the Symposium on Global Labs of International Commercial Dispute Resolution' (2021) 115 AJIL Unbound 1 (as well as the other contributions in the 'Global Labs of International Commercial Dispute Resolution' symposium).

jurisdiction for all domestic matters.[2] They further coexist with international arbitration, which is arguably the preferred forum for the adjudication of commercial disputes with a transnational character. Starting as 'exotic novelties'[3] only a couple of years ago, ICommCs are currently proliferating and finding their own place in the system of domestic and international adjudication:[4] they have spread from the Middle East to the whole of Asia as well as Europe, with even more countries discussing the idea of establishing such courts.[5] This chapter identifies three different categories of ICommCs: 1) ICommCs that form part of a Special Economic Zone, such as the Dubai International Financial Centre (DIFC) Courts, the Qatar International Court and Dispute Resolution Centre (QICDRC) and the Abu Dhabi Global Market (ADGM) Courts; 2) Stand-alone ICommCs that try cases that are 'international' and 'commercial' in nature such as the Singapore International Commercial Court (SICC) and China International Commercial Court (CICC); 3) International chambers within ordinary domestic courts such as the chambers in the courts of Frankfurt, Paris and Amsterdam.[6]

International commercial courts form part of the judicial globalization trend that started with the proliferation of international courts and tribunals in the post–World War II era and the effort on behalf of

[2] There are specialist commercial courts that are not international in this sense; see Justice Ian Kawaley, 'The Role of Specialist Commercial Courts' (2010) 18 Journal of the Commonwealth Magistrates' and Judges' Association 16. On the contemporary roles of commercial courts see Sir William Blair, Contemporary Trends in the Resolution of International Commercial and Financial Disputes, Institute of Commercial and Corporate Law Annual Lecture 2016, Durham University (21 January 2016); see also The Right Hon. The Lord Thomas of Cwmgiedd, Lord Chief Justice of England and Wales, Commercial Justice in the Global Village: The Role of Commercial Courts, DIFC Academy of Law Lecture, Dubai 1 February 2016.

[3] The explanatory memorandum of the now abandoned project to establish a Brussels International Business Court (BIBC) used the term *nouveautés exotiques* to describe ICommCs; see Exploratory Memorandum of the Projet de loi instaurant la *Brussels International Business Court*, www.dekamer.be/flwb/pdf/54/3072/54K3072001.pdf, p. 12.

[4] On the diversity of the current system of international adjudication see W. Michael Reisman, 'The Diversity of Contemporary International Dispute Resolution: Functions and Policies' (2012) 3 Journal of International Dispute Settlement 1.

[5] One example is Australia; see The Hon Justice A. S. Bel, An Australian International Commercial Court – Not a Bad Idea Or What a Bad Idea?, 2019 ABA Biennial International Conference, Singapore (12 July 2019), www.supremecourt.justice.nsw.gov.au/Documents/Publications/Speeches/2019%20Speeches/Bell_20190712.pdf, accessed 1 November 2020.

[6] See also Georgios Dimitropoulos, 'International Commercial Courts in the "Modern Law of Nature": Adjudicatory Unilateralism in Special Economic Zones' (2021) 24 Journal of International Economic Law 361.

international organizations to promote international best practice in domestic courts.[7] International commercial courts follow the trend of internationalization of dispute resolution, while at the same time reversing it: as domestic institutions with an international outlook, that contribute towards the promotion of international commerce and investment, as well as the resolution of cross-border disputes, they contribute to economic and legal globalization in a bottom-up way.[8]

At the intersection between the spheres of the international and the domestic, ICommCs are hybrid institutions; they integrate design features that are usually attributable to international arbitration together with traditional court characteristics. At the same time, while institutionally embedded within a national jurisdiction, ICommCs serve an international function. This function is twofold: in the absence of dispute resolution fora designed for the resolution of cross-border disputes among individuals, ICommCs have been established to cover this gap in international and transnational adjudication. From a political economy perspective, ICommCs are an important feature in government strategies to internationalize their domestic legal orders with a view to attracting foreign direct investment (FDI) and establishing themselves as worldwide or region-wide dispute resolution hubs.

It is ICommCs' functions that allows them the characterization 'international'. The organizational hybridity of ICommCs is conditioned upon their functional internationalism. Accordingly, the bench of an ICommC is composed of judges who are not necessarily nationals of the host jurisdiction; they use sets of rules other than those used in the ordinary courts of the host jurisdiction; the default language of proceedings is English and not the official language of the host jurisdiction. The rise of a domestic institution with international functions has spearheaded the development of a series of mechanisms of functional interoperability between ICommCs and the other fora of domestic and international adjudication.

Section 10.2 discusses the internationalism of ICommCs. It presents the contemporary spread of ICommCs, as well as a typology of the emerging institution. It explains that ICommCs may be seen as both organizationally and functionally international. The organizational internationalism is conditioned upon the international functions ICommCs

[7] See also Georgios Dimitropoulos and Stavros Brekoulakis, 'International Commercial Courts' (Introduction), in this volume.

[8] Cf. also Jayanth K. Krishnan and Priya Purohit, 'A Common Law Court in an Uncommon Environment: The DIFC Judiciary and Global Commercial Dispute Resolution' (2015) 300 Am Rev Int'l Arb 497, 498.

are serving. Section 10.3 discusses ICommCs as hybrid institutions that draw their design both from ordinary domestic courts and international arbitration. Beyond their hybridity, ICommCs have been established to play a new function in international and transnational adjudication, and as a result mechanisms of interoperability between them and other domestic and international dispute resolution fora are in the process of being established.

10.2 The Internationalism of International Commercial Courts: Organizational and Functional

International commercial courts may be classified under three categories depending on where they stand organizationally in the overall court structure of the jurisdiction that establishes them. There are ICommCs that are attached to a Special Economic Zone (SEZ); international commercial stand-alone courts that form part of a broader national jurisdiction; international commercial chambers within the ordinary national court structure. While they are both organizationally and functionally international, it is their function within current systems of global and domestic governance that qualifies ICommCs of all three types as a truly 'international' institutional phenomenon.

10.2.1 A Typology of International Commercial Courts

International commercial courts have seen a very rapid rise. They came into existence and rose to prominence in the Gulf Region and quickly spread towards first the east and then the west, facing in this journey important successes – as well as some failures – thus establishing themselves as a new paradigm in international and transnational adjudication. This section presents the three different types of international commercial courts.

Special Economic Zone Courts

The trend of establishing ICommCs started in 2004 in Dubai with the Dubai International Financial Centre (DIFC) Courts.[9] The DIFC Courts are established within the free financial zone of the DIFC, and now form

[9] The DIFC Courts were established in 2004 and started operating in 2006; see Dubai Law No. 12 of 2004: The Law of the Judicial Authority at Dubai International Financial Centre, as amended. See generally Jayanth K. Krishnan, *The Story of the Dubai International Financial Centre Courts: A Retrospective* (Motivate 2018).

part of the DIFC's Dispute Resolution Authority (DRA).[10] The DIFC Courts feature a Court of First Instance (CFI) – with a Small Claims Tribunal (SCT) – and a Court of Appeal (CA). While the jurisdiction of the DIFC Courts originally was limited to the geographical area of the DIFC dealing with zone-related disputes, their jurisdiction was extended in 2011 by allowing them to hear any domestic or international case commercial dispute with the consent of all parties.[11] DIFC Courts have jurisdiction *ratione materiae* over cases governing civil and commercial matters. Unless otherwise agreed by parties, DIFC law is applicable before the courts. The DIFC law is largely based on the English common law.[12] The bench has an international composition with a focus on judges coming from common law jurisdictions. Accordingly, the language of proceedings is English.

Five years later, the Civil and Commercial Court of the Qatar Financial Centre was established within the Qatar Financial Centre (QFC) in the State of Qatar.[13] The QFC Civil and Commercial Court became known as the Qatar International Court and Dispute Resolution Centre (QICDRC) in 2012. The QICDRC has a First Instance Circuit and an Appellate Division. The First Instance Circuit has jurisdiction over civil and commercial disputes arising between parties that have a connection to the QFC.[14] The QICDRC applies as a default the laws and regulations of the QFC, unless the parties have agreed to the application of the substantive law of a different jurisdiction.[15] The default language of proceedings is English,[16] but the parties may also choose Arabic, while the Court's decisions are announced publicly online in English and Arabic on the

[10] See Articles 3 and 8 of Dubai Law No. 9 of 2004: The Law Establishing the Dubai International Financial Centre.

[11] See Article 5 of Law No. (16) of 2011 Amending Certain Provisions of Law No. (12) of 2004 Concerning Dubai International Financial Centre Courts.

[12] Alejandro Carballo, 'The Law of the Dubai International Financial Centre: Common Law Oasis or Mirage within the UAE?' (2007) 21 Arab Law Quarterly 91.

[13] See Article 8(3) of the QFC Law – Law No. (7) of 2005 – as amended by Law No. 2 of 2009 (Amending Certain Provisions of the Qatar Financial Centre (QFC); see generally Gerald Lebovits and Delphine Miller, 'Litigating in the Qatar International Court', 28 (1) NYSBA International Law Practicum 54 (2015), https://papers.ssrn.com/sol3/papers.cfm?abstract_id=2616475, accessed 30 September 2020; Andrew Mazen Dahdal and Francis Botchway, 'A Decade of Development: The Civil and Commercial Court of the Qatar Financial Centre' (2019) 34 Arab Law Quarterly 1.

[14] See Article 8(3) of the QFC Law.

[15] Articles 11.1.1. and 11.1.2 of The Qatar Financial Centre Civil and Commercial Court Regulations and Procedural Rules.

[16] Ibid., Article 3.2.

Court's website.[17] Judges come from all over the world, with an emphasis on England and the common law world.

Similar developments have been taking place in the Emirate of Abu Dhabi and its Abu Dhabi Global Market (ADGM) financial zone that hosts the ADGM Courts.[18] The ADGM Courts were established in 2013 and have operated since 2015. They also have two instances, a Court of First Instance and a Court of Appeal. The ADGM Courts hear civil and commercial cases arising out of the ADGM; they moreover have jurisdiction conferred on them by any request of the parties to have the Court of First Instance determine the claim or dispute.[19] English common law finds direct application in the ADGM based on the ADGM 'Application of English Law Regulations' 2015. The bench entertains an international composition with a focus on judges with a common law background, and the language of proceedings is English.

Kazakhstan has been leading similar initiatives to the ones in the Gulf Region by establishing the Astana International Financial Centre (AIFC) that features the AIFC Court.[20] The AIFC Court was formally established in 2015, and started operating in 2018. Following the example of the DIFC Courts, it has a Court of First Instance, which has a fast-track procedure for small claims, and a Court of Appeal. The AIFC Court hears commercial and contractual disputes adjudicating all claims arising out of the AIFC and its operations, and other claims in which all parties to the dispute agree in writing to the jurisdiction of the AIFC Court. Applicable law is AIFC law, which is essentially English common law. The bench of this court is also composed of international judges with a common law focus. In fact, for the time being the judges have been drawn exclusively from the UK. The language of proceedings is English.

All four of the aforementioned courts are established within an SEZ. According to a World Bank definition, 'SEZs are generally defined as geographically delimited areas administered by a single body, offering certain incentives ... to businesses which physically locate within the

[17] See www.qicdrc.com.qa/the-courts/judgments, accessed 30 September 2020.

[18] Abu Dhabi Law No. (4) of 2013 Concerning Abu Dhabi Global Market, as amended.

[19] Section 16(2)(e) of the ADGM Courts, Civil Evidence, Judgments, Enforcement and Judicial Appointments Regulations 2015.

[20] See Constitutional Statute no. No 438-V ZRK of 7 December 2015: Astana Financial Services Authority (AFSA); AIFC Court; AIFC International Arbitration Centre (IAC); see generally Nicolas Zambrana-Tevar, 'The Court of the Astana International Financial Center in the Wake of Its Predecessors' (2019) Erasmus Law Review 122.

zone.'[21] The zone laws apply only within the bounds of the relevant zone, and the registered companies are only allowed to operate within the limits of the relevant zones.[22] The default jurisdiction of the courts refers to cases arising out of the relevant SEZ.

In addition to being part of a free zone, the courts of this first category have other common features: first, they have international benches comprised of judges coming from different parts of the world. Their benches are currently composed of eminent judges and practitioners with great experience in their home jurisdictions, particularly in dealing with commercial and financial matters; second, the default language of proceedings is English; third, their procedural rules are based on the Commercial Court of England and Wales; fourth, the law of the SEZ is applicable law before these courts; in the case of all courts of this category, the law of the relevant zone is a transposition of English common law or otherwise English law.

Stand-Alone International Commercial Courts

A second category of ICommCs includes courts that are stand-alone, while at the same time forming part of the regular court structure of the host country. The first and prime example of this category is the Singapore International Commercial Court (SICC), which was established in 2015 as a division of the High Court of Singapore.[23] Chief Justice Sundaresh Menon was inspired by the success of the English Commercial Court and decided to initiate the process of establishing a similar court in Singapore in 2012.[24] While institutionally embedded

[21] World Bank, *Special Economic Zone: Performance, Lessons Learned, and Implication for Zone Development* (World Bank 2008) 2.

[22] The QFC is sometimes identified as an 'onshore zone' given that at least at the moment all QFC registered entities are allowed to operate anywhere in the State of Qatar; see Article 2 of the QFC Law. The other zones are geographically bound.

[23] See Section 18A, Supreme Court of Judicature Act (Cap 322); Report of the Singapore International Commercial Court Committee' (*SICC*, November 2013), www.sicc.gov.sg/documents/docs/Annex%20A%20-%20SICC%20Committee%20Report.pdf, accessed 1 November 2020; Man Yip, 'The Resolution of Disputes before the Singapore International Commercial Court' (2016) 65 ICLQ 439 (hereinafter: Yip, 'The Resolution of Disputes'); Andrew Godwin, Ian Ramsay and Miranda Webster, 'International Commercial Courts: The Singapore Experience' (2017) 18 Melbourne Journal of International Law 219; Sundaresh Menon, 'The Rule of Law and Singapore International Commercial Court' (*SICC*, 10 January 2018), www.sicc.gov.sg/docs/default-source/modules-document/news-and-article/b_58692c78-fc83-48e0-8da9-258928974ffc.pdf, accessed 1 November 2020 (hereinafter: Menon, 'The Rule of Law and SICC').

[24] See Menon, ICommCs: Towards a Transnational System.

into the Singapore High Court, its jurisdictional rules are different as the SICC does not hear domestic cases: According to Chief Justice Menon, 'the SICC is an institution that seeks to harness the best aspects of court litigation for the resolution of transnational commercial disputes in the region'.[25] In order to accommodate this, an organizational innovation is that the bench of the SICC comprises two groups of judges: domestic judges – namely, Singapore Supreme Court judges from both the Court of Appeal and the High Court – as well as 'international judges' drawn from the common as well as the civil law world.[26]

The institutional embeddedness of the SICC in the High Court of Singapore means that this court is serviced by the ordinary court structure in cases, for example, of enforcement or appeal as the judgments of the SICC may be appealed before the Court of Appeal of the Supreme Court of Singapore. Applicable law is that of Singapore unless otherwise determined by the parties, and the language of proceedings is English as the official language of the Republic of Singapore.[27]

The real innovation of the SICC is its jurisdiction. The SICC legislation has envisaged a novel jurisdiction for claims that are of an 'international and commercial' nature.[28] The court has been created for the litigation of international commercial disputes, including those governed by foreign law with only tenuous connections to Singapore – if the claims are of an international and commercial nature and the parties have submitted to the court's jurisdiction under a written jurisdiction agreement.[29]

China has a long history of what would be identified today as international commercial courts.[30] During the 19th National Party Conference of the Communist Party of China, the 'Opinions on the Establishment of International Commercial Dispute Resolution Mechanism and Institutions Concerning the Belt and Road Initiative' was released by the Office of the Central Party Committee and the Office of State Council announcing the establishment of an international commercial court for China. On 29 June 2018, the First International Commercial Court and the Second International Commercial Court of

[25] Menon, 'The Rule of Law and SICC', at 11 (emphasis in the original).

[26] See www.sicc.gov.sg/about-the-sicc/judges, accessed 1 November 2020.

[27] According to Chief Justice Menon, the common law of Singapore is increasingly domestic; Menon, ICommCs: Towards a Transnational System, at 17 (with further references).

[28] See Section 18D(1)(a) of the Supreme Court of Judicature Act.

[29] Yip, 'The Resolution of Disputes', at 446.

[30] See, for example, Par Kristoffer Cassel, *Grounds of Judgment: Extraterritoriality and Imperial Power in Nineteenth-Century China and Japan* (Oxford University Press 2013).

the Supreme People's Court (SPC) were respectively inaugurated in Shenzhen and Xi'an and started to operate officially.[31] They are referred to as the China International Commercial Court (CICC). The CICC has been established by the SPC to hear international commercial cases.[32] The Fourth Civil Division of SPC is responsible for coordinating and guiding the CICC. In contrast to all other ICommCs, its judgments are not subject to appeal.

On 27 October 2017, the Belgian Council of Ministers approved the establishment of the Brussels International Business Court (BIBC).[33] The BIBC was scheduled to become operational by 1 January 2020, aiming to attract potential cases arising from Brexit as well as any other type of international business disputes. Organizationally, the BIBC was scheduled to have a president, a vice president, professional judges and 'Judges in the BIBC' – namely, judges who would be experts in international business law, university professors or lawyers, with proceedings taking place in the English language, and governed by the United Nations Commission on International Trade Law (UNCITRAL) Arbitration rules – not the Belgian Judicial Code. After some concerns expressed by the Conseil supérieur de la Justice (CSJ), this court never saw the light of the day.[34]

Courts discussed under this section form part of the general structure of the ordinary courts of the host jurisdiction. The main feature of this type of ICommC is the *ratione materiae* identification of a new jurisdiction for 'international commercial' cases. According to section 18D of the Supreme Court of Judicature Act, the SICC has jurisdiction to hear an

[31] Matthew S. Erie, 'The China International Commercial Court: Prospects for Dispute Resolution for the "Belt and Road Initiative"', ASIL Insights (31 August 2018); Zachary Mollengarden, '"One-Stop" Dispute Resolution on the Belt and Road: Toward an International Commercial Court with Chinese Characteristics' (2019) 36(1) UCLA Pacific Basin Law Journal 65; Sheng Zhang, 'China's International Commercial Court: Background, Obstacles and the Road Ahead' (2020) 11 Journal of International Dispute Settlement 150; Julien Chaisse and Xu Qian, 'China International Commercial Court' (Chapter 19), in this volume.

[32] See generally Zhengxin Guo and Man Yip, 'Comparing the International Commercial Courts of China with the Singapore International Commercial Court' (2019) 68 Int'l & Comp L Q 916.

[33] 'Draft Bill for Brussels International Business Court (German, French)' (Belgium Chamber of Representatives, 15 May 2018), www.dekamer.be/FLWB/PDF/54/3072/54K3072001.pdf, accessed 1 November 2020; see generally Erik Peetermans and Philippe Lambrecht, 'The Brussels International Business Court: Initial Overview and Analysis' (2019) Erasmus Law Review 42.

[34] See Conseil supérieur de la Justice, Avis d'office – Avant-projet de loi instaurant la Brussels International Business Court (March 2018).

action if the following conditions are satisfied: (a) the action is international and commercial in nature; (b) the action is one that the High Court may hear and try in its original civil jurisdiction; (c) the action satisfies such other conditions as the Rules of Court may prescribe. Similar provisions are found in the CICC,[35] as well as in the draft documents of the BIBC.[36] While these courts are part of the overall court structure of the host country, they create at the same time a separate jurisdiction for the adjudication of matters that are not part of the standard domestic case repertoire of national courts. This is not to say that ordinary domestic courts do not have the power to hear cases that are international and commercial. This can be done by any court based on a jurisdiction agreement between parties. What is new is that these courts are specifically designed to accommodate 'international commercial' cases.

Apart from the identification of their jurisdiction as international and commercial, these courts have further common characteristics: they feature a mix of domestic and international judges. Given the procedural constraints of appointing non-Chinese nationals as judges, the CICC does not have an international bench per se but rather an International Commercial Law Expert Committee, the members of which may be called to offer their services in different stages of the proceedings. Finally, both in the SICC and the CICC domestic law is the default choice.

International Chambers within Ordinary Courts

The BIBC was only one among many efforts to internationalize domestic courts in Europe. Some countries in the European Union (EU) have started developing their own type of ICommC. Given political as well as constitutional constraints, they have taken the path of establishing international chambers within the ordinary courts.[37]

[35] Article 2 of the Provisions of the Supreme People's Court on Several Issues Regarding the Establishment of the International Commercial Court (promulgated by the Supreme People's Court, 27 June 2018, effective July 1, 2018).

[36] See for example Article 15 of the draft, proposing to introduce a new Article 576/1 in the relevant Belgian legislation.

[37] See generally Xandra Kramer, 'The Domino Effect of International Commercial Courts in Europe – Who's Next?' (Conflict of Laws, 20 February 2018), http://conflictoflaws.net/2018/the-domino-effect-of-international-commercial-courts-in-europe-whos-next, accessed 1 November 2020; Marieke Witkamp, 'Internationalizing Domestic Courts in Europe' (Chapter 11), in this volume.

A special chamber for commercial law cases operates in the German State of Hesse as of January 2018.[38] It is based in the *Landgericht* (LG) Frankfurt am Main in Hesse. The main novelty of the German chamber is allowing hearings to be conducted in English if agreed upon by both parties. There are otherwise no major changes in court structure.

In February 2018, two agreements were signed between the French Minister of Justice and the Head of the Paris Bar Association at the Paris Court of Appeal for the purpose of creating an international chamber within the Paris Court of Appeal, and regarding the procedural rules of the Paris Commercial Court and the Paris Court of Appeals.[39] The agreements specify the conditions under which the already existent International Chamber of the Paris Commercial Court and the newly established International Chamber of the Paris Court of Appeals (CICAP) should operate to hear international commercial disputes. As of 1 March 2018, the new court chamber allows parties to plead in English, as it features English-speaking French judges who may have expertise in common law systems. The written submissions and other procedural documents provided for in the French civil procedure have to be in French;[40] final judgments are also issued in French.[41]

In 2018, the Dutch Code of Civil Procedure was amended to provide for the use of English as the language of proceedings within 'an international commercial chamber' of the Amsterdam District Court (NCC District Court) and the Court of Appeal (NCC Court of Appeal), commonly referred to as the Netherlands Commercial Court (NCC).[42] The

[38] Jenny Gesley, 'Germany: Regional Court of Frankfurt Establishes English-Speaking Chamber for Commercial Matters' (Library of Congress, 6 December 2017), www.loc.gov/law/foreign-news/article/germany-regional-court-of-frankfurt-establishes-english-speaking-chamber-for-commercial-matters, accessed 1 November 2020; see generally Burkhard Hess and Timon Boerner, 'Chambers for International Commercial Disputes in Germany' (2019) Erasmus Law Review 33.

[39] PRECONISATIONS SUR LA MISE EN PLACE À PARIS DE CHAMBRES SPECIALISEES pour le traitement du contentieux international des affaires (3 May 2017), www.justice.gouv.fr/publication/Rapport_chambres_internationales.pdf, accessed 1 November 2020; see generally Alexandre Biard, 'International Commercial Courts in France: Innovation without Revolution?' (2019) Erasmus Law Review 24.

[40] Exhibits may be exchanged in English without the need for translation. Pleas, expert testimonies and similar statements are allowed in English with simultaneous interpretation. This is to ensure compliance with Article 2 of the French Constitution of 1958 as well as the Ordinance of Villers-Cotterêts (25 August 1539) that identify French as the language of proceedings before French courts; ibid., at para. 36.

[41] See ibid., at para. 51.

[42] See generally Eddy Bauw, 'Commercial Litigation in Europe in Transformation: The Case of the Netherlands Commercial Court' (2019) Erasmus Law Review 15.

institutional arrangements are similar to those of the courts in Frankfurt and Paris.

The chambers in Frankfurt, Paris and Amsterdam build on the existing court structure of the host jurisdictions and introduce changes in comparison to the ordinary domestic court structure with the intention of making them more attractive for the adjudication of cross-border disputes. The main idea is to introduce English as the language of proceedings for the facilitation of hearings of cross-border disputes. This organizational change within the ordinary courts has been accompanied in the Netherlands and to some extent in France by a major branding effort for the new chambers. Procedurally, the ICommCs of this third category mostly rely on the ordinary rules of civil procedure.

10.2.2 Internationalism in International Commercial Courts

Given the variety and diversity of ICommCs, it is not straightforward to identify what qualifies these courts as 'international'. Courts of all three categories are domestic and form part of a domestic legal order; on the other side, they are different from the ordinary courts of the host jurisdiction. It is the departure from the domestic normalcy that allows their characterization as 'international'. The present section discusses the features of internationalism of ICommCs distinguishing between organizational and functional internationalism.

Organizational Internationalism

The international legal order was until recently not court-centred. But globalization and global governance have been accompanied by a process of 'international judicialization', leading to the establishment and proliferation of judicial and quasi-judicial bodies for the adjudication of international disputes.[43] An international judicial body is (i) a permanent

[43] International judicialization is also referred to as 'judicial globalization'; see generally Alec Stone Sweet, 'Judicialization and the Construction of Governance' (1999) 32 Comparative Political Studies 147; Robert O. Keohane, Andrew Moravcsik and Anne-Marie Slaughter, 'Legalized Dispute Resolution: Interstate and Transnational' (2000) 54 International Organization 457; Jenny S. Martinez, 'Toward an International Judicial System' (2003) 56 Stanford Law Review 429; Karen J. Alter, *The New Terrain of International Law: International Courts in International Politics* (Princeton University Press 2014); Cesare P. R. Romano, Karen J. Alter and Yuval Shany (eds.), *The Oxford Handbook of International Adjudication* (Oxford University Press 2015); William A. Schabas and Shannonbrooke Murphy (eds.), *Research Handbook on International Courts and Tribunals* (Edward Elgar 2017); see also on the ends of international

institution, (ii) established under an international treaty, which (iii) relies on public international law to resolve cases, (iv) following set rules of procedure, and (v) issues legally binding judgments.[44] Moreover, international courts often form part of an international organization,[45] while their jurisdiction usually depends on party consent.[46] International commercial courts satisfy some of the criteria of this definition as they are (i) permanent institutions that generally (iv) follow set rules of procedure and (v) issue legally binding judgments. They are of course not established under an international treaty or in the frame of an international organization; instead, they are creatures of a sovereign act under domestic law. International commercial courts do not also rely on international law to resolve disputes. Their internationalism is different.

International commercial courts are organizationally international. In the words of Lucy Reed: 'Their *international* profile comes from their case load, bench, bar and/or rules'.[47] The cases of ICommCs have a cross-border element in the way discussed in Section 10.2.1 for the different categories of courts.[48] The parties that appear before them will usually not have a connection with the ordinary jurisdiction of the host country. Their judges are drawn from various jurisdictions or are familiar with foreign laws, especially English law. The rules on legal representation are more liberal as well, providing rights of audience to lawyers from many systems.[49] In addition, the default language of most ICommCs is

judicialization Philippe Sands, 'Reflections on International Judicialization' (2016) European Journal of International Law 885.

44 Cesare P. R. Romano, 'The Proliferation of International Judicial Bodies: The Pieces of the Puzzle' (1999) 31 NYU J Int'L L & Pol 709; see also Christian Tomuschat, 'International Courts and Tribunals', Max Planck Encyclopedia of Public International Law [MPEPIL] https://opil.ouplaw.com/view/10.1093/law:epil/9780199231690/law-9780199231690-e35 (Article last updated February 2011); Wong, note 1 above, at 214–15.

45 Tomuschat, note 44 above, at para. 7.

46 James Crawford and Joe McIntyre, 'The Independence and Impartiality of the "International Judiciary"', in Shimon Shetreet and Christopher Forsyth (eds.), *The Culture of Judicial Independence: Conceptual Foundations and Practical Challenges* (Brill 2012) 189, at 191. On the 'new generation' of international courts that exercise compulsory jurisdiction – and have powers to render enforceable judgments – see Gary B. Born, 'A New Generation of International Adjudication' (2012) 61 Duke LJ 775.

47 Lucy Reed, 'International Dispute Resolution Courts: Retreat or Advance? 10th John E. C. Brierley Memorial Lecture' (2017–18) 4 McGill Journal of Dispute Resolution 129, 137 (emphasis in the original).

48 See, for example, the first cryptocurrency case before the SICC: *B2C2 Ltd* v. *Quoine Pte Ltd* [2019] SGHC(I) 03.

49 See Zachary R. Calo, 'Counsel Ethics in Transnational Lawyering' (Chapter 13), in this volume.

English – either for oral hearings and/or written submissions. Finally, most ICommCs use some version of the (English) common law, or other foreign law, instead of the ordinary law of the host jurisdiction, or at least welcome the use of foreign law.

The major and fundamental difference between ICommCs and an international court according to the aforementioned definition of an international court is that the former have jurisdiction to and aim at resolving private and commercial disputes between private parties, while the latter resolve public international law disputes involving a State as at least one of the parties. Thus, while these courts do not necessarily satisfy the formal definition of an international court, they could be understood as international courts from a more functional perspective. The next section argues that the main criterion that qualifies these courts as international is their function.

Functional Internationalism

According to V. K. Rajah, ICommCs are 'domestic courts rooted in the legal system of their home jurisdictions, but specially created and tailored in terms of structure and personnel to meet the needs of transnational commercial disputes'.[50] The same is also reflected in the vision and mission of ICommCs as described by Chief Justice of Singapore Sundaresh Menon, according to whom their mission should be 'to facilitate international commerce in a flattened world marked by an extremely high degree of economic interconnectedness. They should support international commerce by enforcing bargains and resolving disputes across national boundaries'.[51]

International commercial courts are international in that they perform an international function – and the international function spills over into their organization. They are functionally international in the following double sense. First, the courts of all three categories are domestic courts for international commercial disputes, or international business, more broadly defined. In this, they cover a gap in (the existing structure of) international and transnational adjudication.[52] They are created to

[50] V. K. Rajah, SC, 'W(h)ither Adversarial Commercial Dispute Resolution?' (2017) 33 Arbitration International 17, 26.

[51] Menon, ICommCs: Towards a Transnational System, at para. 66.

[52] See also Lance Ang, 'International Commercial Courts and the Interplay between Realism and Institutionalism: A Look at China and Singapore', Harvard International Law Journal Online, https://harvardilj.org/2020/03/international-commercial-courts-and-the-interplay-between-realism-and-institutionalism-a-look-at-china-and-singapore, accessed 1 November 2020.

adjudicate cross-border commercial disputes between private parties – a function so far not undertaken by an intergovernmental institution.[53]

Second, they are functionally international in that they allow the internationalization of domestic legal orders. From a political economy perspective, two main rationales may be identified as driving forces behind the initiatives of different countries around the world to create ICommCs: first, attracting foreign capital. Economic growth depends on the performance of the judicial system.[54] Most ICommCs are established to attract FDI by presenting the host jurisdictions as independent and impartial for foreign investors that are less acquainted with them.[55] This is specifically the case with ICommCs attached to a free financial zone. The zones are governed by different institutions than the ordinary governance institutions of the host country, and apply a different set of rules. International commercial courts are part of a broader institutional framework of the SEZ that separate administrative agencies and the use of laws that investors are familiar with. A similar observation may be made about the second and third categories of ICommCs, where the judges, domestic or international, are selected based on their knowledge of the common law and the English language – the law and lingua franca of international business.

The second rationale is that of making the host country a preferred destination in the global and regional competition for dispute resolution services. In this respect, ICommCs are viewed as complementary to rather than competing with international commercial arbitration.[56] This rationale is more explicit in the case of the courts of the second and third categories. Singapore, for example, has very successfully placed itself as a global and regional dispute resolution hub[57] featuring a very robust and efficient national court system,[58] the Singapore International

[53] See Jan H. Hendrik Dalhuisen, 'The Case for an International Commercial Court' (Posted: 7 May 2014 Last revised: 8 January 2015), https://papers.ssrn.com/sol3/papers.cfm?abstract_id=2433513, accessed 1 November 2020 (on a proposal for the creation of a 'global' international commercial court).

[54] See, for example, Giuliana Palumbo, Giulia Giupponi, Luca Nunziata and Juan Mora-Sanguinetti, Judicial Performance and Its Determinants: A Cross-Country Perspective: A Going for Growth Report, OECD Economic Policy Paper 5 (2013), 8.

[55] See also Krishnan and Purohit, note 8, above. On the interplay between rule of law and ICommCs see Susan L. Karamanian, 'International Commercial Courts, Dispute Resolution, and the Rule of Law' (Chapter 22), in this volume.

[56] See Section 10.3.2.

[57] See Menon, 'The Rule of Law and SICC', at 2; Reed, note 47, above, at 140.

[58] Waleed Haider Malik, *Judiciary-Led Reforms in Singapore* (World Bank 2007).

Arbitration Centre (SIAC) as a world class arbitration centre, and the Singapore International Mediation Centre (SIMC) as an independent mediation centre that offers mediation services tailored to the needs of Asian businesses. Singapore is already one of the most preferred seats of arbitration in the world.[59] The creation of the SICC is one more step in the process of further enhancing the role of the country as a forum for the resolution of international and Asian disputes.[60]

The CICC is also established with the primary goal of serving as the forum for cases arising out of the Belt and Road Initiative. The international chambers in Europe are the result of an effort to attract judicial business in the post-Brexit era.[61] The same observations could be made about the courts of the first category, as most zone courts are no longer restricted to adjudicating cases coming out of the geographical boundaries of an SEZ.

10.3 Hybridity and Interoperability in the System of International Commercial Courts

Globalization as an economic and social phenomenon that intensified at the end of the twentieth century was characterized by the increasing hybridity of social and legal institutions, as well as legal categories and norms: the national and the international, the public and the private, the formal and the informal.[62] International commercial courts are phenomena of economic and legal globalization, for which hybridity is an organizational feature as well.

Globalization in its most recent versions is no longer about hybridization. The old and new institutions and norms now coexist, and need to be made interoperable.[63] International commercial courts are also

[59] *Report of the Singapore International Commercial Court Committee* (November 2013), at para. 6, www.mlaw.gov.sg/content/dam/minlaw/corp/News/Annex%20A%20-%20SICC%20Committee%20Report.pdf, accessed 1 November 2020.

[60] Menon, 'The Rule of Law and SICC', at 12, 15. According to Chief Justice Menon, 'the sheer volume of disputes that accompany the growth in trade and investment fuels the need for a neutral and well-regarded transnational dispute resolution centre in Asia'; Sundaresh Menon, 'Origins and Aspirations: Developing an International Construction Court' (2014) International Construction Law Review 341, at 344.

[61] See Geert van Calster, 'Brexit and the Competition of Dispute Resolution Fora in Europe', (Chapter 21), in this volume.

[62] See generally Georgios Dimitropoulos, *Zertifizierung und Akkreditierung im Internationalen Verwaltungsverbund* (Mohr Siebeck 2012).

[63] See generally on regime collisions Andreas Fischer-Lescano and Gunther Teubner, 'Regime-Collisions: The Vain Search for Legal Unity in the Fragmentation of Global Law' (2004) 25 Michigan Journal of International Law 999.

institutions of this more advanced globalization era of interoperability, and are developing mechanisms of coexistence with the domestic and international political and legal systems and infrastructures.

10.3.1 Hybridity

Dispute resolution systems are often caught in a conundrum between two arguably opposed systems of justice: the public and the private, the formal and the informal.[64] International commercial arbitration and other forms of alternative dispute resolution (ADR) were developed to deal with problems of formal State justice – namely, the sometimes excessive backlog of cases before national courts which are only becoming worse in times of diminishing public budgets. With its more informal approach to dispute resolution and procedure, international arbitration is often seen as more efficient. Proceedings before arbitral tribunals usually lead to faster resolution by avoiding unnecessary litigation, and in a confidential setting that might help preserve good relations between the parties.[65] The informal nature of arbitration – and other ADR mechanisms – may also lead to greater acceptance of final results by the disputing parties, and thus greater voluntary compliance rates with less need to rely on external enforcement.[66] International commercial arbitration also accommodates cross-border dispute resolution, achieving an equivalent standard of dispute resolution for private parties everywhere in the world.[67] In addition, international commercial arbitration relies on a well-tested system of enforcement. The Convention on the Recognition and Enforcement of Foreign Arbitral Awards of 1958 (New York Convention) gives effect to private agreements to arbitrate and to recognize and enforce foreign arbitral awards.

[64] Compare Owen M. Fiss, 'Against Settlement' (1984) 93 Yale Law Journal 1073, 1075 with Jean R. Sternlight, 'Is Alternative Dispute Resolution Consistent with the Rule of Law? Lessons from Abroad' (2007) 56 DePaul Law Review 569.

[65] See, for example, the Decision of High Court in London: Re AI and MT [2013] EWHC 100 (Fam).

[66] See generally Rebecca Hollander-Blumoff and Tom R. Tyler, 'Procedural Justice and the Rule of Law: Fostering Legitimacy in Alternative Dispute Resolution' (2011) Journal of Dispute Resolution 1, 10.

[67] It has been suggested that fears of bias, unfamiliarity with the local language and proceedings, expediency, as well as some preference for uniformity in the drafting of their agreements led international business to commercial arbitration; see W. Laurence Craig, 'Some Trends and Developments in the Laws and Practice of International Commercial Arbitration' (2016) 50 Texas International Law Journal 699, 700.

Informality has its own downsides. It does not give, for example, a chance to parties for a second review, as arbitral awards are only reviewable by courts on a limited number of grounds.[68] At a more systemic level, the private nature of arbitration cannot accommodate the public functions courts typically play in society. Arbitration does not produce precedent, thus not ensuring the development of a system of justice that guarantees consistency and predictability. The informal setting may also arguably be conducive to possible disregard of public interests by arbitrators.[69] In addition, arbitrators are selected by the parties, and may be seen as biased in favour of private corporations – as arbitrators are repeat players in arbitrations in the same way as private corporations are. Overall, informality may be seen as undermining the delivery of justice, the public's confidence in the role of the judiciary, and eventually the rule of law.

In an era of cross-border business transactions and government operations, the lines between domestic and international as well as formal and informal dispute resolution have become increasingly blurred.[70] The difference between a court and a tribunal as well as between a judgment and an award have become blurred as well.[71] Disputes in international commercial arbitration may involve parties that originate in the same jurisdiction. International investment arbitration replaces dispute resolution by domestic courts, and involves private parties appearing as claimants against respondent States.

International commercial courts as a phenomenon of commercial and legal globalization are hybrids in their organization, as well as procedure.[72] They are hybrids between domestic and international, as well as between public and private, and formal and informal

[68] See, for example, Article V of the Convention on the Recognition and Enforcement of Foreign Arbitral Awards (New York, 1958).

[69] See, for example, the dissent of Justice Stevens in US Supreme Court, *Mitsubishi Motors Corp.* v. *Soler Chrysler-Plymouth* (1985).

[70] See also Lord Sumption's *obiter* in *Abela* v. *Baadarani*, [2013] UKSC 44, [2013] 1 WLR 2043, [53]: 'Litigation between residents of different states is a routine incident of modern commercial life.'

[71] See Case C-284/16, *Slowakische Republik (Slovak Republic)* v. *Achmea BV*; see generally Christopher Vajda, 'Transnational Adjudication and the Court of Justice of the European Union' (Chapter 3), in this volume.

[72] The relevant literature has repeatedly highlighted the hybrid nature of ICommCs; see, for example, Reed, note 47, above, at 137; see Michael Patchett-Joyce, 'Private Autonomy in International Commercial Dispute Resolution' (Chapter 16), in this volume; see also for an international law perspective Salvatore Caserta and Mikael Rask Madsen, 'Hybridity in International Adjudication' (Chapter 18), in this volume.

adjudication. They feature design elements of both public and private justice – that is, both traditional domestic courts and arbitral tribunals.

The design of ICommCs has been informed by the more informal organizational and procedural design of arbitration. The ICommC organization and procedure show flexibility in ways that are more characteristic of arbitration in allowing greater space to party autonomy in the dispute resolution process than in the regular court setting.[73] Speaking for the SICC, Judge Stephen Chon said that the procedure of this court is 'a careful marriage between litigation and arbitration, which allows it to strike a middle ground between the two'.[74] The SICC rules of evidence, for example, are relaxed to exclude the application of Singapore's rule of evidence, and allow the application of other rules of evidence.[75] Deviating from the standard rules on applicable law, SICC rules allow foreign laws to be determined on the basis of submission instead of proof.[76] Proof would have necessitated the use of expert witnesses, while submission is to be made by a lawyer representing the party so long as the SICC considers that 'all parties are or will be represented by counsel who are competent to submit on the relevant questions of foreign law'. The SICC rules also allow a party to a dispute to be represented by a foreign lawyer or law expert who is registered in accordance with the Singapore Legal Professional Act.[77] The SICC also permits parties to agree in writing to limit or restrict the scope of appeal or even to waive the right to appeal.[78]

At the same time, ICommCs retain the important design elements that are characteristic of an ordinary domestic court. Judges at ICommCs are generally independently appointed, and not for the purposes of specific cases. Moreover, proceedings take place as a default in open court.[79]

[73] Yip, 'The Resolution of Disputes', at 446.

[74] Steven Chong, 'The Singapore International Commercial Court: A New Opening in a Forked Path', Speech delivered at the British Maritime Law Association Lecture and Dinner (21 October 2015), 31, www.supremecourt.gov.sg/Data/Editor/Documents/J%20Steven%20Chong%20Speeches/The%20SICC%20-%20A%20New%20Opening%20in%20a%20Forked%20Parth%20-%20London%20(21.10.15).pdf, accessed 1 November 2020.

[75] Article 18K of the Singapore Supreme Court of Judicature Act; SICC, Order 110, r. 23 (2014).

[76] SICC, Order 110, r. 25 (2014).

[77] Article 18M of the Singapore Supreme Court of Judicature Act.

[78] Singapore International Commercial Court Practice Directions (Effective 20 July 2020), para. 139, www.supremecourt.gov.sg/docs/default-source/default-document-library/rules/singapore-international-commercial-court-practice-directions-v2.pdf, accessed 1 November 2020.

[79] See Article 28.3 of The Qatar Financial Centre Civil and Commercial Court Regulations and Procedural Rules.

Their judgments are publicly available, and published online on the websites of the courts allowing their judgments to gain precedential value for future cases.[80] The right to appeal is generally preserved, giving parties a second chance to have their case reviewed. Finally, ICommCs retain powers that are not shared by arbitral tribunals, such as joining third parties to the proceedings and consolidating cases.[81] Overall, the organizational hybridity of ICommCs seems to be overcoming the formality/informality conundrum in the comparison between ordinary domestic courts and international commercial arbitration.

10.3.2 Interoperability

The image of organizational hybridity of ICommCs reveals only part of the picture of their overall role and function in the system of transnational adjudication. International commercial courts are not only hybrids. They also present a different paradigm in domestic, international and transnational dispute settlement; that of a domestic court that resolves international disputes. International commercial courts serve their functions in parallel with other domestic and international dispute resolution fora. The coexistence of multiple fora has led to the emergence of systems of functional interoperability.

International Commercial Courts and Ordinary Domestic Courts

International commercial courts are embedded within a broader national judicial structure.[82] International commercial courts and ordinary domestic courts are meant, though, to serve different functions, as well as have different organizational priorities relating both to formal legality and operational efficiency. The establishment of ICommCs has potential substantive and procedural implications, raising issues of interoperability between ICommCs and ordinary domestic courts.

[80] See also Mateja Durovic and Franciszek Lech, 'Harmonization of Commercial Law Based on the Common Law' (Chapter 8), in this volume.

[81] On the SICC's jurisdiction to join additional parties to the proceedings see Order 110 rule 9 of the Rules of Court; see generally Drossos Stamboulakis and Blake Crook, 'Joinder of Non-consenting Parties: The Singapore International Commercial Court Approach Meets Transnational Recognition and Enforcement' (2019) Erasmus Law Review 98.

[82] See Reed, note 47, above, at 137; V. K. Rajah, SC, 'W(h)ither Adversarial Commercial Dispute Resolution?, (2017) 33 Arbitration International 17; cf. also Krishnan and Purohit, note 8 above, at 510 (regarding the DIFC Courts).

International commercial courts of all three categories were developed on the example of the Commercial Court of England and Wales, which has a long tradition in adjudicating cross-border disputes with no connection to England. The new ICommCs will replace to some extent ordinary domestic courts in the adjudication of cross-border cases – as well as possibly more domestic cases. National judges are also partly replaced by judges coming from foreign jurisdictions – mostly from England and the common law world.[83] The same is true for procedural rules, as ICommCs' procedural rules try to approximate those of the English common law system.[84] The default applicable law of most ICommCs is either the English common law or some version thereof, or other foreign law, instead of the law of the ordinary jurisdiction of the host country.[85]

The existence of international and ordinary domestic courts in the same jurisdiction may give rise to dispute bifurcation and the accompanying separation between categories of parties. Similar disputes will have the tendency to be separated in one country depending on whether the parties are international or domestic.[86] It remains to be seen whether this will have further systemic repercussions in the legal orders hosting ICommCs.[87]

International commercial courts operate based on a different set of organizational principles and priorities than those of ordinary domestic courts. Domestic court systems have been in the past decades subject to

[83] The DIFC Courts, for example, make familiarity with the common law a requirement for judicial appointment; see Article 9(3)(b) DIFC Law No. 10 of 2004 (DIFC Court Law).

[84] The procedural rules of the QICDRC, for example, are a more simplified version of the Civil Procedure Rules used in England and Wales; see Lebovits and Miller, note 13 above, at 54.

[85] Former Chief Justice of the DIFC Courts and Head of the DRA, Dr Michael Hwang, famously called the DIFC in 2008 'a common law island in a civil law ocean' referring to the operation of the DIFC Courts within the United Arab Emirates, a civil law jurisdiction; see Michael Hwang, The Courts of the Dubai International Finance Centre: A Common Law Island in a Civil Law Ocean (1 November 2008), www.difccourts.ae/2008/11/01/the-courts-of-the-dubai-international-finance-centre-a-common-law-island-in-a-civil-law-ocean, accessed 1 November 2020; see generally Damien P. Horigan, 'The New Adventures of the Common Law' (2009) 1 Pace Int'l L Rev Online Companion 1; Tiba, note 1 above, at 49.

[86] See Krishnan and Purohit, note 8 above, at 519 (discussing the situation in the UAE).

[87] See, for example, Sylvie Gallage-Alwis, France's Attractiveness: Will the International Chamber of the Paris Court of Appeal Open the Door to a New Way to Litigate in France?, Expert Guides, www.expertguides.com/articles/frances-attractiveness-will-the-international-chamber-of-the-paris-court-of-appeal-open-the-door-to-a-new-way-to-litigate-in-france/arnavgfw, accessed 1 November 2020.

various waves of reform with a view to improving their efficiency.[88] The goal of improving efficiency has led to changes in judicial and court management; targets of quantitative efficiency have more recently started giving way to changes in overall quality of justice management, whereby quality is measured based on indicators like clearance rates, case turnover ratios and disposition time.[89]

International commercial courts operate relatively detached from these organizational considerations. Neither cost-efficiency or measurability, nor new public management are primary considerations in the same way as in ordinary domestic courts. This is not to say that efficiency is not part of their overall gamut of objectives. The QICDRC, for example, must issue its decisions within ninety days from the day the respondent received official notice of the claim.[90] Expediency is one of the most attractive features of ICommCs.[91] In the broad picture, the overall priorities of ICommCs are still different. Organizational and design considerations for ICommCs and ordinary domestic courts diverge largely. As explained in Section 10.2.2, this is the result of the different functions ICommCs serve.[92]

The potentially conflicting relationship between ICommCs and ordinary domestic courts manifested itself in the effort of the Belgian government to establish the BIBC. The Supreme Judicial Council (Conseil supérieur de la Justice (CSJ)) of Belgium opined in March 2018 that establishing the BIBC would violate the Belgian constitution. The CSJ presented three grounds of unconstitutionality. First, the CSJ expressed doubts about the independence of the BIBC given that the proposed bill gave the power of judicial appointment to the executive branch – not to the CSJ as per the constitution; second, the creation of the BIBC raised concerns of an 'institutional' equality of arms between the parties in cases

88 See Klaus Decker, Christian Möhlen and David F. Varela, *Improving the Performance of Justice Institutions* (World Bank 2011), http://siteresources.worldbank.org/INTECA/Resources/librojusticiaING-cian.pdf, accessed 1 November 2020 (identifying a period of economization, a period of cost-efficiency and a service-oriented period). Reforms were often spearheaded by international organizations such as the World Bank and the Organisation for Economic Co-operation and Development (OECD); see generally Dimitropoulos and Brekoulakis, note 7 above.

89 See generally Gar Yein Ng, *Quality of Judicial Organisation and Checks and Balances* (Intersentia 2007); Gar Yein Ng, 'A Discipline of Judicial Governance?' (2011) 7 Utrecht Law Review 102.

90 See Article 32.1 of The Qatar Financial Centre Civil and Commercial Court Regulations and Procedural Rules in conjunction with paras. 10 and 13 of Schedule 6 to the QFC Law.

91 Krishnan and Purohit, note 8 above, at 522.

92 See Section 10.2.2.

before the ordinary national courts and the BIBC; finally, the transparency of the new institution was questioned – especially when it came to its financing. This led eventually to abandoning the idea of establishing an ICommC in Belgium.

Various responses have been provided so far by different legal orders with a view to resolving issues of systemic compatibility and achieving interoperability between the systems. Some countries have tried to improve compatibility and interoperability by giving constitutional recognition to ICommCs. In the United Arab Emirates (UAE), for example, there was an amendment to the UAE constitution in 2004 authorizing the creation of the DIFC and ADGM with the DIFC Courts and the ADGM Courts.[93] Singapore amended its constitution in 2014, allowing the SICC to appoint foreign judges to hear cases.[94] An amendment of the constitution of the Kazakh Republic in 2017 allowed the establishment of a jurisdiction in the financial field in Astana.[95]

The establishment of the QFC and the QICDRC was not accompanied by a constitutional amendment. But this SEZ and ICommC are 'onshore' institutions. They are parallel jurisdictions not separated geographically from the ordinary jurisdiction of the State of Qatar. Given legal constraints in China, the SPC decided to establish an international panel of experts rather than appoint international judges per se.[96]

Mechanisms of coexistence and coordination at the level of streamlining the caseload of international commercial and ordinary domestic courts are also in place in various jurisdictions. One may distinguish between two types of systems of case coordination: case transferals and conflict-of-jurisdiction mechanisms. Transferal is for example addressed in the rules of the SICC and the QICDRC. Under the SICC rules, the SICC can decide that it has no jurisdiction or it can decline to assume jurisdiction. It must transfer the proceedings to the Singapore High Court if it considers that the High Court has jurisdiction in the case and all parties consent to the proceedings being heard in the High Court. If the proceedings are not transferred to the Singapore High Court, the SICC may dismiss or stay

[93] Article 121 of the United Arab Emirates constitution. This was accompanied by the enactment of various federal and local laws. See, for example, Federal Law No. 8 of 2004 Regarding the Financial Free Zones, in particular ibid., at Article 3(2) (exempting free financial zones from the UAE's 'Federal civil and commercial laws').

[94] See Article 95(4)(c) of the Constitution of the Republic of Singapore.

[95] Article 2(3-1) of the Constitution of the Republic of Kazakhstan.

[96] Article 12 of Judge's Law of the People's Republic of China (PRC) of 2019 requires judges to have Chinese citizenship.

proceedings, or make any other order it sees fit.[97] Likewise, the QICDRC rules also provide that the Court may decline jurisdiction or refer any proceedings to another court in the State of Qatar.[98]

Separate institutions may be called upon to decide on the resolution of jurisdictional conflicts. In Dubai, the Judicial Committee of the Dubai Courts and the DIFC Courts was established in 2016 to resolve conflicts of jurisdiction between the DIFC Courts and the ordinary courts that has started playing an active role in defining their relationship.[99]

As the institution of ICommCs proliferates, and the caseload before them will continue growing, the common law or common law-inspired solutions will have the tendency to replace other domestic law. Some systems and courts have introduced balancing safeguards to bridge the differences between common and civil law in otherwise primarily civil law jurisdictions. For example, although the QICDRC follows procedural rules and principles drawn from common law, its decisions are not binding – they are treated as persuasive precedents for later cases.[100] Moreover, the Appellate Division of the QICDRC made clear in its *Chedid* judgment that litigants should not structure their arguments around English case law when Qatari law is applicable.[101] The court has also explained that the applicable law is interpreted with 'regard to the circumstances in Qatar'.[102]

Beyond the institutional mechanisms of interoperability, ICommCs may still help domestic courts become more efficient by relieving their dockets, as well as by serving as good examples of court management.[103]

International Commercial Courts and Arbitration

International commercial courts are sometimes viewed as competitors to international commercial arbitration, sometimes as complementary

[97] 64 r 10(1), O 110, Rules of Court.

[98] Article 9.4 of The Qatar Financial Centre Civil and Commercial Court Regulations and Procedural Rules.

[99] See Julian Bailey, 'The Interplay between International Commercial Courts and Ordinary Courts' (Chapter 15), in this volume.

[100] Article 12.1 of QICDRC, Official Practice Guide, www.qicdrc.gov.qa/media-centre/publications, accessed 1 November 2020.

[101] *Chedid & Assoc. Qatar LLC* v. *Said Bou Ayash*, 3 May 2015, Case No. 02/2015, ¶18 (Appellate Circ.).

[102] *Qatar Financial Centre Auth.* v. *Silver Leaf Capital Partners LLC*, 1 June 2009, Case No. 0001/2009, at ¶33 (First Instance Cir.); see also Faris Elias Nasrallah, 'Applicable Laws in the International Commercial Courts of the Gulf' (Chapter 9), in this volume.

[103] See Krishnan and Purohit, note 8 above, at 518–19 (regarding the DIFC Courts).

alternatives.[104] International commercial courts find themselves in the global competition for cases that are of a cross-border transnational nature. They may also partly be seen as a response to the more recent critique against arbitration.[105] But the relationship between ICommCs and international arbitration is much more complex. It is gradually becoming one of interoperability.

The institutional developments championed by ICommCs have sometimes led to significant spillovers in the broader host jurisdiction. The UAE, for example, building on the experience of the DIFC and the DIFC Courts, adopted after many years of discussions a new UNCITRAL Model Law–based arbitration law for 'mainland' Dubai.[106] Moreover, a new form of 'free zone arbitration' is starting to emerge in SEZs that feature ICommCs.[107] Free zone arbitration is different from 'onshore' arbitration as it is managed by zone-specific institutions, as well as takes place based on zone-specific arbitration rules.[108] This interplay between ordinary-jurisdiction and zone-specific institutions eventually helps shape very strong dispute resolution institutions for the whole jurisdiction.

The most important development in the evolving relationship of interoperability between ICommCs and international arbitration are

[104] See generally Menon, ICommCs: Towards a Transnational System, at 8–11; Reed, note 47 above, at 147; Hwang, note 86; Akira Saito, 'International Commercial Arbitration and International Commercial Courts: Towards a Comparative and Cooperative Relationship', in Bruno Zeller (ed.), *Harmonising Trade Law to Enable Private: Sector Regional Development*, Hors Serie Volume XX (CLJP Hors Serie 2016) 33; Dalma R. Demeter and Kayleigh M. Smith, 'The Implications of International Commercial Courts on Arbitration' (2016) 33 Journal of International Arbitration 441; Dorothee Ruckteschler and Tanja Stooss, 'International Commercial Courts: A Superior Alternative to Arbitration?' (2019) 36 Journal of International Arbitration 431; Patchett-Joyce, note 72, above.

[105] See generally The Right. Hon. The Lord Thomas of Cwmgiedd, Lord Chief Justice of England and Wales, Developing Commercial Law through the Courts: Rebalancing the Relationship between the Courts and Arbitration, THE BAILII LECTURE 2016 (9 March 2016), www.judiciary.gov.uk/wp-content/uploads/2016/03/lcj-speech-bailli-lecture-20160309.pdf, accessed 1 November 2020; Susan L. Karamanian, 'Courts and Arbitration: Reconciling the Public with the Private' (2017) 9 Arb L Rev 65; Thomas Schultz, 'The Ethos of Arbitration', in Thomas Schultz and Federico Ortino (eds.), *The Oxford Handbook of International Arbitration* (Oxford University Press 2020).

[106] UAE Federal Law No. (6) of 2018 on Arbitration.

[107] See, for example, Gordon Blanke, 'Free Zone Arbitration: The Mechanics' (2017–18) 6 Indian J Arb L 56.

[108] For example, arbitration in the DIFC is governed by the DIFC Arbitration Law; see DIFC Law No. 1 of 2008.

the powers that ICommCs are gaining as curial courts in arbitration. The QICDRC was conferred such powers in 2017 under the new arbitration law of the State of Qatar.[109] In 2018, the SICC was given the power 'to hear any proceedings relating to international commercial arbitration that the High Court may hear and that satisfy such conditions as the Rules of Court may prescribe'.[110] The DIFC Courts have gained powers over recognition and enforcement of the mainland Dubai International Arbitration Centre (DIAC) awards issued in mainland Dubai, as well as of foreign arbitral awards under the New York Convention.[111] The relationship between ICommCs and international commercial arbitration is thus developing beyond dichotomies towards a complicated relationship of interoperability.

International Commercial Courts and International Courts and Tribunals

One of the rationales for the creation of ICommCs is to attract FDI by presenting the relevant jurisdictions as independent and impartial for foreign investors that are less familiar with the host jurisdiction. This role has been played since the 1960s by the web of bilateral investment treaties with investor-State arbitration clauses. The creation of ICommCs suggests that (at least some) cases are supposed to move from the international realm to the national jurisdiction of the States hosting an ICommC. International commercial courts have the potential to 'domesticate' disputes by diverting them from the international realm to a national jurisdiction. International commercial courts are thus to some extent in a competitive relationship with the international investment law regime. Given the 'backlash' against investment arbitration, ICommCs may start increasingly appearing as a more appealing solution for the role international investment tribunals have played in the effort of governments to attract foreign investment.[112] One may expect countries that have ICommCs in their jurisdiction to rely less on international investment agreements (IIAs) to attract investment. International

[109] Law No. 2 of 2017 Promulgating the Civil and Commercial Arbitration Law.

[110] Section 18D(2) of the Supreme Court Judicial Act.

[111] See generally Mischa Balen, 'Using the DIFC's Off-Shore Jurisdiction to Enforce Arbitration Awards in On-Shore Dubai' (2016) 82(3) Arbitration 233. These new powers assumed by the DIFC Courts have led to the establishment of the Dubai–DIFC Joint Judicial Committee.

[112] Michael Waibel, Asha Kaushal, Kyo-Hwa Chung and Clair Balchin (eds.), *The Backlash against Investment Arbitration* (Wolters Kluwer 2010).

commercial courts may assume jurisdiction even when there is no IIA between two or more countries.

Mechanisms of coordination and interoperability between ICommCs and international courts and tribunals are yet to be developed. On one hand, CICC officials, for example, have clarified that the court does not have jurisdiction over cases concerning investor-State or State-State investment or trade disputes.[113] Other ICommCs have adopted broader interpretations of the terms 'international' and 'commercial' by potentially allowing investor-State disputes.[114] Finally, one cannot exclude the involvement of ICommCs in future IIAs either explicitly or through exhaustion-of-local remedies or fork-in-the-road clauses.

Conclusion

The design of ICommCs of all three presented categories has been determined by the needs that the courts have been established to cover in the field of transnational adjudication: the organizational internationalism of ICommCs is conditioned upon their functional internationalism. While organizational internationalism highlights the hybridity of ICommCs, this chapter suggests a reorientation of the focus towards growing issues of interoperability of ICommCs with ordinary domestic courts, international commercial arbitration, as well as international courts and tribunals. The success of the mechanisms of interoperability will eventually determine the success of ICommCs as well.

113 CICC, 'The State Council Information Office Held a Press Conference on the "Opinion on the Establishment of 'The Belt and Road' International Commercial Dispute Settlement Mechanism and Institutions"' (28 June 2018), http://cicc.court.gov.cn/html/1/219/208/210/769.html, accessed 1 November 2020.

114 See Godwin, Ramsay and Webster, note 23 above, at 226; Saito, note 111 above, at 54.

11

Internationalizing Domestic Courts in Europe

A Comparative Analysis on Procedure, Function, Organization

MARIEKE WITKAMP

11.1 Introduction

Asia, and the Gulf region especially, is very familiar with international commercial courts (ICommCs). The international courts in the Gulf have been around since 2004 when Dubai opened the doors of the Dubai International Financial Centre (DIFC) Courts. Qatar and Abu Dhabi followed with their own ICommCs in 2009 and 2015 respectively and Singapore opened the doors to its ICommC in 2015 as well. Kazakhstan established its ICommCs in 2017 and China in 2019. It took some time, but Continental Europe is now following Asia's example by establishing its own ICommCs. In 2018, France and Germany established new ICommCs in Paris and Frankfurt respectively and the Netherlands Commercial Court (NCC) was established on 1 January 2019 in Amsterdam.[1] Belgium was also working on creating its own ICommC, but these plans have been discontinued.

All of these ICommCs are different in nature and have been designed to serve different purposes. Accordingly, there is no uniform definition of an ICommC. For the purposes of this chapter, I use this term to refer to courts that seek to attract international commercial disputes and do that by (partially) providing for court procedures in the English language and by having an international or bilingual bench. This sets these international courts apart from their domestic civil and commercial counterparts.

This chapter first discusses in Section 11.2 the reasons for establishing the three new European ICommCs; Brexit being an important one, but not the only justification. Becoming more attractive as an international

[1] Where the abbreviation NCC is used in this chapter, reference is made to both the Netherlands Commercial Court in first instance and on appeal.

business and legal hub was also an important reason to set up these courts. This chapter then sets out how the three European countries position their ICommCs, looking at the different procedures, functions and organization. After establishing in Section 11.3 that the three European countries have well-regarded civil justice systems, but have not been very attractive forums for international disputes, Sections 11.4 and 11.5 discuss what distinguishes these courts from their Asian counterparts and how they compare to each other. This is done by looking at changes of legislation, whether English is used for the full procedures or only partially, by reviewing the courts' rules of procedure, and by discussing their (online) accessibility. The last part of the court comparison consists of a short review of the caseload these courts have generated in their short existence and how they have functioned so far, which is set out in Section 11.6.

I conclude this chapter by listing the essentials of what international users are looking for in international dispute resolution in Section 11.7 and contend that all essentials are offered by the three European ICommCs. They are promising additions to the existing international dispute resolution scene. The NCC in particular, being the only truly English-speaking court of the three, is very well equipped to become a true player in the field of international dispute resolution.

11.2 Rationale behind the Establishment of European International Commercial Courts

An obvious answer to the question of how to explain the trend of European ICommCs is Brexit. In short, by stepping out of the European Union, the United Kingdom – and therefore the London Commercial Court – will lose the advantages of being part of the European Judicial Union, which could make enforcement of its judgments more difficult – but also obtaining means of evidence and serving documents.

In Europe, and perhaps even globally, the London Commercial Court is the most popular judicial forum for the resolution of international commercial disputes. Each year, 80 per cent of the cases submitted have at least one foreign party, and in almost 50 per cent of these cases, both parties are foreign companies.[2] *The court hears annually around two*

[2] Portland Communications, 'Commercial Courts Report 2020' (2020), https://portland-communications.com/publications/commercial-courts-report-2020, accessed 20 July 2020.

hundred cases, of which nearly 20 per cent involve parties from the Continent.[3] Moreover, in the United Kingdom, the commercial litigation legal services market represents a total of approximately 16 billion euros per year.[4] These numbers show the value of being an international litigation hub and it is not strange that other countries wanted to have a piece of that as well. Brexit was in that respect a good opportunity to start competing with the London Commercial Court.

Although both Germany and France already had international chambers that handled commercial disputes of an international nature, Brexit has been an important trigger for these two countries to launch new plans for their ICommCs and to rebrand their existing ones. Brexit was also the reason for Belgium to come with a plan to set up an ICommC.

The International Chamber in Paris was created in 2010 by the Commercial Court of Paris.[5] At that time, no special rules were in place to conduct (part of the) proceedings in English, and there was no international chamber in the appeal court. The International Chamber was intended solely as a specialized chamber to handle complex international commercial cases at the first instance according to the standard French procedural rules. In May 2017, at the request of the French Minister of Justice, the High Legal Committee of the Financial Market in Paris rendered a report with recommendations on why and how to raise the standards of the capital's commercial courts and how to rapidly set up specialized tribunal sections within the civil and commercial courts in Paris to hear international commercial cases.[6] The report points out that in international contracts, contracting parties can

> choose both the law applicable to their business relationship and the courts that will resolve any disputes such relationship may generate. As a result, there is a worldwide, as well as European, competition between courts that, in order to protect the sovereignty of our judicial system and for economic reasons, requires French courts with jurisdiction in various business law

[3] Prof. Dr Dres. h.c. Burkhard Hess, 'The Justice Initiative Frankfurt am Main 2017' (Conflictoflaws.net, 31 March 2017), http://conflictoflaws.net/2017/the-justice-initiative-frankfurt-am-main-2017-law-made-in-frankfurt, accessed 20 July 2020.

[4] Orchard Reports, 'UK Legal Services Market Trends Report 2019' (February 2019), www.researchandmarkets.com/research/pcpfrc/uk_legal_services?w=4, accessed 20 July 2020.

[5] Legal High Committee for Financial Markets in Paris, 'Recommendations for the Creation of Special Tribunals for International Business Disputes' (3 May 2017), https://publications.banque-france.fr/sites/default/files/rapport_07_a.pdf, accessed 20 July 2020.

[6] Ibid.

> fields to project authority and attractiveness by the quality of the service they provide.

It goes on to state that Brexit has made it more important to improve the international competitiveness of the French commercial courts.

Following the report, the Paris Court of Appeal created a new chamber specialized in disputes relating to international commercial contracts to 'meet the expectations of international market participants seeking the benefits of an attractive judicial system'.[7] In February 2018, the Paris Bar and the Paris Commercial Court and Paris Court of Appeal signed two protocols that set out the procedures applicable to the International Chamber of the two chambers and the use of English during these procedures.[8] These protocols are discussed in what follows.

Germany has had a few international commercial chambers since 2010. From that time, it has been possible to conduct oral proceedings in English, if so requested by parties, before the regional courts in Cologne, Bonn, Düsseldorf and Aachen and the higher regional courts in Cologne and Düsseldorf.[9] In November 2017, it was the regional court of Frankfurt am Main that put itself in the spotlight by announcing it will establish the English-speaking Chamber for International Commercial Matters as of 1 January 2018. The reasons given by the so-called *Justizinitiative Frankfurt* for establishing this chamber in Frankfurt were similar as for the Paris international chambers.[10] Reference was made to the popularity of the London Commercial Court as a forum for international disputes. It was felt that this might change after Brexit and that Germany could become a competing judicial hub. Frankfurt's Chamber for International Commercial Disputes is Germany's best known ICommC and the subject of this chapter.

Belgium announced the establishment of the Brussels International Business Court (BIBC) in October 2017, which was clearly inspired by Brexit. One of the main reasons given for the BIBC was to fend off

7 'Protocol Relating to Procedural Rules Applicable to the International Chamber of the Court of Appeal of Paris' and 'Protocol Relating to Procedural Rules Applicable to the International Chamber of the Paris Commercial Court' (February 2018), www.cours-appel.justice.fr/paris/presentation-generale-ccip-ca-iccp-ca, accessed 20 July 2020.

8 Ibid.

9 Matthias Lehmann, 'Law Made in Germany: The Export Machine Stutters', in Xandra Kramer and John Sorabji (eds.), *International Business Courts* (Eleven International 2019) 85–6.

10 Prof. Dr Dres. h.c. Burkhard Hess, 'The Justice Initiative Frankfurt am Main 2017' (Conflictoflaws.net, 31 March 2017), http://conflictoflaws.net/2017/the-justice-initiative-frankfurt-am-main-2017-law-made-in-frankfurt, accessed 20 July 2020.

competition from English courts, whose current success 'will not be facilitated' by Brexit, and also to compete with commercial arbitration.[11] Belgium's BIBC proposal was different from the other European courts and would have led to an international court that was part court and part arbitral tribunal; a true hybrid court.[12] The BIBC proposal required legislative changes, and that is where things went wrong. First, the Council of State Council and the Belgian Council of the Judiciary had some serious concerns relating to the reasons for establishment, the constitutionality of the BIBC and its financials. After that, the legislation lost support in the parliament, where the largest Flemish party referred to the BIBC as a 'caviar court' and the BIBC plans have been discontinued.[13] Belgium therefore will not have its own ICommC anytime soon.

For the Netherlands, Brexit was not the trigger. It was 2014 when the chairman of the Dutch Council for the Judiciary made a plea to establish such an ICommC.[14] The subsequent legislative proposal to establish the NCC gives a couple of reasons underpinning the requirement for an English-speaking commercial court.[15] It firstly points out that, because of ongoing globalization, there is a growing demand for international (English-speaking) dispute resolution processes. Since English is the lingua franca in international business, contracts and communications between parties (and their advisors) are frequently conducted in English. It would facilitate international business greatly if English-speaking litigation would be possible in the Netherlands as well. Language barriers would disappear and translation of (court) documents would no longer be necessary, which would save time and costs.

[11] Geert van Calster, 'The Brussels International Business Court. A Carrot Sunk by Caviar', in Xandra Kramer and John Sorabji (eds.), *International Business Courts* (Eleven International 2019) 108.

[12] Ibid.

[13] Ibid.

[14] Harriet Schelhaas, 'The Brand New Netherlands Commercial Court: A Positive Development?', in Xandra Kramer and John Sorabji (eds.), *International Business Courts* (Eleven International 2019) 45, Raad voor de Rechtspraak, 'Plan tot oprichting van de Netherlands Commercial Court' (November 2015), www.rechtspraak.nl /SiteCollectionDocuments/plan-netherlands-commercial-court.pdf, accessed 20 July 2020.

[15] Explanatory Memorandum to the Legislative Proposal for Enabling English-Language Court Proceedings (Memorie van Toelichting bij het wetsvoorstel 'Wijziging van het Wetboek van Burgerlijke Rechtsvordering en de Wet griffierechten burgerlijke zaken in verband met het mogelijk maken van Engelstalige rechtspraak bij de internationale handelskamers van de rechtbank Amsterdam en het gerechtshof Amsterdam'), TK 2016–17, 34761/3, at 1–3.

The legislative proposal further acknowledges that a well-functioning, independent and predictable judiciary strengthens the investment climate in a country and enhances its prosperity. It was furthermore considered that international arbitration has become very expensive, especially for small and medium-sized companies. For these kind of companies, international arbitration has become a less interesting option. Local English-speaking litigation would offer these companies an attractive alternative for arbitration. A final reason given in the legislative proposal related to the fact that the resolution of complex international cases takes up a lot of time and finances of the judiciary. If these international cases would be handled by a dedicated court and a higher court fee would be charged, it would relieve the other courts, which would be beneficial for the handling of their normal caseload.

So, regardless of Brexit, the Netherlands determined there was a need to introduce English-speaking litigation to facilitate international business and to make the Netherlands more attractive as an international business and legal hub for international parties. This led to the launch of the NCC in 2019.

11.3 Status of European Civil Court Systems

Germany, the Netherlands and France have established and well-regarded legal systems. This is consistently confirmed by the annual Rule of Law Index of the World Justice Project – an independent non-profit organization that promotes the rule of law around the world. Every year, it publishes its Rule of Law Index that provides data on how the rule of law is experienced by the general public and experts. In 2020, it did that relating to 128 countries around the globe.[16] The World Justice Project looks at the rule of law per country from eight different perspectives, including how the civil justice system works in each country.

For the assessment of rule of law in civil justice systems, the World Justice project examines and measures whether:

- ordinary people can resolve their legal problems peacefully and effectively through the civil justice system;

[16] World Justice Project, 'WJP Rule of Law Index 2020' (June 2020), https://worldjusticeproject.org/our-work/research-and-data/wjp-rule-law-index-2020, accessed 20 July 2020.

- civil justice systems are accessible, affordable and free of discrimination, corruption and improper influence by public officials;
- court proceedings are conducted without unreasonable delays, and if decisions are enforced effectively;
- courts are accessible and impartial.

For a number of years in a row, the Dutch and German civil justice systems have ranked in the top three.[17] France is ranked a bit lower – in the eighteenth place in 2020 – but it still has a respectable position. To compare this with other countries that are popular for the resolution of international commercial disputes: Singapore was ranked fifth in 2020, Hong Kong eleventh, the United Kingdom seventeenth and the United States thirty-sixth.

Within the European Union (EU), the EU Justice Scoreboard Monitor provides comparative data regarding the quality, independence and efficiency of national justice systems to assist the EU and EU Member States in improving the effectiveness of their national justice systems.[18] The EU Justice Monitor stresses that where judicial systems guarantee the enforcement of rights, creditors are more likely to lend, businesses are dissuaded from opportunistic behaviour, transaction costs are reduced, and innovative businesses are more likely to invest. The EU Justice Monitor looks into, amongst other things, the efficiency of justice systems, and ranked the Netherlands third in 2020 (which included non-litigious cases), Germany thirteenth and France twentieth. Although the Netherlands, Germany and France have highly ranked legal systems, they are not always regarded as an attractive forum for international commercial disputes – at least not compared to courts in, for example, London, New York and Singapore.[19]

An important reason for this unpopularity of the Continental European courts is that their official court language is not English: when all dealings of a company are conducted in English, it makes things more complicated, time-consuming and costly if all court-related documents, communications and witness statements have to

[17] Ibid.

[18] European Commission, 'EU Justice Scoreboard Monitor 2020' (July 2020), https://ec.europa.eu/info/policies/justice-and-fundamental-rights/upholding-rule-law/eu-justice-scoreboard_en, accessed 20 July 2020.

[19] See Sir William Blair, 'The New Litigation Landscape: International Commercial Courts and Procedural Innovations' (2019) 2 International Journal of Procedural Law 215.

be translated for parties and their international advisors. Another significant reason relates to the applicable local laws and procedural rules: research by the International Chamber of Commerce in 2014 has shown that English law and US state laws were the two most popular sets of applicable laws for contracts.[20] New York, London and Singapore are some of the world's most important commercial and financial hubs and they are all common law jurisdictions. Many international businesses are simply more familiar with common law than with civil law and accordingly prefer English or at least common law–based fora, and not civil law fora. But with the arrival of ICommCs in Europe, this might start to change.

11.4 Comparison of Asian and European International Commercial Courts

Although the first Asian ICommCs set an example for the three European countries that are the subject of this chapter, the set-up and structure of these Asian ICommCs differ from the European International Commercial Courts. Table 11.1 illustrates the main differences:[21]

As the table shows, the first area where the European ICommCs distinguish themselves from most of the Asian ICommCs is how they fit into their home court system. All three European countries have established their international courts within their existing court system as a specialized chamber. Germany, France and the Netherlands have all created a new chamber within their biggest domestic commercial district court. France and the Netherlands have done that both on the district level and the appellate level and Germany has done that in Frankfurt, on the district level only. Of the discussed Asian ICommCs, only the Singapore International Commercial Court is set up in a comparable way as the European courts as it is a division of the Singapore High Court, which is part of the Supreme Court of Singapore, and is therefore part of the existing local court system.

This is in contrast to the Asian ICommCs in the Gulf and Kazakhstan that are all part of a separate economic and legislative zone in their

[20] ICC, 'ICC 2014 Statistics', ICC Dispute Resolution Bulleting 2015/1.

[21] For the purposes of comparison, I focus in this table on the Asian ICommCs that have been in existence for a number of years. The Chinese ICommC is therefore not included. For more information about this court, I refer to Julien Chaisse and Xu Qian, 'China International Commercial Court' (Chapter 19), in this volume.

Table 11.1 *International Commercial Courts Compared*

Country	Place in local court system	Bench: nationality of the judges	Bench: home jurisdiction of the judges
Gulf countries[22]	Special economic zone	Predominantly international	Predominantly common law
Kazakhstan[23]	Special economic zone	International	Common law
Singapore[24]	Division of Singapore High Court	Local and international	Predominantly common law
France[25]	Chamber of Paris court (district + appeal)	Local	Civil law
Germany[26]	Chamber of Frankfurt court (district only)	Local	Civil Law
The Netherlands[27]	Chamber of Amsterdam court (district + appeal)	Local	Civil law

countries.[28] The reason for the creation of these special economic zones was to set up a legal and economic jurisdiction that is separate and different from the home country's legal and economic regime. This was done to facilitate the investment of international businesses. Each special economic zone has its own ICommC to resolve the commercial disputes

[22] See 'DIFC Courts', www.difccourts.ae, 'Qatar International Court and Dispute Resolution Centre', www.qicdrc.com.qa, 'ADGM Courts', www.adgm.com/adgm-courts, accessed 20 July 2020.

[23] See 'Welcome to the AIF Court', www.aifc-court.kz, accessed 20 July 2020.

[24] See 'Singapore International Commercial Court', www.sicc.gov.sg, accessed 20 July 2020.

[25] See 'Tribunal de Commerce de Paris', www.tribunal-de-commerce-de-paris.fr/fr/accueil; Cour d'Appel de Paris, www.cours-appel.justice.fr/paris, accessed 20 July 2020.

[26] See Chamber for International Commercial Disputes at the Landgericht Frankfurt am Main, https://ordentliche-gerichtsbarkeit.hessen.de/ordentliche-gerichte/lgb-frankfurt-am-main/lg-frankfurt-am-main/chamber-international, accessed 20 July 2020.

[27] See Netherlands Commercial Court (NCC), www.ncc.gov.nl, accessed 20 July 2020.

[28] See also Georgios Dimitropoulos, 'International Commercial Courts in the "Modern Law of Nature": Adjudicatory Unilateralism in Special Economic Zones' (2021) 24 Journal of International Economic Law 361.

that businesses, which are part of that economic zone, may encounter during their business dealings.

A major advantage of the European approach is that judgments from these ICommCs, or chambers, have the same status as other domestic judgments. Enforcement of judgments of the European ICommCs should therefore not be more complicated than a judgment in a local case, both within and outside the country. Dubai serves as an example where the execution of judgments from the DIFC Courts was successfully challenged, which is a scenario a court would like to avoid.[29]

Another significant difference between the European ICommCs and the Asian ICommCs is the composition of the bench. The European courts only use their own, local judges. The local judges are selected based on their experience with handling big and complex international commercial disputes and their English-language skills. The Asian ICommCs on the other hand have a predominantly international bench.

The last difference is, of course, that the three European countries have civil law–based systems, while all Asian international courts have a common law basis, and their bench also predominantly comes from common law countries. This is the case even for the Gulf countries and Kazakhstan. Although the legal system of these countries is not common law based, the English common law has strongly influenced the legal regime of the special economic zones in which the ICommCs operate. This also applies to the procedural rules of the ICommCs of the Gulf countries and Kazakhstan, which are modelled on the Civil Procedure Rules of England and Wales.[30] Although one could point to many differences between common law and civil law, which could mean that, inherently, there are significant differences between the practices of Asian ICommCs and European ICommCs, I consider these differences in practice rather relative.

First, the ICommCs of Amsterdam, Frankfurt or Paris will have to apply the law deemed applicable to the case, which can be a different law than that of the court's home jurisdiction. Often, the contract will specify the law applicable to the dispute and – if that is not the case – international private law conflict rules will enable the court to determine the applicable law. Accordingly, a civil law–based court may have to apply the laws of, for example, England and Wales. Judges are trained to apply not only their local laws, but also foreign laws. The court will also

[29] Julian Bailey, 'The Interplay between International Commercial Courts and Ordinary Courts' (Chapter 15), in this volume.

[30] Blair, 'The New Litigation Landscape'.

be informed by parties on foreign law aspects through expert briefs and/or foreign counsel, who will generally be allowed to argue a case before the French, German and Dutch ICommCs, alongside the local counsel of the case.

Secondly, even though the procedural rules the European ICommCs will apply will be based on their local legislation – and therefore be civil law based – France, Germany and the Netherlands have shown willingness to use best practices from common law procedures in their ICommCs. By doing this, the European ICommCs have taken a similar approach as has happened in international arbitration, where civil law practitioners, who practise in an inquisitorial and more paper-based (evidence) system, meet common law practitioners, who practise in an adversarial system that values oral evidence highly. In international arbitration, practitioners from both backgrounds have found a middle ground, as well as their way to allow for their practices to converge – the International Bar Association Rules on the Taking of Evidence in International Arbitration illustrate this.[31]

11.5 The Organizational Features of European International Commercial Courts

Although the European ICommCs are similar in nature, there are also some important differences, discussed in what follows and demonstrated in Table 11.2.

11.5.1 Start Date, Change of Legislation and Court Fees

Germany and France have not changed their existing legislation and could therefore act swiftly after announcing that they would set up an ICommC. They took advantage of the possibility that their existing legislations provided to have a hearing in a different language than the official language of the court as used for pleadings and judgments.

The Netherlands, on the other hand, did decide to change its existing legislation to be able to offer more than oral hearings in English. The legislative process in the Netherlands was not particularly quick – the preparatory work started in 2015 and the final legislative hearing was held in December 2018. The topic discussed the most was

[31] IBA, IBA Rules on the Taking of Evidence in International Arbitration (2010), www.ibanet.org/publications/publications_iba_guides_and_free_materials.aspx, accessed 20 July 2020.

Table 11.2 *Features of the European International Commercial Courts*

Feature	Germany[32] (Frankfurt)	France[33] (Paris)	The Netherlands[34] (Amsterdam)
Start date	1 January 2018	1 March 2018	1 January 2019
Change of legislation	No	No	Yes
Court fee	Substantial court fee, depending on value of case	Low fee: €235	A flat court fee, ranging from €7,500 to €20,000
Use of English	Only oral proceedings + exhibits	Only oral proceedings + exhibits	Both oral and written proceedings
Judgment	In German (with an English translation if requested)	In French (with an English translation if requested)	In English
Rules of Procedure	Standard provisions of civil procedure	Specific set of Rules of Procedure	Specific set of Rules of Procedure
e-Filing	No	No	Yes
website	Very limited English content	No English content (district level), informative website (appeal level)	Very informative

not so much the establishment of the ICommC itself, but the increase of the standard court fee from €3,000 to €15,000 for first instance.[35] The €15,000 court fee per party is, at least from an international arbitration perspective, relatively insignificant. In the Netherlands,

[32] Chamber for International Commercial Disputes at the Landgericht Frankfurt am Main, https://ordentliche-gerichtsbarkeit.hessen.de/ordentliche-gerichte/lgb-frankfurt-am-main/lg-frankfurt-am-main/chamber-international, accessed 20 July 2020.

[33] 'Tribunal de Commerce de Paris', www.tribunal-de-commerce-de-paris.fr/fr/accueil; Cour d'Appel de Paris, www.cours-appel.justice.fr/paris, accessed 20 July 2020.

[34] Netherlands Commercial Court (NCC), www.ncc.gov.nl, accessed 20 July 2020.

[35] Schelhaas, 'The Brand New Netherlands Commercial Court', 55–6, 58–60.

this increase, however, led to concerns that this higher fee might make the NCC less accessible to smaller companies and could also open the door for court fee increases for domestic proceedings. Ultimately, the legislation was approved, including the higher court fee, in December 2018.

As far as court fees are concerned, all three courts have a different approach. The court fees in France are exceptionally low – just €235, which is the standard fee for the commercial court in Paris. In Frankfurt, the court fee depends on the value of the case and could be rather substantial; a €10 million claim comes with a court fee of €113,000 in first instance. The NCC has a fixed fee of €7,500 for summary proceedings, €15,000 for first instance and €20,000 for appeal.[36]

11.5.2 How 'English' Are the Procedures and Judgment?

As explained earlier in this chapter, in Germany and France, only the oral part of the hearings can be done in English. Additionally, exhibits in English don't need to be translated. Written pleadings must, however, still be submitted in French and German and the judgments and any court orders will be rendered in the local language as well. An official translation of the judgment in English can be provided to the parties upon request. This means that there are two versions of one judgment, which could lead to conflicts in interpretation, but the official judgment in either French or German will prevail.

In the NCC, every part of the proceedings is done in English, including both oral and written submissions. This also includes the judgment, which is rendered in English. The NCC is therefore the only truly English-speaking court on the Continent.

11.5.3 Rules of Procedure

The ICommCs of Germany, France and the Netherlands all use their own local, civil law–based procedural rules. France and the Netherlands have both used the flexibility that their standard rules of procedure offer to come up with their own set of rules for their ICommCs. France has its own protocols,[37] one for each instance of the international court, and the

[36] NCC, 'NCC and Other European Courts', www.rechtspraak.nl/SiteCollectionDocuments/Other_European_commercial_courts.pdf, accessed 20 July 2020.

[37] 'Protocol Relating to Procedural Rules Applicable to the International Chamber of the Court of Appeal of Paris' and 'Protocol Relating to Procedural Rules Applicable to the

Netherlands has its NCC Rules that apply to both the district and appellate levels.[38] In these special procedure rules, both countries have implemented best practices from international arbitration and the common law systems into their international court procedures. The following sets out the main innovations to their standard civil law procedures:

1. Both France and the Netherlands recognize the importance of safeguarding fast and efficient proceedings. In an early phase of the procedures, case management conferences will be organized to discuss preliminary matters, motions, fact-finding and a timetable. In the Netherlands, as soon as a claim is submitted, a case will be assigned to a designated judge and a designated clerk who will be in charge of case management.[39] That case management may start directly after the submission of the claim and in most cases will involve a case management conference.[40] The French protocols require that in each case a case management conference will be held after which the court will set a timetable for the full proceedings, including date of the judgment.[41]
   With their focus on case management, both countries make tailor-made proceedings possible, in a similar way that parties are used to in international arbitration. In the Netherlands, this starts even in an earlier phase than in arbitration, since a judge will already be designated at the time of the statement of claim, where arbiters still need to be appointed at that stage.
   A last point to make is that courts generally make sure that proceedings stay on track to avoid unnecessary delays. The NCC confirms on its website that it can and will sanction dilatory tactics and other types of obstruction, so NCC proceedings in any case will be kept moving.[42]
2. France and the Netherlands have both adapted their evidentiary practices to focus more on oral submissions and evidence than is typically the case in civil law procedures, where written pleadings form the core of a case. Written witness statements may be submitted in advance of

International Chamber of the Paris Commercial Court' (February 2018), www.cours-appel.justice.fr/paris/presentation-generale-ccip-ca-iccp-ca, accessed 20 July 2020.

38 'NCC Rules', www.rechtspraak.nl/English/NCC/Pages/rules.aspx, accessed 20 July 2020.

39 Ibid., art. 3.5.

40 Ibid., art. 7.1.

41 'Protocol Relating to Procedural Rules Applicable to the International Chamber of the Court of Appeal of Paris', art. 4.3 and 'Protocol Relating to Procedural Rules Applicable to the International Chamber of the Paris Commercial Court', art. 3.

42 Factsheet NCC and arbitration, www.rechtspraak.nl/SiteCollectionDocuments/factsheet-netherlands-commercial-court-and-arbitration.pdf#search=dilatory, accessed 20 July 2020.

an oral witness testimony.[43] Both countries have also expressly stipulated in their rules the possibility of cross-examination of witnesses and experts by counsel.[44] While it is possible for counsel in standard proceedings to ask questions to a witness or an expert, cross-examination generally does not happen in France or the Netherlands in the adversarial way as in common law countries. In both the NCC Rules and the French protocols, counsel however appears to be given more room to conduct a cross-examination in the way they want, under the supervision of the court. The NCC Rules further acknowledge that parties can enter into an evidentiary agreement in which they can customize their proceedings from an evidentiary perspective and can deviate from the statutory rules of evidence.[45]

3. Both France and the Netherlands have included provisions on obtaining evidence from the other party or a third party and thereby acknowledging the importance of disclosure requests to parties.[46] While there will be no room for fishing expeditions, it is expected that both courts may be more open to disclosure-of-documents requests than is usually the case in civil law procedures. Both courts may also fall back on the IBA Rules on the Taking of Evidence in International Arbitration.

The NCC Rules are overall more elaborate than the French protocols and include other interesting elements, like the possibility of having a court reporter prepare a verbatim transcript of a hearing instead of the usual, more concise summary of the hearing drawn up by the court.[47] The NCC Rules also make it possible to have a combined hearing with a closely connected foreign case, so counsel can argue both cases at the same time.[48]

[43] NCC Rules, art. 8.5.2, Protocol Relating to Procedural Rules Applicable to the International Chamber of the Court of Appeal of Paris', art. 5.3; 'Protocol Relating to Procedural Rules Applicable to the International Chamber of the Paris Commercial Court', art. 4.

[44] NCC Rules, arts. 8.5.3 and 8.6.1, 'Protocol Relating to Procedural Rules Applicable to the International Chamber of the Court of Appeal of Paris', arts. 5.4 and 5.5; 'Protocol Relating to Procedural Rules Applicable to the International Chamber of the Paris Commercial Court', art. 4.

[45] NCC Rules, art. 8.3.

[46] NCC Rules, art. 8.4, 'Protocol Relating to Procedural Rules Applicable to the International Chamber of the Court of Appeal of Paris', art. 5.1; 'Protocol Relating to Procedural Rules Applicable to the International Chamber of the Paris Commercial Court', art. 4.

[47] NCC Rules, art. 7.7.3.

[48] Ibid., art. 7.8.

Lastly, an interesting element in the NCC Rules is the allocation of costs at the end of the proceedings. The standard rule is that the unsuccessful party will bear the costs of the proceedings and that the lawyers' fees will be calculated based on fixed fees per process act. However, parties can deviate from these standard rules with an agreement on costs.[49]

11.5.4 (Online) Accessibility of the Court

Accessibility to the court and easy access to court information, including judgments, is an important feature of a court to make transparent its rules and practices. (Online) accessibility is furthermore relevant for both local as well as international lawyers so that they can familiarize themselves with the court and know how they can submit documents or reach out to clerks. All three European ICommCs have in this respect a different online presence.

The ICommC of Frankfurt am Main has one page on the website of the State of Hessen[50] that contains general information about the court and about the proceedings under the German Code of Civil Procedure. There are no judgments posted nor is any contact information for the court available, so its use is rather limited.

The French ICommCs do not have a shared website but have their own pages on the website of their host court. The Paris International Chamber has its own link on the Tribunal de Commerce de Paris website.[51] The French version of the website contained general information about the International Chamber, its procedures and its judges, but no judgments. The English website did not contain any information other than contact information at the time of writing this chapter. The International Chamber of the Court of Appeal does have a better website with information in French and English about the background of the International Chamber, the protocols and the judges.[52] It also contains a list of judgments of the appeal court with a short summary of the case in French and English and a link to the French judgment and, for most, but not all, cases, also the English translation.

Finally, the (English) website of the NCC contains detailed information about the court, its procedures and its judgments.[53] The NCC

[49] Ibid., art. 10.2.

[50] See https://ordentliche-gerichtsbarkeit.hessen.de/ordentliche-gerichte/lgb-frankfurt-am-main/lg-frankfurt-am-main/chamber-international, accessed 20 July 2020.

[51] See www.tribunal-de-commerce-de-paris.fr/fr/accueil, accessed 20 July 2020.

[52] See www.cours-appel.justice.fr/paris, accessed 20 July 2020.

[53] See www.ncc.gov.nl, accessed 20 July 2020.

furthermore uses e-filing (referred to as 'eNCC') for all court procedures and submissions so cases are easily started and pleadings submitted, with little extra paperwork. The NCC reaches out to the legal market itself as well with news updates and webinars, and in that sense resembles a well-oiled arbitration institute and not so much a governmental court.[54]

11.6 Experience, So Far

In the last part of my comparison of the three courts, I look into what these courts have accomplished during their short existence.

The launch of the Frankfurt Chamber for International Commercial Disputes generated a reasonable amount of publicity in 2018.[55] Against the backdrop of Brexit and the announcement of new European ICommCs there was significant interest in Germany's international chamber in Frankfurt. There is, however, little to no new published information that relates to the practices of the newly established Frankfurt Chamber for International Commercial Disputes. According to Burkhard Hess and Timon Boerner,[56] there was a first case transferred there in December 2018, but it is unknown how this case proceeded. Matthias Lehmann tries to explain in an interesting article why the Frankfurt ICommC has not generated any more cases yet and why the earlier international chambers established in Bonn and Cologne have only heard two cases since 2010.[57] In his view, Germany is, at least at the moment, not an attractive hub for transnational dispute resolution, but things might of course change in the future.

The Paris International Commercial Courts appear to have been busier than the Frankfurt court in the almost two and a half years of their existence in their current form. Since the judgments of the International Chamber of the Paris Commercial Court are not published on their

[54] The NCC organized in June 2020 its first webinar to discuss case management, videoconference hearings and the eNCC during COVID-19; see www.rechtspraak.nl/English/NCC/news/Pages/NCC-News-Updat-nr-9-Webinar-invitation-COVID19–.aspx, accessed 20 July 2020.

[55] See, for example, Christoph Just, 'Landmark in International Commercial Litigation? The Frankfurt High Court Installed a Specialized Chamber for International Commercial Matters', www.schulte-lawyers.com/schulteblog/2882017-6y2e6, Burges Salmon, 'Plans afoot for English-Speaking Commercial Courts in Europe Post-Brexit', www.burges-salmon.com/news-and-insight/legal-updates/plans-afoot-for-english-speaking-commercial-courts-in-europe-post-brexit, accessed 20 July 2020.

[56] Burkhard Hess and Tilman Boerner, 'Chambers for International Commercial Disputes: The State of Affairs' (2019) Erasmus L Rev 33.

[57] Lehmann, 'Law Made in Germany', 86.

website, nor are to be found on other websites, it is unclear what the caseload is of this court at the district level. More is known about the International Chamber of the Paris Court of Appeal. At the time of writing this chapter, there were thirty four judgments published on the website of the International Chamber of the Court of Appeal.[58] Of these thirty-four cases, twenty cases were appeals against judgments from a chamber of the Paris Commercial Court. The appeal judgment did in most cases not specify from which chamber of the Commercial Court the appealed judgment came – it is thus unclear whether they came from the International Chamber. Of the remaining fourteen cases, seven cases were appeals against judgments from courts outside Paris and the last seven judgments related to challenges against arbitration awards. The International Chamber of the Paris Court of Appeal has been given jurisdiction to decide on the challenge and enforcement of arbitral awards, so these cases can be brought directly to the International Chamber.

The Court of Appeal's judgments do not specify whether any part of the (oral) proceedings were conducted in English. Although all cases were international disputes, this does not necessarily mean that the oral proceedings will have been conducted in English, which is optional for parties. This will especially not be the case when the district-level proceedings have been fully conducted in French. Emmanuel Jeuland notes in this respect that very few hearings are held in English before the Paris International Commercial Courts.[59] While it is clear that the Paris International Commercial Courts have been handling cases since early 2018, a big question remains as to how much of the caseload was conducted in English.

The NCC has had to date a modest caseload of five cases in which final rulings were given since the start of its operations on 1 January 2019.[60] In all these cases, there was one Dutch party (either claimant or defendant) and an international counterparty. Of these five cases, four were summary proceedings and one was a standard claim procedure. The governing law of the latter case was English law. Both parties were supported by an English barrister or Queen's Counsel to brief the court on some aspects of English law.[61]

[58] Décisions CCIP-CA / ICCP-CA Judgment, www.cours-appel.justice.fr/paris/decisions-ccip-ca-iccp-ca-judgment, accessed 20 July 2020.

[59] Emmanuel Jeuland, 'The International Chambers of Paris: A Gaul Village', in Xandra Kramer and John Sorabji (eds.), *International Business Courts* (Eleven International 2019) 78.

[60] Judgments NCC, www.rechtspraak.nl/English/NCC/Pages/judgments.aspx, accessed 20 July 2020.

[61] Information provided by NCC Registrar Willem Visser.

Of the four summary proceedings, one case was particularly interesting; it was a COVID-19–related case between a US-based party (claimant) and a Dutch party (defendant). They had been in negotiations for several months about a deal to take over the claimant's 50 per cent stake in an equestrian show-jumping business for €169 million when COVID-19 started to change the world and the defendant wanted to walk away from the deal without further payment. This case led to two judgments in April 2020, the first an interim judgment regarding the jurisdiction of the NCC.[62] The defendant argued that there was no agreement to refer summary proceedings to the NCC and, alternatively, the NCC had no jurisdiction because arbitration was not yet pending. The NCC held that there was a valid NCC clause in which parties had agreed that 'any Party may apply to the [NCC] in Summary Proceedings for preliminary injunctive relief or similar interim measures necessary to preserve its rights pending resolution of any dispute arising out of or in connection with this [agreement] through arbitration'. The NCC furthermore held that the summary proceedings were 'within the scope of the NCC clause because the ordinary meaning of the word "pending" in the present circumstances is that an interim measure precedes and is without prejudice to the resolution of the dispute in arbitration'.[63] Following the interim judgment, a second videoconference hearing was held and one week later the final judgment was issued.[64] The NCC dismissed the claim to compel the transfer of the claimant's 50 per cent stake to defendant but granted payment of the agreed walk-away fee of €30 million instead to the claimant. The NCC was not persuaded by defendant's arguments to modify or reduce this fee given the COVID-19 circumstances. The NCC relied in this respect on the parties' judgment, who were considered 'experienced professionals, well guided and ably counselled by an array of experts. They set the fee and expressed their considered view that it was reasonable. They set their contractual equilibrium. The payment of the fee will preserve that equilibrium'.[65] The NCC therefore honoured the terms the parties had agreed on in their letter of intent.

After the NCC's first case, the lawyers who represented the parties were asked to participate in a survey. The respondents to the survey were

[62] *McCourt Global Sports & Media LLC* v. *Tennor Holding B.V.* [14 April 2020], ECLI:NL:RBAMS:2020:2277.

[63] Ibid.

[64] *McCourt Global Sports & Media LLC* v. *Tennor Holding B.V.* [29 April 2020], ECLI:NL:RBAMS:2020:2406.

[65] Ibid.

positive about the way the court handled the case.[66] One of the lawyers stated that '[e]specially the professionalism, speed, quality of the judge and quality of the decision were impressive', and his colleague praised the court for being 'responsive, flexible and quick. The judge had obviously read the documents and (in my view successfully) directed the debate to address only the relevant issues. The – for Dutch standards – novel use of the first person in the decision was quite convincing'.

Considering all of this, it is clear that both France and the Netherlands have been able to put their plans for an ICommC into action and their ICommCs are open for business. The caseload of the French and Dutch courts may be modest at this time, but this can be explained by the fact that it is only since the start date of these ICommCs that forum selection clauses can be included in international commercial contracts to designate the International Chamber of the Paris Commercial Court or the NCC as their forum of choice. It can therefore be expected that their caseload will increase over time. It is unclear whether the same can be said about Frankfurt's Chamber for International Commercial Disputes, since this court does not appear to be very active.

11.7 Conclusion

The question is frequently posed of whether ICommCs can really compete with international arbitration.[67] There are advantages to both forms of dispute resolution and it will depend on what the parties in question are looking for. The cases handled so far by Paris and Amsterdam in any case show that ICommCs complement international arbitration by offering summary proceedings where this is not always a (viable) option in arbitration, and by offering an English-speaking forum in case an award of an international arbitration tribunal is challenged.

Sir William Blair gave a lecture in 2016 at Durham University in which he talked about what international users are looking for from international commercial dispute resolution.[68] He suggested the following eight

[66] NCC News Update #6, www.rechtspraak.nl/English/NCC/news/Pages/NCC-Update-nr-6.aspx, accessed 20 July 2020.

[67] See, for example, Janet Walker, 'Specialized International Courts: Keeping Arbitration on Top of Its Game' (2019) 85 Arbitration 2–23, Dorothee Ruckteschler and Tanja Stooss, 'International Commercial Courts: A Superior Alternative to Arbitration?', (2019) 36 Journal of International Arbitration 431–50.

[68] Sir William Blair, 'Contemporary Trends in the Resolution of International Commercial and Financial Disputes' (January 2016), www.judiciary.uk/wp-content/uploads/2016/01/blair-durham-iccl-lecture-2016.pdf, accessed 20 July 2020.

components: (1) certainty – application of ascertainable legal principles to the underlying dispute; (2) accessibility of justice; (3) predictability – application of known procedures; (4) transparency – party awareness of the process; (5) independence; (6) experience and expertise of the court or tribunal; (7) efficient case management; (8) effective outcome and enforcement; adding reasonable cost of procedure as a possible ninth component.

European ICommCs tick all these boxes. Because of the very fact that we are dealing with courts instead of tribunals, they offer more safeguards in that their judges are independent and impartial, comply with known ethics standards and, last but not least, have the coercive power to manage cases efficiently or join parties. The European ICommCs therefore provide the essentials of what international users are looking for in international dispute resolution, and are a useful addition to the existing international dispute resolution scene. The NCC in particular, being the only real English-speaking court of the three European ICommCs, is very well equipped to become a true player in the field of international dispute resolution. Let us follow them closely and give them a chance to live up to their potential.

12

The Legitimacy and Ethics of International Commercial Court Judges

CATHERINE A. ROGERS

12.1 Introduction

The role of international arbitrators has long been the subject of debate among scholars and commentators: are they service providers or justice providers?[1] In other words, are arbitrators more akin to accountants or plumbers who provide contractual services,[2] than to judges, meaning that any resemblance between arbitration and litigation is quaint, superficial and perhaps even just coincidental?[3] Or are they justice providers, who serve the same adjudicatory function as the judges who would decide the case in the absence of an arbitration agreement?[4]

[1] Peter B. Rutledge, 'Toward a Contractual Approach for Arbitral Immunity', (2004) Ga L Rev (39)151, 160 (noting that theories of arbitration take one of two forms: the 'regulatory model, which emphasizes that active role of the state in defining the contours and boundaries of arbitration', and the 'market-based model', which 'rests on the basic belief that the form and structure for resolving a dispute should be left to private choice, unencumbered by a regulatory scheme').

[2] Paul D. Carrington and Paul H. Haagen, 'Contract and Jurisdiction' (1996) Sup Ct Rev 331, 337; Edward M. Morgan, 'Contract Theory and the Sources of Rights: An Approach to the Arbitrability Question' (1986–7) S Cal L Rev (60)1059, 1069 ('[T]he legitimacy of arbitral proceedings flows directly from a vision of private autonomy as the conceptual basis of contract law.').

[3] See, for example, Andrew Guzman, 'Arbitrator's Liability: Reconciling Arbitration and Mandatory Rules' (2000) Duke LJ (49)1279, 1316–24 ('Despite its superficial similarity to a court action . . . an arbitration proceeding is more properly viewed as the product of contract.').

[4] See, for example, *Mitsubishi Motors Corp.* v. *Soler Chrysler-Plymouth, Inc.*, 473 U.S. 614, 628 (1985) ('By agreeing to arbitrate a statutory claim, a party does not forgo the substantive rights afforded by the statute; it only submits to their resolution in an arbitral, rather than a judicial, forum.'); *Succula Ltd and Pomona Shipping Co. Ltd* v. *Harland and Wolff Ltd*, [1980] 2 Lloyd's Rep. 381, 388 (an 'arbitrator accepts an appointment . . . he becomes

Even if these questions about arbitrators' role are still open to debate, we now have a newly evolved creature to contend with – the international commercial judge. This new player evolved because the two alternatives – international arbitrator or national court judge – do not fully satisfy the perceived range of adjudicatory needs of international commercial actors.[5] This innovation, however, raises new questions about the nature of this new type of decision maker and the ethical obligations that accompany their role.[6]

International commercial judges have many features in common both with traditional judges and with international arbitrators. On one hand, they are appointed by a State to a standing court funded by tax dollars. They have plenary powers to compel compliance, including from third parties, which are borrowed from the host government's sovereign powers.

On the other hand, these decision makers generally only have jurisdiction when parties agree to submit disputes to them. They are often jurists who are foreign to the host State, a quality that is unusual in State-appointed, taxpayer-funded officials. These judges preside over proceedings in English, which is usually not the host State's local language, but an important adaptation to attract international parties.[7]

International commercial judges generally administer proceedings under international procedures and law selected by the parties. These procedures often have much in common with procedures followed in

a judicial officer, with exactly equal duties towards both parties. It is unnecessary to discuss whether the relationship is contractual in nature').

[5] Some commentators may challenge whether there is a need for this new form of international adjudication. Gary Born, 'A New Generation of International Adjudication' (2012) 61 Duke Law Journal 775.

[6] Some new efforts at international regulation aim to address the ethics of all adjudicators, both judges and arbitrators, in a unified code. See Draft Code of Conduct for Adjudicators in Investor-State Dispute Settlement, https://icsid.worldbank.org/sites/default/files/amendments/Draft_Code_Conduct_Adjudicators_ISDS.pdf (last visited 3 November 2021). The impetus for this effort is tied to proposed reforms in investor-State arbitration, which some hope will result in an international investment court. See Chiara Giorgetti and Mohammed Wahab, 'A Code of Conduct for Arbitrators and Judges', Academic Forum on ISDS Concept Paper 2019/12, 13 October 2019. Comments received as of the drafting of this chapter included several that questioned the wisdom of seeking to address both arbitrators and judges in a single source.

[7] Georgios Dimitropoulos, 'National Sovereignty and International Investment Law: Sovereignty Reassertion and Prospects of Reform' (2020) 21 Journal of World Investment and Trade 71, at 91–2; Georgios Dimitropoulos, 'International Commercial Courts in the "Modern Law of Nature": Adjudicatory Unilateralism in Special Economic Zones' (2021) 24 Journal of International Economic Law 361.

international arbitration.[8] Meanwhile, even if appointed by a host State, these decision makers are designed to adjudicate disputes that are often unrelated to people, events or issues related to that State. Ordinarily, a State's national courts would not have the jurisdiction to adjudicate or any interest in adjudicating such disputes.

These courts are created 'to provide efficient and credible means of commercial dispute resolution' for international disputes, but often 'in support of a particular centre with some of the characteristics of a free trade zone' or 'in support of the court processes already provided by the State'.[9] In creating such courts, host States' incentives are understood as signalling that they are savvy international actors attracting more inward investment.[10]

An essential requirement for these courts to succeed is internationally recognized legitimacy, which in turn implicates the identity and conduct of their judges.[11] It is accepted wisdom that '[f]oreign judges help establish the credibility and impartiality of [international commercial courts]'.[12] While the meaning and nature of legitimacy can be uncertain, it is generally accepted that, at a minimum, legitimacy requires that international judges act ethically and with professional integrity. Many sources acknowledge the link between legitimacy and ethics,[13] but few international courts or tribunals translate that link into meaningful ethical standards and enforcement regimes.

This chapter examines the link between the legitimacy of international commercial courts and the ethics of their judges. It starts from the premise that professional ethics are not only a matter of the personal

[8] For example, although now defunct, '[i]n its draft proposal, the Brussels International Business Court (BIBC) provides that, although the court remains a state court, the procedure will be based on the UNCITRAL Model Law on International Arbitration.' Alexandre Biard, 'International Commercial Courts in France: Innovation without Revolution?' (2019) Erasmus Law Review 24, at 29.

[9] Sir William Blair, 'The New Litigation Landscape: International Commercial Courts and Procedural Innovations' (2019) International Journal of Procedural Law 212, at 215.

[10] Ibid.

[11] Pamela K. Bookman, 'Arbitral Courts' (2021) 61 Va J Int'l L 161.

[12] Aarshi Tirkey, 'The Inconvenient Truth about China's International Commercial Courts', Observer Research Foundation (August 2020), www.orfonline.org/expert-speak/inconvenient-truth-china-international-commercial-courts (last visited 10 February 2021); see also Pamela K. Bookman, 'The Adjudication Business' (2019) 44 Yale Journal of International Law 231, at 264 ('basic levels of fairness and impartiality, which are widely considered markers of legitimacy').

[13] William ('Rusty') W. Park, 'Arbitrator Integrity: The Transient and the Permanent' (2009) 46 San Diego Law Review 629, at 630.

and professional integrity of adjudicators. Instead, their professional conduct requires more clear and deliberate delineation and effective enforcement mechanisms.

Formally delineated enforceable ethics rules are important because, in several areas, what constitutes appropriate judicial conduct may vary from jurisdiction to jurisdiction around the world. In national legal systems, judges are assigned different interrelationship roles, which can affect what is considered appropriate and inappropriate conduct in their systems. When parties and adjudicators from different systems end up in the same proceedings, ambiguity may arise. That ambiguity (and resulting confusion) has certainly been the observed situation with international arbitrators, which suggests it may also be the case for international commercial judges.[14]

This chapter begins by analysing the relationship between legitimacy in a legal system and ethical conduct of its actors. Next, the chapter examines how differing roles may affect what is considered appropriate. Finally, the chapter looks at the example of *ex parte* communication between judges and parties or counsel. The differences among national ethics regulation regarding this same issue illustrate the link between ethical obligations and the culturally differentiated roles that may be assigned to judges. It concludes by calling on States that host international commercial courts to commit energy and resources to developing separate codes of conduct for the judges in the courts they have created.

12.2 The Link between Legitimacy and Ethics

Both the founders of international commercial courts and commentators who analyse creation of those courts share a conviction that their success depends on establishing their legitimacy.[15] While they may disagree about

[14] For a detailed discussion of confusion about applicable and appropriate ethics rules among participants from different cultures, see generally Catherine A. Rogers, 'Regulating International Arbitrators: A Functional Approach to Developing Standards of Conduct', (2005) 41 Stanford International Law Review 53 (2005); Catherine A. Rogers, 'Fit and Function in Legal Ethics: Developing a Code of Attorney Conduct for International Arbitration', (2002) 23 Michigan International Law Journal 392.

[15] Many have challenged investment arbitration as subject to a crisis of legitimacy. Susan D. Franck, 'The Legitimacy Crisis in Investment Treaty Arbitration: Privatizing Public International Law through Inconsistent Decisions' (2005) 73 Fordham L Rev 1521. Many of these challenges focus on critiques of arbitrators and concerns about their bias, real and perceived; see Stavros Brekoulakis, 'Systemic Bias and the Institution of International Arbitration: A New Approach to Arbitral Decision-Making' (2013) 4 Journal of International Dispute Settlement 553 (discussing the link between perceived arbitrator bias and legitimacy of investment arbitration); see also Joost Pauwelyn, 'The Rule of Law

how to ensure legitimacy,[16] one thing they tend to agree on is that legitimacy inevitably relates to the integrity and ethical conduct of the judges.[17]

For example, the mission statement of the Qatar International Court provides that it aims:

> [t]o provide a world-class international court and dispute resolution Centre that will maintain the *highest ethical standards*, act in accordance with internationally recognized best practices and deliver justice fairly and efficiently with a firm commitment to upholding the Rule of Law.[18]

In a similar vein, Singapore Supreme Court Chief Justice Sundaresh Menon, chief architect of the Singapore International Commercial Court (SICC), explains that one reason for creating international commercial courts is that international arbitration cannot 'adequately address such things as the harmonisation of substantive commercial laws, practices and *ethics*'.[19]

Other individuals commenting on legitimacy and the professional conduct of international judges have echoed this point. Former South

without the Rule of Lawyers? Why Investment Arbitrators Are from Mars, Trade Adjudicators from Venus' (2015) 109 American Journal of International Law 761, at 763, 768, 780, 783 (positing that investment arbitrators themselves account for concerns about investment arbitration's legitimacy).

16 There is a distinction between what might be considered institutional legitimacy and procedural legitimacy. Institutional legitimacy is tied to the source of an adjudicatory body's authority, which is party consent for arbitration and government endowed powers for courts; see Bookman, Arbitral Courts (n. 11). While the two cannot always be teased apart, this contribution focuses on procedural legitimacy.

17 The 'stigma of illegitimacy' haunted arbitration in earlier eras, when English law 'allowed courts to reform or to revise completely an arbitrator's ruling on the legal questions that arose during the arbitration'. Thomas E. Carbonneau, 'Arbitral Justice: The Demise of Due Process in American Law' (1996) 70 Tulane Law Review at 1948. The development of clearer ethical regulation for international arbitration has been facilitated by increased opportunities for meaningful debate about arbitrator conduct and clearer guidance for arbitrators. For a discussion of these developments, see Catherine A. Rogers, 'Regulating International Arbitrators: A Functional Approach to Developing Standards of Conduct' (2005) 41 Stan. Int'l L. Rev. 53; see also Rogers, *Ethics in International Arbitration* (Oxford University Press 2014), at 11 ('International arbitration claims to provide modern, sophisticated, fair and legitimate adjudication. The *ethical* conduct of its participants is an implicit part of that claim.').

18 Qatar International Court and Dispute Resolution Centre, Mission Statement, available at www.qicdrc.gov.qa/about-us (last visited 10 February 2021) (emphasis added).

19 Sundaresh Menon, 'International Commercial Courts: Towards a Transnational System of Dispute Resolution', available at www.supremecourt.gov.sg/docs/default-source/default-document-library/media-room/opening-lecture–difc-lecture-series-2015.pdf (last visited 3 November 2021) (Opening Lecture for the DIFC Courts Lecture Series 2015) (emphasis added).

African Supreme Court Justice and international law commentator Richard J. Goldstone has explained:

> Creating viable long-term ethical standards lies at the heart of the fairness of international judicial proceedings. Its importance for the standing and respect for these courts cannot be overemphasized.[20]

Despite consensus that judicial ethics is a priority, this insight has not necessarily translated into specific, meaningful regulation of judges in international commercial courts.

Descriptions of and rules for international commercial courts regularly confirm that their judges are independent and impartial.[21] Although obvious in importance to judicial ethics, the terms 'independence' and 'impartiality' are concepts that mean little in the abstract.[22] Despite the fact that such general commitments have little meaning, rarely do these international commercial courts have an independent or detailed code of conduct that puts meat on these conceptual bones. In some respects, the absence of express codes of conduct in international commercial courts is symptomatic of a larger problem – the vast majority of international courts and tribunals (other than international criminal tribunals) are lacking similar codes of conduct that are binding on their judges.[23]

In addition to ethical regulation of judges, numerous non-judicial actors who are involved in litigation processes, and confirm and establish the role assigned to the judges, should also be subject to clear ethics regulations. These individuals include registry staff, tribunal secretaries, law clerks and translators.[24] As all these actors contribute to smooth and efficient administration of justice, it is essential that professional

[20] Richard J. Goldstone, 'International Judges: Is There a Global Ethic?', Ethics & International Affairs, September 2015, available at www.ethicsandinternationalaffairs.org/2015/international-judges-global-ethic/#:~:text=Judges%20shall%20uphold%20the%20independence,affect%20confidence%20in%20their%20independence (last visited 3 November 2021).

[21] See, for example, Astana International Financial Centre, Court Regulations, art. 11, available at https://aifc.kz/files/legals/68/file/3.-legislation-aifc-court-regulations-2017.pdf (last visited 3 November 2021).

[22] See Rogers, *Ethics in International Arbitration*, at p. 42.

[23] Jeffrey L. Dunoff and Chiara Giorgetti, 'Introduction to the Symposium: A Focus on Ethics in International Courts and Tribunals', 113 (2019) 279–83 (noting the absence of any code of ethics for the International Tribunal for the Law of the Sea, international human rights courts, or in investor–state dispute settlement); see also Chiara Giorgetti and Mohammed Wahab, 'A Code of Conduct for Arbitrators and Judges', Academic Forum on ISDS Concept Paper 2019/12, 13 October 2019 (noting that only a few international arbitration centres have codes of ethics for arbitrators).

[24] Jeffrey L. Dunoff and Chiara Giorgetti, 'Introduction to the Symposium: A Focus on Ethics in International Courts and Tribunals' (2019) AJIL Unbound 113, at 279–83

obligations be clarified and affirmed. Their obligations and the sources of those obligations may differ from those of the judges, particularly to the extent that they are filled by civil servants of the host State. But the need for clear and transparent guidance remains.

Professional regulation of these individuals must include, among other things, an obligation to protect confidentiality, ensure neutral principles of administration, and prevent or report corruption. As Jeffrey L. Dunoff and Chiara Giorgetti explain, the importance of these actors cannot be overstated.[25] Even the most honourable judge cannot properly administer justice if undermined by supporting staff working with contrary motivations or contrary perception of the judge's role.

The exception to the general absence of ethical regulation in international commercial courts is the SICC. This court has a separate code of judicial conduct[26] which is admirable in its detail and related commentary, as well as a separate code for counsel. The code for judges identifies and provides guidance on a number of sub-issues that contribute to the real and perceived impartiality of judges. For example, the SICC code addresses details about such issues as concurrent service on other tribunals, statements made in social media and *ex parte* communications.[27] The remainder of this chapter analyses why all international commercial courts should, at a minimum, have codes of conduct for their judges. It also identifies considerations and strategies for developing those codes, and illustrates the potential for confusion if that work is not undertaken.

12.3 The Judge's Role and Ethical Obligations

Ethics and professional rules of conduct should not be confused with personal or professional integrity.[28] Two judges may both have established reputations for professional integrity. They may, nevertheless, have very different ideas about how their integrity and commitments to impartiality translate into conduct imperatives in particular situations. The reason for these potential differences, even among upstanding judges, is that different legal systems assign different interrelational

[25] Ibid.

[26] Judicial Code of Conduct for International Judges of the Supreme Court of Singapore, available at www.sicc.gov.sg/docs/default-source/guide-to-the-sicc/sicc-code-of-conduct–22-february-2019.pdf (last visited 22 February 2019).

[27] Ibid., at 6 and 15.

[28] See Deborah L. Rhode and David Luban, *Legal Ethics* (Aspen 2nd ed. 1995), at 112.

roles to their judges. These different roles are determined, among other things, by different legal cultures.

For judges who serve on international courts that share a legal culture that is similar to their own, the differences may be small and limited. For example, an Austrian judge appointed to serve in an international commercial court founded in Germany or France may find the procedures and expectations so similar that little or no adjustment is needed. For judges whose systems come from significantly different legal traditions, however, the differences may be consequential. As Joshua Karton explains, legal culture 'both shapes and is shaped by the conduct of [a] community's members'.[29] Clarifying judges' interrelational roles is important because their ethical duties cannot be completely delineated without a clear understanding of their role.

This observation about judges is an example of the broader proposition that moral agency 'is embodied in roles' assigned to actors, who are 'mutually interdefined in terms of types of relationship'.[30] Alasdair MacIntyre illustrates this point by considering the question of whether a person has a moral obligation to feed a certain child. This query cannot be answered in the abstract. The precise answer depends on whether the person is the child's parent, neighbour, babysitter or a complete stranger (and perhaps even whether the child is on the street in front of the person's house or in a far-off land).[31] The point of this analysis is that situation-specific moral and ethical obligations cannot be analysed outside the context of the specific role assigned to an actor in relation to other relevant agents.

Under this reasoning, the ethical obligations of judges in international commercial courts must be determined by first examining their interrelational roles in the specific courts in which they operate. In national

[29] Joshua Karton, *The Culture of International Arbitration and the Evolution of Contract Law* (Oxford University Press 2013) 19; see also Tom Dannenbaum, 'Nationality and the International Judge: The Nationalist Presumption Governing the International Judiciary and Why It Must Be Reversed,' (2012) 45 Cornell International Law Journal 3, at 130 ('In . . . transnational legal communities future international judges develop skills of legal analysis and simultaneously adopt and create the legal culture within which the duty of impartial judging is articulated and emphasized.').

[30] Alasdair MacIntyre, *After Virtue: A Study in Moral Theory*, 2nd ed. (University of Notre Dame Press 1984) 23 ('[E]very moral philosophy offers explicitly or implicitly at least a partial conceptual analysis of the relationship of an agent to his or her reasons, motives, intentions, and actions, and in so doing generally presupposes some claim that these concepts are embodied or at least can be in the real social world.').

[31] Larissa MacFarquhar, *Strangers Drowning: Grappling with Impossible Idealism, Drastic Choices and the Overpowering Urge to Help* (Penguin 2015).

legal systems, the roles of judges are determined by numerous variables. Some of the most influential determinants are the processes by which they are appointed, their decisional methodology, and the procedural arrangements used for gathering proof.[32] Some aspects of these features are quite distinct as between common law and civil law judges, as has already been analysed extensively elsewhere.[33]

In international courts and tribunals, differences become more subtle or opaque because their very existence is an effort to harmonize different procedural traditions and legal cultures, and the roles they portend. The nature of international commercial judges is further complicated because their status, and hence their role, is a mix of public and private features.

Role differentiation among adjudicators does not mean that they do not have in common some universally recognized obligations that all judges share. All adjudicators, both judges and arbitrators, share certain core features, which derive from the nature of adjudication itself. These shared features help discern the role of judges in international commercial courts.

A good place to start defining the role of the archetypal judge is Lon Fuller's classical definition of adjudication. Fuller's universal definition of adjudication is 'a process of decision that grants to the affected party a form of participation that consists of the opportunity to present proofs and reasoned arguments'.[34] This core definition of adjudication, in turn, implies certain fundamental procedural functions that must be performed by an adjudicator in relation to other actors in the adjudicatory process. An adjudicator must be a third party empowered to render authoritative and reason-based decisions after considering arguments from both sides.

From this definition of an adjudicator's functional role, in turn, it becomes clear that an adjudicator must, at some level, be impartial. Bringing reasoned analysis to bear on legal problems necessarily requires being detached enough to engage in rational analysis of the problem as well as an ability to consider arguments from both sides. These functions

[32] See Catherine A. Rogers, 'Regulating International Arbitrators: A Functional Approach to Developing Standards of Conduct' (2005) 41 Stanford Journal of International Law 53, 59.

[33] For the seminal discussion of these differences, see Mirjan R. Damaška, *The Faces of Justice and State Authority: A Comparative Approach to the Legal Process* (Yale University Press 1986), at 130.

[34] Lon Fuller 'The Forms and Limits of Adjudication' (1978) 92 Harvard Law Review 353, at 369.

necessarily imply an obligation of impartiality. Absent impartiality, outcomes would not be based on reasoned application of legal rules or premised on parties' evidence and arguments. Outcomes would instead be based on the personal interests or preferences of the adjudicator.

From these features of the archetypal adjudicator, legal systems differ regarding what constitutes appropriate judicial conduct with respect a host of specific issues that define the extent and nature of adjudicators' impartiality obligations. Painting with very broad brushstrokes, the civil law judge could be characterized as 'the engine of the adjudication machine'.[35] The classic model of the civil law judge has broad managerial powers and 'schedules, sets the agenda for, and presides over a series of hearings, any one of which may ultimately decide the case'.[36] The civil law judge also, in consultation with the parties, 'decides which witnesses and documents will be presented, and the order of such proof'.[37]

This role generally includes taking a leading role in the interrogation of witnesses and in both clarifying the issues and encouraging settlement.[38] As the case progresses, a civil law judge will typically discuss the case with the litigants, including indicating the judge's provisional views regarding the likely outcome. This process occasionally even includes 'encouraging a litigant to abandon a case that is turning out to be weak or hopeless, or to recommend settlement'.[39]

In contrast to these civil law arrangements, common law systems are built around the concept of a 'judicial tabula rasa'.[40] In other words, the common law judge 'is supposed to obtain only through the party dialectic all evidence that must be evaluated and legal arguments that must be analyzed, and ... are to remain completely neutral until it is time to render the final judgment'.[41] In light of this judicial role, attorneys in

35 Rogers, 'Fit and Function in Legal Ethics', 396.

36 Ibid.

37 Ibid.

38 Ibid.

39 John H. Langbein, 'The German Advantage in Civil Procedure' (1985) 52 U Chi L Rev 823, 832 and 862.

40 See Mirjan R. Damaška, 'Presentation of Evidence and Factfinding Precision', (1975) 123 University of Pennsylvania Law Review 1083 at 1088–9 ('"Coaching" witnesses [in inquisitorial systems] comes dangerously close to various criminal offenses of interfering with the administration of justice' as well as being contrary to professional canons of ethics); see also John C. Reitz, 'Why We Probably Cannot Adopt the German Advantage in Civil Procedure' (1990) 75 Iowa Law Review 987, at 994.

41 Rogers, 'Fit and Function in Legal Ethics', 392.

common law systems also have a different role than attorneys in civil law systems.

As a consequence of the relatively passive role of common law judges, attorneys are given a more active role in managing the proceedings, at least relative to their civil-law counterparts. The attorney in US litigation, for example, gathers evidence for the client's case, shapes the issues for trial, and presents evidence at trial, including developing expert testimony and examining and cross-examining witnesses. Because the judge only rules on particular requests presented by the parties, attorneys act as the clients' strategists, evaluating the case and advising when and how various procedural tactics should be used.

In international commercial courts, some of these differences between civil law and common law judges may be ameliorated. Even if judges on international commercial courts come from distinct legal cultures, they generally share what might be called a professional culture (as opposed to a legal culture) that comes from their background as former commercial law judges and lawyers,[42] and their experience on the international stage. Nevertheless, it is difficult to imagine that any judge becomes truly separate from the legal culture in which they were educated and trained.[43] In fact, some international commercial courts appear to intentionally draw judges from a range of different systems, including both common law and civil law.

A good way to understand how different national legal cultures and training among judges and the attorneys who appear before them is to examine a more specific example. *Ex parte* communications among judges, on one side, and parties and counsel, on the other side, provides a helpful illustration of how differences in role determined by legal culture translate into different judicial ethical obligations.

[42] Daniel Terris, Cesare Romano and Leigh Swigart, 'Toward a Community of International Judges', (2008) 30 Loy. L.A. Int'l & Comp. L. Rev. 419, 420–1(describing among international judges a shared 'understanding of the judicial function, and what it entails … [a]nd a common commitment to the aims of international justice animates their growing sense of belonging to a single professional group'). For similar analysis behind the creation of international commercial courts, see Standing International Forum of Commercial Courts, sifocc.org, available at https://sifocc.org/about-us (last visited 1 March 2021).

[43] Paul Schiff Berman, 'The Enduring Connections between Law and Culture: Reviewing Lawrence Rosen, *Law As Culture*, and Oscar Chase, *Law, Culture, and Ritual*' (2019) 57 American Journal of Comparative Law 101, at 102 ('[C]ulture is not simply a set of customs we can choose to put on or take off like clothing; it is woven into the fabric of our being.').

12.4 The Example of *Ex Parte* Communications

Differing approaches to regulating *ex parte* communications illustrate how national legal systems differ in how they interpret and apply impartiality obligations, and the relationship between ethics and role.[44] These differing approaches also illustrate why clearer guidance and more express regulation is needed to avoid ethical misunderstandings and improve the perceived legitimacy of international commercial courts.

12.4.1 Ex Parte *Communication in Civil and Common Law Systems*

Judicial impartiality is generally understood as requiring limitations on an adjudicator's ability to communicate *ex parte* with parties or their lawyers. All systems acknowledge generally that judicial impartiality implies treating parties equally, which in turn suggests limiting the range of permissible communications between parties and judges. The reason for these limitations is obvious: 'Inappropriate' communications might give one side an unfair opportunity to influence the judge or create a perception of partiality. Despite consensus on this basic principle, however, different legal systems draw in a different place the line between what is appropriate and inappropriate with regard to *ex parte* communications.

In the classical model of the civil law system, it is not necessarily presumed that both parties will always be present during proceedings with the judge. If, for example, a German attorney arrived at a hearing at which opposing counsel was either absent or late in arriving, it would be considered perfectly appropriate for the judge to discuss with the present attorney various aspects of the case.[45] In the United States (and many other common law systems), the same conduct might well result in a motion to disqualify the judge and an ethics complaint against the lawyer.

[44] Detlev Vagts, 'International Legal Ethics and Professional Responsibility' (1998) 92 Am Soc'y Int'l L Proc 378, at 379 (discussing a hypothetical case involving contrasting approaches to *ex parte* communication with arbitrators and the need for regulation of such issues).

[45] See, for example, Code of Conduct – Germany, § 8.3 ('A lawyer may contact or submit documents or exhibits to a judge without the knowledge of the lawyer(s) or the opposing client(s) in the case'), cited in Laurel S. Terry, 'An Introduction to the European Community's Legal Ethics Part I: An Analysis of the CCBE Code of Conduct' (1993) 7 Geo J Legal Ethics 1, 36 n. 159, 37–8, and n. 158 (noting that in many European countries '*ex parte* contact with the court on "nonfundamental" issues is not prohibited').

American judicial ethics entail almost absolute restrictions against *ex parte* communications, except in rare procedural contexts.[46] This near absolute prohibition is consistent with the expectation in common law systems about the role of the judge. As alluded to previously, the role of the judge in common law systems is to be 'a blank slate on which the parties, in heated contest, draw their dispute. The system permits no stray renderings by one party that might unfairly alter the tableau.'[47]

The best explanation for the German (and more generally civil law) tolerance for what Americans would consider unethical communication is that the German judge performs a more managerial role. This role may imply that the judge is less susceptibility to lopsided efforts at persuasion and that observers would be less inclined to regard communications as disrupting the delicate equipoise expected of judges in common law systems.[48]

Another context in which *ex parte* traditions may differ as among judges and lawyers from different legal cultures is in the interplay of mediation or settlement and adjudication. Similar to German and other judges trained in civil law, Chinese judges and arbitrators often act as a mediator in the same case in which the person presides as ultimate arbiter.[49] Under this practice, the Chinese judge-turned-mediator may elicit information from the parties in what – from an American perspective – are improper *ex parte* conversations. The substance of these *ex parte* conversations may be (but is not necessarily) communicated to other parties, and '[i]f mediation fails and the court elects to try the case, it may without further investigation rely solely on the information acquired by the judge while he acted as a mediator'.[50]

[46] See, for example, Wolfram, *Modern Legal Ethics* (1986), § 11.3.3, 605–6 (1986).

[47] Rogers, 'Fit and Function in Legal Ethics', 392.

[48] Oscar G. Chase, 'Legal Processes and National Character' (1997) 5 Cardozo J Int'l & Comp L 1, at 4–5.

[49] Jun Ge, 'Mediation, Arbitration and Litigation: Dispute Resolution in the People's Republic of China' (1996) 15 UCLA Pac Basin LJ 122, 127 (noting that the Chinese Civil Procedure Law requires judges to conduct mediation if the parties do not object).

[50] Stanley B. Lubman, 'Dispute Resolution in China after Deng Xiaoping: "Mao and Mediation" Revisited', 11 Colum J Asian L 229, 337 (1997) (quoted in Philip J. McConnaughay, 'Rethinking the Role of Law and Contracts in East–West Commercial Relationships' (2001) 41 Va J Int'l L 427, at 444).

By contrast, an American-trained attorney historically would regard these same *ex parte* mediation efforts as creating a risk that 'the arbitrators may become biased or even corrupted'.[51] Put even more starkly:

> [The] role [of a mediator is] fundamentally repugnant to, and inconsistent with, that ascribed by law to the traditional Anglo-Australian arbitrator. ... [For the same individual to serve both as mediator, and then, if unsuccessful, as arbitrator is] fundamentally contrary to the requirements of natural justice.[52]

This view has changed somewhat in the United States. In recent years, US judges have evolved to assume a more 'managerial' function, which includes encouraging settlement.[53] These procedural changes, however, have not been clearly addressed in modified ethics rules for judges or counsel.[54] As a result 'the ethics rules are unclear as to the judge's proper role in ... in helping to encourage settlement'.[55] More concisely, how can 'a judge ... realize when an ethical line has been crossed if the line has never been drawn in the first place'?[56]

As the US experience demonstrates, even judges from the same national background can morph in their role, with attendant ethical implications. Functional roles can be influenced by pragmatism, which can occur on an ad hoc basis. The development of managerial judging in the United States is a perfect example. The managerial judge's new role in promoting settlement was a practical response to the perceived need to streamline court dockets.[57]

[51] Randall Peerenboom, 'The Evolving Regulatory Framework for Enforcement of Arbitral Awards in the People's Republic of China' (2000) 1 Asian-Pac. L. & Pol'y J 12, 23.

[52] J. D. Fine, 'Continuum or Chasm? Can West Meet East?' (1989) 6 J Int'l Arb 27, 30 (quoted in McConnaughay, 'Rethinking the Role of Law and Contracts in East–West Commercial Relationships', at 452).

[53] See Judith Resnik, 'Managerial Judges' (1982) 96 Harv L Rev 374, at 390, 425–7 (demonstrating and criticizing the modern trend of 'managerial judging').

[54] For a thoughtful discussion of the changes to ethics rules that have been made and arguments against those changes, see Ellen E. Deason, 'Beyond "Managerial Judges": Appropriate Roles in Settlement' (2018) 78 Ohio St L J 73, at 105–27; see also Nancy A. Welsh, 'Magistrate Judges, Settlement and Procedural Justice' (2016) 16 Nev L J 983, at 1004–14, 1018–23, 1028–35.

[55] Sylvia Shaz Shweder, 'Judicial Limitations in ADR: The Role and Ethics of Judges Encouraging Settlements' (2007) 20 Geo. J. Legal Ethics 51, 57.

[56] Ibid.

[57] Of course, not everyone agreed that settlement promotion was itself a worthy goal. For the seminal work opposing settlement as an independent value, see Owen M. Fiss, 'Against Settlement' (1984) 93 Yale Law J 1073, at 1085–7 (opposing facilitation as settlement for, among other reasons, securing peace at the expense of justice and denying the court the opportunity to interpret the law).

In contrast to procedural evolutions, ethical assumptions and expectations tend to more constant over time. This potential lack of alignment can provoke not only criticisms of judges, but more broadly concerns about the fairness or legitimacy of the cases over which they preside. This latter point brings us back to international commercial courts' concerns about their own real and perceived legitimacy and their focus on judges as a source for that legitimacy.

12.4.2 Ex Parte *Communications in International Commercial Courts*

As examined earlier in this chapter, new roles, including those created by new types of judicial appointments, may portend new ethical obligations. Those new ethical obligations, however, may not always fit well-perceived roles and related assumptions. The lesson from this insight is that role, ethics and perceived legitimacy must be engineered, not left to chance.

The emergence of the US managerial judge illustrates how the original judicial role to which ethical obligations were tethered has slipped from its moorings. When that slippage occurs, actors whose role has shifted and those who interact with them in court proceedings may retain background assumptions about what constitutes proper professional conduct.[58]

The differing common law and civil law limits on *ex parte* communication are both regarded as legitimate, ethical judicial practices in their respective systems. If German and American attorneys appear together before an international commercial judge, however, things get more complicated. Presumably the American judges, arbitrators or attorneys would studiously avoid *ex parte* contacts, whereas lawyers, arbitrators or judges trained in civil law might demonstrate a greater willingness to engage in such communications. In fact, not so long ago differing approaches to *ex parte* communication were identified in international arbitration as a problem that needed fixing.[59]

Notably, the otherwise excellent code of conduct for SICC judges does not specifically comment on judicial efforts to aid in settlement and

[58] Rogers (n. 16), at 397.

[59] Vagts, 'International Legal Ethics and Professional Responsibility', at 379 (reporting a panel discussion of a hypothetical case involving European and American lawyers in an arbitration in Geneva that was governed by Swiss law); Ambassador Malcolm Wilkey, 'The Practicalities of Cross-Cultural Arbitration', in Stefan N. Frommel and Barry A. K. Rider (eds.), *Conflicting Legal Cultures in Commercial Arbitration: Old Issues and New Trends* (Kluwer Law International 1999) 79, 86 (describing differing approaches to *ex parte* communication as a problem in international arbitration that must be overcome).

related issues regarding *ex parte* communication. The related SICC Code of Ethics for foreign lawyers, however, has specific and detailed regulation of *ex parte* communication, which are in line with the strict prohibitions typical in common law procedural traditions.[60]

Most (though not all) judges on the SICC are from common law backgrounds, which may suggest shared implicit understandings including with respect to *ex parte* communications and settlement efforts by judges. But with counsel and parties from other legal traditions, even the (mostly) shared background of the judges may not be enough to ensure shared understandings of what is considered appropriate conduct.

It is easy to imagine disruption and potential damage to the perceived legitimacy of an international commercial court if a judge from a civil law background engaged in *ex parte* communications regarded as perfectly acceptable in that judge's legal system. However, that same conduct was regarded as wholly inappropriate to counsel or parties from a common law background. Similarly, it would be easy to imagine a judge trained in common law taking umbrage if an attorney trained in civil law sought to engage the judge in *ex parte* communication that the judge considered ethically impermissible.[61]

To avoid these and other similar potential pitfalls to their legitimacy, international commercial courts should not rely on generalized concepts of integrity or impartiality as a substitute for detailed, formal judicial regulation. Specific guidance is needed, as are clear mechanisms for enforcement. That guidance requires clear codes of conduct for judges.

12.5 Conclusion

This chapter has examined why, for new international courts to establish and enjoy the benefits of legitimacy, they must develop and enforce a clear set of ethical rules for their judges. Those rules must go beyond general exhortations for judges to act with personal integrity. Instead, they must grapple concretely with several issues on which parties and counsel from different legal backgrounds may have different perspectives and expectations about what conduct is ethical and, related, required for an adjudication to be considered fair and legitimate.

[60] See Code of Ethics, S 851/2014, art. 7, available at www.sicc.gov.sg/docs/default-source/guide-to-the-sicc/code-of-ethics_revised.pdf (last visited 10 February 2021).

[61] To some extent, this problem is ameliorated by the Code of Ethics for lawyers, which by its terms pre-empts conflicting foreign ethical rules; ibid., at Article 16.

13

Counsel Ethics in Transnational Lawyering

The Case of International Commercial Courts

ZACHARY R. CALO

Introduction

This chapter considers legal ethics in the context of transnational lawyering, with a focus on the regulation of counsel. While the main concern is to understand regulation of lawyers within international commercial courts (ICommCs), challenges confronting transnational legal ethics extend beyond these specialized institutions. The issues confronting commercial courts are rather endemic to transnational lawyering that takes place across national boundaries, legal systems and regulatory codes.[1] New questions have arisen because of the growing use and importance of dispute resolution mechanisms outside the bounds of domestic civil courts. While the central question in a domestic context is what attorney conduct is to be regulated, the more fundamental questions in the transnational context concern who is to be regulated, by whom, and how these regulations should relate to other ethical obligations that apply to lawyers in jurisdictions of professional licensure.

International arbitration is one area in which examination of these issues is highly developed, at least in terms of the discussion amongst stakeholders, even though implementation has been slower to take shape. By contrast, no meaningful attention has been given to ethics in the context of ICommCs. This reflects, among other factors, the relative novelty of these institutions, their small number, and their independence from each other. There is not a unity of concern that holds together the work of commercial courts in the same way there is with international arbitration. Given this state of affairs, the sizeable ethics literature within

[1] On the internationalization of legal practice see Matthew S. Fronk, 'Making Mistakes Abroad: How the Global Delivery of Legal Services Created a Need for a Uniform Ethics Code' (2013) 21 Michigan State International Law Review 496.

international arbitration offers a useful starting point for identifying and assessing similar issues confronting commercial courts.

While there are discrete concerns specific to these two contexts, there are also common challenges relating to counsel ethics in transnational lawyering. This chapter considers how these different contexts address such matters as the interaction between domestic regulation of the legal professional and regulation within specialized tribunals, the problem of conflict between different ethical norms, the interaction between norms within specialized tribunals and those generally applicable within the jurisdiction, determinations about the scope of regulation, and whether uniformity of norms across institutions is advisable. With particular focus on courts in Qatar, Dubai, Abu Dhabi, and Singapore, the chapter offers a typology of different models for regulating counsel. Even as there are important similarities in form and function among these institutions, these diverse approaches to counsel ethics reveal different institutional structures, needs, and tendencies.

13.1 Counsel Ethics in International Arbitration

Ethics is a frequent topic of discussion within the international arbitration community.[2] Debate around the issue has acquired particular momentum in recent years, but first took shape in the 1980s when a number of international arbitration tribunals issued codes of conduct for arbitrators (although not for counsel). This trend has continued with an increasing number of codes and guidelines being issued. Yet, as Carrie Menkel-Meadow points out, '[t]here remain virtually no rules for the conduct of lawyers, parties, witnesses, etc. in international arbitration'.[3] The focus has rather been almost exclusively on ethical standards for arbitrators. This is beginning to change, with various stakeholders now assessing whether and how counsel in arbitration should also be regulated.[4] While the implementation of regulatory schemes has been

[2] Iris Ng, 'Rethinking Counsel Ethics in International Arbitration', *Kluwer Arbitration Blog* (12 December 2019). http://arbitrationblog.kluwerarbitration.com/2019/12/12/rethinking-counsel-ethics-in-international-arbitration/?doing_wp_cron=1593969066.5437951087951660156250

[3] Carrie J. Menkel-Meadow, 'Are Cross-Cultural Ethics Standards Possible or Desirable in International Arbitration?', in Peter Gauch, Franz Werro, and Pascal Pichonnaz, eds., *Melanges en L'Honneur de Pierre Tercies* (Schulthess 2008) 891–2.

[4] Edna Sussman and Solomon Ebere, 'All's Fair in Love and War – Or Is It? Reflections on Ethical Standards for Counsel in International Arbitration' (2011) 22 American Review of International Arbitration 611.

slow, important developments have taken place that reveal the outlines of movement to translate concepts into action.

The debate about counsel ethics in arbitration revolves around a number of central problems:

13.1.1 Domestic Regulation of the Legal Profession and Unclear Standards

Many of the challenges surrounding counsel ethics in international arbitration arise because of the established practice of regulating lawyers at the national or state level. This localized system of regulation is ill-suited to a transnational practice. What rules govern? Do home rules from the jurisdiction of licensure apply during an international arbitration? If a lawyer is licensed in multiple jurisdictions, as if often the case with international arbitration practitioners, what is the applicable home jurisdiction? Do rules from the seat apply in an international arbitration? Counsel potentially are governed by multiple norms, including those of the jurisdiction of licensure, the jurisdiction in which the arbitration is occurring, and the rules of the arbitral tribunal. It might also be the case that lawyers are subject to no identifiable regulatory scheme, resulting in what Catherine Rogers notably called an 'ethical no man's land'.[5] In a humorous illustration of the problem, Doak Bishop, in his 2010 keynote address at the meeting of the International Council of Commercial Arbitration, asked, 'What are the professional rules applicable to an Indian lawyer in a Hong Kong arbitration between a Bahraini claimant and a Japanese defendant represented by New York lawyers?'[6] It might well be the case that the lawyers themselves do not know.[7]

5 Catherine A. Rogers, 'Fit and Function in Legal Ethics: Developing a Code of Conduct for International Arbitration' (2002) 23 Michigan Journal of International Law 341.

6 Doak Bishop, 'Ethics in International Arbitration', International Council for Commercial Arbitration (2001) 1. www.arbitration-icca.org/media/0/12763302233510/icca_rio_keynote_speech.pdf

7 See Silvano Domenico Orsi, 'Ethics in International Arbitration: New Considerations for Arbitrators and Counsel' (2013) 3 The Arbitration Brief 109–10. Cyrus Benson notes that '[o]ne might well ask 50 arbitration practitioners to describe the professional conduct principles applied by them and one would receive 50 different answers'. 'Can Professional Ethics Wait? The Need for Transparency in International Arbitration' (2009) 3 Dispute Resolution International 79.

13.1.2 *Conflicting Standards (The Problem of Double Deontology)*

A related problem is that an attorney might be subject to conflicting ethical requirements. This is commonly referred to as the problem of double deontology. In this situation, a lawyer could violate a rule of ethics regardless of the conduct taken. For instance, Rogers recounts an incident in which a German attorney was imprisoned for failing to disclose information required under English law but which disclosure would have subjected the attorney to professional discipline for violating client confidentiality.[8] A similar situation could arise because of conflict with the rules of a tribunal. As Jane Wessel and Gordon McAllister note, '[i]t is a confusing and wholly unsatisfactory situation when a lawyer needs to be concerned with potentially competing and contradictory ethical regulations when conducting an international arbitration'.[9] In such situations, the problem of ethics in transnational lawyering results not merely in ethical ambiguity but ethical incoherence. Efforts to regulate counsel ethics in arbitration could have the paradoxical effect of increasing the likelihood of just such a conflict.

13.1.3 *Inequality and Unfairness*

Even if there is clarity about the ethical rules that apply to counsel, another problem that can arise concerns fairness among lawyers who are subject to different governing norms. For one thing, applying rules of conduct with which a lawyer is not familiar, such as those of the arbitral seat, imposes an undue burden.[10] An even more problematic situation involves strategic inequality, for instance, between common and civil law lawyers who are subject to different standards with respect to such matters as the scope of discovery, taking of witness statements, or preparing witnesses. At its extremes, this potential divergence in ethical obligations might precipitate a 'Machiavellian cost-benefit analysis' of what strategically advantageous conduct can be pursued.[11]

There is widespread agreement that these are among the main issues concerning counsel ethics in international arbitration. This agreement

[8] Catherine Rogers, *Ethics in International Arbitration* (Oxford University Press 2014) 107.

[9] Jane Wessel and Gordon McAllister, 'Towards a Workable Approach to Ethical Regulation in International Arbitration' (2015) 10 Canadian International Lawyer 5.

[10] Richard M. Mosk, 'Attorney Ethics in International Arbitration' (2010) 5 Berkeley Journal of International Law Publicist 32.

[11] Cyrus Benson, 'Can Professional Ethics Wait? The Need for Transparency in International Arbitration' (2009) 3 Dispute Resolution International 79.

aside, little consensus remains about what response, if any, should be advanced. Little progress has been made in systematically regulating counsel at any level. One reason is that many stakeholders remain of the opinion that the current system works reasonably well and that problems are not of a serious and widespread enough nature to justify a strong-handed interventionist approach.[12] The proposed remedies could be worse than the disease.[13] It has also been argued that imposing more systematized ethical norms would create unnecessary burdens that undermine the flexible and contractual nature of the arbitral process. Gary Born has expressed concern that further regulation could create a potential basis for challenging arbitral awards on the basis of unethical attorney conduct.[14] There also continues to be some confidence that conduct within international arbitration can be adequately governed by informal norms of conduct – which Cyrus Benson terms 'subjective "internationalized" versions of national codes'.[15] These shared values about ethical conduct provide a means of self-governance without the need for formalized rules. This approach might have worked efficiently when the arbitration community was smaller, more closed, and more homogenous.[16] However, many commentators are now of the opinion that greater legal and cultural diversity renders such informal arrangements increasingly untenable. Along these lines, Rogers has argued that '[i]nternational arbitration cannot continue to operate with uncertain, unwritten, and culturally variable assumptions about what constitutes proper conduct for attorneys'.[17]

These concerns aside, there is significant support for establishing some means of regulating attorney conduct within international arbitration. A 2018 Queen Mary University survey found 73 per cent of respondents

[12] Wessel and McAllister, 'Towards a Workable Approach to Ethical Regulation in International Arbitration', 12.

[13] Charlie Caher and Jonathan Lim, 'Regulation of Counsel and Professional Conduct in International Arbitration', in *The International Comparative Legal Guide to International Arbitration* 2019. https://iclg.com/practice-areas/international-arbitration-laws-and-regulations/1-regulation-of-counsel-and-professional-conduct-in-international-arbitration

[14] Wessel and McAllister, 'Towards a Workable Approach to Ethical Regulation in International Arbitration', 6.

[15] Benson, 'Can Professional Ethics Wait?', 80.

[16] Sundaresh Menon, 'The Special Role and Responsibility of Arbitral Institutions in Charting the Future of International Arbitration', Keynote Address (SIAC Congress, 17 May 2018). www.supremecourt.gov.sg/Data/Editor/Documents/SIAC%20Congress%202018%20Keynote%20Address%20%20(Checked%20against%20delivery%20with%20footnotes%20-%20170518).pdf

[17] Rogers, *Ethics in International Arbitration*, 137.

agreed that arbitration rules (whether institutional or ad hoc) should address the 'conduct of parties and/or their counsel'.[18] Sundaresh Menon observes that there is 'an emerging sense that perhaps something ought to be done'.[19] But what? A range of positions have been advanced that tend to centre around the following options: (1) establishing a binding international code of conduct; (2) developing institutional codes of conduct; (3) utilizing ethical checklists agreed to by the parties in order to establish a contract-based code of conduct.

The idea of establishing an international code of conduct represents the most ambitious response to the problem of counsel ethics. Rather than relying on a patchwork regulatory framework at the institutional or party level, proponents of an international code propose that a uniform and universally applicable set of norms, along with a centralized means of enforcement, represents the more effective and efficient approach. Global practice requires a global regulatory system.

There are different schemes for implementing such a universal code. The most serious proposal came from the Swiss Arbitration Association (ASA), which called in 2014 for the creation of a Global Arbitration Ethics Council.[20] This entity, to be composed of representatives from arbitration associations, would develop a code of core ethical principles and also have enforcement and sanctioning power. The ASA proposal aimed to build upon the recently promulgated IBA Guidelines and LCIA Rules. Elliott Geisinger, the president of the ASA at the time, stressed the importance of both the rule-making and enforcement functions. By centralizing rule-making, a global council avoids 'fragmentation' and the impression that 'there are no generally recognized minimum standards of ethical behavior'.[21] Moreover, by vesting enforcement in a neutral institution, the proposal would avoid problems associated with having arbitrators deciding

[18] Queen Mary University of London and School of International Arbitration, '2018 International Arbitration Survey: The Evolution of International Arbitration', 34. www.arbitration.qmul.ac.uk/media/arbitration/docs/2018-International-Arbitration-Survey–The-Evolution-of-International-Arbitration-(2).PDF

[19] Menon, 'The Special Role and Responsibility of Arbitral Institutions in Charting the Future of International Arbitration'.

[20] 'ASA Proposes Global Arbitration Ethics Counsel to Apply and Enforce Ethical Principles' (16 September 2014). www.arbitration-ch.org/en/asa/asa-news/details/979.asa-proposes-global-arbitration-ethics-counsel-to-apply-and-enforce-ethical-principles.html?querystart=11

[21] Elliott Geisinger, '"Soft Law" and Hard Questions: ASA's Initiative in the Debate on Counsel Ethics in International Arbitration', *ASA Special Series* No. 37 (2015): 26–7.

matters of counsel ethics.[22] The proposal received widespread attention, but a subsequent report of the ASA Working Group on Counsel Ethics concluded that creation of the Global Arbitration Ethics Council 'is an idea whose time has not yet come'.[23] The idea has not been revisited.

A second approach to regulating counsel ethics focuses on developing rules of conduct at the institutional level. While this approach would not achieve the more totalizing uniformity envisioned by the ASA's Global Arbitration Ethics Council, it would have a norm-shaping influence on international practice. If spearheaded by leading arbitral institutions and legal organizations, perhaps with some degree of coordination, this modality could achieve a soft consensus on the norms and processes that should regulate counsel.[24] Along these lines, one commentator argues that 'there is a compelling need for an internationally standardized code' and that 'enforcement of any future standardized code should be done by the major arbitral institutions'.[25]

Dozens of such ethical codes have been issued.[26] Perhaps the most significant effort to move the process forward was achieved through the 2013 IBA Guidelines on Party Representation in International Arbitration.[27] The IBA Guidelines establish a detailed framework for regulating counsel within arbitration, consisting of twenty-seven rules and extensive comments to the rules. These rules cover a range of issues relating to attorney conduct including *ex parte* communication, document production, and preparation of witness statements or testimony. With respect to remedies for misconduct, Rule 26 provides that the arbitral tribunal may, among other sanctions, admonish counsel and consider misconduct in appropriation of costs. The IBA Guidelines are

[22] Ibid., 22–5.

[23] 'Report of the ASA Working Group on Counsel Ethics'. www.arbitration-ch.org/en/asa/asa-news/details/993.asa-working-group-on-counsel-ethics-releases-latest-findings.html

[24] Stephen Schill proposes that international tribunals could utilize working groups and consultations with administering institutions to 'coordinate their work so as not to impose starkly diverging obligations concerning counsel conduct'. Stephan Schill, 'The Case for Public Regulation of Professional Ethics for Counsel in International Arbitration' (*Kluwer Arbitration Blog*, 7 July 2017). http://arbitrationblog.kluwerarbitration.com/2017/07/07/case-public-regulation-professional-ethics-counsel-international-arbitration/?doing_wp_cron=1596142856.9383389949798583984375

[25] Orsi, 'Ethics in International Arbitration', 108–9.

[26] Menon, 'The Special Role and Responsibility of Arbitral Institutions in Charting the Future of International Arbitration'.

[27] International Bar Association, 'Guidelines on Party Representation in International Arbitration' (2013). www.ibanet.org/Publications/publications_IBA_guides_ and_free_materials.aspx

not a comprehensive code of conduct but do touch on many important and sometimes contested issues. Moreover, the IBA Guidelines address potential conflicts that might arise with other ethical obligations in a prudential rather than rule-based manner. For instance with respect to witness preparation, Comments to Guidelines 18–25 note that domestic conduct norms sometimes impose higher standards and that conflicts should be addressed with the other party and/or the arbitral tribunal. By so proposing, the IBA Guidelines aim to skirt the double deontology problem by delegating responsibility to the parties and the tribunal to achieve a proper remedy.

The IBA Guidelines have no juridical force as such. It is a model code for what norms might govern arbitration. As noted in the Preamble, these rules are of a 'contractual nature' and 'parties may thus adopt the Guidelines or a portion thereof by agreement'.[28] Not only parties but also institutions may adopt the rules, and the Australian Centre for International Commercial Arbitration and the Lagos Chamber of Commerce International Commercial Arbitration Centre did so in 2016.[29] A similar approach involves arbitral tribunals establishing their own ethics rules for counsel, the most notable instance being the London Court of International Arbitration's 2014 'General Guidelines for the Parties' Legal Representatives'. These Guidelines, incorporated as an Annex to the LCIA Arbitration Rules, address such matters as making false statements, concealing documents, and ex parte communications.[30]

[28] See also Guideline 1: 'The Guidelines shall apply where and to the extent that the Parties have so agreed, or the Arbitral Tribunal, after consultation with the Parties, wishes to rely upon them after having determined that it has the authority to rule on matters of Party representation to ensure the integrity and fairness of the arbitral proceedings.'

[29] Ng, 'Rethinking Counsel Ethics in International Arbitration'.

[30] LCIA Rule 18.6 provides that: 'In the event of a complaint by one party against another party's legal representative appearing by name before the Arbitral Tribunal (or of such complaint by the Arbitral Tribunal upon its own initiative), the Arbitral Tribunal may decide, after consulting the parties and granting that legal representative a reasonable opportunity to answer the complaint, whether or not the legal representative has violated the general guidelines. If such violation is found by the Arbitral Tribunal, the Arbitral Tribunal may order any or all of the following sanctions against the legal representative: (i) a written reprimand; (ii) a written caution as to future conduct in the arbitration; and (iii) any other measure necessary to fulfil within the arbitration the general duties required of the Arbitral Tribunal under Articles 14.4(i) and (ii).' This rule is significant in authorizing the tribunal to order sanctions against an attorney found to be in violation. By so doing, the LCIA establishes a self-governing ethical ecosystem that offers a potential model for future regulation at the institutional level. Concerns have been raised, however, about vesting arbitrators with the authority to make determinations on matters of ethics. While arbitral institutions arguably are in the best position to make these determinations,

The LCIA Guidelines, in contrast to the IBA Guidelines, are narrow in scope.[31] Their limited reach creates fewer potential conflicts with other attorney obligations and affords greater space for parties to agree on matters of conduct.[32] At the same time, the minimalist approach taken by the LCIA, and the failure to take a position on some of the more challenging and complicated ethical questions confronting counsel in arbitration, raise questions about the overall impact of these rules.

A final model emphasizes party autonomy by relying on a contract-based approach to regulating attorney conduct . Rather than imposing standardized norms, this approach gives parties control over the rules that govern the arbitration based on their particular needs and interests. Cyrus Benson has advanced the idea of an 'ethical checklist' to be utilized at the outset of an arbitration. The checklist allows parties to reach agreement on norms of conduct and to ensure that there is no inequality because of differing national rules that bind counsel. Benson describes this in terms of 'procedural fairness' that establishes a 'level playing field' between the parties.[33] The model checklist addresses rules on a variety of issues around legal submissions, evidence, disclosure, and communications which the parties agree to either adopt or reject. There is, of course, no reason the parties need to operate with a prefabricated checklist. They can also devise their own agreed upon terms. Benson's checklist, along with other similar initiatives, represent a pragmatic and low-cost way to bring ethics more formally into the arbitral process but in a way that emphasizes flexibility, fairness, and party autonomy.[34]

this responsibility falls outside the proper scope of authority for the arbitrators. This model also invites questions about whether arbitrators would be willing to take the professional risk of imposing ethical sanctions on attorneys.

31 Vincent S. Dattilo, 'Ethics in International Arbitration: A Critical Examination of the LCIA General Guidelines for the Parties' Legal Representatives' (2016) 44 Georgia Journal of International and Comparative Law 652.

32 Paragraph 1 of the General Guidelines for the Parties' Legal Representatives provides that: 'Nothing in these guidelines is intended to derogate from the Arbitration Agreement or to undermine any legal representative's primary duty of loyalty to the party represented in the arbitration or the obligation to present that party's case effectively to the Arbitral Tribunal. Nor shall these guidelines derogate from any mandatory laws, rules of law, professional rules or codes of conduct if and to the extent that any are shown to apply to a legal representative appearing in the arbitration.' Whereas the IBA Rules address the double deontology problem by directing an affected party to address the other party and/or the arbitral tribunal, the LCIA Guidelines establish a hierarchy of obligation.

33 Benson, 'Can Professional Ethics Wait?', 89.

34 Rogers, *Ethics in International Arbitration*, 262.

13.2 Counsel Ethics in International Commercial Courts

13.2.1 Current Regulatory Models

Debate about counsel ethics within international arbitration provides a starting point for assessing similar issues within ICommCs. Because international arbitration and ICommCs operate in a similar transnational space and share similar aims, the assessment of counsel ethics in the former can illuminate the latter. However, while international arbitration and ICommCs both provide mechanisms for dispute resolution outside the boundaries of traditional domestic litigation, important differences remain that bear on the regulation of counsel. As such, while debate about ethics within international arbitration might properly inform that within commercial courts, the two should not be overly conflated.

International commercial courts are often characterized as a third way of resolving disputes that adopt characteristics of both arbitration and traditional civil litigation.[35] Moreover, international arbitration and commercial courts are both promoted as mechanisms for establishing an investment friendly environment that bypasses local courts and concerns about the enforceability of judgments.[36] While countries hosting commercial courts are also likely to have invested in arbitration infrastructure, they have much more control in using commercial courts to advance particular aims. Decisions regarding the scope of a court's jurisdiction, the composition of its judiciary including the extent to which it utilizes foreign judges, decisions about language and governing law, the relationship to domestic courts, and procedures for enforcing judgments all impact the role a given court has within a country's overall judicial system. The key point is that commercial courts, for all their outward-facing profile, are creations of domestic law and remain embedded within the domestic legal infrastructure. As Lucy Reed observes, '[i]t bears emphasis that international commercial courts … are part of the relevant *municipal* legal order. Their *international* profile comes from their case load, bench, bar and/or rules'.[37] International arbitration, by contrast, remains in significant respects a form of private dispute

[35] Steven Chong describes the Singapore International Commercial Court as a 'careful marriage between litigation and arbitration'. 'The Singapore International Commercial Court: A New Opening in a Forked Path', speech delivered at British Maritime Association Lecture and Dinner (October 2015), 52.

[36] Cf. Georgios Dimitropoulos, 'International Commercial Courts in the "Modern Law of Nature": Adjudicatory Unilateralism in Special Economic Zones' (2021) 24 Journal of International Economic Law 361.

[37] Lucy Reed, 'International Dispute Resolution Courts: Retreat or Advance,' (2017–18) 4 McGill Journal of Dispute Resolution 137 (emphasis in original).

resolution largely dissociated from the court system.[38] A country can invest in the development and promotion of its arbitration infrastructure, cultivate a favourable reputation for ease of enforcement, and hold other strategic advantages but, in the end, remains at a fundamental remove from the arbitration process itself.

International commercial courts hold different relationships to their respective domestic courts and legal systems. Most importantly, they have different degrees of autonomy and different jurisdictional mandates that, in turn, inform approaches to counsel ethics. The Qatar International Court and Dispute Resolution Centre (QICDRC) and the Dubai International Financial Centre (DIFC) Courts, for instance, are both located within international financial centres and operate at significant distance from the domestic legal regime. The original jurisdictional mandate of the DIFC Courts was to resolve disputes that arose in relation to the financial centre, although the jurisdiction has been expanded to now permit parties to contract to their jurisdiction.[39] The QICDRC continues to have more limited jurisdiction only over matters involving Qatar Financial Centre (QFC) entities.[40] It is not a general commercial court to which parties without such points of contact can freely contract to grant jurisdiction. Yet while these courts operate outside the domestic civil court system, judgments of the commercial courts are enforceable in their respective country's civil courts.[41] The Singapore International Commercial Court (SICC), by contrast, is organized as a division of the High Court of Singapore and, as such, is embedded within the domestic legal framework. The SICC has a broader jurisdiction in that it can also hear disputes of parties who consent to jurisdiction in a written agreement as well as cases the High Court directly refers to it. As a division of the High Court, SICC judgments are enforceable as judgments of the High Court. Because the SICC is also located within the domestic judicial system, there should be greater ease in enforcing its judgments in other jurisdictions.

These differences aside, all commercial courts share the general characteristic of being 'something of a hybrid' between arbitration and traditional

[38] Domestic courts retain the prerogative under domestic law and international obligations to refuse enforcement of arbitral awards on certain defined bases.

[39] Law No. (16) of 2011 Amending Certain Provisions of Law No. (12) of 2004 Concerning Dubai International Financial Centre Courts, Article 5.

[40] The Qatar Financial Centre Civil and Commercial Court Regulations and Procedural Rules, Article 9.

[41] On enforcement of awards see Michael Hwang, 'Commercial Courts and International Arbitration – Competitors or Partners?' (2015) 31 Arbitration International 193–212.

litigation, operating from within an outward-facing domestic legal framework.[42] The structure of these institutions as specialized domestic courts frames their approach to counsel ethics. Many of the same ethical challenges within international arbitration apply to international commercial courts. What ethical norms govern foreign counsel practising before them? Are attorneys subject to multiple and potentially conflicting norms that give rise to the double deontology problem? Are there problems with equality and fairness because attorneys are subject to different ethical norms? Who should regulate, if at all, and with what degree of specificity and breadth?

Ethical issues arise because of the distinctive location of these institutions within the domestic legal system. By one measure, commercial courts have severed, or at least complicated, the traditional link between geography and regulation of the legal profession, much in the way that arbitration has. At the same time, these international institutions remain rooted in a domestic system. The semi-independent character of ICommCs – creations of domestic law yet existing at a remove from the domestic judicial system – establishes the context within which counsel is regulated. Questions arise as a consequence. Who should make decisions about whether and how to regulate lawyers? Should foreign lawyers have a right of appearance before these institutions and, if so, subject to what conditions? To what extent should general norms regulating attorney conduct apply to foreign lawyers appearing before a specialized commercial court? These in turn feed into broader questions concerning the structure and aims of the institutions. What degree of autonomy does a given commercial court hold in relation to the domestic legal system? Should there be coordination among commercial courts with respect to ethical norms? Some of these questions arise from the specific structure of a given legal system. Others invite a more general discussion about the future role of ICommCs. They collectively establish the context within which to assess different approaches to counsel ethics.

A number of models exist for regulating counsel within ICommCs. Three such approaches are detailed next, with reference to courts in Qatar, Dubai, Abu Dhabi, and Singapore.[43] These can be categorized as no regulation, court-level regulation, and state-level regulation.

[42] Dalma R. Demeter and Kayleigh M. Smith, 'The Implications of International Commercial Courts on Arbitration' (2016) 33 Journal of International Arbitration 442.

[43] A fuller analysis would need to also take account of ethics provisions in other recently opened ICommCs. For instance, the Astana International Financial Centre (AIFC) Court provides a Code of Conduct for lawyers holding rights of audience. 'AIFC Court – Code of Conduct for Legal Practitioners', https://court.aifc.kz/uploads/AIFC%20Court%20-%

The QICDRC has adopted the approach of not expressly regulating attorney conduct. The Qatar Financial Centre Civil and Commercial Court Regulations and Procedural Rules provide that '[t]he Court, acting by the President may issue Practice Directions or Practice Guides in relation to any aspect of the procedures to be followed by the Court'.[44] While authority exists, no such regulations have been promulgated. Regulations at the QFC, within which the QICDRC is located, include a Legal Services Code that applies to all QFC lawyers.[45] These rules address certain key issues including conflicts of interest and confidentiality but are not intended to serve as a comprehensive code of legal ethics. However these Rules apply only to 'QFC Lawyers' providing legal services on behalf of a firm licensed to provide services in or from the QFC.[46] While this includes many of the international firms operating in Qatar, it is not a general regulation that applies to all lawyers appearing before the QICDRC. Non-QFC lawyers appearing before the Court are not bound by the Code or any other ethical regulations emanating from a Qatari legal authority.[47]

The QICDRC approach relies largely on regulations that apply to lawyers based on professional licensure in another jurisdiction. Although QFC lawyers are subject to regulations of the Legal Services Code, they must also report 'any matter which may affect their good standing with their Legal Professional Body or their ability to remain a member of their Legal Professional Body'.[48] Such a provision has the

20Code%20of%20Conduct%20for%20Legal%20Practitioners.pdf. The AIFC Code of Conduct is minimalist in content and addresses only general duties to the Court, other lawyers and clients. The new Netherlands Commercial Court (NCC) does not appear to have promulgated ethical rules specific to the institution. The NCC also has more restrictive protocols on foreign lawyers, allowing them to represent a client before the Court only when holding a cooperation agreement with a domestically registered lawyer. See Ioana Knoll-Tudor, 'The European and Singapore International Commercial Courts: Several Movements, a Single Symphony' (*Kluwer Arbitration Blog*, 6 March 2019), http://arbitrationblog.kluwerarbitration.com/2019/03/06/the-european-and-singapore-international-commercial-courts-several-movements-a-single-symphony. It likewise does not appear that the China International Commercial Court has established any specific ethical rules for counsel.

44 The Qatar Financial Centre Civil and Commercial Court Regulations and Procedural Rules, Article 37.2.

45 QFCA Rules, Part 6 (3 February 2020). https://qfcra-en.thomsonreuters.com/sites/default/files/net_file_store/QFCRA_5172_VER8.pdf

46 Ibid., Part 6.1.

47 Unless the lawyer is a member of the Qatari bar and subject thereby to the rules of professional conduct established in Law 23 (2006) of the Civil Code.

48 QFCA Rules (3 February 2020), Part 6.9.12. The QFC Legal Services Code provides that a conflict between QFC rules and those of another professional body 'shall be referred to the

effect of incorporating these norms indirectly into the QFC governance structure. There are no such express requirements for non-QFC lawyers practising before the QICDRC, although the Court would likely report certain ethical violations to external professional bodies. In this respect, regulation of counsel is largely outsourced.

Whereas the QICDRC has not established a code of ethics for counsel, the DIFC Courts and the Abu Dhabi Global Markets (ADGM) Courts have developed binding codes of conduct that apply to all lawyers practising before them. Like the QFC, the DIFC Courts are located within an international financial centre, address disputes arising out of entities or activities related to the financial centre, and have adopted a common law–based system of adjudication.[49] Rights of appearance before the DIFC Courts are open to international practitioners who are duly registered, although the process favours lawyers from common law jurisdictions.[50]

The right to practise before the DIFC Courts is conditioned upon observance of a Code of Conduct.[51] While not a totalizing code of ethics on par with those that apply in a domestic context, the Code addresses issues ranging from duties owed to clients, the Court, other practitioners, and parties such as witnesses. A notable feature is that the Code provides a formalized system for receiving and assessing complaints. Parties found in violation are subject to private or public admonition, monetary fines, and suspension or removal from the Register of Practitioners. In addition, the Code provides that when imposing a sanction other than a private admonition, the Court may notify the bar association or other regulatory body to which the lawyer is subject.[52] This provision provides additional teeth to the Court's enforcement authority.

The ADGM Courts have taken a similar approach to the DIFC Courts by promulgating their own Rules of Conduct that 'apply to lawyers

QFCA for resolution'. QFCA Rules (3 February 2020), Part 6.9.3. This less-determined approach to addressing conflicts contrasts with those of other courts which establish a hierarchy of obligation. The Legal Services Code, by contrast, prioritizes flexibility over clarity.

49 On the legal structure of the DIFC, see www.difc.ae/business/laws-regulations.

50 On requirements for registration of legal practitioners within the DIFC Courts see www.difccourts.ae/guidelines-registration-practitioners.

51 DIFC Courts' Order No. 4 of 2019, Mandatory Code of Conduct for Legal Practitioners in the DIFC Courts. www.difccourts.ae/wp-content/uploads/2019/09/DIFC_Courts_Order_No._4_of_2019_Mandatory_Code_of_Conduct_for_Legal_Practitioners_in_the_DIFC%20Courts.pdf

52 See Mandatory Code of Conduct for Legal Practitioners in the DIFC Courts, Part F, Sanctions for Breach of the Code.

appearing before the ADGM Courts'.[53] The aim of the Rules 'is to assist lawyers to act ethically and in accordance with the principles set out in these Rules'.[54] The ADGM Rules cover many of the same subjects as the DIFC Code, although they are less detailed and exhaustive. A significant feature of the ADGM's approach is a requirement that '[l]awyers must comply with the Rules, notwithstanding any provision to the contrary in any rules of conduct to which they are subject in any other jurisdiction in which the lawyers are duly authorized to practice law'.[55] By pre-empting other rules to which a lawyer is subject, the ADGM Rules avoid ambiguity as to the scope of authority. Perhaps it is assumed that because the Rules are of a general nature they are unlikely to prompt a conflict with specific obligations arising from another jurisdiction. All the same, while the ADGM Rules aim to bypass the problem of double deontology, their approach accentuates potential tensions.

The SICC offers yet another model for regulating attorney conduct. There are similarities between the SICC approach and that of the courts in Dubai and Abu Dhabi, particularly concerning the content of regulations. Yet, whereas regulations at the latter are made by the courts and exist apart from the regulatory structure that applies to the domestic legal system, those which apply to the SICC are derived from legislation governing Singapore's judiciary and legal profession. The SICC rules reflect its location within the domestic judicial framework. Under the SICC system, a registered foreign attorney may represent parties under statutorily defined conditions.[56] Every registered foreign lawyer must comply with the Code of Ethics set forth in the Legal Professions Act.[57] Although encompassing only sixteen provisions, the Code of Ethics covers a number of fundamental and contested issues. Of the ethics codes under consideration, the SICC Code most mirrors that of a domestic legal regime. Its rules are more substantial than merely supplementary. Among issues addressed are *ex parte* communications, false submissions, document disclosure, and preparation of witnesses.[58]

[53] ADGM Courts, Rules of Conduct Rule 1.1.

[54] Ibid., Rule 1.2.

[55] Ibid., Rule 1.3.

[56] Registration of Foreign Lawyers before the SICC. www.sicc.gov.sg/registration-of-foreign-lawyers

[57] Legal Profession Act, Chapter 161, Rule 38. https://sso.agc.gov.sg/SL/LPA1966-S851-2014#pr38-

[58] SICC Code of Ethics, Rules 7, 8, 10, 13. www.sicc.gov.sg/docs/default-source/guide-to-the-sicc/code-of-ethics_revised.pdf

In addition, as with Abu Dhabi, the SICC Code of Ethics provides that its rules trump any other rules of conduct to which a lawyer might be obligated.[59]

13.2.2 Future Challenges

These are different models, all of which have advantages and limitations. Qatar has adopted a minimalist approach of not directly regulating counsel appearing before the tribunal. Dubai and Abu Dhabi have adopted a more intensive approach, creating a clear set of applicable norms but ones which do not attempt to be overly systematic in their coverage and which might be viewed as primarily complementary in nature. These courts moreover have issued rules pursuant to their regulatory authority. Finally, Singapore provides an even more complete code of ethics for foreign lawyers through legislation. This diversity not only reflects strategic choices made by individual courts but the different location of these courts within domestic legal systems. As international courts continue to grow in number, importance, and visibility, additional issues are likely to arise about the most appropriate means of regulating counsel ethics.

One issue is whether there is need for more extensive regulation. Across the courts discussed, there is a general tendency to regulate counsel selectively, if at all. The ethical codes cover different aspects of legal conduct, albeit it with a significant degree of overlap, but in no instance do they approach a comprehensive set of standards. They are prudential efforts to regulate issues of particular concern to the court and of central importance to the litigation process. The various codes are designed to complement existing systems of domestic regulation of the legal professional rather than offer a totalizing parallel alternative. This tendency mirrors that seen within the international arbitration community, where ethical guidelines issued by institutions and associations typically address a limited set of essential attorney duties and do not approach resembling a fully developed ethical code. Even when court rules provide that its guidelines trump other obligations, there is an

[59] Rule 16 of the SICC Code of Ethics provides that '[w]here a registered foreign lawyer acts in any relevant proceedings before the Court, the registered foreign lawyer must comply with the provisions of this Code of Ethics, despite any provision to the contrary in any rules of ethics or professional conduct to which the registered foreign lawyer is subject in any other state or territory in which the registered foreign lawyer is duly authorised or registered to practise law'.

implicit reliance on the larger ethical infrastructure within existing domestic regulatory regimes.

The circumscribed scope of the ethics guidelines reflects their supplementary nature. It also represents an accommodation to the needs of foreign lawyers who practise before the courts. The competitiveness and attractiveness of these institutions depends in part on there not being onerous and opaque rules to which lawyers are bound. While regulation has the benefit of establishing and equalizing standards, it can also impede the dynamic and flexible character of the institutions. The autonomy commercial courts have from the domestic system makes it possible to maintain a regulatory model that preserves these characteristics. Pressure to more fully integrate courts, or to subject them to greater regulation, will have important implications for the treatment of foreign lawyers and attorney conduct.

Another issue concerns whether efforts should be taken to synchronize standards across commercial courts. Strong voices within the international arbitration community advocate coordination of ethical standards. Although the Swiss Arbitration Association (ASA) did not succeed in establishing a Global Arbitration Ethics Council, initiatives such as the IBA Guidelines have had some measurable impact on conversation about the proper scope of regulation. Do these same considerations apply to international commercial courts? A number of leading commentators have begun speaking in favour of greater harmonization. For instance, Justice John Middleton of the Federal Court of Australia has addressed 'the important issue of consistency and . . . "harmonisation" of substantive laws, practices and ethics' within commercial courts.[60] For the Chief Justice of Singapore, Sundaresh Menon, harmonization would allow courts to more effectively develop a *lex mercatoria*. Along these lines, he proposed in a 2015 lecture that ICommCs 'can be instrumental in facilitating the harmonization of commercial law and practices'.[61]

[60] John E. Middleton, 'The Rise of the International Commercial Court', address at the 2018 Hong Kong International Commercial Law Conference. www.fedcourt.gov.au/digital-law-library/judges-speeches/justice-middleton/middleton-j-20180921

[61] Sundaresh Menon, 'International Commercial Courts: Towards a Transnational System of Dispute Resolution', Opening Lecture for the DIFC Courts (2015), www.supremecourt.gov.sg/docs/default-source/default-document-library/media-room/opening-lecture–difc-lecture-series-2015.pdf. A similar perspective was offered by Singapore Supreme Court Justice Kannan Ramesh, who identified international commercial courts as uniquely positioned to foster 'the holy grail – harmonization of substantive commercial law'. Kannan Ramesh, 'International Commercial Courts: Unicorns on a Journey of a Thousand Miles', Lecture presented at the Conference on the Rise of International

It is beyond the scope of this chapter to assess whether it is appropriate or feasible to seek a strategic convergence of substantive law among these courts by, for instance, fostering a self-referential jurisprudence. The question of whether procedural and ethical norms should be harmonized can, however, be considered independently of this larger issue. Commercial courts might well play an important role, alongside arbitral institutions, mediation organizations, and other international bodies in addressing new challenges confronting counsel ethics in transnational lawyering. At the same time, synchronizing norms across commercial courts might not be as appropriate as synchronizing norms within international arbitration. Indeed, while certain efficiencies could be gained through harmonizing norms and enforcement mechanisms, commercial courts have reasons for wanting to maintain maximal control over their governing rules. More than that, commercial courts are located in different jurisdictions, with different forms of organization, different strategic objections, different jurisdictional mandates, and different relationships to domestic courts such that a unified code of ethics might well run counter to the structure and needs of a given institution.

From this perspective, the current situation is not a problem but an appropriate reflection of institutional diversity. The experiences of commercial courts might properly inform each other but not necessarily with the goal of advancing regulatory synchronicity. In light of this situation, an approach to ethics centred at the institutional level is most apt, whether regulations are created through a court's own authority or through an authority external to the court. There is often an impulse to seek more and better coordinated regulation, yet in this instance such ambitions should be limited by a posture of modesty.

Such modesty might be understood in two respects. First, there is modesty with respect to resisting a push to achieve a more integrated regulatory model. The issues confronting counsel ethics in commercial courts are different from those within international arbitration in a particularly important respect. While international arbitration can exist within an 'ethical no man's land', this is not the case with ICommCs.[62] All of the commercial courts under consideration have adopted an approach to regulating attorney conduct and have the capacity to enact new regulations as needed. Rather than pushing

Courts, Doha, Qatar (13 May 2018). www.sicc.gov.sg/docs/default-source/modules-document/news-and-article/international-commercial-courts-unicorns_23108490-e290-422f-9da8-1e0d1e59ace5.pdf

[62] Rogers, 'Fit and Function in Legal Ethics', 341.

a coordinated regulatory schema, it is better to respond as issues emerge. Some form of coordination or overlapping engagement could in the longer term prove valuable but, unlike with international arbitration, the conditions for pursuing such a project lack significant justification at the present moment. While debate within arbitration often focuses on specific ethical problems, such as the use of guerrilla tactics, there is no such similar issue that is endemic to commercial courts and for which regulation is needed. In the absence of such common problems, it is all the more proper to defer to the judgment of individual institutions.

Second, there is modesty with respect to the scope of regulation. Commercial courts regulate lawyers to varying degrees but all of the models reflect the structures, aims, and location of the respective courts within their domestic system. Regulation in commercial courts follows institutional form. As a type of domestic court, these institutions do not face the ethical void that can define international arbitration. At the same time, imposing overly exacting standards of conduct would inhibit the very flexibility, openness, and efficiency that make them internationally attractive and competitive. Higher barriers of entry to foreign lawyers, including more detailed and unfamiliar ethical provisions, run counter to these objectives. As such, ethical obligations that apply to foreign lawyers appearing before these tribunals tend to focus on essential issues. They are supplemental, not comprehensive, codes of ethics. Commercial courts operate as ethical halfway houses between arbitration and domestic courts, adopting an approach to regulation that focuses on best practices that cut across different ethical systems. This approach appropriately balances the character of these institutions as both domestic and transnational entities.

In the longer term, effective institutional codes of conduct within commercial courts will need to take fuller account of how existing approaches to regulating lawyer conduct at the state and national levels interface with the globalization and pluralization of legal practice. For instance, existing approaches to regulating counsel ethics do not untangle the problems of fairness and double deontology. This cannot be accomplished at the institutional level alone but rather will require broader international cooperation across states, particularly with respect to choice of law.[63] For the time being, debate about counsel ethics in

[63] More integrated and comprehensive approaches to counsel ethics in a transnational context will require addressing conflicts of laws issues. To create a universal regime, or even one which has widespread effectiveness across jurisdictions and institutions, will

transnational lawyering occurs largely in isolated silos. Stakeholders within international arbitration, international commercial mediation, and international commercial courts assess needs and debate solutions without much consideration to the larger shared landscape. Should efforts to devise more integrated solutions occur in the future, commercial courts are uniquely positioned to play a central role in that process.

Conclusion

This chapter has developed a preliminary typology for identifying different ways in which ICommCs have regulated counsel ethics. Utilizing debate within international arbitration as a background, the analysis identifies a number of regulatory challenges that confront international courts. Issues unique to these courts arise because of their location within domestic legal regimes and their strategic role in providing efficient, flexible, and internationally attractive dispute resolution forums. In response, courts in Qatar, Dubai, Abu Dhabi, and Singapore have developed a range of regulatory approaches. It is argued that this diversity is not itself problematic but reflects different strategic needs and choices as well as different institutional forms. At the same time, across this diversity a shared understanding exists that ethics rules should exist in a modest and supplementary relationship with those that otherwise govern foreign lawyers. It might also be the case that this state of affairs is the beginning rather than the end of a process. The ongoing emergence of ICommCs will only further amplify challenges with regulating lawyers in a transnational environment increasingly dependent on various forms of alternative dispute resolution. The impulse to impose greater and more coordinated regulations, which has found some resonance within the international arbitration community, could grow among ICommCs as well.

require a degree of coordination across domestic regulatory regimes. This is by no means an unachievable aim but is also not something likely to take shape in the short term. Wessel and McAllister, 'Towards a Workable Approach to Ethical Regulation in International Arbitration', 12.

14

The Use of Technology at International Commercial Courts

PIETRO ORTOLANI

14.1 Introduction: Dispelling Two Myths

Technology can be used in a multitude of dispute resolution fora. Among these disparate settings, international commercial courts (ICommCs) seem to be a particularly promising environment, for at least two reasons. First, given the special nature of the disputes ICommCs aim to resolve, it is particularly desirable to devise bespoke and efficient solutions, so as to address the numerous challenges cross-border litigation structurally entails. Second, since many of the cases pending before ICommCs concern high values in dispute,[1] it is likely that parties, judges and administrators will adopt an ambitious approach to technology, harnessing its full potential.[2] In light of this, the use of technologies is a key challenge for all ICommCs.[3] This chapter investigates the topic from a comparative perspective.

[1] To be sure, ICommCs do not aim at resolving exclusively high-value disputes. To the contrary, some ICommCs expressly envisage special small claims procedures: the DIFC Courts, for instance, include the Small Claims Tribunal for cases of value up to USD 136,000. See https://sct.difccourts.ae, accessed 1 February 2020. Nevertheless, many cross-border cases involve significant amounts in dispute, and some ICommCs are especially tailored for high-value claims: the NCC, for instance, cannot be used for low-value disputes, which fall within the competence of a Dutch Subdistrict Court (Art. 1.3.1 of the NCC Rules). For a taxonomy of ICommCs see Georgios Dimitropoulos, 'The Design of International Commercial Courts' (Chapter 10), in this volume.

[2] From this point of view, Sir William Blair distinguishes among practitioner-driven innovation, innovation in court practice and technological assistance in decision-making: Sir William Blair, 'The New Litigation Landscape: International Commercial Courts and Procedural Innovations' (2019) 2 International Journal of Procedural Law 230.

[3] The procedural rules of some ICommCs make express reference to the importance of technology: by way of example, Art. 4.3.4. of the Regulations and Procedural Rules of the QICDRC states that 'dealing with all cases justly includes, so far as practicable ... making

Before delving into the core of the topic, it is necessary to dispel two 'myths' – that is, two oft-repeated tropes concerning the use of technology in courts. First, despite the frequent claims to the contrary, the use of technology in courts is nothing new. Technology, in fact, has always been both a catalyst and a limit for the administration of justice. Throughout the history of adjudication, the influence of technology on adjudication has retained its importance, irrespective of the level of technological advancement. Even rudimentary and archaic types of justice reflect and embrace the type of technologies prevailing within the society that generated them.[4] Investigating the use of technologies in ICommCs is not an exercise in futurology, but rather an attempt to unveil the latest developments of an everlasting dialogue between technology and justice.

According to the second oft-repeated trope, technology is a neutral force that can be introduced in the courtroom to enhance the efficiency of the proceedings and save costs. Once inserted in the context of adversarial litigation, however, technology will unavoidably live a life independent of its creators, and it must be expected that the parties will use it not necessarily to enhance the efficiency of proceedings, but rather to further their case and, in some cases at least, to try to disrupt the functioning of the court. Introducing a new technology may often mean opening new avenues for 'procedural guerrilla', and potentially also generating points of discussion that can be used in appellate and/or recognition and enforcement proceedings. This chapter looks at technology not only as a driver of innovation in proceedings before ICommCs, but also as a potential 'strategic weapon' for the parties to use.

The remainder of this chapter proceeds in three sections. Section 14.2 discusses the emergence of ICommCs, illustrating in particular the important connections between technological evolution and the factors triggering the ideation and recent proliferation of these courts. It is shown that ICommCs are themselves a product of technology. Subsequently, Section 14.3 offers a comparative overview of the use of technology during proceedings conducted before ICommCs, with insights and examples elucidating how these technologies can be

appropriate use of information technology'; see 'Regulations and Procedural Rules of the Qatar Financial Centre Civil and Commercial Court' (Qatar International Court and Dispute Resolution Centre), www.qicdrc.gov.qa/sites/default/files/s3/wysiwyg/qfc_civil_and_commercial_court_regulations_date_of_issuance_15_december_2010_0.pdf, accessed 29 January 2020.

4 See, for example, James B. Thayer, 'The Older Modes of Trial' (1891) 5(2) Harvard Law Review 45.

operationalized in practice. Finally, Section 14.4 puts forth normative recommendations and proposals for the future technological evolution of ICommCs.

14.2 The Rise of International Commercial Courts and the Influence of Technology

This section of the chapter considers three factors that have contributed to the recent rise of ICommCs: (1) the ever-growing success of international arbitration; (2) the uncertainties brought about by Brexit (with specific respect to ICommCs instituted by EU Member States); and (3) the need to guarantee certainty for commercial actors in a world characterized by mounting instability. All three of these factors have strong ties with the use of technology at ICommCs.

14.2.1 Technology As a Differentiating Criterion in the Competition between International Commercial Courts and Arbitration

International commercial courts have emerged, to a certain extent, as an alternative and a response to international arbitration.[5] The ever-increasing caseload of the leading arbitration institutions demonstrates the existence of a strong demand for neutral and reliable fora where complex cross-border disputes can be resolved.[6] Hence, the decision of many national legal systems to institute ICommCs can be seen as an attempt on the part of States to have a more meaningful presence in this particular segment of the market for dispute resolution services. More specifically, it is possible to understand the relationship between ICommCs and arbitration in terms of 'monopolistic competition' – that is, a market structure where State courts and arbitral institutions offer similar, but not identical services.[7] Under conditions of monopolistic competition, a competitor acquires market power inasmuch as it manages to differentiate its product from the ones offered by the other

[5] Zhengxin Huo and Man Yip, 'Comparing the International Commercial Courts of China with the Singapore International Commercial Court'(2019) 68(4) International & Comparative Law Quarterly 903; Michael Hwang, 'Commercial Courts and International Arbitration: Competitors or Partners?'(2015) 31(2) Arbitration International 193.

[6] See, for example, International Chamber of Commerce, '2018 ICC Dispute Resolution Statistics' (2019) 1 ICC Dispute Resolution Bulletin 12; LCIA, '2018 Annual Casework Report', www.lcia.org/News/2018-annual-casework-report.aspx, accessed 6 December 2019.

[7] Edward Hastings Chamberlain, *The Theory of Monopolistic Competition: A Re-orientation of the Theory of Value*, 8th ed. (Harvard University Press 1962).

competitors. For the purposes of this chapter, it is crucial to notice that one of the key elements of differentiation, in the particular market of cross-border commercial dispute resolution, is the use of technology.

Traditionally, arbitration is deemed to offer fundamental and widely discussed advantages as compared to court litigation: neutrality, flexibility, finality and enforceability are just some of the many well-known factors discussed in the literature.[8] However, the impermanent nature of arbitral tribunals has recently given rise to claims that, in certain scenarios, arbitration may struggle to provide structures sufficient for the management of complex disputes.[9]

Technology can be a key differentiating factor between ICommCs and arbitration: the former may prove to have a capacity-building advantage over the latter, as the permanent nature of State courts can facilitate the development of technological solutions (for instance, for the filing of mass claims in the financial sector) which would not be easily replicable by arbitral tribunals.

14.2.2 Technology As a Differentiating Criterion in the Wake of Brexit

In addition to the ever-growing relevance of international arbitration, an additional factor has undoubtedly contributed to triggering the creation of ICommCs, with specific respect to Europe: Brexit. Historically, the London Commercial Court has played a central role in the resolution of complex cross-border commercial disputes. Parties with no geographical link to the territory of England routinely insert choice-of-court agreements in their contracts, conferring jurisdiction upon English courts; choice-of-court agreements of this type can be found, for instance, in Loan Market Association (LMA) agreements[10] and in the International Swaps and Derivatives Association (ISDA) Master Agreement.[11] However, the United Kingdom's exit from the European Union (EU) may partially endanger the centrality of London in the market for international commercial litigation. Within the EU, the enforcement of

[8] Gary B. Born, *International Commercial Arbitration*, 2nd ed. (Kluwer 2014) 73–93.

[9] A case in point is *Abaclat and Others* v. *Argentine Republic*, ICSID Case No. ARB/07/5 (formerly *Giovanna A. Beccara and Others* v. *The Argentine Republic*); see Ridhi Kabra, 'Has *Abaclat v Argentina* left the ICSID with a "Mass"ive Problem?' (2015) 31(3) Arbitration International 425.

[10] See, for example, LMA Multicurrency Term and Revolving Facilities Agreements, for intra-EU loans, www.lma.eu.com/documents-guidelines/documents#, accessed 10 December 2019.

[11] See Art. 13(b)(i)(1) of the 2002 ISDA Master Agreement, if the agreement is governed by English law.

choice-of-court agreements selecting the London Commercial Court, as well as the recognition and enforcement of the resulting judgments, is currently governed by the Brussels I *bis* Regulation, which sets forth a uniform and friendly regime of recognition and enforcement.[12] Once the applicability of this regulation comes to an end, there is uncertainty as to the regime applicable to (especially non-exclusive) choice-of-court clauses, and the resulting judgments.[13] The uncertainty has been perceived in many EU Member States (in particular Germany, France, the Netherlands and Belgium)[14] as an opportunity to challenge the primacy of London in the European market for cross-border commercial litigation.[15]

Technology is likely to play a pivotal role in the competition between the London Commercial Court and the other, newly instituted ICommCs. While widely praised for its expertise and commercial sensibility, the London Commercial Court is also often criticized for the significant costs of litigation.[16] It is hence unsurprising that, when devising their own services, the other European ICommCs attempt to contain costs while at the same time ensuring high-quality dispute resolution. Technology is key to ensuring efficient case and cost management: electronic filing of submissions and production of evidence, as well as the possibility to conduct hearings via videoconference or tele-presence, are just some of the techniques ICommCs can deploy to enhance their cost-effectiveness. In sum, technology may help the ICommCs that have been recently established in many European jurisdictions to compete

[12] Arts. 25 and 31(2) of Regulation no. 1215/2012 of 12 December 2012 on jurisdiction and the recognition and enforcement of judgments in civil and commercial matters.

[13] Andrew Dickinson, 'Back to the Future: The UK's EU Exit and the Conflict of Laws' (2016) 12(2) Journal of Private International Law 195; Sara Masters and Belinda McRae, 'What Does Brexit Mean for the Brussels Regime?' (2016) 33(7) Journal of International Arbitration 483; Mateusz Pilich, 'Brexit and EU Private International Law: May the UK Stay In?'(2017) 24(3) Maastricht Journal of European and Comparative Law 382.

[14] See, in Germany, the Chamber for International Commercial Disputes at the District Court Frankfurt/Main; in France, the International Commercial Chambers of Paris; in the Netherlands, the Netherlands Commercial Court; in Belgium, the project of the Brussels International Business Court. For a comparative overview of European ICommCs see the special issue (2019) 1 Erasmus Law Review.

[15] See, for example, Legal High Committee for Financial Markets of Paris, 'Recommendations for the Creation of Special Tribunals for International Business Disputes', https://publications.banque-france.fr/sites/default/files/rapport_07_a.pdf, accessed 10 December 2019 5, expressly referring to Brexit as a reason for the institution of ICommCs in France.

[16] Sir Geoffrey Vos, 'A View from the Business and Property Courts in London' (2019) 1 Erasmus Law Review 10, 12, para 24.

with the English courts, by both enhancing procedural efficiency and minimising language barriers.

14.2.3 *Technology As a Tool for Neutral Dispute Resolution in Times of Growing Protectionism*

A third important incentive for the creation of ICommCs is the tension between the persistence of cross-border trade and investment, on one hand, and the growing climate of protectionism existing in many legal and political systems, on the other. Given the mounting uncertainties surrounding international trade and investment, it is unsurprising that commercial actors demand reliable and neutral dispute resolution fora, leading to enforceable results. If ICommCs are to provide such fora, though, they must isolate themselves from external influences, striving to stay immune from interferences, concerns of protectionism, home bias and/or lack of neutrality. In other words, ICommCs can only be successful if they rely on a resilient regulatory and organizational infrastructure, capable of preserving their autonomy and neutrality vis-à-vis outside influence. To this end, technology can play a crucial role.

The cornerstone of such an infrastructure is obviously constituted by the treaties ensuring that the jurisdiction of ICommCs be respected, and that the resulting judgments be recognized and enforced internationally. As the 1958 New York Convention has demonstrated with respect to arbitration, the success of any mechanism of international adjudication hinges first and foremost on the presence of a friendly and simple international regime of recognition and enforcement.[17] As far as court litigation is concerned, such a framework is provided by the 2005 Hague Convention on Choice-of-Court Agreements,[18] which aims at ensuring the enforceability of exclusive choice-of-court agreements, as well as setting forth a regime for the recognition and enforcement of judgments. Since the jurisdiction of ICommCs will often derive from exclusive choice-of-court agreements, the aforementioned instrument seems to be (at least partially) suitable for cross-border litigation before ICommCs. Furthermore, where the jurisdiction of ICommCs is not based on an exclusive choice-of-court agreement, the 2019 Hague Judgments Convention may in the future ensure the recognition and

[17] Katia Fach Gomez and Ana M. Lopez Rodriguez, *60 Years of the New York Convention: Key Issues and Future Challenges* (Kluwer 2019).

[18] Convention of 30 June 2005 on Choice-of-Court Agreements.

enforcement of judgments issued by ICommCs.[19] The Hague instruments provide the minimum legal infrastructure, guaranteeing that clauses conferring jurisdiction upon ICommCs be respected by other courts in the States which are parties to the instruments, and that the judgments rendered by ICommCs can circulate across borders. International commercial courts have recently undertaken initiatives aimed at fostering judicial cooperation in this area, encouraging the mutual recognition and enforcement of each other's judgments: an interesting example, in this respect, is the Multilateral Memorandum published by the Standing International Forum of Commercial Courts.[20] However, while such an infrastructure is necessary to make litigation before ICommCs practically viable, it is far from sufficient. Other efforts are necessary to ensure that ICommCs are effectively protected against external 'protectionist' influences. To this end, it is crucial for ICommCs to embrace new technologies, as the following two examples illustrate.

A first illustrative example concerns the taking of evidence: in cross-border commercial litigation, pieces of evidence as well as oral witnesses are likely to be located in different jurisdictions; as a consequence, it may be impossible for ICommCs to examine that evidence (e.g. ordering an inspection) or to compel the attendance of witnesses without the collaboration of the State where the evidence or witness are geographically based. For the reasons illustrated earlier in this chapter, however, ICommCs should manage the extent to which they depend on the cooperation of foreign courts, which may not always be willing to provide assistance. In order to overcome this obstacle, witness examination at ICommCs may be conducted via videoconference. Section 14.3 of this chapter expounds on this point, describing in further detail how ICommCs can use the technologies at hand.

A second important example regards the recognition and enforcement of judgments. The prospect that foreign courts may decline jurisdiction and enforcement is in and of itself enough to potentially undermine the practical attractiveness of ICommCs. Apart from the cases where the intra-EU circulation of judgments is governed by the Brussels I *bis* Regulation, the aforementioned Hague instruments aim at minimizing

[19] Convention of 2 July 2019 on the Recognition and Enforcement of Foreign Judgments in Civil or Commercial Matters; see, in particular, Art. 5(1)(m).

[20] Standing International Forum of Commercial Courts, 'Multilateral Memorandum on Enforcement of Commercial Judgments for Money', www.sifocc.org/wp-content/uploads/2019/11/Multilateral-Memorandum-on-Enforcement-Nov-2019.pdf, accessed 29 January 2020.

such a risk of denial of recognition and enforcement.[21] Technology, however, can also play a crucial role in ensuring the effectiveness of ICommCs judgments, by making them largely self-enforcing. Technologies such as smart contracts make it increasingly possible for adjudicators (be they national judges or arbitrators) to allocate disputed assets to the prevailing party without relying on the cooperation of the authorities of the place where the assets are located.[22] When the judgment awards monetary compensation, a 'smart escrow' mechanism may potentially be devised, ensuring the automatic payment of the compensation.[23] In general, self-enforcing technologies could be applied not only at ICommCs, but also in 'ordinary' domestic court proceedings, as well as in commercial arbitration.[24] Nevertheless, among the different possible use cases, ICommCs seem particularly promising, for the reasons presented previously.

14.3 A Procedure Naturally Infused with Technology? Evidence from a Comparative Analysis

This section of the chapter provides a comparative overview of the possible uses of technology in proceedings before ICommCs, following the typical development of a case before this type of court, in chronological order, starting from the conclusion of a choice-of-court agreement, until the recognition and enforcement of the resulting judgment.

14.3.1 Choice-of-Court Agreements

The jurisdiction of ICommCs is likely to be based on a choice-of-court agreement. Therefore, a possible use of technology concerns the

[21] See in particular Art. 35 of the Regulation (n. 12).

[22] Pietro Ortolani, 'The Impact of Blockchain Technologies and Smart Contracts on Dispute Resolution: Arbitration and Court Litigation at the Crossroads' (2019) 24(2) Uniform Law Review 430; Pietro Ortolani, 'The Judicialization of the Blockchain', in Philipp Hacker, Ioannis Lianos, Georgios Dimitropoulos and Stefan Eich (eds.), *Regulating Blockchain: Techno-social and Legal Challenges* (Oxford University Press 2019) 289; Pietro Ortolani, 'Self-Enforcing Online Dispute Resolution: Lessons from Bitcoin' (2016) 36(3) Oxford Journal of Legal Studies 595.

[23] For a more detailed explanation see Section 14.3.9.

[24] In fact, companies such as Jur envisage the development of blockchain-based infrastructures supporting the conduct of commercial arbitration proceedings: see Jur, 'Whitepaper', https://jur.io/wp-content/uploads/2019/05/jur-whitepaper-v.2.0.2.pdf, accessed 29 January 2020.

electronic conclusion of such an agreement. Within the European Union, a basic distinction must be drawn between business-to-business (B2B) contracts, on one hand, and consumer contracts, on the other. As far as the former category is concerned, a choice-of-court agreement concluded electronically complies, in principle, with the requirement that such agreement be 'in writing or evidenced in writing':[25] pursuant to Article 25(2) of the Brussels I *bis* Regulation, 'any communication by electronic means which provides a durable record of the (choice-of-court) agreement shall be equivalent to "writing"'. Expounding on these rules, the Court of Justice of the European Union (CJEU) has clarified that the notion of 'communication by electronic means which provides a durable record of the agreement' comprises the case of 'click-wrapping' – that is, the technique whereby general terms and conditions are accepted by ticking a box, but only displayed if the party adhering to the contract clicks on a special link.[26] Therefore, there do not seem to be obstacles against the conclusion of an electronic choice-of-court agreement in the context of a B2B contract. This solution, by contrast, is not applicable to consumer contracts, which are governed by a more protective regime;[27] more specifically, Article 19(1) of the Brussels I *bis* Regulation largely precludes consumers from validly entering into pre-dispute choice-of-court agreements, be they concluded online or via more 'traditional' means.[28]

Whenever the Brussels I *bis* Regulation is not applicable, an important point of reference to assess the validity of electronic choice-of-court agreements in favour of ICommCs is the 2005 Hague Convention.[29] The Convention, which does not apply to agreements concluded by consumers, prescribes that choice-of-court agreements must be 'concluded or documented … in writing, or … by any other means of communication which renders information accessible so as to be usable for subsequent reference'.[30] The requirement of usability for subsequent reference is, in many respects, comparable to the notion of 'communication … providing a durable record of the agreement',

[25] Article 25(1)(a) of the Brussels I *bis* Regulation (n. 12).

[26] Case C-322/14, *Jaouad El Majdoub* v. *CarsOnTheWeb.Deutschland GmbH*, ECLI:EU:C:2015:334.

[27] *CarsOnTheWeb* (n. 26), para. 37, distinguishing the case of B2B contracts from the hypotheses governed by Directive 97/7/EC on the protection of consumers in distance contracts, with reference to *Content Services*, case C-49/11, ECLI:EU:C:2012:419.

[28] Subject to the exceptions of Art. 19(2) and (3).

[29] Convention of 30 June 2005 on Choice-of-Court Agreements (n. 18).

[30] Art. 2(1)(a) (n. 18).

relevant under the Brussels I *bis* regulation. Hence, similarly to what has been observed with reference to the Brussels regime, the Hague Convention ensures the enforceability of choice-of-court agreements concluded electronically.

14.3.2 Electronic Filing and Exchange of Written Submissions and Documents

The electronic filing of claims, as well as the subsequent electronic exchange of submissions and documents, is increasingly available not only before ICommCs, but in general before a host of national courts. In principle, this sort of development seems to constitute one of the least controversial applications of technology in civil proceedings, allowing for an increase in efficiency without imposing any macroscopic structural transformation of the way in which a court functions. Furthermore, the digitalization of filing is widely encouraged: among the various criteria the EU Justice Scoreboard uses to evaluate the quality of justice systems in different EU Member States, an important role is played by the possibility to file a case electronically, to exchange written defences online, and to monitor the progress of a case.[31] Along similar lines, the World Bank's Doing Business Report looks at 'court automation' as a predictor of strength of legal institutions.[32]

An interesting example of online filing is the DIFC Courts, which offer counsel and judges detailed guidelines on the use of electronic bundles (so-called e-bundles). While many of these indications (concerning the numbering and naming of the files, bookmarking, searchable text format etc.) may seem trivial, they do significantly enhance the quality of the proceedings, avoiding the otherwise frequent problem of voluminous filings containing electronic exhibits in different formats, and without a logical order.

Despite the general desirability of digitalization in this context, additional questions arise with specific respect to electronic filings at ICommCs. A first, interesting problem is whether ICommCs should use the same electronic mechanisms (e.g. online portals for the uploading of documents) that may be available in a given jurisdiction for the other

[31] European Commission, 'The 2019 EU Justice Scoreboard', https://ec.europa.eu/info/sites/info/files/justice_scoreboard_2019_en.pdf, 4–7, accessed 13 December 2019.

[32] World Bank Group, 'Doing Business 2019: Training for Reform', www.doingbusiness.org/content/dam/doingBusiness/media/Annual-Reports/English/DB2019-report_web-version.pdf, 4, accessed 13 December 2019.

courts, or whether tailor-made solutions should be devised instead.[33] An important distinction, in this respect, is whether foreign counsel are authorized to represent parties appearing before a certain ICommC. If that is the case, then the portal/platform created for the 'ordinary' courts may require some adaptation, so as to ensure that the filing of submissions is not dependent on the provision of information that can only be given by local counsels (e.g. registration numbers proving membership of the national bar association).[34]

From the early 2000s on, it has often been repeated that electronic filing offers the advantage of around-the-clock availability, as compared with human clerks and registrars.[35] In the case of international commercial disputes, such as the ones dealt with by ICommCs, this feature is particularly important, as it may significantly facilitate the work of counsels working in different time zones. At the same time, however, the geographical complexity of the dispute should be taken into account by ICommCs, when giving deadlines for the parties' submissions. If, for instance, an ICommC repeatedly sets deadlines at a time that is the end of the working day for the counsel of one of the parties, and the end of the night for the counsel of the opposing party, this may be seen as a possible encroachment on the latter party's right to present its case, giving rise to concerns of potential violation of due process and the principle of equality of arms. Disputes on such procedural aspects may not only complicate the litigation before the ICommC, but also potentially lead to an annulment of the resulting judgment, and/or endanger its prospects of recognition and enforcement abroad.[36] International commercial courts should be adaptive and cautious in this respect, using their electronic filing tools in a way that scrupulously respects due process. Useful guidance, in this respect, may be found in the techniques commonly

[33] See, for example, DIFC Courts, 'General Guidelines for Electronic Bundles in the DIFC Courts', www.difccourts.ae/e-bundle, accessed 13 December 2019; QICDRC, 'e-Court', www.qicdrc.gov.qa/the-courts/e-filing, accessed 13 December 2019; SICC, 'Electronic Filing Service', www.sicc.gov.sg/forms-and-services/electronic-filing-service, accessed 13 December 2019. On the topic of electronic filing see also Blair (n. 2) 231.

[34] See, for example, para. 26 of the Practice Directions of the SICC, allowing (under certain circumstances) representation by foreign lawyers or foreign experts; see also the list of Registered Practitioners at the DIFC Courts.

[35] See, for example, Kyla Kitajima, 'Electronic Filing and Informational Privacy' (2000) 27 (3) Hastings Constitutional Law Quarterly 563; William A. Fenwick and Robert D. Brownstone, 'Electronic Filing: What Is It? What Are Its Implications?' (2002) 19(1) Computer and High Technology Law Journal 181.

[36] See the reference to the fundamental principles of procedural fairness of the requested State, in Article 9(e) of the 2005 Hague Convention (n. 18).

adopted by international arbitral tribunals: while detailed discussions of such minute procedural aspects are sometimes dubbed as the result of so-called due process paranoia, they ultimately form part of a mentality that protects the outcome of the adjudication against possible challenges.[37] As such, it serves the interest of both the disputing parties and the ICommC itself. Several ICommCs expressly foster the involvement of the parties when procedural orders and case-management decisions must be issued.[38]

Finally, electronic filing of submissions and documents at ICommCs can raise complex questions concerning cybersecurity. It is not uncommon for parties involved in an international commercial dispute to rely on documents which contain confidential information (e.g. industrial secrets). Whenever this is the case, it is vital that the contents of the documents not be divulged to the general public, despite the general prevalence of the principles of transparency and publicity in State court litigation.[39] This in turn requires ICommCs to take adequate cybersecurity measures to ensure that these documents remain adequately protected once filed electronically. These concerns should also be taken into account by ICommCs currently exploring the possibility to transition to blockchain-based technologies:[40] if, on one hand, the use of blockchain

[37] Klaus Peter Berger and J. Ole Jensen, 'Due Process Paranoia and the Procedural Judgment Rule: A Safe Harbour for Procedural Management Decisions by International Arbitrators' (2016) 32(3) *Arbitration International* 415.

[38] Interestingly, in proceedings pending before the London Commercial Court, Rule 58.13 of the Civil Procedure Rules sets forth a specific case-management regime, different from that of other English courts. While many of the ordinarily applicable rules are excluded (i.e. Part 26 and the majority of Part 29 of the Rules), Rule 58.13 ensures the applicability of Rule 29.3(2), which in turn requires the parties' legal representatives (under certain conditions) to attend case-management conferences. Along similar lines, the procedural rules of some ICommCs expressly envisage the possibility of soliciting the parties' submissions when procedural orders must be issued, while at the same time respecting due process and the equality of arms: see, for example, Article 15 of the Regulations and Procedural Rules of the QICDRC (n. 3), with reference to the parties' right to make representations before any procedural order is made.

[39] An especially interesting provision is Rule 30 of the SICC Rules, whereby the Court may (upon application of a party) make a variety of orders concerning confidentiality, including an order that the case be heard *in camera*, a confidentiality order preventing publication or divulgation of information related to the case, and/or an order that the court file be sealed. See also Art. 8.4.2. of the NCC rules, envisaging the possibility of a 'confidentiality ring' created upon the agreement of the disputing parties.

[40] This possibility is currently being explored in Dubai by the DIFC Courts and the Dubai Future Foundation: 'Court Tech Lab Launched by DIFC Courts and the Dubai Future Foundation', www.difccourts.ae/2019/10/30/court-tech-lab-launched-by-difc-courts-and-the-dubai-future-foundation, accessed 13 December 2019.

guarantees immutability and tamper-resistance of the data, on the other, it does presuppose the existence of a distributed ledger, rather than a centralized server, thus potentially making certain pieces of information more easily visible and traceable from the outside.[41] Hybrid solutions, such as the so-called permissioned blockchains, are currently being developed in an attempt to combine immutability with confidentiality.[42] A particularly promising experience in this respect is the Dubai Court Tech Lab, one of whose purposes is the development of a blockchain infrastructure aimed at verifying court judgments (with a view to their cross-border enforcement) and avoiding the duplication of documents, as well as other inefficiencies.[43]

14.3.3 Electronic Case-Management Techniques

A relatively uncontroversial use of technology at ICommCs concerns basic case-management techniques, such as the creation of an electronic calendar of the proceedings and terms of reference. At this stage, technology can be key to enhancing efficiency and ensuring frictionless exchange of information. Among the many examples of ICommCs using technology to facilitate communication between the parties and the court, the Singapore International Commercial Court (SICC) allows the parties to access the entire case file remotely through its electronic filing system.[44] Since 2017, approximately 90 per cent of the filings made by parties at the DIFC Courts have been completed electronically.[45] Along similar lines, the Rules of the NCC envisage the Court's electronic platform (called eNCC) as the 'only means of communication with the court', to be 'used for all purposes'.[46]

[41] Primavera de Filippi and Aaron Wright, *Blockchain and the Law: The Rule of Code* (Harvard University Press 2018) 35–8.

[42] Ibid., 31–2.

[43] Dubai Future Foundation, 'Courts of the Future', www.courtsofthefuture.org/#courts-of-blockchain, accessed 29 January 2020.

[44] SICC Practice Directions, Effective 22 July 2019, www.supremecourt.gov.sg/docs/default-source/default-document-library/sicc-practice-directions–amended-version-(15-july -2019).pdf, accessed 31 January 2020, para. 20.

[45] H. E. Justice Ali Shamis Mohamed Shamis Al Madhani, 'Technology Should Enable, not Define, Modern Commercial Courts', www.difccourts.ae/2017/06/15/technology-enable-not-define-modern-commercial-courts, accessed 31 January 2020.

[46] Rules of Procedure for the International Commercial Chambers of the Amsterdam District Court (NCC District Court) and the Amsterdam Court of Appeal (NCC Court of Appeal), Art. 3.2.1.

14.3.4 Videoconferencing and Electronic Cross-Examination

Conducting (at least parts of) the hearings via videoconference can be a desirable solution for any court in order to enhance efficiency and save costs. Videoconferencing, for instance, has recently been adopted by China in the context of three 'Internet courts', in Hangzhou, Beijing and Guangzhou, established to deal mainly with low-value, high-volume e-commerce disputes.[47] Nevertheless, of all possible settings within which videoconferencing can be introduced, ICommCs are a particularly suitable environment, given the international nature of the disputes these courts aim to resolve, and the significant costs and complications the physical presence of counsels, judges and witnesses at the same location would unavoidably entail.

In practice, most ICommCs envisage the possibility of conducting hearings through long-distance communication technology; however, not all of them follow the same approach. On one hand, the rules of some ICommCs enable parties and judges to conduct the entire hearing via videoconference: at the SICC, for instance, videoconferencing technologies can be used not only to conduct hearings,[48] but also to contact the registrar and to file urgent applications.[49] The Rules of the Qatar International Court and Dispute Resolution Centre (QICDRC) expressly envisage that the possibility to use videoconference extends to 'any hearings' conducted at the Court,[50] and analogous possibility are contemplated at numerous other ICommCs as well, such as the Frankfurt Chamber for International Commercial Disputes.[51] On the other hand, the rules of other ICommCs mainly allow videoconferencing with reference to a particular activity to be conducted during the hearing, or to a specific category of cases: at the London Commercial Court, for instance, the use of a video link is foreseen for the purpose of taking of oral evidence,[52] and at the Netherlands Commercial Court (NCC), a hearing may be conducted via videoconference when the case is 'closely

[47] Sophie Hunter, 'China's Innovative Internet Courts and Their Use of Blockchain Backed Evidence' (*Conflict of Laws*, 28 May 2019), http://conflictoflaws.net/2019/chinas-innovative-internet-courts-and-their-use-of-blockchain-backed-evidence, accessed 13 December 2019.

[48] SICC Practice Directions (n. 44) para. 57.

[49] Ibid., para. 15.

[50] Art. 28(7) of the Regulations and Procedural Rules of the QICDRC.

[51] Landgericht Frankfurt Am Main, 'Chamber for International Commercial Disputes', https://ordentliche-gerichtsbarkeit.hessen.de/ordentliche-gerichte/lgb-frankfurt-am-main/lg-frankfurt-am-main/chamber-international, accessed 31 January 2020.

[52] HM Courts and Tribunals Service, 'The Commercial Court Guide', https://assets.publishing.service.gov.uk/government/uploads/system/uploads/attachment_data/file/672422/

connected' with a foreign case, so that a joint oral discussion may become desirable.[53]

The use of videoconferencing techniques can undoubtedly help limit costs for the disputing parties and facilitate the practical organization of the hearing. However, the use of videoconferencing at ICommCs also comes with some significant challenges. One of the most interesting use cases concerns the examination of witnesses, as the possibility of long-distance communication facilitates the participation of witnesses unlikely to attend in person. In a typical cross-border commercial dispute, unavailability can constitute a considerable obstacle given the number of witnesses whose testimony the parties will normally seek to rely on. In some sensitive cases, videoconferencing may also make it possible to examine witness whose physical presence at the venue of the court would be altogether unfeasible – for instance, due to the impossibility to obtain a visa. Furthermore, videoconferencing can reduce travel and accommodation costs, making litigation as a whole more affordable.

The taking of oral evidence via videoconference can also entail some drawbacks. First of all, being connected via technological means is not the same as being physically present at the hearing. Even if an ICommC relies on sophisticated and perfectly functional technologies, the video connection constitutes a certain barrier and may take away some of the spontaneity of direct interaction. In addition, it is difficult to rule out the concern that a witness may consult materials 'offscreen', limiting the court's ability to assess the sources of information on which the answers are based. By contrast, in a traditional court setting, it is relatively easy for the court to verify whether the witness is reading from a certain document and, if yes, what documents (often included in a trial bundle) are being used.

Furthermore, the psychological impact of videoconferencing on judges and witnesses should not be underestimated.[54] Being present at the courtroom entails a significant psychological pressure for the witness; by contrast, such a psychological effect may partially fade if the witness is connected electronically. This difference in turn may make it easier for witnesses who participate via videoconference to sustain a cross-examination, thus potentially giving rise to complaints of unequal

The_Commercial_Court_Guide_new_10th_Edition_07.09.17.pdf, accessed 31 January 2020, Section H.3.

[53] NCC Rules (n. 46) Art. 7.8.

[54] Anthony Garofano, 'Avoiding Virtual Justice: Video-Teleconference Testimony in Federal Criminal Trials' (2007) 56 Catholic University Law Review 683, 700–2.

treatment of the parties once the judgment is rendered. In order to alleviate this type of concern, it would be desirable for an ICommC to clarify as early as possible in the proceedings and well in advance of the hearing which witnesses will be heard via videoconference, and which ones (if any) will appear in person. Against this background, the parties' explicit consent should be elicited; if a consensus cannot be found, the ICommC should at least aim to strike a balance between the parties – for example, avoiding that one of them will exclusively rely on witnesses participating via videoconference, while the other one will exclusively submit witnesses who attend the hearing in person.

In sum, the use of videoconferencing at ICommCs is certainly desirable and can bring about significant advantages in terms of efficiency and cost-saving. Nevertheless, ICommCs should scrupulously ensure that the use of this technology does not result in potential violations of due process, which may in turn endanger the finality and enforceability of the resulting judgment.

14.3.5 Virtual Site Inspections

The need to assess the state of a site arises often – for example, in the context of construction disputes. In this respect, a particularly promising technology is virtual reality (VR). Virtual reality tools are increasingly used for the taking of evidence, and in particular for forensic reconstructions in criminal justice, and criminal courts frequently rely on 3D reconstructions and visualisation – for example, to virtually inspect a crime scene.[55] The SICC has experimented with VR in the context of a conference held in 2019,[56] a Beijing court has already taken oral evidence via VR,[57] and a more practical adoption in the day-to-day operations of ICommCs seems likely in the future, given the advantages VR can bring about. The use of VR in particular has the obvious benefit of enabling an inspection even years after the facts have taken place and the site has undergone modifications. Witnesses can be asked to wear a VR

[55] Ross Tredinnick, Simon Smith and Kevin Ponto, 'A Cost-Benefit Analysis of 3D Scanning Technology for Crime Scene Investigation'(2019) Forensic Science International: Reports (advance access). For recent examples of application of 360-degree photographical technology in US courts see *State* v. *Banks*, No. M201800264CCAR3CD, 2019 WL 4917164, at *5 (Tenn. Crim. App., 4 October 2019); *State* v. *Vandenburg*, No. M201701882CCAR3CD, 2019 WL 3720892, at *5 (Tenn. Crim. App., 8 August 2019).

[56] 'Singapore Judicial College Annual Report 2019', www.supremecourt.gov.sg/docs/default-source/default-document-library/sjc/sjc-ar-2019.pdf, accessed 31 January 2020, 13.

[57] Blair (n. 2) 231.

headset and 'walk through' the site, pointing out specific locations and linking their recollection of the facts to the site's morphology. This technique allows the blending of witness examination and site inspection, ensuring that the narratives witnesses offer are spatially contextualized.

The adoption of this type of technology in international litigation can often have beneficial effects. In the aforementioned example of a construction dispute, VR could allow the parties, the experts and the judges to inspect the site around which the case revolves. This use of technology would bring about at least four advantages, enhancing the quality and efficiency of litigation before ICommCs. First of all, VR can limit the costs associated with an inspection, thus making this evidence-taking method viable even in cases where the amount in dispute is relatively small. Second, VR allows the court, the parties and the witnesses to visualize different versions of the same location as they existed at different points in time. This sort of diachronic comparison would enhance the accuracy of fact-finding and the overall quality of adjudication. Third, VR can help the court compare and assess the reliability of witnesses without necessarily relying on techniques such as 'hot-tubbing', which may have the unintended consequence of discouraging the participation of less-experienced witnesses.[58] Fourth, VR can make it possible to inspect a site located in a foreign jurisdiction, where the local authorities would not be likely to support the evidence-taking activities.

If, on one hand, virtual site inspections can offer significant advantages, on the other, they also give rise to a number of doubts which should not be underestimated. First of all, under many systems of civil procedure, there may be a *numerus clausus* of admissible means of evidence.[59] This restriction (which is not generally present in international arbitration), may determine the inadmissibility of VR site inspections, given the hybrid nature of this evidence-taking technique (somewhat at the crossroads between inspection, documentary evidence and oral testimony). Needless to say, lengthy debates as to the admissibility of the evidence may destroy the efficiency technology aims to bring about in the first

[58] Roland Ziadé, 'Proactivité et diversité dans la conduite de l'audience: "Mega hot tubbing" ou quand le tribunal arbitral mène la danse', in Bernd Ehle and Domitille Baizeau (eds.), *Stories from the Hearing Room: Experience from Arbitral Practice: Essays in Honour of Michael E. Schneider* (Kluwer 2015) 243.

[59] Matthias Scherer, Bernd Ehle and Samuel Moss, 'Construction Arbitration in Switzerland', in Manuel Arroyo (ed.), *Arbitration in Switzerland: The Practitioner's Guide*, 2nd ed. (Kluwer 2018) 1017, 1034.

place, and potentially cast doubts as to the validity and/or enforceability of judgments.

Furthermore, the use of VR in ICommC litigation presupposes the development of a 3D model of a given site, which judges, parties and witnesses will then be able to inspect through immersive technology. This in turn requires a high level of accuracy in the creation of the model. In complex cross-border disputes, the parties may wish to oversee the development of such a 3D model – for example, by appointing their own experts who will assist and consult with the court technicians responsible for the VR technology. As a result, the costs and complexities associated with this evidence-taking technique should not be underestimated.

14.3.6 Legal Analytics

Recent developments in machine learning and natural language processing have made it possible for researchers and practitioners to develop tools which analyse case law.[60] The analysis of judicial precedent through algorithm is often referred to as 'legal analytics'.[61] On one hand, legal analytics can be used for descriptive purposes – that is, to draw a comprehensive picture of the current state of the case law on a certain topic and to identify prevailing trends and lines of reasoning in the judgments a given court has issued so far. On the other hand, however, it is also possible to use artificial intelligence in a predictive fashion, to foresee how future cases will be decided on the basis of the information that can be drawn from past cases.

Legal analytics is progressing at an increasing pace. In 2016, a group of researchers presented the results of a study predicting the outcome of cases heard by the European Court of Human Rights (ECtHR), exclusively on the basis of textual content, with an average accuracy of 79 per cent.[62]

60 Geneviève Vanderstichele, 'The Normative Value of Legal Analytics: Is There a Case for Statistical Precedent?' (MPhil Thesis, University of Oxford, 2019), https://papers.ssrn.com/sol3/papers.cfm?abstract_id=3474878&download=yes, accessed 13 December 2019; Daniel Martin Katz, 'Quantitative Legal Prediction – or – How I Learned to Stop Worrying and Start Preparing for the Data-Driven Future of the Legal Services Industry, (2013) 62 Emory Law Journal 909.

61 Kevin D. Ashley, *Artificial Intelligence and Legal Analytics: New Tools for Law Practice in the Digital Age* (Cambridge University Press 2017) 73–126.

62 Nikolaos Aletras, Dimitrios Tsarapatsanis, Daniel Preoţiuc-Pietro and Vasileios Lampos, 'Predicting Judicial Decisions of the European Court of Human Rights: A Natural Language Processing Perspective' (2016) PeerJ Computer Science 1.

Along similar lines, a study in 2019 described the results obtained by a natural language-processing tool which was able to predict violations of Article 9 of the European Convention on Human Rights with an average accuracy of 75 per cent.[63] Doubts have been cast as to what value should be given to the insights provided by predictive algorithms, and national regulators have sometimes reacted negatively to these attempts to use machine learning with the purpose of predicting case outcomes.[64] France, most notably, enacted a law which prevents the reuse of judges' and clerks' personal data for the purpose of 'evaluating, analysing, comparing or predicting their real or supposed professional practices'.[65]

In principle, ICommCs constitute an ideal breeding ground for predictive legal analytics, for at least two reasons. First, the relatively high value in dispute of many (albeit not all) ICommC cases makes it likely that parties will make significant efforts to predict the outcome of their case and mitigate risk. Since the development of legal analytics is a complex and costly venture, this technology seems best suited for parties willing to go to great lengths to prevail in the litigation. Second, ICommCs are envisaged as standing adjudicative bodies; as such, even in the absence of a binding *stare decisis* rule, ICommC judges can reasonably be expected to follow precedent more closely than adjudicators operating within other mechanisms for the resolution of international commercial disputes.[66]

In the future, parties to ICommC litigation may increasingly use this set of tools to persuade the court to adopt a certain solution. Whenever legal analytics insights are provided by the disputing parties, the ICommC should require the disclosure of the algorithm on which the prediction is based so that its reliability can be subject to verification. In principle, a widespread use of these tools may create the interesting dilemma of whether ICommCs and other courts will still be able to develop their case law, potentially diverging from precedent, or whether they will progressively become constrained by their own precedent – that

63 Masha Medvedeva, Michel Vols and Martijn Wieling, 'Using Machine Learning to Predict Decisions of the European Court of Human Rights' (2019) Artificial Intelligence and Law (advance access).

64 Vanderstichele (n. 60).

65 Art. 33 of law no. 2019-222 of 23 March 2019.

66 More specifically, the composition of arbitral tribunals varies from case to case; this in turn makes it more difficult to predict the outcome of a case, especially in the field of commercial arbitration, where case-by-case economic considerations may play a significant role in the reasoning of the tribunal.

is, forced to adhere to the approach legal analytics demonstrate have been prevailing so far.

In principle, it may be possible for ICommCs themselves to develop their own legal analytics tools, both for descriptive purposes (i.e. to map the status and evolution of their case law to date), and to assist the judges in the adjudication of future disputes. Nevertheless, while the use of legal analytics may certainly help parties and judges in the identification of relevant precedent, algorithms should not replace human adjudicators in the resolution of complex international disputes.

14.3.7 Electronic Deliberations

Most ICommCs rely on a roster of experienced adjudicators who do not necessarily reside in the territory or the State where the Court is located. As a consequence, videoconferencing and tele-presence, but also more 'traditional' technologies such as email, may be useful not only during the hearings, but also at the deliberations stage, when the judges (who may be located in different parts of the world) need to discuss the case, exchange viewpoints and elaborate their decision. While it is unusual for the Rules and Practice Directions of an ICommC to regulate this aspect in detail, the use of technologies at the deliberations stage seems to be commonly accepted in practice.

Electronic deliberations raise significant cybersecurity concerns. In principle, deliberations should always be conducted confidentially so as to protect the judges from external influences and preserve an unconstrained environment where decision-making activities can be conducted freely. It is therefore crucial that ICommCs implement adequate cybersecurity measures and educate judges, clerks and employees about the precautions that should be taken to avoid hacks and data leaks.

As the field of investor-State arbitration demonstrates, the way in which the deliberations are conducted may be relied upon by the unsuccessful party in order to obtain the setting aside of the award and/or to resist its enforcement.[67] In principle, similar attempts at challenging the outcome of a case may become possible also with respect to ICommCs. It is indispensable for judges and administrative personnel involved in

[67] See, in particular, the Russian Federation's challenge to the *Yukos* award, based on the role allegedly played by the tribunal's secretary in the drafting of the award: Hague District Court, judgment of 20 April 2016, *Russian Federation* v. *Veteran Petroleum Limited, Yukos Universal Limited and Hulley Enterprises Limited*, C/09/477160/ HA ZA 15-1, C/ 09/477162 / HA ZA 15-2 and C/09/481619 / HA ZA 15-112.

proceedings before ICommC not to underestimate the importance of adopting security measures sufficient to preserve the confidentiality of the deliberative process.

14.3.8 *Digital Delivery of Judgment*

The delivery of the judgment via electronic means may appear like an efficient communication technique. In practice, however, the digital delivery of an ICommC judgment may entail significant complications at the recognition and enforcement stages, especially in cases where digital delivery is not immediately followed by the delivery of a physical, authentic copy of the judgment. If the judgment only exists in the form of an electronic file, in particular, it may be difficult for the prevailing party to obtain recognition and enforcement of the judgment in a different jurisdiction. In this respect, it is necessary to draw a distinction between ICommCs where the final judgment is typically rendered in the form of an arbitral award, for the purposes of its international circulation under the 1958 New York Convention, and ICommCs that do not deploy such techniques of conversion.

In the vast majority of ICommCs, the final rulings of the court are expected to circulate in their original form of court judgments. Therefore, in order to determine whether a judgment can be delivered in electronic format only, it is necessary to look at the (domestic or international) laws governing the recognition and enforcement of the judgment. While these laws may change depending on the place of enforcement as well as a number of other factors, the electronic delivery of the judgment is often not a viable option without the contextual issuance of certified, physical copies. The 2005 Hague Convention, for instance, requires the party seeking recognition and enforcement to produce, inter alia, 'a complete and certified copy of the judgment'.[68]

As mentioned earlier, there are exceptional instances of ICommCs where, once the Court renders a final decision, the latter may be converted into an arbitral award so as to enable recognition and enforcement under the 1958 New York Convention: this is the case, in particular, at

[68] Art. 13(1)(a) of the 2005 Hague Convention (n. 18). It is telling that the Convention envisages the possibility of choice-of-court agreements concluded electronically, but does not mention the electronic delivery of the judgment: Trevor Hartley and Masato Dogauchi, *Explanatory Report on the 2005 Hague Choice of Court Agreements Convention* (HCCH 2005) para. 211. The Convention's silence in this respect therefore should be read as a requirement of 'physical' delivery.

the DIFC Courts.[69] Article IV of the Convention requires that the party seeking recognition and enforcement of an award provide 'the duly authenticated original award or a duly certified copy thereof'. Therefore, if the procedural rules of an ICommC envisage the conversion of the judgment into an arbitral award, the Court should deliver a 'physical' version of its ruling for the purposes of enforcement.[70]

14.3.9 Blockchain-Based Enforcement of Judgment

Finally, technology can play an important role at the stage of enforcement, after the conclusion of ICommC litigation. More specifically, technology increasingly allows for the so-called self-enforcement of dispute resolution outcomes. Inasmuch as the disputed assets are digital in nature, it is in principle possible to devise systems whereby the adjudicators (arbitrators, or ICommC judges) allocate those assets to the prevailing party. In this scenario, the rendering of the decision and its enforcement chronologically coincide, although they continue to be theoretically distinguishable as two separate phases. A practical example may help explain the potential of self-enforcement: many blockchain-based systems allow private parties to conclude a contract denominated in a digital currency, and store a sum of money in escrow.[71] These systems are typically attached to an online dispute resolution procedure, so that, if a dispute arises and a dispute resolution procedure takes place, the disputed sum can be unlocked and directed to the prevailing party. As a consequence, the need for recognition and enforcement is largely bypassed.

Although the use of escrow accounts to guarantee compliance with dispute resolution outcomes is far from new, the magnitude of the

[69] See Practice Direction no. 2 of 2015 of the DIFC Courts. This technique, whereby a document other than an arbitral award is converted into an arbitral award in order to ensure its enforceability, is commonly associated with the case of settlement agreements reached by the disputing parties, which can be recorded in the form of an 'award by consent' or 'award on agreed terms': Giacomo Marchisio, 'A Comparative Analysis of Consent Awards: Accepting Their Reality'(2016) 32(2) Arbitration International 331.

[70] This limitation, of course, does not rule out the possibility for tribunals and arbitral institutions to provide the parties with PDF 'courtesy copies' – that is, copies created for the mere purposes of informing the parties, which cannot be used to seek recognition and enforcement.

[71] Orna Rabinovich-Einy and Ethan Katsch, 'Blockchain and the Inevitability of Disputes: The Role for Online Dispute Resolution' (2019) Journal of Dispute Resolution (advance access).

current phenomenon is unprecedented.[72] In the future, inasmuch as contracts will be denominated in a digital currency, it will be possible to devise a self-enforcing mechanism. The widespread adoption of self-enforcing escrow mechanisms would have a disruptive effect on the current reality of dispute resolution, eroding the monopoly the State currently maintains over recognition and enforcement procedures and, ultimately, over the use of force.[73]

To date, no ICommC has implemented a blockchain-based escrow system to streamline the enforcement of the judgment rendered by the court. Some ICommCs, however, are currently exploring the possibility of using blockchain technologies to 'verify' judgments, so that it may be possible to enforce a judgment across national borders at a click of the mouse, simplifying the bureaucratic procedure that recognition and enforcement traditionally require.[74]

14.4 The Way Forward: Four Practical Recommendations

Observing the current (and potential future) uses of technology in ICommC litigation, one central lesson can be drawn: in the context of international commercial dispute resolution, technology is never neutral. Rather than being an uncontroversial, efficiency-enhancing factor, technology necessarily comes with challenges. On one hand, ICommCs can harness technology to reduce costs and significantly improve the quality of adjudication. On the other hand, however, technology triggers concerns, especially as far as due process and the right to present one's case are concerned. In light of this, four practical recommendations can be put forth in an attempt to delineate a reliable way forward concerning the integration of technological tools in ICommC litigation.

First, whenever ICommC judges consider the use of technologies that may potentially prove controversial (e.g. because they are not routinely adopted in court proceedings or because they are used in a non-ordinary fashion), the parties' consent to the use of those technologies should be elicited. This, of course, may not always be enough: in cases of serious violations of due process, an expression of consent will typically not prevent the unsuccessful party from seeking the annulment of the judgment or from resisting its recognition and enforcement. Nevertheless,

[72] See *supra* note 22and accompanying text.

[73] Ortolani, 'The Judicialization of the Blockchain' (n. 22).

[74] See the 'Courts of the Future' initiative of the DIFC Courts (n. 43).

reaching a consensus at an early stage can certainly help an ICommC streamline its proceedings and avoid complaints and challenges at a later stage. The case-management stage envisaged by the Rules of most ICommCs can prove crucial to ensure the consensus of all involved parties. An interesting question in this respect is whether the judges sitting at ICommCs will be ready to adopt such a 'consent-focused' approach, aimed at obtaining (whenever possible) the parties' agreement, rather than at imposing procedural decisions on them. Such an approach is traditionally typical of arbitration, more than court litigation. While it is impossible to make comprehensive forecasts in this respect, it seems reasonable to draw a distinction among different ICommCs based on the background and expertise of the judges. More specifically, in ICommCs where the adjudicators are selected from a specialized roster with extensive expertise in cross-border dispute resolution, such a cross-fertilization between arbitration and litigation appears feasible, with the result that ICommC judges will seek the opinion of the parties as to the ways in which they wish to deploy technology in the proceedings. By contrast, in those ICommCs where the roster of adjudicators is composed of judges who typically deal with domestic cases and only occasionally may be entrusted with the task of adjudicating an international dispute, it may be more difficult to switch to such a consent-centred approach to the management of technology-assisted litigation.[75]

Second, the comparative analysis undertaken in the previous section demonstrates that, when it comes to the use of technology in court litigation, one size does not fit all. There is an evident fallacy in most attempts to devise a technological infrastructure for domestic cases and then transposing it to the 'niche' of international commercial dispute resolution. If states are to create effective procedures for the adjudication of international commercial disputes, they must take the specificities of those disputes seriously. Lawmakers should be mindful of these obstacles and peculiarities of ICommCs, rather than trying to hastily 'repackage' their domestic procedures into ICommCs. Technology in this respect

[75] In theory, most ICommCs are expected to be composed of judges with bilingual abilities and experience in international commercial disputes. However, in practice, a 'domestic' judicial mindset may still prevail, especially in cases where all ICommC judges share the same nationality and legal background. An interesting example in this regard may be the China International Commercial Court; see Matthew S. Erie, 'The China International Commercial Court: Prospects for Dispute Resolution for the "Belt and Road Initiative"' (*ASIL Insights*, 31 August 2018), www.asil.org/insights/volume/22/issue/11/china-international-commercial-court-prospects-dispute-resolution-belt#_edn10, accessed 1 February 2020.

should mainly be seen not as a tool to save costs, but rather as an instrument that can allow lawmakers to respect the specificities of cross-border dispute resolution and devise adequate solutions to the largely unique problems international commercial cases pose.

Third, when deciding whether a certain technology can be employed in the context of an ICommC, the prospects of future circulation of ICommC judgments should be taken into account by lawmakers, judges and court administrators. The necessity to protect any future judgment from denials of recognition and enforcement seems to be the overarching goal around which the entire procedure of an ICommC must be shaped. To this end, as already mentioned, ICommC judges should not underestimate the importance of consensus in the management of the procedure and the parties' agreement to the use of technology. In addition, ICommCs should adopt a comparative approach to due process and procedural public policy: when deciding whether the use of a given technology is desirable, an ICommC should consider how widely accepted that technology is in different legal systems, taking into particular account the judicial attitudes at the likely place(s) of enforcement of the judgment.[76]

Fourth, ICommCs should not be seen as a field of unconstrained experimentation. There is a superficial appeal in the idea of using ICommCs as a 'laboratory' to develop innovative, cost-efficient solutions which can then be transposed into general civil procedure and applied to all sorts of cases.[77] However, the technological solutions employed in ICommC litigation are not necessarily suitable for domestic disputes, and vice versa. Caution is necessary so as not to undermine the core mission of ICommCs, which is to render valid and enforceable judgments.

[76] A case in point is the QICDRC, whose Regulations and Procedural Rules (n. 3) expressly refer to 'fundamental international principles and international best practice', at Art. 9.2.

[77] Eddy Bauw, 'Commercial Litigation in Europe in Transformation: The Case of the Netherlands Commercial Court' (2019) 1 Erasmus Law Review 15, 22.

PART IV

The Interplay between International Commercial Courts and Other Dispute Resolution Fora

15

The Interplay between International Commercial Courts and Ordinary Courts

JULIAN BAILEY

15.1 Introduction

The subject of this chapter is the interaction between 'hybrid' international commercial courts in those jurisdictions which have created them, and the pre-existing 'ordinary' courts of those jurisdictions.[1] Before considering the interplay between the two styles of court, this chapter begins by discussing a slightly broader subject – namely, how courts interact with each other – for better or (on occasion) for worse.

It may be wrong to suggest, at least as a matter of generality, that courts display human traits. But to some extent this may well be right. On the virtuous side, courts exist to dispense justice. And doing justice, by seeking to redress wrongs as far as a judicial system is able to do so, resonates with the inherent sense of fairness that burns inside all of us.

On the less virtuous side, courts may be protective of their jurisdiction and try to prevent other courts from hearing cases or making orders which conflict with or may lead to an ascendancy of power. Self-preservation, if not self-interest, is a powerful motivation. A court with more business is likely to attract greater standing, and (if relevant) greater income, than one that hears only the occasional case.

We can find examples of courts engaging in measures to guard their jurisdiction, and therefore their power and influence, throughout history. This chapter begins by considering an English example of a 'turf war', from four centuries ago, to illustrate the point. It then proceeds to consider more recent examples taken from Dubai, where there have been several cases in which jurisdictional conflicts have arisen between the international Dubai International Financial Centre (DIFC) courts

[1] 'Ordinary' is not used in any pejorative sense here.

and the pre-existing 'onshore' courts of Dubai.[2] The chapter concludes with some reflections on measures that can be taken to reduce the probability of 'international' and 'ordinary' courts clashing with each other.

15.2 *The Earl of Oxford's Case* (1615)

To set the scene: English judge-made law developed from medieval times through three primary courts, referred to as the common law courts. These courts were the King's Bench, the Common Pleas and the Exchequer. The common law courts were created pursuant to and exercised the power of the English monarch. Between them, these three courts developed principles of law referred to as 'the common law'. As we shall see further down, English common law plays a significant part in many hybrid court legal systems.

But that was not all, because the English monarch created another source of legal authority, through the office of the Lord Chancellor. The Lord Chancellor would typically be an ecclesiastic, but from around the time of the Reformation in the sixteenth century onwards, the Lord Chancellor would be a secular officer of government, akin to a modern-day prime minister. The powers the Lord Chancellor exercised were numerous and not well defined. But one type of power the Lord Chancellor could exercise, as a facet of the monarch's prerogative powers, was judicial power, which was deployed through the Court of Chancery. He could hear suits and make orders which were enforced throughout the land.[3]

One of the touchstones for the exercise of the Lord Chancellor's powers was correcting injustices which had been brought about – or

[2] By contrast, similar conflicts have not become apparent between the more recently created (and comparable) Qatar Financial Centre, Abu Dhabi Global Market and AIFC (Nur-Sultan, Kazakhstan) courts and their respective national courts. It may be conjectured as to why this is the case – for example, that the existence of smaller case loads of those courts compared with the DIFC courts yields a lower probability of conflicts issues arising. Whatever the true explanation, the absence of 'conflicts cases' from those legal systems necessarily limits their utility for the purposes of a chapter such as this, which is focussed upon the existence of conflicts between courts.

[3] Although the office of Lord Chancellor has existed for around a thousand years, there has only ever been one female Lord Chancellor: the Rt Hon. Elizabeth Truss MP, who held the office of Lord Chancellor from July 2016 to June 2017. See 'Liz Truss Sworn in As First Female Lord Chancellor', *BBC News* (London, 21 July 2016) www.bbc.com/news/uk-36857331, accessed 1 August 2019.

would otherwise be brought about – by operation of the rules of the common law. Conceptually, this suggested the Lord Chancellor could wield power to, as it were, override an order made by a common law court. However, England did not have a formal, written constitution, so understanding whether the Lord Chancellor would have any overriding power was not clear in English law, until the early seventeenth century, with the *Earl of Oxford's case*.[4]

The *Earl of Oxford's case* involved a dispute over rights concerning property in central London. The land in question was acquired by Magdalen College, Cambridge, in the early part of the sixteenth century. Later in the sixteenth century, the land was sold, through intermediaries, to the Earl of Oxford. The Earl of Oxford then built houses on the land and leased them to tenants for particular rents. So far, this is fairly straightforward. But what complicated matters was that in 1571 a statute was passed which in its application would operate to render the transfer of land void.[5] The import of the statute had perhaps not been appreciated when the transfer of land took place. And when a later Master of Magdalen College (one Barnabas Gooch) became apprised of the statute and its significance, he took action to try to recover the land on behalf of the College, and to seize it back from the Earl.

And the matter then proceeded before the English courts. First it went to the common law courts, before a jury who upheld the Earl's rights. But the jury's decision was then overturned by Sir Edward Coke, who was Chief Justice of the Common Pleas – that is, one of the common law courts. Coke held that the statute of 1571 took effect on its own terms as an Act of Parliament, and no court could go against an Act of Parliament. But then the Earl of Oxford sought relief from the Lord Chancellor (Lord Ellesmere) against this judgment, appealing to the injustice that would flow from the Earl losing title to land he had bought in good faith and improved through building on the land.

The Lord Chancellor went against Sir Edward Coke's judgment, and held that the statute did not strike down the transfer of land. In doing so, he relied upon the Old Testament (Deuteronomy), holding that 'The Law

[4] *The Earl of Oxford's Case* [1615] 1 Ch Rep 1, [1615] 21 ER 485. Much has been written about the background to the case and about the case itself. For an illuminating discussion of the political dynamic of early Stuart England, see John Baker, 'The Common Lawyers and the Chancery: 1616' (1969) 4 Irish Jurist 368.

[5] See Ecclesiastical Leases Act 1571 (13 Eliz 1 c 10).

of God speaks for the Plaintiff [the Earl]. . . . By the Law of God, he that builds a House ought to dwell in it,' and similar catechisms.[6]

So there was a deadlock. Two judges from different courts reached opposing conclusions on the same matter. How was the deadlock resolved? In this case, it was by the King himself, consulting with his attorney-general, Sir Francis Bacon. On Bacon's advice, James I decided the Lord Chancellor's judgment took precedence over that of the Court of Common Pleas.[7] And so it was that the supremacy of the Court of Chancery over the common law courts was established.

Although the *Earl of Oxford's case* is centuries old and largely relates to political and constitutional issues in England in the early seventeenth century, it provides a striking indication of the potential for conflict to arise between national courts over questions of curial power. As we shall see, the potential for such conflicts exists even today, and indeed such conflicts have been encountered in the paradigm of international commercial courts. Before we consider such matters, we need to start with some basic concepts and definitions.

15.3 'Hybrid' International Commercial Courts

15.3.1 Definition

The expression 'hybrid court' is a neologism. It is unfamiliar to most lawyers and judges. It is not found in any standard dictionary of the English language.

As a matter of concept and etymology, the idea of a hybrid court being a court which includes a mix of domestic and international elements originates from the early part of the twenty-first century. The germ of the idea comes from the sphere of international criminal justice, primarily in relation to tribunals created to address atrocities committed in conflicts

[6] *Earl of Oxford's Case* (n. 4) [486].

[7] Bacon himself was appointed Lord Chancellor in 1618. Although a few years later, Sir Edward Coke exacted revenge on Sir Francis Bacon by having him tried and convicted for corruption. As a judge, Bacon had accepted certain 'gifts' from litigants who appeared before him, although he claimed these gifts did not influence his judgment. It was postulated by a twentieth-century law lord, Lord Simon of Glaisdale, that a large part of Coke's motivation for usurping the Court of Chancery as the dominant juridical power was that 'Chief Justices – indeed all the Judges – derived a substantial part of their emoluments from fees paid by the litigants before them; if litigation went elsewhere their emoluments fell; and Coke was notorious for combining his vast learning with attachment to mundane rewards': Jocelyn Simon, 'Dr Cowell' (1968) 26 Cambridge Law Review 265, 266.

in different parts of the world including the Balkans, Lebanon, Sierra Leone, Sri Lanka, Cambodia and East Timor. Special, ad hoc, hybrid courts and tribunals have been created in each of these countries, where the 'hybrid' courts and tribunals provide a blend of local and international judges and laws. The nature of these courts and tribunals has been pithily summarised by Professor Laura Dickinson as follows:

> Hybrid domestic-international tribunals offer an important approach to transitional justice, the process by which societies provide accountability and reconciliation for mass atrocity. Hybrid courts are courts in which the institution and the applicable law consist of a blend of the international and the domestic: foreign judges sit alongside their domestic counterparts to try cases prosecuted and defended by teams of local lawyers working with those from other countries; and at the same time, the judges apply domestic law that has been reformed to include international standards. These courts have developed in an ad hoc way, the result of on-the-ground innovation rather than grand institutional design.[8]

There have been a number of reasons for the development of such hybrid criminal courts and tribunals, which include the following.

First, in some jurisdictions there is an absence of sufficient skilled and *impartial* judges and lawyers to address the particular criminal cases. This has necessitated the utilisation of international judges and lawyers.

Secondly, there may be an issue of what might be referred to as 'process legitimacy', at least when viewed from an international perspective. If a defendant is charged with crimes against humanity by the application of the local criminal law, this may lead to justice in local terms, but for the types of crimes involved, which (rightly) have attracted significant international attention, there may be a perception (rightly or wrongly held) that the local criminal laws fall short of an international benchmark. By applying international criminal laws with local laws as part of the 'hybrid' process, the perception may develop that justice has been served at two levels: locally and internationally.

Thirdly, there is the matter of 'institutional legitimacy'. This too is grounded in perception, although it may also be grounded in actual fact. If serious crimes are claimed to have been committed by persons associated with the government of country X, and they are then tried before the national courts of country X, a suspicion could well be held that the national courts are likely to be unduly lenient upon those who are

[8] Laura Dickinson, 'The Relationship between Hybrid Courts and International Courts: The Case of Kosovo' (2003) 37 New England Law Review 1059; see also Ilias Bantekas, International Commercial Courts: Lessons from International Criminal Tribunals (Chapter 4), in this volume.

charged with the particular crimes.[9] To counterbalance any such impression, the introduction of recognised neutral and respected international judges or persons into the judicial process may act to strengthen the perceived credibility of the institution itself (i.e. the hybrid court/tribunal).

What these matters boil down to is *capacity* and *trust*. For any judicial process to be effective, it has to be resourced with capable and respected judges able to discharge their tasks with skill and efficiency. And both the process and the institution require recognition and trust, ultimately so that the outcome of the process (i.e. the judgments delivered by the court) are seen to be fair and thorough so 'justice' is done.

These considerations are paramount for any court, whether it be a criminal court, a civil court (including a commercial court) or an administrative court. The court must have credibility, otherwise its judgments will be treated as of little value, and ultimately as an institution it is likely to fail.

15.3.2 International Commercial Courts

If one were to search for a list of the various 'hybrid' international commercial courts that have sprouted around the world over the past two decades or so, a useful starting point would be the website of the Standing International Forum of Commercial Courts (SIFoCC).[10] The SIFoCC was established in 2016, following an invitation from Lord Thomas (a former Lord Chief Justice of England and Wales, and the current President of the Qatar International Court), 'to enable the judiciary worldwide to share experiences and discuss subjects of mutual interest' in relation to commercial courts.[11]

The SIFoCC defines 'commercial courts' as courts which 'hear and resolve domestic and/or international disputes over business and commerce'.[12] That is an entirely apt description of what a 'commercial court' is – that is, a court that decides business cases. But taken literally such a description would apply to a huge range of courts without discriminating between their relevant features.

9 Ibid., 1065.
10 'Standing International Forum of Commercial Courts' (SIFoCC), www.sifocc.org, 1 August 2019.
11 www.sifocc.org/about-us.
12 Ibid.

To elaborate, taking Australia as an example, the SIFoCC's members currently include the Federal Court of Australia, the Supreme Court of New South Wales and the Supreme Court of Victoria. The workload of each of these courts includes a significant volume of 'business cases'. The courts include specialist judges and divisions to handle these business cases, which are sometimes very complicated and high-value cases. And the judgments produced by those courts in 'business cases' are of the highest quality. But those courts also handle a huge variety of other business, including criminal cases and other non-commercial cases. It would not be accurate to describe those Australian courts as purely 'business courts'. Nor would it be accurate to describe them as 'international' courts – even just taking 'business cases' as a subset of judicial work. The work of those courts is varied not only as to its subject matter, but as to its domestic and international character. Perhaps, to use the language of the title of this chapter, such courts may be described as 'ordinary courts'.

If, therefore, we are to zero in on what a 'hybrid' international commercial court is, we need to understand what the essential features are of such a court, and therefore whether any particular court falls within the description of being such a court. For it is only by demarcating between 'hybrid' international commercial courts and 'ordinary' courts that we may begin to see how issues concerning the interplay of these courts can arise.

15.3.3 Features of 'Hybrid' International Commercial Courts

If we are to identify the common features of 'hybrid' international commercial courts, we may seek assistance in our characterisation by considering the salient features of 'hybrid' criminal courts and tribunals discussed earlier in this chapter. Moreover, we must also understand the purpose that international courts, whether of a commercial or a criminal variety, seek to fulfil. For international courts, it is possible to identify two broad objectives of such courts.

The first broad objective of 'hybrid' international courts is to create a forum located in a particular jurisdiction which is comfortably accessible, in a legal and practical sense, to persons who are not from that jurisdiction. International courts seek to proffer a court system which is conducted in a familiar way, according with common practices in other jurisdictions, or perhaps even in accordance with norms (if international 'norms' may be said to exist for commercial cases). There are various ways in which 'hybrid' international commercial courts attempt to accommodate the customs and practices of outsiders. They include through the use of a common language (e.g. English), conferring rights of audience upon foreign counsel, the appointment of respected and recognised judges from outside of the jurisdiction and perhaps even the adoption of a system of substantive law (e.g. English common law) to regulate commercial dealings between parties contracting within the particular jurisdiction. These are all powerful measures which attempt to break down the legal and psychological barriers to a particular jurisdiction, as if to say to the world, 'we are open for business with you'.

The second broad objective, which is implicit – but rarely stated – is to provide a legally clear and effective means of deciding cases and enforcing the orders made by the court within the particular jurisdiction where the court is located. For 'hybrid' international criminal courts, this may mean that the court is able (and without inordinate difficulty) to accept jurisdiction, and to make orders punishing convicted criminals that will be given effect – for example, a war criminal convicted by the 'hybrid' international criminal court or tribunal will be sent to gaol. For international commercial courts, the effective assumption of jurisdiction and enforceability of orders means, among other things, that the judgment of the court, which (in commercial cases) will usually be for a monetary amount, is enforceable against the judgment debtor (and the assets of the judgment debtor) within the jurisdiction where the court is located.

It is primarily in relation to aspects of jurisdiction and enforcement that issues can arise in the interplay between international commercial courts and 'ordinary courts' in a particular jurisdiction.

15.4 Conflict Issues

Issues of conflict may arise in various ways and between various jurisdictions. A conflict may arise, for example, if one takes a judgment from an international commercial court in country A and tries to enforce it in country B. Whether the judgment is enforceable in country B is a function of the laws of country B itself, including whether countries A and B have any applicable treaty or convention between them which countenances the recognition and enforcement of judgments between jurisdictions.

The same conflict, or indeed other conflicts, may, however, also arise purely in the context of country A itself. There are numerous possibilities as to where conflicts may arise between the international commercial courts and ordinary courts of a particular jurisdiction. Ultimately, the possibility for conflicts is driven by the constitutional laws of the jurisdiction in question, including those laws which establish and regulate the relationship between international commercial courts and ordinary courts.

The number and type of conflict issues that may arise are manifold, and are perhaps incapable of being fully delineated or prognosticated. Particular examples one may conjecture are:

- If a claimant is successful in its claim before the international commercial court, and it thereby obtains a judgment from that court, is that judgment recognised and enforceable before the ordinary courts of the particular jurisdiction? Is it treated as if it were a judgment of the country in question, or is it regarded as a foreign judgment?
- A claimant is unsuccessful in its claim before the ordinary courts of a particular jurisdiction. May the claimant then bring the same action before the international commercial court in the hope of a favourable outcome? To what extent do concepts of *res judicata* and abuse of process apply in this instance?
- A commences proceedings against B in the international commercial court of a jurisdiction. B brings countervailing proceedings against A concerning the same subject matter in the ordinary courts of that jurisdiction. Are both sets of proceedings able to continue? If they are, and they do, what happens if the international commercial court and the ordinary court reach different conclusions on the underlying matter in issue?

It is impossible to proffer answers to each of these questions in any general or other sense, because, as indicated, in every case the outcome is purely a function of the applicable national laws and constitutional arrangements where the courts exist. There are no international treaties, cases or legal norms that can – at present at least – determine outcomes here.

It is perhaps unsurprising, given the recent creation of many international courts, that there is a general paucity of examples that one may refer to for conflicts between hybrid and ordinary courts. There is one jurisdiction which provides a recent abundance of Byzantine cases involving a 'turf war' of sorts between its international commercial courts and ordinary courts. That jurisdiction is the Emirate of Dubai in the United Arab Emirates (UAE).

15.5 Dubai

15.5.1 Constitutional Background

Dubai was one of the first jurisdictions in the world to experiment with 'hybrid' international commercial courts. To understand the legal nature of the courts created in Dubai, it is first necessary to consider the constitutional arrangements and legislation of the UAE.

The UAE may be described as a single country, although it is constituted by seven nations known as 'Emirates'. Each Emirate has a Ruler or 'Emir'. The Ruler of each Emirate is a monarch, and the Ruler's decrees are law. Although each Emirate is sovereign and therefore able to pass its own laws, the UAE as a whole comprises a federation of the seven Emirates.[13] There is a federal government of the UAE, which in structural terms functions in a similar way to federal governments in other countries, such as the United States, Australia and Canada. Each Emirate also has its own legislature, which may enact laws for that particular Emirate.

Dubai is the largest of the seven Emirates by population, and it may be regarded as the most 'international' Emirate as well, being a regional centre for international trade and banking as well as tourism. As part of its objective of attracting international trade and business to Dubai, the government of Dubai, in 2004, created a 'special economic zone' or so-called free zone known as the Dubai International Financial Centre (DIFC).[14] The DIFC describes itself as a 'global financial centre strategically located between the East and West, providing a stable and secure platform for businesses and financial institutions to tap into the emerging markets of the Middle East, Africa and South Asia'.[15]

What is presently of interest regarding the DIFC is that it contains 'hybrid' international commercial courts, which are known as the DIFC Courts.[16] The DIFC Courts were established pursuant to Dubai

[13] The seven Emirates are Abu Dhabi, Dubai, Sharjah, Ajman, Ras Al Khaimah, Umm Al Quwain and Fujairah. The Constitution of the UAE (1971) Article 1 provides (in translation) that 'The United Arab Emirates is an independent, sovereign, federal state' comprised of those seven Emirates. See 'United Arab Emirates's Constitution of 1971 with Amendments through 2004' (Constitute Project, 17 January 2018), www.constituteproject.org/constitution/United_Arab_Emirates_2004.pdf, accessed 1 August 2019.

[14] Dubai Law No. (9) of 2004 (Dubai International Financial Centre), www.difc.ae/files/4414/5735/7076/Dubai_Law_No_9_of_2004_-_English.pdf, accessed 1 August 2019.

[15] 'Dubai International Financial Centre' (DIFC), www.difc.ae, accessed 1 August 2019.

[16] Ibid. The DIFC Courts consist of a Court of First Instance and a Court of Appeal. The Court of Appeal is the apex court from which there is no appeal. There is also a DIFC

legislation in 2004.[17] Some of the salient features of the DIFC Courts which give them a 'hybrid' and 'international' character include the following:

- Proceedings before the DIFC Courts are conducted in English.
- Foreign practitioners who are sufficiently fluent in the English language and are sufficiently experienced in advocacy in their home jurisdictions may obtain rights of audience before the DIFC Courts.[18]
- The judges of the DIFC Courts represent a mixture of highly respected UAE and international judges (currently from England and Wales, Malaysia and Australia). The immediate past Chief Justice of the DIFC Courts was Michael Hwang SC (a Singaporean), a vastly experienced judge and arbitrator, particularly in relation to commercial disputes. His successor is Justice Tun Zaki Bin Azmi, a former Chief Justice of Malaysia.
- The substantive laws of the DIFC largely replicate English law.[19]

The DIFC Court of First Instance exercises jurisdiction over civil or commercial cases connected with the DIFC, for instance where a contract is to be performed within the DIFC, or where contracting parties have otherwise agreed to their dispute being heard before the DIFC Courts.[20] Judgments of the DIFC Courts are to be issued in the name of the Ruler of Dubai.[21]

The system of the DIFC Courts is self-contained, in the sense that the DIFC Courts constitute their own hierarchy of courts, separate from those of the legal system in Dubai (and in the UAE itself) outside of the DIFC.

Courts Small Claims Tribunal, which has jurisdiction over any claim up to 500,000 AED (US $136,000).

17 Dubai Law No. (12) of 2004 (Dubai Financial Services Authority), www.dfsa.ae/Documents/Dubai%20Law%20No%2012%20of%202004.pdf, accessed 1 August 2019. The power of the government of Dubai to create the DIFC was, in turn, conferred by a combination of (i) UAE Federal Law No. 8 of 2004, which allows for the creation of a financial free zone in any Emirate of the UAE by a federal decree; and (ii) Federal Decree No. 35 of 2004, which (among other things) sets out the geographical boundaries of the DIFC within Dubai. Physically, the DIFC covers an area of approximately 110 hectares within the main business district of Dubai.

18 'DRA Order No. 1 of 2016' (DIFC Courts, 20 September 2016) Articles 4 and 5, www.difccourts.ae/2016/09/20/dra-order-no-1-2016-respect-rights-audience-registration-part-ii-academy-laws-register-practitioners, accessed 1 August 2019.

19 See, for example, 'DIFC Law No. 6 of 2004' (DIFC Courts, 2004), www.difc.ae/files/9014/5448/9175/Contract_Law_DIFC_Law_No._6_of_2004.pdf, accessed 1 August 2019 [hereinafter DIFC Contract Law].

20 Dubai Financial Services Authority (n. 19), Article 5(A).

21 Ibid., Article 3(5).

This, as we shall see, creates the possibility for conflict between the DIFC courts and the ordinary courts in Dubai which sit outside of the DIFC.

15.5.2 Dubai's 'Offshore' and 'Onshore' Courts

It is evident that the purpose and set-up of the DIFC Courts (which are commonly referred to as Dubai's 'offshore' courts)[22] is to provide an 'international' or 'hybrid' commercial court to persons engaged in commerce in Dubai who choose to conduct their business in – or in connection with – the DIFC so as to be distanced from the 'onshore' courts of Dubai.

Why, it may be asked, might a (foreign) party prefer to litigate in the 'offshore' DIFC courts instead of the 'onshore' Dubai courts? There could be a number of reasons, including that proceedings before the courts of Dubai are:

- Conducted in Arabic, meaning that all pleadings and evidence, if not originally in Arabic, need to be translated into Arabic. Further, the judgment of the court will be given in Arabic, which may necessitate its translation into another language for non-Arabic speakers. For a non-Arabic-speaking litigant, this may make the process of litigation all the more intimidating (beyond what it usually is), as the litigant will be unable to follow the court proceedings without the aid of a translator.
- Conducted pursuant to rules of procedure which, although not unusual, may be unfamiliar to a foreign party.

As a further matter, where commercial contracts are entered into in relation to Dubai, the parties have the opportunity to agree upon the substantive laws of the DIFC governing the contract, as opposed to the substantive laws of Dubai itself.[23] The DIFC's laws[24] are largely based on

[22] Although the reference to the DIFC Courts as 'offshore' courts is a little misleading. As mentioned, the DIFC is an area physically located in the main business district of Dubai. So, in a physical sense, the DIFC Courts are not 'offshore' to Dubai – they are 'onshore'. The metaphysical reference to the DIFC being 'offshore' is presumably used to denote the separateness, in legal terms, of the DIFC's laws and jurisdiction from those of the rest of Dubai.

[23] Indeed, contracting parties may agree upon the application of the laws of many other nations – for example, they may agree that English law should apply to their contract. However, for contracts which concern a subject matter in Dubai, there may be a strong inclination for the laws of Dubai – whether the 'onshore' or the 'offshore' laws – to be referenced in the particular contract.

[24] Which includes UAE federal law as it applies to Dubai.

English common law,[25] whereas Dubai law is based (as is common in Middle East countries) on civil law and Sharia law principles. If one were to contrast these two different systems in a commercial context, the variances found would not be overly significant. Nevertheless, to a person unfamiliar with the laws of Dubai, especially a person only familiar with English common law, the apprehension of 'the unknown' legal world of Dubai may make the DIFC legal system, with its common law basis, a more attractive haven for transacting business in Dubai.

15.5.3 Conflicts between Dubai's 'Offshore' and 'Onshore' Courts

The operation of dual court systems in Dubai, with the 'offshore' and the 'onshore' courts of that Emirate, self-evidently creates the capacity for conflicts between the two systems. And this capacity for conflict has in the past four years[26] led to situations where there have been actual conflicts between the 'onshore' and the 'offshore' courts, giving rise to a 'turf war' of sorts, but more significantly creating an unfavourable impression of the systems operating in the Emirate of Dubai.[27] Before considering these 'turf war' cases, it is necessary to say something regarding the constitutional arrangements of the UAE and the Emirate of Dubai itself as regards conflicts of jurisdiction.

[25] See Michael Hwang, 'The Courts of the Dubai International Finance Centre: A Common Law Island in a Civil Law Ocean' (DIFC Courts, 1 November 2008), www.difccourts.ae/2008/11/01/the-courts-of-the-dubai-international-finance-centre-a-common-law-island-in-a-civil-law-ocean, accessed 1 August 2019; former Chief Justice Michael Hwang SC described the DIFC as a 'common law island in a civil law ocean' (although perhaps this gives rise to an oxymoron of sorts, if one is to regard the DIFC as an 'offshore' jurisdiction). Within the UAE, the DIFC is not the only common law island, because there also exists the Abu Dhabi Global Market (ADGM) special economic zone, which (like the DIFC) follows a common law system in the absence of any other applicable law; and by contrast with the DIFC Courts, which include judges who are from the UAE, all of the current judges of the ADGM Courts are from common law jurisdictions outside of the UAE: see 'Judges' (ADGM Courts), www.adgm.com/doing-business/adgm-courts/judges, accessed 1 August 2019. The same is also true of Kazakhstan's recently established 'hybrid' commercial court, the Astana International Financial Centre (AIFC) Court: see 'Justices' (AIFC Courts), http://aifc-court.kz/justices, accessed 1 August 2019 (Astana has since been renamed 'Nur-Sultan', but the AIFC acronym has been retained, for now at least).

[26] This chapter is concerned with the period leading up to November 2018, and not thereafter.

[27] The title of the following recent article concerning the conflicts between Dubai's 'onshore' and 'offshore' courts provides an indication of the perception being generated: Andrew Bodnar and Martin Kenney, 'Jurisdiction and the Dubai Courts: Self-Immolation or Order out of (Potential) Chaos?' (2018) 19 *Business Law International* 125.

Under the UAE's constitution, which applies to the DIFC Courts, the apex court of the UAE[28] – being the Union Supreme Court – is vested with the power to resolve conflicts of jurisdiction between (a) federal and local judicial authorities; and (b) the local judicial authorities of one Emirate and another Emirate.[29] However, it will be noted that (b) relates to *inter*-Emirate conflicts. Although the UAE constitution addresses such conflicts, it makes no provision for the resolution of intra-Emirate conflicts between courts, such as may occur between the offshore courts of the DIFC and the onshore courts of Dubai – both types of courts being courts of the Emirate of Dubai.

The government of Dubai, being alive to this position – that is, that solutions to intra-Emirate conflicts must be found within the Emirate itself, has therefore taken steps to avoid or at least resolve conflict between its courts. Two principal measures have been taken in this regard.

First, the Dubai law enacted in 2004 creating the DIFC Courts provides for the recognition and enforcement of the 'offshore' judgments of those courts in onshore Dubai.[30] This law has been supplemented by a 2009 'Protocol of Jurisdiction' between the DIFC Courts and the Dubai courts which, among other things, provides for the mutual recognition and enforcement between the courts of each jurisdiction of 'final' judgments.[31] To some extent, the 2004 law and the 2009 Protocol do assist in resolving conflict issues where a judgment of either the onshore or offshore courts is unchallenged as a judgment. But the Protocol did not (and probably could not) resolve the 'turf war' over which court system has jurisdiction to consider a case in the first place, and therefore whether the judgment rendered by the particular court should be enforceable under the Protocol in the other court system. The government sought to address this issue some years later, as elaborated upon next.

[28] But not of the DIFC Courts, which represent a self-contained legal system within Dubai. The DIFC Court of Appeal is the apex court within the DIFC jurisdiction.

[29] UAE Constitution (n. 15) Articles 99(8) and 99(9).

[30] Dubai Financial Services Authority (n. 19) Article 7.

[31] 'Protocol of Jurisdiction' (DIFC Courts, 2009) Article 5, www.difccourts.ae/wp-content/uploads/2018/01/DIFCC_protocol_dubaicourts.pdf, accessed 1 August 2019. In February 2018, an equivalent agreement was reached between the Abu Dhabi Global Market Courts and the Justice Department of the Emirate of Abu Dhabi: see 'MoU between ADJD and ADGM Courts' (ADGM Courts, 2018), www.adgm.com/media/256642/executed-mou-for-reciprocal-enforcement-between-adjd-and-adgm-courts-11022018.pdf, accessed 1 August 2019.

Secondly, in 2016 the government of Dubai issued a decree which sought to address conflicts of jurisdiction between the onshore and offshore courts of Dubai.[32] The rationale for the decree appears to have been an emerging realisation that the constitutional arrangements of Dubai's courts required an additional, interfacing measure to resolve conflicts without the need for parties resorting to the Union Supreme Court.[33] The Decree of 2016 created a Judicial Committee of the Dubai Courts and the DIFC Courts. The 'Joint Judicial Committee' consists of senior judges representing the Dubai and the DIFC Courts in equal numbers. [34] Its remit is to determine, upon application, conflicts of jurisdiction between the DIFC and Dubai courts.[35] The Joint Judicial Committee's deliberations are final and binding,[36] meaning that they cannot be appealed to the Union Supreme Court.[37] Since its creation, the Joint Judicial Committee has (at the time of writing)[38] delivered seventeen decisions, including four with dissenting opinions from the DIFC judges.[39] Curiously all four of the dissenting opinions of the Committee have involved the three DIFC members disagreeing with the Committee members from the Dubai courts. Under the decree, in the case of an equally divided view taken by the members of the Committee, the Chief Justice of the Dubai Court of Cassation has the casting vote.[40]

[32] Being Decree No. (19) of 2016 forming the Judicial Committee of the Dubai Court and the DIFC Courts, 9 June 2016.

[33] Indeed the case of *Meydan Group LLC* v. *Banyan Tree Corporate Pte Ltd* [2014] DIFC CA 005, discussed in what follows, could well have been a catalyst for the creation of the Joint Judicial Committee.

[34] Which may also be referred to as the 'Judicial Tribunal'. The decisions of the Committee describe it as the 'Judicial Tribunal for Dubai Courts and DIFC Courts'. Nothing turns on the nomenclature of the Committee/Tribunal.

[35] See n. (33), Article 2.

[36] See n. (33), Article 7.

[37] Although perhaps there is some scope for argument as to whether a decree of one Emirate (in this case, the Emirate of Dubai) is capable, as a matter of UAE constitutional law, of occluding the jurisdiction of the UAE's apex court. However, it is understood that there is a decision (in Arabic) of the Union Supreme Court which confirms the conclusive jurisdiction of the Joint Judicial Committee: see Muhammad Mahmood, 'Conflicts of Jurisdiction Resolved? Dubai Decree No. 19 of 2016 and the Judicial Tribunal's Initial Decisions' (Al Tamimi & Company, February 2017), www.tamimi.com/law-update-articles/conflicts-of-jurisdiction-resolved-dubai-decree-no-19-of-2016-and-the-judicial-tribunals-initial-dec, accessed 1 August 2019.

[38] November 2018.

[39] See 'Joint Judicial Committee Decisions' (DIFC Courts), www.difccourts.ae/judgments-and-orders/joint-judicial-commitee-decisions, accessed 1 August 2019.

[40] See n. (33), Article 3. Because of this decree, the 'onshore' courts have the upper hand when it comes to decisions over conflicts of jurisdiction between the 'onshore' and 'offshore' courts.

Thus the constitutional, legislative and judicial framework of the UAE and Dubai possesses mechanisms to resolve conflicts between the various courts of the UAE. The provision of such mechanisms is naturally desirable, if not a necessity. But for the foreigner seeking to 'do business' in Dubai, it is undesirable to be in a position whereby it is necessary to invoke such mechanisms in the first place.

15.5.4 *Conflict Cases*

There have been a number of cases concerning the DIFC Courts where conflict issues between it and the onshore courts of Dubai (and indeed other Emirates) have arisen. The four most notable cases of this group are discussed next.

Case 1 Meydan v. Banyan Tree

The first of our cases concerned an attempt to enforce an onshore arbitral award in the offshore DIFC Courts.[41] The underlying subject matter of the dispute was a hotel management agreement between a hotel operator (Banyan) and a hotel owner (Meydan). Meydan terminated the hotel management agreement, and Banyan thereupon commenced an arbitration pursuant to the agreement. The provisions of the agreement specified for the arbitration to be conducted in Dubai pursuant to the Dubai International Arbitration Centre (DIAC) rules. At the time, the DIAC was purely an onshore arbitration centre in Dubai.[42]

Banyan was successful in the arbitration, and the arbitrator determined that Meydan had wrongfully terminated the agreement, and that Banyan was entitled to approximately US $19.4 million in damages.[43] Banyan then sought to enforce the award through the DIFC Courts. In parallel, Meydan brought proceedings in the courts of Dubai, seeking (among other things) an annulment of the arbitrator's award.

One of the striking features of the case was that neither the parties, nor the subject matter of the dispute (i.e. the hotel, and the hotel management agreement), had any connection with the DIFC. Meydan was incorporated

[41] *Meydan Group LLC* v. *Banyan Tree Corporate Pte Ltd* [2014] DIFC CA 005.

[42] See 'Dubai International Arbitration Centre', www.diac.ae/idias. The DIAC, established in 1994, is the largest arbitration centre in the Middle East. It opened a representative office in the DIFC in 2016.

[43] Mr Alexis Mourre, the current president of the International Chamber of Commerce (ICC).

in Dubai, but outside of the DIFC. Banyan was incorporated in Singapore. And the hotel itself was (and is) not located in the DIFC.[44]

Notwithstanding this lack of connecting factors, the DIFC Courts enforced the 'onshore' arbitration award in its 'offshore' jurisdiction. In doing so, the DIFC Court of Appeal relied upon Article 42 of the DIFC Arbitration Law, which provides as follows:[45] 'An arbitral award, irrespective of the State or jurisdiction in which it was made, shall be recognised as binding within the DIFC and, upon application in writing to the DIFC Court, shall be enforced.' As the Court of Appeal observed, although Article 42 was based on the New York Convention:[46]

> On its face the article imposes an obligation on the DIFC court to recognise and to enforce an award irrespective of the state or jurisdiction in which it was made. Having been made in Dubai, the present award is not one falling within the provisions of the New York Convention. But in this respect the article draws no distinction between a domestic and a foreign award.[47]

The Court of Appeal then went on to hold that, in order for the DIFC Courts to exercise jurisdiction over the case:

> The presence of assets [within the DIFC] is no longer put forward as a requirement [for jurisdiction to arise]. . . . I likewise find nothing to support the proposition that enforcement of awards within the DIFC is dependent upon some form of personal jurisdiction over the respondent within the jurisdiction.[48]

Thus, the DIFC Court of Appeal held that it had jurisdiction over the matter, and proceeded to enforce the onshore award in its offshore legal ecosystem. The logic of the approach taken by the Court of Appeal is, with respect, sound.

A person unfamiliar with Dubai's legal system may well ask the question: what was the purpose of the claimant's conduct in the DIFC

[44] The Meydan Hotel is situated next to the Meydan Racecourse, which itself has been the subject of litigation in the English Technology and Construction Court: *Honeywell International Middle East Ltd* v. *Meydan Group LLC* [2014] EWHC 1344 (TCC).

[45] 'DIFC Arbitration Law No. 1 of 2008' (DIFC Courts, 2008), www.difc.ae/files/9014/5449/8249/DIFC_Arbitration_Law_2008_0_1.pdf, accessed 1 August 2019.

[46] That is, the Convention on the Recognition and Enforcement of Foreign Arbitral Awards, 10 June 1958, 330 UNTS 38, entered into force 7 June 1959 (New York Convention); Article 45 of the DIFC Arbitration Law is based upon Article III of the New York Convention.

[47] *Meydan Group LLC* v. *Banyan Tree Corporate Pte Ltd* [2014] DIFC CA 005 at [14], per Sir David Steel DCJ (Justices Giles and Al-Madhani concurred).

[48] Ibid., [17].

proceedings? That is to say, if the respondent did not possess any assets within the DIFC against which enforcement could be executed, and there was otherwise no connection with the DIFC, why go to the trouble and expense of bringing proceedings in the DIFC at all?

The answer to this question, at least in relation to the circumstances prevailing in Dubai at the time,[49] was that the enforcement of an arbitral award – whether it be a domestic (i.e. onshore Dubai) or a foreign award – was more efficiently conducted, with less scope for challenge to the enforcement of the award, if the award were (a) first enforced offshore in the DIFC; and then (b) the judgment thus created would be enforced onshore in Dubai, where it would simply be treated as a (final) DIFC judgment which the Dubai courts would be bound to recognise and enforce.[50] The mechanism thus described is sometimes referred to as the DIFC Courts' 'conduit jurisdiction', because the DIFC Courts' jurisdiction is invoked not for the purposes of pursuing a party (including its assets) located *in the DIFC*. Rather, the DIFC Courts are used as a conduit for pursuing a party (and perhaps ultimately enforcing against its assets) *outside of the DIFC*.

The DIFC Courts' so-called conduit jurisdiction *could*, therefore, represent a basis upon which the DIFC Courts' power may, in substance, have extraterritorial effect in onshore Dubai due to the requirement, under Dubai law, for the Dubai courts to enforce the DIFC Courts' judgments without (subject to very exceptions) scrutinising or reopening the matter adjudicated upon by the DIFC Courts.

However, the apparent consequence of the existence of this 'conduit jurisdiction', and of the DIFC Court of Appeal taking an 'expansionist' approach to its jurisdiction (as in *Meydan* v. *Banyan Tree*) was to bring about the creation of the Joint Judicial Committee in 2016 which, in practice, has had the effect of reining in the 'expansionist' approach taken by the DIFC Courts to their jurisdiction (on which, see cases 3 and 4 later in this chapter).

[49] Earlier in 2018, the UAE passed a new arbitration law, which brings the UAE's laws closer to 'international norms' for arbitration: Federal Law No. (6) of 2018 on Arbitration. The 2018 law replaced an earlier arbitration law under which enforcement procedures for arbitral awards, and the grounds upon which challenges could be made to arbitral awards, could not readily be characterised as 'pro-enforcement'. The UAE arbitration laws (both before and since the reforms of 2018) do not, however, apply to the DIFC, which has its discrete set of arbitration laws that substantially accord with the New York Convention.

[50] That is, pursuant to Law No. 12 of 2004 of the Judicial Authority of the Dubai International Financial Centre, Article 7 (DFSA, 2004), www.dfsa.ae/Documents/Dubai%20Law%20No%2012%20of%202004.pdf, accessed 20 September 2020.

Case 2 Investment Group

The second case concerned a lending arrangement between a bank, Standard Chartered Bank (SCB), and a borrower, Investment Group Private Limited (IGPL).[51] The borrower defaulted under the relevant loan agreements, and the bank brought proceedings in the DIFC Courts to enforce its rights against the borrower.

In the meantime the borrower, which was incorporated in the Emirate of Sharjah, commenced court proceedings in that Emirate, seeking damages against the lender for breach of various loan agreements. The Sharjah Federal Court of First Instance dismissed the claim on the basis that the court had no jurisdiction to consider it. The court held that it had no jurisdiction on the basis that the lender was headquartered in Dubai (and had a registered branch in the DIFC), and the relevant agreements were to be performed in Dubai. The borrower appealed this decision to the highest court in the UAE, the Union Supreme Court. The Supreme Court's judgment was pending at the time the DIFC Court of Appeal, in the parallel proceedings, considered the matter.

Returning to the DIFC proceedings: the borrower took the principal position that the DIFC Courts should decline jurisdiction on *forum non conveniens* grounds, on the basis of the extant proceedings in Sharjah which were being appealed.

Both the first-instance judge and the DIFC Court of Appeal refused the borrower's application. There were certainly compelling grounds for doing so, given that the courts of Sharjah had dismissed the proceedings on the basis that they lacked jurisdiction. Only the speculative possibility of a revival of those proceedings by the Union Supreme Court could change the position. Thus, the reality was that there were no extant parallel proceedings in respect of which the DIFC proceedings should be stayed. Accordingly, there was ultimately no conflict of jurisdiction to be resolved.

Although the outcome of this case was the correct one, for the foreign lender seeking to enforce its loan and security agreements, this satellite litigation must have been unwelcome, to say the least. One of the principal purposes of hybrid courts and special economic zones is to create a space for foreign investors, which allows them to conduct business in an efficient manner without becoming embroiled in issues over 'local' laws and litigation before ordinary courts. The *Investment Group* litigation clearly consumed considerable time and resources on the lender's part,

[51] *Investment Group Private Ltd* v. *Standard Chartered Bank* [2015] DIFC CA 004.

with the case on the putative conflict of courts proceeding before the DIFC Court of First Instance and then to the Court of Appeal. The issues covered in the case are several, and the judgment of the Court of Appeal runs to some 198 paragraphs. It may be that there is no simple way under the UAE's constitutional arrangements of preventing such litigation from arising. Whether or not that is so, cases like *Investment Group* do not send out a 'pro-investment' message to foreign businesses.

Case 3 Daman

The third case arises from the period just after the creation in Dubai of the Joint Judicial Committee, the purpose of which, as previously mentioned, is to resolve conflict issues between the Dubai courts and the DIFC Courts.[52] This case involves the first decision of the Committee.

The underlying facts concerned a contract between a developer (Daman) and a contractor (Oger) for the construction of a tower (Daman Tower, now known as the 'Burj Daman') within the precinct of the DIFC.[53] Furthermore, the developer company itself was located and licensed in the DIFC. The contract between the developer and the contractor provided for disputes to be resolved by arbitration through the DIAC.

Disputes concerning the project arose between the contractor and the developer, and those disputes were referred to arbitration. The DIAC produced an arbitral award in favour of the contractor. The contractor sought to enforce its award against the developer in the DIFC Courts. However, in parallel the developer brought onshore court proceedings in the Dubai courts to seek to have the award set aside.

There was thus a conflict of jurisdiction between the onshore and offshore courts, ripe for resolution by the Joint Judicial Committee. Which court should determine the enforceability (or otherwise) of the award?

The Joint Judicial Committee decided unanimously that because the arbitration was seated onshore, only the courts of Dubai should decide

[52] *Daman Real Estate Capital Partners Company LLV* v. *Oger Dubai LLC*, Joint Judicial Committee Cassation No. 1/2016, decision of 25 January 2017 (DIFC Courts), www.difccourts.ae/wp-content/uploads/2017/08/Cassation-No-1-of-2016-with-Dissenting-Opinion.pdf, accessed 1 August 2019.

[53] The building, by coincidence, is the home in Dubai for a number of international law firms, including the author's law firm. The Burj Daman is on a street renamed 'Happiness Street', although subsequently it was renamed 'Al Mustaqbal Street' or 'the Street of the Future'. Paradise has been postponed, it would seem.

whether the award should be annulled. In this respect, the Committee's decision is clearly an orthodox one. The parties had agreed to an onshore-seated arbitration, and thereby implicitly agreed to the supervisory jurisdiction of the onshore Dubai courts.

Nevertheless, there was disagreement between the judges comprising the Committee as to whether the DIFC Courts could exercise jurisdiction over the contractor's enforcement action. The onshore judges comprising the Committee[54] held, without elaborating, that 'the DIFC should cease from entertaining the case'.[55]

In a dissenting joint decision, the offshore DIFC judges comprising the Joint Judicial Committee[56] held that:

> The DIFC has compulsory and exclusive jurisdiction to entertain an application for recognition and enforcement [of the arbitral award] within the DIFC. There are therefore two competent courts to decide this case, each court deciding the matters concerning this case within its jurisdiction according to the relevant laws governing its jurisdiction.

Although the overall conclusion of the case was correct – that is, that the matter be resolved by the onshore courts, given the onshore seat of the arbitration, it is a little remarkable to see such a sharp division of approaches taken by the onshore and offshore judges as to whether the DIFC Courts should ever have assumed jurisdiction over the case. In this regard, one can appreciate the force of the DIFC judges' reasoning. After all, the project that was the subject of the arbitration took place physically within the DIFC, and the developer of the project was located and licensed in the DIFC. Given this strong DIFC connection, and given the DIFC Courts' statutory jurisdiction over DIFC-related matters, why would it be said that the DIFC should not accept jurisdiction over the enforcement proceedings?

Leaving aside the apparent 'turf war' between Dubai's onshore and offshore courts, which manifested themselves in the decision of the Joint Judicial Committee, there is an anterior issue of why, given the offshore, DIFC-centric nature of the parties and the project, the contract between the developer and the contractor specified onshore arbitration. The simple expedient, to avoid the conflict which later emerged, would have been for the contracting parties to agree to the arbitration being seated in

[54] Being Dr Ali Ibrahim Al Imam, Chief Justice of the Cassation Court; Mr Essa Mohammad Sharif, Chief Justice of the Appeal Court; and Mr Jassim Baqer, Chief Justice of the Court of First Instance.

[55] See fn. 53.

[56] Being Michael Hwang CJ, Sir David Steel DCJ, and Omar Al Muhairi J.

the DIFC itself. Perhaps there was a reason the parties did not follow such a course, although any such reason is not readily apparent.

Case 4 Mishmish

The final case in our quartet also concerns an onshore DIAC arbitral award.[57] Sweet Homes was successful in the arbitration, and brought proceedings in the DIFC Courts to enforce the award against the unsuccessful Mr Mishmish.[58]

Mr Mishmish, however, brought proceedings in the Dubai courts, seeking to have the arbitral award annulled. Mr Mishmish also sought a decision of the Joint Judicial Committee that the Dubai courts, and not the DIFC Courts, could exercise jurisdiction over the matter.[59] He was successful in his application to the Committee; however, the DIFC members of the Committee dissented.

As with the *Daman* case, the majority of the Joint Judicial Committee held that the Dubai courts were the competent ones to exercise jurisdiction in the matter, because the arbitration was an 'onshore', Dubai-seated arbitration.[60] And again, the majority went on to hold that 'The CIFC [*sic*] Court must cease from entertaining the case.'

The dissent of the DIFC judges focussed upon the statutory powers of the DIFC Courts pursuant to Article 42 of the DIFC Arbitration Law.[61] In a Parthian shot, the DIFC Court judges held:

> We have read the decision of the majority. We respectfully disagree with its reasoning. The decision is based on the general principle of law that the Dubai Courts have the general jurisdiction and thus are the competent courts to decide the case. This implies that, whenever there is there are [sic] two cases being adjudicated in relation to one arbitral award, [the DIFC Courts] must give precedence to Dubai Courts. There is no such principle in Dubai law.[62]

57 *Ramadan Mousa Mishmish* v. *Sweet Homes Real Estate LLC* (2017) Joint Judicial Committee Cassation No. 3/2017, decision of 5 June 2017 (DIFC Courts), www.difccourts.ae/wp-content/uploads/2017/08/Cassation-No-3-of-2017-with-Dissenting-Opinion.pdf, 1 August 2019.

58 Ibid., Dissenting Opinion, para. 3. The amount awarded (by DIAC) to Sweet Homes was AED 77,000, or approximately US $21,000. On top of that, Sweet Homes awarded costs in the amount of AED 1.2 million, or approximately US $325,000.

59 At the time of the Joint Judicial Committee's decision, the Dubai courts had not decided the annulment challenge.

60 Comprising the members of the Committee from the Dubai courts.

61 DIFC Arbitration Law No. 1 of 2008, (DIFC Courts), www.difc.ae/files/9014/5449/8249/DIFC_Arbitration_Law_2008_0_1.pdf, accessed 1 August 2019.

62 *Mishmish* (n. 62), para. 10 of the dissent.

Despite the relatively strong protestations of the DIFC Court judges, the picture which has emerged in Dubai is relatively clear: the onshore court judges, who ultimately control the Joint Judicial Committee, will not permit the so-called conduit jurisdiction of the DIFC Courts for enforcing arbitral awards to be used to trump any extant, parallel proceedings in the Dubai courts regarding the underlying arbitration. By dint of the 2016 decree, the onshore courts have won the 'turf war' with the offshore DIFC Courts.

15.6 Conclusions

15.6.1 The Future for the DIFC Courts

What the future looks like for the DIFC Courts is unclear. Certainly, the DIFC Courts include amongst their judiciary some of the most astute and capable commercial judges in the world. And the laws of the DIFC are, as mentioned, grounded in established international commercial norms. There is certainly much that is attractive about the DIFC Courts as 'hybrid' international commercial courts.

Be that as it may, the popularity of the DIFC Courts for international persons wishing to do business in Dubai may well be impacted by the *perceptions* arising from the recent series of cases, of which a sample has been presented in this chapter, in which Dubai's onshore and offshore courts have come into conflict over the limits of their respective jurisdictions. It is highly unlikely that international persons of business have any appetite for becoming involved in judicial 'turf wars' of the kind Dubai has seen in recent times.

However, what is not clear is the extent to which these 'turf wars' will have the effect of causing international people of commerce to take their business elsewhere. It may be that lawyers become exercised, or even perplexed, by the interfacing issues in recent times between Dubai's onshore and offshore courts, but perhaps there are many businesspeople who are not fazed by such matters.

In any case, what we can deduce with some measure of certainty is that the recent episodes of conflict between Dubai's onshore and offshore courts would better have been avoided, if that was at all possible. To reflect upon the implications of the Dubai 'turf war' for international commercial courts more generally, we now turn to wider thoughts and conclusions.

15.6.2 *Jurisdictional Harmonisation*

The ability for a 'turf war' to arise between international commercial courts and ordinary domestic courts is essentially a function of the constitutional arrangements of the relevant jurisdiction in which those courts exist.

The system of international DIFC Courts created in Dubai sets those courts apart, in jurisdictional terms, from the ordinary courts of onshore Dubai. No doubt there were understandable reasons for doing so – that is, to attempt to insulate foreign persons wishing to do business in Dubai from the unfamiliar local courts. But for practical purposes what has been created is two, parallel court systems which have not easily interfaced with each other.

What is an alternative approach? One possibility could be for the offshore, international courts to form part of *the same* judicial hierarchy, and indeed *the same* family of courts, as the onshore courts. In other words, the international commercial court could exist as a division of the courts of Dubai, thus (for juridical purposes) obliterating the distinction between the onshore and offshore courts. The international commercial court itself would be an onshore court, albeit a court which carried all of the international features of a 'hybrid' court (e.g. proceedings would be conducted in English, foreign counsel would be entitled to appear, etc.). The court would be empowered to render judgments effective throughout the jurisdiction, thus doing away with any need (as presently exists in Dubai) for reciprocity or mutual enforcement as between the onshore and offshore courts. And there would never be any 'turf war' between courts because the international court would form part of same court as the ordinary courts. At most, the contest would be over which division of the court should decide the matter, rather than whether the court should consider the matter at all.

Such a model has been followed in Singapore, with the Singapore International Commercial Court (SICC).[63] The SICC is a division of the Singapore High Court, which is a part of the Singapore Supreme Court.[64] Although the SICC has only been in existence for a short space

[63] There may, indeed, be other legal systems which have followed a similar approach to 'hybrid' international commercial courts. No doubt examples of the models used in the various legal systems that have created 'hybrid' courts are discussed in various chapters of this book.

[64] Supreme Court of Judicature Act (Cap. 322, 2007 rev. ed.) (Sing) sections 18A–18M. See also Andrew Godwin, Ian Ramsay and Miranda Webster, 'International Commercial Courts: The Singapore Experience' (2017) 18 *Melbourne Journal of International Law* 1.

of time (since 2015), no particular 'interfacing' issues have emerged of the magnitude of those faced in Dubai.

We may also observe that the model of a 'unitary' system, whereby international and ordinary courts form part of the same court system, is not a new one. If we return to the 'turf war' manifested in *The Earl of Oxford's case* (1615), the 'clash of courts' was between the common law courts and those of the courts of equity.[65] Even though the courts of equity came to assume a dominant position over the common law courts, the 'clash of courts' continued in various ways, resulting in litigating parties being sent from court to court as their cases were non-suited on what now may seem matters of pedantry or triviality.[66] The end of the division between the common law courts and equity occurred in England in the early-mid 1870s with the Judicature Act reforms.[67] The reforms created a single court – the Supreme Court of Judicature – which included divisions for common law and chancery matters. By merging the courts into a single system for the administration of justice, the English 'turf war' had finally come to an end.

'Hybrid' international commercial courts are a recent invention, created for the purposes of promoting and facilitating investment, trade and commerce in the jurisdictions in which those courts are made. Given their novelty, it is inevitable that conflicts will, to a greater or lesser extent, emerge between these international commercial courts and the pre-existing ordinary courts in any particular jurisdiction. And through experience and interaction with colleagues across the world working in international commercial courts, we may by degrees understand the features of what works and what doesn't for international commercial courts.

65 (1615) 1 Ch Rep 1 [21 ER 485].

66 This egregious feature of the English system was perhaps most vividly illustrated, at least in a popular sense, by Charles Dickens in his novel *Bleak House* (1852–3).

67 Supreme Court of Judicature Act 1873 (UK) and Supreme Court of Judicature Act 1875 (UK). The fusion of the administration of the common law and equity is now reflected in Senior Courts Act 1981 (UK) section 49. See also Dyson Heydon, Mark Leeming and Peter Turner (eds.), *Meagher, Gummow and Lehane's Equity: Doctrines and Remedies* (LexisNexis, 5th edition, 2015), chapter 2.

16

Private Autonomy in International Commercial Dispute Resolution

International Commercial Arbitration and International Commercial Courts

MICHAEL PATCHETT-JOYCE

This chapter looks at the current relationship between international commercial courts (ICommCs) and international commercial arbitration (ICA). It first covers the historical background and current drivers for international dispute resolution. It finds ICommCs are of complex identity whose utility will be tested by market choice. The chapter then discusses what is meant by autonomy in the present context, and continues by looking at the needs and requirements of international dispute resolution ('imperatives') from a number of perspectives: those of the consumer (the 'business imperative'), of governments (the 'political imperative') and of non-arbitral decision makers (the 'jurisprudential imperative'). From that review, a measure of interdependence between ICA and ICommCs emerges. The chapter ends with the conclusion that ICA and ICommCs will enjoy a competitive and collaborative, but not a hybrid, relationship.

16.1 Introduction

At the end of the nineteenth century, commercial dispute resolution took two big steps forward in England and Wales. The City of London Chamber of Arbitration (the original name of the London Court of International Arbitration (LCIA)) was established in 1892. The London Commercial Court was created in 1895.[1] The aim of both was to meet better the needs of the business community: one cause, two effects.

[1] A specialist chamber of the High Court of Justice, Queen's Bench Division. From 4 July 2017, the High Court specialist jurisdictions, including the Commercial Court, have collectively become known as the Business and Property Courts of England and Wales. The Commercial Court continues as a court under that umbrella; see *The Business*

The relationship between international commercial arbitration (ICA) and commercial courts, now including international commercial courts (ICommCs), is nuanced. It is both symbiotic and competitive. International commercial arbitration and commercial courts share the same goal, to administer justice for the benefit of parties and the good functioning of society. Each is quite distinct from the other, yet notions of coordination and interdependence abound. International commercial arbitration depends on speed, cost-efficiency and privacy to meet commercial needs. Party autonomy empowers the parties to tailor the process to suit their circumstances and gives them a say in who should resolve their dispute. Commercial courts rely on legal certainty (often backed by binding precedent), together with judicial calibre and integrity. The primary virtues of ICA and commercial courts – including ICommCs – are different: two routes, one end.

In the century that passed after the LCIA and London Commercial Court were set up, ICA flourished and London remained the only international commercial court of note. Both prospered because of private autonomy. Party choice is a core principle of ICA, but parties with no connection to the UK who chose to litigate in the London Commercial Court also did so as an exercise of party choice.[2]

In the second half of the twentieth century, the fortunes of ICA were boosted, first, by the Convention on the Recognition and Enforcement of Foreign Arbitral Awards ('the New York Arbitration Convention') in 1958 and, secondly, by the UNCITRAL Model Law on International Commercial Arbitration, published in 1985 ('the UNCITRAL Model Arbitration Law'). Over the remainder of the century, the New York Arbitration Convention established a global enforcement norm for ICA while the UNCITRAL Model Arbitration Law created a legislative norm for ICA, inspiring many domestic arbitration statutes in jurisdictions around the world.

Although, broadly speaking, ICA continued to grow throughout that time (sometimes exhibiting exponential growth), the London Commercial Court had a bumpier ride and ploughed a solitary furrow. In 1956, the London Commercial Court sat for only fifty-six days and

and Property Courts of England & Wales: An Explanatory Statement, www.judiciary.uk/wp-content/uploads/2017/03/bpc-explanatory-statement-final-20170518-v2.pdf.

[2] See, for example, Julian Lew, Loukas Mistelis and Stefan Kröll, *Comparative International Commercial Arbitration*, (Kluwer 2003), chapter 2 [2–41], p. 28: '[T]he primacy of the principle of party autonomy, as embodied in the [UNCITRAL] Model Law, [has] now been recognised in all modern arbitration laws.'

heard only twenty-nine cases.[3] It was thought to be dying. It had fallen back into bad court habits of long pleadings and extensive evidence, costly in time and expense. It was reformed through the work of a Users' Conference which reported in 1962 and revived by more active case management.[4] As Mark Twain observed, history may not repeat itself but it often rhymes. The dip in the fortunes of the London Commercial Court was directly attributable to its taking too long and becoming too costly, a salutary note ICA should bear in mind as it faces similar accusations with increasing frequency.

The reason no other court followed in the footsteps of the London Commercial Court is less evident until the nature of that court is appreciated. At heart, it was and remains a domestic court, albeit a court with attractive attributes in terms of judicial calibre and incorruptibility, availability of highly skilled advocates and some extraterritorial reach in enforcing its judgments under reciprocal enforcement legislation, first passed in England and Wales in 1922. Other domestic commercial courts, being the public good of particular nation states, did not fully meet the transnational needs of globally pioneering business.

International agencies such as the World Bank and the International Chamber of Commerce also advocated the use of ICA as an instrument for generating economic benefit.[5] For all these reasons, it is no surprise that, during the twentieth century, business embraced ICA as a dispute resolution mechanism more to its liking.

When international dispute resolution was, essentially, a binary choice between ICA and domestic courts, the market decided. International commercial arbitration won hands down (possibly, in no small measure, because of the greater enforceability of international arbitral awards under the New York Arbitration Convention). That overwhelming victory came, however, at a price. The development of commercial law was taking place behind closed doors. In the absence of court judgments and

[3] Thomas (Cayman), ¶[22] (see further *infra* fn. [64]), derived from The Report of the Commercial Court Users' Conference (1962, Cmnd. 1616). Also, see Lord Hamblen JSC, Annual COMBAR Lecture, 'The Commercial Court: Past, Present and Future', 13 October 2020, www.supremecourt.uk/docs/speech-201013.pdf.

[4] Thomas (Cayman), ¶[23]

[5] Thomas K. P. Schultz and Clement Bachmann, 'A Wig for Arbitrators: What Does It Add?' in Rashid Bahar, Rita Trigo Trindade, and Giulia Neri-Castracane (eds.), *Vers les sommets du droit, Liber Amicorum pour Henry Peter* (Schulthess 2019), 105; King's College London Law School Research Paper No. 2019–33, https://ssrn.com/abstract=3405350 or http://dx.doi.org/10.2139/ssrn.3405350 [hereinafter Schultz and Bachmann, 'A Wig for Arbitrators' (2019)], at pp. 109–10.

precedent-creating case law to provide a full picture, jurisprudential visibility and accessibility were jeopardised.

Charting a course for economic development and diversification in the interconnected world of the first quarter of the twenty-first century has required a wholesale political shift for many countries. Nation states are no longer self-contained markets, but now need to trade with each other around the world. An open but regulated financial market provides vital support. The establishment or development of such a market underpins wider diversification and creates jobs and opportunities in its own right. To realise that objective, economic diversification cannot simply be wished for; it requires an infrastructure. That infrastructure includes new laws, new regulations and a new financial tribunal which can easily be (and, in several instances, has been) transmuted into a 'new' commercial court.

Since the start of the twenty-first century, new arbitration institutions and centres have sprung up with apparent increasing frequency around the world but another noticeable feature is that those new centres have often been accompanied by new commercial courts. That may, in part, simply be a natural consequence of globalisation; as trade and business expand so does the need for commercial dispute resolution.[6] But, in combining new arbitration centres *with* courts, other factors may be discernible.

Such 'new' commercial courts, rooted in international finance, need to be differentiated from 'ordinary' domestic commercial courts; hence, the label 'international commercial courts'. But, as has been pointed out, these new courts are, like the London Commercial Court, not international in the sense of the International Court of Justice (ICJ).[7] They are 'municipal' or – to adopt Professor Reed's thought-provoking

[6] For an interesting contrast drawn between the Westphalian concept of national sovereignty and interconnectedness of trade and commerce through globalisation and the rise of connective technology, see Chief Justice Sundaresh Menon, *International Commercial Courts: Towards a Transnational System of Dispute Resolution*, DIFC Courts Lecture (19 January 2015), www.supremecourt.gov.sg/docs/default-source/default-document-library/media-room/opening-lecture–difc-lecture-series-2015.pdf [hereinafter, Menon, *International Commercial Courts*, DIFC Lecture (2015)].

[7] See Lucy Reed, '"International Dispute Resolution Courts: Retreat or Advance?", John E. C. Brierley Memorial Lecture (September 2017)' (2017–18) 4 McGill Journal of Dispute Resolution 127 [hereinafter, Reed, 'Retreat or Advance?' (2017)]; Stephan Wilske, 'International Commercial Courts and Arbitration: Alternatives, Substitutes or Trojan Horse?' (2018) 11 Contemporary Asia Arbitration Journal, 153, at 157 [hereinafter, Wilske, 'Alternatives, Substitute or Trojan Horse?', (2018)].

oxymoron – 'domestic international' commercial courts.[8] For this reason, ICommCs can be regarded as institutions with a complex identity.

That complexity of identity lies at the heart of a present-day conundrum. It is easy to find features that differentiate an *international* commercial court from a *domestic* commercial court – use of English even if not the language of the host state, judges drawn from other jurisdictions, non-domestic legal representation, streamlined case management and more flexible procedures etc. It is, however, much more difficult to explain why any of those features marks out an ICommC as substantively different – *in specie* – from its domestic counterpart.

This chapter looks at international commercial dispute resolution through the lens of private autonomy and how the market for international commercial dispute resolution is influenced by three powerful imperatives: the business imperative, the political imperative and the jurisprudential imperative. A consideration of those imperatives explains the enduring popularity of ICA as well as the recent emergence of ICommCs. It is suggested that ICommCs are to be differentiated from domestic commercial courts not so much through their substance as by their origins. International commercial courts are best understood as the result of a new (post-Westphalian) political imperative, whereas domestic commercial courts were established when an older (Westphalian) political imperative held sway.

So understood, ICommCs are updating (and, therefore, making more relevant to users' needs) the court offering for international commercial dispute resolution. Recalling that history often rhymes, ICommCs are doing so by simplifying court processes and procedures, often by taking a leaf out of ICA's book. Paradoxically, the current trend in ICA may be to complicate things, with cost and time advantages being lost or growing 'elusive'.[9]

Ultimately, however, international commercial dispute resolution cannot be boiled down to a one-size-fits-all solution. There are sufficient bright-line differences between ICA and resolution of commercial disputes by courts for the two forms of dispute resolution not to merge. Those differences preclude hybridity. Without hybridity, there will be no single victor. Once the notion that one form of dispute resolution might triumph over – or even dominate – another is rejected, ICA and

[8] See Reed, 'Retreat or Advance?' (2017) at pp. 133, 137.

[9] Doug Jones, 'Using Costs Orders to Control the Expense of International Commercial Arbitration', Roebuck Lecture 2016, https://dougjones.info/content/uploads/2017/07/Roebuck-Published-3.pdf; cited in Thomas (Cayman) at ¶[24] (see, further *infra* fn. [64]).

commercial courts will coexist (and domestic and ICommCs will also coexist). Coexistence can be collaborative or competitive or both.

16.2 Autonomy

The *public* autonomy of courts in dispute resolution was challenged during the twentieth century by the *private* autonomy of arbitration, particularly – and with increasing success – in relation to international commercial dispute resolution. More recently, many of the traditional advantages (or 'justifications') of arbitration have been eroded, which raises the question whether ICA's autonomy has, in turn, been rendered more open to challenge.

It is important to have a clear understanding of what autonomy means in this context. Autonomy (derived from *auto-nomos*, i.e., self-rule) may be evaluated from different perspectives. From the perspective of an individual using ICA to resolve a dispute, the question is whether that system accords autonomy to its users. Yet, taking a systemic perspective, the question changes to whether ICA as a means of dispute resolution is autonomous. There are also questions of degree inherent in the concept of autonomy. Some may regard a system that possesses its own identity – that is, its own distinguishing features, as autonomous; others may say simple differentiation is not enough and true autonomy demands a stand-alone capacity – that is, a self-reliant integrity.

16.2.1 Individual (or Particular) Autonomy

Individual autonomy in the context of ICA means party choice. Parties can choose not to litigate, but to arbitrate. Parties can choose whether to arbitrate on an ad hoc basis or subject to institutional rules. Parties can choose to nominate an arbitrator and, through their choice, have a direct say in the constitution of the decision-making body empanelled to determine their particular dispute. Though subject to practical and organisational constraints, parties can, within bounds, choose the procedure whereby their dispute will be settled.

For an individual party to arbitration, ICA is quasi-autonomous. International commercial arbitration is purposeful and particular – 'purposeful' in pursuing the parties' mandate, and 'particular' because any tribunal is limited to resolving the specific dispute within the powers given to it.

International commercial arbitration does not operate in self-contained isolation. When the tribunal's limits are reached, parties (or, indeed, the tribunal itself) may seek external court support when needed, both during the arbitral process and in subsequent enforcement of the award. Here too ICA is only quasi-autonomous, dependent on a symbiotic and collaborative relationship with commercial courts around the world, including ICommCs.

16.2.2 Systemic (or Structural) Autonomy

Whether ICA can be regarded as an autonomous legal order is a question on which profound differences of opinion have been expressed.[10] French courts and academics have been passionate, contending that ICA should be regarded as an autonomous legal order. The French Cour de Cassation in two cases, *Putrabali*[11] and *Ryanair*,[12] had no doubt an arbitral award belonged to 'an autonomous international legal order'. Professor Emmanuel Gaillard has also long advocated that ICA should be granted the 'recognition of the existence of an arbitral legal order'.[13]

Other commentators broadly share that view. Notably, Singaporean jurist and Chief Justice Sundaresh Menon holds the view that ICA has developed its own 'impressive body of adjectival law' and also encompasses 'a growing body of lex arbitralis materialis containing transnational substantive rules'.[14]

[10] Systemic or structural autonomy is a subject of much debate between practitioner-academics; see E. Gaillard, *Legal Theory of International Arbitration* (Martinus Nijhoff 2010) [hereinafter, Gaillard, *Legal Theory* (2010)]; Jan Paulsson, *The Idea of Arbitration* (Oxford University Press 2013) [hereinafter, Paulsson, *Idea of Arbitration* (2013)], esp. chapter 2, 'The Legal Foundations of Arbitration'; Won L. Kidane, *The Culture of International Arbitration* (Oxford University Press 2017); [hereinafter, Kidane, *Culture of International Arbitration* (2017)], esp. chapter 4, 'The Theories and Theoreticians of International Arbitration'. The intention here is simply to point to such that debate, not contribute to it.

[11] Cour de Cassation, 29 June 2007.

[12] Cour de Cassation, 8 July 2015.

[13] See Gaillard, *Legal Theory* (2010) at chapter 1, C.2, pp. [52]–[66]. For a searing critique of Gaillard, see Kidane, *Culture of International Arbitration* (2017) at pp. 65–76.

[14] Chief Justice Sundaresh Menon, 'Transnational Commercial Law: Realities, Challenges and a Call for Meaningful Convergence' (2013) Singapore Journal of Legal Studies 231, https://pdfs.semanticscholar.org/832e/58f6262747e2b1867b37e91091e749ca51b2.pdf?_ga=2.125251208.382653704.1599663775-2015791176.1599663775 [hereinafter, Menon, 'Transnational Commercial Law' (2013)], p. 240.

On the other hand, Lord Mance has appeared antipathetic to the proposition.[15] In a lecture delivered in 2015, he detected a lack of coherence in those advocating such a view.[16]

On further analysis, however, the difference between those two approaches becomes more semantic and less substantive. Although Lord Mance expressed concern that ICA might declare unilateral independence and the view that '[a]rbitration is not, and should not become, a law unto itself', his real concern would seem to be that arbitral awards (rather than arbitration per se) should not be regarded as autonomous of national courts.[17] That is a more modest proposition. Equally, Professor Gaillard's argument contains important qualifications. He sees the autonomous existence of ICA as legitimised through 'the convergence of national legal orders'.[18] He also acknowledges that national jurisdictions have kept the monopoly on enforcement of arbitration awards but sees that as 'in no way undermin[ing] the autonomy of the arbitrators' judicial function and the legal order in which they operate'.[19] For Gaillard, autonomy lies in party choice and independence of process.

It comes down to a question of degree. Gaillard sees ICA as autonomous despite court involvement; Lord Mance regards ICA as not autonomous because of such involvement. Gaillard is content to adopt a less strict definition of autonomy than Lord Mance.

For Prof. Gaillard, autonomy is compatible with coexistence; for Lord Mance, interdependence precludes autonomy. Both would agree that ICA is independent and quasi-autonomous, being:

- a self-standing form of dispute resolution;
- its '*leitmotif*' being '[party] autonomy and consent – as regards the composition and jurisdiction of the tribunal, procedure, evidence, confidentiality etc.' (as Lord Mance has acknowledged);[20]

[15] Formerly Deputy President of the UK Supreme Court, now Chief Justice of the AIFC Courts in Nur-Sultan, Kazakhstan, and an international judge of the Singapore International Commercial Court.

[16] Jonathan (Lord) Mance, 'Arbitration: A Law unto Itself?', School of International Arbitration and Freshfields Bruckhaus Deringer 30th Annual Lecture (4 November 2015), www.supremecourt.uk/docs/speech-151104.pdf [hereinafter, Mance, *Arbitration* (Freshfields Lecture 2015)].

[17] Or, to quote Paulsson, *Idea of Arbitration* (2013) at p. 30: 'The great paradox of arbitration is that it seeks the cooperation of the very public authorities from which it wants to free itself.'

[18] Gaillard, *Legal Theory* (2010) at p. 59.

[19] Ibid.

[20] Mance, 'Arbitration' (Freshfields Lecture 2015) at p.2.

- freely chosen by the vast majority of regional and international businesses;[21]
- supported by well-established regional and international arbitral institutions.

International commercial arbitration is, however, not independent insofar as it relies on court systems to function at each stage of the arbitral cycle, from constitution of the tribunal to enforcement of an award. Courts act as the 'bulwark of public confidence'.[22] They should 'supervise with a light touch but assist with a strong hand'.[23] 'Maximum support. Minimum interference'.[24]

16.3 Imperatives

International commercial dispute resolution, particularly the interaction between ICA and ICommCs, may be better understood by exploring certain current imperatives in play – notably, the business imperative, the political imperative (which has developed as geo-economic circumstances have changed) and (more recent and specifically) the jurisprudential imperative.

16.3.1 Business Imperative: Business Knows Best

The business imperative is clear. Entrepreneurship is pioneering, expansive and transnational, finding and exploiting new markets. Business is business; disputes are a sideshow.

[21] 'Arbitration better meets [businesses'] demands than other readily-available options such as commercial litigation.' See 2015 QMUL Survey, www.arbitration.qmul.ac.uk/media/arbitration/docs/2015_International_Arbitration_Survey.pdf.

[22] Chief Justice James Allsop AO, 'National Courts and Arbitration: Collaboration or Competition?' (2015) 4 Arbitration 434.

[23] See Michael Hwang SC, 'Commercial Courts and International Arbitration: Competitors or Partners? Clayton Utz University of Sydney International Arbitration Lecture, 2014' 31 (2015) Arb. Int'l 193, 194; in leading to that conclusion Michael Hwang said: 'The courts of most Model Law countries agree that curial courts should adopt an "arbitration friendly" policy, that is, to decline to set aside awards for error of law or fact, however gross; instead, courts should read awards generously and not looking assiduously for defects in process, unless really serious violations of due process have occurred which have caused real prejudice. Furthermore, courts should intervene quickly in support of arbitration by issuing court orders enforcing tribunal decisions where judicial assistance is needed.'

[24] See Thomas (Beijing); see, further *infra* fn. [64].

Business also craves certainty. It wants laws that are clear, intelligible and uniformly applied. It wants mechanisms whereby disputes can be avoided, mediated or resolved. It wants those mechanisms to be good (reliable), cheap (i.e. cost-effective) and quick (in relative terms). It may also want to protect legitimate commercial confidences. It wants effective enforcement of decisions made (either awards or judgments). In short, business wants to dispose of disputes – including international disputes – as quickly, cheaply and effectively as possible.

To compete at a transnational level, international business also needs to be commercially agile. Business mobility creates challenges – linguistic, cultural and often a reluctance on the part of one party to submit to the jurisdiction of the other party's courts. It has been said that national legal systems are 'inimical' to international trade.[25] Hence, as noted earlier, ICA has developed to meet business needs in a multi-jurisdictional, multilingual and multicultural environment.

Agility applies to commercial dispute resolution too: 'international commercial disputes are mobile'[26]. Dispute mobility is, again, a matter of party choice. In the more fluid present-day transnational business environment, mobility can take a number of forms – notably (i) *forum* mobility (choice between arbitration and litigation, or choice between a 'domestic' and an 'international' commercial court), (ii) *geographic* mobility (choice of seat, choice of arbitral institution or choice between competing ICommCs) and, as a viral pandemic has shown, (iii) *platform* mobility in which dispute resolution, whether rooted in court, arbitration or mediation, has moved online.

Business will choose the forum, location and medium that is most suitable for the resolution of the particular dispute in which it is involved: 'Ultimately, the preferred mode of dispute resolution depends very much on the needs of the parties.'[27] The broader market context also conditions how specific party needs are met – that is, market perception and market acceptance of dispute resolution means.

[25] See Justice Quentin Loh, 'The UNCITRAL Model Law and the Pro-arbitration Approach: Judicial Internationalism and International Interpretation – The Singapore Experience', in Frédéric Bachand and Fabien Gélinas (eds.), *The UNCITRAL Model Law after 25 Years* (JurisNet 2013), (chapter 9) at p. [190].

[26] Sir William Blair, 'Contemporary Trends in the Resolution of International Commercial and Financial Disputes', Durham University Institute of Commercial and Corporate Law Annual Lecture (21 January 2016), www.judiciary.uk/wp-content/uploads/2016/01/blair-durham-iccl-lecture-2016.pdf [hereinafter Blair, 'Contemporary Trends' (2016)].

[27] Menon, 'International Commercial Courts', DIFC Lecture (2015), ¶[56].

As for market perception, it is easy to stigmatise (as some have) an ICommC as a 'caviar court',[28] a 'court for the super rich',[29] a 'VIP court'[30] or a 'luxury item'[31] that will cause much-needed resources to be diverted from already struggling domestic courts. It is also easy to challenge the necessity for *international* commercial courts when the work can be handled just as well by specialist *domestic* commercial courts or specialist lists in such courts.[32] In some form, those arguments have been levelled at many ICommCs – and put paid to one initiative, the proposed Brussels International Business Court (BIBC).[33] The debate over resource allocation is only set to intensify in these more economically stringent times, when financial austerity has been aggravated by the fallout from a global pandemic. In terms of market perception, now may not be an auspicious time for ICommCs.

International commercial courts face no less a challenge when it comes to market acceptance because of the exceptionally high standing enjoyed by ICA. The 2018 White & Case/Queen Mary University London International Arbitration Survey[34] found that a staggering 97 per cent of respondents said international arbitration was their preferred method of dispute resolution (up from 90 per cent in the previous 2015 survey).[35]

[28] See ConflictsofLaws.net blog, quoted in Sir William Blair, 'The New Litigation Landscape: International Commercial Courts and Procedural Innovations' (2019) 9(2) International Journal of Procedural Law, https://sifocc.org/app/uploads/2020/04/The-New-Litigation-Landscape-International-Commercial-Courts-and-Procedural-Innovations.pdf [hereinafter, Blair, 'The New Litigation Landscape' (2019)], p. 220 (and cf. Geert van Calster, 'The Brussels International Business Court: A Carrot Sunk by Caviar', in Xandra E. Kramer and John Sorabji (eds.), *International Business Courts: A European and Global Perspective* (Eleven International 2019), chapter 6, 107–14 [hereinafter Kramer and Sorabji, *International Business Courts* (2019)].

[29] Blair, 'The New Litigation Landscape' (2019).

[30] Ibid.

[31] See Kramer and Sorabji, *International Business Courts* (2019), p. 8.

[32] Blair, 'The New Litigation Landscape' (2019), giving as an example, Justice A. S. Bell, 'An Australian International Commercial Court: Not a Bad Idea, or What a Bad Idea?, Speech, ABA Conference, Singapore (July 2019), www.supremecourt.justice.nsw.gov.au/Documents/Publications/Speeches/2019%20Speeches/Bell_20190712.pdf [hereinafter Bell (2019)] but, for a riposte to Bell (2019), see Justice Craig Colvin, 'Comment on Bell (2019)', ABA Conference, Singapore (ibid.,), www.fedcourt.gov.au/__data/assets/pdf_file/0003/58890/20190711.pdf.

[33] Van Calster, 'Brussels International Business Court'.

[34] www.arbitration.qmul.ac.uk/media/arbitration/docs/2018-International-Arbitration-Survey–The-Evolution-of-International-Arbitration-(2).PDF

[35] See White & Case/QMUL International Arbitration Survey 2015 at pp. 2 and 5 and Chart 51 on p. 53, www.arbitration.qmul.ac.uk/media/arbitration/docs/2015_International_Arbitration_Survey.pdf. Data relied on by Firew Kebede Tiba, 'The Emergence of Hybrid

The conclusion of the earlier survey that '[t]he strong preference for international arbitration by its users demonstrates that arbitration better meets their demands than other readily available options, such as commercial litigation' still holds good.[36] If arbitration should only feel threatened if courts were better able (than arbitration) to satisfy the reasons to arbitrate, the 7 per cent *increase* from 2015 to 2018 on an already-high preference rating shows the enduring attraction of ICA.[37]

A significant shift is detectible, though: from using ICA alone to its continued use in conjunction with other alternative dispute resolution (ADR). The combination of arbitration and mediation is often viewed as being in sequence (med-arb, arb-med, med-arb-med) but it might equally be a combination in parallel. Though some of the shift between 2015 and 2018 might be explicable by an increase in popularity of a sequential approach to dispute resolution, that would be cumbersome, time-consuming and costly – and, therefore, unrealistic – in all but very high-value cases. That would point to a significant proportion of the shift being accounted for by mediation being used in parallel with ICA. If so, that dynamic would be attributable to knowledgeable and sophisticated users fashioning a dispute resolution mechanism to their liking. It would also indicate that ICommCs might encounter an uphill struggle for substantial market share if there is only *de minimis* resort to cross-border litigation (whether or not in conjunction with ADR) by users who have shown themselves adaptable in pursuit of means of dispute resolution suited to their wishes but whose movement has not been towards ICommCs but in another direction altogether.

Market acceptance is the collective manifestation of individual party choice. The long-standing popularity of ICA reflects the strong and enduring pull of private autonomy in this context. Applying the old adage 'if it ain't broke, don't fix it!' with such high satisfaction ratings ICA would seem to have no cause for concern as regards market acceptance. At the same time, ICA cannot complacently rest on its laurels. If,

International Commercial Courts and the Future of Cross Border Commercial Dispute Resolution in Asia' (2016) 14(1) Loyola University Chicago International Law Review and Chief Justice James Allsop AO and Justice Clyde Croft, 'The Role of the Courts in Australia's Arbitration Regime', Commercial CPD Seminar Series (11 November 2015), www.supremecourt.vic.gov.au/sites/default/files/assets/2017/09/f4/e4e199c14/commercial%2Bcpd%2Bseminar_role%2Bof%2Bthe%2Bcourts_paper.pdf.

36 Ibid., p. 5.

37 Dalma R. Demeter and Kayleigh M. Smith, 'The Implications of International Commercial Courts on Arbitration' (2016) 33 Journal of International Arbitration 441, 445 (2016) [hereinafter Demeter and Smith, 'Implications' (2016)].

despite their complex identity, ICommCs can provide one or more facilities that ICA cannot and can match all the other features of ICA that international business values, then – but only then – ICommCs might wrest some of the market acceptance away from ICA. That will be the acid test. As Sir William Blair recently put it, '[i]n the long term it will be market choice that will ultimately determine the success of the new courts, just as it did with all previous models'.[38]

To flourish, ICommCs must be sufficiently attractive to international business to change what is now a well-established, embedded path of private autonomy. Some disputes will inherently be more suited to resolution by one or other means of international dispute resolution. Cases that are more suited to court resolution (e.g. because it is desirable to set a precedent capable of general application) will naturally gravitate towards ICommCs and the availability of such courts will, for such cases, better meet business needs and market demand. Likewise, disputes better suited to arbitration will stay within the scope of ICA. It would seem very likely that more commercial disputes will always come into the latter category than the former. To avoid being limited to thin gruel, ICommCs will, in all probability, need to persuade some commercial disputants to vote with their feet. To that extent, ICommCs represent competition for ICA but, given ICA's present dominant position, the barrier to entry for any ICommC is high.

In a characterisation that would appeal to business, it is certainly now popular to regard dispute resolution as a 'market'.[39] That suggests a keen competitive environment at several levels: between domestic commercial courts, between domestic commercial courts and ICommCs, and between ICommCs and ICA. This aspect is considered in more detail once the other imperatives have been covered.

16.3.2 Political Imperative

The Westphalian view of the world order regarded the nation state as sovereign and the political realm as responsible for public goods whose objective was to preserve and advance the integrity of each nation state.[40]

[38] Blair, 'The New Litigation Landscape' (2019) at pp. 217–18, referring back to Blair, 'Contemporary Trends' (2016).

[39] See, for example, Marta Requejo Isidro, 'International Commercial Courts in the Litigation Market' (2019) MPILux Research Paper Series 2019(2), esp. at Section 3.

[40] See, for example, Menon, 'International Commercial Courts', DIFC Lecture (2015) at ¶¶[1]–[2]; cf. also Blair, 'The New Litigation Landscape' (2019), p. 219.

The original political imperative, therefore, saw dispute resolution as a public good; hence, the establishment of courts.

The self-contained nature of nation states has, however, come to be seen as increasingly unsuited to the globalised neoliberal world, especially for countries dependent largely on a service economy, or substantially on a finite natural resource. For such nations particularly, the political imperative now looks to a wider horizon in which economic development and diversification feature prominently.

The political imperative has shifted as international commerce has overreached the jurisdictional constraints imposed under the Westphalian doctrine. The political imperative now is to prioritise economic diversification and encourage inward foreign direct investment (FDI). An intrinsic element of this imperative is the establishment of a sound financial system and centre underpinned by rigorous application of the rule of law. As Lord Thomas has observed, economic development cannot take place in a vacuum.[41] It 'depends on more than the rule of law in one or a number of states. It depends upon its development and adherence to it across the world'.[42] It is no surprise, therefore, that 'as the pre-eminent mode of resolving cross-border commercial disputes, international arbitration plays a vital role in facilitating transnational commerce'.[43]

As economic diversification means incentivising entrepreneurship domestically and encouraging FDI, it means not only being open for business, but being seen to be open for business.[44] The post–World War II neoliberal economic agenda, to which Western democratic values were thought to be an essential underpinning, has come under increasing challenge by emerging market economies in the Gulf, in South Asia, in Central Asia, in China and elsewhere. By and large, emerging economies leading the eastward (and southward) gravitational pull of current

[41] Thomas (Cayman), ¶[70]; see further *infra* fn. [64].

[42] '[L]aw is a fundamental instrument of all transnational economic integration' (quoted by Menon, 'Transnational Commercial Law' (2013), 231 at 244.

[43] Justice Steven Chong, 'Singapore International Commercial Court: A New Opening in a Forked Path,' Speech (October 2015), www.supremecourt.gov.sg/Data/Editor/Documents/J%20Steven%20Chong%20Speeches/The%20SICC%20-%20A%20New%20Opening%20in%20a%20Forked%20Parth%20-%20London%20(21.10.15).pdf, ¶[5].

[44] See Blair, 'Contemporary Trends' (2016) p. [11] citing, in support, Cheryl Xiaoning Long, 'Does the Rights Hypothesis Apply to China?' (2010) 3 Journal of Law & Economics 629; see also Thomas (Cayman), ¶[65]; see further *infra* fn. [64]; and Thomas (Singapore), ¶[36], see further *infra* fn. [64].

economic development are not following the Western-style democratic model, but *are*, very definitely, open for business.[45]

Economic diversification through FDI means giving business what it likes. Business has consistently opted for ICA. The political imperative is, therefore, supportive of ICA, but goes further. Financial systems and centres must be properly regulated by law with a concomitant need for court supervision. The present political imperative therefore favours not just ICA but also the creation of commercial courts. Given the globally interrelated nature of finance and FDI, it is but a short step for such new commercial courts to become *international* commercial courts – ICommCs – or, at least, to be badged as such.

That new political imperative acknowledges and accepts the business imperative and seeks better to accommodate commercial needs so as to promote economic development and diversification. Dispute resolution is part of that picture; hence, the greater interest in the establishment of arbitration centres.

The world has changed from one of unipolar constructs in which nation states were sovereign and autonomous to a more multipolar environment in which nation states compete *inter se* to attract trade and investment. In doing so, states have ceded (some) autonomy in response to global influences from the international commercial sector. It is no longer sufficient just to provide courts as a public good; it is also necessary to support and promote arbitration as a private autonomous alternative.

A new ICommC/ICA arbitration centre sends a powerful market message. The establishment of such courts and arbitration centres signals a political understanding of the business imperative.[46] That analysis is confirmed when new ICommCs are considered in more detail. The first wave of ICommCs (Dubai, Qatar, Singapore, Abu Dhabi, Nur-Sultan (Astana)) were clearly established to promote economic diversification – either to move economies away from overreliance on finite natural resources or, in Singapore's case, to further the ambition of a city state to market its strong services sector regionally and internationally. The second wave, the China International Commercial Courts (CICC) established in Shenzhen and Xi'an, is an integral part of an economic project, the Belt and Road Initiative (BRI). The third wave, ICommCs in

[45] See Menon, 'Transnational Commercial Law' (2013), 231 at 234.

[46] See also Georgios Dimitropoulos, 'National Sovereignty and International Investment Law: Sovereignty Reassertion and Prospects of Reform' (2020) 71 Journal of World Investment & Trade 91–2.

Europe – Paris, Amsterdam, Hamburg, Frankfurt, Zurich, Geneva, Dublin and Belgium (now shelved) are again economically inspired, driven by Brexit opportunism.[47] All are products of the new post-Westphalian political imperative (though, in the case of the third wave, that is often done by grafting a 'new' ICommC chamber on to an existing domestic commercial court).

Another, separate but closely related dynamic is at work. If one of the first consequences of a driver to economic diversification was the creation of a dispute resolution environment more to the liking of international commerce (i.e. the establishment of arbitration centres as well as courts), a second consequence is now following fast upon the first: competition *between* new centres to attract the business of international dispute resolution.

The emergence of more international dispute resolution centres has tended to 'foster a competitive environment in which different states and systems and commercial actors seek to create optimal conditions to encourage use of their particular dispute resolution mechanisms'.[48] Competition does mean survival of the fittest (or, at least, the fitter). With so many new ICommCs having recently opened or in the pipeline, a note of caution should be sounded; at least one commentator 'would not put my money on the chances of success for so many [ICommCs], even if their goals are modestly regional'.[49]

A further point might be noted. The City of London was a forerunner in opening up a regulated financial market through the so-called Big Bang in October 1986, which led to clear and comprehensive primary legislation, the Financial Services and Markets Act 2000, with accompanying subordinate legislative instruments, rulebooks etc. Given that laws are open source, it should be no surprise that jurisdictions establishing an ICommC, especially those in the first wave launching a financial market in support of economic diversification, should adapt, adopt and use a statutory framework derived mainly from English law.[50] It is then

[47] 'The BREXIT Wannabe Profiteers' as Wilske, 'Alternatives, Substitute or Trojan Horse?' (2018) has described them, p. 169. On a typology of ICommCs see Georgios Dimitropoulos, 'International Commercial Courts in the "Modern Law of Nature": Adjudicatory Unilateralism in Special Economic Zones' (2021) 24 Journal of International Economic Law 361.

[48] Blair, 'Contemporary Trends' (2016), at p. [4].

[49] Reed, 'Retreat or Advance?' (2017) p. [12].

[50] See, for example, the Application of English Law Regulations 2015 (AELRs), which provide the foundation of the civil and commercial law in the Abu Dhabi Global Market (ADGM) Courts. As the ADGM Courts explain on their website: 'these

but a short step to staff the concomitant specialist tribunals and courts with judges familiar with that regime – that is, common-law, predominantly English, judges.

This development has resulted in a cohesive, skilled, experienced and motivated cadre of judges moving from a national to an international stage. The emergence of this group has coincided with the third important imperative that has been identified, the jurisprudential imperative. Indeed, it may be no coincidence at all. The current high visibility of the jurisprudential imperative may be directly attributable to the emergence of this assemblage of judges with an international platform.

Thus, the present political imperative, in one respect, promotes ICA, thereby protecting and safeguarding its integrity and autonomy. In another, however, it introduces an instrument whereby ICA's autonomy may be challenged by introducing a potential competitor, ICommCs, which are presided over by judges with a clear agenda. At the top of that agenda is their desire to promote commercial jurisprudence (by improving accessibility) as a means of promoting the rule of law internationally.[51]

16.3.3 *Jurisprudential Imperative*

A healthy society adheres to the rule of law. Access to justice is a fundamental tenet of the rule of law. There are two principal elements to access to justice – that is, access both to effective means of dispute resolution and to the law itself. Laws should be certain, and their application predictable. Thus, legislation should be publicly promulgated and the application of law (and, particularly in the common law context, its development through case law precedent) should be publicly available and readily accessible. That is the jurisprudential imperative.

Jurisdictionally, there is considerable overlap between ICommCs and ICA. Jurisprudentially, there is not. It is in a court's DNA to put legal reasoning in the public domain whereas arbitral tribunals are hardwired to keep such analysis for the parties' eyes only. Such privacy poses a challenge to full understanding of the current state of commercial law

Regulations make English common law (including rules and principles of equity) directly applicable in ADGM. In addition, a wide-ranging set of well-established English statutes on civil matters are also made applicable in ADGM'.

[51] For further discussion of the contribution of ICommCs to the Rule of Law, see Susan L. Karamanian, 'International Commercial Courts, Dispute Resolution and the Rule of Law' (Chapter 22), in this volume.

and raises the question whether ICA stands in the way of the continued development of the law. International commercial courts perform a 'public adjudicatory function' whereas ICA acts in private.[52] This fundamental difference must be explored for the future relationship between ICommCs and ICA to be predicted.[53]

International commercial arbitration's contribution to access to justice is, therefore, ambivalent. By adding another effective means of dispute resolution, it makes a very positive contribution but, by doing so behind closed doors, it can be said to impede others' access to justice because legal analysis goes unpublished and potential jurisprudential developments go unnoticed. That concern is a cause recently championed by judges with an international vision, eager to safeguard the orderly development of commercial jurisprudence and promote the rule of law. Such judicial activism is benign and well motivated, but adds muscularity to the present debate over the coexistence of ICA and ICommCs.

International commercial arbitration privacy and confidentiality can thus be seen either as an attribute or a detriment. Similarly, the absence of appeal in ICA is either a virtue or a vice. Business (broadly) likes privacy and confidentiality, and no appeal; judges, mindful of the rule of law and the jurisprudential imperative, (broadly) don't.[54]

Another peculiar feature of the jurisprudential landscape is that, however well suited ICommCs might be to the development of international

[52] See Tiong Min Yeo, 'Staying Relevant: Exercise of Jurisdiction in the Age of the SICC', Eighth Yong Pung How Professorship of Law Lecture 2015, https://law.smu.edu.sg/sites/default/files/law/CEBCLA/YPH-Paper-2015.pdf, at ¶[51], drawing on and summarising M. Keyes, *Jurisdiction in International Litigation* 22–6 (Sydney 2005) at pp. [22]–[26].

[53] In Thomas (Cayman) (see further *infra* fn. [64]), Lord Thomas recognised the stark contrast between the open justice approach of ICommCs and litigation on one hand, and the strict confidentiality that is intrinsic to ICA. Even in what is, quite literally, an open-and-closed debate, he acknowledged signs of movement on both sides, regarding as a 'live and important question' whether judgments might, in some instances, be anonymised or only partially recite the facts. At the same time, the ICA community is actively considering whether the publication of awards – again, suitably anonymised – might go a long way to addressing the criticism that the development of commercial law is being unduly retarded by the prevalence of ICA.

[54] Eighty-seven per cent of respondents to the 2018 International Arbitration Survey by QMUL/White & Case (www.arbitration.qmul.ac.uk/media/arbitration/docs/2018-International-Arbitration-Survey–The-Evolution-of-International-Arbitration-(2).PDF) believed confidentiality in ICA to be of importance. Fifty-seven per cent of in-house counsel surveyed rated confidentiality as 'very important' (Survey, p. 27). In the same survey, only 14 per cent of respondents identified lack of appeal as one of the worst characteristics of ICA (Survey, p. 8). Cf. the view of the judiciary expressed by Lord Thomas in Thomas (BAILII) at ¶[22]; see, further *infra* fn. [64].

commercial jurisprudence, ICA has stolen a march through the New York Arbitration Convention and the UNCITRAL Model Arbitration Law, both of which have proved very attractive to the market. Both have had a global normative effect, inculcating 'judicial internationalism' as regards the recognition and enforcement of ICA awards long before the ICommCs began to follow the same approach.[55] To be a viable alternative to ICA, ICommCs must develop comparable enforcement mechanisms. To do so, ICommCs can emulate or innovate – and seem to be doing both.

Emulation comes in the form of the Hague Conventions (1) in 2005, on choice-of-court agreements[56] ('the Hague CoC Convention'), which aims 'to promote international trade by enhancing certainty for choice of court agreements in terms of allocation of jurisdiction and the enforcement of resulting judgments',[57] and (2) in 2019, on Recognition and Enforcement of Foreign Judgments in Civil or Commercial Matters ('the Hague Judgments Convention').[58] The Hague CoC Convention has been described as a game changer.[59] The more widely the Hague CoC and Judgments Conventions are adopted, the more attractive ICommCs will become.[60]

[55] This argument is derived from a series of articles by Professors Frédéric Bachand and Fabien Gélinas; see Frédéric Bachand and Fabien Gélinas, 'The UNCITRAL Model Law after 25 Years: Global Perspectives on International Commercial Arbitration', in Frédéric Bachand and Fabien Gélinas (eds.), *The UNCITRAL Model Law after 25 Years: Global Perspectives on International Commercial Litigation* (JurisNet 2013), 219; Frédéric Bachand and Fabien Gélinas, 'Interpreting the Model Law: Methodology and the Singapore Experience', in David Foxton and David Joseph (eds.), *Singapore International Arbitration: Law & Practice* (LexisNexis Singapore 2014).

[56] The Hague CoC Convention was concluded on 30 June 2005 and entered into force on 1 October 2015.

[57] Tiong Min Yeo, 'Hague Convention on Choice of Court Agreements 2005: A Singapore Perspective' (2015) 114(1) Journal of International Law and Diplomacy [国際法外交雑誌] 50 ¶[53]. Research Collection School of Law, https://ink.library.smu.edu.sg/sol_research/1688, and Tiong Min Yeo, *Report of the Law Reform Committee on the Hague Convention on Choice of Court Agreements 2005*, Law Reform Committee Report, 1–26 (2013). Research Collection School of Law, https://ink.library.smu.edu.sg/sol.

[58] Which was concluded on 2 July 2019, '[d]esiring to promote effective access to justice for all and to facilitate rule-based multilateral trade and investment, and mobility, through judicial co-operation'.

[59] Sundaresh Menon, 'The Transnational Protection of Private Rights: Issues, Challenges, and Possible Solutions' (2015) 5(2) Asian Journal of International Law, 219 (2015), pp. [17]–[44] at p. [37].

[60] Reed, 'Retreat or Advance?' (2017). It is small wonder, then, that in a survey of practitioners conducted by the American Bar Association before the Hague Convention was adopted, an overwhelming 98 per cent of respondents indicated that such a convention

In the shorter term, greater alignment between ICommCs is being pursued through softer channels: bilateral protocols, bi- and multilateral memoranda and other multilateral initiatives being pursued under the auspices of the Standing International Forum of Commercial Courts (SIFoCC).[61]

If ICommCs can move the dial by having a real effect on the jurisprudential imperative, they might make an invaluable contribution to international commercial dispute resolution, which ICA – by its very nature – is unable to make. This might, then, address current criticisms of ICommCs. International commercial courts would be neither 'a careful marriage between litigation and arbitration'[62] nor 'little more than a national court in an arbitral tribunal's clothing'.[63] Rather, ICommCs would occupy a distinctive place in the spectrum of international dispute resolution.

With the emergence of ICommCs, judges also now have an international platform. International commercial courts have given judges who were troubled by the jurisprudential threat posed by ICA a new base from which to voice their concerns. Prominent amongst them have been Sundaresh Menon, Chief Justice of Singapore, and Lord Thomas, former Lord Chief Justice of England and Wales.

would be useful for their practice; further, more than 70 per cent also indicated that, if such a convention did come into existence, they would be 'more willing to designate litigation instead of arbitration' in their contracts. [Fn.: Louise Ellen Teitz, 'Both Sides of the Coin: A Decade of Parallel Proceedings and Enforcement of Foreign Judgments' (2004) 10(1) Roger Williams University Law Review 1, 63.

61 It is tempting to consider whether use of a model law is more attractive to *codiste*, 'top-down', civil law jurisdictions, and whether 'soft' alignment measures are more attractive to incremental, 'bottom-up', common law jurisdictions. For reasons of time and space, that temptation cannot be further explored here.

62 An expression first coined by Justice Steven Chong, 'Singapore International Commercial Court: A New Opening in a Forked Path', Speech (October 2015), www.supremecourt.gov.sg/Data/Editor/Documents/J%20Steven%20Chong%20Speeches/The%20SICC%20-%20A%20New%20Opening%20in%20a%20Forked%20Parth%20-%20London%20(21.10.15).pdf, at ¶[52]. Chong was speaking with specific regard to the SICC. However, his Singapore Supreme Court colleague Justice Kannan Ramesh applied the expression to ICommCs in general; see Judge Kannan Ramesh, 'International Commercial Courts: Unicorns on a Journey of a Thousand Miles', Conference on the Rise of International Commercial Courts, Qatar University, Doha (May 2018), www.sicc.gov.sg/docs/default-source/modules-document/news-and-article/international-commercial-courts-unicorns_23108490-e290-422f-9da8-1e0d1e59ace5.pdf.

63 See Demeter and Smith, 'Implications' (2016), 466: 'While the new international commercial courts perceive themselves as a hybrid, the current model of both the SICC and DIFC Courts is little more than a national court in an arbitral tribunal's clothing.'

This phenomenon of benign judicial activism in support of the jurisprudential imperative has been witnessed with increasing intensity recently. Judicial activism has been both 'hard' and 'soft': 'hard' in making the point that courts, in particular ICommCs, are better placed to develop commercial case law and jurisprudence than ICA tribunals; 'soft' through the inter-ICommC alignments described earlier in this chapter.

16.3.3.1 Jurisprudential Imperative: The Harder Edge of Judicial Activism

Lord Thomas developed and expounded his views on international commercial dispute resolution in a series of lectures delivered in 2016–17 in Dubai, London, Singapore, Cayman Islands and Beijing.[64]

In his Dubai lecture, he voiced concern that the development of commercial law may be 'retarded by a reduction in authoritative court judgments'. (He also planted the seeds of the initiative that was to germinate as the SIFoCC.) He expanded on his concern in the BAILII Lecture 2016, expressing the view that the widespread use of arbitration clauses had caused 'a serious impediment to the development of the common law by the courts in the UK, particularly through the Commercial Courts in London … and on appeal from them'.[65] Lord

[64] John (Lord) Thomas (i) Dubai – 'Commercial Justice in the Global Village: The Role of Commercial Courts', The DIFC Academy of Law Lecture (1 February 2016), www.judiciary.uk/wp-content/uploads/2016/02/LCJ-commerical-justice-in-the-global-village-DIFC-Academy-of-Law-Lecture-February-2016.pdf, [abbreviated elsewhere herein as Thomas (Dubai)]; (ii) London – 'Developing Commercial Law through the Courts: Rebalancing the Relationship between the Courts and Arbitration', The BAILII Lecture (9 March 2016), www.BAILII.org/BAILII/lecture/04.pdf, [abbreviated elsewhere herein as Thomas (BAILII)]; (iii) Singapore – 'Cutting the Cloth to Fit the Dispute: Steps towards Better Procedures across the Jurisdictions', The Singapore Academy of Law Annual Lecture (September 2016), www.judiciary.uk/wp-content/uploads/2016/10/lcj-speech-singapore-academy-of-law.pdf, [abbreviated elsewhere herein as Thomas (Singapore)]; (iv) Cayman Islands – 'Giving Business What It Wants: A Well-Run Court for Commercial and Business Disputes', Grand Court of the Cayman Islands Guest Lecture (2 March 2017), www.judiciary.uk/wp-content/uploads/2017/03/grand-court-of-the-cayman-islands-guest-lecture-march-2017.pdf, [abbreviated elsewhere herein as Thomas (Cayman)]; (v) Beijing – 'Commercial Dispute Resolution: Courts and Arbitration', Speech at the National Judges College, Beijing (6 April 2017), www.judiciary.uk/wp-content/uploads/2017/04/lcj-speech-national-judges-college-beijing-april2017.pdf, [abbreviated elsewhere herein as Thomas (Beijing)].

[65] Thomas (BAILII), ¶[5]. In this, he seemed to be building on comments he had made in an earlier lecture, 'The Centrality of Justice: Its Contribution to Society and Its Delivery' (10 November 2015).

Thomas' concern was that arbitration ('the resolution of disputes firmly behind closed doors') precluded courts developing and explaining the law, and retarded public understanding of the law and debate over its application.[66]

Lord Thomas was not the first or only voice to express such concerns. Sundaresh Menon in his 2015 DIFC Lecture,[67] Sir Bernard Rix in a March 2015 lecture,[68] and the British Institute of International and Comparative Law 2015 study for the UK Ministry of Justice[69] made the same point. The BAILII Lecture, however, caused a legal brouhaha.

Lord Thomas' diagnosis was 'a wrong turning ... taken in 1979 and 1981'[70] when, respectively, legislative changes (to promote party autonomy in arbitrations, and limit the ability to appeal awards)[71] were introduced, and judicial involvement was substantially curtailed.[72] He regarded those reforms as having 'undermine[d] the means through which a significant part of [London's commercial law] strength – its "excellence" was developed ... to the detriment of the wider interests of the common law'.[73] He delivered a rallying call to 'restore an essential part of the way in which courts are able to continue the development of the law that underpins our trade, financial system and our prosperity'.[74]

In a pithy summary of points made earlier in his lecture, Lord Thomas concluded:[75] 'It is the courts that develop the law. Arbitration does not. Courts articulate and explain rights, including definitive rulings on the scope and interpretation of contractual clauses, financial instruments and so on. Arbitration does not. ... [O]pen court proceedings enable people

66 Thomas (BAILII), ¶[23].

67 Menon, International Commercial Courts, DIFC Lecture (2015).

68 Sir Bernard Rix, 'Confidentiality in International Arbitration: Virtue or Vice?', Jones Day Professorship in Commercial Law Lecture, SMU Singapore (12 March 2015), https://law.smu.edu.sg/sites/default/files/law/CEBCLA/Notes_Confidentiality_in_International_Arbitration.pdf.

69 Eva Lein, Robert McCorquodale, Lawrence McNamara, Hayk Kupelyants and José del Rio, British Institute of International and Comparative Law (for UK Ministry of Justice), 'Factors Influencing International Litigants' Decisions to Bring Commercial Claims to the London Based Courts', Ministry of Justice Analytics Series 2015, https://assets.publishing.service.gov.uk/government/uploads/system/uploads/attachment_data/file/396343/factors-influencing-international-litigants-with-commercial-claims.pdf.

70 Thomas (BAILII), ¶[6]

71 To which Lord Thomas returns at ibid., ¶¶[19]–[21].

72 Ibid., esp. at ¶¶[19]–[21].

73 Ibid., ¶[9].

74 Ibid., ¶[24]

75 See, in particular, ibid., at ¶¶[5], [6], [22], [23] and [45]

to watch, debate, develop, contest, and materialize the exercise of both public and private power. Arbitration does not.'

Those trenchant comments catch the eye, but do not fully reflect his more balanced earlier formulation nor his ultimate conclusion, repeating the words of Lord Parker CJ some fifty years previously that arbitration and litigation should be regarded as 'co-ordinate rather than rival'.[76] It might also not have helped that Lord Thomas saw the problem as stemming from the English Arbitration Acts and long-established case law of high authority, *The Nema* (both totemic in English arbitral lore) with statutory reform being his proposed cure.[77]

Thus it becomes important to differentiate between malady, diagnosis and treatment. The malady was that the development of commercial law was being held back. The diagnosis was that courts needed to play a prominent role and be an attractive forum for international commercial dispute resolution. The treatment was statutory reform of English arbitration law to enable more appeals to be brought from awards to court.

It was Lord Thomas' proposed treatment that drew fire.[78] Lord Saville regarded any proposal to expand the right of appeal in arbitration as a 'wholly retrograde step', and one 'calculated to drive international arbitration away from London'. Sir Bernard Eder made the point that party autonomy included the right to exclude or severely curtail any appeal and drew attention to empirical evidence from the London maritime arbitral community which showed no appetite for legislative change. Sir Peter Gross drew attention to a recent analysis by JUSTICE which had found that 'It is impossible to conclude that the decline in the number of claims issued before English courts is a consequence of the popularity of arbitration. ... This is an area that warrants further research and consideration.'[79]

[76] Ibid. at ¶[49].

[77] *Pioneer Shipping Ltd* v. *BTP Tioxide Ltd* (*The Nema*) (No. 2) [1982] A.C. 724.

[78] Notably from other retired members of the English senior judiciary, including Lord Saville of Newdigate (see Mark (Lord) Saville, 'Reforms Will Threaten London's Place As a World Arbitration Centre', *The Times* (28 April 2016), Sir Bernard Eder (see Sir Bernard Eder, 'Does Arbitration Stifle Development of the Law? Should s.69 Be Revitalised?', Chartered Institute of Arbitrators (London Branch), AGM Keynote Address (28 April 2016)) and Sir Peter Gross (see Sir Peter Gross, 'Courts and Arbitration', 2nd Jonathan Hirst QC Commercial Law Lecture (1 May 2018), www.judiciary.uk/wp-content/uploads/2018/05/speech-by-lj-gross-hirst-lecture-distribution-may-2018.pdf).

[79] See 'The Erosion of Commercial Common Law: The Relative Merits of Litigation and Arbitration', 8 January 2018, at [13], quoted in Gross (2018) at ¶[21(iv)].

Those criticisms may have hit home. In his later Beijing lecture,[80] Lord Thomas stressed the complementary relationship between ICA and commercial courts (ICommCs, in particular) and in a later lecture, he spoke of 'the key point [being] the balance between respect for party choice and the wider state and public interest in ensuring the law is developed and keeps pace with change'.[81] This ultimate exposition of his views is in essence a balance of the imperatives under discussion. '[R]espect for party choice' brings in the business imperative; the 'wider state and public interest' acknowledges the political imperative, with the tension between the two creating a jurisprudential imperative to be resolved by courts as satisfactorily as possible.

The speeches Lord Thomas delivered represent an important contribution to the current discussion of international dispute resolution. He is surely right to see the relationship between ICA and ICommCs as complementary and supportive. International commercial arbitration may be (quasi-)autonomous, but it is not a law unto itself.

16.3.3.2 Jurisprudential Imperative: The Softer Side of Judicial Activism

The jurisprudential imperative is also susceptible to softer judicial influence, exemplified by the founding of the Standing International Forum of Commercial Courts (SIFoCC). Building on his Singapore lecture in which he noted the need for procedural convergence in international commercial court procedures, Lord Thomas created the Forum in 2016 and convened its inaugural meeting in 2017. The establishment of SIFoCC should, however, be put in context.

The business imperative requires not just speed, confidentiality and cost-efficiency in the arbitral process. It also requires international recognition of awards and ease of enforcement. There is a small irony that the success of ICA depends on comity among courts around the world in giving effect to the New York Arbitration Convention and, thus, no surprise that commercial courts, led by ICommCs, have – independently from normative instruments such as the Hague Conventions – sought to make improvements in this regard.

[80] Thomas (Beijing), ¶[4]: 'Today ... I want ... to speak about how we ensure that Commercial Courts and arbitral centres work together to enhance expert, efficient and cost-effective dispute resolution and to keep the law up to date.'

[81] John (Lord) Thomas, 'Keeping Commercial Law Up to Date', The Jill Poole Memorial Lecture, Aston University (8 March 2017), www.judiciary.uk/wp-content/uploads/2017/05/lcj-aston-university-speech-8-march-2017.pdf.

At the instigation and with the active participation of ICommCs, commercial courts around the world have increasingly worked together over the past decade in constructive and innovative ways. Commercial courts have increasingly entered into bilateral memoranda – of guidance, of understanding and/or of agreement – on the recognition and enforcement of each other's judgments. (The DIFC Courts have been a trailblazer in that regard.)[82]

Although such steps are described as 'court' initiatives, the motivating factor is almost invariably the chief justice or presiding judge of the courts involved. It is, accordingly, perfectly permissible to regard such measures as the product of benign judicial activism.

The logical progression from bilateral accords is to a multilateral plane. It is that shift which the recent establishment of the SIFoCC has sought to facilitate. It should come as no surprise that the 'development of an effective, widely respected, recognition and enforcement mechanism for commercial disputes' has been an early work topic undertaken by the SIFoCC.

The first fruit of that work has now been seen in the Multilateral Memorandum on the Enforcement of Commercial Judgments for Money published in June 2019 (the 'Multilateral Memorandum on Enforcement'), and the topic remains under active consideration by the SIFoCC.[83] The Multilateral Memorandum on Enforcement formalises a clearly discernible trend towards cooperation and comity between commercial courts around the world.[84]

[82] See list of DIFC Memoranda of Understanding at www.difccourts.ae/courts-programmes/protocols-and-memorandums-of-understanding.

[83] On the issue of enforcement, it has been noted that: '[e]nforcement is among the subjects in which there is a common interest among commercial courts globally. It is relevant to the broad question of how the commercial courts of the world are to interrelate'; see 'Introduction', SIFoCC Multilateral Memorandum on Enforcement of Commercial Judgments for Money (June 2019), https://sifocc.org/app/uploads/2019/11/Multilateral-Memorandum-on-Enforcement-Nov-2019.pdf.

[84] See, for example, Mance, 'Arbitration' (Freshfields Lecture 2015): 'courts see themselves today as part of an international legal order [and] should respect each other's decisions in the fullest sense . . . so far as possible avoid[ing] duplication, repetition and inconsistency in decision-making' at p. [22]; also, ibid., 'one would expect any enforcement court, in today's world, to pay attention to the reasoning and decision of any other court, particularly the court of the seat on an issue coming before it' at p. [21], citing in support the judgment of Colman J in *Minmetals Germany GMBH* v. *Ferco Steel Limited* and judgments to like effect from Singapore, Hong Kong and Australia. See, for example, *TCL Air Conditioner (Zhongshan) Co Ltd* v. *Castel Electronics Pty Ltd* [2013] HCA 5, 87 ALJR 410; 295 ALR 596 (13 March 2013), in which the High Court of Australia spoke of 'international harmony and concordance of approach'.

Specifically on the relationship between ICommCs and ICA, the SIFoCC has recognised 'the importance of dialogue between commercial courts and arbitral bodies built on mutual respect and the complementary nature of their respective roles' – that is, a symbiotic relationship. As Sir William Blair and Sir Robin Knowles, two leading lights in the SIFoCC, have put it:

> In short, whenever a mandatory intervention [in ICA] is required, recourse will be made to courts. As many arbitrators gladly acknowledge, experienced commercial courts help make arbitration work.[85]

The remit of the SIFoCC is, however, more ambitious. In Beijing, Lord Thomas spoke of building and developing a 'a more systematic and common approach to the provision of dispute resolution, to keep commercial dispute resolution up to date and to see that the law and legal framework is developed in a way that supports international trade, international commerce and the international financial markets'.[86]

It is notable that Lord Thomas referred to 'dispute resolution' generically, not to courts and litigation specifically. The need for a 'more systematic and common approach' might be more directed to courts than arbitration, given the commonality that the New York Convention and the UNCITRAL Model Law has provided to ICA. Keeping 'up to date' and seeing that 'the law and legal framework' is developed in a supportive way is clearly a nod to the role of commercial courts in establishing case law and the need for best practice to be shared by ICommCs and other commercial courts.

But the vision goes yet further. In his Dubai lecture (and subsequently), Lord Thomas has argued that ICommCs and commercial courts have more than a purely legal role. They also contribute significantly to societal values – by promoting the rule of law – and societal functioning – by underpinning global economic development.

In those regards, ICommCs are relevant and influential in a broader, values-based context into which ICA does not seek to venture. The cooperation between commercial courts around the world, including ICommCs, is multifaceted. It is, at the same time, collaborative (sharing experiences and best practices), practical (looking at enforcement, case management, court use of technology and the relationship between commercial courts, arbitration and mediation) and developmental

[85] See Report of First SIFoCC Meeting, www.sifocc.org/app/uploads/2019/02/First-SIFOCC-Report-FINAL.pdf, p. 4.

[86] Thomas (Beijing), ¶[33].

(mentoring commercial courts in developing countries, supporting UN Resolution 70/1 on sustainable development, and encouraging good practices for effective commercial dispute resolution).

The broad importance of ICommCs and commercial courts in combination was well articulated by the Deputy General Counsel of the World Bank, Irina Kichigina, at the second SIFoCC meeting, who spoke of the importance of commercial dispute resolution as a channel for the rule of law and sustainable investment as follows:

> The primacy of the rule of law is a key aspect of an enabling environment that attracts sustained investment from the private sector. The courts, and their role in resolving commercial disputes, are integral. If a country doesn't have functioning and efficient commercial dispute resolution mechanisms, how can it protect property rights or ensure the proper enforcement of contractual obligations between commercial parties?
>
> The better protected property and contractual rights are from government or third parties, the stronger the link between effort and reward, and thus the greater the incentives to open new businesses, to invest more in existing ones, and simply to work harder. In the big picture, a functioning judiciary helps encourage investor confidence and promote public trust.[87]

Those paragraphs speak eloquently to the current need to synthesise the business, political and judicial imperatives discussed at the beginning of this chapter.

16.3.4 The Tensions and Interactions between the Imperatives

The imperatives act both in tension and in tandem, in opposition and in concert. The business imperative is market-chasing and internationally minded. At least in its Westphalian incarnation, the political imperative was self-centred, bounded by state borders. A tension developed between the more adventurous business spirit and more protectionist statecraft, creating a 'turbulence [of] global cross-currents'.[88] More recently, the political imperative has changed to embrace a more international approach encouraging economic diversification and foreign direct investment. The tension between the business and the political imperatives has ebbed in consequence. The business imperative of commercial certainty, favouring privacy/confidentiality and the absence of appeal, is

[87] Report of the Second SIFoCC Meeting, www.sifocc.org/app/uploads/2019/02/Report-of-the-Second-SIFoCC-Meeting-New-York-2018.pdf, pp. 22–4 at 22.

[88] A phrase coined by Chief Justice Sundaresh Menon in Menon, 'International Commercial Courts', DIFC Lecture (2015), [6].

also in tension with the jurisprudential imperative of legal certainty, favouring transparency and accessibility.

A paradox lurks at the heart of this tension in that, through continued market dominance, ICA may fall victim to its own success. A necessary element of certainty is predictability, and predictability thrives on transparency. The cloak of privacy surrounding arbitration, rendering parties oblivious to the existence and outcome of an earlier arbitration, may prevent a useful legal analysis from being accessible or an innovative legal development being known with the result that two materially identical arbitral references duplicate time and cost in going over the same ground twice or, worse, result in different, mutually incompatible and irreconcilable awards.

It was this paradox to which Lord Thomas and other jurists have sought to draw attention. It is, moreover, a paradox which ICA is largely incapable of resolving itself. Public justice depends, essentially, on an open court process and the availability of published judgments.

Other aspects of the business imperative, notably seeking quick and cost-effective dispute resolution, are also under threat. In this regard, the irony is that the threat comes largely from within. Party autonomy has not enabled parties to control the arbitral process sufficiently to prevent sclerosis through widespread 'judicialisation'. (Indeed, the 'one-shot' nature of ICA may create a 'leave-no-stone-unturned' approach conducive to sclerosis developing.) At the same time as ICA has 'complexified', commercial courts – with ICommCs leading the charge – have simplified, borrowing more streamlined procedures and means of receiving evidence (e.g. on foreign law) from ICA, and adopting bilateral and multilateral measures to improve enforcement of foreign judgments.

Another factor that must be recognised is increased party mobility. If parties are faced by a stark choice between dispute resolution in a domestic court or through ICA, parties will choose ICA if they harbour doubts about the competence or independence of the court option. The more readily parties can move away from domestic courts and resolve their disputes in international courts, the reassurance of neutrality (otherwise only achievable through party choice of ICA) can be replicated by party choice of courts of impeccable good standing, including an increasing number of ICommCs.

The traditional virtues of ICA – speed, cost, procedural alignment to business needs, convenience, independence, and ease of recognition and enforcement of awards globally – are now for a variety of reasons under threat from judicialisation, innovative court procedural reforms, objective recognition of court probity and reputation and inter-court cooperation, both informal and formal. In manifold ways, ICA is suffering an erosion of advantage and the reasons for choosing ICA are becoming less clear-cut.

16.4 Conclusion: The Relationship between International Commercial Courts and Domestic Commercial Courts, and International Commercial Courts and International Commercial Arbitration

The relationship between ICommCs and other international dispute resolution mechanisms (notably domestic commercial courts and ICA) has variously been described as 'competitive', 'collaborative', 'interdependent' or 'hybrid'. On analysis, the relationship is not so susceptible to easy labelling and must include a further element, which I term 'flexible convergence'.

As between ICommCs and domestic commercial courts, commentators have found the distinguishing features of ICommCs elusive to identify and define. It is difficult to point to something that only an ICommC, not a domestic commercial court, can do. It is tempting to see ICommCs as needing to act assertively and be jurisdictionally acquisitive to carve out a market niche and survive. On that view, domestic commercial courts would need to beware ICommCs' sharp elbows.

But that would misconstrue the true purpose of ICommCs. International commercial courts are not novel. They are courts just like domestic commercial courts. They are located – obviously – at the litigation end of the dispute resolution spectrum. What ICommCs possess, however, is the capacity to innovate.

The shift in the political imperative to focus on economic diversification has brought a need for regulatory laws which are fit for purpose across a wide range of legal fields. The regulation of financial services is the prime example, but far from alone. Competition policy, procurement, state aid and fiscal regimes – all must be fair. Those branches of law (and many others) are regulated by laws that reflect and embody international best practice. Although national commercial courts are competent to rule on such issues (and do so), *international* commercial courts – ICommCs – may increasingly have a normative role in upholding *international* best practice.[89] If

[89] For a further discussion of the normative effect ICommCs might exert, see Matija Durovic and Franciszek Lech, 'Harmonization of Commercial Law Based on Common Law' (Chapter 8), in this volume.

such norms are maintained, interpreted and developed by supranational courts, it may be easier for domestic courts to follow and adhere to such standards.

When she coined the expression 'domestic international commercial courts', Professor Reed described them as 'a hybrid species and, necessarily a rare species'.[90] Reed's striking juxtaposition of adjectives has been explained by later commentators as '*domestic* in the sense that they are part of a country's judiciary; *international* in the sense that English is their default language, their bench is usually compounded from different countries, and the law they apply is typically foreign, often a variant of Anglo-American law'.[91] International commercial courts may, on that basis, be able to carve out their own niche vis-à-vis domestic commercial courts, but their relationship with ICA must be different.

It is noticeable that the areas of law in which international best practice should prevail are often areas of law in which the focus is 'state (as embodied in the regulator) vs. business' – that is, areas of law in which arbitral resolution of disputes is seldom found and, if it is, it is subject to investor-state arbitration, not ICA. There can be no 'read-across' from the relationship between ICommCs and domestic commercial courts to the relationship between ICommCs and ICA.

What is clear is that the relationship between ICommCs and ICA is dynamic, not static. It is a relationship driven by several strong imperatives – business, political and jurisprudential. In some ways, those imperatives pull in different directions; in others, they are confluent.

As the complexities of international commerce have intensified, a corresponding need for sophisticated dispute resolution processes has arisen: 'international businesses expect and deserve a wide choice of first-class dispute resolution mechanisms'.[92] This statement points to a fundamental truth: the business imperative is paramount and determinative. Equally, it begs several questions. (1) Is there a need to expand the choice of international dispute resolution mechanisms for commercial parties by the addition of ICommCs? (2) Even if ICommCs are not strictly necessary, do ICommCs provide a desirable option for commercial parties? And, if the answer to (1) or (2) is 'yes', (3) are ICommCs confined only to inhabit the litigation end of the spectrum of international dispute resolution mechanisms?

[90] Reed, 'Retreat or Advance?' (2017), p. 137.

[91] See Schultz and Bachmann, 'A Wig for Arbitrators' (2019).

[92] Reed, 'Retreat or Advance?' (2017).

As for the first question, a 'need' would only arise if there were a gap in the market to be plugged. International commercial arbitration has, over a century and more, established itself as a distinct and distinguished means of international dispute resolution. As necessary, ICA has turned to domestic commercial courts for support. The arrangement has worked well and will continue to do so. In the absence of any discernible gap, it is difficult to give a resounding 'yes' to the first question.

If there is no gap as such, the second question considers whether the market would function better with ICommCs. Here, the picture is much more encouraging. A broader choice of international commercial dispute resolution mechanisms will not harm and, if used effectively, will support the business imperative. There are likely to be two impediments to widespread business use of ICommCs. First, some cases (e.g. those involving confidential business information) will always be better suited to the privacy of ICA than the glare of public dispute resolution in court. Secondly, there will be some 'we've-always-arbitrated' inertia and reluctance. Neither impediment is insuperable. There is a flipside to the first impediment. In some circumstances (e.g. disputes over the meaning of a commonly used standard term), the market would benefit from public availability of a published judgment and resultant sectoral clarity. The second impediment will wilt and wither if the market – that is, the parties to a commercial dispute – see advantage to court determination as compared with ICA.

Beyond preference according to circumstance, both ICommCs and ICA are demonstrating a flexibility in approach, an open-mindedness to adaptation and a readiness to 'borrow' and therefore, in practice, to converge. For example, ICommCs have adopted streamlined procedures from ICA, and ICA is looking at anonymised publishing of awards.

Just as it was difficult to make a case for answering 'yes' to the first question, it is difficult to reach any answer other than 'yes' to the second.

As for the third question, the starting point is to identify the spectrum of international dispute resolution mechanisms. Not only are there various means of dispute resolution – in court, by arbitration, through mediation or other forms of ADR – there are also options within those means (domestic or international commercial courts; institutional or ad hoc arbitration; facilitative or evaluative mediation; neutral evaluation/determination etc.). Those means and options are largely separate and distinct but may, in limited instances, be combined – for example, through a 'stepped' dispute resolution clause. In reality, the spectrum comprises a delicate balance of independence, complementarity and interdependence between means and options, with party choice being paramount.

This interweaving range of dispute resolution alternatives resembles a 'market' or an 'ecosystem'.[93] The former emphasises the discrete nature of the means available; the latter, the complementarity of those means. A market is competitive and thrives on party choice. An ecosystem is collaborative and enables party choice to be fine-tuned. Several venues around the world – including all those where ICommCs have been established – now promote themselves as dispute resolution 'hubs', providing ready access and availability to what best meets market demand.[94]

The competitive nature of the market enables the varying needs of business – the business imperative – to be met. There is no one-size-fits-all means of dispute resolution. Some disputes will be more suited to resolution by arbitration; others in court. International commercial arbitration and ICommCs will constantly adapt and evolve, better to meet such needs. Borrowings and adoptions by ICommCs from ICA and vice versa should be seen as a normal and natural incident of systemic development. The ebb and flow between systems of ideas, concepts and initiatives improves both systems. Such systemic dynamism is the badge of a vibrant market in dispute resolution services.

Beyond the fluid interdependence of suitability and assimilation of good practices, there is a further, more hard-edged interdependence between ICommCs and ICA. Arbitration depends on court support to provide efficiency throughout the process and courts depend on arbitration to shoulder a significant volume of commercial dispute resolution which, in turn, contributes to the administrative and procedural efficiency of court systems.

That leaves the question of hybridity. While ICommCs may be a 'hybrid species', it would be wrong, in my opinion, to characterise any approximation between ICommCs and ICA as tending towards hybridity.[95] There are too many bright-line differences between ICommCs and ICA to lump them together under one compendious umbrella of 'hybrid dispute resolution fora'. Nor do ICommCs inhabit some newly discovered 'arb-lit' segment. The evolution of and

[93] Blair, 'The New Litigation Landscape' (2019) at pp. 220, 224; Kramer and Sorabji, *International Business Courts* (2019), esp. chapters 10, 14.

[94] See Kramer and Sorabji, *International Business Courts* (2019), esp. chapters 1, 5, 8–12.

[95] See also Georgios Dimitropoulos, 'The Design of International Commercial Courts' (Chapter 10), in this volume.

interrelationship between, ICommCs and ICA is best characterised as 'flexible convergence'.

Hybridity (if hybridity there be) must lie elsewhere. At a stretch, it may be possible to argue that ICommCs are hybrid in two particular ways: to dispense international justice from within a municipal court system is hybrid, and to depend on party consent (a characteristic shared with ICA) to do so is also hybrid. Those features might demonstrate some 'micro-hybridity' within the commercial court system rather than the 'macro-hybridity' of a new genre of 'hybrid dispute resolution fora'. At that macro level, there is a new-found dynamism, which tends towards flexible convergence through vigorous discussion, debate and even activism, but not hybridity.

There will be no blood-on-the-walls fight to the death between ICommCs and ICA. International commercial courts will take their place in the firmament of international dispute resolution. They will do so both in competition and in collaboration with ICA and other dispute resolution mechanisms. As a 'rare species', it may be that not all ICommCs will thrive but the determining factor for success will not be found in an internecine fight but on the sophisticated (consumer) choice of transnational business.

In a globalised world of international trade, commerce and finance and a market driven by user choice, there is almost certainly a role for a few strategically placed ICommCs. International commercial courts will coexist alongside ICA and domestic commercial courts, without supplanting either. International commercial arbitration, ICommCs and other forms of dispute resolution will therefore coexist and be mutually dependent. Interdependence is the hallmark of an ecosystem and coexistence tends strongly to the development of specialised foci or hubs where the component parts of the ecosystem can come together. As it has been graphically put, 'there is room for co-existence and even partnership between international commercial courts and arbitration, as both are fishing in the same pond while enlarging the pie'.[96]

[96] Winnie Jo-Me Ma, 'Competitive, Collaborative or Cooperative Relations between Litigation, Arbitration and Mediation?' Speech, Taipei International Conference (Kluwer Arbitration Blog, 23 October 2018), cited in Schultz and Bachmann, 'A Wig for Arbitrators', p. 5.

17

Procedure before International Commercial Courts and Ordinary Courts

A Comparative Perspective

GEORGIA ANTONOPOULOU*

17.1 Introduction

International commercial courts are currently mushrooming across the globe.[1] Despite their divergent features, their different stages of evolution and the distinct legal orders in which they are established, international commercial courts have in common the claim to be different from the ordinary courts. However, the literature to date has centred its attention mainly on the surge of international commercial courts as a product of a civil justice systems competition, and has focused on specific international commercial courts and their innovative features.[2] The aim of this chapter is to explain the differences in procedure between international commercial courts and ordinary courts, and to explore the relationship between them. The chapter also examines the added value of international commercial

* This research has received funding from the European Research Council-ERC Consolidator grant agreement no. 726032 ('Building EU Civil Justice: Challenges of Procedural Innovations Bridging Access to Justice', www.euciviljustice.eu). I am particularly grateful to Prof. Xandra Kramer, Priskila P. Penasthika, Dr Jos Hoevenaars, Dr Erlis Themeli and Yihua Chen for their help and comments.

[1] For an overview, see Marta Requejo Isidro, 'International Commercial Courts in the Litigation Market' (2019) 9 International Journal of Procedural Law 4; John Sorabji and Xandra Kramer, 'Introduction: The International Business of Courts', in Xandra Kramer and John Sorabji (eds.), *International Business Courts* (Eleven International 2019); and in this book, see the introduction by the editors.

[2] Xandra Kramer and John Sorabji, 'International Business Courts in Europe and Beyond: A Global Competition for Justice?' (2019) 12 Erasmus Law Review 1; in this book, Geert van Calster, 'Brexit and the Competition of Dispute Resolution Fora in Europe' (Chapter 21). For an analysis of specific courts, see the literature in the footnotes that follow.

courts as 'extraordinary' courts by delving into their distinctive features and, where relevant, drawing on a variety of these courts.

Among the distinctive procedural features of international commercial courts, three stand out across jurisdictions. First, unlike ordinary courts, international commercial courts deal exclusively with international, cross-border disputes. Second, international commercial courts are optional fora, and therefore their jurisdiction is mostly founded on choice of court agreements. Third, some international commercial courts strongly resemble arbitration through having adopted arbitration features that heavily distinguish them from ordinary courts. This chapter unpacks these three distinct procedural features of international commercial courts and uses them as the touchstones for further analysis. It focuses on the Singapore International Commercial Court (SICC), the China International Commercial Courts (CICC), the Dubai International Financial Centre (DIFC) Courts, the proposal for the establishment of the Brussels International Business Court (BIBC), the Netherlands Commercial Court (NCC) and the Frankfurt Chamber for International Commercial Disputes as being most interesting for the present purposes, considering their features or level of advancement.

The remainder of this chapter is structured as follows. Section 17.2 explores the requirement of an international dispute across the SICC, the BIBC proposal, the NCC, and the DIFC Courts. Except for pondering the pertinent legal framework, it aims to divert our attention from ongoing discussions on a competition between states and their civil justice systems towards an issue that so far has attracted less attention – namely, the rise of a domestic competition between international and ordinary courts. The internationality of the dispute and how it may fuel such a competition takes centre stage. Section 17.3 turns to the voluntary jurisdiction of international commercial courts and lays down the provisions pertaining to choice of court agreements in favour of the SICC, the CICC, the Frankfurt Chamber and the NCC. It illustrates that in order to attract disputes, international commercial courts had to ease the establishment of their jurisdiction and loosen their jurisdictional requirements. Lastly, Section 17.4 focuses on the arbitration features of international commercial courts. It illustrates how several international commercial courts attempt to beat the allegedly 'unbeatable' virtues of arbitration and, in particular, the confidentiality and privacy of its proceedings, the flexibility of its rules and the nearly worldwide enforceability of its judgments. The chapter concludes that the internationality of the disputes they handle, and the voluntary establishment of their jurisdiction, not only procedurally distinguish international commercial courts from ordinary courts but also legitimise such a distinction and, in some instances, their detachment from national legal rules and judicial structures. However, the chapter remarks in conclusion that the arbitration features of international commercial courts raise procedural concerns and call into question their attractiveness as a dispute resolution option.

17.2 The Internationality Requirement

By and large, the jurisdiction of international commercial courts depends on the international character of the dispute. Therefore, the internationality of the dispute sets the jurisdictional scope of these courts and draws the line between these and ordinary courts.

Starting with the SICC, the BIBC proposal, and the NCC, this section singles out internationality criteria unique to these courts. Their uniqueness lies in that they are broadly conceived. While such 'exorbitant' internationality criteria bear the power of vesting the emerging courts with a greater number of disputes, it is argued that they overly stretch the definition of an international dispute and may therefore trigger domestic forum shopping. This section subsequently turns to the DIFC Courts. It narrates their jurisdictional development from courts dealing exclusively with DIFC disputes to courts dealing with international disputes lacking a territorial connection to the zone. It is illustrated that although opening up the DIFC Courts to international disputes rightfully lent them the title of international commercial court, it nevertheless sparked a jurisdictional tension between these and the domestic courts.

17.2.1 'Exorbitant' Internationality Criteria: The Singapore International Commercial Court, the Brussels International Business Court, and the Netherlands Commercial Court

The first distinctive features of international commercial courts – the internationality of the dispute – is in practice very broad as well as divergent in its actual definition. The SICC was created in 2015 with the aim of handling international commercial disputes and reinforcing Singapore's status as a popular dispute resolution hub in Asia.[3] Unlike ordinary courts, the SICC deals exclusively with international disputes.[4]

3 Singapore International Commercial Court, Official Website, available at www.sicc.gov.sg/about-the-sicc, accessed April 2021.

4 Supreme Court of Judicature Act, Section 18D (1) (a); Rules of Court, Order 110, rule 1 (2) (a) (hereinafter: Rules of Court).

According to the Rules of Court, a claim is international if, first, the parties had their place of business in different States, or if none of the parties had their place of business in Singapore. Second, a claim is international if the place of performance of a substantial part of the obligations of the parties' commercial relationship or the place with which the subject matter of the dispute is most closely connected is situated outside any State in which at least one of the parties had their place of business. Finally, the last criterion provides that a case is international if the parties to the claim have expressly agreed that the subject matter of the claim relates to more than one State.[5]

The last criterion is the SICC's most noticeable internationality criterion. It allows the parties to turn an otherwise domestic dispute into an international one by their mere agreement, and results in placing their dispute within the court's jurisdictional ambit. By contrast, parties are not allowed to agree on the domestic character of an international dispute and therefore withdraw it from the court's jurisdiction.[6]

The parties' agreement on the international character of the dispute signals a party-friendly court that holds party autonomy and procedural flexibility in high regard. It also expands the pool of disputes eligible to be heard by the SICC.[7] However, this internationality criterion is not exempt from procedural implications. Standing in stark contrast to the definition of an international dispute under the Hague Convention on Choice of Court Agreements,[8] the agreement of the parties as an internationality criterion questions the enforceability of exclusive choice-of-court agreements in favour of the SICC when the dispute's international character rests solely on the will of the parties.[9]

[5] Rules of Court n. (4), Order 110, rule 1 (2) (a).

[6] Yeo Tiong Min, 'Staying Relevant: Exercise of Jurisdiction in the Age of the SICC' (Yong Pung How Professorship of Law Lecture, 2015) para. 14.

[7] Man Yip, 'The Resolution of Disputes before the Singapore International Commercial Court' (2016) 65 International and Comparative Law Quarterly 439, 450.

[8] Art. 1 (2) Hague Conference on Private International Law, Convention of 30 June 2005 on Choice of Court Agreements (hereinafter: Hague Convention).

[9] Man Yip, 'Navigating Singapore's Private International Law Rules in the Age of Innovative Cross-Border Commercial Litigation Framework', in Poomintr Sooksripaisarnkit and Sai Ramani Garimella (eds.), *China's One Belt One Road Initiative and Private International Law* (Routledge 2018), 55, 66; Adeline Chong and Man Yip, 'Singapore As a Centre for International Commercial Litigation: Party Autonomy to the Fore' (2019) 15 Journal of Private International Law 97, 121.

In 2017, the Belgian Minister of Justice announced the intention to establish a court specialised in international commercial disputes and thereby reinforce Belgium's position as the de facto capital of Europe.[10] Lacking the necessary political support and having attracted the negative attention of the Belgian judiciary, the proposal to establish the BIBC was finally shelved in March 2019.[11] Nevertheless, the bill proposed the creation of a court with many innovative features, and its failure illuminates the negative turn the establishment of an international commercial court may take.

Just like the SICC, the BIBC initial legislative proposal provided that the parties may agree on the international character of a dispute and thereby extend the court's jurisdictional reach. Unlike the SICC, the parties' agreement on the international character of the dispute was greeted with scepticism in Belgium.

Driven by the concern that the use of English for some disputes as opposed to others may constitute discrimination according to the Belgian constitution, the Belgian Council of State suggested that the justification for use of the English language should find its expression in the jurisdiction of the BIBC. In the opinion of the Council of State, only disputes that by their nature and according to objective factors are international should come before the BIBC.[12] In response, the final proposal for the establishment of the BIBC adopted a series of objective criteria that qualify a case as international.[13] The parties' agreement on the international character of a dispute was abandoned as a subjective factor unrelated to the dispute. Moreover, such an internationality criterion would open the door to forum shopping between the BIBC and the ordinary courts, allowing

[10] Legislative proposal establishing the Brussels International Business Court (*Wetsontwerp houdende oprichting van het Brussels International Business Court/Project de loi instaurant la Brussels International Business Court*), Parliamentary Documents (*Parl. St./Doc. parl.*): Belgian House of Representatives (*Belgische Kamer van Volksvertegenwoordigers/ Chambre de représentants de Belgique*) 54, 3072/001, Explanatory Statement (*Memorie van Toelichting/Expose de motifs*), 5 (hereinafter: BIBC Legislative Proposal).

[11] Matthias Verbergt, 'Controversiëlle "kaviarrechtbank" van Geens wordt begraven', *De Standaard*, 21 March 2019, available at www.standaard.be/cnt/dmf20190321_04272272, accessed April 2021.

[12] Council of State (Conseil d' État), Legislation section (*section de legislation*), Opinion 62.411 / 2 / AG of 2 March 2018 on a Preliminary Draft Law Establishing the Brussels International Business Court (*Avis 62.411/2/AG du 2 mars 2018 sur un avant-projet de loi instaurant la Brussels International Business Court*), B. The Justification for the Creation of the BIBC (*B. La justification de la création de la BIBC*), paras. 17–27.

[13] BIBC Legislative Proposal n. (10) Art. 20.

parties to circumvent the jurisdiction of the latter by agreeing that the dispute had an international, cross-border character.[14]

The SICC and the BIBC are examples of two courts with opposing understandings of the internationality requirement. While in Singapore the parties' agreement on the international character of the dispute was celebrated as one more step towards party autonomy, in Belgium it was criticised as pushing the boundaries of party autonomy, and it was consequently deleted from the final version of the proposal.

In line with the BIBC, the NCC's definition of internationality lies in objective, dispute-related criteria, and the agreement of the parties does not suffice to turn a domestic dispute into an international one. However, there is an NCC internationality criterion that stands out and questions the alleged immunity of the NCC criteria to the parties' will.

The requirement relating to a dispute with cross-border elements was not always there. When the Dutch Council for the Judiciary first heralded the NCC, it envisioned a court competent for both domestic and international commercial disputes.[15] However, the judiciary's initial plan stumbled upon negative reactions. Fearing that expanding the court's jurisdiction over domestic disputes would gradually decrease the number of commercial disputes litigated before ordinary courts,[16] the legislative proposal for the establishment of the NCC inserted the internationality criterion as one of the court's main jurisdictional requirements.[17]

The Explanatory Notes to the NCC Rules list a series of indicative, alternative criteria that lend to the dispute the required internationality.[18] Internationality criteria such as the application of foreign law, the

[14] Advice of the Council of State nr. 64.312/2/AV of 15 October 2018 (*Avis du Conseil d' état nr. 64.312/2/AG du 15 Octobre 2018*), Parliamentary Documents (*Doc. parl.*): House of Representatives of Belgium (*Chambre de représentants de Belgique*) 54, 3072/003, 3–4.

[15] Council for the Judiciary (*Raad voor de Rechtspraak*), Plan for the Establishment of the Netherlands Commercial Court (*Plan tot oprichting van de Netherlands Commercial Court*), November 2015, 5, 10(hereinafter: Dutch Council for the Judiciary, NCC Plan 2015).

[16] Parliamentary Papers II 2016/2017 (*Kamerstukken II*), 34 761, no. 3, Explanatory Statement (*Memorie van Toelichting*) 11–12 (hereinafter: NCC Explanatory Statement).

[17] Art. 30r (1) Dutch Code of Civil Procedure (*Wetboek van Burgerlijke Rechtsvordering*, hereinafter: Rv), available in English in Alex Burrough, Stephen Machon, Duco Oranje, Lincoln Frakes and Willem Visser (eds.), *Code of Civil Procedure, Selected Sections and the NCC Rules* (Eleven 2018); Art. 1.3.1. (b) Rules of Procedure for the International Commercial Chambers of the Amsterdam District Court (NCC District Court) and the Amsterdam Court of Appeal (NCC Court of Appeal), December 2020 (hereinafter: NCC Rules).

[18] NCC Rules n. (17), Annex I: Explanatory Notes Art. 1.3.1. (b).

company's turnover abroad and any cross-border interest reveal that these are broadly conceived.[19] However, a noteworthy internationality criterion is the use of English in the parties' contractual agreements. It is noteworthy because the language of the contract lacks a substantive connection to the dispute, and because it depends on the parties' will it could be susceptible to manipulation. Merely by drafting their agreement in a language other than Dutch, parties could 'create' an international dispute and thus circumvent the jurisdiction of the ordinary courts. Therefore, such a criterion runs counter to the rationale that underlay the adoption of the NCC's internationality requirement – namely, the establishment of a specialised court desirable in view of the international and therefore complex character of the dispute. It should be noted as well that the foreign language of the contract could be at odds with the definition of an international dispute under the Hague Convention and the Brussels I*bis* Regulation,[20] the key European instrument pertaining to choice-of-court agreements in cross-border civil and commercial disputes.[21]

Nevertheless, the language of the contract as an internationality criterion makes sense if we take into consideration that – contrary to similar initiatives in other continents – the use of English before European courts evolved against a backdrop of dissenting voices. In particular, it raised concerns regarding procedural discrimination;[22] it was feared to threaten the publicity of court hearings;[23] and it was lastly criticised as disadvantaging weaker parties such as small and medium-sized enterprises lacking the power to refuse a trial in a foreign language.[24] Seen from this angle, the use of English in the parties' contract justifies the use of a foreign

[19] Georgia Antonopoulou, 'Defining International Disputes: Reflections on the Netherlands Commercial Court Proposal' (2018) Nederlands Internationaal Privaatrecht 740, 755; Isidro n. (1) 28.

[20] Regulation (EU) No. 1215/2012 of the European Parliament and of the Council of 12 December 2012 on Jurisdiction and the Recognition and Enforcement of Judgments in Civil and Commercial Matters (recast), *OJ* 2012, L 351/1.

[21] Robert Magnus, 'Der grenzüberschreitende Bezug als Anwendungsvoraussetzung im europäischen Zuständigkeits- und Kollisionsrecht' (2018) Zeitschrift für Europäisches Privatrecht 507, 535; Antonopoulou n. (19) 753.

[22] For the BIBC, see earlier in this chapter at Section 2.1.

[23] German Parliament (*Deutscher Bundestag*), Legislative Proposal for the Establishment of Chambers for International Commercial Disputes (*Entwurf eines Gesetzes zur Einführung von Kammern für internationale Handelssachen*), Drucksache 19/1717 of 18 April 2018, Explanatory Statement (*Begründung*), 8–10.

[24] NCC Explanatory Statement n. (16) 10–11, 14. See also Duci Oranje, 'The Coming into Being of the Netherlands Commercial Court' (2016) Tijdschrift voor Civiele Rechtspleging 122, 124–5.

language before the NCC, and prevents weaker parties from being unwillingly caught up in English-language court proceedings they could not possibly foresee.

Although all international commercial courts deal with international disputes, it has so far been shown that different countries opt for divergent definitions of an international dispute and thereby create varying jurisdictions for their international commercial courts. The SICC allows parties to agree on the international character of the dispute, and is therefore a court that adheres to loose internationality criteria. Like the BIBC, the NCC aims to demarcate its jurisdiction strictly and to prevent domestic forum shopping by adopting internationality criteria immune to the parties' will. However, some NCC criteria are broadly conceived and therefore leave room for the parties to manipulate and – as a result – expand the court's jurisdiction.

17.2.2 Domestic Competition between International and Ordinary Courts: The DIFC Courts

The DIFC Courts and the gradual expansion of their jurisdiction serve as a prime example of how loose jurisdictional requirements may foster domestic competition between international and ordinary courts, and ultimately create jurisdictional tensions between them. The DIFC Courts were established in 2004 with the aim of offering foreign investors the reassurance of a trustworthy and efficient dispute resolution system.[25] This rationale driving the creation of the courts found its expression in their jurisdictional reach. Initially, the DIFC Courts had exclusive jurisdiction over all disputes occurring within the DIFC or related to companies registered in it.[26]

However, 2011 marked the beginning of a 'second era' for the DIFC Courts.[27] Dubai Law No. 16 expanded the jurisdiction of the Court of First Instance on any civil or commercial matter as long as the parties

[25] Jayanth Krishnan and Priya Purohit, 'A Common Law Court in an Uncommon Environment: The DIFC Judiciary and Global Commercial Dispute Resolution' (2014) 25 The American Review of International Arbitration 497, 499; Harold Koster and Mark Beer, 'The Dubai International Financial Centre (DIFC) Courts: A Specialised Commercial Court in the Middle East', in Eddy Bauw, Harold Koster and Sonja Kruisinga (eds.), *De Kansen voor een Netherlands Commercial Court* (Boom juridisch 2018), 195, 201.

[26] Art. 5 (A) Law No. 16 of 2011 Amending Certain Provisions of Law No. (12) of 2004 concerning Dubai International Financial Centre Courts.

[27] Jayanth Krishnan, *The Story of the Dubai International Financial Center Courts: A Retrospective* (DIFC Academy of Law 2018) 43, available at https://issuu.com/difc courts/docs/difc_courts_10_years, accessed 5 November 2019.

have expressly agreed on the court's jurisdiction.[28] This opt-in jurisdiction aligned the DIFC Courts with the rest of the international commercial courts, and internationalised these further by adding international disputes to their previously domestic caseload.[29]

However, the expansion of the DIFC Courts' jurisdictional grounds coupled with a pro-forum judicial interpretation[30] sparked tension between these and the Dubai Courts. This tension became especially evident in cases dealing with the recognition and enforcement of foreign judgments. According to Article 7 (2) of the Judicial Authority Law, the Dubai Courts shall enforce DIFC Courts judgments including foreign judgments recognised and enforced or arbitral awards ratified by these.[31] In *DNB Bank ASA*, the DIFC Courts asserted jurisdiction to recognise and enforce a foreign judgment, although the defendant had no assets within the DIFC and there was no other connection to the zone.[32] Parties may therefore resort to the DIFC Courts as a 'conduit' jurisdiction for the recognition and enforcement of foreign judgments and arbitral awards, and then seek execution in the Dubai Courts, thereby taking advantage of the reciprocal enforcement mechanisms provided by the Judicial Authority Law.[33] In June 2016, this jurisdictional overreach of the DIFC Courts, and the resulting tension between them and the ordinary courts, culminated in the establishment of the Judicial Tribunal. The Judicial Tribunal was created with the aim of resolving conflicts of jurisdiction between the DIFC and the Dubai Courts, and of drawing a clear jurisdictional line.[34]

[28] Art. 5 (A) (2) Law No. 16 of 2011.

[29] Michael Hwang, 'Commercial Courts and International Arbitration: Competitors or Partners?' (2015) 31 Arbitration International 193, 202; Sundaresh Menon, 'International Commercial Courts: Towards a Transnational System of Dispute Resolution' (Opening Lecture for the DIFC Courts Lecture Series 2015).

[30] See *National Bonds Corporation PJSC* v. (1) *Taaleem PJSC* and (2) *Deyaar Development PJSC* [2011] DIFC CA 001; *Corinth Pipeworks SA* v. *Barclays Bank Plc* [2011] DIFC CA 002; *Investment Group Private Ltd* v. *Standard Chartered Bank* [2015] DIFC CA 004; *Gavin* v. *Gaynor* [2015] DIFC CFI 017; *Tavira Securities Limited* v. (1) *Re Point Ventures Fzco* (2) *Jai Narain Gupta* (3) *Mayank Kumar* (4) *Saroj Gupta* [2017] CFI 026.

[31] Dubai Law No. 12/2004 in Respect of the Judicial Authority at Dubai International Financial Centre as amended.

[32] *DNB Bank ASA* v. *Gulf Eyadah Corporation & Gulf Navigation Holding PJSC* [2015] DIFC CA 007. For arbitral awards, see (1) *Egan* (2) *Eggert* v. (1) *Eava* (2) *Efa* [2013] DIFC ARB 002; *Meydan Group LLC* v. *Banyan Tree Corporate Pte Ltd* [2014] DIFC CA 005; *Oger Dubai LLC* v. *DAMAN Real Estate Capital Partners Limited* [2016] DIFC CFI 013.

[33] DIFC Courts, Enforcement Guide 2018 13, available at www.difccourts.ae/wp-content/uploads/2019/08/Enforcement_Guide_2019.pdf, accessed April 2021.

[34] Dubai Decree No. 19 of 2016 concerning the Establishment of a Judicial Tribunal for the Dubai Courts and DIFC Courts. See also Michael Black and Tom Montagu-Smith, 'A

The DIFC Courts' transition to this 'second', new era brought about novel controversies. As the DIFC Courts case illustrates, while a broad definition and lenient judicial interpretation of a court's jurisdictional requirements - such as the international character of the dispute - may seem justified in light of the need to increase the number of disputes before court, it could nevertheless create unintended tensions regarding the rest of the domestic courts. Although it might be unlikely that forum shopping and consequently domestic competition between the BIBC or the NCC and the ordinary courts would emerge, the considerations discussed previously have shown that the national legislatures were mindful of such a possibility when drafting the respective jurisdictional provisions.

17.3 Voluntary Jurisdiction

In contrast to the ordinary courts that are additionally vested with mandatory jurisdiction, international commercial courts mostly base their jurisdiction on choice of court agreements.[35] As a result, the voluntary establishment of their jurisdiction is their second distinctive procedural feature. This consensual jurisdiction further underlines the significance international commercial courts place on the parties' will and on party autonomy in general.

However, on the way to becoming the desired venues of choice in international commercial disputes, each court has had to fight its own demons. This section focuses first on the voluntary jurisdiction of the SICC and the CICC, and examines the means employed to enable the establishment of their jurisdiction. In particular, the SICC had to revise or relinquish the *forum non conveniens* doctrine so as to facilitate the establishment of its jurisdiction and comply with the Hague Convention. Similarly, the CICC is confronted with the rigid requirement of an 'actual connection' between the dispute and the chosen forum. What nevertheless unites these Asian courts is the possibility of a transfer of cases from the ordinary courts to the international commercial court, a mechanism that provided their first cases. Attention is then focused on the Frankfurt

Curb on the Jurisdiction of the DIFC Courts?', 4 August 2016, XXIV Barristers' Chambers, available at https://xxiv.co.uk/a-curb-on-the-jurisdiction-of-the-difc-courts, accessed April 2021.

[35] Exceptions are some of the 'SEZ Courts' such as the Qatar International Court and Dispute Resolution Centre that for the moment does not have opt-in jurisdiction; see Art. 8 (3) (c) Qatar Financial Centre Law No. (7) of 2005.

Chamber and the NCC in order to illustrate that, in contrast to other international commercial courts, the requirements relating to agreements in favour of these courts are stricter, and that a transfer against the parties' will is excluded. It is explained that the aim of these requirements is to protect procedurally weaker parties from the use of English before the court as well as the NCC's higher – when compared to the ordinary courts – court fees, and thereby reveals these courts' more social agenda.

17.3.1 The SICC and the Forum Non Conveniens *Doctrine*

The SICC has jurisdiction when each of the parties has submitted to the court's jurisdiction under a written agreement or where the case has been transferred from the High Court to the SICC.[36] What differentiates the SICC from the ordinary Singaporean courts is that in the presence of a written jurisdiction agreement no leave to serve on a foreign defendant is required, thereby making it easier for parties to commence proceedings at the court.[37]

Turning to the SICC's exercise of jurisdiction, the Rules of Court do not distinguish between an exclusive and a non-exclusive jurisdiction agreement.[38] In the event of an exclusive jurisdiction agreement the court may not decline to exercise its jurisdiction unless strong cause is shown.[39] By contrast, in the event of a non-exclusive jurisdiction agreement the SICC may apply the *forum non conveniens* doctrine as crystallised in the *Spiliada* ruling,[40] albeit more restrictively than the ordinary courts, and decline jurisdiction.[41] While determining whether Singapore is an appropriate forum in which to hold a trial, the SICC and its unique features are one of the factors considered.[42] For exclusive choice-of-court agreements falling under the Hague Convention, the strong cause or *Spiliada* test are irrelevant and the chosen court must decide the dispute unless the agreement is null and void according to its laws.[43]

[36] Rules of Court n. (4) Order 110, rules 7 (1) (b) and 12.
[37] Ibid., rule 6 (2) and (2A).
[38] Ibid., rule 8.
[39] *Amerco Timbers Pte Ltd* v. *Chatsworth Timber Corp Pte Ltd* [1977–8] SLR(R) 112.
[40] House of Lords *Spiliada Maritime Corp* v. *Cansulex Ltd* [1987] AC 460.
[41] Yeo n. (6) para. 32; Chong and Yip n. (9) 107–8.
[42] Singapore Court of Appeal *Rappo* v. *Accent Delight International Ltd* [2017] 2 SLR 265 [116].
[43] Section 11 Choice of Court Agreements Act 2016; Yip n. (9) 64.

The narrow grounds for declining jurisdiction give away the fact that the SICC places considerable weight on the parties' choice of court, and is generally disinclined to refuse jurisdiction. Against those who raise concerns of international comity, it is asserted that the SICC's unique features, the parties' voluntary submission and the formal requirements upon agreements in favour of the court - such as the written form - ensure the parties' will to litigate before the SICC and justify the court's positive stance towards its own jurisdiction.[44]

During its nascent years, however, the SICC was only seized in cases transferred from the Singapore High Court. In February 2018, three years after establishment of the SICC, the first case in which the parties directly chose the court finally knocked on its door.[45] Consequently, this referral mechanism fed the SICC with cases during its first years of functioning and allowed the newly established court to showcase its first judgments. For agreements concluded after 1 October 2016, the date on which the legislation implementing the Hague Convention entered into force in Singapore, a choice-of-court agreement in favour of the Singapore High Court is considered to include the SICC as well.[46] Such a provision dispenses with the requirement set by the Convention that every party must consent to a transfer.[47] In addition, such a provision implies that a choice-of-court agreement does not need to explicitly specify the SICC as the chosen court. For cases falling outside the scope of the Hague Convention, the High Court may still transfer them to the SICC of its own motion and despite the parties' opposing will.

The SICC has thus employed various procedural devices that facilitate the establishment of its jurisdiction. It has dispensed with the requirement of an express jurisdiction clause and accepts cases transferred by the ordinary courts. Lastly, the SICC gave up the *forum non conveniens* doctrine, and consequently secured the recognition and enforcement of choice of court agreements under the Hague Convention. For cases falling outside the scope of the Hague Convention, the *forum non conveniens* doctrine remains applicable. However, the SICC considers itself and its features, such as its international bench, one of the factors that

[44] Chong and Yip n. (9) 109.

[45] SICC News, 'A Landmark First Case Filed in the Singapore International Commercial Court', Issue no. 11/April 2018, available at www.sicc.gov.sg/docs/default-source/modules-document/media-resources/sicc-newsletter-issue-no-11_8239f5c5-8e7f-42bf-81b0-cb581c33a349.pdf, accessed April 2021.

[46] Rules of Court n. (4) Order 110, rule 1 (2) (ca).

[47] Hague Convention n. (8) 8 (5).

plead in favour of its jurisdiction. The involvement of foreign judges familiar with the application of foreign law is in particular considered a factor rendering the SICC a convenient forum for cases requiring the application of foreign law.[48]

17.3.2 The CICC and the 'Actual Connection' Requirement

In mid-2018, China established the First and Second China International Commercial Courts. Like other courts of its kind, the CICC deals with international commercial disputes and aims to promote the 'Belt and Road Initiative'.[49] According to Article 2 (1) of the Provisions of the Supreme People's Court on Several Issues regarding the Establishment of the International Commercial Court, the CICC accepts first-instance international commercial cases in which the parties have chosen, pursuant to Article 34 of the Civil Procedure Law (hereinafter: CPL), the Supreme People's Court, and the amount in dispute is at least RMB300 million.[50] As a consequence, Article 2 roots the court's jurisdiction in choice-of-court agreements, and brings it in line with the rest of the international commercial courts.[51] However, apart from the CICC's high financial threshold, the reference to Article 34 CPL implies that the court's consensual jurisdiction is not boundless.

Article 34 CPL stipulates that parties to a contractual dispute or any other property dispute may agree in writing to be subject to the jurisdiction of the people's court in the place that has a connection with the dispute; these include where the defendant is domiciled, where the contract is performed, where the contract is signed, where the plaintiff is domiciled, where the subject matter is located and so on. The condition, however, is that such an agreement does not violate the provisions regarding court-level and exclusive jurisdictions.[52] Article 34 CPL fleshes out the principle of 'actual connection', which requires parties to choose

48 n (42).

49 China International Commercial Court, Official website, available at http://cicc.court.gov.cn/html/1/219/193/195/index.html, accessed April 2021.

50 Provisions of the Supreme People's Court on Several Issues regarding the Establishment of the International Commercial Court.

51 David Holloway, 'The New Chinese International Commercial Court and the Future of Dispute Resolution in the Belt and Road Initiative' (2018) The Vindobona Journal of International Commercial Law and Arbitration 96, 110.

52 Art. 34 Civil Procedure Law of the People's Republic of China (Revised in 2017); and Art. 531 of the Supreme People's Court, 'Interpretation of the Supreme People's Court on the Application of the People's Republic of China Civil Procedure Law'.

a forum that has a substantial connection with the dispute.[53] Consequently, when it comes to the jurisdiction of the CICC, party autonomy does not suffice to establish its jurisdiction; as a territorial connection to the forum is also required.[54]

The principle of 'actual connection' has been criticised as unnecessarily restrictive as well as incompatible with international trade practices. It has therefore raised voices pleading for its abolition.[55] As regards the CICC, the requirement of an 'actual connection' restrains the court's reach. It could, in particular, prevent offshore disputes from reaching the CICC and hamper agreements in favour of this court as a neutral forum.[56] However, judicial practice has in essence dropped the requirement of an 'actual connection' when it comes to choice-of-court agreements in favour of a Chinese court.[57] The practice to uphold choice-of-court agreements in favour of a Chinese court despite the absence of an 'actual connection' is primarily owed to the tendency of Chinese courts to favour national jurisdiction in international disputes.[58] Furthermore, taking into consideration that China has signed – but

[53] Guangjian Tu, *Private International Law in China* (Springer 2016) 131; Bo Yuan, *Foreign-Related Commercial Dispute Resolution in China: A Focus on Litigation and Arbitration* (Erasmus University Rotterdam 2017) 46–9, available at https://repub.eur.nl/pub/101798, accessed April 2021; Yong Gan, 'Jurisdiction Agreements in Chinese Conflict of Laws: Searching for Ways to Implement the Hague Convention on Choice of Court Agreements in China' (2018) 14 Journal of Private International Law 295, 304.

[54] It is unclear how cases are divided between the First and Second International Commercial Courts. According to Yu Chen, 'The First Anniversary of China International Commercial Courts', *China Justice Observer*, 18 August 2019, available at www.chinajusticeobserver.com/a/review-the-first-anniversary-of-china-international-commercial-courts, accessed April 2021, cases are divided in accordance with the routes of the 'Belt and Road Initiative'. Cases involving the 'the Road' route are heard by the First International Commercial Court in Shenzhen, and cases involving 'the Belt' route are handled by the Second International Commercial Court in Xi'an.

[55] Zheng Sophia Tang, Yongping Xiao and Zhengxin Huo, *Conflict of Laws in the People's Republic of China* (Elgar 2016) 3.42–3.44.

[56] Zhengxin Huo and Man Yip, 'Comparing the International Commercial Courts of China with the Singapore International Commercial Court' (2019) 68 International and Comparative Law Quarterly 903, 922; Ning Zhao, 'The CICC: An Endeavour towards the Internationalization and Modernization of Chinese Courts', in Xandra Kramer and John Sorabji (eds.), *International Business Courts* (Eleven International 2019), 161, 177.

[57] Supreme People's Court, 'Answers to Questions Arising out of Trial Practice of Commercial and Maritime Cases with Foreign Elements' (*Shewai Shangshi Haishi Shenpan Shiwu Wenti Jieda*); Gan, n. (53), 304–6.

[58] Another example is the tendency to interpret jurisdiction clauses as non-exclusive, especially when a foreign court is chosen, and, reversely, to interpret non-exclusive jurisdiction clauses as exclusive when a Chinese court is chosen; see Zheng Sophia Tang, 'Effectiveness of Exclusive Jurisdiction Clauses in the Chinese Courts:

not yet ratified - the Hague Convention,[59] it will be its treaty obligation to respect choice-of-court agreements in favour of an unrelated court falling under the convention's scope unless it makes a declaration to the contrary.[60]

Lastly, it merits mention that disputes may be transferred to the CICC from the ordinary courts.[61] Just as in the case of Singapore, this referral mechanism has provided the newly established court with its first cases despite the absence of an agreement in its favour.[62]

Similar to the SICC, the CICC has to secure the recognition and enforcement of choice-of-court agreements, especially in light of the Hague Convention, by dropping national legal obstacles such as the 'actual connection' requirement. The transfer of cases from the ordinary courts to the CICC has proved to be a useful tool that channelled cases to the court and allowed it produce its jurisprudential footprint. The future ratification of the Hague Convention may, however, put an end to the transfer of cases to the CICC despite the parties' opposing will.[63]

17.3.3 The Frankfurt Chamber, the Netherlands Commercial Court and the Protection of Weaker Parties

Unlike their name suggests, European international commercial courts are not self-standing courts but chambers.[64] Being chambers within

A Pragmatic Study' (2012) 61 International and Comparative Law Quarterly 459; Tang et al. n. (55) 3.48.

59 For the treaty's current ratification status, see the official website of the Hague Conference on Private International Law, available at www.hcch.net/en/instruments/conventions/status-table/?cid=98, accessed April 2021.

60 Hague Convention n. (8) Art. 19.

61 Arts. 2 (2) and (5) Provisions of the Supreme People's Court on Several Issues regarding the Establishment of the International Commercial Court.

62 Matthew Errie, 'Update on the China International Commercial Court', *OpinioJuris*, 13 May 2019, available at http://opiniojuris.org/2019/05/13/update-on-the-china-international-commercial-court%EF%BB%BF; Yu Chen, 'CICC Case Tracking Series – 01: China's First International Commercial Court (As of 20190821)', *China Justice Observer*, 29 September 2019, available at www.chinajusticeobserver.com/a/cicc-case-tracking-series-01; Guodong Du and Yu Chen, 'CICC Case Tracking Series – 03: China's Second International Commercial Court (As of 20190821)', *China Justice Observer*, 27 October 2019, available at www.chinajusticeobserver.com/a/cicc-case-tracking-series-03, all accessed April 2021.

63 Hague Convention n. (8) Arts. 5 (3) and 8 (5).

64 Georgios Dimitropoulos, 'International Commercial Courts in the "Modern Law of Nature": Adjudicatory Unilateralism in Special Economic Zones' (2021) Journal of International Economic Law 1, 8.

courts, their international, territorial and subject-matter jurisdiction rests upon the international, territorial and subject-matter jurisdiction of the court of which they form a part. Thus, the jurisdiction of the Frankfurt Chamber for International Commercial Disputes depends on the jurisdiction of the Regional Court of Frankfurt am Main.[65] In a similar vein, the NCC is a chamber of the Amsterdam District Court, and therefore its jurisdiction presupposes the jurisdiction of the latter.[66]

However, agreements in favour of the court of which they form a part are not enough to establish the jurisdiction of the Frankfurt Chamber and the NCC. The parties' agreement to litigate before these chambers is also required. Parties wishing to litigate before the Frankfurt Chamber shall *declare before the end of the deadline for the statement of defence that they would like to plead in the oral hearing in English, and waive the right to have an interpreter.*[67] Turning to the NCC, parties should have explicitly agreed in writing on the use of the English language and the application of the NCC Rules.[68] By agreeing on the NCC Rules, the parties also implicitly agree to bear the higher NCC court fees amounting to €15,000 for each party in first instance and €20,000 on appeal.[69]

In the case of the European international commercial courts their institutional design as chambers within courts hinges their jurisdiction on the jurisdiction of the latter. By way of background, the choice to establish these courts as chambers lay predominantly in the desire to avoid laborious and time-consuming legislative amendments. In fact, in Germany the previous unsuccessful legislative proposals for the establishment of Chambers for International Commercial Disputes underlined that if Germany wanted to keep up with other European Member States establishing international commercial courts and thus 'stay on the map' of international commercial dispute resolution, it should expeditiously

[65] Regional Court Frankfurt am Main, Chamber for International Commercial Disputes, 'Which Proceedings Are Eligible?' https://ordentliche-gerichtsbarkeit.hessen.de/ordentliche-gerichte/lgb-frankfurt-am-main/lg-frankfurt-am-main/chamber-international, accessed April 2021.

[66] Art. 30r (1) Rv; Art. 1.3.1 (c) NCC Rules n. (17).

[67] See n. (65).

[68] Art. 30r (1) Rv; Art. 1.3.1. (d) NCC Rules n (17); *Elavon Financial Services DAC* v. *IPS Holding B.V. and others* [2019] NCC 19/003 ECLI:NL:RBAMS:2019:1637, at 6.3 (d).

[69] Art. 9a Act on Court Fees for Civil Cases (*Wet griffierechten in burgerlijke zaken*); NCC Explanatory Statement 17.

set up a court of its own.[70] The Frankfurt Chamber allows for the use of English during the oral hearing based on a lenient interpretation of the existing rules of civil procedure, and is therefore mostly an organisational measure without any legislative cost.[71] By the same token, when the Dutch judiciary introduced the idea of the NCC, it relied on a market survey conducted by the Boston Consulting Group and highlighted the uncertain and in any case small number of cases coming before the NCC during its initial years.[72] The uncertainty of such a start-up phase did not justify broad legislative amendments and vast expenses.[73] Therefore, the NCC law restricted itself to two main amendments regarding the use of English before the court and the higher NCC fees.[74] It was decided that the NCC should be a chamber of the Amsterdam District Court, to make use of existing facilities and tap into Amsterdam's prime location.[75]

The provisions pertaining to the jurisdiction of the Frankfurt Chamber and the NCC are stricter when compared to other international commercial courts. Except for a choice-of-court agreement, the parties shall explicitly agree in writing to litigate before the newly established chambers in English and according to the

[70] German Parliament (*Deutscher Bundestag*), Legislative Proposal for the Establishment of Chambers for International Commercial Disputes (*Entwurf eines Gesetzes zur Einführung von Kammern für internationale Handelssachen*), Drucksache 17/2163 of 16 June 2010, available at http://dipbt.bundestag.de/dip21/btd/17/021/1702163.pdf; German Parliament (*Deutscher Bundestag*), Legislative Proposal for the Establishment of Chambers for International Commercial Disputes (*Entwurf eines Gesetzes zur Einführung von Kammern für international Handelssachen*), Drucksache 18/1287 of 30 April 2014, available at http://dipbt.bundestag.de/dip21/btd/18/012/1801287.pdf, all accessed April 2021.

[71] Burkhard Hess, 'The Justice Initiative Frankfurt am Main 2017', conflictoflaws.net, 31 March 2017, available at conflictoflaws.net/2017/the-justice-initiative-frankfurt-am-main-2017-law-made-in-frankfurt, accessed April 2021. For a 'head start' advantage of establishing the Frankfurt Chamber before Brexit, see ' Es könnte der Beginn eines ganz neuen Kapitels sein' (2018) 2 Deutscher AnwaltSpiegel 17.

[72] The Boston Consulting Group, 'Market Survey Netherlands Commercial Court (*Marktverkenning Netherlands Commercial Court*)'.

[73] Dutch Council for the Judiciary, NCC Plan 2015, 4, 9, 12; NCC Explanatory Statement 4; Eddy Bauw, 'Ondernemerschap in de Rechtspleging. Over de Kansen van een Netherlands Commercial Court' (2016) Ars Aequi 97; Eddy Bauw, 'Procederen in Internationale Handelszaken bij een Netherlands Commercial Court' (2016) Trema 182.

[74] Art. 30r Rv; Art. 9a Act on Court Fees for Civil Cases (*Wet griffierechten in burgerlijke zaken*).

[75] Dutch Council for the Judiciary, NCC Plan 12, 14; NCC Explanatory Statement 3, 8; Oranje n. (24) 123.

chambers' rules.[76] By contrast, the parties' explicit agreement is not necessary in the case of the SICC or the DIFC Courts, where an agreement in favour of the Singapore High Court or the Dubai Courts is deemed to include the former as well.[77] Moreover, unlike the SICC and the CICC, a dispute cannot be transferred to the Frankfurt Chamber or the NCC without the parties' agreement. These stricter requirements forecast a lower number of cases for the Frankfurt Chamber and the NCC, especially during their initial years of operation.

However, more comment is warranted on what prompted these requirements. As mentioned earlier, various concerns and objections accompanied the establishment of international commercial courts in Europe. While the German Chambers for International Commercial Disputes were criticised mainly for the use of English as the language of court proceedings,[78] the NCC attracted negative attention for its higher, when compared to the ordinary courts, court fees.[79] It was feared that procedurally weaker parties such as small and medium-sized enterprises might find themselves unwillingly caught up in an expensive trial in a foreign language. Therefore, the requirement of an explicit and written agreement to litigate in English before the Frankfurt Chamber and the

[76] Georgia Antonopoulou, 'Requirements upon Agreements in Favour of the NCC and the German Chambers: Clashing with the Brussels Ibis Regulation'? (2019) 12 Erasmus Law Review 56.

[77] For the SICC, Rules of Court, Order 110, rule 1 (2) (ca); for the DIFC Courts, *IGPL* v. *Standard Chartered Bank* [2015] DIFC CA 004 (19 November 2015), paras. 123–54; *Sunteck Lifestyles Limited* v. *Al Tamimi and Co Ltd* [2017] DIFC CFI 048 (15 November 2017), para. 24.

[78] See, for example, Axel Flessner, 'Deutscher Zivilprozess auf English - Der Gesetzentwurf des Bundesrats im Lichte von Staatsrecht, Grundrechten und Europarecht' (2011) Neue Juristische Online-Zeitschrift 1913; Christopher Bisping, 'Conquering the Legal World: The Use of English in Foreign Courts' (2012) 20 European Review of Private Law 541; Wolfgang Hau, 'Fremdsprachengebrauch durch deutsche Zivilgerichte - vom Schutz legitimer Parteiinteressen zum Wettbewerb der Justizstandorte', in Ralf Michaels and Dennis Solomon (eds.), *Liber Amicorum Klaus Schurig* (Sellier European Law 2012) 49, 61–2.

[79] Senate (*Eerste Kamer*), Report of the Meeting of 4 December 2018 (*Verslag van de vergadering van 4 december 2018*) (2018/2019 nr. 10); Parliamentary Papers I 2017/18 (*Kamerstukken* I 2017/18), 34 761, B Reply to the Statement of Objections (*Memorie van Antwoord*) 3–5; Parliamentary Papers I 2017/18 (*Kamerstukken* I 2017/18), 34 761, C Detailed Report from the first Commission for Justice and Security (*Nader voorlopig verslag van de vaste commissie voor Justitie en Veiligheid*), 2–3; Parliamentary Papers I 2018/19 (*Kamerstukken I 2018/19*), 34 761, D Further Reply to the Statement of Objections (*Nadere Memorie van Antwoord*), 3–5, all available at www.eerstekamer.nl /wetsvoorstel/34761_engelstalige_rechtspraak, accessed April 2021.

NCC reflects concerns of an unfair trial that were eventually cast in terms of venue. The European courts are concerned about the impact of their innovative features on the procedural rights of weaker parties, and consequently their jurisdictional provisions are stricter and driven by a more social agenda.

17.4 Arbitration Features

One of the innovative procedural features of some international commercial courts that heavily distinguishes them from the ordinary courts are their arbitration features. Although in the case of some international commercial courts these arbitration features are merely 'buzz words' aimed at appealing parties favouring arbitration, they nevertheless go against common perceptions of ordinary, state courts that are strictly distinguished from arbitration. Therefore, the focus of this section is to explore the last but arguably most fascinating feature of international commercial courts: their arbitration features.

More specifically, this section addresses a persistently recurring question: how could international commercial courts beat the confidentiality and privacy of arbitration, the flexibility of its proceedings and lastly the nearly worldwide enforceability of its awards?[80] To answer this question, it focuses on three international commercial courts and explores how each one of them tackles each one of the arguably 'unbeatable' virtues of arbitration. It begins with the SICC and introduces the term 'offshore cases'. These are cases that bear no connection to Singapore, and are therefore allowed to be conducted confidentially and in private. On the flexibility front, this section focuses on the BIBC, which, although a state court, would apply not the Belgian rules of civil procedure but the UNCITRAL Model Law on International Commercial Arbitration.[81] Lastly, the DIFC Courts and their innovative experiment of turning DIFC Courts judgments into arbitral awards demonstrates how international commercial courts strive to enhance and improve the recognition and enforcement of their judgments abroad.

[80] See White & Case and Queen Mary University of London, 2018 International Arbitration Survey: The Evolution of International Arbitration, Chart 3, available at www.whitecase.com/sites/whitecase/files/files/download/publications/qmul-international-arbitration-survey-2018-19.pdf, accessed April 2021.

[81] UNCITRAL Model Law on International Commercial Arbitration 1985 with amendments as adopted in 2006 (hereinafter: Model Law).

17.4.1 *Confidentiality and Privacy: The SICC*

Previously, the notion of an international dispute under the SICC procedural rules was examined. The SICC rules do not distinguish only between international and domestic disputes; they have, in addition, coined the term 'offshore cases'. An offshore case is an action that has no substantial connection to Singapore. A substantial connection is lacking when Singapore law is not the law applicable to the dispute; where the subject matter of the dispute is not regulated by or otherwise subject to Singapore law; or the only connections between the dispute and Singapore are the parties' choice of Singapore law as the law applicable to the dispute and the parties' submission to the jurisdiction of the court.[82] Due to their tenuous link to the forum, offshore cases enjoy certain procedural privileges. First, while ruling on a confidentiality order, the court will take into consideration whether the case is an offshore case.[83] Second, parties in offshore cases may be represented by a foreign lawyer who is registered for this purpose.[84]

The SICC proceedings are by default heard in open court. Open court proceedings and the publication of SICC judgments create after all a body of jurisprudence and enhance the predictability of SICC judgments to interested parties.[85] Nevertheless, parties may apply for their case to be heard confidentially under certain criteria. According to the Rules of Court, there are three kinds of confidentiality orders: parties may apply for an order that the case be heard *in camera*, an order that no person

[82] Rules of Court n. (4), Order 110, rule 1 (2) (f). See also *Teras Offshore Pte Ltd* v. *Teras Cargo Transport (America) LLC*, [2016] 4 SLR 75, para. 8.

[83] Rules of Court n. (4), Order 110, rule 30 (2) (a); Johannes Landbrecht, 'The Singapore International Commercial Court (SICC): An Alternative to International Arbitration?' (2016) 34 ASA Bulletin 112, 121; Man Yip, 'Singapore International Commercial Court: A New Model for Transnational Commercial Litigation', in Ying-jeou Ma (ed.), *Chinese (Taiwan) Yearbook of International Law and Affairs* (Martinus Nijhoff 2014) 155, 161.

[84] Supreme Court of Judicature Act, Section 18M; Legal Profession Act, Section 36P; Singapore International Commercial Court Practice Directions n. (82), para. 26; Landbrecht n. (83) 123; Andrew Godwin, Ian Ramsay and Miranda Webster, 'International Commercial Courts: The Singapore Experience' (2017) 18 Melbourne Journal of International Law 1, 17–19. See also Singapore International Commercial Court, Register of Foreign Lawyers, available at www.sicc.gov.sg/registration-of-foreign-lawyers/foreign-lawyers, accessed April 2021.

[85] Speech by Senior Minister of State for Law, Indranee Rajah, at the Litigation Conference 2015, 16 March 2015 para. 40, available at www.mlaw.gov.sg/news/speeches/speech-by-senior-minister-of-state-for-law–indranee-rajah–at-t, accessed April 2021; Man Yip, 'The Singapore International Commercial Court: The Future of Litigation?' (2019) 12 Erasmus Law Review 81, 89.

may reveal or publish any information or document relating to the case, and an order that the court file be sealed.[86] While ruling on such an order, the court will take into consideration whether the case is an offshore case and whether both parties agree.[87]

It is asserted that in offshore cases the public interest in maintaining open court proceedings is less critical than in other cases bearing stronger connections to Singapore.[88] Offshore cases and their weak link to the forum weaken in turn the potential of a clash with national public policy, and therefore justify a departure from the principle of open justice. However, one might still object that apart from a national public policy there is a transnational public policy mandating that court proceedings be held in public.[89] In addition, even if private and confidential proceedings at the SICC could escape the restraints of a transnational public policy, they would still stumble upon the national public policy of other states. The recognition and enforcement of SICC judgments, where publicity was excluded, could be refused for violating the national public policy of the state of recognition and enforcement.

17.4.2 Procedural Flexibility: The BIBC Proposal

Most of the international commercial courts underline the flexibility of their civil procedure rules. In particular, several courts base their rules on arbitration rules often perceived as granting parties greater freedom to design proceedings than national procedural rules.[90] In this respect, the BIBC proposal was the most remarkable. Although a state court, the BIBC would apply not the Belgian rules of civil procedure but the Model Law. The Belgian rules would apply only if expressly referred to.[91]

[86] Rules of Court n. (4), Order 110, rule 30 (1).

[87] Ibid., rule 30 (2).

[88] Yip n. (83) 155, 160.

[89] Art. 14 (1) 1966 United Nations Covenant on Civil and Political Rights; Art. 6 European Convention on Human Rights; Art. 47 Charter of Fundamental Rights of the European Union.

[90] For the SICC evidence rules that are largely based on the IBA Rules on Taking of Evidence in International Arbitration 2010, see Teh Hwee Hwee and Justin Yeo, 'The Singapore International Commercial Court in Action: Illustrations from the First Case' (2016) 28 Singapore Academy of Law Journal 692, 701.

[91] BIBC Legislative Proposal, 13–14; Amendment no. 24 by Sonja Becq and others, Parliamentary Documents *(Doc. parl.)*: Belgian House of Representatives (*Chambre*) 54, 3072/009, 2.

The choice for the Model Law was based on the consideration that it reconciles civil and common law approaches especially with regard to evidence rules,[92] and is attractive especially to international parties who are familiar with its provisions.[93] The aim of applying the Model Law further was to 'unplug' the new court from Belgian law. Switching off the application of the Belgian civil procedure would free the BIBC from a set of rules that were not developed primarily for international commercial disputes. Reminiscent in a way of the SICC and its offshore cases, the explanatory statement to the BIBC legislative proposal underscored that the exclusion of Belgian civil procedure law made all the more sense in international disputes lacking a connection to Belgium.[94]

The exclusion of Belgian civil procedure law and the application of the Model Law invited criticism. The BIBC was characterised as an arbitral tribunal in the guise of a state court and, therefore its very identity as a court was questioned. The application of arbitration rules additionally raised questions as to the BIBC's added value. The fact that the Belgian arbitration law was already based on the Model Law called into question the BIBC's distinctive and therefore attractive features.[95]

Owing to these and other objections mainly targeting the use of English as the language of court proceedings, the court's unclear funding and the appointment procedure of its judges, the BIBC proposal was finally withdrawn. Despite its short lifespan, however, the BIBC remains interesting. It was the court that got the closest to arbitration, and its rise and fall illuminate the possible flipsides of transplanting arbitration rules to state courts.

17.4.3 Enforcing Judgments As Arbitral Awards: The DIFC Courts

Turning lastly to the recognition and enforcement of court judgments, the DIFC Courts came up with an innovative experiment to enhance the

92 BIBC Legislative Proposal, Explanatory Statement, 11.

93 Philippe Lambrecht and Erik Peetermans, 'The Brussels International Business Court: Initial Overview and Analysis' (2019) 12 Erasmus Law Review 42, 52.

94 BIBC Legislative Proposal, Explanatory Statement, 10–11.

95 André Henkes, 'About Cross-Border Taxation, Other International Economic Issues and the Contribution of the Supreme Court' (*Over grensoverschrijdende fiscaliteit, andere internationale economische vraagstukken en de bijdrage van het Hof van Cassatie*), Ceremonial Opening Session of the Belgian Supreme Court (*Plechtige openingszitting van het Hof van Cassatie van België*), 3 September 2018, II. Incidental Considerations on the Brussels International Business Court and Crypto-currencies, para. 35; Open Letter from the Magistrates of the Brussels Court of Appeal (*Lettre ouverte des magistrats de la cour d'appel de Bruxelles*), 1 December 2018.

enforceability of their judgments. The DIFC Courts' judgments may be enforced outside the United Arab Emirates (UAE) just like judgments of the Dubai Courts. The UAE have in particular entered into treaties with foreign jurisdictions providing for the reciprocal recognition and enforcement of court judgments. These treaties are the Gulf Cooperation Council Convention (1996), the Riyadh Convention (1983) and bilateral treaties with Tunisia (1975), France (1992), India (2000), Egypt (2000), China (2004) and Kazakhstan (2009). Moreover, the DIFC Courts have signed Memoranda of Guidance with various jurisdictions, which although lacking a binding legal effect, set out a 'mutual understanding' of the applicable laws and judicial processes governing the enforcement of final money judgments.[96]

So as to further enhance the enforceability of the DIFC Courts judgments especially in offshore disputes, the DIFC Courts experimented in 2015 with the 'conversion' of their judgments into arbitral awards. According to Practice Direction No. 2, parties may agree that any dispute arising out of or in connection with the non-payment of any money judgment given by the DIFC Courts may, at the option of the judgment creditor, be referred to arbitration under the Arbitration Rules of the DIFC-LCIA Arbitration Centre.[97] In this way, the DIFC Courts aim to profit from the extensive territorial reach of the New York Convention and lend to their judgments nearly worldwide enforceability. The Practice Direction further clarifies that such an arbitration agreement provides the creditor with an additional option to enforce the judgment and does not preclude his right to seek execution before any national court. Accordingly, the judgment debtor may not invoke this arbitration agreement against execution before a national court.[98]

The enforcement through arbitration is presented as the last resort for a creditor seeking enforcement of its judgment. If in particular the debtor's assets are located in Dubai, the creditor should then resort to the Dubai Courts. If the debtor has assets in a common law jurisdiction, he is then advised to sue on the DIFC Courts judgment as a foreign judgment in this jurisdiction. If, lastly, the debtor has assets in a country with which the UAE has a treaty providing for the mutual recognition and enforcement of judgments, priority should be given to enforcement

[96] DIFC Courts, Protocols and Memoranda, available at www.difccourts.ae/about/protocols-memoranda, accessed April 2021.

[97] Amended DIFC Courts Practice Direction No. 2 of 2015 – Referral of Judgment Payment Disputes to Arbitration.

[98] DIFC Courts, Enforcement Guide 2018 n. (33) 14.

under the treaty provisions. Therefore, a creditor should refer to arbitration only if none of these options are available.[99]

However, doubts have been expressed as to whether the non-payment of a court judgment constitutes a dispute under the New York Convention and is therefore arbitrable.[100] Nonetheless, the rubber-stamping of court judgments as arbitral awards along with the dual nature of the resulting DIFC judgment award blur the fine distinction between court judgments and arbitral awards and depict the growing approximation of court litigation and arbitration.

17.5 Conclusion

By exploring the international character, the voluntary jurisdiction and the arbitration features of international commercial courts, this chapter substantiates the claim that international commercial courts are procedurally different from ordinary courts. Two main procedural features that distinguish international commercial from ordinary courts are the international character of the disputes they handle and the voluntary establishment of their jurisdiction. At the same time, these features legitimise the creation and proliferation of these courts and the rest of their distinctive features that this chapter has failed to address.[101] In particular, the complexity of cross-border disputes and the wilful involvement of the parties justify the different procedural rules applicable before international commercial courts and in some instances their detachment from the national legal orders and the judicial systems surrounding them.

Furthermore, some international commercial courts adopt arbitration-like court proceedings. However, creating courts in the image and likeness of arbitration raises procedural concerns and challenges the added value of international commercial courts as well as their potential as an attractive dispute resolution option.

[99] Amended DIFC Courts Practice Direction No. 2 of 2015 n. (97).

[100] Michael Hwang, 'The DIFC Courts Judgment: Arbitration Protocol, Referral of Judgment Payment Disputes to Arbitration', DIFC Courts Lecture, 19 November 2014 1, 5–7; Anselmo Reyes, 'Recognition and Enforcement of Interlocutory and Final Judgments of the Singapore International Commercial Court' (2015) 2 Journal of International and Comparative Law 337, 345–8; Dalma R. Demeter and Kayleigh M. Smith, 'The Implications of International Commercial Courts on Arbitration' (2016) 33 Journal of International Arbitration 441, 457–61; David Isidore Tan, '"Enforcing" National Court Judgments As Arbitration Awards under the New York Convention' (2018) 34 Arbitration International 415, 428–9.

[101] Kramer and Sorabji n. (1).

PART V

International Commercial Courts and Global Governance

18

Hybridity in International Adjudication

How International Are International Commercial Courts?

SALVATORE CASERTA AND MIKAEL RASK MADSEN*

18.1 Introduction

How international are international courts (ICs)? And, related, how international are international commercial courts (ICommCs)? Among lawyers, the notion of ICs comes with a strong public international law connotation. The standard definition of ICs only highlights this.[1] International courts are defined as (i) permanent institutions (ii) composed of independent judges (iii) that adjudicate disputes between two or more entities, at least one of which is either a state or an international organisation, (iv) work on the basis of predetermined rules of procedure and (v) render decisions that are binding. This definition, and notably its third component, makes it apparent that the standard view of ICs is heavily inspired by public international law in terms of the centrality of states and international organisations. Thereby, ICommCs such as the Qatar International Court, the Dubai International Financial Centre (DIFC) Courts, the Singapore International Commercial Court (SICC)

* This research is funded by the Danish National Research Foundation Grant no. DNRF105 and conducted under the auspices of the Danish National Research Foundation's Centre of Excellence for International Courts (iCourts).

[1] See the discussions in Cesare P. R. Romano, 'The Proliferation of International Tribunals: Piecing together the Puzzle' (1999) 31 NYU Journal of International Law and Politics 709; Cesare P. R. Romano, 'A Taxonomy of International Rule of Law Institutions' (2011) 2 Journal of International Dispute Settlement 241; Cesare P. R. Romano, Karen J. Alter and Yuval Shany, 'Mapping International Courts and Tribunals, the Issues and Players', in Cesare P. R. Romano, Karen J. Alter and Yuval Shany (eds.), *The Oxford Handbook of International Adjudication* (Oxford University Press 2014).

or the Netherlands Commercial Court are in fact not ICs, as they do not adjudicate conflicts involving states and international organisations.[2] Yet these new judicial institutions – ICommCs – engage with international conflicts and make use of foreign law as well as judges, and for these reasons are often portrayed as hybrid courts.[3] But they are not alone in being hybrid. As we show in this chapter, even among those courts that fulfil all the elements of this definition of ICs, hybridity is also prevalent. Hybridity is thus not a phenomenon reserved for domestic courts engaging international dimensions of law, but also a characteristic of many 'proper' ICs as they engage and employ a variety of domestic legal features.

This is in some ways unsurprising in light of the evolution of international law and its only gradual and recent autonomisation from domestic law to become a distinct field of law.[4] This is visible in the fact that many ideas related to the architecture of international law and courts have been borrowed and adapted from domestic law, most strikingly the very notion of courts. The idea of juridical conflict resolution via courts is a distinct cultural institution dating back hundreds of years in European societies and beyond.[5] Moreover, domestic law, particularly in the context of federal states, has also a number of attributes we commonly associate with international law and courts. The European Court of Human Rights (ECtHR) and its famous doctrine of margin of appreciation is in many ways a replica of the various tools that federal systems use to balance centralised and decentralised legal and political power.[6] A key feature of European Union (EU) law, the procedure of preliminary references, is also to an extent borrowed from federal legal systems. Finally, the jurisdictions of some ICs include purely domestic conflicts,

[2] For a typology of international commercial courts see Georgios Dimitropoulos and Stavros Brekoulakis, 'Introduction', in this volume; Georgios Dimitropoulos, 'International Commercial Courts in the "Modern Law of Nature": Adjudicatory Unilateralism in Special Economic Zones' (2021) 24 Journal of International Economic Law 361.

[3] See Georgios Dimitropoulos, 'The Design of International Commercial Courts' (Chapter 10), in this volume.

[4] See for example Martti Koskenniemi, *The Gentle Civilizer of Nations: The Rise and Fall of International Law 1870–1960* (Cambridge University Press 2001).

[5] See for example on early English courts in Alan Harding, *The Law Courts of Medieval England* (Routledge 2019).

[6] Mikael Rask Madsen, '"Unity in Diversity" Reloaded: The European Court of Human Rights' Turn to Subsidiarity and Its Consequences' (2020/1) 15 Law & Ethics of Human Rights 93–123.

as in the case of the Central American Court of Justice (CACJ) and the Caribbean Court of Justice (CCJ).

Interestingly, this varied hybridity of ICs is largely unexplored in existing scholarship. Seeking to remedy this gap, the chapter paraphrases Anthea Roberts' research question of 'how international' international law is,[7] and asks the related but different question of 'how international' international courts are.[8] We further ask the same question in relation to ICommCs in an effort to demonstrate how, different from what is often suggested, these share a number of features with ICs. More specifically, we explore the hybridity of ICs and ICommCs by focusing on three interrelated dimensions. These have been drawn up from the comparative enterprise of analysing the institutionalisation of ICs across the globe, which has been conducted at iCourts, the Centre of Excellence for International Courts at the University of Copenhagen.[9] The specific dimensions we focus on with regard to ICs and ICommCs are professional, institutional and legal forms of hybridity. *Professional hybridity* refers to the mixed professional backgrounds of international judges (diplomacy, legal academia, the bench, private practitioners etc.). In terms of *institutional hybridity* we explore the mixed jurisdiction of ICs and ICommCs and how this often blurs the boundaries between domestic law and international law. To the same form of hybridity belongs the admixing of legal and political features in the institutional context of many ICs and ICommCs, most notably the operation of commissions as part of the international court systems, and the often blurred boundaries between judicial and arbitral roles among the competences delegated to many of these institutions. The final dimension of hybridity we investigate, *legal hybridity*, refers to the mixed legal knowledge used by ICs and ICommCs (national and international law, different legal traditions etc.). Importantly, as we explain in what follows, legal hybridity is often closely linked to professional and institutional forms of hybridity.

In this chapter we trace examples of such hybridity in international adjudication. We first examine hybridity in international adjudication by looking back in history to some of the antecedents of contemporary ICs such as the first CACJ and the Permanent Court of International Justice

[7] Anthea Roberts, *Is International Law International?* (Oxford University Press 2017).

[8] We have explored some elements of this relative internationalism in a previous publication. See Mikael Rask Madsen, 'Who Rules the World: The Educational Capital of the International Judiciary' (2018) 3 UC Irvine Journal of International, Transnational and Comparative Law 97.

[9] https://jura.ku.dk/icourts.

(PCIJ). We then zoom in on some particularly pertinent examples of current ICs in Europe, the Americas and the Caribbean. Due to space limits we leave out a number of subregional and regional African ICs, which however also supply ample evidence of hybridity.[10] We also leave out the recent surge of hybrid international criminal courts. We conclude by applying the findings on the three forms of hybridity in ICs to ICommCs. In the conclusion we argue that regardless of what the formal definition of ICs suggests, hybridity is present not only in ICommCs but also ICs. This also means that although ICommCs such as the Qatar International Court are not strictly speaking ICs, they have many features in common with the more classic ICs and can be viewed as part of the same proliferation of international dispute resolution.

18.2 Historical Antecedents: Hybridity at the First International Courts

Historians of international law typically date the origins of international adjudication to the use of international arbitration in the Anglo-American conflict in 1794, yet the first real IC was the Central American Court of Justice – also known as the Cartago Court. Created in 1907 and in operation until 1918 in Costa Rica, this first IC was characterised by a remarkably broad and hybrid jurisdiction. The court was, in fact, not only empowered to rule upon interstate disputes and conflicts between a government and a national of another state as a typical IC, but had also the power to decide over conflicts between the legislative, executive and judicial branches of government of its member states.[11] Thereby, it had the competence to oversee that the separation of powers was respected at the national level. This turned

[10] See for example Karen J. Alter, Laurence R. Helfer and Jacqueline R. McAllister, 'A New International Human Rights Court for West Africa: The ECOWAS Community Court of Justice' (2013) 107 American Journal of International Law 737; Laurie Nathan, 'The Disbanding of the SADC Tribunal: A Cautionary Tale' (2013) 35 Human Rights Quarterly 870; James Thuo Gathii, 'Variation in the Use of Subregional Integration Courts between Business and Human Rights Actors: The Case of the East African Court of Justice' (2016) 79 Law & Contemporary Problems 37; Mihreteab Taye, 'The Role of the East African Court of Justice in the Advancement of Human Rights: Reflections on the Creation and Practice of the Court' (2019) 27 African Journal of International and Comparative Law 359.

[11] Convention for the Establishment of a Central American Court of Justice, Articles 1, 2 and 4. The 'Constitutional Competence' of the Cartago Court was included in an optional clause ratified by all member states except Costa Rica.

this institution into a de facto constitutional review court, at least for issues related to the most fundamental aspects of the operation of the state, the separation of powers. The Cartago Court was, however, short-lived. Becoming embroiled in geopolitical issues that greatly divided the member states, it did not survive its eleventh year of operation. The court was left to expire under a sunset clause after having ruled against the United States and Nicaragua on matters directly linked to US interests in securing exclusive rights to build an interoceanic canal in Nicaragua.[12] Attempts at relaunching the court would not bear fruit until much later. We return to that in the next section.

It is perhaps because of the short life of the Cartago Court that most scholars tend to associate the genesis of international adjudication with the establishment of the PCIJ – known as the World Court at the time – in The Hague in 1922. From a formal perspective, the PCIJ fulfilled almost to perfection all criteria laid out in the standard definition of ICs. It is indeed quite possible that the PCIJ provided the original benchmark against which the standard definition of ICs has later been articulated. A closer look at the PCIJ beyond its formal competences and jurisdiction, however, reveals that even this court, possibly the most archetypical of ICs, was influenced by an attempt at fusing different domestic traditions of law with building a genuinely international institution.

A telling example comes from the negotiations of the court and the debate that took place concerning who would be eligible for the job as international judges. In other words, who should – and could – be appointed to act as the judge of sovereign states? Unsurprisingly, diplomats argued that it was a matter for diplomats. After all, international relations and law had until this point been mainly an issue handled by diplomats. But international law professors also claimed a stake. Academic lawyers had long been at the forefront of the intellectual debate on the creation of international courts and institutions, an issue that due to the lack of institutional progress had been largely academic in nature. Then, of course, there were those who advocated for the idea that judges from national apex courts were the natural candidates for undertaking the task of operating as international judges.[13] The outcome of all of this

[12] Freya Baetens, 'First to Rise and First to Fall: The Court of Cartago (1907–1918)', in Ignacio Rasilla and Jorge E. Viñuales (eds.), *Experiments in International Adjudication: Historical Accounts* (Cambridge University Press 2019).

[13] Antoine Vauchez, 'The International Way of Expertise. The First World Court and the Genesis of Transnational Expert Fields' (2014) EUI Working Paper RSCAS.

was that the first bench of the PCIJ consisted of 'three judges, three legal advisers and five professors'.[14] While this dominance of academic lawyers caused some consternation among the other contenders for the spots on the bench, the law professors turned out to be good at the delicate job of balancing law and politics and the court experienced a successful first decade of operation.[15]

This reveals that one of the most pronounced forms of hybridity of ICs is the mixing of professional backgrounds on the bench. And although most of the involved states generally converge on the delineation of the different legal-professional categories, the interplay of these categories differs in the mode of production of law in different countries. While for instance barristers and judges are closely linked in the operation of the justice system in the English tradition, in many civil law countries there is a much closer link between the judiciary and civil servants or between the judiciary and academia. This added another dimension of implicit hybridity to the PCIJ. In addition, even differences in court appearance and dress code made it into the debate. Although it was eventually decided that judges should wear black robes, an earlier proposal that they should also wear a kind of small hat led to an outcry from the UK Foreign Office, arguing it would make them look like a cross 'between bishops and clowns'.[16] This must likely have made some of the other participants smile, particularly if images of Old Bailey and wigs and gowns crossed their minds.

This particular form of hybridity of ICs – namely, the admixing of different legal professional profiles and forms of knowledge – has had an enduring effect on ICs. The contemporary configuration of the agency of the international judiciary is clearly influenced by these original forms of hybridity. In 2006, there were some 215 international judges who came from 86 different countries with 136 of them being European.[17] In terms of professional background, they resembled very much the bench of the PCIJ more than ninety years earlier: they were dominantly former legal researchers, judges or civil servants: 40 per cent of the international

[14] Ole Spiermann, 'The Legacy of the Permanent Court of International Justice: On Judges and Scholars, and also on Bishops and Clowns', in Christian J. Tams and Malgosia Fitzmaurice (eds.), *Legacies of the Permanent Court of International Justice* (Nijhoff 2013).

[15] Mikael R. Madsen, 'The International Judiciary As Transnational Power Elite' (2014) 8 International Political Sociology 332.

[16] Spiermann (n. 14).

[17] Daniel Terris, Cesare P. R. Romano and Leigh Swigart, *The International Judge: An Introduction to the Men and Women Who Decide the World's Cases* (Oxford University Press 2007).

judges surveyed in 2006 had predominantly pursued an academic legal career and 33 per cent were former judges, followed by 27 per cent who were former civil servants.[18] Six years later, in 2012, the number of international judges had grown to 304 judges employed at 21 different ICs.[19] This international judiciary comprised 111 different nationalities, including a growing number of Africans (consequential to the spread of regional ICs) and a continuous over-representation of Europeans. In 2012, 26 per cent had a background primarily as judges, 19 per cent as legal academics, 21 per cent mainly as civil servants and 11 per cent in private practice or 'other legal capacity' (prosecutor, arbitrator etc.). The rest had worked in a combination of these categories.[20]

A final example from historic ICs are the two war crimes tribunals set up in the aftermath of the Second World War in respectively Tokyo and Nuremberg. In terms of hybridity, these war crimes tribunals are interesting. First, they tried individuals and not states, which itself was an innovation in international law and clearly an import from domestic criminal law. That said, the criminal acts being pursued were novel and reflected an international innovation.[21] Secondly, and perhaps more interesting for our purposes, these tribunals became a melting pot of legal knowledge – above all different traditions of criminal law and procedural law from the allied countries involved in the prosecution and adjudication. As scholars studying the Nuremberg tribunal have shown, the dominant American prosecutors pursued the Nazi leaders precisely the same way they had pursued Al Capone and others in their prior life as domestic prosecutors fighting the Mob. There was nothing particularly international about that – they might as well have done it in Chicago instead.[22] The evolution of current international criminal courts and tribunals has also shown that core concepts have been distilled from many national traditions of criminal law.[23] This mixing of national legal

[18] Ibid., 17.

[19] Leigh Swigart and Daniel Terris, 'Who are International Judges?', in Cesare P. R. Romano, Karen J. Alter and Yuval Shany (eds.), *The Oxford Handbook of International Adjudication* (Oxford University Press 2014).

[20] Ibid., 626.

[21] Philippe Sands, *East West Street: On the Origins of 'Genocide' and 'Crimes against Humanity'* (Vintage 2017).

[22] Sara Dezalay, John Hagan, and Ron Levi, 'International Courts in Atypical Political Environments: The Interplay of Prosecutorial Strategy, Evidence, and Court Authority in International Criminal Law' (2016) 79 Law and Contemporary Problems 289.

[23] Elies van Sliedregt, *Individual Criminal Responsibility in International Law* (Oxford University Press 2012).

traditions and forms of knowledge and its distillation at international courts is perhaps the single most important form of hybridity in international courts. It links directly to the agency of ICs and its varied professional backgrounds. This is both a historic and contemporary feature of practically all ICs, as we will show in the following sections of this chapter.

18.3 Hybridity in Contemporary Regional International Courts

In what follows, we discuss hybridity in the context of regional courts in Europe, Latin America and the Caribbean. As it emerges from our analysis, all ICs under scrutiny are characterised by three interrelated forms of hybridity: (i) professional, relating to the mixed background of the judges; (ii) institutional, relating to central features of these courts that they have borrowed from national and/or federal systems; and (iii) legal, relating to the mixing of national, regional and international legal norms in the jurisprudence of these ICs. Although all three forms of hybridity are present in the ICs included in the analysis, we limit the analysis to emblematic examples of these different features.

18.3.1 Hybridity in European International Courts

The World Court was at the vanguard of the development of international law, particularly in the 1920s. Yet, in the period following the Second World War, the biggest innovation in terms of ICs occurred at the regional level. At the international level, the International Court of Justice was largely a continuation of the PCIJ, while the mentioned war crimes tribunals were ad hoc courts that expired once they had delivered a series of judgments against a series of war criminals. A much more enduring effect on the field came from the European continent, notably from the new regional courts set up in Luxembourg and Strasbourg. Thus it was the courts set up under the auspices of the European Economic Community (at the time the Coal and Steel Community) and the Council of Europe that provided impetus for the proliferation of international courts in the subsequent decades.[24] The idea of supranational law provided new political and legal tools that had the double effect of granting more power to regional institutions and simultaneously ensuring that the

[24] Karen J. Alter, 'The Global Spread of European Style International Courts' (2012) 35 West European Politics 135.

national levels of law and politics were only increasingly deeper integrated with the supranational level. The two European ICs thereby advanced a uniquely transnational form of law, which overcame some of the shortcomings of traditional international law and the way it hinged on the will of states to implement judgments. In the European supranational variant, the coupling of national and European judicial levels ensured a close operation of domestic and international levels.[25]

In EU law, this transnational coupling is done primarily via the procedure of preliminary references where domestic courts, when in doubt about the interpretation of EU law (lack of *acte clair*), send a request to the common European court in Luxembourg to provide an interpretation.[26] This raises the basic question of whether that procedure and institutional architecture is unique to EU law or it is an international hybridisation of pre-existing legal ideas and practices. Some of its core elements undoubtedly originate from continental constitutional law, and particularly continental constitutional courts. The basic idea of abstract review – different from the implied powers of the US Supreme Court to perform concrete constitutional review – was first launched by Hans Kelsen, the legal philosopher and later judge at the world's first constitutional court in Vienna. This idea was further sophisticated in the mandate given to the *Bundesverfassungsgericht* established in Karlsruhe after the Second World War. Some of the same ideas, even some of the same people, were included in the comparative studies on federalism that channelled similar concepts into the making of the European Court of Justice during the same period.[27]

The origins of this competence, however, can also in part be found in international law, most notably in the competence to give advisory opinions – a power the PCIJ already had. Advisory opinions from international courts provides also a means for a kind of preliminary

[25] This is most explicit in the context of EU law, but it is also a feature of contemporary European human rights as operationalised via the ECtHR and underlying European Convention of Human Rights. Because of the way in which the European Convention has been incorporated in domestic legal orders it has today become akin to EU law: directly applicable and with a claim to supremacy via the ECtHR.

[26] Morten Broberg and Niels Fenger, *Preliminary References to the European Court of Justice* (Oxford University Press 2014).

[27] Antonin Cohen, 'Le Plan Schuman de Paul Reuter. Entre Communauté Nationale et Fédération Européenne' (1998) Revue Française de Science Politique 645; Antonin Cohen, 'Constitutionalism without Constitution: Transnational Elites between Political Mobilization and Legal Expertise in the Making of a Constitution for Europe (1940s–1960s)' (2007) 32 Law & Social Inquiry 109.

abstract review. Such a competence is today found at most ICs, including the ECtHR which via its most recent additional protocol has been given the power to issue advisory opinions (Additional Protocol No. 16). Thus the institution of preliminary references has elements of both federal and international law. Interestingly, such competences are today found in most regional ICs.[28]

Another form of hybridity in EU law is the notion of subsidiarity which resembles how many federal systems have explicit or implicit institutional brakes to counter tendencies of overcentralisation by the common federal institutions. The EU's long-standing political objective is 'an ever-closer union', which since 2000, when the telling motto 'united in difference' was adopted, has been translated into a form of further integration respectful of national-cultural differences.[29] Legally, although the EU seeks a uniform application of its laws across the member states, it also operates under the principle of subsidiarity which first saw its light in the 1992 Maastricht Treaty. As codified in the current Article 5(3) of the Treaty on the European Union, subsidiarity is a general principle of law that fuses elements of proportionality with elements of proximity.[30]

This kind of balancing act is hardly unique to EU law and resembles what is found in federal and con-federal law and practices. For example, in US law, one speaks about federalism when a balance has to be struck between common federal regulation and the relative autonomy of the states making up the federation. As in EU law, this is a dynamic relationship but based on a premise of toleration of relative difference and pluralism.[31] At the other ICs, we also find such balancing tools. Most

[28] Alter (n. 24).

[29] See https://europa.eu/european-union/about-eu/symbols/motto_en (last visited 20 October 2020).

[30] The difference between the EU's main legislative means, notably between Regulations and Directives, operationalises the notion in practice. While regulations are binding legislative acts and must be applied uniformly across the EU, directives have to be transposed into national law and the member states are to devise their own laws as to how to reach the EU goals. Subsidiarity is, thus, controlled *ex ante* at the political level during the lawmaking process and controlled *ex post* by the Court of Justice of the EU (CJEU) in cases brought before it. In practice, however, the *ex ante* control has turned out to be by far the most important. In *ex post* arguments before the CJEU, the general tendency is that the push for 'an ever-closer union' most often trumps subsidiarity arguments in favour of domestic law or lawmaking. Illustratively, see the opinion of General Advocate Maduro in paragraphs 27–31 in Case C 58/08 (*Vodafone Ltd, Telefónica O2 Europe plc, T Mobile International AG, Orange Personal Communications Services Ltd* v. *Secretary of State for Business, Enterprise and Regulatory Reform* (delivered on 1 October 2009).

[31] Judith Resnik, 'Federalism(s)' Forms and Norms: Contesting Rights, De-essentializing Jurisdictional Divides, and Temporizing Accommodations' (2014) 55 Nomos 363, 364.

strikingly, the ECtHR has developed its doctrine of margin of appreciation to reflect the subsidiary role of the court vis-à-vis the member states as the primary subjects of the Convention.[32] The doctrine concerns, essentially, whether the member states have or do not have the liberty to find local solutions to realise the common catalogue of rights. While the doctrine has helped balance the different levels of European law for decades, the past ten years have seen a call for increasingly more robust subsidiarity in the system.[33] Resembling typical federal rhetoric, critics of the ECtHR have argued that new and better brakes were needed to secure the member states against over-centralisation and over-intervention from ECtHR. During the negotiation of the 2012 Brighton Declaration, it was eventually agreed that subsidiarity should be written directly into the preamble of the European Convention of Human Rights in order to highlight the subsidiary role of the ECtHR.[34]

18.3.2 Hybridity in Latin American and Caribbean International Courts

Latin American and Caribbean ICs not only replicate the forms of hybridity seen in European ICs, but also have other more pronounced forms of hybridity. As we argue in what follows, this is in part the result of the particular histories of these regions, all characterised by postcolonial reminiscences and, as concerns Latin America, periods of turmoil within and between the states of each region. In turn, these contexts have made the regions prone to serve as venues for experimenting various forms of international adjudication and/or of other forms of international dispute settlement mechanisms than what is found at the ICs already examined.

One court with a particularly high level of hybridity is the CACJ, which was created – or resurrected – as the judicial arm of the Central American Integration System (SICA) in the 1990s. Interestingly, in addition to granting the court with competences imitating the CJEU to rule upon economic disputes of the Central American common market, the CACJ's statute also transferred some of the competences of the original Cartago

[32] Dean Spielmann, 'Whither the Margin of Appreciation?' (2014) 67 Current Legal Problems 49, 51.

[33] Mikael Rask Madsen, 'Rebalancing European Human Rights: Has the Brighton Declaration Engendered a New Deal on Human Rights in Europe?' (2018) 9 Journal of International Dispute Settlement 199.

[34] See Additional Protocol No. 15 Article 1.

Court to the present court.[35] Thus, in addition to its jurisdiction to rule upon SICA market law, the CACJ was also empowered to act as an arbitral tribunal, as an interstate international court (if designated by the parties) and, most controversially, as a supranational constitutional court with jurisdiction to review conflicts over the separation of powers in the member states. In other words, the court was created to operate with a unique mixture between purely international and supranational competences as well as tasks usually assigned to national constitutional courts. This institutional hybridity was further cemented by the mixed competences of the judges eventually elected to sit on the CACJ's bench, who were a combination of former diplomats and national judges, many of whom had very significant experience with constitutional law. What was however absent during the first two decades of the court's operation were judges with relevant knowledge on regional market law.

The institutional and professional hybridity of the CACJ is further reflected in the court's rulings, particularly in its involvement as an apex court on constitutional matters of the member states. In 2005, for example, the court got involved in the constitutional crisis between the Nicaraguan parliament and President of the Republic Enrique Bolaños. The parliament – at that time controlled by the leftist Sandinista Party – sought to pass a number of constitutional reforms aimed at disempowering the president. Regardless of the many critical voices raised in the region concerning the court's involvement in such a mega-political national conflict, the CACJ delivered one of its most known rulings, which, while not directly resolving the constitutional crisis in Nicaragua, contributed to mediating the conflict.[36]

When read in conjunction with other developments taking place at the court, this landmark ruling reveals the CACJ's inclination to act not only as the judge of the Central American economic integration, but also as a hybrid institution at the crossroads of supranational, international and constitutional law. In the court's docket, in fact, we find rulings as diverse as disputes related to territorial disputes between its member states, the validity of national elections and appointments of members of the regional Parliament (PARLACEN), inter-institutional disputes among

[35] The historical and sociopolitical dynamics accounting for this unique transfer of competences among two institutions that existed almost a hundred years from one another have been expounded in Salvatore Caserta, *International Courts in Latin America and the Caribbean: Foundations and Authority* (Oxford University Press 2020).

[36] *Enrique Bolaños* v. *the Parliament of Nicaragua*, CACJ n. 69–01–03–01–2005.

regional organs and more classic issues of tariffs and trade matters.[37] All of this suggests that, regardless of its role in the system of economic integration, the CACJ has developed a form of jurisprudential hybridity that ranges from Central American Community law, classic international law, fundamental rights of individuals, structural constitutional issues, electoral matters and even environmental law and implementation of unexecuted national judgments.

This voluminous and differentiated docket differs considerably from how community law developed in Europe under the aegis of the CJEU. European Union Law – at least in the early days of the Community – was deliberately developed as an, in principle, apolitical, technical, yet hierarchically strong system of regional norms capable of having structural precedence over national norms. The prominent role of the principles of direct effect and supremacy derive precisely from this situation. Conversely, the institutional and professional hybrid nature of the CACJ has pushed the court to create a much thicker version of regional law, which seeks not only to enable and enforce free trade, and therefore trumps inconsistent national laws, but also seeks to contribute to the democratisation and pacification processes of the region and the member states. In short, the CACJ has taken a path more akin to a federal supreme court than to a classic public international law IC.[38]

Another regional IC characterised by a striking level of hybridity is the CCJ. A result of the particular colonial and postcolonial trajectory of the English-speaking Caribbean, the CCJ was established in 2005 with a unique double jurisdiction consisting of both an original and an appellate jurisdictions.[39] In its original jurisdiction, the court is empowered to rule over community law matters stemming from CARICOM community interactions. In this conjunction, it has imported various EU-like dimensions of supranational law yet transformed them to fit its local context. In its appellate jurisdiction the court is intended to replace the last remnant of colonial rule in the region – namely, the appeals to the Judicial Committee of the Privy Council in London – which at the time of the establishment of the CCJ many countries of the

[37] For a general review of the Court's activity, see Caserta (n. 35).

[38] A similar view was already expressed in Salvatore Caserta, 'Regional Integration through Law: The Central American and Caribbean Cases' (2017) 30 Leiden Journal of International Law 579.

[39] Salvatore Caserta and Mikael R. Madsen, 'Between Community Law and Common Law: The Rise of the Caribbean Court of Justice at the Intersection of Regional Integration and Post-colonial Legacies' (2016) 79 Law and Contemporary Problems 89.

region still maintained as their highest court. To date, the appellate jurisdiction of the CCJ has been ratified only by four states: Barbados, Guyana, Belize and Dominica.[40] This means that the court only acts in this capacity for those countries, while it acts as a community court for all member states of the CARICOM in its original jurisdiction. Thus the CCJ combines both domestic and international law under the same roof by being both a court of regional integration and an apex court for national legal matters. Similar to the CACJ, this institutional hybridity is reflected in the professional backgrounds of the judges so far elected. Since its opening in 2005, the judges of the CCJ have constituted a perfect mix of lawyers with expertise in regional law, national judges from the different legal traditions of the region (notably common law and civil law) and international lawyers, as well as diplomats.

The institutional and professional hybridity of the CCJ is further reflected in the court's adjudicatory practices. In, for example, *Myrie* v. *Barbados*,[41] a seminal freedom-of-movement case decided by the court in 2013, the CCJ expanded its original jurisdiction to encompass not only CARICOM-related economic disputes, but also fundamental individual rights. In this decision, the court also developed a unique principle of community law, which, while being inspired by the doctrines of direct effect and supremacy of the CJEU, differs from them in important ways and as such constructs a hybrid system of regional laws. Among other things, in *Myrie*, the CCJ was called to address the issue of whether unimplemented international treaties had legal effects in national law. To respond to this highly sensitive question, which is particularly contentious in the many Caribbean member states which subscribe to a strong notion of dualism in their approach to international law, the CCJ developed a doctrine we elsewhere have labelled *indirect effect*.[42] According to this doctrine, in the context of the CARICOM, unimplemented treaties do not produce legal effects nationally, but are nevertheless binding at the international level, and are therefore directly applicable before the CCJ at the request of private parties. In other words, the court has developed a doctrine that bypasses dualist approaches to international law, a unique hybrid conceptualisation of community law as directly available and

[40] For an overview of the trajectory of institutionalisation of the CCJ, see Caserta (n. 35).

[41] *Shanique Myrie* v. *Barbados* [2012] CCJ 3 (OJ and [2013] CCJ 1 and 3 (OJ).

[42] Salvatore Caserta and Mikael Rask Madsen, 'Consolidating Supranational Authority: The Caribbean Court of Justice Decisions in the *Tomlinson* Cases' (2016) 110 American Journal of International Law 1, 7.

judiciable at the international level regardless of whether it is implemented domestically.

These legal developments were confirmed by the court in a number of subsequent original jurisdiction cases. Exemplary in this regard are the two *Tomlinson* cases.[43] Both cases concerned freedom of movement and specifically whether domestic statutory law prohibiting homosexuality was a reason for denying entrance into the countries of Belize and Trinidad and Tobago under CARICOM law. In both cases, the court explicitly acknowledged its hybrid function as both an international and national court. In terms of law, the court rejected the cases on the grounds that in the practices of the two states these laws had not been applied for long time. At the same time, the CCJ reminded that the mere existence of laws that violate the basic rights of CARICOM (i.e. the freedom of movement of individuals within the Community) should be enough to embark on national legal reforms to strike down these laws. Most importantly, the CCJ put forward a rather controversial principle – at least from a classic public international law point of view – the principle in point being that when called to rule upon in its original jurisdiction against a state that had accepted its appellate jurisdiction, the CCJ has the capacity to interpret national law when assessing whether Community obligations had been infringed. This hybrid status creates a rather unusual situation for an IC, but also raises the question of how the CCJ should act under its appellate jurisdiction when judging a case concerning community law – a question thus far not addressed by the court.

Regardless of how these unique features will be operationalised in the future practices of the court, these doctrines show how the CCJ has thus far strived to create a hybrid version of supranational law in the CARICOM, which both resembles and differs from the one developed in the context of the EU by the Luxembourg Court as well as the CACJ. In particular, the CCJ's strong emphasis on *indirect effect* – and not on direct effect as in the EU – has a number of practical implications that make the CARICOM into a hybrid supranational legal system with semi-constitutional features. Perhaps the most important manifestation of this can be seen in the fact that in the CARICOM private parties – and neither states nor the regional secretariat – have been turned into the primary engines of integration. The result is a hybrid supranational system with

[43] *Maurice Arnold Tomlinson* v. *Belize and Trinidad and Tobago*, [2014] CCJ 2 (OJ) and [2016] CCJ 1 (OJ).

constitutional features characterised by direct applicability at the domestic and supranational levels and by direct effect and direct access to the CCJ at the supranational level.

Another Latin American court which has developed unique forms of hybridity is the Mercosur dispute settlement system, which fuses elements of a court and an arbitral tribunal. It operates with a rather complex system of access, limiting the access of private parties. Individuals can only file complaints before the national section of the Common Market Group (CMG), which means that they cannot bring their own state before the regional dispute settlement mechanism.[44] In addition, disputes must be solved primarily through direct and informal diplomatic negotiations. Only when and if interstate negotiations have failed, and if there is common agreement between the two states parties of the dispute, can the CMG intervene through the formulation of non-binding recommendations aimed to resolve the conflict.[45] If the dispute cannot be resolved by the CMG, any party to the dispute may communicate to the secretariat of the Mercosur their will to use the arbitral system in the form of an ad hoc arbitral tribunal or, if there is agreement between the parties, to directly present a suit before the Mercosur Permanent Review Court (PRC).[46] In the case in which the ad hoc arbitral tribunal has intervened, the parties of the dispute can file an appeal to the PRC, but its analysis is limited to the legal questions of the controversy and to an evaluation of the interpretations developed by the arbiters in their decision.[47]

What can be observed is a distinct mixing of arbitration and court like-structures. Such hybridity is not unknown beyond this court. It is an implicit and sometimes explicit understanding in most international legal systems that conflicts should first be sought to be resolved by other means before courts get involved. Even human rights courts like

[44] Paula Wojcikiewicz Almeida, 'The Case of MERCOSUR', in Robert Howse, Hélène Ruiz-Fabri, Geir Ulfstein and Michelle Q. Zang (eds.), *The Legitimacy of International Trade Courts and Tribunals* (Cambridge University Press 2018).

[45] Olivos Protocol, articles 4, 5, 6, 7 and 8.

[46] Ibid., articles 9 and 23.

[47] It must be, however, mentioned that the PRC has also an original jurisdiction, also called *per saltum*. When this is activated states can have direct access to the court, but only if diplomatic negotiations have not been successful. A similar form of direct access to the PRC is granted to states in cases of urgency and there is the possibility that the dispute would cause irreparable damages to the parties if not solved rapidly. Marcelo H. Granillo Fernández, 'El Sistema de Solución de Controversias en el MERCOSUR. Protocolo de Olivos' (2003) 5 Revista de Derecho Internacional y del Mercosur.

the ECtHR seek to settle disputes before the court gets involved. And, as shown, other courts have arbitral competences if called upon – for example, the CACJ. But what makes Mercosur distinct is the integration of arbitral and court structures in a single institution. In domestic law, arbitration is typically an alternative to judicial means and not a first step towards a judicial resolution. But at the international level these otherwise distinct forms of dispute resolution might be merged as demonstrated by the Mercosur.

18.4 Comparison: Hybridity in International Commercial Courts

It follows from this survey that hybridity in ICs is a recurrent phenomenon since the genesis of ICs in the beginning of the twentieth century. Although formal definitions of ICs make a distinct claim to the public international law nature of ICs, there is considerable evidence that even some of the most 'international' ICs have significant elements derived directly and indirectly from domestic law and legal thinking. Of course one element sets ICs apart from other courts, including ICommCs – namely, the presence of states or international organisations as one of the parties in litigation. This produces a particular political dimension in the proceedings of these courts which is not found in, for example, commercial disputes among private parties. Thus, formally speaking, the growing number of ICommCs that have emerged over the past decade do not, regardless of their designation, qualify as ICs since they do not always involve states and even less so international organisations. But this dimension apart, the three forms of hybridity observed across the examined ICs are also found in many of these new courts. As we briefly survey in this concluding part of the chapter, this goes for the mixed professional backgrounds of their judges, the mixed legal knowledge and the mix of judicial and arbitral roles. In the following, we address and compare three distinct forms of ICommCs, using the typology developed by Georgios Dimitropoulos: ICommCs embedded in Special Economic Zones, Stand-Alone ICommCs and International Commercial Chambers within Ordinary Courts.[48]

Among ICommCs embedded in Special Economic Zones (SEZs), the DIFC Courts are probably the most well-known institutions. The DIFC Courts were established in 2004 and are now part of the integrated

[48] See Dimitropoulos n. 2.

DIFC's Dispute Resolution Authority (DRA), which also includes an arbitration institute. The DIFC Courts were originally created to handle disputes over financial services within the SEZ but have since expanded their jurisdiction to cover more generally civil and commercial matters from within the SEZ and since 2011 also from outside of it if the parties have so agreed. Thus, institutionally, we immediately observe a sort of mixed jurisdiction which both extends beyond its immediate context of the SEZ and is placed right next to an arbitration centre. Just as ICs in various ways have encroached on domestic law, the DIFC Courts are arguably following a similar pattern with its new competence to adjudicate cases from outside of the SEZ.

Another well-known SEZ-embedded ICommC is the Qatar Financial Centre's (QFC) Civil and Commercial Court which was set up in 2009. It subsequently became known as the Qatar International Court and Dispute Resolution Centre (QICDRC) in 2012, which also performs arbitration functions. In terms of jurisdiction, although embedded in an SEZ, the court's reach goes beyond the economic zone as the entities of the QFC can operate across the State of Qatar and thereby bring the jurisdictional reach of the court beyond the zone's formal limits. For our purposes, it suffices to note that the international commercial court of the QFC, like the DIFC Courts, is part of a broader dispute resolution centre and has developed jurisdiction that encroaches on local law. Other comparable institutions, such as the Abu Dhabi Global Market (ADGM) Courts, created in 2013, operate in a way similar to the DIFC Courts. The Astana International Financial Centre (AIFC) Court, created in 2015, also follows this model.[49]

All of these courts are also marked by a relative mix of professional backgrounds of the appointed judges as well as usage of legal knowledge. All four courts are to various degrees open to common law and particularly English common law and operate, by default, in English. The DIFC law, for example, is largely based on English common law, and the same is the case of the AIFC. At the ADGM, English common law is directly applicable before the court. At the QICDRC, the applicable law is the laws and regulations of the QFC, which also imports common law and English law elements. The influence of common law is further accentuated by the recruitment to the benches of these courts. All of them have seen a high number of judges from common law jurisdictions, particularly from England, appointed to their bench. Other traditions and nationalities

[49] Ibid.

are, however, also featured, including judges from countries of the seat of the courts. All of this is contributing to a unique melting pot of law and lawyers where local regulations of the SEZs are being interpreted in light of common law principles and case law as well as various forms of civil law.

The same high level of hybridity is, however, not replicated when we move the focus to stand-alone ICommCs. These courts are set up within existing domestic court structures but with a distinct jurisdiction over international commercial disputes. Established in 2015, the SICC is part of the High Court of Singapore but it caters only to international commercial disputes, also those with only little connection to Singapore and governed by foreign law. Its international dimension is underlined by its mixed bench consisting of Singaporean judges from the higher courts and international judges coming from both civil and common law traditions. The SICC basically seeks to attract international commercial disputes by offering a distinct internationalised court based on the established framework of the Singaporean judicial system.

China has recently created a slightly different variant of stand-alone ICommCs intended to cater to potential international commercial conflicts stemming from the Belt and Road Initiative. Two ICommCs set up in Shenzhen and Xi'an, known as the China International Commercial Court (CICC), started operating in 2019 with a narrower jurisdiction than the SICC and governed by local procedural law.[50] The bench is not mixed as in the case of the SICC, requiring the judges to be current judges at Chinese courts and Chinese nationals with experience in international commerce. In all cases, it is required that they can work in English as well as Chinese, but proceedings are in Chinese. To remedy this national orientation of an otherwise international commercial court, the court operates with the International Commercial Expert Committee to assist it with regard to foreign law as well as provide advice. The Committee includes legal experts from around the world in matters pertaining to international commercial law.

The CICC resembles in many ways the third group of ICommCs – namely, what Dimitropoulos calls 'International Commercial Chambers within Ordinary Courts'.[51] These are ICommCs created in Europe over the past two to three years which in reality are mostly international

[50] See further in Julien Chaisse and Xu Qian, 'China International Commercial Court'(Chapter 19), this volume.

[51] Dimitropoulos n. 2.

chambers of existing commercial courts, where English language is allowed for proceedings but the bench remains local. Currently, three of these courts are taking off: the *Landgericht* (LG) Frankfurt am Main, the International Chamber of the Paris Court of Appeals (CICAP), and the Netherlands Commercial Court (NCC). They clearly seek a stake in the growing market of international commercial disputes and are above all continental competitors to the Chancery Division of the High Court of England and Wales and its long-standing position in handling international commercial conflicts. The main international hybridity of these courts is their usage of foreign language (English) and openness to adjudicate foreign law. Their assumed strength is that they capitalise on the legitimacy of the public court systems of the involved countries. But by lowering the language barrier, they enter a different space of adjudication – that of ICommCs – and are likely influenced by developments at those other courts.

18.5 Conclusion

This survey of the three dominant forms of ICommCs suggest that mainly the courts embedded in SEZs and, to some extent, the stand-alone ICommCs are marked by the kind of hybridity which has marked the evolution of ICs since the beginning of the twentieth century. The new international commercial chambers of continental European courts are only to a very limited extent hybrid in this sense. Hence, it is particularly in the first category of ICommCs we find hybridity in terms of law, institutional reach and combinations of legal knowledge which resembles what was developed at ICs. Due to the specific nature of commercial disputes, however, some of the fundamental quasi-federal issues facing many ICs are not replicated at ICommCs. Here we find a clear difference between public and private law also at the international level. That said, the ICommCs are likely going to be inspired and influenced by development relating to – directly and indirectly – to private law taking place at ICs. Another key difference is that the international commercial courts embedded in SEZs, although international in outlook and in recruitment of judges, tend to lean towards (English) common law as the preferred *lex mercatoria*. At ICs, such legal preference is, at least in principle, never the case and the common reference point is public international law and international customary law as well as comparative law from similar ICs. Finally, the presence of states and international organisations in the disputes before ICs differentiates ICs from ICommCs.

This raises the question whether ICommCs are not only conceptually but also materially a different phenomenon than ICs. Basically, not only can these new commercial courts not feature as ICs under the standard public international law definition introduced in this chapter, but they are also materially different from ICs with regard to important aspects of their operation and hybridisation of law and legal knowledge. However, if we view these developments as a matter of transnational and global governance by law, ICommCs might well be seen as yet another stage in the ongoing proliferation of institutions of international dispute resolution. Taking this broader view, our analysis suggests that ICs and ICommCs in fact share a number of features in their ambition of being international: the mixed legal cultural agency, the explicit and implicit hybridisation of domestic and international law and the legal architectures that combine judicial functions. Thus the convergence primarily occurs at the level of internationalisation in terms of a cultural intermingling of institutional frameworks and forms of knowledge and actors than at the legal conceptual level of what is 'international'. Part of the reasons for this pathway towards convergence is that although most experts have a general idea of what constitutes a court of law, there is in reality no universal model of a court. No court can claim true 'courtness' but rather exhibit and assemble a set of features that makes their claim to being a court acceptable to others. And this this is only exacerbated at the international and transnational levels of legal governance.

19

China International Commercial Court

Architecture, Pitfalls and Promises

JULIEN CHAISSE AND XU QIAN

19.1 Introduction

China is a unique laboratory for legal innovation and hybridization. The hybrid nature of China's legal system is remarkably evidenced by the use of both common law and civil law on its territory. In accordance with the Sino-British (1984) and Sino-Portuguese (1987) Joint Declarations, Hong Kong and Macau were handed over to the People's Republic of China (PRC) in 1997 and 1999 respectively and are known as Special Administrative Regions (SARs) of the People's Republic of China (PRC). The two SARs retain 'a high level of autonomy',[1] with their social, economic and legal systems 'basically unchanged' for fifty years under the implementation of 'One Country, Two Systems'.[2] Article 31 of the

[1] Basic Law of the Hong Kong Special Administrative Region of the People's Republic of China, 3rd Session, 7th National People's Congress (NPC), 4 April 1990, Art. 2, 29 ILM 1511, www.basiclaw.gov.hk [hereinafter HK Basic Law]; Basic Law of the Macau Special Administrative Region of the People's Republic of China, 1st Session, 8th NPC, 31 March 1993, Art. 2 (unofficial English translation available online: http://bo.io.gov.mo/bo/i/1999/leibasica/index_uk.asp) [hereinafter Macau Basic Law].

[2] Joint Declaration of the Government of the United Kingdom and the Government of China on the Question of Hong Kong, 19 December 1984, 1399 UNTS 33, Art. 3(3), 3(5), 3(12) [hereinafter Sino-British Joint Declaration]. These articles list the 'basic policies' that the Chinese government undertakes to implement in the Region. China undertook similar obligations regarding Macau: Joint Declaration of the Government of Portugal and the Government of China on the Question of Macau,13 April 1987, 1498 UNTS 195, Art. 2(2), 2(4), 2(12) (unofficial English translation at 229) [hereinafter Sino-Portuguese Joint Declaration]. Article 5 of both the HK Basic Law and the Macau Basic Law provide that '[t]he socialist system and policies shall not be practiced in the [Hong Kong/Macau] Special Administrative Region, and the previous capitalist system and way of life shall remain unchanged for 50 years'. This amounts more to an obligation not to introduce the Chinese socialist system than one to leave the previous systems unchanged.

Chinese constitution stipulates the fundamental legal connection between the PRC and the two SARs.[3] Each SAR has its basic law, which has been drafted by mixed committees of experts from the PRC, Hong Kong and Macau and enacted with a 'quasi-constitutional nature and supra-legal hierarchical level'.[4] The two SARs are vested with legislative and independent judicial power, including that of final adjudication. The laws, decrees and regulations currently in force remain basically unchanged.[5] This peculiar status is reflected in the hybrid nature of China's legal system featuring both common law and civil law.[6] In this respect, the interface and interaction of the common law and the PRC's civil law system has been abundantly discussed in the literature from a comparative perspective.[7]

Even though a larger portion of the territory and the population are subject to civil law, it is also a fact that the nature of Chinese civil law has constantly evolved to reach a high degree of hybridization over the past decades. China's socialist market economy is a market economy co-existing with a large public sector, which was symbolized by the Communist Party of China's (CPC) at its 14th Congress in October 1992, and by the 1993 amendment of Article 15 of the

[3] Constitution of the People's Republic of China, promulgated by the First Session of the 13th National People's Congress of the People's Republic of China on 11 March 2018 [hereinafter Constitution]. Article 31 reads: 'The State may establish special administrative regions when necessary. The systems to be instituted in special administrative regions shall be prescribed by law enacted by the National People's Congress in the light of specific conditions'. Ignazio Castellucci, 'Legal Hybridity in Hong Kong and Macau' (2012) McGill Law Journal 57(4), 665–720, 674.

[4] Castellucci, 'Legal Hybridity in Hong Kong and Macau', 674.

[5] HK Basic Law Art 8; Macau Basic Law.

[6] HK Basic Law Art 8; Macau Basic Law.

[7] Chenguang Wang and Guobin Zhou, 'A Tale of Two Legal Systems: The Interaction of Common Law and Civil Law in Hong Kong' (1999) 4 Revue internationale de droit comparé 918. It states, 'These problems and issues are particularly perplexed by the fact that the two systems are of drastically different legal traditions and political nature. At the macro level, Hong Kong needs to construct a new constitutional framework that is based on the Basic Law of the Hong Kong SAR and that, through the Basic Law, is posited within the Chinese constitutional structure. The role and function of the Court of Final Appeal (the "CFA") of the Hong Kong SAR, the relation between the Central Authorities and SAR governments and their respective powers, the interpretation of the Basic Law, the effects of legal rules of the Mainland in Hong Kong, etc. are issues of controversies triggered by such reinstitutionalization and tensions between two legal traditions. At the micro level, legal practitioners and judges in Hong Kong in dealing with cross-border business transactions and other matters, have to use constantly not only Hong Kong legal terms and rules, but also those pertinent to the mainland legal system. It is of no exaggeration that most of lawyers and judges in Hong Kong should know how to deal with and live with the legal rules and systems that are foreign to them. In short, the hand-over offers rich opportunities to boost comparative law study and practice in Hong Kong.'

Constitution. Article 15 of the Constitution declared that 'the state practices a social market economy',[8] replacing the reference to the 'supplementary role' of the market.[9] China's affiliation with a 'civil law' system is affected by globalization, international trade and economic reform. China has referred to and learned from other countries' experience in legislation both from the common law and civil law countries, such as for the protection of intellectual property rights and the environment. In the fields of civil and commercial legislation, the basic systems of both civil and common law countries have influenced the general principles of civil law and contract and property rights. In addition, China has adopted the principle of legal certainty and proportionality of modern administrative law in an effort to further promote the rule of law.[10]

This chapter provides the first comprehensive analysis of the China International Commercial Court (CICC), which is the latest legal innovation in the constantly evolving Chinese legal system. The objective of this chapter is to contribute to the emerging literature on hybrid courts by critically reviewing the establishment of the CICC. The chapter submits that the CICC corresponds to a new stage of regulatory (and economic) development reached by China which demonstrates the country's ambition to strengthen the rule of law for a number of economic transactions which are key for the country's future economic development. This chapter also critically reviews the genesis of the CICC, its anatomy and its problematic features. The analysis places the CICC in the broader context of China's economic and regulatory development, in particular, with respect to the existing domestic courts and arbitration centres in China as well as in other Belt and Road Initiative (BRI) countries.[11]

[8] Constitution Article 15. It reads, 'The State practices [a] socialist market economy. The State strengthens economic legislation, improves macro-regulation and control. The State prohibits in accordance with law any organization or individual from disturbing the socio-economic order.'

[9] Donald C Clarke, 'China: Creating a Legal System for a Market Economy' (Asian Development Bank, 2007) 8, https://scholarship.law.gwu.edu/cgi/viewcontent.cgi?article=2258&context=faculty_publications. Last accessed 13 December 2019.

[10] Cheng-Yi Huang and David S. Law, 'Proportionality Review of Administrative Action in Japan, Korea, Taiwan, and China', in Francesca Bignami and David Zaring (eds.), *Research Handbook in Comparative Law and Regulation* (Edward Elgar 2014) 25.

[11] See 'The Belt and Road Initiative' (Hong Kong Trade Development Council), http://china-trade-research.hktdc.com/business-news/article/The-Belt-and-Road-Initiative/The-Belt-and-Road-Initiative/obor/en/1/1X3CGF6L/1X0A36B7.htm. Last accessed 13 December 2019. For more information on BRI countries, see 'The Belt and Road Initiative: Country Profiles' (Hong Kong Trade Development

19.2 From Economic to Legal Globalization

The CICC has to be understood in the context of the BRI, which itself corresponds to a specific stage of China's engagement with economic globalization with consequences for its *legal globalization*. In fact, the CICC is the latest legal instrument designed to provide China greater influence and a larger role in economic globalization – a goal the BRI should boost. In this respect, we review the evolution of the Chinese economy (and its globalization) under the policy of 'Reform and Opening Up' before turning to the BRI as a global policy.

19.2.1 From the Reform and Opening Up Policy to Now

At the 2013 Third Plenum, the Communist Party under the leadership of President Xi Jinping made a decisive commitment to further China's Reform and Opening Up policy, thirty-five years after the launch of Deng Xiaoping's reform in 1978.[12] The Plenum issued 'The Decision on Major Issues concerning Comprehensively Deepening Reforms', which 'allow(s) the market to play a decisive role in resource allocation'.[13] For instance, China has moved from an approval-based system to a negative list-based system in terms of foreign direct investment (FDI),[14] in order to ease restrictions, as the new system does not require a government review for all inbound FDI.[15] In addition, the Free Trade Zones (FTZs) provide a wide range of FDI incentives to further ease investment restrictions – for example, a higher level of autonomy, preferential employment policies

Council), http://china-trade-research.hktdc.com/business-news/article/The-Belt-and-Road-Initiative/The-Belt-and-Road-Initiative-Country-Profiles/obor/en/1/1X000000/1X0A36I0.htm. Last accessed 13 December 2019.

12 'Communiqué of the Third Plenary Session of the 18th Central Committee of the Communist Party of China', China Internet Information Center (15 January 2014), www.china.org.cn/china/third_plenary_session/2014-01/15/content_31203056.htm. Last accessed 13 December 2019.

13 Kevin Rudd, 'China's Economic Reforms: Cannot, Should Not Stop' (Caixin, 12 November 2018), https://asiasociety.org/policy-institute/chinas-economic-reforms-cannot-should-not-stop. Last accessed 13 December 2019.

14 Dorcas Wong, 'China's New Negative List Targets Unified Market Access, China Briefing' (China Briefing, 9 January 2019), www.china-briefing.com/news/chinas-new-negative-list-targets-unified-market-access. Last accessed 13 December 2019.

15 Mark Preen, 'Economic Reform in China: Current Progress and Future Prospects' (China Briefing, 3 April 2019), www.china-briefing.com/news/economic-reform-china-opening-up-future-prospects. Last accessed 13 December 2019.

and a variety of tax exemptions.[16] In June 2018, the Ministry of Commerce (MOFCOM) and the State Administration for Industry and Commerce (SAIC) implemented the 'One Window, One Form' policy for registering foreign-funded enterprises. The reform strengthens data exchange and information sharing between relevant government departments to simplify the registration process.[17]

These efforts partly explain why China moved from the seventy-eighth to the forty-eighth position in 2018 in the World Bank's 'Ease of Doing Business' rankings compared with 2017.[18] With regard to trade facilitation reforms, in 2015, China became the sixteenth member to formally accept and ratify the WTO's Trade Facilitation Agreement (TFA).[19]

China has been influenced by the most sophisticated international models of the difference between common law and civil law through its participation in the international economy and fulfilling its international commitments.[20] The principle of rule of law is increasingly taking a more prominent position in the country; therefore, the Belt and Road Initiative will undoubtedly change China's role in international relations in a comprehensive manner.[21]

19.2.2 Role of Domestic Courts in International Dispute Settlement

The concrete example can be found in Article 158 of the Hong Kong Basic Law, where the highest court in Hong Kong lacks the definitive interpretation of its respective basic laws. In the circumstances, the interpretation of rules of the Hong Kong Basic Law can be done within

[16] Joseph Percy, 'Investing in China's Economic Development Zones' (China Briefing, 19 March 2019), www.china-briefing.com/news/chinas-economic-development-zones-types-incentives. Last accessed 13 December 2019.

[17] 'China's "One Window, One Form" to Streamline Foreign Business Registration' (China Briefing, 13 March 2018), www.china-briefing.com/news/china-implement-one-window-one-form-foreign-business-registration. Last accessed 13 December 2019.

[18] Preen, 'Economic Reform in China'.

[19] 'China Ratifies Trade Facilitation Agreement' (World Trade Organization, 4 September 2015), www.wto.org/english/news_e/news15_e/fac_04sep15_e.htm. Last accessed 13 December 2019.

[20] Rodolfo Sacco, 'Legal Formants: A Dynamic Approach to Comparative Law' (1991) 39 American Journal of Comparative Law 4, 1–34, 343–401.

[21] Yun Zhao, 'Introduction', in Yun Zhao (ed.), *International Governance and the Rule of Law in China under the Belt and Road Initiative* (Cambridge University Press 2018) 2. See also Mark Feldman, '"One-Stop" Commercial Dispute Resolution Services: Implications for International Investment', in Julien Chaisse, Leila Choukroune and Sufian Jusoh (eds.), *Law Handbook of International Investment Law and Policy* (Springer 2021).

the authority of local courts because it does not 'involve falling under the authority of the PRC's central government or relating to the relations between the SARs and the Mainland'.[22] In Chinese tradition and theory, the interpretation is considered to be law-making in nature and belongs to the lawmaker, which is different from the Hong Kong's common law tradition which implies the doctrine of *stare decisis*.[23]

This perception was brought to the fore in the 'Congo case', which related to the execution of an award against a state's assets in Hong Kong. The frozen assets belonged to Chinese state-owned enterprises (SOEs).[24] The actual scope of 'acts of State' was in dispute and the argument was that the narrower concept of 'acts of State' established under common law were subject to the jurisdiction of Hong Kong courts, whereas the Chinese government followed the absolute doctrine of state immunity. When the case reached the Court of Final Appeal (CFA), the government of Hong Kong solicited the court to require an interpretation by the National People's Congress Standing Committee (NPCSC).[25]

19.2.3 The Belt and Road Initiative As a Global Economic Policy

In 2013, Chinese President Xi Jinping announced the Belt and Road Initiative (BRI), broadly viewed as a commercial and geopolitical project to link China with Southeast, Southern and Central Asia, Russia and Europe by land and a twenty-first-century Maritime Silk Road.[26] This project involves more than US$1 trillion in investments, largely in infrastructure development for roads, ports, railways and airports, as well as telecommunication networks and power plants.[27] The BRI marks China

[22] Ignazio Castellucci, 'Legal Hybridity in Hong Kong and Macau' (2012) McGill Law Journal 57(4), 665–720, 677.

[23] Article 158 of the Hong Kong Basic Law stipulates: 'The Standing Committee of the National People's Congress shall authorize the courts of the Hong Kong/Macau Special Administrative Region to interpret on their own, in adjudicating cases, the provisions of this law which are within the limits of the autonomy of the region.' Chien-huei Wu, 'One Country, Two Systems, and Three Memberships: Legal and Economic Integration between China and Its Two SARs' (2007) 7(3) Global Jurist. Doi: 10.2202/1934-2640.1253.

[24] *Democratic Republic of the Congo* v. *FG Hemisphere Associates LLC* [2012] HKEC 20.

[25] The Congo case (CA leave to appeal), at para. 13; Castellucci, 'Legal Hybridity in Hong Kong and Macau', 687.

[26] 'Belt and Road Initiative' (European Bank for Reconstruction and Development), www.ebrd.com/what-we-do/belt-and-road/overview.html. Last accessed 13 December 2019.

[27] Ibid.

as a major source of outward international investment while exposing Chinese investors to various legal systems.

There is a well-developed international legal framework that may apply to BRI projects, depending on where they are located. Most participating countries are party to a significant number of international agreements, such as bilateral investment treaties (BITs), multilateral and bilateral free trade agreements, other multilateral agreements (such as the Energy Charter Treaty), World Trade Organization (WTO) agreements (such as the WTO Trade Facilitation Agreement[28]) and UN Conventions (such as the UN Convention on Contracts for the International Sale of Goods (CISG)[29]). Many countries have adopted some variation of the model laws provided by the United Nations Commission on International Trade Law (UNCITRAL) as their domestic laws, including the Model Laws on Public Procurement, Secured Transactions, International Credit Transfers, and International Commercial Arbitration.[30]

Due to the complex nature of construction deals and project finance, it is envisaged that BRI will generate an abundance of disputes which may be covered by the traditional BIT investor-state dispute settlement clauses, whereas some of them may fall within the ambit of domestic and transnational jurisprudence and rules. In these circumstances, it has become necessary to develop China-based institutions to streamline and control the flow of these disputes.[31]

[28] The WTO Trade Facilitation Agreement's (TFA) 2017 entry into force was very timely for the BRI. According to the WTO, 'The TFA contains provisions for expediting the movement, release and clearance of goods, including goods in transit. It also sets out measures for effective cooperation between customs and other appropriate authorities on trade facilitation and customs compliance issues. It further contains provisions for technical assistance and capacity building in this area.' See 'Trade Facilitation' (World Trade Organization), www.wto.org/english/tratop_e/tradfa_e/tradfa_e.htm. Last accessed 13 December 2019.

[29] According to UNCITRAL, 'The purpose of the CISG is to provide a modern, uniform and fair regime for contracts for the international sale of goods.' See 'United Nations Convention on Contracts for the International Sale of Goods' (UNCITRAL, 1980), www.uncitral.org/uncitral/en/uncitral_texts/sale_goods/1980CISG.html. Last accessed 13 December 2019.

[30] 'United Nations Commission on International Trade Law: Texts and Status', (UNCITRAL), www.uncitral.org/uncitral/en/uncitral_texts.html. Last accessed 13 December 2019.

[31] Matthew S. Erie, 'The China International Commercial Court: Prospects for Dispute Resolution for the "Belt and Road Initiative"'(2018) 22 American Society of International Law, www.asil.org/insights/volume/22/issue/11/china-international-commercial-court-prospects-dispute-resolution-belt. Last accessed 13 December 2019.

19.3 Anatomy of the China International Commercial Court

The Provisions of the Supreme People's Court on Certain Issues concerning the Establishment of International Commercial Courts became effective on 1 July 2018.[32] The regulations set out the scope and operation of two new international commercial courts (ICommCs) in China (the CICCs) in Shenzhen and Xi'an respectively. The establishment of the CICCs is driven by the intention to facilitate dispute resolution related to BRI projects. It is anticipated that the Shenzhen CICC, which is in the Greater Bay Area, will focus on disputes involving infrastructure along maritime routes. On the other hand, the Xi'an CICC will focus on disputes arising from projects on land.[33]

19.3.1 Object and Purpose of the China International Commercial Court

According to the CICC, its 'objective is to try international commercial cases fairly and timely in accordance with the law, protect the lawful rights and interests of the Chinese and foreign parties equally, create a stable, fair, transparent, and convenient rule of law international business environment'.[34] These courts mark the first attempt of China to create a legal institution for the world as part of China's ambitions for global influence.[35]

According to the Provisions, the establishment of the CICC emphasizes its ability to serve transnational players with the objective of better managing international commercial disputes, creating a better judicial environment and facilitating BRI construction. This highlights that the objective of CICC is to serve BRI parties instead of attracting new investment opportunities or other parties seeking to adjudicate their

[32] Wei Sun, 'International Commercial Court in China: Innovations, Misunderstandings and Clarifications' (*Kluwer Arbitration Blog*, 4 July 2018), http://arbitrationblog.kluwerarbitration.com/2018/07/04/international-commercial-court-china-innovations-misunderstandings-clarifications. Last accessed 13 December 2019.

[33] Freshfields Bruckhaus Deringer, 'China Establishes International Commercial Courts to Handle Belt and Road Initiative Disputes' (*Oxford Business Law Blog*, 17 August 2018), www.law.ox.ac.uk/business-law-blog/blog/2018/08/china-establishes-international-commercial-courts-handle-belt-and. Last accessed 13 December 2019.

[34] 'About China International Commercial Court' (China International Commercial Court), http://cicc.court.gov.cn/html/1/219/193/195/index.html. Last accessed 13 December 2019.

[35] Pamela K. Bookman, 'The Adjudication Business' (2020) 45(2) Yale Journal of International Law 227.

disputes before the CICC.[36] Some of the reforms are unprecedented, and parties can voluntarily submit their disputes to the CICC, which could be a good 'starting point' for China to be considered an attractive place for BRI disputes.[37]

19.3.2 The China International Commercial Court and the Supreme People's Court of China

The CICC was established under the authority of the Supreme People's Court of China (SPC), which is China's highest court. Provisions of the Supreme People's Court on Several Issues regarding the Establishment of the International Commercial Court came into effect on 1 July 2018.[38]

The SPC has now released further rules for the operation of CICC. The Procedural Rules for the China International Commercial Court of the Supreme People's Court (For Trial Implementation)[39], the Working Rules of the International Commercial Expert Committee of the Supreme People's Court (for Trial Implementation) came into force[40] and the Notice of the Supreme People's Court on Inclusion of the First Group of International Commercial Arbitration and Mediation Institutions in the 'One-Stop' Diversified International Commercial Dispute Resolution Mechanism were simultaneously issued on 5 December 2018.[41]

[36] Li Huanzhi, 'China's International Commercial Court: A Strong Competitor to Arbitration?' (*Kluwer Arbitration Blog*, 30 September 2018), http://arbitrationblog.kluwerarbitration.com/2018/09/30/chinas-international-commercial-court-a-strong-competitor-to-arbitration. Last accessed 13 December 2019.

[37] Ibid.

[38] 《最高人民法院关于设立国际商事法庭若干问题的规定》 Provisions of the Supreme People's Court on Several Issues concerning the Establishment of the International Commercial Courts, passed by the Adjudication Committee of the Supreme People's Court on 25 June 2018, issued on 27 June 2018, effective as of 1 July 2018, Article 1 [hereinafter Provisions].

[39] 《最高人民法院国际商事法庭程序规则(试行)》 'Procedural Rules for the China International Commercial Court of the Supreme People's Court (For Trial Implementation) effective as of 5 December 2019' (CICC, 5 December 2018), http://cicc.court.gov.cn/html/1/219/208/210/1183.html. Last accessed 13 December 2019. [hereinafter Procedural Rules].

[40] 《最高人民法院国际商事专家委员会工作规则(试行)》 Working Rules of the International Commercial Expert Committee of the Supreme People's Court (For Trial Implementation), effective as of 5 December 2019, http://cicc.court.gov.cn/html/1/219/208/210/1183.html. Last accessed 13 December 2019. [hereinafter Expert Committee Rules].

[41] 《最高人民法院办公厅关于确定首批纳入'一站式'国际商事纠纷多元化解决机制的国际商事仲裁及调解机构的通知》 Notice of the Supreme People's Court on Inclusion of the First Group of International Commercial Arbitration and

These rules provide further details about the operation and procedures of the CICC. The CICC Rules of Procedure are formulated in accordance with Civil Procedure Law of the People's Republic of China, the Provisions and other laws and judicial interpretations. However, the CICC rules are rather brief (containing only forty articles) and they do not specify whether other laws include international arbitration rules. It is likely that when applying these rules in practice, Chinese civil procedure law will be referred to frequently.[42]

19.3.3 The CICC Two Courts (Shenzhen and Xi'an) and Their Coordination

The CICC comprises two courts which are permanent branches of the SPC. The First International Commercial Court is in Shenzhen, Guangdong Province, and the Second International Commercial Court is in Xi'an, Shaanxi Province. The Fourth Civil Division of the SPC in Beijing is responsible for 'coordinating and guiding the two courts'.[43]

The CICC is intended to create a 'one-stop' ICommC – that is, a 'one stop' international commercial dispute resolution platform.[44] This is one of the most innovative mechanisms of Chinese initiative given the 'organically integrated' dispute mechanism, which combines mediation, arbitration and litigation.[45] Matthew S. Erie has characterized the consolidation of dispute resolution services as part of a larger 'multi-door courthouse' tradition.[46] Feldman

Mediation Institutions in the 'One-Stop' Diversified International Commercial Dispute Resolution Mechanism, effective as of 5 December 2018, http://cicc.court.gov.cn/html/1/219/208/210/1144.html. Last accessed 13 December 2019.

[42] 'Supreme People's Court Issues Rules of Procedure for the China International Commercial Courts' (Herbert Smith Freehills, 7 December 2018), https://hsfnotes.com/asiadisputes/2018/12/07/supreme-peoples-court-issues-rules-of-procedure-for-the-china-international-commercial-courts. Last accessed 13 December 2019.

[43] 'About China International Commercial Court' (China International Commercial Court), http://cicc.court.gov.cn/html/1/219/193/195/index.html. Last accessed 13 December 2019.

[44] Notice of the Supreme People's Court on Inclusion of the First Group of International Commercial Arbitration and Mediation Institutions in the 'One-Stop' Diversified International Commercial Dispute Resolution Mechanism.

[45] Bookman, 'The Adjudication Business'.

[46] Erie, 'The China International Commercial Court'. Mariana Hernandez-Crespo Gonstead, 'Transcript, a Dialogue between Professors Frank Sander and Mariana Hernandez Crespo: Exploring the Evolution of the Multi-door Courthouse' (2008) 5

views the potential development of a CICC as 'significant and exciting'.[47] In contrast, Zihao Zhou highlights that the arbitration and mediation institutions selected to work with CICC are Chinese institutions, which may raise concerns that the system will be biased in favour of Chinese companies.[48] Bookman also warns that the offered alternative dispute resolution (ADR) will 'become mandatory or that the parties will feel forced into them, which is contrary to the consent-based foundations of arbitration and mediation'.[49]

19.3.4 China International Commercial Court Judges and Expert Committee

Cases will be heard by a panel of three or more judges.[50] The practice is 'First Instance being Final', which means there are no appeals of decisions. The CICC's decisions are final and legally binding on the parties.[51] The SPC will appoint judges who will be familiar with international commerce and investment and will able to work in English[52]. The first group of eight judges was appointed by the CICC on 3 July 2019.[53] In accordance with the work demands of the SPC, the second group of seven judges was appointed by the

University of St. Thomas Law Journal 665, 670. Frank Sander conceptualized the 'multi-door courthouse' as a platform for considering 'different forms of dispute resolution – mediation, arbitration, negotiation, and med-arb' and developing 'some kind of taxonomy of which disputes ought to go where, and which doors are appropriate for which disputes'.

[47] Mark Feldman, 'The New York Convention and International Dispute Resolution' (China Arbitration Summit, Beijing, September 2018), http://dx.doi.org/10.2139/ssrn.3251091. Last accessed 13 December 2019.

[48] Zihao Zhou and Nathan Harpainter, 'Survey Results: Rules on China's International Commercial Courts' (Stanford Law School: China Guiding Cases Project, December 2018), https://cgc.law.stanford.edu/commentaries/clc-3-201812-26-zhou-harpainter-cao. Last accessed 13 December 2019.

[49] Bookman, 'The Adjudication Business'.

[50] Provisions, Article 5.

[51] Wei Cai and Andrew Godwin, 'Challenges and Opportunities for the China International Commercial Court' (2019) 68 International and Comparative Law Quarterly 869, 897.

[52] Wei Sun, 'International Commercial Court in China'.

[53] The eight judges are Wang Chuang, Zhu Li, Sun Xiangzhuang, Du Jun, Shen Hongyu, Zhang Yongjian, Xi Xiangyang and Gao Xiaoli. See 'Eight Judges of the China International Commercial Court were Appointed' (China International Commercial Court, 3 March 2018), http://cicc.court.gov.cn/html/1/219/208/210/821.html. Last accessed 13 December 2019.

CICC on 7 December 2019[54] and the third group of three judges was appointed on 21 July 2020.[55] According to Art. 4 of the Provisions, the CICC judges are professional Chinese judges 'experienced in trial work, familiar with international treaties, international usages, and international trade and investment practices, and capable of using Chinese and English proficiently as working languages'.[56] The CICC possesses a select team of highly qualified senior judges with extensive experience in adjudicating transnational commercial disputes. In addition, nine judges out of the fifteen also hold law degrees from common law jurisdictions.[57]

Although it is different from the courts in Qatar and Singapore, which employ international jurists,[58] some commentators still view the provisions as likely to represent a significant step forward in the professionalization of the Chinese courts.[59]

Article 12 of the Provisions specifies that if the parties choose to mediate the dispute through the CICC, the CICC may entrust members of the International Commercial Expert Committee (the Expert Committee) or an international commercial mediation institution to mediate the dispute.[60] The members of the Expert Committee may act as mediators in CICC's international cases, provide advisory opinions in international commercial disputes at the instruction of CICC or various levels of People's courts and give advice and suggestions for the CICC and SPC.[61] Currently, the first group of the Expert

[54] The seven judges are Wang Shumei, Wei Wenchao, Song Jianli, Zhang Xuemei, Yu Xiaohan, Ding Guangyu and Guo Zaiyu. See 'The Second Group of Judges of the China International Commercial Court Were Appointed by the Supreme People's Court' (China International Commercial Court, 7 December 2018), http://cicc.court.gov.cn/html/1/219/208/210/1134.html. Last accessed 13 December 2019.

[55] The three judges are Ren Xuefeng, Hu Fang and Huang Xiwu. See 'The Third Group of Judges of the China International Commercial Court Were Appointed by the Supreme People's Court' (China International Commercial Court, 21 July 2020), http://cicc.court.gov.cn/html/1/218/149/192/1620.html. Last accessed 29 August 2020.

[56] CICC Article 4.

[57] Zhou and Harpainter, 'Survey Results'.

[58] Susan Finder, 'China International Commercial Court Starts Operating' (*Supreme People's Court Monitor*, 14 January 2019), https://supremepeoplescourtmonitor.com/2019/01/14/china-internationalcommercial-court-starts-operating. Last accessed 13 December 2019.

[59] Zhou and Harpainter, 'Survey Results'.

[60] CICC Article 12.

[61] 《最高人民法院关于⊠任国际商事专家委员会⊠批专家委员的决定》 Decision of the Supreme People's Court on the Appointment of the First Group of Members of the International Commercial Expert Committee, issued on and effective as of 24 August 2018, http://cicc.court.gov.cn/html/1/218/149/192/949.html. Last accessed 13 December 2019.

Committee consists of thirty-two practitioners, scholars and judges, more than half of whom are from foreign jurisdictions.[62] The term of their engagement is four years and may be renewed upon expiry.[63]

In some ways, the CICC is designed with an eye towards establishing an alternative solution that will allow the court to leverage international experts from diverse backgrounds. It enhances 'the professionalism and sophistication of PRC courts', and helps present a 'more impartial image of CICC to the international community'.[64] However, since the CICC operates under Chinese law, following a modified set of procedures that draws on the civil law system, CICC judges accordingly will have less discretion and flexibility than judges in other jurisdictions. In addition, the parties may have less control over the proceedings.[65]

19.4 Will the China International Commercial Court Work? The Two Major Issues on the Road Ahead

Despite (or perhaps, because of its innovative character, the CICC seems to be facing a number of challenges to its viability and capacity to function. After all, many other Chinese legal innovations have in the past encountered problems, which obliged the country to adjust and refine the legal and policy aspects of special economic zones or the status of Hong Kong and Macao. It is also true that hybrid courts are a relatively new global legal phenomenon, and many jurisdictions seem to be learning by doing. With respect to the CICC, two major challenges need to be discussed: firstly, the CICC's jurisdiction, and secondly, the enforceability of CICC judgments.

[62] The Expert Committee comprises twelve Chinese and twenty-one non-Chinese. See 'The Supreme People's Court Established the International Commercial Expert Committee' (China International Commercial Court, 26 August 2018), http://cicc.court.gov.cn/html/1/219/208/209/981.html. Last accessed 13 December 2019.

[63] CICC Article 5.

[64] Zhou and Harpainter, 'Survey Results'.

[65] Bookman, 'The Adjudication Business'; for a description of the Chinese legal system and the difficulties Western scholars face in trying to understand it, see Donald Clarke, 'Puzzling Observations in Chinese Law: When is a Riddle Just a Mistake?' in Stephen Hsu (ed), *Understanding China's Legal System* (New York University Press 2003).

19.4.1 *The Question of the China International Commercial Court's Jurisdiction*

The CICC will hear only international civil and commercial matters; it will not hear investor-state disputes or interstate trade disputes.[66] The CICC jurisdiction is limited to international commercial disputes which involve one or more foreign parties or relevant foreign objects or legal facts.[67] The CICC has jurisdiction for the following disputes[68]:

(1) First-instance international commercial cases in which the parties have chosen the jurisdiction of the Supreme People's Court according to Article 34 of the Civil Procedure Law, with an amount in dispute of at least 300,000,000 Chinese yuan;
(2) First instance international commercial cases which are subject to the jurisdiction of the higher People's courts that nonetheless consider that the cases should be tried by the Supreme People's Court, and for which permission has been obtained;
(3) First instance international commercial cases that have a significant nationwide impact;
(4) Cases involving applications for preservation measures in arbitration, for setting aside or enforcement of international commercial arbitration awards according to Article 14 of the Provisions;
(5) Other international commercial cases that the Supreme People's Court considers appropriate to be tried by the International Commercial Court.

The most common way for the CICC to assume jurisdiction is over disputes with monetary value over RMB 300 million through parties' consent. Article 8(1) of the CICC Rules of Procedure specifies that the parties' consent must be in written form. There are also less common ways for CICC to establish its first instance jurisdiction; for instance, by

[66] Wei Sun, 'International Commercial Court in China'.

[67] See CICC Article 3, 'A commercial case with one of the following situations can be regarded as an international commercial case under these Provisions:

(a) one or both parties are foreigners, stateless persons, foreign enterprises or other organizations;
(b) one or both parties have their habitual residence outside the territory of the People's Republic of China;
(c) the object in dispute is outside the territory of the People's Republic of China;
(d) legal facts that create, change, or terminate the commercial relationship have taken place outside the territory of the People's Republic of China'.

[68] CICC Article 2.

referral from higher courts, or at the instruction of the SPC if the cases have significant national impact.[69] Notably, the CICC is not limited to consent-based jurisdiction, which may raise the concerns that parties may feel compelled to submit to mediation or arbitration.[70] Especially, if consent to CICC jurisdiction becomes a pre-condition of Chinese investment along the BRI, the CICC may gain prominence quickly. For now, the CICC only cooperates with Chinese arbitration centres.[71] The test rests on how the CICC will operate as a court, meaning also to what extent it will operate as a Chinese or international institution.[72]

However, such a jurisdictional approach may pose difficulties in practice. The first difficulty would be how to draft an effective dispute resolution clause in order to choose the CICC as the dispute resolution forum. In addition, there is not always a positive correlation between the total value of the contract and the amount in dispute.[73] That is to say, one cannot predict the 'size of the dispute' when drafting an effective dispute resolution clause, which produces too much uncertainty.[74] In these circumstances, some practitioners propose the adoption of a 'non-exclusive' choice of forum clause clarifying that disputes with monetary value exceeding RMB 300 million will be submitted to the CICC; otherwise they will be submitted to an arbitral tribunal or other Chinese courts.[75]

It is also noted that, at first glance, the quantifiable threshold might lighten the CICC's workload. Nevertheless, as Wei Sun has pointed out, cases exceeding RMB 300 million may still have trouble in reaching CICC, either due to change in the claims by the claimant or the filing

[69] 'Supreme People's Court Issues Rules of Procedure for the China International Commercial Courts'.

[70] Zhou and Harpainter, 'Survey Results'.

[71] See the CICC, where it is mentioned. 'According to applications made by relevant institutions, and after taking into account the number of international commercial cases accepted, the international influence and the construction of informatization, it is hereby determined that the China International Economic and Trade Arbitration Commission, the Shanghai International Economic and Trade Arbitration Commission, the Shenzhen Court of International Arbitration, the Beijing Arbitration Commission, the China Maritime Arbitration Commission, the Mediation Center of China Council for the Promotion of International Trade and the Shanghai Commercial Mediation Center [are] to be included in the first group of arbitration and mediation institutions in the "one-stop" diversified international commercial dispute resolution mechanism ("the Mechanism").'

[72] Bookman, 'The Adjudication Business'.

[73] Wei Sun, 'International Commercial Court in China'.

[74] Li Huanzhi, 'China's International Commercial Court'.

[75] Ibid.

of counterclaims by the defendant.[76] In some cases, parties may be deprived of autonomy if the higher courts or the SPC transfers the disputes to the CICC.[77] Under Art. 2(3) of the Provision, the CICC may also encourage use of arbitration for BRI disputes, given the judicial assistance for the enforcement of preservation measures and awards of international arbitration.

It is essential to read Art. 2 of the Provisions in conjunction with Chinese Civil Procedure Law (CPL), particularly Art. 34 of the CPL,[78] which stipulates several locations that might have 'connection with the disputes' where parties may agree, in writing, to jurisdiction of a court. Li argues that the CICC 'would have difficulty satisfying the demands of parties seeking a neutral forum' for BRI disputes. In other words, the 'CICC might only facilitate the resolution of cases which are already under Chinese jurisdiction'.[79] This practice differs from the Singapore International Commercial Court (SICC) and the Dubai International Financial Centre Courts (DIFCCs), which do not require that the dispute have an actual connection with Singapore or Dubai.[80]

The numerous advantages of international arbitration over litigation in national courts for international commercial disputes are well known, and include neutrality (no 'home court advantage' for one party), flexibility of procedure, confidentiality, finality of the decision (no appeals), the ability to select arbitrators who are knowledgeable about the subject matter of the dispute and the enforceability of arbitral awards in 159 countries[81] (based on the Convention on the Recognition and Enforcement of Foreign

[76] Wei Sun, 'International Commercial Court in China'.

[77] CICC Article 2(2), Article 2(5).

[78] 'The parties to a contractual dispute or any other property dispute may agree in writing to be subject to the jurisdiction of the People's court at the place having connection with the dispute, such as where the defendant is domiciled, where the contract is performed, where the contract is signed, where the plaintiff is domiciled or where the subject matter is located, etc., provided that such agreement does not violate the provisions of the Law regarding court-level jurisdictions and exclusive jurisdictions.' The Chinese version emphasizes the 'actual connection with the dispute'. See ≪中华人民共和国民事诉讼法≫ 'Civil Procedure Law of the People's Republic of China (Revised in 2017)' (China International Commercial Court, June 29 2017) Article 34, http://cicc.court.gov.cn/html/1/219/199/200/644.html. Last accessed 13 December 2019.

[79] Li Huanzhi, 'China's International Commercial Court'.

[80] Ibid.

[81] 'Status: Convention on the Recognition and Enforcement of Foreign Arbitral Awards' (UNCITRAL, 2019), www.uncitral.org/uncitral/en/uncitral_texts/arbitration/NYConvention_status.html. Last accessed 13 December 2019.

Arbitral Awards (the New York Convention)).[82] The parties' ability to select arbitrators who are knowledgeable about the subject matter of the dispute is particularly important for construction, infrastructure and energy disputes, which tend to be very technical and complex, often involving multiple parties, multiple contracts and voluminous documentation.

Several international arbitral institutions are positioning themselves to attract BRI-related disputes. The International Court of Arbitration of the International Chamber of Commerce (ICC), the world's leading international arbitral institution, announced in March 2018 the establishment of a commission to consider how the ICC can best respond to dispute resolution opportunities arising from BRI projects.[83] The ICC emphasized that its existing procedures are already well suited to BRI disputes, and that it can also provide the necessary mediation, commercial as well as investor-state arbitration.[84]

Furthermore, the Hong Kong International Arbitration Centre (HKIAC) announced the creation of a Belt and Road Advisory Committee and an online resource platform dedicated to the BRI in April 2018.[85] While the HKIAC has offered a model dispute resolution clause that calls directly for arbitration,[86] it has been suggested that this clause would be improved by making it a 'hybrid clause', combining both mediation and arbitration, since there is a long-standing culture of mediating disputes in Asia, given that arbitration may still be perceived as expensive and detrimental to parties' commercial relations.[87]

[82] Convention on the Recognition and Enforcement of Foreign Arbitral Awards (New York Convention 1958) 330 UNTS 38 (1959), www.uncitral.org/uncitral/en/uncitral_texts/arbitration/NYConvention.html. Last accessed 13 December 2019.

[83] 'ICC Court Launches Belt and Road Initiative Commission' (International Chamber of Commerce, 5 March 2018), https://iccwbo.org/media-wall/news-speeches/icc-court-launches-belt-road-initiative-commission. Last accessed 13 December 2019.

[84] Ibid.

[85] 'Press Release: HKIAC Announces Belt and Road Programme' (Hong Kong International Arbitration Centre, 26 April 2018), www.hkiac.org/news/hkiac-announces-belt-and-road-programme. Last accessed 13 December 2019.

[86] 'Model Clauses for Belt and Road Contracts' (Hong Kong International Arbitration Centre), www.hkiac.org/Belt-and-Road/model-clauses-belt-and-road-contracts. Last accessed 13 December 2019.

[87] Stephanie Tang, 'HKIAC's New Belt and Road Programme: Does More Need to be Done?' (*Kluwer Arbitration Blog*, 27 June 2018), http://arbitrationblog.kluwerarbitration.com/2018/06/27/hkiacs-new-belt-road-programme-need-done. Last accessed 13 December 2019.

Additionally, the Singapore International Arbitration Center (SIAC) is a strong contender for resolving BRI disputes; as Singapore is currently the most popular seat for arbitration in Asia and the third most popular seat for arbitration in the world.[88] Compared with the SIAC, as illustrated previously, only Chinese citizens can serve as judges on the CICC, even if the applicable law is foreign law, and only Chinese admitted lawyers can act as legal representatives.[89] As discussed earlier in this chapter, the CICC has established the Expert Committee as an institutional innovation within a rigid and traditional legal system. Whereas the practical value of this Committee remains to be seen, it is obvious that the CICC may not possess the same attractiveness in terms of referring to leading international experts and flexible rules of representation for foreign lawyers.

However, the CICC will not have automatic jurisdiction over BRI-related disputes: participants in BRI projects will have to select the CICC in the dispute resolution clauses of their contracts or agree to its jurisdiction once a dispute arises. The memorandums of understanding (MOUs) that China signed with participating countries may require that BRI-related disputes be submitted to the CICC; this does not appear to be the case, and is to be evaluated on a case-by-case basis.[90] However, foreign parties may not want to have their disputes with Chinese parties heard by Chinese courts, whose independence and impartiality they may doubt. They also may not want their dispute to be decided based on Chinese law, which is relatively unknown outside of China. Parties to cross-border projects and transactions often select an established and well-known law, such as English or New York law, as the law governing their contract.

Much is still unclear about how the CICC will function. The proceedings will be in Chinese, but evidence can be submitted in English without translation, if the opposing party consents.[91] The CICC also offers translation at the parties' expense.[92] The CICC needs to establish strong

[88] '2018 International Arbitration Survey: The Evolution of International Arbitration' (Queen Mary University of London, 9 May 2018), www.arbitration.qmul.ac.uk/research/2018. Last accessed 13 December 2019.

[89] Article 9 of Chinese Judges Law.

[90] 'China Briefing: Confusion over Dispute Resolution at China's New Belt and Road Courts' (Dezan Shira & Associates, 2 February 2018) 1, www.china-briefing.com/news/bilateral-confusion-dispute-resolution-chinas-new-belt-road-courts. Last accessed 13 December 2019.

[91] CICC Article 9.

[92] Ibid. Article 6.

procedures for reviewing and interpreting laws and regulations, as there are numerous non-English-speaking countries along the BRI.

There are also difficulties posed by higher Chinese laws. In the absence of a 'full-scale' revision of the current laws, establishing some special procedures for the CICC would not eliminate parties' concerns regarding the Chinese judicial system as a whole. For instance, Art. 27 (6) of the CICC Rules provides general regulations concerning the exchange of evidence in a pretrial conference; however, the Chinese CPL does not provide any compulsory requirement for evidence disclosure before the start of a hearing. The possibility of facing surprising evidence may become one of the biggest obstacles for common law lawyers to trust Chinese judicial proceedings.[93]

Finally, there are concerns about the finality of mediated settlements and arbitral awards. Article 16 of the Provision applies to the retrial of a 'legally effective judgment, ruling or conciliation statement made by the International Commercial Court'[94]. This clause should be read together with Art. 201 of CPL if a party can prove the conciliation is not voluntary or the consent of the parties violates the law.[95] However, the application for setting aside or enforcement of an arbitral award is regulated separately by Art. 14 of the Provisions.[96] In this regard, Art. 274 of the Chinese CPL comes into play.[97] The foregoing analysis highlights the confusion

93 Li Huanzhi, 'China's International Commercial Court'.

94 CICC Article 16.

95 CPL Article 201, where it is stated, 'With respect to a legally effective conciliation statement, if evidence furnished by a party proves that the conciliation violates the principle of voluntariness or that the content of the conciliation agreement violates the law, the party may apply for a retrial. If the foregoing proves true after its examination, the People's court shall retry the case.'

96 CICC Article 14 states, 'Where a party makes an application to the International Commercial Court for setting aside or enforcement of an arbitral award rendered by an international commercial arbitration institution under Article 11 paragraph 1 of these Provisions, the International Commercial Court shall review the application in accordance with provisions of the Civil Procedure Law and other related legal provisions.

97 CPL Article 274 states, 'A People's court shall, after examination and verification by a collegial panel of the court, make a written order not to allow the execution of the award rendered by an arbitral organ of the People's Republic of China handling cases involving foreign element, if the party against whom the application for execution is made furnishes proof that:

(1) the parties have not had an arbitration clause in the contract or have not subsequently reached a written arbitration agreement;
(2) the party against whom the application for execution is made is not given notice for the appointment of an arbitrator or for the inception of the arbitration proceedings or is unable to present his case due to causes for which he is not responsible;

which may arise due to the language of the Provisions, especially for many foreign parties who are not familiar with Chinese CPL.

19.4.2 The Question of Enforceability of China International Commercial Court Judgments

For all courts and hybrid courts, a major issue is enforceability of their judgments. There is no international treaty for the recognition and enforcement of foreign court judgments comparable to the New York Convention for foreign arbitral awards. This means that even if a foreign party prevailed against a Chinese party in the CICC, the foreign party would likely have difficulty getting that Chinese court judgment recognized and enforced by a court outside of China. To improve the enforceability of CICC judgments, China is party to the negotiations over the Hague Convention on the Recognition and Enforcement of Foreign Judgments.[98] Additionally, China is considering ratifying the Hague Convention on the Choice of Court Agreements (COCA).[99] Currently, cross-border enforcement of Chinese court judgments can be achieved in a limited number of foreign jurisdictions through international treaties, bilateral treaties and the principle of reciprocity. As of September 2018, China has entered into twenty Sino-foreign treaties on judicial assistance in civil and commercial matters, covering only a small number of the BRI countries and regions.[100]

As for the reciprocity, though, is unlikely to provide a reliable basis to seek enforcement of CICC judgments abroad because the issue of reciprocity would be determined solely by the court in the foreign jurisdiction. This uncertainty may hinder the development of CICC as the parties will not be able to reliably predict whether a foreign jurisdiction would recognize a CICC judgment.

(3) the composition of the arbitration tribunal or the procedure for arbitration is not in conformity with the rules of arbitration; or
(4) the matters dealt with by the award fall outside the scope of the arbitration agreement or which the arbitral organ is not empowered to arbitrate.

If the People's court determines that the execution of the award goes against the social and public interest of the country, the People's court shall make a written order not to allow the execution of the arbitral award.'

98 Freshfields Bruckhaus Deringer, 'China Establishes International Commercial Courts to Handle Belt and Road Initiative Disputes'.

99 Ibid.

100 A list of the judicial assistance treaties that China has entered into is posted online at the website of the Ministry of Foreign Affairs of the People's Republic of China, at http://treaty.mfa.gov.cn/Treaty/web/index.jsp.

19.5 Conclusion

The CICC represents a major legal innovation in China. However, the CICC is still at an embryonic stage of development in the broader context of hybrid courts. It might be too early to judge its success as it seems to be a deeply Chinese court in many ways, such as the proceedings are in Chinese, subject to Chinese procedure rules and adjudicated by Chinese judges. The enforcement of the judgment also poses a certain risk for the development of the CICC. There are also a number of features and characteristics that suggest a great potential for the CICC. For instance, as the chapter discussed, the court is likely to have a positive effect on the competence of the Chinese judiciary in terms of international trade and investment issues.[101]

It is also important to highlight very recent developments, in particular, the publication of the CICC Rules of Procedure, which is a key step in the development of the institution following the establishment of CICC in July 2018. The CICC Rules of Procedure place great emphasis on the efficiency in the meanwhile facilitating alternative dispute resolution for instance arbitration and mediation. However, it is still unclear about how the CICC Rules of Procedure will be used in practice and how popular the CICC would be as a judicial forum for resolving international commercial disputes. The CICC Rules of Procedure, the CICC Expert Committee Rules, and the nomination of one-stop-shop institutions indicate the ambition of the CICC to serve China's Belt-and-Road Initiative.

In this twilight, the CICC will also have to be assessed with respect to its capacity to abide by the international standards of due process and to what extent the parties to the dispute can truly voluntarily consent to the court' s jurisdiction. It remains uncertain to what extent the CICC will enable China to expand its institutional influence in the world.[102] The parties' willingness to arbitrate and the standard of due process which, far from casting doubts as to the potential role of the CICC, in fact, reveal the considerable role the CICC could play in the further engagement of China with economic and legal globalization. In this respect, the CICC is undoubtedly a major addition to the different hybrid courts that already exist in the world, and might well become a benchmark of Chinese involvement with legal globalization.

[101] Finder, 'China International Commercial Court Starts Operating'.
[102] Bookman, 'The Adjudication Business'.

20

The Emergence of International Commercial Courts and Dispute Resolution Centres in Frontier Markets

A Perspective from Kazakhstan

THE RT. HON. THE LORD WOOLF CH AND CHRISTOPHER CAMPBELL-HOLT

20.1 Introduction

The formation of international financial centres has become a common strategic focus for rapidly developing and modernising states.[1] The presence of such centres assists with the creation and redistribution of world financial income, attracting capital, generating income from taxes, contributing to the innovative development of economies and increasing the role of states in global governance. By eliminating barriers between domestic and global financial markets, developing ties between them, these centres can positively contribute to attracting foreign investment.[2]

The creation of the Astana International Financial Centre (AIFC) in Kazakhstan is one recent example of an initiative to assist a rapidly developing frontier market, Kazakhstan, to become a more competitive economy regionally and globally. What follows in this chapter is the perspective of what has been achieved in Kazakhstan with unique first-hand insight and analysis of what is required to successfully create international standard dispute resolution systems in frontier markets. It is hoped that the contents of this chapter will assist other frontier

[1] See, for example, Georgios Dimitropoulos and Stavros Brekoulakis, 'Introduction', in this volume; Georgios Dimitropoulos, 'International Commercial Courts in the "Modern Law of Nature": Adjudicatory Unilateralism in Special Economic Zones' (2021) 24 Journal of International Economic Law 361.

[2] See, for example, Sir William Blair, 'The New Litigation Landscape: International Commercial Courts and Procedural Innovations', International Journal of Procedural Law 2019 no. 2, p. 221.

markets, including other countries in Central Asia, to create their own international dispute resolution systems.

20.2 Establishing a New Dispute Resolution System

Since 2018, the AIFC has been officially operating in Nur-Sultan, formerly Astana, the capital city of Kazakhstan. The AIFC Court and the International Arbitration Centre (IAC) are two distinct and important independent bodies providing international standard commercial dispute resolution at the AIFC.[3]

The Article of the First President of the Republic of Kazakhstan, 'The Nation's Plan: The Road to the Kazakhstani Dream', stated that 'The central question of the third direction of the Nation's Plan is the creation of the Astana International Financial Centre with an independent judicial system, a separate jurisdiction based on the principles of English law, with the application of English language and the introduction of the investment residency principle.'[4] The full significance of this initiative has to be seen against the background of the changes that had already taken place in Kazakhstan's legal system. This is not a common law system but a civil law system, bearing close relation to the systems found in the majority of centres on the mainland of Europe.

The judiciary of the Republic of Kazakhstan had already been the subject of reform. In 2000, the Decree of the First President was adopted. This separated the executive from the existing judiciary and transferred the operation of the courts in Kazakhstan from the Ministry of Justice to the Committee of Court Administration under the Kazakhstan Supreme Court. That court was already established in the Supreme Court's building in Nur-Sultan. However, the effect of the announcement of the First President at the opening of the Congress meant inevitably there was to be a new system of justice to support the AIFC.

[3] The Elbasy of the Republic of Kazakhstan, Nursultan Nazarbayev, showed great vision in creating the AIFC. The Elbasy is the First President of the independent Republic of Kazakhstan and the 'Father of the Nation'. His intention to create the AIFC was reflected in the Plan of the Nation, '100 Concrete Steps', which was the next step to implement five institutional reforms. The Plan was announced at the XVI Congress of the Nur Otan Party on 11 March 2015 with the aim to achieve 'a modern state for all'. There would be an international financial centre in Astana (Nur-Sultan). The international centre was to include a court founded on the principles of English law.

[4] See Nursultan Nazarbayev, 'The Nation's Plan: The Road to the Kazakhstani Dream', *Astana Times*, 12 January 2016: Plan of the Nation: The Path to the Kazakhstan Dream (astanatimes.com).

It would mean two systems of justice in Kazakhstan – its traditional system and a new system supported by the AIFC Court and the IAC. Both the AIFC Court and the IAC now provide critical support for the role of the AIFC and ensure that the AIFC is a flagbearer for the rule of law. This flag is a huge support for the commercial activities of the AIFC.

From February 2017, Lord Woolf and Christopher Campbell-Holt were engaged by the AIFC to advise on the establishment of the AIFC Court and the IAC. From 1 January 2018, the AIFC Court and the IAC had been established in a record time as separate independent legal entities and became fully operational. The AIFC Court and the IAC were established following the approval of the AIFC Court Regulations 2017 and the AIFC Arbitration Regulations 2017 by the AIFC Management Council.[5]

Before this could happen, the Parliament of Kazakhstan enacted the AIFC Constitutional Statute 2015, which provided for the establishment of the AIFC. More specifically, the AIFC Constitutional Statute 2015 provided for the establishment of the AIFC Court in Article 13, which provides that the AIFC Court shall be 'independent in its activities and is not part of the judicial system of the Republic of Kazakhstan', and Regulation 11 of the AIFC Court Regulations 2017 provides for the judges of the AIFC Court to have 'complete independence' and to 'act independently and impartially' when performing their judicial functions. Article 14 of the AIFC Constitutional Statute provided for the establishment of the IAC and the AIFC Arbitration Regulations 2017 and IAC Arbitration and Mediation Rules 2018 provided the requirements of independence and impartiality for arbitrators. In March 2017 the Constitution of Kazakhstan was amended in order to enable a legal regime for a financial centre, the AIFC, in Nur-Sultan, in Kazakhstan.[6]

Now at the heart of the AIFC is a legal system that has been created to apply common law and international best practices so as to attract investment by enabling effective commercial practices and providing

[5] See AIFC Court Regulations (Resolution of the AIFC Management Council) 2017 (https://aifc.kz/files/legals/68/file/3.-legislation-aifc-court-regulations-2017.pdf) and AIFC Arbitration Regulations (Resolution of the AIFC Management Council) 2017 (https://aifc.kz/files/legals/73/file/aifc-arbitration-regulations-2017.pdf).

[6] Lord Woolf became the AIFC Court's first Chief Justice from 1 January 2018. He retired on 31 January 2020 and from 1 February 2020 The Rt. Hon. The Lord Mance, the former Deputy President of the UK Supreme Court, was appointed to be the new Chief Justice of the AIFC Court. Since 1 January 2018 Barbara Dohmann QC has been the IAC Chairman and Christopher Campbell-Holt has been the Registrar and Chief Executive of the AIFC Court and the IAC.

robust protection of investor rights. The AIFC Court and the IAC are the ultimate safeguards to protect investor rights at the AIFC and they provide justice that accords with the rule of law.

The rule of law is a concept whose precise meaning is difficult to define. It has been defined in a book by the same name by one of the UK's most distinguished judges, the late Lord Bingham.[7] He noted that the rule of law takes its identity from its context so it is important to ascertain its meaning from the context in which it is being considered.[8] The rule of law has many requirements. In particular it requires that every individual is entitled to access to a court or dispute resolution forum for the determination of his or her rights and to be treated equally and fairly in the same way as anyone else subject to the court's or dispute resolution forum's jurisdiction. Every party in a dispute deserves to have his or her case determined in accordance with the law of the land. This includes having fair consideration of the dispute by independent and incorruptible judges, arbitrators or other types of dispute resolution professionals, who conduct the case and give a decision with reasonable expedition. Citizens who live in a country which adheres to the rule of law can be confident that their disputes will be resolved in a just manner and that justice will not only be done but it will also be seen to be done.

The reason the AIFC Court and the IAC were established is relevant to the consideration of what the rule of law requires. The AIFC required the creation of a special court and arbitration centre because it appreciated that its prospect of success as a commercial centre would be greatly increased if investors involved with the AIFC, many of whom are expected to come from outside Kazakhstan, are satisfied that the AIFC is a safe environment in which to invest. International investors look to invest in jurisdictions which recognise and apply the rule of law. Any commercial decision outside of an investor's home jurisdiction involves increased risk. Investors know that from time to time disputes in business will arise and they may well require the assistance of a court or arbitration centre to resolve them. When this happens, they want the protection the rule of law provides. Risk is significantly reduced if a court and arbitration centre exist which complies with the requirements of the rule of law.

In recent times courts and arbitration centres similar to what has been established in the AIFC have been established in other countries where new commercial centres have been created to attract investment,

[7] Tom Bingham, *The Rule of Law* (Penguin, 2011).

[8] Ibid.

including in Singapore, Hong Kong, Qatar, Dubai and Abu Dhabi. Other countries inherited common law systems including commercial law from the UK, including Australia, Canada, India, Malaysia and New Zealand. Like the AIFC, these jurisdictions have systems of justice which are substantially based on the common law system of justice designed to operate in accord with the rule of law. The models of commercial dispute resolution institutions in these jurisdictions were considered when deciding upon the model which should be adopted at the AIFC.

The AIFC Court and the IAC are still in their early years of operation but outstanding results have been achieved ahead of time and more quickly than at any other international financial centre. By the end of February 2021, the AIFC Court had given seventeen judgments and orders and additional cases were ongoing. All resolved cases had been enforced in Kazakhstan to 100 per cent satisfaction.[9] Seven hundred eighty-six arbitration and mediation cases had been successfully resolved at the IAC.[10] The cases at the IAC were predominantly mediation cases, reflecting the appetite for commercial parties in disputes in Kazakhstan to resolve their disputes amicably via mediation without needing to pursue more formal arbitration or litigation. The case parties came from Kazakhstan, the UK, Russia, China, Uzbekistan, Poland, Azerbaijan, Turkey and India. The law applied in the cases was predominantly the law of the AIFC, Kazakhstan and Russia. The nature of the disputes covered all areas of commercial practice including finance, sales, property, land and general contract matters. Three hundred thirteen lawyers from twenty-nine jurisdictions around the world (twenty-five countries) had registered with the AIFC Court for rights of audience.[11] The AIFC Court and the IAC were included in the dispute resolution clauses of thousands of business contracts of businesses in Kazakhstan and elsewhere.

The AIFC and the IAC are playing a central role in establishing Kazakhstan as a successful commercial centre with all of the facilities and international standards that investors expect such institutions to have. The establishment of the AIFC Court and the IAC will significantly increase the attractiveness of investment in the AIFC, Kazakhstan and the wider Central Asia region where at present there are no comparable commercial dispute resolution institutions.

[9] See the AIFC Court website: https://court.aifc.kz/enforcement.
[10] See the IAC website: https://iac.aifc.kz.
[11] See the AIFC Court website: https://iac.aifc.kz.

20.3 The Key Features of a New Dispute Resolution System

Judges, Arbitrators, Mediators and Other Dispute Resolution Professionals

The current Chief Justice of the AIFC Court, Lord Mance, is supported by nine judges. The judges are amongst the most experienced and distinguished judges from the common law world. The IAC has, in addition to Chairman Barbara Dohmann QC, a panel of outstanding arbitrators and mediators comprising highly experienced and multilingual professionals from around the world.

The judges, arbitrators, mediators and other dispute resolution professionals at the AIFC Court and the IAC have global reputations for absolute independence, impartiality, integrity and incorruptibility. They are committed to the rule of law and uphold the same judicial standards and legal principles that have been developed and applied over many years by commercial dispute resolution centres in the UK and elsewhere. In particular, they all have considerable experience and interactions over many years with commercial entities and individuals who they represented as lawyers. That background gives them experience and understanding of the commercial world and they understand the need for commercial law to reflect the needs of the business community. They ensure that the AIFC Court and the IAC meet the expectations of the international business community by ensuring provision of predictable legal protection in a timely manner. Disputes will be decided only on their merits without regard to nationality, politics, religion or race.

Services

The AIFC Court provides litigation proceedings with application of the most modern procedural rules modelled on the rules of other common law courts including the courts of England and Wales. It also provides judicial mediation – that is, mediation of a dispute before litigation by a judge of the AIFC Court.[12] That judge would not then consider the case as a judge of the AIFC Court if the case progressed to litigation at the AIFC Court. The judges of the AIFC Court also have considerable experience in commercial arbitration and the AIFC Court provides limited supervision of IAC arbitration cases guided by the principle of non-intervention.

[12] See the AIFC Court website: https://court.aifc.kz/judicial-mediation.

The IAC provides four main dispute resolution services: 1. Arbitration – exclusive administration of arbitrations governed by the IAC Arbitration and Mediation Rules, subject to the agreement of the parties to a case; administered arbitrations governed by UNCITRAL Arbitration Rules and ad hoc arbitration rules subject to the agreement of the parties to a case; 2. Mediation – mediations governed by the IAC Arbitration and Mediation Rules and ad hoc mediation rules subject to the agreement of the parties to a case, as well as other forms of alternative dispute resolution subject to the agreement of the parties to a case; 3. Appointments – an appointment authority, assisting with the appointment of arbitrators and mediators to arbitrations and mediations conducted at the IAC or elsewhere; and 4. Fundholding – fundholding, holding and disbursing advances in relation to costs associated with use of the IAC's services and facilities.[13]

Jurisdiction, Levels, Precedent and Rights of Audience

The AIFC Court has the sole power to determine the proper scope of its jurisdiction within the limits of its competence given by AIFC law. It does not have jurisdiction to hear administrative[14] or criminal cases but it does have jurisdiction to: 1. Interpret AIFC regulations; and 2. Adjudicate any disputes: (a) between AIFC registered companies (AIFC Participants), AIFC bodies and/or their foreign (i.e. non-Kazakh nationals) employees; (b) relating to operations carried out in the AIFC and regulated by the AIFC Acting Law; and (c) transferred to the Court by agreement of the parties (i.e. 'opt-in' jurisdiction for parties who do not otherwise have any connection to the AIFC).[15] Parties may file applications to the AIFC Court applying any law, whether it is common law or civil law, AIFC law or otherwise, provided all of the parties to the case agree and the AIFC Court decides that it is appropriate for it to have jurisdiction.

[13] See the IAC website: https://iac.aifc.kz/our-services.

[14] The term 'administrative' is used to refer to matters such as road traffic offences or immigration issues which are dealt with by the RK Administrative Court. It is not intended to limit the review by the AIFC Court or an AIFC body such as AFSA, the AIFC regulator. It differs from its meaning in English law. See AIFC Court Regulations 2017, Article 26(5), which provides that 'The [AIFC] Court of First Instance has jurisdiction to hear and determine an appeal from the decision of an AIFC Body . . . where the appeal relates to: (a) a question of law; (b) an allegation of a miscarriage of justice; (c) an issue of procedural fairness; or (d) a matter provided for in or under AIFC law.'

[15] See AIFC Constitutional Statute 2015, Article 13.

Similar to other international arbitration centres, the IAC considers disputes where the governing law of the dispute is AIFC law or any other law as agreed by the parties to the dispute. The AIFC Arbitration Regulations provide the AIFC as the seat in an arbitration at the IAC where the seat has not been agreed by the parties. But parties can agree to have an alternative jurisdiction as the seat in their arbitration proceedings at the IAC if they agree to do so.[16] This flexibility has been provided to the IAC to give case parties maximum choice and flexibility and to enable dispute resolution on legal and procedural terms that most appropriately fits the needs of the parties and justice in each individual case.

The AIFC Court has three different levels: 1. The Small Claims Court is a division of the AIFC Court of First Instance, with specialist judges and procedures for cost-effective and timely resolution of disputes valued up to USD 150,000. 2. The AIFC Court of First Instance is the first court where disputes are heard applying the AIFC Court's Rules. It also considers appeals from the AIFC Small Claims Court. 3. The AIFC Court of Appeal will hear appeals from the AIFC Court of First Instance. Its decisions are final and not subject to appeal.[17] To appeal to the AIFC Court of Appeal requires litigants to have been given permission to appeal by the AIFC Court of First Instance or the AIFC Court of Appeal. The AIFC Court has already successfully resolved numerous small claims, first-instance claims and a permission to appeal application.

The AIFC Court may consider final judgments of the AIFC Court in related matters and final judgments of the courts of other jurisdictions when deciding cases.[18] While there is no automatic binding precedent of previous AIFC Court decisions on future AIFC Court decisions,[19] it is expected that the flexibility inherent in the procedures and the approach that is expected to be adopted at the AIFC Court will enable the AIFC common law system to develop principles incrementally and keep up to date without producing uncertainty.

Within the framework of AIFC statute or written AIFC law, the AIFC law is being developed by the judges of the AIFC Court through their

[16] See AIFC Arbitration Regulations 2018, Regulation 30.

[17] See AIFC Constitutional Statute 2015, Article 13(7).

[18] See ibid., Article 13(6).

[19] See ibid., Article 13(6) which says, 'the AIFC Court . . . may also take into account final judgments of the AIFC Court in related matters and final judgments of the courts of other common law jurisdictions'. The provision of 'may' enables the AIFC Court to take into final judgments of other common law courts. It does not require the AIFC Court to do so.

decisions in cases at the AIFC Court with application of legal principles to new circumstances in a way that is sensitive to the particular commercial context of the case in dispute. AIFC Court decisions also continue to be made accessible and transparent via the AIFC Court website and in law reports, textbooks and media which analyse the effect of the decisions with a view to identifying the principles that underlie them. This will assist parties and their lawyers to understand their legal positions under the AIFC law and to be able to make a reasonable prediction of the outcome of any disputes that will be considered by the AIFC Court.

The AIFC Court has extremely wide rights of audience. All lawyers have rights of audience provided the lawyer has a practising certificate from anywhere in the world, or in the case of Kazakhstan lawyers, qualified by a law degree and some court experience.[20] Similar to other frontier markets, in Kazakhstan there is no centrally administered regulatory body to regulate the training and practices of Kazakhstani lawyers and without this special rights of audience provision they would not be able to represent parties in cases at the AIFC Court. By comparison, the IAC is accessible to all lawyers and professionals to represent parties in cases at the IAC.

Rules

The procedural rules of the AIFC Court and IAC were drafted by leading dispute resolution professionals including Lord Woolf, Barbara Dohmann QC, Tom Montagu-Smith QC and Christopher Campbell-Holt. When creating a new judicial system, it is all too easy to overcomplicate matters by underestimating the importance of a court and arbitration centre having the appropriate powers and avoiding unnecessary complexities which can delay or restrict justice. With this in mind practical procedural rules were drafted for the AIFC Court and IAC that foster predictability and enable cases to be dealt with in a way that is proportionate to their complexity. The procedural rules include all of the modern innovations of other international dispute resolution institutions and are sensitive to the unique needs of commercial court and dispute resolution institution users but in as short a number of rules as possible to avoid unnecessary complexity.

[20] The special rights of audience provision for Kazakhstani lawyers was developed to create a level playing field. See AIFC Court website: https://court.aifc.kz/rights-of-audience.

The procedural rules of the AIFC Court and IAC clearly set out their approach. The AIFC Court Rules 2018 provide at Rule 1 that the AIFC Court has the overriding objective to deal with cases justly. Dealing with cases justly includes, so far as practicable: ensuring that the system of justice is accessible and fair; ensuring the parties are on an equal footing; ensuring that litigation takes place expeditiously and effectively, using no more resources than is necessary; dealing with cases in ways that are proportionate to the amount of money involved, the importance of the case, the complexity of the issues, facts and arguments, and the financial position of each party; and making appropriate use of IT. The IAC Arbitration and Mediation Rules 2018 provide at Rule 2.1 that the overriding objective of the IAC is to obtain the fair resolution of disputes by an impartial tribunal without unnecessary delay or expense.

There are other more specific rules in the AIFC Court and IAC Rules but they do no more than amplify or illustrate the overriding objectives. They give the judges of the AIFC Court and the arbitrators and mediators of the IAC the wide discretion and flexibility they need to do justice in individual cases.

Enforcement of AIFC Court and IAC Decisions and Awards

Enforcement of AIFC Court decisions and IAC arbitration awards is critically important. If this cannot happen, the successful party in a dispute resolution will be left with a sense of injustice. It is this fear of injustice that deters investors who could profitably do business with a particular country from doing so, to the economic disadvantage of the country with which they could have otherwise done business.

Enforcement of AIFC Court decisions within Kazakhstan is carried out in the same manner as the enforcement of decisions of other courts in the Kazakhstan legal system.[21] Translations of the AIFC Court's decisions into the Russian and Kazakh languages are authorised by the AIFC Court in accordance with the AIFC Acting Law and provided to the Kazakhstan authorities for enforcement purposes. In practice, enforcement of AIFC Court decisions in Kazakhstan is ensured by the implementation of step-by-step procedures of the AIFC Court and the enforcement authorities in Kazakhstan. The procedures are implemented with the closest supervision of the AIFC Court Registry and the enforcement agents, and the result by the end of February 2021 was that all AIFC

[21] See AIFC Constitutional Statute 2015, Article 13(8).

Court decisions had been enforced within Kazakhstan to 100 per cent satisfaction.[22]

Enforcement of AIFC Court decisions in countries outside of Kazakhstan will happen with the support of the Kazakhstan authorities in accordance with international agreements that provide for mutual recognition and enforcement of court decisions. The AIFC Court is also a member of the Standing International Forum for Commercial Courts and works in close cooperation with the many jurisdictions that are represented by the membership of that organisation including on enforcement of court decisions.

The IAC arbitration awards are enforced in Kazakhstan as Orders of the AIFC Court.[23] The procedure to convert an IAC arbitration award into an Order of the AIFC Court for enforcement purposes is simple and expedient. The IAC arbitration awards have been recognised by the AIFC Court and judgments and execution orders of the AIFC Court have been given within a matter of hours of such applications being filed at the AIFC Court Registry. Kazakhstan acceded to the New York Convention 1958 and enforcement of IAC arbitration awards in countries outside of Kazakhstan shall happen in accordance with that Convention.

Premises and Information Technology

The AIFC Court and IAC have international standard physical premises at the EXPO-2017 site in Nur-Sultan with advanced meeting and conference rooms, hearing rooms and office facilities for all lawyers, judges, arbitrators and mediators.

The AIFC Court and IAC also have innovative modern digital technology to assist with timely and cost-effective case management and overall dispute resolution. eJustice was launched at the AIFC Court and IAC in February 2019. It provides immediate 24/7 access to all documents in a given case to the parties, judges, arbitrators and mediators working on that case from initiation to final disposition of the case. Video technology is used for oral hearings when a judge, arbitrator or mediator decides that an in-person hearing is not necessary or appropriate.

[22] See the AIFC Court website: https://court.aifc.kz/enforcement.

[23] See AIFC Court Regulations 2018, Regulation 26(8), and see AIFC Arbitration Regulations 2018, Regulations 45(1) and 46(1).

20.4 Conclusion

The successful establishment and operation of the AIFC Court and IAC has ensured that the AIFC has a dispute resolution system that applies the strictest standards of the rule of law. With proven case resolution numbers, enforcement of decisions, inclusion in the dispute resolution clauses of business contracts, and significant outreach, promotions and training programmes, both institutions are quickly becoming the model for other countries in Central Asia and frontier markets to adopt. This is a powerful signal to the international commercial world that Kazakhstan has a modern international dispute resolution system that is committed to the strictest adherence to the rule of law and that can be trusted by investors. It is the model to which other countries in Central Asia and frontier markets will turn.

21

Brexit and the Competition of Dispute Resolution Fora in Europe

Whither the Rush to English Courts Post Withdrawal?

GEERT VAN CALSTER

21.1 Introduction

The United Kingdom's prime position as a forum of choice in international commercial dispute resolution is well documented, including by contributors to this volume. This enviable position of UK (in particular English) courts predates UK membership in the European Union (EU). However, it is clear that following that membership, the attraction of a United Kingdom court judgment has been increased, given the swift, near-automatic recognition and enforcement of judgments from UK courts across the European continent.

This chapter reviews some core points on the impact on the competition for dispute resolution in Europe, of the withdrawal of the United Kingdom from the EU – a process colloquially known as 'Brexit', given that with UK EU membership, the aforementioned recognition and enforcement mechanism will no longer apply. This chapter is structured as follows. In Section 21.2 I discuss the EU's overall view on forum shopping in international litigation. In Section 21.3 I highlight the UK's role in the same. Section 21.4 discusses in detail the impact of Brexit on the formal arrangements with UK judgments. Section 21.5 concludes.

21.2 Regulatory Competition in Civil Procedure and Private International law

European Union Member States, as well as indeed States all over the world, have the tendency to employ their courts system as one element of a State's regulatory structure which may lead parties to litigate in that State as opposed to others.[1] The coinciding phenomenon of selecting one particular court rather than another is referred to as 'forum selection' if one is inclined to see the attractive side of this competition.[2] Alternatively those who take issue with the practice tend to refer to it as 'forum shopping'.[3] The applicable law side of the debate is referred to not so much as applicable law shopping, rather as 'party autonomy'.

The EU is somewhat ambivalent on whether to support or suspect the practice. Its core instrument for civil and commercial litigation, the Brussels Ia Regulation,[4] supports choice of court for many issues, with specific protective rules for a limited number of contracts (consumer, employment and insurance contracts). Yet:

- It has struggled to provide sufficient support for choice-of-court agreements, in the event one of the parties sues first in another court rather than in the court to which parties agreed.
- It fails properly to consider whether party autonomy should extend to choice of court for a court outside of the EU (the so-called reflexive effect of choice of court agreements).
- It struggles to find a harmonised approach to the substantive validity of choice-of-court agreements (including the issue of whether 'unilateral', 'optional', 'assymetric' or 'hybrid' choices of court should be accepted).[5]

[1] See G. Dimitropoulos and S. Brekoulakis, 'Introduction', in this volume; G. Dimitropoulos, 'International Commercial Courts in the "Modern Law of Nature": Adjudicatory Unilateralism in Special Economic Zones' 24 (2021) Journal of International Economic Law 361; see also S. Francq, 'Regulatory Competition in Civil Procedure between Member States', in G. van Calster and J. Falconis (eds.), *European Private International Law at 50*, Cambridge, Intersentia, 2018, 13–31; X. Kramer, 'Competitie in de Europese civiele rechtsruimte. Een spanningsveld in de Europese civiele rechtsruimte?', TPR – tijdschrift voor Privaatrecht, 4/2014, 1745–1806.

[2] A. Mukarrum, *The Nature and Enforcement of Choice of Court Agreements*, Oxford, Hart, 2017, chapter 2.

[3] T. Thiede, 'Bier, Shevill und eDate — Aegrescit medendo?', *Zeitschrift für das Privatrecht der Europäischen Union*, 4/2012, 219–22.

[4] Regulation (EU) No. 1215/2012 on jurisdiction and the recognition and enforcement of judgments in civil and commercial matters (recast) [2012] OJ L351/1 (Brussels I Regulation Recast or 'Brussels Ia').

[5] M. Keyes (ed.), *Optional Choice of Court Agreements in Private International Law* (Proceedings of the 20th Conference of the International Academy of Comparative Law) Springer, 2020.

In the area of insolvency, forum shopping is actively discouraged by the EU,[6] albeit that by choosing one's corporate seat (which is a decision itself protected by the EU's rules on free movement of establishment and of services[7]), some forum shopping is in fact possible. On applicable law for contracts, the EU's Rome I Regulation fully supports party autonomy.[8] More broadly, there is plenty of scope in particular in business-to-business relations for parties to profit fully from the regulatory competition offered by the Member States.

21.3 The United Kingdom As a Winner in Regulatory Civil Procedure Competition

The use of UK courts, in particular the courts of England and Wales, as well as the use of the English law as a favourite *lex contractus*, is well documented, and the reasons are numerous.[9] The English bench is invariably incorruptible and generally extremely knowledgeable, including at the first instance stage. This is to an important degree the result of the selection (from the experienced Bar) and promotion of judges. English courts work fast by comparison with many of their European counterparts. Judgments are published transparently and almost instantly; many European States struggle to publish properly the case law even of their courts of appeal, let alone first-instance courts. The English court system in commercial cases has not stopped innovating since the introduction of the London Commercial Court in 1895. The London Courts continue to try out various new procedures and areas of specialisation in a tireless way against which even the most modern continental business courts pale. English civil procedure rules harbour a number of most interesting and relevant ways to speed up procedure, such as in particular the case-management conference at which parties and the judge streamline the core issues to be discussed in the case. The

[6] G. van Calster, 'COMIng, and Here to Stay. The Review of the European Insolvency Regulation', European Business Law Review, 2016, 735–53.

[7] G. van Calster, *European Private International Law. Third*, thoroughly revised and updated edition, London, Bloomsbury/Hart, in print for 2021; second, revised edition, 2016.

[8] Regulation (EC) No. 593/2008 on the law applicable to contractual obligations ('Rome I') [2008] OJ L177/6, as applied to the UK by Commission Decision 2009/26/EC [2009] OJ L10/22.

[9] X. E. Kramer and J. Sorabji (eds.), *International Business Courts: A European and Global Perspective*, The Hague, Eleven, 2019; C. Grout and Sir W. Blair, 'The Role of International Commercial Courts in Commercial Dispute Resolution' (Chapter 1), in this volume.

possibility of application for summary proceedings enables courts quickly to process cases which have no proper chance of success. Provisional measures are issued fast and creatively, with a high expectation for counsel to come to court with clean hands and under full and frank disclosure. Awarding costs against the losing party, and flexibly allowing third party funding,[10] all arguably assist in the bringing of cases which otherwise might not be brought.[11]

The latter element of course also comes with certain disadvantages: the very threat of being sued in London and awarded costs against one may be an effective way to force a party to settle. Moreover the speed and so forth of commercial litigation may not in fact be realised for criminal law.[12] Selection of judges from the (often commercial) Bar may lead to an overemphasis on commercial direction rather than the principled nature of the law (on which of course the English courts and the Court of Justice of the European Union (CJEU) have clashed in cases such as *West Tankers*).[13] Access to the courts may in practice not be open to all, as in the well-known saying among English lawyers: 'In England, Justice is open to all, like the Ritz hotel.'[14] The need to apply for permission to appeal and cross-appeal, and subsequent submissions in appeal, leads to considerable duplication in legal services and the ensuing invoices. Most importantly perhaps, many EU Member States do have similarly attractive propositions, such as the use of modern civil procedure rules, but are simply less adroit at marketing it.[15]

[10] Relevant also, for example, for modern 'human rights due diligence' and environmental cases. See, for instance, the Supreme Court in *Vedanta* [[2019] UKSC 20 *Vedanta and Konkola* v. *Lungowe*] and G. van Calster, 'Private International Law and Environmental Protection', in E. Lees and J. Viñuales (eds.), *Comparative Environmental Law*, Oxford, Oxford University Press, 2019, 1139–59.

[11] See the comments of Lord Briggs in *Vedanta, supra* note 10, with respect to England being sustained as a forum. Zambia was found not to be an appropriate forum for reasons of 'substantial justice', among others because of the absence of conditional fee agreements, and given the unavoidable scale and complexity of this case (wherever litigated), the trial judge was right that it could not be undertaken at all with the limited funding and legal resources the evidence led him to conclude were available within Zambia.

[12] The Secret Barrister, *Stories of the Law and How It's Broken*, London, Macmillan, 2018.

[13] G. van Calster, 'Kerpow! The United Kingdom Courts, West Tankers, and the Arbitration "Exception" in the Brussels I Regulation', *European Review of Private Law*, 2013, 205–20.

[14] Attributed to Sir James Mathew by R. E. Megarry in *Miscellany-at-Law*, London, Stevens and Sons, 1955).

[15] See, inter alia, the German 'Law Made in Germany' project: www.lawmadeingermany.de/Law-Made_in_Germany_EN.pdf, last accessed 10 September 2020.

21.4 The Situation post Brexit

In this section I look in a bit more technical detail to the impact Brexit will have on the attraction of UK courts. I do so by first outlining the exact way in which the UK has been integrated with EU civil procedure and private international law.

21.4.1 The Position of the United Kingdom vis-à-vis European Union Private International Law prior to Brexit

'Brexit' has been causing headaches for many a practitioner and observer of international and EU law, including in the field of private international law.[16] The transition period under the EU–UK Withdrawal Agreement (WA) came to an end on 1 January 2021.[17] I summarise the WA's provisions with respect to European private international law later in this section.

The United Kingdom joined the EU on 1 January 1973 and it joined the first instrument of EU private international law, the 1968 'Brussels Convention', in 1978. This Convention was a classic instrument of public international law – not European law. The UK Civil Jurisdiction and Judgments Act 1982 implemented the Convention into UK law (a crucial step given the UK's dualist approach to public international law implementation).

Since 1978, the UK has been subject to all of the core of EU private international law (PIL) in the area of commercial litigation, as well as the early instruments on parental responsibility, partially aligned with the Hague Conventions in the area. However, in the institutional arrangements on the further harmonisation of EU private international law,[18] the UK – like Ireland[19] – secured a flexible 'opt-in'. This means that in

[16] See also generally the European Commission Notice to Stakeholders of 27 August 2020, Withdrawal of the UK and EU rules in the field of civil justice and private international law, https://bit.ly/32hQJut, last accessed 10 September 2020. The Notice had already been amended twice and may be again.

[17] [2019] OJ CI 384/1.

[18] Specifically, in Article 3 of the Protocol on the position of the United Kingdom and Ireland annexed to the 1992 Treaty on European Union and the Treaty establishing the European Communities, OJ [2006] C321/E, 198–200.

[19] Denmark negotiated a less flexible opt-out: it does not take part in this part of EU law at all, unless it negotiates and ratifies a specific, PIL protocol for every time it wants to have the specific instrument apply to it. This is a heavy procedure and despite the treaty provision for Denmark unilaterally to decide to leave it, this system so far continues unchanged.

principle it is not bound by further EU PIL instruments, unless it notifies, by 'simple' letter to the EU institutions, that it does wish to be so subject to the EU law at issue. By use of this flexible mechanism, the UK is bound of its own volition inter alia by the successors to the Brussels Convention: the Brussels I and Brussels Ia Regulations, as well as the commercially highly relevant Rome I and II Regulations on applicable law for contractual and non-contractual obligations, and the Insolvency Regulation. Overall, the UK is subject to twelve of the current eighteen EU law instruments in the area of PIL.[20]

Arguably, the UK's (and Ireland and Denmark's) principle of exclusion of EU PIL was not the result of an objection against the very area of harmonisation in PIL. Rather, PIL instruments were seen as part and parcel of the 'area of freedom, security and justice' which the Member States adopted as an aspiration in the Treaty of Maastricht. The focus of that Title of the Treaty – Title IV – was on 'Visas, asylum, immigration and other policies related to free movement of persons'. It was the prospective of further cooperation on migration policies to which these States did not wish to adhere. The resulting complexity for PIL arguably was collateral damage. It is also important to point out that other Member States have hesitated to extend the reach of EU harmonisation in those areas of family law which touch upon core societal choices such as marriage and divorce. It is no coincidence that the area of private international law is the biggest single user so far of the EU's 'enhanced cooperation' mechanism, a procedure where a minimum of nine Member States may establish advanced integration or cooperation in an area within EU structures but without the other EU countries being involved, let alone be bound.

21.4.2 The EU–UK Withdrawal Agreement and Private International Law

The WA deals with judicial cooperation in civil and commercial matters in its Articles 66–9. In essence, the WA extended the temporal scope of

[20] M. Poesen, 'Civil and Commercial Private International Law in Times of Brexit: Managing the Impact, and Fostering Prospects for a Future EU–UK Cooperation', in M. Sacco (ed.), *Brexit and EU Law: A Way Forward*, Delaware, Vernon Press, 2019 (253) 257, footnote 10, referring to J. Ungerer, 'Brexit von Brüssel und den anderen Verordnungen zum Internationalen Privat- und Verfahrensrecht', in M. Kramme, C. Baldus and M. Schmidt-Kessel (eds.), *Brexit und die Juristischen Folgen*, Baden-Baden, Nomos, 2017, 296–306.

application of those European PIL rules to which the UK was committed as a result of the opt-in discussed earlier. Consequently, the WA extended the application of the jurisdictional rules of the main 'Brussels Ia' Regulation to legal proceedings 'instituted before the end of the transition period'. Brussels Ia's recognition and enforcement provisions will continue to apply to 'judgments given in legal proceedings instituted before the end of the transition period'.[21] Provided that the relevant European Enforcement Order (EEO) Certificate was applied for before the end of the transition period, the EEO Regulation (on uncontested claims) will also continue to apply. It is clear that Brussels Ia and related Regulations will echo in the UK courts for a while after the UK has left.

Generally, prior to the potential no-deal Brexit in March 2019, the UK government had issued the Civil Procedure Rules (CPR) 1998 (Amendment) (EU Exit) Regulations 2019. These rules clearly set out the UK government's thinking on the practice impact of a break from the EU rules on civil procedure. The thinking was to make the pending proceedings fully subject to existing (EU) law and case law as it existed prior to Brexit, with respect to, inter alia, service of documents and recognition and enforcement of judgments:

> The approach to transitional and saving provision is to follow the provision for these matters made in the statutory instruments listed in paragraph 7.1 (which can be summarised as allowing for proceedings started in a court in England and Wales before exit day to be concluded after exit day under the rules as they stood immediately before exit day).[22]

The DNA of these proposed CPR amendments was clearly to continue to apply pre-existing EU law and case law to pending proceedings and it is no surprise the WA's provisions confirmed as much.

The WA also provides that the Rome I Regulation on applicable law for contracts shall apply in the UK in respect of contracts concluded before the end of the transition period (31 December 2020), and that the Rome II Regulation on applicable law for non-contractual obligations shall apply in the UK in respect of events giving rise to damage, where such events occurred before the end of the transition period.

[21] [2019] OJ CI 384/1.

[22] Explanatory Memorandum, at 7.5, https://bit.ly/2xspiRH, last accessed 10 March 2020.

21.4.3 The Situation post Transition

Clearly anyone writing on the impact of Brexit on civil procedure, including PIL, post 31 December 2020 did so with a degree of clairvoyance.[23] Support for commentators' analysis has been found in public international law, including the provisions on treaty termination, acquired rights (a much overestimated mechanism) etc. under the Vienna Convention on the Law of Treaties (VCLT).

Of a certain stable nature is the (UK) European Union Withdrawal Act 2018 which includes – among others – provisions with respect to courts being able to depart from any retained EU case law. This has excited common law conflicts lawyers for they immediately see the *forum non conveniens* doctrine resurrected, to name but one obvious distinction between the common law of conflicts and EU PIL.[24]

The modus operandi with respect to the variation of retained case law by the courts does not rely so much on the Supreme Court's own initiatives and parameters as suggested by s.6(4)(a) of the 2018 Act. Rather, that section is subject to ministerial decree which will set out the criteria to be used for the Supreme Court and the lower courts to deviate from that case law. That is because both in the 2018 Act and in the 2020 Act s.6 is dependent upon s.26 and its ministerial clarification – the

[23] J. Basedow, 'Brexit Und Das Privat- Und Wirtschaftsrecht' (2016) *Zeitschrift für Europäisches Privatrecht* 567; J. M. Carruthers, 'Brexit: The Implications for Civil and Commercial Jurisdiction and Judgment Enforcement', *Scots Law Times*, 2017, 105; A. Dickinson, 'Back to the Future :The UK's EU Exit and the Conflict of Laws' (2016) *Journal of Private International Law* 195; A. Dickinson, 'Close the Door on Your Way Out: Free Movement of Judgments in Civil Matters – A "Brexit" Case Study' (2017) *Zeitschrift für europäisches Privatrecht* 539; B. Hess, 'Back to the Past: BREXIT Und Das Europäische Internationale Privat- Und Verfahrensrecht' (2016) *Praxis des Internationalen Privat- und Verfahrensrechts* 409; E. Lein, 'Unchartered Territory? A few Thoughts on Private International Law post Brexit', in A. Bonomi and G. P. Romano (eds.), *Yearbook of Private International Law*, Cologne, Dr Otto Schmidt, 2016, 39; S. Masters and B. McRae, 'What Does Brexit Mean for the Brussels Regime?' (2016) *Journal of International Arbitration* 483; M. Pilich, 'Brexit and EU Private International Law' (2017) *Maastricht Journal for European and Comparative Law* 382; Poesen, 'Civil and Commercial Private International Law in Times of Brexit', 253; H. Raulus, 'Brussels Falling: The Relationship between the UK and the EU post Brexit', in G. van Calster and Jura Falconis (eds.), *European Private International Law at 50*. Series Jura Falconis Libri, Cambridge, Intersentia, 2018, 109; G. Rühl, 'Judicial Cooperation in Civil and Commercial Matters after Brexit: Which Way Forward?' (2018) *International and Comparative Law Quarterly* 104.

[24] Compare relevant cases held under the *forum non conveniens* doctrine in business and human rights cases: L. Roorda, *Jurisdiction over Foreign Direct Liability Claims against Transnational Corporations in EU Member States*, Utrecht, Ridderprint, 2019, 119ff.

direction of which is entirely uncertain.[25] Whatever the direction this future ministerial and Supreme Court intervention will take, it is clear that the very possibility of case-law authority upending principles long established, and the need and scope for distinguishing existing authority will not improve predictability of outcome and hence may make UK courts less attractive.

21.4.3.1 At the Level of Jurisdiction and Recognition

Of greater likelihood at the level of jurisdiction and recognition and enforcement is the currently non-materialised, yet potential future accession of the United Kingdom to the Lugano II Convention 2007. On 28 January 2020 the UK government clearly signalled its intention of the same by securing support for this option from Norway, Iceland and Switzerland, being the current non-EU Lugano States,[26] and it filed a formal request of accession in April 2020.[27] Since that intention was aired, however, it became clear that the UK's accession to Lugano was blocked by the EU (a co-signatory and in a position of veto), as part of the post-Brexit relationship between the UK and the EU.

The alternative path, which would have done away with the need for EU approval, would be for the UK to become part of the European Free Trade Area (EFTA). Not all EFTA States are party to Lugano (Liechtenstein, at the time of writing, was not), however under Article 70(1) a of the Lugano Convention 2007, an EFTA Member State may accede to the Convention without other Lugano Members being able to object. This route, however, presupposes UK EFTA Membership which, given its impact on the UK's sovereignty to conclude external trade agreements (I will not go into detail here as to why that is the case), is not at all a realistic option.

Under Lugano, the CJEU has no jurisdiction to hear cases involving the interpretation of the Lugano Convention, at least when the case is pending in a non-EU Member State. This is an attractive position for the UK because its government has indicated CJEU jurisdiction in any post-Brexit UK–EU relations as a so-called red line. There is, however, a protocol annexed to the Lugano Convention which obliges Lugano

[25] Sections 25 and 26, in particular the 'Relationship with the EUWA 2018', in particular on 'saved EU law' and 'retained EU law'.

[26] Ministry of Justice statement of 28 January 2020, available at www.gov.uk/government/news/support-for-the-uks-intent-to-accede-to-the-lugano-convention-2007, last accessed 12 September 2020.

[27] Available at https://bit.ly/3jTQ2O6, last accessed 9 September 2020.

States courts to take 'due account' of (inter alia) CJEU case-law when interpreting the Convention.[28] 'Due account' of course is not as strong as given the CJEU case law the force of authority.[29]

Unlike the flagship Brussels Ia Regulation, neither Lugano I or II contain an Article 33–34-type rule which now allows Member State courts to stay the case in the event the same or a related case is already pending in a court outside the EU. The CJEU's 'Owusu' absolute exclusion of *forum non conveniens* applies to Lugano II. Argument for that is clear in the accompanying Report to the Convention:

> The ad hoc working party discussed whether Article 28 [on lis pendens, GAVC], ought to be made more flexible by granting the court first seized the right to decline jurisdiction in favour of the court seized subsequently, where the circumstances of the case would make that advisable, but it decided against this course. Providing such a right would have introduced into the Convention a further application of the doctrine of *forum non conveniens* that is alien to the legal tradition of most of the States bound by the Convention.[30]]

The UK in the meantime has acceded to the 2005 Hague Choice of Court Convention which will give some certainty to reciprocal respect for choice of court agreements across the Hague Convention area.[31] That certainty has issues attached. In the business-to-business context, the Hague Convention and the Brussels regime largely align – with important question marks such as on the applicable law for the substantive validity of the agreement. In the business to consumer context, and in the competition law ('antitrust') context, by contrast, the Hague regime works quite differently than the EU's. There are other important differences which I do not discuss here.[32]

Both the UK and the EU might also at some point in the future be bound by the 2019 Hague Judgments Convention.[33] That Convention

[28] Article 1 Protocol 2 to Lugano 2007, [2007] OJ L339/3.

[29] Leading, inter alia, one of the authorities on EU civil procedure, Professor Burkhard Hess, to argue against the Lugano route post Brexit; see B. Hess. 'The Unsuitability of the Lugano Convention (2007) to Serve As a Bridge between the UK and the EU after Brexit', MPI Luxembourg Working paper, January 2018, https://bit.ly/2TJgeR3, last accessed 11 September 2020.

[30] Report Fausto Pocar to the Lugano 2007 Convention, OJ [2009] C319/1, para. 123.

[31] Its December 2018 Accession was withdrawn for technical reasons on several occasions given the WA with the EU. A new notification was effected on 2 October 2020.

[32] See, inter alia, M. Poesen, *supra* note 20.

[33] 2019 Convention on the Recognition and Enforcement of Foreign Judgments in Civil or Commercial Matters.

has many caveats and uncertain definitions, scope for unilateral reservations, indirect only use of jurisdictional rules, and no oversight mechanism which can secure uniform application such as the CJEU does within the EU.[34]

Finally there has been some attention to the existence of bilateral treaties on recognition and enforcement which were in force prior to the 1968 Brussels Convention and which may or may not have led a sleeper existence from which they may be woken or resurrected.[35] Over and above the wildly varying substantial content of these treaties, discussion on the possibility of this route centres upon EU institutional law, and domestic constitutional law as well as the impact of the posterior EU regimes on the pre-existing Treaties by virtue of the VCLT.

Whatever the specific regimes on jurisdiction and/or recognition and enforcement the UK may or may not adhere to, it is clear that with Brexit the near-automatic, swift and in practice largely incontestable recognition and enforcement of UK judgments in EU Member States has come to an end. Even if the EU and the UK will find themselves bound by bilateral or multilateral agreements at some point in the future, none of these will come close to the by now relatively smooth operation of recognition and enforcement under Brussels IA.

I do not believe that continental judges will somehow use this renewed 'freedom' (see, however, the caveat of bilateral conventions) routinely or even liberally to refuse to recognise UK judgments. I appreciate that continued adherence to the rule of law must not be taken for granted.[36] However it is most unlikely that the UK legal order and the functioning of the UK courts post Brexit would be of such nature seriously to change from a substantive point of view the overall reception which continental courts give to UK judgments even outside of the Brussels regime. Clearly there will be instances where such judgments will be refused recognition – as

[34] G. van Calster, 'The November 2015 Draft Hague "Judgments" Project. A Powerful Potion or a Cauldron Full of Jurisdictional Spells?' (GAVC Law), https://gavclaw.com/2016/02/15/the-november-2015-draft-hague-judgments-project-a-powerful-potion-or-a-cauldron-full-of-jurisdictional-spells, last accessed 10 September 2020.

[35] A. Dickinson, 'A View from the Edge', Oxford Legal Studies Research Paper No. 25/2019. https://ssrn.com/abstract=3356549, last accessed 12 October 2020.

[36] The UK government admitted that its September 2020 UK Internal Market Bill (https://publications.parliament.uk/pa/bills/cbill/58-01/0177/20177.pdf, last accessed 10 September 2020) amounted to a breach of international law 'in a very specific and limited way': B. Lewis, North Ireland Secretary, 8 September 2020 in the House of Commons. See Hansard 8 September 2020 column 509, https://bit.ly/33pGLa3, last accessed 2020.

they can be under the current rules, for instance using the order public exception, or for judgments which were issued in spite of concurrent proceedings in an EU court. That latter element is of course more conceivable now that the UK will no longer be using identical jurisdictional rules, including the guillotine-like *lis alibi pendens* regulation in Brussels Ia. One very important commercial area of note in this respect is the English 'Schemes of arrangement' (and since June 2020, the 'Restructuring Plan'). These are restructuring mechanisms that have been used in great numbers by continental corporations and enforced on the continent on sometimes unwilling creditors. The UK courts have been relying for years on *arguendo* cover of these schemes under Brussels Ia, which largely insulates them from jurisdictional scrutiny, and even recalcitrant creditors have not pushed the point too vigorously.

An interesting example of the negative impact of Brexit on the attraction of the English courts as a litigation destination is *Graham Woloff eaor Calzaturificio Zengarini eaor re Akkurate Ltd.*[37] It concerned the question of whether the court has the power under section 236(3) of the Insolvency Act 1986 to require persons resident in the EU to produce books and papers and an account of their dealings with a company being compulsorily wound up in England and Wales. (It is not disputed that Akkurate's centre of main interests (COMI) was in England and Wales under the European Insolvency Regulation (EIR)).

European Insolvency Regulation 2000 applies to this case because the winding up of Akkurate was before 26 June 2017; however, the issue is not materially different in the new Regulation. There are inconsistent first-instance decisions which Vos C reviews, inter alia, at 27 ff. At 54 after consideration, he considers s236(3) does *not* have extraterritorial effect on the basis of what he considers to be binding authority, however that following the EIR 2000 (unchanged in EIR 2015) the European regime can and does extend the territoriality of purely domestic insolvency provisions. The CJEU authority cited is in particular C-339/07 *Seagon* v. *Deko Marty Belgium* (at 58 ff. – it is not in fact certain whether the CJEU so clearly held in this direction). Vos C also decides that he can and should apply his discretion to grant the relevant orders. Clearly, post Brexit, the situation will revert to Tucker, which would make the English courts less attractive than their continental counterparts – although of course one would have to wait for CJEU authority to confirm the issue less equivocally.

[37] [2020] EWHC 1433 (Ch). www.bailii.org/ew/cases/EWHC/Ch/2020/1433.html

Overall, in the landscape of regulatory competition for judicial services, and the prestige and turnover they generate, there are plenty of instances where speed is of the essence. Despite my expectation that no dramatic changes ought to be expected at the substantive recognition level (UK judgments eventually will not en masse be refused recognition), clearly with Brussels Ia falling away, so too does its speed of recognition and enforcement. That is important for instance for provisional measures (albeit Brussels Ia has limited their inclusion in the enforcement title). It might also mean that parties may be encouraged to look beyond UK courts for litigation. It is in this context of course that so many continental EU Member States have been looking to set up international commercial courts (ICommCs) of all shapes and sizes.[38]

21.4.3.2 At the Level of Applicable Law

For applicable law the situation is quite different. Looking first from the point of view of the EU Member States, the most important international commercial PIL instruments have a 'universal' nature, meaning that their mechanisms identify an applicable law regardless of the 'nationality' of that law. Particularly in the case of the laws of England and Wales, many contracts (subject to the Rome I Regulation) will continue to be subject to English law and that will be fully accepted under EU rules. Parties will simply have to ponder whether they want English courts to apply these laws, or instead opt for choice of court in favour of a court in the EU.

Conversely, English conflict of laws has no great objection to accepting foreign law as the *lex contractus*. Indeed in the aforementioned European Union Withdrawal Act 2018 existing EU law is retained, including Rome I and Rome II. Clearly, this retention may be changed at any time. Moreover, the prospect of UK courts independently applying retained EU law without CJEU oversight may lead to awkward results in the future.[39]

[38] See X. E. Kramer and J. Sorabji (eds.), *International Business Courts: A European and Global Perspective*, The Hague, Eleven, 2019.

[39] See also M. Poesen, *supra* note 20; for an example of how EU private international law applied ex-EU might lead to odd outcomes, see G. van Calster, 'Bauer v. QBE Insurance. Brussels Ia, Rome I and Rome II in Western Australia', https://gavclaw.com/2020/09/01/bauer-v-qbe-insurance-the-cjeu-inspires-in-western-australia, last accessed 10 September 2020.

21.5 Conclusion

United Kingdom courts have been serial providers of national case law on European private international law. In the immediate post-Brexit period, little will change in practice, as explained earlier in this chapter. Readers and practitioners in the UK will continue to find retained EU private international law to be of great importance. They will also find of course that knowledge of EU PIL is relevant to anyone doing business with the EU. Litigants will continue to flock to UK courts and these will therefore continue to be a formidable competitor to ICommCs the world over.

However, depending upon the direction which UK case law will take post Brexit, and particularly in the absence of a formal arrangement with the EU which would tie together the continent's and the UK's civil procedure regime, continental courts are likely to discontinue their automatic recognition and enforcement of UK judgments. Such a development would give ICommCs on the continent and elsewhere a formidable opportunity to take litigation away from the UK. There is one important condition for that to happen: these ICommCs themselves, within the EU, need to ensure a proper integration with the judiciary. For ICommCs outside the EU, negotiated guarantees on recognition and enforcement of ICommC judgments will be a crucial factor.

22

International Commercial Courts, Dispute Resolution and the Rule of Law

SUSAN L. KARAMANIAN*

22.1 Introduction

The increased flow of transborder goods, services and people since the 1980s has resulted in important developments within States.[1] One of the more creative and resource-intensive responses involves an aspect of a State's identity, the judicial system. Specifically, as States or subdivisions within them seek to attract foreign investment and associated activity, they have enabled the removal of resolution of certain commercial disputes from their long-established municipal courts. They have shifted this authority to stand-alone courts with no or limited ties to the national judicial system or they have created specialized commercial courts within the existing judicial system. The new international commercial courts (ICommCs) are associated with terms such as *efficiency, judicial integrity and independence* and *transparency*.

The establishment of ICommCs has broad implications for the rule of law. States have allocated limited public resources to create new courts rather than addressing perceived shortcomings in existing courts. In their founding, some of the new courts accept that dispute resolution is a 'business'. What are the implications of these developments for justice?

* I thank my colleague Professor George Dimitropoulos for his careful guidance on many of the issues raised in this chapter.

[1] Although to the contrary in recent years, the long-term trend in trade and foreign direct investment has been upward; see for example Esteban Ortiz-Ospina and Diana Beltekian, 'Trade and Globalization' (October 2018), https://ourworldindata.org/trade-and-globalization#trade-from-a-historical-perspective, accessed 15 June 2020; World Bank, 'Foreign Direct Investment, Net Inflows (% of GDP): 1970–2018', https://data.worldbank.org/indicator/BX.KLT.DINV.WD.GD.ZS, accessed 15 June 2020 (showing more than 300 per cent increase from 1980 to 2018).

Further, do the new courts operate in silos or are they setting new standards to guide municipal courts and other relevant actors?

Answering these and related questions is difficult given the variety of ICommCs and their unique operating circumstances. Further, the emergence of the courts is a relatively new development, so one should proceed with caution in rushing to judgment. These are not obstacles, however, to making a general assessment and specific observations. In this light, Section 22.2 provides an overview of the new courts. The description focuses more on aspects relevant to the rule of law given the descriptions in other chapters of this book. Section 22.3 examines the meaning of the rule of law, a concept that has both substantive and procedural aspects. In Section 22.4, the principles examined in Section 22.3 elucidate the work of the courts to understand aspects that promote and those that challenge the rule of law.

22.2 International Commercial Courts: What, Why and How

22.2.1 Overview

International trade and investment have prompted the rise of global commercial hubs and within them new ICommCs. The courts have two major forms: (1) courts within a financial centre with the latter being a self-contained legal regime; and (2) courts that are established or otherwise associated within existing municipal legal systems.

Examples of the first model are the Qatar International Court (QIC),[2] the Dubai International Financial Centre Courts (DIFC Courts),[3] the Abu Dhabi Global Market Courts (ADGM Courts)[4] and the Astana International Financial Centre (AIFC) Court.[5]

Examples of the second model are the Singapore International Commercial Court (SICC), a division of the Singapore High Court,[6] and the China International Commercial Court (CICC), established by the Supreme People's Court of China (SPC) in 2018 and operating under

[2] The website for the QICDRC, home to the QIC, is at www.qicdrc.gov.qa, accessed 15 June 2020. The QIC is located in the Qatar Financial Centre (QFC).

[3] The DIFC Courts' website is at www.difccourts.ae, accessed 15 June 2020. The DIFC Courts are located in the Dubai International Financial Centre (DIFC).

[4] The ADGM Courts' website is at hwww.adgm.com/adgm-courts, accessed 15 June 2020. The ADGM Courts are located in the Abu Dhabi Global Market (ADGM).

[5] The AIFC Court's website is at https://court.aifc.kz, accessed 15 June 2020. The AIFC Court is located in the Astana International Financial Centre (AIFC).

[6] The SICC website is at www.sicc.gov.sg, accessed 15 June 2020.

the Fourth Civil Division of SPC with judges from China.[7] In recent years, anticipating a post-Brexit environment in which London may not be a desirable dispute resolution centre, ICommCs have emerged as offshoots of courts in Europe.[8] Two examples are the Chamber for International Commercial Disputes at the Landgericht Frankfurt am Main[9] and the Netherlands Commercial Court in Amsterdam, a chamber of the Amsterdam District Court.[10] Building on the specialized chamber within the Paris Commercial Court, the Paris Court of Appeals in 2018 launched the International Chamber of the Paris Court of Appeal.[11]

22.2.2 *Courts within International Financial Centres*

22.2.2.1 Qatar International Court

In 2009, Qatar enacted a law to establish the Qatar International Court (QIC) within the existing Qatar Financial Centre (QFC).[12] The QFC, created in 2005,[13] is an 'onshore business and financial' centre designed to attract business to Qatar.[14] Entities within the QFC have 100 per cent ownership rights and can repatriate 100 per cent of their profits.[15] The

[7] The CICC website is at cicc.court.gov.cn/html/1/219/index.html, accessed 15 June 2020.

[8] See Stephan Wilske, 'International Commercial Courts and Arbitration: Alternatives, Substitutes or Trojan Horses?' [2018] 11(2) Contemp. Asia Arb 153, 169–70.

[9] The website of the Chamber for International Commercial Disputes is at https://ordentliche-gerichtsbarkeit.hessen.de/ordentliche-gerichte/lgb-frankfurt-am-main/lg-frankfurt-am-main/chamber-international, accessed 15 June 2020.

[10] The website of the Netherlands Commercial Court is at www.rechtspraak.nl/English/NCC/Pages/default.aspx, accessed 15 June 2020.

[11] See Wilske (n. 8) 170.

[12] QFC Law No. (7) of 2005, amended by Law No. (2) of 2009 art. 8 (3), https://qfcra-en.thomsonreuters.com/sites/default/files/net_file_store/QFC_Law-V2-April09.pdf, accessed 15 June 2020 [hereinafter 'Amended QFC Law No. (7)'].

[13] Law No. (7) of Year 2005 on the promulgation of Law for the Qatar Financial Centre (Version No. 1) (24 May 2005), https://qfcra-en.thomsonreuters.com/sites/default/files/net_file_store/QFC_Law_7_0f_2005-V1.pdf, accessed 15 June 2020 [hereinafter 'QFC Originating Law'].

[14] 'Qatar Financial Centre: About', www.qfc.qa/en/about, accessed 15 June 2020. The QFC seeks to 'promote Qatar as an attractive business destination at the crossroads between East and West' (ibid.).

[15] 'Qatar Financial Centre: Our Organisation', www.qfc.qa/en/about/our-organisation, accessed 15 June 2020. Outside of the QFC, restrictions on foreign ownership and repatriation in Qatar have eased yet they are still subject to other legislation; see Law No. 1 of 2019 on Regulating Non-Qatari Capital Investment in the Economic Activity, https://investmentpolicy.unctad.org/investment-laws/laws/314/qatar-law-no-1-of-2019, accessed 15 June 2020.

QFC has its own regulatory regime, including an oversight body, the QFC Regulatory Authority.[16] From the outset, it has had an Appeals Body to hear challenges to decisions of the QFC Regulatory Authority.[17]

The QIC consists of a first-instance court and a court of appeals. The former has jurisdiction over civil and commercial disputes with links to the QFC. The disputes could arise from 'transactions, contracts, arrangements or incidences taking place in or from the QFC between entities established' in the QFC.[18] They could involve QFC authorities or institutions or an entity established within the QFC.[19] The disputes could be between QFC entities 'and contractors therewith and employees thereof' unless otherwise agreed.[20] They could be 'arising from' business dealings 'between entities established within The QFC' and Qatar residents or 'entities established' in Qatar but outside of the QFC, unless otherwise agreed.[21]

Of note, under Rule 9.2 of the QIC's procedural rules, consent to QIC jurisdiction is permissible:

> Consistently and in accordance with fundamental international principles and international best practice, the Court will take into account the expressed accord of the parties that the Court shall have jurisdiction.[22]

Rule 9.2 reaffirms that choice of forum is an entrenched, international principle which the QIC embraces.

Appeals from the first-instance court are to the Appellate Division, subject to permission from the first-instance court or another established court.[23] Appeals are limited to cases in which 'a judgment or decision is

[16] QFC Originating Law (n. 13) art. 8(1). The QFC Regulatory Authority regulates, licenses and supervises 'banking, financial and insurance-related business carried on in or from the QFC' (ibid.).

[17] Ibid. art. 8(2).

[18] Amended QFC Law No. (7) (n. 12) art. 8 (3)(c)(1).

[19] Ibid. art. 8 (3)(c)(2).

[20] Ibid. art. 8 (3)(c)(3). Under this article, the QIC has jurisdiction over a contract dispute between the Claimant and the Defendant based solely on the fact that the Claimant, licensed and regulated by the QFC, entered into a contract with the Defendant, a non-QFC entity. *NASCO Qatar LLC* v. *MISR Insurance (Qatar Branch)* [2020] QC(F) f (10 May 2020), www.qicdrc.gov.qa/sites/default/files/s3/judgments/english/judgment_case_no_3_of_2020_10_may_2020.pdf, accessed 15 June 2020.

[21] Amended QFC Law No. (7) (n. 12) art. 8(3)(c)(4).

[22] QFC Civil and Commercial Court Regulations and Procedural Rules art. 9.2, www.qicdrc.gov.qa/sites/default/files/s3/wysiwyg/qfc_civil_and_commercial_court_regulations_date_of_issuance_15_december_2010_0.pdf, accessed 15 June 2020 [hereinafter 'QIC Regulations and Procedural Rules'].

[23] Ibid. art. 35.1.

erroneous and there is significant risk that it will result in serious injustice'.[24] Further, the Appellate Division can hear appeals from the QFC Regulatory Tribunal, which has replaced the original Appeals Body.[25]

The QIC judges, appointed 'based on their expertise in resolving civil and commercial disputes' are from civil law and common law jurisdictions.[26] They are subject to the QICDRC's Judicial Code of Conduct, premised on four principles being 'fundamental to the rule of law and to a fair trial': independence, impartiality, integrity, and propriety.[27]

The applicable law depends upon the dispute. QFC law and QFC regulations apply as to transactions that emanate from a QFC-registered entity.[28] Yet, the parties could select other governing law so long as it does not violate public policy.[29]

22.2.2.2 DIFC Courts and ADGM Courts

An amendment to the UAE constitution in 2004, along with the enactment of various federal and local laws, enabled the creation of 'financial free zones' in the UAE, such as the DIFC and the ADGM, which then established the DIFC Courts and the ADGM Courts, respectively.[30]

[24] Ibid.

[25] Amended QFC Law No. (7) (n. 12) art 8(3)(d).

[26] QICDRC: The Court Overview, www.qicdrc.gov.qa/the-courts/overview, accessed 15 June 2020. The first president was Lord Phillips of Worth Matravers, former president of the Supreme Court of the United Kingdom (ibid.). The current president is Lord Thomas of Cwmgiedd, the former Lord Chief Justice of England and Wales (ibid.). Current judges from the region include Dr Hassan Al-Sayed, former dean of Qatar University Faculty of Law, Hon. Rashid Al Badr, former Qatari judge, including having served as the chief justice of the Court of Appeal of Qatar, and Dr Rashid Hamad Al-Anezi, a professor of international law at Kuwait University (ibid.).

[27] 'QICDRC Judicial Code of Conduct', www.qicdrc.gov.qa/sites/default/files/s3/wysiwyg/judicial_code_of_conduct.pdf, accessed 15 June 2020.

[28] Amended QFC Law No. (7) (n. 12) Schedule 6, art. 8. See also QIC Regulations and Procedural Rules (n. 22) art. 11.1.1.

[29] Amended QFC Law No. (7) (n. 12) Schedule 6, art. 8. See also QIC Regulations and Procedural Rules (n. 22) art. 11.1.2(a). Consumer protection provisions of the QFC Law and QFC Regulations are mandatory law (ibid. art. 11.1.2(b)).

[30] Constitution of the United Arab Emirates art. 121. A new federal law enabled the establishment of Financial Free Zones exempt from 'Federal civil and commercial laws'; see Federal Law No. 8 of 2004 regarding the Financial Free Zones art. 3(2), www.difc.ae/files/5314/5449/7480/Federal_Law_No_8_of_2004_English.pdf, accessed 15 June 2020. Both Dubai and Abu Dhabi passed laws to establish their respective centres and courts; see for example Dubai Law No. 9 of 2004 In respect of the Dubai International Financial Centre, www.difc.ae/files/4414/5735/7076/

Like the QIC's first-instance court, the DIFC court of first instance has jurisdiction over civil and commercial disputes linked to the DIFC, such as those involving a DIFC entity or an entity licensed in the DIFC or a contract or incident linked to the DIFC, as well as appeals from DIFC bodies.[31] The DIFC Courts also have jurisdiction based upon the parties' agreement.[32] The DIFC has an array of laws and regulations based on common law, so judges of the DIFC Courts mainly apply it or the law selected by the parties.[33] Judges of the DIFC Courts, like those in the QIC, come from diverse jurisdictions such as the UAE, the UK and Malaysia.[34]

The ADGM Courts consist of a court of first instance with three divisions: civil, employment, and small claims and a court of appeals. The jurisdiction of the civil division is akin to that of the QIC and DIFC Courts, which hear civil or commercial cases 'involving the Global Market' or its Authorities or Establishments as well as appeals of decisions of Global Market Authorities.[35] Further, it has jurisdiction over disputes 'arising out of or relating to a contract or a transaction conducted in whole or in part in the Global Market or to an incident occurring' therein.[36] By amendment in 2020 to the ADGM Founding Law, parties unrelated to the ADGM may 'opt in' to the jurisdiction of the ADGM Courts.[37] The 2020 amendments also confirm that the ADGM Courts are courts of Abu Dhabi, which is important 'to the enforcement of ADGM

Dubai_Law_No_9_of_2004_-_English.pdf, accessed 15 June 2020; Dubai Law No. 12 of 2004 The Law of the Judicial Authority at Dubai International Financial Centre, as amended by Law No. (16), www.difccourts.ae/wp-content/uploads/2017/10/Dubai12of2004_amended2011.pdf, accessed 15 June 2020 [hereinafter 'Amended DIFC Courts Law']; Law No. (4) of 2013 Concerning Abu Dhabi Global Market, www.adgm.com/documents/legal-framework/abu-dhabi-legislation/abu_dhabi_law_no_4_of_2013.pdf, accessed 15 June 2020 (establishing the ADGM and the ADGM Courts).

31 Amended DIFC Courts Law (n. 30) art. 5(A)(1).

32 Ibid. art. 5(A)(2).

33 DIFC Authority Laws & Regulations, www.difc.ae/business/laws-regulations/difc-laws-regulations, accessed 15 June 2020 (the DIFC has 'its own civil and commercial legal framework, inclusive of financial services regulation and a courts system modeled closely on international standards and principles of common law').

34 DIFC Courts: Judges, www.difccourts.ae/court-structure/judges, accessed 15 June 2020.

35 Law No. (4) of 2013 Concerning Abu Dhabi Global Market art. 6, www.adgm.com/documents/legal-framework/abu-dhabi-legislation/abu_dhabi_law_no_4_of_2013.pdf, accessed 15 June 2020.

36 Ibid.

37 ADGM Courts: Guide to amendments to Article 13 of the Abu Dhabi Law No. 4 of 2013 pp. 2–3, www.adgm.com/documents/courts/legislation-and-procedures/guidance-papers/adgm-courts-guide-to-amendments-to-article-13-of-the-founding-law.pdf, accessed 15 June 2020.

Courts' judgments and awards under international treaties and conventions' to which the UAE is a party.[38] Further, the 2020 amendments specify that judgments are to be 'issued in the name of the Ruler of Abu Dhabi', again to ease their enforcement outside of Abu Dhabi.[39]

The ADGM Courts are 'a fully independent common law framework to adjudicate civil and commercial disputes' as the 'ADGM's legal framework' is the 'direct application of English common law'.[40] Their applicable rules and regulations reflect critical values such as judicial independence, integrity of the judiciary, transparency and access to justice.[41] The judges were previously judges in common law jurisdictions – namely, the UK, Australia, New Zealand and Hong Kong.[42]

22.2.2.3 AIFC Court

The most recent ICommC within a financial centre is the AIFC Court in Astana, Kazakhstan, self-described as 'an independent common law court operating to the highest international standards'.[43] The AIFC Court consists of nine justices, all from the United Kingdom and most of whom had been judges there.[44] It exercises exclusive jurisdiction over disputes involving AIFC entities, relating to 'operations carried out in the AIFC and regulated by the law of the AIFC' or 'the interpretation of AIFC Acts'.[45] Further, it has exclusive jurisdiction based on the parties' agreement.[46]

The applicable law is that of the AIFC, the law selected by the parties or 'such law as appears to the Court to be the most appropriate in the facts and circumstances of the dispute'.[47] Under AIFC Court regulations, the Court 'in determining a matter or proceeding, shall be guided by decisions of the Court and decisions made in other common law

38 Ibid. p. 7 (referencing Article 13(1) of the Amended Founding Law).
39 Ibid. pp. 7–8 (referencing Article 13(2) of the Amended Founding Law).
40 'ADGM Courts: English Common Law', www.adgm.com/adgm-courts/english-common-law, accessed 15 June 2020.
41 Ibid.
42 ADGM Courts: Judges, www.adgm.com/adgm-courts/judges, accessed 15 June 2020.
43 AIFC Courts (n. 5).
44 Ibid. The chief justice is Lord Mance, a former justice of the UK Supreme Court.
45 Astana International Financial Centre: AIFC Court Regulations Resolution of the AIFC Management Council art. 26(1)(a), (b), and (d) (5 December 2017), https://aifc.kz/files/legals/68/file/3.-legislation-aifc-court-regulations-2017.pdf, accessed 15 June 2020.
46 Ibid. art. 26(1)(c).
47 Ibid. art. 29(1). The AIFC law includes 'the AIFC Constitutional Statute, AIFC Regulations including the AIFC Courts Regulations, and AIFC Court Rules' (ibid. art. 29(1)(a)).

jurisdictions'.[48] This provision mandates a system of precedent within the AIFC Court and authorizes the court to cite to decisions from other common law jurisdictions in establishing its own jurisprudence.

22.2.3 *International Commercial Courts within Municipal Legal Systems*

The second form of an ICommC is one with closer ties to municipal legal system. The most notable is the Singapore International Commercial Court (SICC). An amendment to the Constitution of Singapore in 2014 launched the SICC, which opened its doors on 5 January 2015.[49] The SICC was established to provide 'efficient and effective resolution of international commercial disputes'.[50]

The SICC exercises jurisdiction over claims of 'an international and commercial nature' based on party consent.[51] The founders contemplated that a case could be 'offshore' – namely, lacking a substantial connection to Singapore.[52] In such circumstance, foreign counsel may appear before the SICC after registering as foreign lawyers under Singapore's Legal Profession Act.[53]

The applicable law depends upon the case, and as many cases involve contracts, it is likely based on the parties' choice. As the SICC is a division

[48] Ibid. art. 29(2).

[49] See Lawrence Teh, 'The Singapore International Commercial Court' [2017] 11 Dispute Resol Int'l 143, 144–45 (discussing the constitutional amendment to enable Singapore's president 'to appoint international judges to the SICC', the amendment of the Supreme Court of Judicature Act 'to establish the SICC as a division of the High Court of Singapore and its jurisdiction', the amendment of the Rules of Court to establish procedural rules for the SICC and the amendment of the Legal Profession Act to enable foreign lawyers to appear before the SICC).

[50] 'SICC Brochure', www.sicc.gov.sg/docs/default-source/about-sicc/sicc-brochure.pdf, accessed 15 June 2020.

[51] Supreme Court of Judicature Act, Rules of Court (Amendment No. 6) Rules 2014, New Order 110 art. 7(1), www.supremecourt.gov.sg/docs/default-source/default-document-library/s-850-2014–rules-of-court-(amendment-no-6)-rules-2014.pdf, accessed 15 June 2020 [hereinafter 'SICC Rules of Court']. The Rules of Court define a claim 'international in nature' (ibid. Rule 1 (2)(a)). They also define a claim 'commercial in nature' (ibid. Rule 1(2)(b)). Excluded from jurisdiction are cases in which a party seeks 'relief in the form of, or connected with, a prerogative order' (ibid. Rule 7(1)(c)).

[52] Ibid. Rule 1 (defining an offshore case); Rule 1(2)(f) (expanding the definition of offshore case and elaborating on when an action 'has no substantial connection to Singapore').

[53] See Singapore International Commercial Court Practice Directions art. 26 (1)(a), www.supremecourt.gov.sg/docs/default-source/default-document-library/sicc-practice-directions–amended-version-(15-july-2019).pdf, accessed 15 June 2020.

of the Singapore High Court, which in turn is part of the Supreme Court of Singapore, all appeals are to the Court of Appeal of Singapore.[54] Unlike the courts in the international financial centres, the judges consist of sitting local judges (e.g. Singapore High Court judges, the chief justice of Singapore, judges of appeal) as well as an array of international judges from both common law and civil law jurisdictions.[55] The chief justice has the authority to appoint judges to hear specific cases.[56]

A distinguishing feature of the SICC is its development of the legal profession in Singapore beyond arbitration. The brainchild of Chief Justice of Singapore Honourable Sundaresh Menon, the SICC was designed 'to grow the legal services sector and to expand the scope for the internationalization and export of Singapore law'.[57] In other words, the SICC had an entrepreneurial purpose beyond dispute resolution, and it has sought to take advantage of Singapore's reputation 'as a neutral third party venue for resolving disputes between parties from different jurisdictions'.[58] In fact, the SICC boldly states that it is '[a] prime destination for international commercial dispute resolution'.[59] Consistent with this theme is the role of foreign law and its proof before the SICC. In contrast to many rules, foreign law may 'be determined on the basis of counsel's submissions' instead of by expert witness proof.[60] Second, the parties may agree to apply evidence rules from a jurisdiction outside of Singapore.[61]

Similarly, in 2018, the Supreme People's Court of China (SPC) established the China International Commercial Court (CICC) under the guidance of the Fourth Civil Division of the SPC.[62] Two CICCs exist, one in Shenzhen, Guangdong Province, and the second in Xi'an, Shaanxi Province.[63] Unlike the other ICommCs, the judges of the CICC are judges from China, yet there is the International Commercial Expert

54 'SICC: Judges', www.sicc.gov.sg/about-the-sicc/judges, accessed 15 June 2020.
55 Ibid.
56 Ibid.
57 Report of the Singapore International Commercial Court Committee 3 (November 2013), www.mlaw.gov.sg/files/Annex-A-SICC-Committee-Report.pdf, accessed 15 June 2020.
58 Ibid.
59 SICC (n. 6).
60 Teh (n. 49) 146.
61 SICC Rules of Court (n. 51), Rule 23.
62 See n. (7).
63 Lance Ang, 'International Commercial Courts and the Interplay between Realism and Institutionalism: A Look at China and Singapore' Harv. Int'l L J, https://harvardilj.org/2020/03/international-commercial-courts-and-the-interplay-between-realism-and-institutionalism-a-look-at-china-and-singapore></int_u, accessed 15 June 2020.

Committee, consisting of thirty-one Chinese and foreign experts, to help 'CICC judges in ascertaining the content of foreign laws and preside over mediation[s]'.[64] The CICC's jurisdiction is based on consent subject to a minimum amount in controversy, as well as other grounds related to some link to China.[65] Of note, decisions of the CICC are final with full binding legal effect.[66] The CICC is not without controversy as it was established principally to address disputes related to the 'One Belt, One Road' project, which could benefit Chinese entities.[67]

22.3 The Rule of Law in Context

Understanding the rule of law implications of ICommCs, created to remove commercial disputes from existing municipal courts, necessitates clarity about the phrase 'rule of law'. As has been observed, the rule of law is 'a much celebrated, historic ideal, the precise meaning of which may be less clear today than ever before'.[68]

Some understand 'rule of law' to mean adherence to the law of a specific state grounded in efficiency and fairness, or as Thomas Carothers has described it as 'rule by law'.[69] Robert McCorquodale has referenced A. V. Dicey and his three elements of the rule of law: supremacy of the law, equality, and enforcement before the courts.[70] These minimalist or 'thin' notions of the rule of law recognize that a State has an established legal system and the ability to enforce adherence to the law emanating from that system. Yet the definition is far from satisfactory as the law itself may be divorced from critical normative elements.

[64] Ibid.

[65] Ibid.

[66] See n. (7).

[67] Zhengxin Huo and Man Yip, 'Comparing the International Commercial Courts of China with the Singapore International Commercial Court' [2019] 68 ICLQ 903–42.

[68] Richard H. Fallon Jr, 'The "Rule of Law" As a Concept in Constitutional Discourse' [1997] 97 Columb L Rev 1, 1.

[69] Thomas Carothers, 'Rule of Law Temptations' [2009] 33 The Fletcher Forum of World Affairs 49, 53.

[70] Robert McCorquodale, 'Defining the International Rule of Law: Defying Gravity' (2016) 65 ICLQ 277, 279 (citing A. V. Dicey, *An Introduction to the Study of the Law of the Constitution* (Macmillan 1885) Pt II). See also ibid. 288 (citing Simon Chesterman, 'An International Rule of Law' [2008] 56 AJCL 331, 342 that a national rule of law is grounded in a government of laws, supremacy of the law, and equality before the law).

So if the rule of law is to reflect values beyond the existence of the law itself, what are they? The World Justice Project (WJP) recognizes that the rule of law embraces two distinct principles: (1) limits on the power of the State and others;[71] and (2) when exercising these limits, the State protects its citizens and ensures access to means to resolve disputes.[72] Accordingly, the rule of law 'is a framework of laws and institutions that embodies four universal principles': accountability, just laws, open government, and accessible and impartial dispute resolution.[73] This approach, set out in more detail in what follows, conforms to Professor McCorquodale's 'international rule of law', or a 'thick' approach that embraces 'legal order and stability; equality of application of the law; protection of human rights; and the settlement of disputes before an independent legal body'.[74]

Accountability means that all actors, government or private, are subject to the laws.[75] This understanding comports with the UN Secretary-General's 2012 report, 'Delivering Justice: Programme of Action to Strengthen the Rule of Law at the National and International Levels', which recognizes that under the rule of law, 'all persons, institutions and entities, public and private, including the State itself, are accountable to laws'.[76] Inherent within the concept of accountability is the fundamental notion of supremacy of the law.[77]

The concept of 'just laws' includes certain foundational concepts. For example, 'publicly promulgated, equally enforced and independently adjudicated' standards are critical, as are clarity and stability.[78]

[71] World Justice Project, Rule of Law Index 2019 8 (2019), https://worldjusticeproject.org/sites/default/files/documents/WJP-ROLI-2019-Single%20Page%20View-Reduced_0.pdf, accessed 15 June 2020 [hereinafter 'WJP Index'] (asking 'whether the law imposes limits on the exercise of power by the state and its agents, as well as individuals and private entities').

[72] Ibid. (examining whether the law 'fulfills its basic duties towards its population so that the public interest is served, people are protected from violence, and all members of society have access to dispute settlement and grievance mechanisms').

[73] Ibid., at 9.

[74] McCorquodale (n. 70) p. 292.

[75] Ibid.

[76] 'Delivering Justice: Programme of Action to Strengthen the Rule of Law at the National and International Levels', Report of the Secretary General, UN Doc A/66/749 (2012) para. 2 [hereinafter 'Delivering Justice'].

[77] Ibid.

[78] Ibid.

As important is that the substantive standards are consistent with fundamental rights and international human rights norms.[79] As the Council of Europe has noted, the rule of law must show respect for human rights.[80] An essential aspect is 'equality before the law.'[81] In sum, this element of the rule of law goes beyond procedural safeguards and 'embrac[es] the protection of human rights'.[82]

The third aspect of the rule of law, open government, entails a process of promulgation, administration and enforcement of laws that is 'accessible, fair, and efficient'.[83] At the heart of open government is public engagement. For the latter to be substantial, an informed citizenry is required, which supposes an open (transparent) system of governance.

Finally, critical to a legal system grounded in justice, equality and fairness is a means for resolving disputes that is reliable in terms of quality, accessibility and impartiality. The WJP has elaborated on dispute resolution as follows:

> Justice is delivered timely by competent, ethical, and independent representatives and neutrals who are accessible, have adequate resources, and reflect the makeup of the communities they serve.[84]

Two aspects of dispute resolution merit focus. First, there are the structural aspects of the system, such as a neutral forum that has qualified judges and other personnel who uphold the highest ethical standards and do so free of outside pressures. Second, as Stephan Schill has observed in the context of investor-state arbitration tribunals, the rule of law is the benchmark for assessing the practice of tribunals.[85] In other words, in their work, does a court or tribunal promote the values of the rule of law as reflected in 'just laws'?

[79] Ibid. (under the rule of law, laws 'are consistent with international human rights norms and standards').

[80] European Commission for Democracy through Law (Venice Commission), Report on the Rule of Law, adopted at its eighty-sixth plenary session (Venice, 25–26 March 2011), hwww.venice.coe.int/webforms/documents/default.aspx?pdffile=CDL-AD(2011)003rev-e, accessed 15 June 2020.

[81] Chesterman (n. 70) at 360.

[82] Thomas Bingham, *The Rule of Law* (Penguin 2010) 66–7.

[83] WJP Index (n. 71) 9.

[84] Ibid.

[85] Stephan W. Schill, 'International Investment Law and the Rule of Law' 15, ACIL Research Paper 2017–15, available at SSRN.

22.4 International Commercial Courts: Promoting or Challenging the Rule of Law?

22.4.1 Overview

Given this broad understanding, the rule of law implications of ICommCs are multifold and complex. They could be far-reaching, such as involving a critique of the role of courts in general and their specific relationship to society, including the host State and even beyond. They could be narrower, such as examining the means by which a specific court's operations set the gold standard for promoting efficiency and transparency in dispute resolution. Between these two extremes are multiple layers, and depending on one's perspective, they could be considered as either promoting or challenging the rule of law.

22.4.2 International Commercial Courts in Relationship to Host States

A threshold issue is whether the establishment of an ICommCs is an indicator that the rule of law in a specific State is impaired. The answer is, arguably, no. Of note, the courts, whether within a financial centre or embedded in the existing systems, were authorized under the constitutions or other applicable legal standards of the respective States. The existing legal framework enabled new laws or amendments to existing ones to create the courts. In sum, their establishment was law-based.

Further, jurisdictions around the world have legal mechanisms to authorize the creation of specialized courts.[86] Having a dedicated court to resolve discrete differences between defined parties comports with the recognized practice of specialized courts or divisions in specific areas, such as family law, labour law and criminal law.[87] Establishment of commercial courts is no different.[88]

[86] See for example Richard L. Revesz, 'Specialized Courts and the Administrative Lawmaking System' [1990] 138 Univ of Penn L Rev 1111 (recognizing that Articles I and III of the US Constitution enable the establishment of specialized courts); Eric Armour Beecroft, 'Courts of Specialized Jurisdiction in Australia' [1931] 79 Univ of Penn. L. Rev. 1021, 1022 (various powers under the constitution of Australia, such as the ability to regulate trade and commerce, enable the federal parliament to create specialized courts).

[87] Diane P. Wood, 'Generalist Judges in a Specialized World' [1997] 50 SMU L Rev 1755, 1761–2 (discussing the development of specialized courts in Germany, France and the United Kingdom); Diane P. Wood, 'Judges of All Trades: Further Thoughts on Specialized Courts' [2015] 99 Judicature 11, 11–12 (describing specialized courts in the United States).

[88] T. E. Scrutton, 'The Work of the Commercial Courts' [1921–3] 1 Cambridge L J 6, 17–18; Geoffrey Kiryabwire, 'The Development of the Commercial Judicial System in Uganda:

A State may have a large volume of commercial disputes in its existing courts or lack requisite expertise, so the new courts, with their specialized focus, can more efficiently address the backlog.[89] For example, recent judgments of the QIC and the DIFC Courts concern standard commercial disputes. The cases were resolved in short order (sometimes virtually) with a comprehensive, accessible judgment.[90]

Continuing with this analysis, the concern that ICommCs are co-opting municipal courts arguably rings hollow. For years, States have abdicated dispute resolution to private actors such as arbitrators, or they have encouraged settlement through mandatory mediation before private neutrals, all done behind closed doors. They have given broad deference to choice-of-courts clauses.[91] They have respected choice-of-law clauses of commercial actors, even when the applicable law may have little relationship to the parties or transactions at issue.[92]

The rise of arbitration, however, is not without controversy. Commercial disputes, while usually involving businesses, have social consequences, as US federal judge Patrick E. Higginbotham has noted, and the privacy of arbitration removes them from public scrutiny.[93] Yet,

A Study of the Commercial Court Division, High Court of Uganda' [2009] J. Bus, Entrepreneurship & the Law 349; Ember Reichgott Jung, 'Business Courts: Efficient Justice or Two-Tiered Elitism' [1998] 24 William Mitchell L Rev 315.

89 Scrutton (n. 88), 17–18 (discussing the advantages of the then newly established Commercial Court in England).

90 See for example *Obayashi Qatar LLC & HBK Contracting Co WLL* v. *Qatar First Bank LLC* (Public), [2020] QIC (F) 5 (31 May 2020) (ruling in favour of claimant due to defendant's breach of performance bond; judgment entered less than one year after the claim was filed); *Luerd Commercial Bank (PJSC)* v. *Ladern*, 2020 [DIFC] SCT 068 (4 May 2020) (ruling in favour of claimant due to defendant's breach of loan agreement; judgment entered within three months of filing of the claim).

91 Various states are signatories or parties to a multilateral treaty that seeks to respect the choice of court. See Hague Convention on Choice of Courts Agreements [30 June 2005] 44 ILM 1294.

92 See EU Commission Regulation 593/2008 (Rome I), On the Law Applicable to Contractual Obligations, 2008 O.J. (L. 177) 6.

93 Patrick E. Higginbotham, 'Judge Robert A. Ainsworth, Jr. Memorial Lecture, Loyola University School of Law: So Why Do We Call Them Trial Courts?' [2002] 55 SMU L. Rev. 1405, 1415 (acknowledging that '[l]arge commercial disputes have consequences for investors and communities dependent on their presence and success, not to mention their safety record and good citizenship'). See also Judith Resnik, 'Diffusing Disputes: The Public in the Private of Arbitration, the Private in Courts, and the Erasure of Rights' [2014–15] 124 Yale LJ 2804, 2811 (challenging US jurisprudence in favour of arbitration as unconstitutional unless measures are adopted 'to protect opportunities for voice and participation' and 'to require public access to the processes and outcomes, making the alternatives transparent and accountable').

as discussed earlier, transparency and public participation are hallmarks of the rule of law.

The new ICommCs, however, offer unique opportunities to promote the rule of law in dispute resolution beyond those realized by arbitration. As Lord Thomas has observed, courts 'promote the development of the law to keep pace with the ever increasing pace of change in international markets, trade and commerce'.[94] They 'develop the law'; they 'articulate and explain rights' to help guide future parties.[95] They issue detailed, reasoned decisions. The decisions of ICommCs readily cite to precedent, and either rely on or distinguish it based on the facts of the case. In other words, they contribute to order and stability, additional hallmarks of the rule of law.

Further, as courts, they work in the open, in contrast to arbitrators.[96] Most of the judges of the new courts are subject to judicial codes of conduct, readily accessible on the courts' websites. The dockets, orders, judgments and other developments in the cases are also easily available. Transparency and accountability are defining features of the new courts.[97]

This general and relatively favourable overview of ICommCs, however, ignores an overriding and critical fact about courts associated with financial centres: is the rule of law promoted or undermined by the presence of two distinct legal systems in a single State? Underlying the question are additional critical facts as the legal systems involve different substantive and procedural rules, operate in different languages, have different standards for the appointment of judges, and have different standards for admission of counsel to appear in their respective courts.

The existence of two legal systems within a single State could cause confusion and thus undermine the rule of law's aim of clarity and predictability. Nevertheless, federal States around the world, such as the United States, Australia, India or the United Arab Emirates, manage multiple courts and differing laws and, in many instances, across great geographical distance. The key to promoting certainty is that each legal

[94] Right Hon. Lord Thomas of Cwmgiedd, 'Developing Commercial Law through the Courts: Rebalancing the Relationship between the Courts and Arbitration', The Bailii Lecture 2016 para. 6 (9 March 2016), www.judiciary.uk/wp-content/uploads/2016/03/lcj-speech-bailli-lecture-20160309.pdf, accessed 15 June 2020.

[95] Ibid., at para. 49.

[96] Ibid.

[97] There are, however, some exceptions. For example, the SICC Rules of Court authorize the Court, upon request of a party, to issue orders to have a case heard in camera as well as impose other confidentiality measures. Rule 30 (1)(a)(b).

regime understands its role within the State and its relationship to the other legal regime. Further, citizens and other actors must appreciate the role of different courts, so the message to them needs to be understandable and consistent.

In line with building capacity and promoting understanding, the DIFC Courts have entered into agreements, principally memoranda of understanding, with entities within their respective States.[98] The agreements seek to facilitate cooperation and belie the notion that the regimes operate in silos. For example, the DIFC Courts' MoU with the UAE Ministry of Justice focuses principally upon the exchange of ideas and cooperation to build 'a mutual understanding of each other's founding laws, procedures, rules, policies and ambitions'.[99]

Second, there could be instances in which the State mandates application of certain standards within the international financial centre. For example, Kazakhstan's Ministry of Finance and the AIFC entered into a joint order in 2018 acknowledging that the AIFC would comply with Kazakhstan's anti-money-laundering legislation.[100] Likewise, entities operating in the QFC are subject to Qatar anti-money-laundering law as well as QFC rules and regulations.[101] The QFC clearly signals that certain Qatari criminal laws, including the Qatari penal code, apply within the QFC.[102]

Third, the judges of the ICommCs have the ability to exercise respect for the municipal legal system. An example is the QIC's decision in a judgment referenced earlier, *Obayashi Qatar LLC*, in which the court examined the law of Qatar and that of the QFC to establish that there was no material difference between the two as the law relates to a bond

[98] See for example Memorandum of Understanding between Ministry of Justice and DIFC Courts (26 April 2010), www.difccourts.ae/wp-content/uploads/2018/01/DIFCC_MoU_MOJ.pdf, accessed 6 August 2020 [hereinafter 'MOJ-DIFC Courts MoU']; Memorandum of Understanding between Ras Al Khaimah Courts Department and Abu Dhabi Global Markets Courts Concerning the Reciprocal Enforcement of Judgments (5 May 2019), www.adgm.com/documents/courts/memorandum-of-understanding/united-arab-emirates/mou-between-rak-courts-and-adgm-courts-on-enforcement–signed-5-may-2019.pdf, accessed 6 August 2020.

[99] MOJ-DIFC Courts MoU (n. 98) para. C(1).

[100] Joint Order between Astana International Financial Centre and Ministry of Finance of the Republic of Kazakhstan (19 July 2018), https://aifc.kz/files/legals/127/file/joint-order-between-aifc-and-mof-on-aml.pdf, accessed 15 June 2020. The Joint Order is unsigned, yet it is on the AIFC website.

[101] 'QFC Regulatory Authority: AML Law and Legislation', www.qfcra.com/aml-law-and-legislation, accessed 15 June 2020.

[102] Ibid.

dispute.[103] As another example, in *Karin Berardo* v. *Stumpf Energy Limited*, the ADGM Court put on a hold a proceeding given the possibility of a related criminal proceeding in the 'onshore court', presumably the courts of Abu Dhabi.[104]

A different way to consider the presence of two legal regimes operating within a single State is to recognize that one with expertise in a certain area could lead the development of the law beyond its jurisdiction. For example, the QFC has a comprehensive scheme to tackle money laundering. Enforcement is through the QFC Regulatory Authority, with an aggrieved party having the right to appeal the decision of the latter to the Regulatory Tribunal (RT), and with the right to request a further appeal of the RT's decision to the QIC Court of Appeals. In *Horizon Crescent Wealth LLC* v. *Qatar Financial Centre Regulatory Authority and Qatar Financial Centre Authority*, the applicant sought to appeal the RT's decision in which, among other issues, it held that the applicant had not established a due diligence program to comply with anti-money-laundering rules and requirements to combat the financing of terrorism.[105] The RT fined the applicant 25 million Qatari riyals.[106] The Court of Appeals denied applicant's permission to appeal the RT's decision. As for the anti-money-laundering claim, the Court of Appeals deferred to the RT's finding that the authority was not required to prove that the relevant funds were 'unlawfully acquired abroad' but that liability can arise due to the failure to establish 'arrangements for due diligence before handling monies from abroad which were, on any view, highly suspect'.[107] The decisions of both the RT and the QIC Court of Appeals are notable for two reasons. First, the establishment of a financial system that prevents illicit use of funds is consistent with substantive rule-of-law principles.[108] Second, the QIC has taken the lead on an important area of

103 *Obayashi Qatar LLC and HBK Contracting Co. WLL* v. *Qatar First Bank LLC (Public)* [2020] QIC (F) 5, www.qicdrc.gov.qa/sites/default/files/s3/judgments/english/case_no_8_of_2019_judgment_31_may_2020_1.pdf, accessed 15 June 2020.

104 *Karin Berardo* v. *Stumpf Energy Limited* [20 April 2018] ADGMCFI-2017-004, www.adgm.com/documents/courts/judgments/adgmcfi-2017-004-judgment-on-application-for-stay-and-costs-of-justice-sir-michael-burton-20042018.pdf, accessed 15 June 2020.

105 *Horizon Crescent Wealth LLC* v. *Qatar Financial Centre Regulatory Authority and Qatar Financial Centre Authority* [2020] QIC (A) on appeal from [2020] QIC (RT) 1, www.qicdrc.gov.qa/sites/default/files/s3/judgments/english/case_nos_5_and_6_of_2020_judgment_7_june_2020.pdf, accessed 15 June 2020.

106 Ibid. para. 6(a)(ii).

107 Ibid. para. 6(a)(i).

108 Money laundering enables 'various forms of transnational organized crime' which pose 'a serious threat to security, democracy, the rule of law and political and financial

the law that could set the guiding norm outside of QFC. In this sense, the work of the QIC is promoting the rule of law.

22.4.3 International Commercial Courts As Destination Fora

A State's promotion of ICommCs to encourage investment and other economic activity, including the growth of the legal profession, in itself is arguably not at odds with at least a thin conception of the rule of law. Many of the ICommCs afford efficient and accessible decision-making before independent and respectable international and local judges in line with accepted legal standards. As to the SICC, the parties also have some leeway to 'customize' the dispute resolution platform, which further serves the needs of the litigants.[109]

A possible outlier is the CICC in China. That court consists of Chinese judges who apply procedure law drawn largely from Chinese law.[110] Hence, to 'improve the credibility of the judicial system and, more generally, help in the development of the rule of law in China' it will need to 'absorb international standards and practices'.[111]

Does a somewhat favourable analysis of ICommCs change when the doors to the courthouse are open to parties or disputes unrelated to the forum? The World Bank's annual 'Doing Business' assessment of States has looked favourably upon creative techniques to expedite dispute resolution.[112] Specialized commercial courts fit within the 'good practices' category in terms of the 'enforcing contracts' indicator.[113] The mere fact that the forum resolves 'off-shore' disputes, which is possible as to the

stability'. Herbert V. Morais, 'Fighting International Crime and Its Financing: The Importance of Following a Coherent Global Strategy Based on the Rule of Law' [2005] 50 Vill L Rev 583, 593 (referencing the purpose of the United Nations Convention against Transnational Organized Crime, G.A. Res. 55/25, U.N. GAOR, 55th Sess., U.N. Doc. A/55/383 (2000)).

109 Hon. Kannan Ramesh, 'International Commercial Courts: Unicorns on a Journey of a Thousand Miles', para. 23 [13 May 2018], www.sicc.gov.sg/docs/default-source/modules-document/news-and-article/international-commercial-courts-unicorns_23108490-e290-422f-9da8-1e0d1e59ace5.pdf, accessed 4 August 2020.

110 CICC (n. 7).

111 Wei Cai and Andrew Godwin, 'Challenges and Opportunities for the China International Commercial Court' [2019] ICLQ 869, 902.

112 The World Bank, 'Doing Business 2020', 12–13, http://documents.worldbank.org/curated/en/688761571934946384/pdf/Doing-Business-2020-Comparing-Business-Regulation-in-190-Economies.pdf, accessed 15 June 2020.

113 The World Bank, 'Doing Business, Measuring Business Regulations', www.doingbusiness.org/en/data/exploretopics/enforcing-contracts/good-practices, accessed 8 August 2020.

SICC, for example, does not mean that the SICC detracts from protecting contracts. It may reflect poorly on other possible venues such as the place of performance of the contract, but it does not mean that the rule of law in Singapore, for example, is undermined.

A possible, perhaps stretched analogy is the emergence of international human rights courts that may be located away from the place of the alleged human rights violations. These courts have limited jurisdiction – namely, to hear cases due to the failure of States to protect human rights under a specific treaty and usually after exhaustion of local remedies. They have emerged due to shortcomings in municipal systems. They have prompted the development of a cadre of lawyers who are skilled in appearing before them; in other words, due to these courts a new type of legal practice has emerged. Along with this development is the emergence of human rights hubs, such as Strasbourg, France (home to the European Court of Human Rights) and San José, Costa Rica (home to the Inter-American Court of Human Rights). The courts have developed an extensive body of jurisprudence in their areas of specialty. To suggest that the rule of law is somehow impaired due to their location or the desire of their founders to have them build capacity would miss their valuable contributions.[114]

Further, by attracting 'off-shore' cases, the ICommCs and those acting within them are not the exclusive beneficiaries of the work. Various ICommCs take advantage of the presence of judges and lawyers from around the world and conduct open events to inform the broader legal community on a wide range of issues. Such engagement enhances understanding about the law and enables the healthy exchange of ideas. Indeed, given the emergence of multiple ICommCs, a thriving network has developed leading to the harmonization of commercial law.[115] These results are in line with the rule of law's focus on predictability and clarity of the law. Further, it demonstrates that the courts have the ability to shape the law and practices well beyond their respective borders.

When examining the issue from a broader understanding of the rule of law, however, concerns are apparent. First, the notion that dispute resolution is a business with the measure of its success being the volume of cases filed and resolved, while appealing from an efficiency perspective, is arguably inimical to the principles embedded in an expansive notion of the

[114] See for example Merris Amos, 'The Value of the European Court of Human Rights to the United Kingdom' [2017] 28 Eur. J Int'l L 763, 784–5 (concluding that as to the United Kingdom, 'it is not possible to have a commitment to protecting human rights through law and also dismiss the value of the [European Court of Human Rights]').

[115] Ramesh (n. 109) at paras. 9–14.

rule of law. Specifically, it challenges values such as equal access to justice and affordability of dispute resolution, as surely not everyone can engage counsel to get qualified in a foreign court and pursue claims thousands of miles away.

Second, the use of public resources to establish a more 'favourable' forum for commercial entities could signal a special status for commercial entities. In short, fundamental issues of equality come to the fore. For example, the proposed Brussels International Business Court, akin to the other European special commercial courts, has been taken off the table, apparently due to concerns from the political left that the court would be a 'caviar court' for the 'super rich'.[116] This argument mirrors the backlash against investor-state dispute settlement (ISDS), which some consider inimical to the rule of law as it a special process designed to protect major corporations.[117] Further undermining the cause were Belgian judges, who apparently expressed concern about a 'two-tiered justice' system, the costs of setting up a new 'VIP court' and the possibility that litigants would not find the court attractive.[118]

The backlash against special courts for special litigants reflects the growing antiglobalization sentiment. A fundamental tenet of the rule of law is the substantive principle of equality, which could be in jeopardy when legal institutions are established or structured to benefit a specific category of actors.

22.5 Conclusion

Analysing ICommCs from the rule-of-law perspective, whether it be thin or thick, national or international, enables a better understanding of their current role, benefits and possible shortcomings. A second functional value is that the rule of law serves as a yardstick on a going forward basis. Drawing upon Professor Schill's approach to examining ISDS from a rule of law perspective, a meaningful approach would be to understand

[116] Xander Kramer, 'The International Business Courts Saga Continued: NCC First Judgment-BIBC Proposal Unplugged', Conflict of Laws.net (27 March 2019), https://conflictoflaws.net/2019/the-international-business-courts-saga-continued-ncc-first-judgment-bibc-proposal-unplugged, accessed 15 June 2020.

[117] See for example Letter from Professor Erin Chemerinsky et al. to Senator Mitch McConnell et al. (11 March 2015), www.citizen.org/wp-content/uploads/lawyers-isds-letter-march-2015.pdf, accessed 15 June 2020 (contending that ISDS 'weakens the rule of law by giving corporations special legal rights').

[118] Kramer (n. 116).

ICommCs and their associated legal regimes as instruments to promote the rule of law, nationally and internationally.[119] In other words, they are means to a laudable end, and like any institution, they sometimes fulfil that objective and other times they do not.

Considering ICommCs as instruments in a broader societal context, rather than an end in themselves, enables the courts and host States to remain focused on the rule of law and the associated responsibilities of each under it. As this chapter has observed, the courts are already doing this to a certain extent, particularly as to transparency, judicial integrity, supremacy of the law and accountability.

On a prospective basis, three areas are ripe for focus due to their implications for the rule of law. Accordingly, as they continue with their work, ICommCs should allocate time and attention to them.

First, party accessibility to the courts will likely become more important as the activity of the courts increases. Notably, some of the courts, such as the QIC and the DIFC Courts, have instituted pro bono programs to help litigants that otherwise cannot afford counsel. This type of awareness and preparedness is essential to ensuring that dispute resolution is affordable, an aspect of the rule of law.

Second, disputes under review will invariably touch on issues that extend beyond the parties to the case. For example, in the context of enforcement of anti-money-laundering laws, defences relating to fundamental rights could likely come to the fore. As another example, non-parties may have an interest in the outcome of a case and seek to play a role as *amicus curiae*. In short, the courts must anticipate that even commercial disputes affect the public and with that comes the need for each court to appreciate its role beyond the specific case at hand.

Third, an area of likely regular activity will be the evolving relationship between ICommCs and municipal courts of the host State. From the perspective of the rule of law, clarity and predictability are a priority. Further, a dialogue between the two legal regimes, along the lines that now exists between courts of different States, would promote further harmony and enable the development of legal principles aligned with 'just law'.

International commercial courts are still in their early stages. Their healthy respect for the rule of law, both as a constraint and as an aspiration, will enable them to play a more meaningful role in fulfilling important societal objectives.

[119] Schill (n. 85) at 5.

INDEX

Abu Dhabi Global Market (ADGM)
  overview, 31, 228, 232, 256
  establishment of, 519
  Founding Law, 130
Abu Dhabi Global Market Court (ADGMC)
  generally, 4, 21–2, 117, 375, 492–3
  applicable law
    generally, 229, 247–8, 521
    Application of English Law Regulations 2015, 12, 243–4, 256
    English common law, 34–5, 139, 141, 155–6, 218, 223–4, 234–5, 236–7, 243–4, 256, 287, 464–5, 521
    hybridity in, 464–5
    legislation pertaining to, 242–3
    other foreign law, application of, 145
    symbolic capital and, 230
    UAE law, 243
  application of English Law Regulations 2015, 141
  Belt and Road Initiative and, 32
  British judges in, 35
  caseload, 237
  counsel ethics in, 316, 328–9, 330, 334
  Court of Appeal, 12, 256, 520–1
  Court of First Instance, 12, 130, 256, 520–1
  Court Regulations, 154
  Court Rules, 120–1
  DIFCC compared, 218
  domestic courts, conflicts with, 364
  dual legal system, effect of, 531
  enforcement of judgments
    generally, 218, 520–1
    bilateral regimes for, 154
    foreign judgments, 46, 47–8
    regional regimes for, 154
  establishment of, 12, 120–1, 232–3, 256, 273, 278, 519
  Financial Services and Markets Regulations, 141
  hybrid nature of, 464
  international commercial arbitration in, 236
  judges, 35, 121, 145, 256, 464–5, 521
  jurisdiction
    generally, 12, 33, 256, 520–1
    additional parties or claims, capacity to accept, 136–7
    both parties choosing forum, capacity to accept cases, 130
    defendant accepting plaintiff's choice of forum, capacity to accept cases, 134
    subject matter jurisdiction, 164, 165
  language in, 218
  London Court of International Arbitration (LCIA) and, 47
  as 'off-shore' jurisdiction, 232–3
  pro bono services in, 50
  purpose of, 32, 120–1
  QICDRC compared, 218, 234, 245
  rule of law and, 531
  Rules of Conduct, 328–9
  SICC compared, 218, 329–30
  special economic zones (SEZs) and, 210, 252, 256, 464, 516, 519
  as stand-alone court, 160, 174, 285–7
access to justice
  generally, 49
  CETA and, 84
  DIFCC, 535

international commercial arbitration, lack in, 71, 405
language issues, 49–50
powers of ICommCs, 49
pro bono services, 50
QICDRC, 535
rule of law and, 535
accountability, rule of law and, 525
Achmea, 79–80
ADGM. *See* Abu Dhabi Global Market (ADGM)
ADGMC. *See* Abu Dhabi Global Market Court (ADGMC)
'adjudicative offer', 55
adjudicators, judicial ethics and, 307–8
advantages of ICommCs
generally, 54, 72
'adjudicative offer' and, 55
competitive nature of, 61–4
'court' as signalling word, 56–7, 59
as latest product, 61–4
legitimacy and, 56–7
political system, ICommCs in, 58–9
power and, 55–6
public interest and, 57–9
'race to the top', 63
state interests and, 59–61
AIFC. *See* Astana International Financial Centre (AIFC)
AIFCC. *See* Astana International Financial Centre Court (AIFCC)
Allsop, James, 40
Alvarez, Jose, 247
American Bar Association, 406–7
Amos, Merris, 533
Antonopoulou, Georgia, 23–4
applicable law. *See also specific tribunal*
generally, 20, 21
accommodation by ICommCs, 369–70
Brexit, effect of, 513
comparative analysis, 116, 156–7, 287–8
diversity of, 138, 229
English common law as, 138 (*See also specific tribunal*)
function of, 228–9
symbolic capital and, 229, 230, 235–6
arbitration. *See* International commercial arbitration
Astana International Arbitration Centre (IAC)
generally, 500
Arbitration and Mediation Rules, 491
arbitrators, 494
caseload, 493
dual legal system, effect of, 491
enforcement of awards, 498, 499
establishment of, 490, 491
international commercial arbitration, 495
jurisdiction, 496
mediation, 495
New York Convention and, 499
premises, 499
procedural rules, 497–8
purpose of, 492
rule of law and, 491–2
services, 495
success of, 493
technology in, 499
Astana International Financial Centre (AIFC)
arbitration regulations, 491, 496
constitutional statute, 130, 146, 491, 496
court registry, 498–9
court regulations, 130, 146, 491, 495, 521–2
court rules, 146, 496, 497–8
establishment of, 256
Management Council, 491
Astana International Financial Centre Court (AIFCC)
generally, 4, 24, 117, 209, 375, 489–90, 500
applicable law
generally, 521–2
English common law, 35, 139, 142, 155–6, 223–4, 256, 287, 464–5
hybridity in, 464–5
Astana Council Resolution, 142
attorneys in, 497
British judges in, 35

Astana International (cont.)
caseload, 493
choice-of-court clauses, 167
constitution, 220
counsel ethics in, 326–7
Court of Appeal, 14, 256, 496
Court of First Instance, 14, 256, 496
development of law in, 496–7
domestic courts, conflicts with, 364
dual legal system, effect of, 491, 530
economic diversification and, 402
enforcement of judgments
generally, 498
bilateral regimes for, 154
in Kazakhstan, 498–9
outside of Kazakhstan, 499
regional regimes for, 154
establishment of, 14, 121–2, 219–20, 256, 273, 278, 490, 491
hybrid nature of, 464
judges, 121–2, 220, 256, 464–5, 494, 521–2
jurisdiction
generally, 14, 33, 256, 495, 521–2
additional parties or claims, capacity to accept, 137
both parties choosing forum, capacity to accept cases, 130
defendant accepting plaintiff's choice of forum, capacity to accept cases, 134
other foreign law, application of, 146
language in, 220, 498
mediation, 494
precedent and, 496
premises, 499
pro bono services in, 50
procedural rules, 497–8
purpose of, 32, 121–2, 490, 492
reciprocity and, 156
rule of law and, 491–2, 530
services, 494
Small Claims Court, 496
special economic zones (SEZs) and, 210, 219–20, 256, 464, 516, 521–2
as stand-alone court, 160, 174, 285–7
success of, 493
technology in, 499
Australia
commercial courts in, 493
Federal Court, 153, 369
federalism in, 529–30
Supreme Court of New South Wales, 153, 369
Supreme Court of Victoria, 369
Australian Centre for International Commercial Arbitration, 322

Bachmann, Clément, 20
Bacon, Francis, 366
Bailey, Julian, 23
Bangladesh, child labour in, 102
Bantekas, Ilias, 20–1
Banyan Tree Corporate Pte Ltd, 378–9
Barbados, CCJ and, 460
Beatson, Jack, 220
Belgium. *See also* Brussels International Business Court (BIBC) (proposed)
constitution, 272–3, 425
Council of State, 425
Judicial Code, 16, 163, 170, 259
Supreme Judicial Council (CSJ), 272–3, 282
Belize, CCJ and, 460, 461
Bell, Gary, 57–8
Belt and Road Initiative
generally, 24, 142
ADGMC and, 32
bilateral regimes for enforcement of judgments and, 155
CICC and, 177, 181, 193, 195, 258–9, 266, 402, 433, 434, 465, 471, 475, 485, 488, 523–4
as global economic policy, 473–4
Hong Kong International Arbitration Centre (HKIAC) and, 484
International Chamber of Commerce (ICC) and, 484
Singapore International Arbitration Centre (SIAC) and, 485
Benelux Court of Justice, 77

Benson, Cyrus, 319, 323
Berman, Paul Schiff, 309
Bianchi, Andrea, 68
BIBC. *See* Brussels International Business Court (BIBC) (proposed)
bilateral investment treaties (BITs), 79–80, 276, 474
Bingham, Tom (Lord), 492
Bishop, Doak, 317
Blair, William, 20, 36–7, 40, 54, 297–8, 335, 400, 413
Blockchain technology
  electronic filing and, 346–7
  enforcement of judgments and, 356–7
Boerner, Timon, 294
Bolaños, Enrique, 458
Bookman, Pamela K., 52, 62, 63, 478
Born, Gary, 319
Bosnia and Herzegovina, hybrid criminal court in, 7, 107, 366–7
Boston Consulting Group, 437
Botchway, Francis, 236
Bretton Woods system, 203
Brexit
  generally, 24–5, 501
  attractiveness of UK as litigation destination, effect on, 512, 514
  Commercial Court of England and Wales, impact on, 185–6, 212, 279
  common law, impact on, 87
  European ICommCs, impact on, 280, 281–2
  private international law, effect on
    generally, 514
    applicable law, 513
    enforcement of judgments, 509–13, 514
    harmonization of international commercial law, 505–6
    jurisdiction, 509–13
    'opt-in', 505–6
    post-Brexit situation, 508–9
    pre-Brexit situation, 505–6
  technology in ICommCs, impact on, 338–40
  Withdrawal Agreement (WA), 506–7
Briggs, Michael (Lord), 205, 224, 504
Brighton Declaration (2012), 457
British Institute of International and Comparative Law, 409
Brussels I Regulation
  generally, 182–3
  choice of court clauses and, 170–1, 338–9
  Commercial Court of England and Wales and, 128–9, 182–4, 185–6, 198
  enforcement of judgments and, 152
  'forum shopping' and, 502
  NCC and, 427
  technology and, 342–4
  transfer jurisdiction and, 171
  UK and, 506
Brussels Ia Regulation, 506, 507, 510, 511–12, 513
Brussels Convention (1968), 505, 511
Brussels International Business Court (BIBC) (proposed)
  generally, 5, 16, 124–5
  applicable law
    English common law, 143
    UNCITRAL Arbitration Rules, 259, 301
    UNCITRAL Model Law, 439, 441–2
  Brexit, impact of, 280, 281–2
  choice-of-court clauses, 170
  conflict with domestic courts, 272–3
  criticism of, 534
  economic diversification and, 402–3
  failure to create, 158, 278
  Hague Choice of Court Convention and, 149
  international commercial arbitration, procedural similarities with ICommCs, 439, 441–2
  jurisdiction
    generally, 260
    both parties choosing forum, capacity to accept cases, 132

Brussels International (cont.)
defendant accepting plaintiff's choice of forum, capacity to accept cases, 133
party agreement on nature of case, 425
subject matter jurisdiction, 163, 166–7
language in, 442
party autonomy and, 426
procedure
generally, 422
flexibility of, 441–2
international commercial arbitration, procedural similarities with ICommCs, 439, 441–2
internationality requirement, 425–6, 428
rationale for establishment, 281–2
as stand-alone court, 161, 259
Burnett, Ian (Lord), 205
business imperative
generally, 392
agility and, 397
creativity and, 396–400
interactions between imperatives, 414–16
market acceptance and, 398–400
market perception and, 398
party mobility and, 415
political imperative and, 402, 414–15
tensions between imperatives, 414–16
business-to-business (B2B) contracts, 343
Butcher, Christopher (Justice), 197

CACJ. *See* Central American Court of Justice (CACJ)
Calo, Zachary R., 22–3
Cambodia, hybrid criminal court in, 7, 102, 107, 108, 366–7
Campbell-Holt, Christopher, 24, 491, 497
Canada
CETA (*See* Comprehensive Economic and Trade Agreement between the EU and Canada (CETA))
commercial courts in, 493
Caribbean Court of Justice (CCJ)
CJEU compared, 460
hybridity in, 459–62
indirect effect and, 460, 461
institutional hybridity in, 460–1
jurisdiction, 448–9
professional hybridity in, 460–1
CARICOM, 459–62
Carothers, Thomas, 524
Cartago Court. *See* Central American Court of Justice (CACJ)
Casablanca
commercial courts in, 37, 38
Finance City (CFC), 38
International Mediation and Arbitration Centre (CIMAC), 38
case management
comparative analysis, 291
electronic case management, 346, 347
technology and, 346, 347
Caserta, Salvatore, 24
CCJ. *See* Caribbean Court of Justice (CCJ)
Central American Court of Justice (CACJ)
CJEU compared, 457–8, 459
historical background, 450–1
hybridity in, 449–50, 457–9
institutional hybridity in, 458
jurisdiction, 448–9
jurisprudential hybridity in, 458–9
professional hybridity in, 458
Central American Integration System (SICA), 457, 458
Centre of Excellence for International Courts, 449
CETA. *See* Comprehensive Economic and Trade Agreement between the EU and Canada (CETA)
Chaisse, Julien, 24

characteristic features of ICommCs, 210–11
China
  Belt and Road Initiative (*See* Belt and Road Initiative)
  Civil Procedure Law (CPL), 156, 193, 194, 433–4, 477, 483, 486–7
  Communist Party of China, 16–17, 258–9, 469–70, 471
  constitution, 468–70
  domestic courts, role of, 472–3
  economic evolution of, 471–2
  ex parte communication in, 311
  foreign direct investment (FDI) in, 471
  Foreign Investment Law, 219
  Free Trade Zones (FTZs), 471–2
  Hague Choice of Court Convention and, 149, 199
  Higher People's Courts, 173, 193, 219
  hybrid nature of legal system, 468–70
  Law of the People's Republic of China on the Laws Applicable to Foreign-Related Civil Relations, 146
  Maritime Silk Road, 16–17, 473
  Ministry of Commerce (MOFCOM), 472
  National People's Congress Standing Committee (NPCSC), 473
  'One Window, One Form' Policy, 472
  Provisions of the Supreme People's Court on Several Issues regarding the Establishment of the International Commercial Court, 433, 475, 476
  Silk Road Economic Belt, 122
  Special Administrative Regions (SARs), 468–9
  State Administration for Industry and Commerce (SAIC), 472
  State Council, 16–17, 258–9
  Supreme People's Court (SPC)
    generally, 131, 193–4
    Belt and Road Initiative and, 16–17
    CICC as division of, 181, 197, 258–9, 476–7, 523–4
    experts, 273
    transfer of cases to CICC, 173, 199
  UAE, bilateral treaty with, 443
  videoconferencing in, 348
  virtual site inspections in, 350
China International Commercial Court (CICC)
  generally, 4, 21, 24, 117, 158, 470, 488
  applicable law, 142
  Belt and Road Initiative and, 177, 181, 193, 195, 258–9, 266, 402, 433, 434, 465, 471, 475, 485, 488, 523–4
  Commercial Court of England and Wales compared, 183–4, 195
  coordination of courts, 477–8
  DIFCC compared, 483
  dispute resolution clauses, 482
  as division of existing court, 160, 174, 181, 516–17, 523–4
  economic diversification and, 402
  enforcement of judgments
    bilateral regimes for, 155
    finality of judgments, 486–7
    outstanding questions regarding, 487
    reciprocity, 487
  establishment of, 16–17, 180–1, 218–19, 278, 475
  Frankfurt Court compared, 438
  Hague Choice of Court Convention and, 434–5, 487
  Hague Judgments Convention and, 487
  hybrid nature of, 218–19, 465
  internationalization and, 196–7
  international nature of, 30
  judges
    generally, 123, 219, 478–80
    diversity of, 41
    hybridity and, 465
    International Commercial Law Expert Committee, 196–7, 219, 260, 273, 465, 479–80, 485, 488, 523–4
  judicial interpretation, 193, 194, 195

China International (cont.)
jurisdiction
generally, 219, 260
additional parties or claims, capacity to accept, 137
both parties choosing forum, capacity to accept cases, 130–1
consensual jurisdiction, 194–5, 481–2
defendant accepting plaintiff's choice of forum, capacity to accept cases, 134
international commercial cases, 193–4, 481
jurisdiction agreements, 197
monetary amount of claims, 195, 482–3
other foreign law, application of, 146–7
outstanding questions regarding, 481–7
subject matter jurisdiction, 166–7
transfer jurisdiction, 173, 195, 199
voluntary jurisdiction, 430, 433–5
language in, 219, 465, 485–6
as modern ICommC, 196–7
NCC compared, 438
Notice of the Supreme People's Court on Inclusion of the First Group of International Commercial Arbitration and Mediation Institutions in the 'One-stop' Diversified International Commercial Dispute Resolution Mechanism, 476
party autonomy and, 195, 434
procedure
generally, 422
'actual connection' requirement, 430, 433–5
evidence, 486
purpose of, 122–3, 177, 199, 219, 475–6
QICDRC compared, 479
reciprocity and, 156
Rules of Procedure, 137, 476, 477, 481–2, 488
SICC compared, 195, 435, 465, 479, 483
SPC and
CICC as division of, 181, 197, 258–9, 476–7, 523–4
transfer of cases to CICC, 173, 199
as stand-alone court, 252, 258–9, 465
Working Rules of the International Commercial Expert Committee of the Supreme People's Court (for Trial Implementation), 476
choice-of-court clauses
generally, 21, 174, 175 (*See also specific tribunal*)
Brussels I Regulation and, 170–1, 338–9
Hague Choice of Court Convention and, 149, 170–1, 340
ICommCs and, 167–71
technology and, 342–4
Chon, Stephen, 269
CICAP. *See* Paris Chambers
CICC. *See* China International Commercial Court (CICC)
Cicero, 201, 227
CISG. *See* Convention on Contracts for the International Sale of Goods (CISG) (1980)
civil law systems
comparative analysis, 287
ex parte communication in, 310, 311
judicial ethics in, 308
CJEU. *See* Court of Justice of the European Union (CJEU)
Clancy, Michael, 234–5
'click-wrapping', 343
coexistence of ICommCs with other tribunals, 5
Coke, Edward, 365, 366
comity, 411
Commercial Court of England and Wales
generally, 3–4, 21, 116, 159, 209, 493
advantages of, 503–4
applicable law, 138–40, 155–6, 184–5
Brexit, impact of, 185–6, 212, 279

Brussels I Regulation and, 128–9, 182–4, 185–6, 198
caseload, 179
CICC compared, 183–4, 195
Civil Procedure Rules, 128–9, 182, 184–5
Commercial Court Guide, 139
commercial nature of, 32–3
dedicated premises, 35–6
DIFCC compared, 211
disadvantages of, 504
enforcement of judgments, bilateral regimes for, 153
English Commercial Court, 117
establishment of, 178, 211, 388
forum non conveniens, 184–5
Hague Choice of Court Convention and, 149, 185–6
historical background, 389–90
'home advantage' in, 207
influence of, 34, 176, 179, 257, 271
innovation in, 503–4
international commercial arbitration, relation to, 118
internationalization and, 195–6
international nature of, 30
jurisdiction
  additional parties or claims, capacity to accept, 135–6
  both parties choosing forum, capacity to accept cases, 128–9
  commercial claims, 182
  defendant accepting plaintiff's choice of forum, capacity to accept cases, 133
  international jurisdiction, 182–6
  other foreign law, application of, 143–4
  subject matter jurisdiction, 164, 166–7
  transfer jurisdiction, 186
London Court of International Arbitration (LCIA) and, 118
other tribunals as challenge to, 339, 465–6
party autonomy and, 138–9, 389
popularity of, 279–80, 281
purpose of, 177, 199–200, 211
regulation, 198
restructuring of, 178
SICC compared, 183–4, 211
Spillada principles and, 184–5
success of, 195–6
Technology and Construction Court (TCC), 117–18
technology in
  Brexit, impact of, 338–40
  electronic case management, 346
  videoconferencing, 348–9
as traditional ICommC, 195–6
underutilization of, 389–90
Commercial nature of ICommCs, 32–3
Commission on International Trade Law (UNCITRAL)
  adoption of model laws, 474
  Arbitration Rules, 16, 259, 389, 495
  comity and, 411
  harmonization of international commercial law and, 208
  jurisprudential imperative and, 405–6
  Model Law on International Commercial Arbitration, 121, 124–5, 143, 163, 275, 301, 413, 439, 441–2
common law. *See* English common law
Common Market Group (CMG), 462
communicative skills
  generally, 90–1
  channel, 91–2
  elements of communication, 97
  of ICommCs, 92, 93
  of international criminal tribunals, 92
  message, 91–2
  receiver, 91–2
  signification contrasted, 92
comparative analysis. *See also specific tribunal*
  applicable law, 116, 156–7, 287–8
  case management, 291
  civil law versus common law, 287
  court fees, 290
  discovery, 292
  division of existing court versus stand-alone court, 285–7

comparative analysis (cont.)
enforcement of judgments, 116, 156–7, 287
judges, 287
jurisdiction, 115–16, 156–7, 176–7, 199–200
language, 290
online access, 293–4
organizational features, 289
procedure, 288, 290–3
tables, 286, 289
technology, 342
witnesses, 291–2
Comprehensive Economic and Trade Agreement between the EU and Canada (CETA)
generally, 75
access to justice and, 84
adoption of, 80–2
appellate tribunal, 81–2, 83–4
independence requirement and, 83–4
Joint Committee, 83–4
party autonomy and, 82–3
referral to CJEU, 82
tribunal, 81–2, 83–4
confidentiality, international commercial arbitration lacking, 226, 405
Context of ICommCs, 20
Convention on Contracts for the International Sale of Goods (CISG) (1980)
generally, 474
harmonization of international commercial law and, 208
public purpose and, 110
purpose of, 474
Convention on the Recognition and Enforcement of Foreign Arbitral Awards (New York Convention) (1958)
generally, 18, 413, 487
adoption of, 389
advantages of international commercial arbitration, 483–4
comity and, 411
DIFCC and, 276, 379, 380, 443, 444
digital delivery of judgment and, 355–6
enforcement of awards, 45–6, 148, 267, 340, 390–1
Hague Choice of Court Convention compared, 149
jurisprudential imperative and, 405–6
Convention on the Recognition and Enforcement of Foreign Judgments in Civil or Commercial Matters (Hague Judgments Convention) (2019)
generally, 46, 341–2
comity and, 411
comparative analysis, 150–1
ICommCs and, 340–1
jurisprudential imperative and, 406
Cooke, Jeremy, 240
Council of Europe, 454, 526
counsel ethics. *See also specific tribunal*
generally, 22–3, 315, 316, 334
in ICommCs
current regulatory models, 324–30
diversity of approaches, 330
future challenges, 330–4
harmonization of, 331–2
hybrid nature of ICommCs and, 325–6
international commercial arbitration compared, 324–5
lack of attention to, 315–16
modesty in, 332–3
need for more regulations, 330–1
in international commercial arbitration
generally, 315, 316–17
conflicting standards, 318
domestic regulation, 317
double deontology problem, 318
ICommCs compared, 324–5
inequality and, 318–23
unfairness and, 318–23
universal code of conduct, proposals for, 320–3
court fees, 290
Court of Justice of the European Union (CJEU)

generally, 75
CACJ compared, 457–8, 459
CETA, compatibility of ISDS provisions with EU law, 80–4
establishment of, 73
ICommCs applying law of, 87–8
ISDS arbitral tribunal not deemed court or tribunal for purposes of TFEU, 79–80
jurisdiction, 73
Lugano Convention II and, 509–10
public purpose and, 103
references by ICommCs, 85–7
referrals to, 74, 78–9, 87–8
subsidiarity and, 456
technology and, 343
UK and, 504, 513
uniform interpretation of law and, 74
validity of EU law, referrals regarding, 86, 87–8
COVID-19 pandemic
enforcement of foreign judgments, effect on, 46–7
harmonization of international commercial law and, 201
NCC and, 296
SICC and, 214
Cyprus, common law in, 87

Dahdal, Andrew, 236
Daman Real Estate Capital Partners Company LLV, 382
Damaska, Mirjan, 308
definition of ICommC, 89–90, 278, 368–9
Demeter, Dalma, 55
Deng Xiaoping, 471
Denmark, private international law and, 505, 506
Dezalay, Yves, 62
Dickinson, Laura, 367
DIFCC. *See* Dubai International Financial Centre Court (DIFCC)
digital delivery of judgment, 355–6
Dimitropoulos, Georgios, 22, 196, 463, 465
disadvantages of ICommCs
generally, 54, 72
backlash, potential of, 70–1
common public interest, neglect of, 71–2
as latest product, 64
legitimacy, lack of, 64–5
new social orders created by, 66–8, 69–70
representativeness, lack of, 71
undemocratic nature of, 71
discovery, comparative analysis, 292
dispute resolution. *See also specific tribunal*
generally, 20
essential elements of, 297–8
historical background, 448
international commercial arbitration (*See* International commercial arbitration)
rule of law and, 526
disruptive effect of ICommCs, 52–3
divisions of existing courts, 285–7, 465–6, 516–17. *See also specific tribunal*
Dohmann, Barbara, 494, 497
Doing Business Indicators, 9
Doing Business Report, 344
domestic courts. *See also specific tribunal*
generally, 23
conflicts with ICommCs
DIFCC (*See* Dubai International Financial Centre Court (DIFCC))
examples, 370–1
future trends, 385
harmonization of law, possibility of, 386–7
co-option by ICommCs, 528
elements of in ICommCs, 269–70
harmonization of international commercial law, unsuitability for, 226–7
ICommCs compared
generally, 391–2, 416
hybridity, 417
innovation, 416

domestic courts (cont.)
international commercial arbitration versus, 417
normative role of ICommCs, 416–17
international commercial arbitration versus, 268
interoperability with ICommCs, 270–4
judges of ICommCs, domestic court judges compared, 300–1
judicial ethics in, 306–7
reforms in, 271–2
rule of law, ICommC relations with host states and, 527–32, 535
TFEU, under, 74
Dominica, CCJ and, 460
Dubai International Arbitration Centre (DIAC), 276, 378, 382, 384, 443
Dubai International Financial Centre Court (DIFCC)
generally, 4, 21–2, 117, 492–3
access to justice in, 535
ADGMC compared, 218
advantages of litigating in, 374–5
applicable law
generally, 229, 237–8, 247–8, 255, 373, 520
advantages of litigating in, 374–5
case law regarding, 239–42
English common law, 34, 139, 140–1, 155–6, 224, 235, 236–7, 287, 464–5
flexibility of, 239–40
hybridity in, 464–5
legislation pertaining to, 238–9
non-DIFC law, 241–2
parties agreeing on, 374–5
symbolic capital and, 230
UAE law, 238, 241–2
caseload, 237
CICC compared, 483
Code of Conduct, 328
Commercial Court of England and Wales compared, 211
counsel ethics in, 316, 325, 328, 330, 334
Court of Appeal (CA), 11, 215, 232, 241–2, 255, 372–3, 379, 381–2, 520
Court of First Instance (CFI), 11, 129, 215, 232, 255, 372–3, 381–2, 428–9, 520
Court Rules, 136
domestic courts, conflicts with
generally, 363–4, 371, 375
Daman Real Estate Capital Partners Company LLV v. *Oger Dubai LLC* (2017), 382–4
enforcement of judgments, 429
future trends, 385
harmonization of law, possibility of, 386–7
Investment Group Private Ltd v. *Standard Chartered Bank* (2015), 381–2
Joint Judicial Committee and, 377, 382–4, 385
Meydan Group LLC v. *Banyan Tree Corporate Pte Ltd* (2014), 378–80
Protocol of Enforcement and, 376
Ramadan Mousa Mishmish v. *Sweet Homes Real Estate LLC* (2017), 384–5
resolution of, 376–8
'turf wars', 375, 385
dual legal system, effect of, 530
economic diversification and, 402
enforcement of judgments
generally, 216
bilateral regimes for, 153, 154
comparative analysis, 287
domestic courts, conflicts with, 429
foreign judgments, 46, 48
Protocol of Enforcement, 216, 233
regional regimes for, 154
establishment of, 11, 119–20, 232, 254–5, 273, 278, 372–3, 428, 519
Frankfurt Court compared, 438
funding of, 97
as hybrid court, 224, 373
hybrid nature of, 447–8, 463–4
international commercial arbitration

generally, 236
enforcement of awards, 276
procedural similarities with ICommCs, 439, 442–4
international nature of, 30
Joint Judicial Committee, 377, 382–4, 385
judges
generally, 119–20, 145, 215, 255, 373
British judges, 35
diversity of, 41
hybridity and, 464–5
jurisdiction
generally, 31–2, 11, 33, 215–16, 255, 520
additional parties or claims, capacity to accept, 136
based on other grounds, 174
both parties choosing forum, capacity to accept cases, 129
'conduit jurisdiction', 380, 385
conflicts of, 274
defendant accepting plaintiff's choice of forum, capacity to accept cases, 133
opt-in jurisdiction, 428–9
other foreign law, application of, 144–5
subject matter jurisdiction, 164–5
language in, 215, 255, 373, 374
Memoranda of Guidance, 443
NCC compared, 438
New York Convention and, 276, 379, 380, 443, 444
as 'off-shore' jurisdiction, 232–3, 374
Practice Direction No. 2, 443
pro bono services in, 50
procedure
generally, 216, 422
advantages of litigating in, 374
international commercial arbitration, procedural similarities with ICommCs, 439, 442–4
internationality requirement, 428–30
Protocol of Enforcement, 216, 233, 376
purpose of, 38, 119–20, 215, 428
QICDRC compared, 217–18, 234, 245, 464
Register of Practitioners, 328
rule of law and, 528, 530
as self-contained system, 373–4
SICC compared, 215
Small Claims Tribunal (SCT), 11, 255
special economic zones (SEZs) and, 210, 214, 215, 252, 254–5, 463–4, 516, 519
as stand-alone court, 160, 174, 285–7
Tech Lab, 347
technology in
digital delivery of judgment, 355–6
electronic case management, 347
electronic filing, 344, 347
user-friendly aspirations of, 95
Dubai International Financial Centre (DIFC)
generally, 11, 31, 228, 254–5
Arbitration Law, 379, 384
Authority, 239
Court Law, 140–1, 214
Dispute Resolution Authority, 232, 254–5, 463–4
establishment of, 214, 232, 372, 519
Real Property Law, 240–1
regulations, 239
Regulatory Authority, 239
Dunoff, Jeffrey L., 305
Durovic, Mateja, 21

Earl of Oxford's Case (1615), 364–6, 387
Easton, David, 58
ECHR. *See* European Convention on Human Rights (ECHR) (1959)
ECJ. *See* European Court of Justice (ECJ)
Eco Swiss, 78–9
ECtHR. *See* European Court of Human Rights (ECtHR)
Eder, Bernard, 410
Egypt, bilateral treaty with UAE, 443
electronic deliberations, 354–5

electronic filing, 344–7
Ellesmere, Lord (Lord Chancellor), 365
emergency of ICommCs, 3–4
Energy Charter Treaty, 474
enforcement of judgments. *See also specific tribunal*
  generally, 20, 21, 147–8
  Belt and Road Initiative, bilateral regimes for enforcement of judgments and, 155
  bilateral regimes, 152
  Blockchain technology and, 356–7
  Brexit, effect of, 509–13, 514
  Brussels I Regulation and, 152
  comparative analysis, 116, 156–7, 287
  conflicts regarding, 370
  as feature of ICommCs, 370
  foreign judgments, 45–8
  Hague Judgments Convention (*See* Convention on the Recognition and Enforcement of Foreign Judgments in Civil or Commercial Matters (Hague Judgments Convention) (2019))
  ICommCs' own judgments, 48
  by international commercial arbitration, 148
  in international criminal tribunals, 370
  local enforcement, 148
  New York Convention (*See* Convention on the Recognition and Enforcement of Foreign Arbitral Awards (New York Convention) (1958))
  other bases of enforcement, 155–6
  reciprocity and, 156
  regional regimes, 152
  technology and, 341–2, 356–7, 359
England. *See also* United Kingdom
  common law (*See* English common law)
  Court of Chancery, 364, 366
  Court of Common Pleas, 364, 366
  Earl of Oxford's Case (1615), 364–6, 387
  Exchequer, 364
  jurisdictional conflicts in, 364–6
  King's Bench, 364
  Lord Chancellor, 364
English Commercial Court. *See* Commercial Court of England and Wales
English common law. *See also specific tribunal*
  generally, 264
  as applicable law, 138 (*See also specific tribunal*)
  Brexit, impact of, 87
  civil law versus, 287
  ex parte communication in common law systems, 311
  flexibility of, 205
  good faith in, 105
  harmonization of international commercial law and, 211–12, 224
  historical development of, 234–5
  impartiality of, 205
  influence on ICommCs, 34–5
  judicial ethics in common law systems, 308–9
  multinational corporations and, 205–6
  pragmatic nature of, 204–5
  widespread nature of, 204
Erie, Matthew S., 477
ethics
  counsel ethics (*See* counsel ethics)
  judicial ethics (*See* judicial ethics)
European Banking Authority, 163–4
European Coal and Steel Community (ECSC) Treaty (1952), 73
European Convention on Human Rights (ECHR) (1959)
  hybridity and, 455
  legal analytics and, 352–3
  subsidiarity and, 456–7
European Court of Human Rights (ECtHR)
  hybridity in, 455
  legal analytics and, 352–3
  margin of appreciation, 448, 456–7
  rule of law and, 533

subsidiarity and, 456–7
European Court of Justice (ECJ)
hybridity in, 455
public purpose and, 103
European Economic Community, 73, 454
European Free Trade Area (EFTA), 509
European Judicial Union, 279
European Stability Mechanism (ESM), 103
European Union
Brussels I Regulation (*See* Brussels I Regulation)
Brussels Ia Regulation, 506, 507, 510, 511–12, 513
CETA, compatibility of ISDS provisions with EU law, 80–4
Charter of Fundamental Rights, 76, 83, 84–5, 103
CJEU (*See* Court of Justice of the European Union (CJEU))
competition law, 78–9
Directives, 456
Enforcement Order Regulation, 507
European Insolvency Regulation (EIR), 512
on 'forum shopping', 502–3
Insolvency Regulation, 506
Justice Scoreboard Monitor, 284
preliminary references, 448, 455
regulations, 456
Rome I Regulation, 503, 506, 507, 513
Rome II Regulation, 506, 507, 513
subsidiarity, 456–7
TFEU (*See* Treaty on the Functioning of the European Union (TFEU) (1958))
unitary court system in, 73–4
US compared, 73–4
validity of EU law, referrals to CJEU regarding, 86, 87–8
Euskadi Ta Askatasuna (ETA), 92–3
evidence
in CICC, 486
discovery, comparative analysis, 292
in SICC, 269
ex parte communication
judges of ICommCs, 302, 313–14
judicial ethics and
generally, 310
in civil law systems, 310, 311
in common law systems, 310–11
in mediation, 311–12

federalism, 529–30
Feldman, Mark, 477–8
Fine, J.D., 312
Fiss, Owen M., 312
Fitzmaurice, Gerald, 53
foreign direct investment (FDI)
in China, 471
funding of ICommCs and, 97
ICommCs and, 253
political imperative and, 402
forum non conveniens, 184–5
'forum shopping'
generally, 501–2
Brussels I Regulation and, 502
party autonomy and, 501–2
France. *See also* Paris Chambers
civil law system, status of, 283–5
commercial courts in, 29
Cour de Cassation, 85, 394
High Legal Committee of the Financial Market in Paris, 280–1
legal analytics in, 353
Paris Bar, 281
Paris Commercial Court, 15
Paris Court of Appeal, 15
UAE, bilateral treaty with, 443
Frankfurt District Court
generally, 522, 523, 5, 158
appeals from, 85
applicable law
comparative analysis, 287–8
English common law, 143, 223–4
attractiveness of, 298
Brexit, impact of, 280
Chamber for Commercial Disputes, 172
Chamber for International Commercial Disputes, 85, 172, 294, 297

Frankfurt District Court (cont.)
  Charter of Fundamental Rights, subject to, 84–5
  CICC compared, 438
  Commercial Court of England and Wales, as challenge to, 339, 465–6
  court fees, 290
  DIFCC compared, 438
  as division of existing court, 285, 435–6, 465–6, 517
  economic diversification and, 402–3
  establishment of, 14–15, 124, 222–3, 278
  EU law, application of, 84
  as international chamber within domestic court, 252, 261
  judges, 223
  jurisdiction
    both parties choosing forum, capacity to accept cases, 132
    defendant accepting plaintiff's choice of forum, capacity to accept cases, 134–5
    subject matter jurisdiction, 162
    transfer jurisdiction, 172
    voluntary jurisdiction, 430–1, 435–9
  language in, 223, 261, 290, 436–9, 465–6
  legislative changes, 288
  online access, 293
  Paris Chambers compared, 281
  procedure
    generally, 223, 422
    case management, 291
    comparative analysis, 288, 290–3
    discovery, 292
    protection of weaker parties, 430–1, 435–9
    witnesses, 291–2
  purpose of, 124, 222–3
  rationale for establishment, 281
  record of, 294, 297
  SICC compared, 438
  technology in, 348
  videoconferencing in, 348
Free Trade Zones (FTZs), 471–2
free zone international commercial arbitration, 275
Fuller, Lon, 307
functional internationalism, 22, 253–4, 264–6
function of ICommCs, 20
funding
  generally, 91
  foreign direct investment (FDI) and, 97
  of ICommCs, 96–8, 100–1
  of international criminal tribunals, 98, 100, 101
  legitimacy, importance of, 98, 101
  'value for money', 101

Gadamer, Hans-Georg, 68
Gaillard, Emmanuel, 394, 395
Garth, Bryant, 62
Geisinger, Elliott, 320–1
General Agreement on Tariffs and Trade (GATT), 62
Germany. *See also* Frankfurt District Court
  Chambers for International Commercial Disputes (proposed), 436–7, 438
  civil law system, status of, 283–5
  Code of Civil Procedure, 223, 293
  commercial courts in, 29
  Courts Constitution, 223
  ex parte communication in, 310, 311
  Federal Constitutional Court (Bundesverfassungsgericht), 455
  Frankfurt Court of Appeal, 85
  Stuttgart Commercial Court, 164
Giorgetti, Chiara, 305
global administrative law, 2
global governance, 20
globalization
  harmonization of international commercial law and, 203
  ICommCs and, 252–3, 266–7
Goldstone, Richard J., 303–4
good faith, 105
Grice, Paul, 93–4
Gross, Peter, 410

groupthink, 60–1
Grout, Christopher, 20
Gulf Cooperation Council (GCC) Judgments Convention (1996), 154, 216, 443
Guyana, CCJ and, 460
Guzman, Andrew, 299

Hague Choice of Court Convention (2005). *See also specific tribunal*
  choice-of-court clauses and, 149, 170–1, 340
  comity and, 411
  digital delivery of judgment and, 355
  enforcement of judgments and, 46
  jurisdiction and, 128–9
  jurisprudential imperative and, 406
  New York Convention compared, 149
  technology and, 343–4
  transfer jurisdiction and, 171–2, 173
Hague Judgments Convention. *See* Convention on the Recognition and Enforcement of Foreign Judgments in Civil or Commercial Matters (Hague Judgments Convention) (2019)
Hamblen, Nicholas (Lord), 205
Hamburg Rules on Carriage of Goods by Sea (1978), 208
harmonization of international commercial law
  generally, 21, 202
  Brexit, effect of, 505–6
  confidentiality and, 225
  contractual method, 208–9
  COVID-19 pandemic and, 201
  DIFCC, possibility for, 386–7
  domestic courts, unsuitability of, 226–7
  efficiency and, 207, 225
  English common law and, 211–12, 224
  explanatory method, 208
  globalization and, 203
  as goal itself, 207–8
  historical background, 203
  'home advantage', reducing, 207
  ICommCs and, 202, 224–7
  inadequacy of traditional dispute resolution mechanisms, 201–2
  international commercial arbitration, unsuitability of, 224–6
  joinder of parties and, 225
  legislative method, 208, 226
  lower costs and, 206–7
  need for, 201, 206
  publication of opinions and, 225
Hensler, Deborah, 63
Hess, Burkhard, 294
Higginbotham, Patrick E., 528–9
Hong Kong
  commercial courts in, 492–3
  as common law jurisdiction, 204
  Court of Final Appeal (CFA), 3–4, 473
  Court of First Instance, 29
  domestic courts, role of, 472–3
  Hong Kong Basic Law, 472–3
  ranking of legal system, 284
  Special Administrative Region (SAR), 468–9
Hong Kong International Arbitration Centre (HKIAC), 484
Hope, David (Lord), 218
Human Development Index (HDI), 101
human rights, rule of law and, 525–6, 533
Hwang, Michael, 55, 61–2, 71, 232, 239–40, 241, 271, 396
hybrid criminal courts, 7
hybridity. *See also specific tribunal*
  in divisions of existing courts, 465–6
  domestic versus international, 268–9
  formal versus informal, 268–9, 270
  of ICommCs
    generally, 19, 24, 253, 254, 466–7
    counsel ethics and, 325–6
    domestic courts, elements of, 269–70
    domestic courts compared, 417
    international commercial arbitration, elements of, 269

hybridity (cont.)
precluding merger with international commercial arbitration, 392–3, 419–20
institutional hybridity, 449, 454
in international courts and tribunals, 448, 449–50
judges and, 451–4
legal hybridity, 449, 454
margin of appreciation, 448, 456–7
preliminary references, 448, 455
professional hybridity, 449, 451–4
public versus private, 268–9
special economic zones (SEZs), ICommCs associated and, 463–5
in stand-alone courts, 465
subsidiarity, 456–7

ICC. *See* International Chamber of Commerce (ICC); International Criminal Court (ICC)
Iceland, Lugano Convention II and, 509
ICJ. *See* International Court of Justice (ICJ)
ICTR. *See* International Criminal Tribunal for Rwanda (ICTR)
ICTY. *See* International Criminal Tribunal for the former Yugoslavia (ICTY)
India
commercial courts in, 493
federalism in, 529–30
UAE, bilateral treaty with, 443
institutional hybridity, 449, 454
institutional legitimacy, 303, 367–8
Inter-American Commission on Human Rights, 533
Inter-American Court of Human Rights, 533
International Bar Association
Guidelines on Party Representation in International Arbitration, 320, 321–2, 323, 331
Rules on the Taking of Evidence in International Arbitration, 288, 292
International Centre for Settlement of Investment Disputes (ICSID)
economic diversification and, 402–3
QICDRC and, 111
International Chamber at the Paris Court of Appeal (CICAP). *See* Paris Chambers
International Chamber of Commerce (ICC), 39, 110, 208, 389–90, 484
International commercial arbitration. *See also specific tribunal*
generally, 2–3, 23
'abject retreat', 60–1
access to justice, lack of, 71, 405
backlash against, 53–4, 276
business imperative, 396–400 (*See also* business imperative)
comity and, 411
complexity of, 392, 415
confidentiality, lack of, 226, 405
counsel ethics in
generally, 315, 316–17
conflicting standards, 318
domestic regulation, 317
double deontology problem, 318
ICommCs compared, 324–5
inequality and, 318–23
unfairness and, 318–23
universal code of conduct, proposals for, 320–3
domestic courts versus, 268
elements of in ICommCs, 269
enforcement of judgments by, 148
free zone international commercial arbitration, 275
harmonization of international commercial law, unsuitability for, 224–6
ICommCs compared
generally, 388, 420
advantages of ICommCs, 418
advantages of international commercial arbitration, 390–1, 483–4
business imperative, 396–400 (*See also* business imperative)
competition with, 297

competitive nature of ICommCs, 61–4
counsel ethics, 324–5
domestic courts versus, 417
dynamic nature of relationship, 417
flexibility, 418
hybridity precluding merger of forms, 392–3, 419–20
interoperability with, 274–6
interweaving of dispute resolution functions, 418–19
judges of ICommCs, arbitrators compared, 300–1
jurisprudential imperative, 404–14 (*See also* jurisprudential imperative)
legitimacy, 56–7, 64–5
need for multiple forms of dispute resolution, 418
nuanced differences, 389
political imperative, 400–4 (*See also* political imperative)
political system, 58–9
power, 55–6
procedural similarities, 422, 439
public interest, 57–9
relation between, 38–41, 265–6
state interests, 59–61
technology, 337–8
transparency, 529
informality of, 18–19, 267–8
ISDS (*See* Investor–State Dispute Settlement (ISDS))
jurisprudential imperative, 392, 404–14 (*See also* jurisprudential imperative)
lack of access to, 71
mediation and, 399
New York Convention (*See* Convention on the Recognition and Enforcement of Foreign Arbitral Awards (New York Convention) (1958))
party autonomy and
generally, 389
ICommCs compared, 269
individual autonomy, 393–4
judicialization, 415
particular autonomy, 393–4
private autonomy, 393
structural autonomy, 394–6
systematic autonomy, 394–6
patriarchal nature of, 68
political imperative, 400–4 (*See also* political imperative)
precedent, lack of, 224–5, 226
procedural similarities with ICommCs, 422, 439
published opinions, lack of, 224
role of arbitrators, 299
state justice compared, 18, 267
'stigma of illegitimacy' and, 303
transparency, lack of, 528–9
UNCITRAL Arbitration Rules, 259, 389
international commercial courts (ICommCs). *See specific court or topic*
international commercial law, 202–3
International Consortium for Court Excellence, 9–10
International Court of Justice (ICJ)
generally, 202
Article 38 ICJ Statute, 7
as continuation of PCIJ, 454
hybridity in, 454
as prime example of international court, 7
public purpose and, 102–3
shortcomings of, 1
United States and, 102–3
international courts and tribunals. *See also specific court or tribunal*
defined, 447
domestic law in, 448–9
evolution of, 1–2, 5–8
hybridity in, 448, 449–50
ICommCs distinguished, 264, 463, 467
judicial ethics in, 307
modern courts and tribunals, 2, 7–8
traditional model of, 1–2
International Criminal Court (ICC), 98, 102, 202

International Criminal Tribunal for Rwanda (ICTR), 98, 102, 108
International Criminal Tribunal for the former Yugoslavia (ICTY), 98, 101, 102, 107, 108
international criminal tribunals. *See also specific tribunal*
  generally, 20–1
  capacity of, 368
  communicative skills of, 92
  defined, 90
  enforcement of judgments in, 370
  funding of, 98, 100, 101
  healing, contributing to, 109
  historical records of conflict, compiling, 108
  impartiality in, 367
  institutional legitimacy, 367–8
  jurisdiction, 370
  lessons for ICommCs, 90, 111–12
  local justice institutions, fortifying, 109
  procedural legitimacy, 367
  public purpose and, 104–5, 106–7
  rise of, 366–7
  transitional justice, 109–10
  trust and, 368
  user-friendly aspirations of, 94, 95–6
  victims, giving voice to, 108–9
international financial centres (IFCs). *See specific centre*
International Institute for the Unification of Private Law (UNIDROIT)
  Convention on Agency in the International Sale of Goods (1983), 208
  harmonization of international commercial law and, 208
International Investment Agreements (IIAs), 276–7
internationality requirement
  generally, 422
  competition with domestic courts, 423, 428–30
  'exorbitant' internationality, 423–8
internationalization of domestic courts, 6, 8–10
international judicial bodies, 6–7, 262–3
international judicialization, 6, 262
International Monetary Fund (IMF), 9
international nature of ICommCs, 30–2
International Swaps and Derivatives Association (ISDA), 163–4, 338
interoperability of ICommCs
  generally, 270, 277
  dispute bifurcation, 271
  domestic courts, with, 270–4
  international commercial arbitration, with, 274–6
  international courts and tribunals, with, 276–7
  Investor–State Dispute Settlement (ISDS), with, 276–7
Investment Group Private Limited (IGPL), 381
Investor–State Dispute Settlement (ISDS)
  backlash against, 534
  CETA, compatibility of ISDS provisions with EU law, 80–4
  Draft Code of Conduct for Adjudicators in Investor-State Dispute Settlement, 300
  electronic deliberations in, 354
  interoperability with ICommCs, 276–7
  rule of law and, 534–5
  TFEU, arbitral tribunal not deemed court or tribunal for purposes of, 79–80
Iraq, hybrid criminal court in, 107
Ireland
  common law in, 87
  private international law and, 505, 506
ISDS. *See* Investor–State Dispute Settlement (ISDS)
Ive, Jony, 52, 55

James I (England), 366
Jeuland, Emmanuel, 295
judges of ICommCs. *See also specific tribunal*
  generally, 22, 41–2, 210, 263

accommodation by ICommCs, 369–70
arbitrators compared, 300–1
comparative analysis, 287
diversity of, 36, 41–2
domestic court judges compared, 300–1
'domestic judicial mindset', 358
ex parte communication, 302, 313–14
historical development of, 300
impartiality of, 304
independence of, 304
judicial ethics
generally, 302, 314
court personnel, 304–5
ex parte communication and, 302, 313–14
importance of, 302
legitimacy, relation to, 301–2
legitimacy
generally, 301, 314
judicial ethics, relation to, 301–2
judicial activism
'hard' judicial activism, 408–11
'soft' judicial activism, 408, 411–14
judicial ethics
adjudicators, 307–8
in civil law systems, 308
in common law systems, 308–9
court personnel, 304–5
in domestic courts, 306–7
ex parte communication and
generally, 310
in civil law systems, 310, 311
in common law systems, 310–11
mediation and, 311–12
ICommCs, judges of
generally, 302, 314
court personnel, 304–5
ex parte communication and, 302, 313–14
importance of, 302
legitimacy, relation to, 301–2
integrity distinguished, 305–6
in international courts and tribunals, 307
legal culture, relevance of, 306, 309
legitimacy, relation to, 302–5
role, relevance of, 306–7
judicial globalization, 6, 262
judicialization, 415
jurisdiction. *See also specific tribunal*
generally, 20, 21, 125, 263
additional parties or claims, capacity to accept, 126–8, 135
assumption by ICommCs, 370
based on other grounds, 173–5
both parties choosing forum, capacity to accept cases, 125–6, 128
Brexit, effect of, 509–13
'clash of courts', 387
comparative analysis, 115–16, 156–7, 176–7, 199–200
conflicts between ICommCs and domestic courts
DIFCC (*See* Dubai International Financial Centre Court (DIFCC))
examples, 370–1
future trends, 385
harmonization of law, possibility of, 386–7
courts protecting, 363–4
defendant accepting plaintiff's choice of forum, capacity to accept cases, 126, 132–3
Earl of Oxford's Case (1615), 364–6, 387
international and domestic cases, 164–5
international commercial cases, 162–4
international courts and tribunals, ICommCs distinguished, 264
international criminal tribunals, 370
jurisdiction agreements, 187, 189–91, 197–9 (*See also specific tribunal*)
matters with strong connection to forum, capacity to accept, 128, 137–8
party agreement on nature of case, 165–6
subject matter jurisdiction

jurisdiction (cont.)
generally, 162
international and domestic cases, 164–5
international commercial cases, 162–4
party agreement on nature of case, 165–6
value of claim, 166–7
transfer jurisdiction
generally, 174–5
Brussels I Regulation and, 171
party autonomy and, 199
transfer as basis of jurisdiction, 171–3
'turf wars', 363–4
value of claim, 166–7
voluntary jurisdiction
generally, 422, 430–1
'actual connection' requirement, 433–5
forum non conveniens, 431–3
protection of weaker parties, 435–9
jurisprudence of ICommCs, 42–5
jurisprudential imperative
generally, 392
'hard' judicial activism and, 408–11
interactions between imperatives, 414–16
political imperative and, 404
rule of law and, 404, 413
'soft' judicial activism and, 408, 411–14
tensions between imperatives, 414–16
just laws, rule of law and, 525–6

Karamanian, Susan L., 25
Karton, Joshua, 305–6
Kazakhstan
AIFC (*See* Astana International Financial Centre (AIFC))
AIFCC (*See* Astana International Financial Centre Court (AIFCC))
as civil law system, 490
Committee of Court Administration, 490
constitution, 273, 491
judicial reforms in, 490
Ministry of Finance, 530
Ministry of Justice, 490
Supreme Court, 153, 490
UAE, bilateral treaty with, 443
Keene, David, 36–7
Kelsen, Hans, 455
Kenya High Court, 153
Keynes, John Maynard, 62
Khatam, Damira, 63
Kichigina, Irina, 414
Kiev Convention on Settling Commercial Disputes (1992), 154
Knowles, Robin, 413
Kosovo, hybrid criminal court in, 7, 107, 366–7
Kuwait, DIFCC and, 216

Lagos Chamber of Commerce International Commercial Arbitration Centre, 322
Landgericht (LG) Frankfurt am Main District Court. *See* Frankfurt District Court
Lando, Ole, 247
language. *See also specific tribunal*
generally, 263–4
access to justice, language issues, 49–50
accommodation by ICommCs, 369–70
comparative analysis, 290
Laswell, Harold, 58
Lauterpacht, Hersch, 247
Law Society of England and Wales, 38
Lebanon
hybrid criminal court in, 102, 107, 366–7
Special Tribunal for Lebanon, 107
Lech, Franciszek, 21
Le Gal, Jean-Francois, 209
legal analytics, 352–4
legal hybridity, 449, 454
legitimacy

generally, 91
assessments and, 65
funding, importance to, 98, 101
ICommCs, judges of
generally, 301, 314
judicial ethics, relation to, 301–2
institutional legitimacy, 303, 367–8
international commercial arbitration
as advantage of ICommCs versus, 56–7
as disadvantage of ICommCs versus, 64–5
'stigma of illegitimacy' and, 303
international criminal tribunals, 367–8
judicial ethics, relation to, 302–5
lack of as disadvantage of ICommCs, 64–5
normative legitimacy, 98–9
perceptions and, 65
procedural legitimacy, 303, 367
public interest and, 100
rationalchoice theory and, 65
sociological legitimacy, 98–9
Lehmann, Matthias, 294
Lein, Eva, 21
lex mercatoria, 201, 203, 204, 226–7
LG. *See* Frankfurt District Court
Liechtenstein, Lugano Convention II and, 509
Li Huanzhi, 483
Loan Market Association (LMA), 338
locally administered justice, 37–8
Loh, Quentin, 59
London Commercial Court. *See* Commercial Court of England and Wales
London Court of International Arbitration (LCIA)
generally, 39
ADGMC and, 47
Arbitration Rules, 322–3, 443
Commercial Court of England and Wales and, 118
counsel ethics and, 320
establishment of, 388
General Guidelines for the Parties' Legal Representatives, 322–3
London Maritime Arbitration Association (LMAA), 118
Lugano Convention II (2007), 185–6, 509–10

Maastricht Treaty (1992), 456, 506
Macau Special Administrative Region (SAR), 468–9
MacIntyre, Alasdair, 306
Madsen, Mikael Rask, 24
Malaysia, commercial courts in, 493
Malmström, Cecilia, 81
Malta, common law in, 87
Mance, Jonathan (Lord), 395, 412, 494
Mansfield, Lord (William Murray), 204
margin of appreciation, 448, 456–7
Mauritius, commercial courts in, 37, 38
McAllister, Gordon, 318
McCorquodale, Robert, 524, 525
mediation
AIFCC, 494
Astana IAC, 495
ex parte communication in, 311–12
international commercial arbitration and, 399
QICDRC, 37
Menkel-Meadow, Carrie, 316
Menon, Sundaresh (Chief Justice), 407, 409, 12–13, 50–1, 179, 199–200, 205, 213, 214, 227, 257–8, 264, 303, 320, 331, 394, 523
Mercosur Permanent Review Court (PRC), 462–3
Meydan Group LLC, 378–9
Middleton, John (Justice), 331
Minsk Convention on Legal Assistance (1992), 154
Mishmish, Ramadan Mousa, 384
mission of ICommCs, 50–1
money laundering, 530, 531–2, 535
monopolistic competition, 337–8
Montagu-Smith, Tom, 497
Morgan, Edward M., 299
Mounin, Georges, 92
al-Muhairi, 'Ali, 231
Multilateral Memorandum on the Enforcement of Commercial

Judgments for Money, 10, 46, 152, 341, 412
Murray, William (Lord Mansfield), 204

Nasrallah, Faris Elias, 21–2
Nazarbayev, Nursultan, 490
NCC. *See* Netherlands Commercial Court (NCC)
Netherlands
  civil law system, status of, 283–5
  Code of Civil Procedure, 5, 15–16, 147, 261–2
  Commercial Court Bill, 5, 15–16
  commercial courts in, 29
  competition law, 78–9
  Council for the Judiciary, 426
  Slovakia, Bilateral Investment Treaty with, 79–80
Netherlands Commercial Court (NCC)
  generally, 522, 523, 5, 29, 117, 158
  appeals from, 85
  applicable law
    comparative analysis, 287–8
    English common law, 142–3, 223–4
  attractiveness of, 298
  Brussels I Regulation and, 427
  choice-of-court clauses, 168–9, 170–1
  CICC compared, 438
  Commercial Court of England and Wales, as challenge to, 339, 465–6
  counsel ethics in, 326–7
  court fees, 290
  Court of Appeal, 15–16, 85, 134, 161, 168–9, 222, 261–2
  COVID-19 pandemic and, 296
  DIFCC compared, 438
  District Court, 15–16, 85, 131, 134, 161, 168–9, 222, 261–2
  as division of existing court, 161, 285, 435–6, 465–6, 517
  economic diversification and, 402–3
  enforcement of judgments, 222
  establishment of, 15–16, 123–4, 222, 278
  Hague Choice of Court Convention and, 149, 427
  hybrid nature of, 447–8
  as international chamber within domestic court, 252, 261–2
  judges, 123–4
  jurisdiction
    additional parties or claims, capacity to accept, 137
    both parties choosing forum, capacity to accept cases, 131
    defendant accepting plaintiff's choice of forum, capacity to accept cases, 134
    other foreign law, application of, 147
    subject matter jurisdiction, 162–3
    transfer jurisdiction, 172
    voluntary jurisdiction, 430–1, 435–9
  language in, 222, 261–2, 290, 427–8, 436–9, 465–6
  legislative changes, 288–90
  online access, 293–4
  procedure
    generally, 222, 422
    case management, 291
    comparative analysis, 288, 290–3
    discovery, 292
    internationality requirement, 426–8
    protection of weaker parties, 430–1, 435–9
    witnesses, 291–2
  purpose of, 123–4
  rationale for establishment, 282–3
  record of, 295–7
  Rules 2020, 162–3, 426, 436
  SICC compared, 438
  technology in
    electronic case management, 347
    videoconferencing, 348–9
New York Convention. *See* Convention on the Recognition and Enforcement of Foreign Arbitral Awards (New York Convention) (1958)

New Zealand, commercial courts in, 493
normative legitimacy, 98–9
Norway, Lugano Convention II and, 509
Nuremberg Tribunal, 453, 454
Nur-Sultan Court. *See* Astana International Financial Centre Court (AIFCC)

Oger Dubai LLC, 382
online access, 293–4
Open government, rule of law and, 526
organizational internationalism, 253–4, 262–4
Organization for Economic Co-operation and Development (OECD), 9
organization of ICommCs. *See also specific tribunal*
  generally, 20, 277
  functional internationalism, 22, 253–4, 264–6, 277
  hybridity
    generally, 19, 24, 253, 254, 466–7
    counsel ethics and, 325–6
    domestic courts, elements of, 269–70
    domestic courts compared, 417
    international commercial arbitration, elements of, 269
    precluding merger with international commercial arbitration, 392–3, 419–20
  international chambers within domestic courts, 260–2
  interoperability (*See* Interoperability of ICommCs)
  organizational internationalism, 253–4, 262–4
  special economic zones (SEZs), associated with, 254–7
  stand-alone courts, 257–60
Ortolani, Pietro, 23

Paris Chambers
  generally, 522, 523, 5, 117, 158, 209
  appeals from, 85
  applicable law
    generally, 221
    comparative analysis, 287–8
    English common law, 143, 222, 223–4
  attractiveness of, 298
  Brexit, impact of, 280
  choice of court clauses, 169
  Commercial Court of England and Wales, as challenge to, 339, 465–6
  court fees, 290
  as division of existing court, 160–1, 285, 465–6, 517
  establishment of, 15, 124, 220, 261, 278
  Frankfurt Court compared, 281
  Hague Choice of Court Convention and, 149
  as international chamber within domestic court, 252, 261
  judges, 221
  jurisdiction
    generally, 221
    both parties choosing forum, capacity to accept cases, 131
    other foreign law, application of, 147
    subject matter jurisdiction, 163–4
  language in, 49, 221, 261, 290, 295, 465–6
  legislative changes, 288
  online access, 293
  procedure
    generally, 221
    case management, 291
    comparative analysis, 288, 290–3
    discovery, 292
    witnesses, 291–2
  purpose of, 124, 220–1
  rationale for establishment, 280–1
  record of, 294–5, 297
Parker, Andrew (Lord), 410
party autonomy
  generally, 7, 392
  BIBC and, 426
  CICC and, 195, 434

party autonomy (cont.)
Commercial Court of England and Wales and, 138–9, 389
counsel ethics and, 323
CTEA and, 82–3
defined, 393
'forum shopping' and, 501–2, 503
international commercial arbitration and
generally, 389
ICommCs compared, 269
individual autonomy, 393–4
judicialization, 415
particular autonomy, 393–4
private autonomy, 393
structural autonomy, 394–6
systematic autonomy, 394–6
internationalization and, 195–6
jurisdiction agreements and, 197–9
public autonomy, 393
SICC and, 177, 180, 188–9, 190–1, 192, 424, 426
transfer jurisdiction and, 199
Patchett-Joyce, Michael, 23
Pauwelyn, Joost, 66–7
Permanent Court of International Justice (PCIJ)
historical background, 451
hybridity in, 449–50
ICJ as continuation of, 454
Phillips, Nick (Lord), 246
political driver of ICommCs, 63
political imperative
generally, 392
business imperative and, 402, 414–15
competition between tribunals and, 403–4
economic diversification and, 401–3
foreign direct investment (FDI) and, 401, 402
interactions between imperatives, 414–16
jurisprudential imperative and, 404
rule of law and, 401
sound financial systems and, 401
tensions between imperatives, 414–16
'post-shame age', 60–1
preliminary references, 448, 455
pro bono services, 50
procedural legitimacy, 303, 367
procedure. *See also specific tribunal*
generally, 20, 23–4, 421–2, 444
overview, 422–3
British rules of procedure, influence of, 35
case management, 291
comparative analysis, 288, 290–3
discovery, 292
evidence
in CICC, 486
discovery, comparative analysis, 292
in SICC, 269
international commercial arbitration, procedural similarities with ICommCs, 422, 439
internationality requirement
generally, 422
competition with domestic courts, 423, 428–30
'exorbitant' internationality, 423–8
voluntary jurisdiction
generally, 422, 430–1
'actual connection' requirement, 433–5
forum non conveniens, 431–3
protection of weaker parties, 435–9
witnesses
comparative analysis, 291–2
technology and, 341
videoconferencing, 348–50
professional hybridity, 449, 451–4
proliferation of ICommCs, 6, 10–11, 252
public purpose
generally, 91, 111–12
as advantage of ICommCs versus international commercial arbitration, 57–9
benefits of institutionalization, 107–8
drawbacks of institutionalization, 106–7

emergence of, 102
healing, contributing to, 109
historical records of conflict, compiling, 108
ICommCs and, 103–4, 105, 106, 110–11
international criminal tribunals and, 104–5, 106–7
legitimacy and, 100
local justice institutions, fortifying, 109
necessary elements, 111–12
neglect as disadvantage of ICommCs, 71–2
transitional justice, 109–10
victims, giving voice to, 108–9
working in partnership with other mechanisms as, 104–5
purpose of ICommCs, 17, 30

Qatar
Arbitration Law in Civil and Commercial Matters, 37
as British protectorate, 230
Civil and Commercial Procedure Law, 245
Commercial Court, 37
complexity of law in, 231
Council of Ministers, 244
hybrid nature of law in, 231
Ministry of Economy and Commerce, 244
Qatar Financial Centre Law, 11–12
Tendering and Bidding Law, 245
Qatar Financial Centre (QFC)
generally, 228, 517–18
Civil and Commercial Court, 11–12, 36, 233, 255
Court Rules, 234, 245
establishment of, 233, 255
Insolvency Regulations, 246
as 'on-shore zone', 257
regulations, 245
Regulatory Authority, 233, 517–18, 531–2
Regulatory Tribunal, 11–12, 36, 233, 518–19, 531–2
Qatar International Court and Dispute Resolution Centre (QICDRC)
generally, 4, 21–2, 34, 117, 492–3
access to justice in, 535
ADGMC compared, 218, 234, 245
Appellate Circuit, 11–12, 255, 518–19, 531–2
applicable law
generally, 229, 234, 247–8, 255, 274, 519
case law regarding, 246
English common law, 34, 139, 141, 155–6, 217, 235, 236–7, 287, 464–5
hybridity in, 464–5
QFC laws, 244–5
symbolic capital and, 230
caseload, 237
CICC compared, 479
communicative skills of, 92
counsel ethics in, 316, 325, 327–8, 330, 334
DIFCC compared, 217–18, 234, 245, 464
dissenting judgments, lack of, 42
domestic courts, conflicts with, 364
dual legal system, effect of, 530–2
economic diversification and, 402
enforcement of judgments
generally, 217–18
bilateral regimes for, 154
foreign judgments, 46
own judgments, 48
regional regimes for, 154
establishment of, 11–12, 36, 120, 216, 255, 278
First Instance Circuit, 11–12, 255, 518
funding of, 97
hybrid nature of, 447–8, 464
ICSID and, 111
international commercial arbitration in, 37, 40, 236, 276
international nature of, 30
judges
generally, 36–7, 120, 217, 235, 256, 519
British judges, 35

Qatar International Court (cont.)
diversity of, 36, 42
enforcement judge, 96
hybridity and, 464–5
judicial ethics, 303
Judicial Code of Conduct, 245, 519
jurisdiction
generally, 11–12, 32, 33, 217, 255, 518
additional parties or claims, capacity to accept, 136
based on other grounds, 173–4
both parties choosing forum, capacity to accept cases, 130
defendant accepting plaintiff's choice of forum, capacity to accept cases, 133–4
other foreign law, application of, 145
transfer jurisdiction, 274
jurisprudence of, 43–5
language in, 49–50, 217, 255–6
Legal Services Code, 327
mediation in, 37
money laundering and, 530, 531–2
as 'on-shore' jurisdiction, 234, 273
pro bono services in, 50
procedural rules, 518
public purpose in, 110, 111
purpose of, 36, 38, 120, 216
reciprocity and, 156
Regulations and Procedure Rules, 35, 42, 48, 49–50, 141, 145, 173–4, 327
rule of law and, 528, 530–2
special economic zones (SEZs) and, 210, 252, 255–6, 273, 464, 516, 517–19
as stand-alone court, 160, 174, 285–7
technology in
generally, 335–6
videoconferencing, 348
time requirements in, 272
user-friendly aspirations of, 95, 96
Qatar Legal Forum, 37
QFC. *See* Qatar Financial Centre (QFC)
QICDRC. *See* Qatar International Court and Dispute Resolution Centre (QICDRC)
Queen Mary University, 319–20, 398–9
Quran, 105

'race to the top', 63
Rajah, V. K., 264
Ramesh, Kannan (Justice), 207, 208, 331–2
rationalchoice theory, 65
Raynaud, Iris, 209
Reed, Lucy, 50, 60, 61, 263, 324, 391–2, 417
representation, 263
Requejo Isidro, Marta, 55, 62
Resnik, Judith, 528
Reyes, Anselmo, 61–2
rise of ICommCs, 391–2
Rix, Bernard, 409
Riyadh Convention (1983), 154, 443
Roberts, Anthea, 449
Rogers, Catherine A., 22, 319
role of ICommCs, 20, 33–4, 50–1
Romano, Cesare, 6–7, 309
Rome I Regulation, 503, 506, 507, 513
Rome II Regulation, 506, 507, 513
rule of law. *See also specific tribunal*
generally, 25, 515–16, 524
access to justice and, 535
accountability and, 525
defined, 492, 524
dispute resolution and, 526
human rights and, 525–6, 533
ICommCs and
generally, 515–16, 527, 534–5
as destination fora, 532–4
dual legal system, effect of, 529–32
host state relations and, 527–32, 535
promoting rule of law, 529
Investor–State Dispute Settlement (ISDS) and, 534–5
jurisprudential imperative and, 404, 413
just laws and, 525–6
limits on state power and, 525
open government and, 526

political imperative and, 401
protection of citizens and, 525
special economic zones (SEZs) and, 105
Rule of Law Index, 283–4
Rutledge, Peter B., 299

sales strategy of ICommCs, 63–4
Sander, Frank, 477–8
Sappideen, Razeen, 208
Saville, Mark (Lord), 410
Scheffler, Samuel, 70–1
Schill, Stephan W., 321, 526, 534–5
Schlag, Pierre, 53, 67
Schultz, Thomas, 20
Schwebel, Stephen, 81
SEZs. *See* Special economic zones (SEZs)
Shari'a, 231
SICC. *See* Singapore International Commercial Court (SICC)
Sierra Leone, hybrid criminal court in, 7, 102, 108, 366–7
SIFoCC. *See* Standing International Forum of Commercial Courts (SIFoCC)
signalling, 56–7, 59
signification, 92
Simon, Jack (Lord Simon of Glaisdale), 366
Singapore
as common law jurisdiction, 204
constitution, 273, 522
Court of Appeal, 522–3
General Division, 173
High Court
generally, 191, 276
confidentiality, lack of, 213
extraterritorial jurisdiction, 189
original jurisdiction, 186–7, 212–13
SICC as division of, 161, 180, 212, 257–8, 285, 325, 386–7, 465, 516–17, 522–3
transfer of cases to SICC, 173, 191–2, 273–4, 431, 432
International Arbitration Act, 187
international commercial arbitration in, 265–6
Legal Professions Act, 269, 329, 522
popularity for international dispute settlement, 284–5
ranking of legal system, 284
Rules of Court, 161
Supreme Court, 13, 14, 153, 258
Supreme Court of Judicature Act (SCJA), 161, 259–60
Singapore International Arbitration Centre (SIAC), 39, 265–6, 485
Singapore International Commercial Court (SICC)
generally, 4, 21, 117, 158, 492–3
ADGMC compared, 218, 329–30
appeals from, 13–14, 258, 522–3
applicable law
generally, 258, 522–3
English common law, 140, 155–6
choice-of-court clauses, 169–70
CICC compared, 195, 435, 465, 479, 483
Code of Ethics, 314, 329–30
Commercial Court of England and Wales compared, 179, 183–4, 211
confidentiality in, 346
contempt, 187
counsel ethics in, 316, 325, 329–30, 334
COVID-19 pandemic and, 214
DIFCC compared, 215
as division of existing court, 160, 161, 174, 180, 212, 285, 516–17, 522–3
economic diversification and, 402
enforcement of judgments
bilateral regimes for, 153
regional regimes for, 153
entrepreneurial purpose of, 523
establishment of, 12, 118–19, 212, 257, 273, 522
Frankfurt Court compared, 438
Hague Choice of Court Convention and, 149, 191–2, 424, 431, 432
harmonization of law and, 386–7
High Court and

Singapore International (cont.)
SICC as division of, 161, 180, 212, 257–8, 285, 325, 386–7, 465, 516–17, 522–3
transfer of cases from, 173, 191–2, 273–4, 431, 432
as hybrid court, 269
hybrid nature of, 447–8, 465
international commercial arbitration
generally, 276
confidentiality, 440–1
procedural similarities with ICommCs, 439, 440–1
internationalization and, 196–7
international nature of, 30
judges
generally, 14, 118–19, 196, 213, 522–3
British judges, 35
code of conduct, 313–14
diversity of, 41–2
domestic judges, 258
international judges, 258
judicial ethics, 305, 313–14
jurisdiction
generally, 13–14, 212–13, 257–8, 259–60, 522
additional parties or claims, capacity to accept, 136
both parties choosing forum, capacity to accept cases, 129
commercial claims, 188
defendant accepting plaintiff's choice of forum, capacity to accept cases, 133
innovative nature of, 258
international claims, 187–8, 423–4
jurisdiction agreements, 187
other foreign law, application of, 144
party agreement on nature of case, 188–9, 424
subject matter jurisdiction, 162, 165–6
transfer jurisdiction, 173, 187, 191–2, 199, 273–4
voluntary jurisdiction, 430, 431–3
jurisdiction agreements, 189–91, 198–9
language in, 258
as modern ICommC, 196–7
NCC compared, 438
party autonomy and, 177, 180, 188–9, 190–1, 192, 424, 426
powers of, 55
procedure
generally, 213–14, 422
evidence, 269
forum non conveniens, 430, 431–3
international commercial arbitration, procedural similarities with ICommCs, 439, 440–1
internationality requirement, 423–4, 426, 428
publication of opinions, 225
purpose of, 118–19, 177, 180, 199, 212, 214
rule of law and, 532–3
Rules of Court, 186–7, 212–13, 276, 346, 424, 431, 440–1, 529
service outside of jurisdiction, 189
Spillada principles and, 192, 431
as stand-alone court, 252, 257–8, 465
technology in
electronic case management, 347
virtual site inspections, 350
Singapore International Mediation Centre (SIMC), 265–6
Sino-British Joint Declaration (1984), 468
Sino-Portuguese Joint Declaration (1987), 468
Slovakia, Bilateral Investment Treaty with Netherlands, 79–80
Smith, Andrew, 244
Smith, Kayleigh, 55
social externalities, 20. *See also* Disadvantages of ICommCs
sociological legitimacy, 98–9
Southern African Development Community (SADC), 103, 107
Soviet Union, collapse of, 203
Spain, Euskadi Ta Askatasuna (ETA) and, 92–3

Special Criminal Court on the Events in Darfur (SCCED), 100
special economic zones (SEZs). *See also specific tribunal*
- common features of ICommCs associated with, 257
- defined, 256–7
- hybridity in ICommCs associated with, 463–5
- ICommCs associated with, 209–10, 254–7, 463–5, 516
- rule of law and, 105

Special Tribunal for Lebanon, 107
Sri Lanka, hybrid criminal court in, 366–7
stand-alone courts, 285–7, 465. *See also specific tribunal*
Standard Chartered Bank (SCB), 381
Standing International Forum of Commercial Courts (SIFoCC)
- generally, 10, 46–7
- definition of ICommC, 368–9
- enforcement of judgments and, 151–2, 341
- judicial activism and, 411, 412–13
- jurisprudential imperative and, 407
- member courts, 209, 369
- Multilateral Memorandum on the Enforcement of Commercial Judgments for Money, 10, 46, 152, 341, 412

state justice, 18
subject matter jurisdiction
- generally, 162
- international and domestic cases, 164–5
- international commercial cases, 162–4
- party agreement on nature of case, 165–6
- value of claim, 166–7

subsidiarity, 456–7
Sumption, Jonathan (Lord), 246
Sun, Wei, 482–3
Sweet Homes Real Estate LLC, 384
Swigart, Leigh, 309
Swiss Arbitration Association (ASA) Global Arbitration Ethics Council, 320–1, 331
Switzerland
- Lugano Convention II and, 509
- proposal for ICommCs in, 158–9

technology in ICommCs. *See also specific tribunal*
- generally, 23, 336–7
- Brexit, impact of, 338–40
- Brussels I Regulation and, 342–4
- choice-of-court clauses and, 342–4
- comparative analysis, 342
- consensus, recommendation regarding, 359
- consent, recommendation regarding, 357–8
- digital delivery of judgment, 355–6
- electronic case management, 346, 347
- electronic deliberations, 354–5
- electronic filing, 344–7
- enforcement of judgments and, 341–2, 356–7, 359
- experimentation, avoiding, 359
- Hague Choice of Court Convention and, 343–4
- importance of, 335
- international commercial arbitration, ICommCs compared, 337–8
- legal analytics, 352–4
- neutrality, myth of, 336
- newness, myth of, 336
- 'one size fits all' approach, avoiding, 358–9
- protection, impact of, 340–2
- videoconferencing, 348–50
- virtual site inspections, 350–2
- witnesses and, 341

Terris, Daniel, 309
TFEU. *See* Treaty on the Functioning of the European Union (TFEU) (1958)
Thomas, John (Lord Thomas of Cwmgiedd), 10, 36–7, 43,

151–2, 217, 401, 405, 407, 408–10, 411, 413, 529
Thomas, Michael, 36–7
Timor Leste, hybrid criminal court in, 7, 102, 107, 366–7
Tokyo Tribunal, 453, 454
Torrens land registration system, 240–1
Trade Facilitation Agreement (TFA), 472, 474
transfer jurisdiction. *See also specific tribunal*
  generally, 174–5
  Brussels I Regulation and, 171
  party autonomy and, 199
  transfer as basis of jurisdiction, 171–3
transitional justice, 109–10
transparency, international commercial arbitration lacking, 528–9
Treaty on European Union (Maastricht Treaty) (1992), 456, 506
Treaty on the Functioning of the European Union (TFEU) (1958)
  generally, 20
  adoption, 73
  arbitral tribunals not deemed court or tribunal, 77–80
  CETA, compatibility of ISDS provisions with EU law, 80–4
  CJEU (*See* Court of Justice of the European Union (CJEU))
  compulsory jurisdiction requirement for court or tribunal, 75–6
  domestic courts under, 74
  established by law, court or tribunal required to be, 75
  ICommCs as court or tribunal, 84–5
  independence requirement for court or tribunal, 76–7
  ISDS arbitral tribunals not deemed court or tribunal, 79–80
  member state requirement for court or tribunal, 77
  permanence requirement for court or tribunal, 75
  uniform interpretation of law and, 74
Trinidad and Tobago, CCJ and, 461
Trucial States of the Emirates, 230–1
Truss, Elizabeth, 364
Tunisia, bilateral treaty with UAE, 443
'turf wars', 363–4, 375, 385
Twain, Mark, 390
Twigg-Flesner, Christian, 208

UNCITRAL. *See* Commission on International Trade Law (UNCITRAL)
UNIDROIT. *See* International Institute for the Unification of Private Law (UNIDROIT)
Uniform Commercial Practices (UCP), 43–5
Uniform Rules for Demand Guarantees (URDG), 43–5, 110
United Arab Emirates
  Abu Dhabi Executive Council, 242
  ADGM (*See* Abu Dhabi Global Market (ADGM))
  ADGMC (*See* Abu Dhabi Global Market Court (ADGMC))
  bilateral treaties, 443
  complexity of law in, 231
  constitution, 140–1, 214, 215, 232, 273, 376, 519
  DIFC (*See* Dubai International Financial Centre (DIFC))
  DIFCC (*See* Dubai International Financial Centre Court (DIFCC))
  Dubai Financial Services Authority (DFSA), 239
  Dubai Law No. 16, 428–9
  federalism in, 529–30
  Federal Law No. (6) of 2018 on Arbitration, 380
  Financial Free Zones, 140–1
  governmental structure of, 372
  hybrid nature of law in, 231
  Institute of Training and Judicial Studies, 235
  international commercial arbitration in, 275
  Judicial Authority Law, 429

Judicial Committee of the Dubai Courts and the DIFC Courts, 274
Law No 12 of 2004 in respect of the Judicial Authority at Dubai International Financial Centre Cases, 174
Ministry of Justice, 153, 530
Ras Al Khaimah Courts, 153
Sharjah Federal Court of First Instance, 381
Union Supreme Court, 376, 381
Value Added Tax, 244

United Kingdom. *See also* Commercial Court of England and Wales; England
- Administration of Justice Act, 153
- Arbitration Act 1996, 39, 410
- Brexit (*See* Brexit)
- Brussels I Regulation and, 506
- City UK Legal Services Report, 139
- Civil Jurisdiction and Judgments Act 1982, 505
- Civil Procedure Rules 1998 (CPR), 35, 216, 244, 287, 346
- Civil Procedure Rules 1998 (Amendment) (EU Exit) Regulations 2019, 507
- CJEU and, 504, 513
- commercial courts in, 29
- common law (*See* English common law)
- as common law jurisdiction, 204
- in EU, 505
- European Union Withdrawal Act 2018, 508–9
- Financial Services and Markets Act 2000, 141, 403–4
- Foreign Judgments (Reciprocal Enforcement) Act 1933, 153
- Hague Choice of Court Convention and, 149, 505, 510
- Hague Judgments Convention and, 505, 510–11
- Insolvency Act 1986, 512
- Joint Stock Companies Winding Up Act 1848, 246
- Judicial Committee of the Privy Council, 459–60
- jurisprudence in, 44
- popularity for international dispute settlement, 284–5
- prominent position in international commercial dispute resolution, 501
- ranking of legal system, 284
- Supreme Court of Judicature, 387
- Supreme Court of Judicature Act 1873, 387
- Supreme Court of Judicature Act 1875, 387

United Nations
- Committee Against Torture (CAT), 102
- *Delivering Justice: Programme of Action to Strengthen the Rule of Law at the National and International Levels*, 525
- UNCITRAL (*See* Commission on International Trade Law (UNCITRAL))
- UNODC Global Judicial Integrity Network, 37

United States
- commercial courts in, 29
- as common law jurisdiction, 204
- District Court for the Southern District of New York, 153
- EU compared, 73–4
- *ex parte* communication in, 310–11, 312
- federalism in, 529–30
- Hague Choice of Court Convention and, 149
- ICJ and, 102–3
- managerial role of judges in, 312, 313
- popularity for international dispute settlement, 284–5
- ranking of legal system, 284

University of Copenhagen, 449

user-friendly aspirations
- generally, 90–1
- defined, 96

user-friendly aspirations (cont.)
of ICommCs, 94–5, 96
of international criminal tribunals, 94, 95–6

Vagts, Detlev, 310, 313
Vajda, Christopher, 20
van Calster, Geert, 24–5
videoconferencing, 348–50
Vienna Convention on the Law of Treaties (1969), 82, 508, 511
Virtual site inspections, 350–2
voluntary jurisdiction
generally, 422, 430–1
'actual connection' requirement, 433–5
forum non conveniens, 431–3
protection of weaker parties, 435–9

Walker, Janet, 21
Wang, Chenguang, 469
Wessel, Jane, 318
White & Case, 398–9
Wilkey, Malcolm, 313
Witkamp, Marieke, 522, 523
witnesses
comparative analysis, 291–2
technology and, 341
videoconferencing, 348–50
Wong, D. H., 30–1
Woolf, Harry (Lord), 24, 36–7, 220, 491, 497
World Bank, 9, 344, 389-90, 472, 532
World Court. *See* International Court of Justice (ICJ)
World Justice Project (WJP), 283–4, 525, 526
World Trade Organization (WTO), 62, 472, 474

Xi Jinping, 471, 473
Xu Qian, 24

Yip, Man, 21

Zapatero, José Luis Rodríguez, 92–3
Zarbiyev, Fuad, 60–1
Zho, Zihao, 478
Zhou, Guobin, 469
Žižek, Slavoj, 68

www.ingramcontent.com/pod-product-compliance
Lightning Source LLC
LaVergne TN
LVHW010339220926
848484LV00004BB/932
9781316519257